Navigating HUD Programs
A Practitioners' Guide to the Labyrinth

Edited by **George Weidenfeller** and **Julie McGovern**

Forum on Affordable Housing and Community Development Law

Cover design by 7G Design LLC.

The materials contained herein represent the opinions and views of the authors and/or the editors, and should not be construed to be the views or opinions of the law firms or companies with whom such persons are in partnership with, associated with, or employed by the American Bar Association, nor of the ABA Forum on Affordable Housing and Community Development Law unless adopted pursuant to the bylaws of the Association.

Nothing contained in this book is to be considered as the rendering of legal advice for specific cases, and readers are responsible for obtaining such advice from their own legal counsel. This book and any forms and agreements herein are intended for educational and informational purposes only.

© 2012 American Bar Association. All rights reserved.

No part of this publication may be reproduced, stored in a retrieval system, or transmitted in any form or by any means, electronic, mechanical, photocopying, recording, or otherwise, without the prior written permission of the publisher. For permission contact the ABA Copyrights & Contracts Department, copyright@americanbar.org or via fax at (312) 988-6030.

16 15 14 13 13   5 4 3 2 1

Library of Congress Cataloging-in-Publication Data

Navigating HUD programs / Julie McGovern and George L. Weidenfeller, Editors.
   p. cm.
   Includes bibliographical references and index.
   1. United States. Dept. of Housing and Urban Development. 2. Public housing—Law and legislation—United States. I. McGovern, Julie S. II. Weidenfeller, George L. III. Title: Navigating Housing and Urban Development programs.
KF5729.N38 2012
363.5'80973—dc23   2012017504

ISBN: 978-1-61438-575-2

Discounts are available for books ordered in bulk. Special consideration is given to state bars, CLE programs, and other bar-related organizations. Inquire at Book Publishing, ABA Publishing, American Bar Association, 321 North Clark Street, Chicago, Illinois 60654-7598.

www.ShopABA.org

Contents

Preface xix
About the Editors xxi
About the Contributors xxiii
Introduction xxix

Chapter 1
FHA Multifamily Programs: General Overview and Recent Developments ...1
Brianne N. Schwanitz and Charles C. Bissinger, Jr.
   I. Introduction 1
  II. Hallmarks of HUD Programs 6
     A. Eligible Projects 6
     B. Eligible Borrowers 6
     C. First-Lien Requirement 7
     D. Mortgageable Interest 7
     E. Maximum Loan Amounts 9
     F. Large Loan Limits 12
     G. Mortgage Term 13
     H. Prepayment Restrictions 14
     I. Cost Certification 15
        1. New Construction and Substantial Rehabilitation Projects 16
        2. Refinancing Projects 17
     J. Reserve for Replacements, Mortgage Insurance Premiums, and HUD Fees 17
        1. Reserve for Replacements 17
        2. Mortgage Insurance Premiums (MIP) 18
        3. Escrowing for Taxes/Property Insurance Premiums/Mortgage Insurance Premiums 19
        4. FHA Application Fee 19
        5. FHA Inspection Fee 20
     K. Defaults 20
     L. Assumability/Transfer of Physical Assets 21
     M. Prevailing Wage Requirements 23
     N. Subordinate Financing 24
     O. Commercial Space 26

III. HUD's Active Insurance Programs 27
   A. Insurance of Advances (New Construction and Substantial
      Rehabilitation) 27
      1. New Construction versus Substantial Rehabilitation 27
      2. Early Start Procedures 29
      3. Borrower Equity and Escrow Requirements 30
         a. Front-Money Escrow 30
         b. Working Capital Escrow 31
         c. Operating Deficit Escrow 32
         d. Off-site Escrow 32
         e. Demolition Escrow 33
      4. Assurance of Completion 33
      5. Minimum Property Standards 33
      6. Procedures for Advances 34
      7. Change Orders 34
      8. Mortgage Increases 35
      9. Final Endorsement 35
     10. Program Variations 36
         a. Section 207 36
         b. Section 220 36
         c. Section 221(d)(3) 37
         d. Section 231 38
   B. Insurance Upon Completion (New Construction or Substantial
      Rehabilitation) 39
   C. Section 223(f) (Acquisition or Refinancing) 40
      1. Eligible Projects 41
      2. Maximum Insurable Mortgage 41
      3. Cash Out Refinance 42
      4. Reserve for Replacements; Repairs 43
      5. Other Requirements and Restrictions 44
   D. Section 223(a)(7) (Acquisition or Refinancing) 45
   E. Section 223(d) (Operating Loss Loan) 46
   F. Section 241 (Supplemental Loan) 47
IV. Approval Process 48
   A. New Construction/Substantial Rehabilitation 48
      1. Pre-application 49
         a. A/E Review 50
         b. Valuation Review 50
         c. Mortgage Credit Review 52
      2. Letter of Invitation 53
      3. Firm Commitment 54
         a. A/E Review 54
         b. Cost Review 55
         c. Valuation Review 55
         d. Mortgage Credit Review 56
         e. Management Review 57

       B. Acquisition or Refinancing under Section 223(f) 58
          1. A/E Review 58
          2. Cost Review 59
          3. Valuation Review 59
          4. Mortgage Credit Review 60
          5. Management Review 60
       C. Issuance of the Firm Commitment 60
  V. Closing Process 60
       A. Borrower Entity's Organizational Documents 61
       B. Title and Survey 61
       C. Closing Documents 62
          1. Security Instrument 62
          2. Note 64
          3. Regulatory Agreement 65
             a. Reserve for Replacements and Residual Receipts 66
             b. Distributions 66
             c. Financial Reporting Requirements 66
             d. Management 67
             e. Actions Requiring HUD Approval 67
             f. Nonrecourse Provisions 68
          4. Lender's Certificate/Request for Endorsement 68
          5. Building Loan Agreement 68
          6. Construction Contract 69
          7. Opinion of Borrower's Counsel 70
          8. Additional Documents 70
       D. Construction Period and Final Closing 71
 VI. Conclusion 72

Chapter 2
Multifamily Housing Preservation 73
  John Daly
  I. FHA Mortgage Insurance—Incontestable? 74
 II. FHA Mortgage Insurance 75
       A. Full Faith and Credit of the United States? 75
       B. Funding for FHA Mortgage Insurance Claims 75
       C. NHA Section 223 76
       D. NHA Section 207 78
       E. Statutes "Related" to NHA 80
       F. Preservation of Rental Assistance Payments 81
       G. Funding Source Transfers 81
       H. NHA Section 220 82
       I. NHA Section 221 83
       J. NHA Section 231 84
       K. NHA Section 236 84
       L. NHA Section 241 87
       M. NHA Section 250 87

III.	Flexible Subsidy Program	88
IV.	Emergency Low Income Housing Preservation Act of 1987	90
V.	Low Income Housing Preservation and Resident Homeownership Act	90
VI.	Portfolio Reengineering Demonstrations and Multifamily Assisted Housing Reform and Affordability Act of 1997	91
VII.	Project Loan Funding Sources	94
VIII.	Low-Income Housing Tax Credits	94
IX.	Conclusion	96

Chapter 3
Health-Care and Hospital Financing 99
Kristin M. Neun and Andrea R. Ponsor

- I. Introduction 99
- II. Section 232 100
  - A. Authority and Guidance 100
  - B. General Terms and Requirements 101
  - C. Eligible Facilities 102
    1. Nursing Homes—also known as Skilled-Nursing Facilities (SNF) 102
    2. Intermediate-Care/Board-and-Care Facilities (IC Facilities) 102
    3. Board-and-Care Facilities 102
    4. Assisted-Living Facilities (ALF) 103
  - D. Types of 232 Loans 103
    1. 232 New Construction and Substantial Rehabilitation 103
    2. 232/223(f) 103
    3. 232/223(a)(7) 104
    4. 232/241 104
  - E. LEAN Processing for New Section 232 Loans 105
    1. Application 105
    2. Application Processing 105
    3. From Commitment to Closing 106
    4. Special Processing—Portfolio Transactions 106
  - F. Special Issues in Underwriting and Closing 232 Loans 108
    1. Owner/Operator/Management Agent Structure 108
       - a. Permitted Structures 108
         - i. Operating Lease 108
           - A. Operating Lease Requirements 108
           - B. Regulatory Agreements for Operators 109
           - C. Operator Security Agreement 109
         - ii. Management Agent 109
    2. Security for the Loan 110
       - a. Deposit Account Control Agreements 110
       - b. Collateral Including License/Certificate of Need 111

　　　　　3. Accounts Receivable Financing 112
　　　　　　　a. General Program Guidance and Requirements 112
　　　　　4. Master Leases/Portfolio Transactions 113
　　　G. Asset Management Issues 114
　　　　　1. REAC 115
　　　　　2. Transfers of Physical Assets 115
　　　　　3. Distressed Assets 115
　II. Section 242 116
　　　A. Authority and Guidance 116
　　　B. General Terms and Requirements 118
　　　　　1. Eligible Facilities 118
　　　　　2. Standard Types of Facilities 118
　　　　　3. Types of FHA-Insured Hospital Loan Products 120
　　　C. Processing/Underwriting Issues 121
　　　　　1. Preliminary Meeting/Inquiry 121
　　　　　2. Preliminary Review 121
　　　　　3. Resolve Issues or Schedule Pre-application Meeting 123
　　　　　4. Application Process 123
　　　　　　　a. Underwriting/Financing Issues 124
　　　　　　　　　i. Mortgage Reserve Fund 124
　　　　　　　　　ii. CON/Financial Feasibility Study 124
　　　　　　　b. Regulatory and Operational Requirements 125
　　　　　　　　　i. Covenants 125
　　　　　　　　　ii. Insurance Requirements 125
　　　　　　　　　iii. Financial Reporting 126
　　　　　　　　　iv. Affiliate Relationships 126
　　　　　5. Construction and Construction Completion/Final
　　　　　　　Endorsement 126
　　　G. Asset Management Issues 126
　　　　　1. TPA 127
　　　　　2. Operating Difficulties/Business Plan 127
　　　　　3. Risk Mitigation/Priority Watch List Default 127
　　　　　4. Problem Solving 127

Chapter 4
HUD Section 202 and Mixed Finance Guide for Development and Operation of Supportive Housing for the Elderly 129
Karen Sherman and Michael Decina
　I. Introduction 129
　II. Statutory, Regulatory, and Programmatic Authority 130
　　　A. Statutory Authority 130
　　　B. Regulatory Authority 131
　　　C. Programmatic Guidance and Authorities 132
　　　D. The Process from NOFA to Closing 132

III. Mixed Finance 133
   A. Ownership Structure 133
   B. Structure of Loan to Partnership 134
   C. Timing of the 202 Capital Advance 134
   D. Additional Unit Projects 135
   E. Structural Issues to Be Addressed to Maximize Tax Credit Equity . 136
   F. Secondary Financing 136
IV. Refinance and Preservation of Projects with Section 202 Direct Loans . 138
V. The Future and New Trends 140
Appendix A: Diagram of NOFA Process 141
Appendix B: Example of Ownership Structure for Mixed Finance Program ... 142
Appendix C: Diagram of Loan Structure 143
Appendix D: Rider to Be Utilized When Using AHP and 202 Funds 146
Appendix E: Refinance Sample Riders Used in Various HUD Field Offices ... 150
Appendix F: HUD-Required Provision Rider 151

Chapter 5
Navigating HUD Programs: The 2530 Previous Participation Approval Process 155
Elizabeth H. Friedgut and Dianne S. Pickersgill
I. General Overview 155
   A. Purpose of Process 155
   B. Legal Authority 156
II. Triggers of the 2530 Process 157
   A. Covered Projects 157
   B. Property Submissions 158
   C. Organization Structure Changes 159
III. Definition of Principal for Whom HUD Approval Is Required 161
IV. Disclosure of Principal Participation History, Certification, and Signature 163
V. Special Situations 166
   A. Limited-Liability Corporate Investors 166
   B. Passive Investors 167
   C. Foreign Nationals 168
VI. Due Diligence and Flags 169
VII. 2530 Application Submission Form—Paper or APPS 171
VIII. 2530 Review by HUD Field Offices and HUD Headquarters 173
IX. Appeal Process 175
X. Continuing Trouble Points for Practitioners 175

Chapter 6
Community Development 177
Robert S. Kenison
I. Scope 177

II. Community Development Block Grants (CDBG) 178
   A. From "Categoritis" to Block Grants 178
   B. Indicia of a Block Grant 179
   C. The Community Development Block Grant Profile 179
   D. Activity Eligibility 179
   E. Programmatic Eligibility 180
   F. Program Administration 182
   G. Program Requirements 182
III. HOME, a "Community Development" Housing Program 183
   A. Fund Allocation 183
   B. Eligible Activities, Costs 184
   C. Community Housing Development Organizations (CHDOs) 184
   D. Program Administration 185
   E. Homeownership 186
IV. Homeless Programs 187
   A. More Community Development Programs 187
   B. Program Typologies 188
   C. Some Recurring Issues, Legal and Policy 189
V. Other Community Development Programs, Other Block Grants 190
VI. "Now vee may perhaps to begin. Yes?" 190
VII. Commonalities 192

Chapter 7
Community Planning and Development: Emerging Neighborhood Stabilization Programs 195
Laura Schwarz
I. Program Overview 197
   A. Neighborhood Stabilization Program 1 197
   B. Neighborhood Stabilization Program 2 199
   C. Neighborhood Stabilization Program 3 200
   D. General Sources of Guidance 201
II. Eligible Partners, Properties, and Uses 202
   A. Eligible Partners 202
      1. Grantees 202
      2. Consortium Members 203
      3. Subrecipients 204
      4. Developers 205
      5. Contractors 206
   B. Eligible Properties 206
      1. Foreclosed Properties 207
      2. Abandoned Properties 209
      3. Vacant Properties 210
      4. Timing Considerations 211
   C. Eligible Uses 212
      1. Eligible Use (A): Financing Mechanisms 213

2. Eligible Use (B): Purchase and Rehabilitation of Foreclosed and Abandoned Properties 214
  3. Eligible Uses (C) and (D): Land Banking and Demolition 215
  4. Eligible Use (E): Redevelopment of Demolished or Vacant Property 216
 III. Affordability Restrictions 217
   A. Rental Housing 218
   B. Homeownership Units 219
   C. Combining NSP Funds with Other Funding Sources 222
 IV. Cross-Cutting Federal Requirements 223
  V. Conclusions 227

Chapter 8
Public Housing Development—Mixed Finance in the Context of Historical Trends 231
Roberta L. Rubin
  I. Introduction 231
 II. The Public Housing Program 231
   A. A False Start: The National Industrial Recovery Act 231
   B. A New Beginning: The United States Housing Act of 1937 232
     1. Original Goals—Slum Clearance and Economic Stimulus 232
     2. Federal Financing—Local Development and Operation 234
     3. Slum Clearance and Public Housing 235
     4. Desirable Housing for the Working Poor 235
   C. Evolution of the Public Housing Program—Decline in the Urban Core 237
     1. Statutory and Regulatory Changes 237
        a. 1940s and 1950s: Slum Clearance and Urban Redevelopment 237
        b. 1961–1983: Brooke Amendment, Federal Preferences and "the Projects" 238
   D. A New World of Public Housing Redevelopment: HOPE VI, QHWRA, and Mixed Finance 243
     1. Traditional Public Housing Development 243
     2. Origins of the HOPE VI Program 244
     3. "Mixed Finance" and HOPE VI 245
     4. Future Funding: HOPE VI and Choice Neighborhoods 247
     5. Capital and RHF Funds: Additional and Continuing Sources .. 248
     6. Basics of "Mixed Finance" 250
        a. Leverage 250
        b. Income Mixing, Reduced Density, and Deconcentration of Poverty 251
        c. Proportionality 252
        d. Applicability of Public Housing Requirements to Mixed-Finance Developments 253

III. Mechanics of Public Housing Redevelopment in the Twenty-First
    Century 253
    A. Statutory Underpinnings 253
    B. Regulatory and Sub-regulatory Guidance 254
    C. HUD Processing in Mixed-Finance Projects 257
        1. HUD Review Process—Disposition, Mixed-Finance
           Proposal, and Project Review Panel 257
        2. Mixed-Finance Evidentiary Review and Funding 260
    D. Mixed-Finance Documentation: Key HUD Regulatory
       Documents 262
        1. Regulatory and Operating Agreement (Rental Developments) . 262
        2. Declaration of Restrictive Covenants (All Mixed-Finance
           Projects) 263
        3. Mixed-Finance ACC Amendment (Rental) and Mixed-Finance
           Addendum to Grant Agreement (Homeownership) 263
        4. Evidence of Cooperation Agreement (Rental) 264
    E. Mixed-Finance Evidentiaries 265
        1. Opinion of Counsel 265
        2. Management and Occupancy Documents 265
        3. Organizational and Financing Documents 266
        4. Site Control and Zoning 266
        5. PHA Certifications 267
    F. Cross-Cutting Legal Requirements 267
    G. Public Housing Authorities as Principals of Mixed-Finance
       Owners 269
    H. Mixed-Finance Homeownership Development 271
IV. Financial and Operational Issues for Mixed-Finance Projects 273
    A. Financial Impact of Public Housing Program Limitations 273
        1. Tenant-Paid Rent and Utility Allowances 273
        2. Operating Subsidy and Calculation of Project Expense Level
           and Utility Expense Level 275
        3. Commencement of Operating Subsidy 276
    B. Using Public Housing Capital to Collateralize Bonds 277
    C. Capital Fund Financings 277
    D. Using Project-Based Vouchers to Enhance Project Feasibility 280
    E. Educating Funders 280
V. Conclusion 281

Chapter 9
Public Housing Operations 283
Melissa K. Worden and William J. Ward
I. Introduction 283
II. History of the Public Housing Program 284
III. Structure of Public Housing Authorities and HUD's Role in
     Their Funding and Regulation 287

      A. General Structure, Powers, and Duties of Housing Authorities 287
      B. Annual Contributions Contracts 288
III. Procurement Requirements for Housing Authorities 290
IV. Form of Housing Authority Contracts and Required Provisions 290
      A. Form of Contracts 291
      B. Fixed-Price Contracts 291
      C. Cost-Reimbursement Contracts 291
      D. Indefinite Delivery Contracts 291
      E. Time and Materials and Labor-Hour Contracts 292
      F. Letter Contracts 292
      G. Prohibited Contracts 292
      H. Mandatory Contract Clauses 293
V. Public Housing Funding 293
      A. Capital Funds 294
      B. Use of Capital Funds 295
      C. Replacement Housing Factor Funds 297
      D. Leveraging Capital Funds 298
      E. Time Line for Use of Capital Funds 298
      F. Operating Funds 299
      G. Operating Subsidy 299
      H. Moving to Work Agencies 302
VI. Operation of Public Housing 303
      A. Admissions and Tenant Selection Policies 303
      B. Designated Housing 305
      C. Determining Tenant Rent and Calculating Tenant Income 305
      D. Determining Income-Based Rent 306
      E. Flat, Market-Based Rent 307
      F. Tenant Utility Expenses 307
      G. Occupancy Standards and Requirements 308
         1. Public Housing Tenant Leases 308
         2. Tenant's Right to Grieve Housing Authority Actions 309
         3. Community-Service and Economic Self-Sufficiency
            Requirements 309
         4. Pet Ownership in Public Housing 310
VII. Demolition, Disposition, and Conversion of Public Housing 311
VIII. Monitoring and Oversight of Public Housing 312
      A. Enforcement through the Annual Contributions Contract and Grant
         Agreements 312
      B. Monitoring through Public Housing Agency Plans 312
      C. Monitoring through the Public Housing Assessment System 314
      D. Physical Condition Assessment 315
      E. Financial Condition Assessment 315
      F. Management Operations Assessment 316
      G. Capital Fund Program Assessment 317

H. HUD Office of Inspector General Audits 317
I. Voluntary Compliance Agreements 317
IX. Conclusion 318

Chapter 10
The Section 8 Housing Assistance Program **319**
Michael H. Reardon and Tatiana Gutierrez Abendschein
I. Project-Based Assistance Programs 320
II. Tenant-Based Assistance Programs 322
III. Common Features of All Section 8 Programs 326
IV. Section 8 Project-Based Contract Renewals 327
V. MAHRA Renewal Options 328
   A. Option 1: Mark-Up-to-Market 329
   B. Option 2: OCAF or Budget-Based 330
   C. Option 3: Referral to OAHP 330
   D. Option 4: Exception Projects 331
   E. Option 5: Preservation and Demonstration Projects 332
   F. Option 6: Opt Out 332
VI. Chapter 15 333
VII. Annual Increases 334
VIII. Other HUD Rental Assistance Programs 334

Chapter 11
Looking to the Future—The Heat Is On: Trimming HUD's Energy Bill for Public and Privately Owned Assisted Housing **337**
N. Linda Goldstein
I. The Mark-to-Market's Green Initiative and the Green Retrofit Program—Early Efforts to Make HUD-Assisted Housing Energy-Efficient 340
Inez Tremain
II. Fannie Mae's Green Refinance Plus Mortgage Program 342
Michael Johnson
III. Practical Guidance for Counsel—More on Green Assessments; Understanding Utility Allowances; Implementation of the HUD/DOE Memorandum of Understanding Related to Weatherization 344
Kevin McMahan and Robert Hazelton
   A. Understand the Green Assessment 344
   B. Understanding Utility Allowances 346
   C. Implementation of the HUD/DOE Memorandum of Understanding Related to Weatherization 348
IV. HUD Requirements for Implementing Energy-Savings Projects at Housing Authorities 350
George Weidenfeller and Mattye Goulsby Jones
V. In Summary 353

Chapter 12
Resolution of Troubled or Defaulted HUD-Insured Multifamily and Health-Care Loans 355
La Fonte Nesbitt and Stephen D. Niles
- I. Introduction 355
- II. Overview of HUD Multifamily and Health-Care Loan Programs 356
- III. Overview of Government National Mortgage Association's Role in HUD's Multifamily and Health-Care Loan Programs 359
- IV. Options 360
- V. Refinancing under § 223(a)(7) 361
- VI. Mortgage Modification 363
- VII. Partial Payments of Claim (PPC) 367
  - 1. The Recent Reemergence of HUD's PPC Approach 368
  - 2. Qualifying for a PPC 368
  - 3. PPC Proposal 369
  - 4. Loan Restructuring Issues 370
  - 5. Tax Considerations 372
  - 6. PPC Processing and Closing Process 373
  - 7. PPC Conclusion 374
- VIII. HUD Note Sales 374
- IX. Conclusion 378

Chapter 13
Cross-Cutting Requirements: Federal Requirements Impacting HUD Programs 379
Mary Grace Folwell, Amy M. Glassman, Amy M. McClain, Joy C. O'Brien, Nydia M. Pouves, Margaret H. Tucker, and Sharon Wilson Géno
- I. Introduction 379
- II. Procurement by HUD Grantees and Subgrantees 380
  - A. Procurement Standards and General Requirements 380
  - B. Competition 382
  - C. Methods of Procurement 383
  - D. Bonding Requirements 384
  - E. Cost and Price Analysis 385
  - F. Required Contract Provisions 385
- III. Labor Provisions 386
  - A. Davis-Bacon Statute 386
  - B. Application of Davis-Bacon Related Acts 386
  - C. Community Development Block Grant Program 386
  - D. HOME 387
  - E. Public Housing and Section 8/Housing Choice Voucher Programs . 388
  - F. Indian Housing Block Grants/NAHASDA 390
  - G. Demolition 390
  - H. Character of the Work 391
  - I. Contract Work Hours and Safety Standards Act 392

		J.	Copeland Act 392

        J. Copeland Act 392
        K. Fair Labor Standards Act 393
   IV. Environmental Requirements 393
        A. Overview 393
        B. Environmental Review Process 394
        C. Exempt Activities 394
        D. Categorical Exclusion 395
        E. Other Environmental Laws and Authorities 395
        F. Environmental Assessment 397
        G. Environmental Impact Statement 398
        H. HUD as Responsible Entity 398
    V. Relocation Requirements 399
        A. Federal Relocation Law 399
            1. Overview 399
            2. Relocation Plans and Surveys 399
            3. Notice Requirements 400
                a. General Information Notice 400
                b. Notice of Eligibility or Notice of Non-displacement 400
                c. 90-Day Notice 401
                d. Other Notices 401
        B. Displaced Persons 401
        C. Exclusions from Displaced Persons Definition 402
        D. Relocation Benefits 404
            1. Business Occupants 404
            2. Residential Occupants 405
                a. Tenants 405
                b. Homeowners 407
            3. Last-Resort Housing 407
        E. Grievances and Waivers of Benefits 408
        F. Section 104(d) 408
   VI. Subsidy Layering 408
  VII. Funding and Grant Issues 410
        A. Grant Application Requirements 410
        B. Funding Decisions 411
        C. The Anti-Deficiency Act 413
        D. The Cash Management Improvement Act 413
        E. Grant Disbursements 414
 VIII. Regulatory Waivers 415
   IX. Energy Star/Energy-Efficiency Programs 415
        A. Public and Indian Housing 416
        B. Affordable Housing Grant Programs 417
    X. Section 3 417
        A. Applicability 418
        B. Thresholds 419

        C. Compliance Requirements 419
        D. Reporting and Monitoring 421
        E. Complaints 421
  XI. Conclusion 421

Chapter 14
Civil Rights Programs Administered and Enforced by HUD 423
    Harry Carey
    I. History of Civil Rights in Housing 423
   II. Current Civil Rights Requirements in Housing and Community
       Development Programs and Activities 426
       A. Title VI of the Civil Rights Act of 1964 426
       B. Section 504 of the Rehabilitation Act of 1973 427
       C. Section 109 of the Housing and Community Development
          Act of 1974 428
       D. The Fair Housing Act 429
          1. Prohibited Conduct under the Fair Housing Act 429
              a. Sale, Rental, and Advertising Practices 430
              b. Reasonable Accommodations and Reasonable
                 Modifications 431
              c. Failure to Design and Construct Certain New
                 Multifamily Housing to Be Accessible to and Usable
                 by Persons with Disabilities 432
              d. Discrimination in Residential Real Estate–Related
                 Transactions 433
              e. Discrimination in the Provision of Brokerage Services 433
              f. Unlawful Interference, Coercion, and Intimidation 433
          2. Exemptions to the Provisions of the Fair Housing Act 433
  III. The HUD Process of Enforcement in Civil Rights Cases 434
       A. Programs of Federal Financial Assistance 434
       B. The Fair Housing Act 435
  IV. Administration of HUD Programs and Activities 439
       A. Executive Order 11,063 439
       B. Affirmatively Furthering Fair Housing 439
          1. HUD Project Site-Selection Criteria 441
          2. Affirmative Fair Housing Marketing 441
          3. Affirmatively Furthering and Public Housing Tenant
             Selection 442
          4. Community Development Programs 443
          5. Fair Housing Poster 444
          6. Economic Opportunities for Low- and Very Low-Income
             Persons 444

Chapter 15
Compliance and Enforcement **445**
  Margarita Maisonet
  I. Introduction 445
  II. Office of Community Planning and Development 447
      A. Community Development Block Grant (CDBG) 447
      B. Home Investment Partnerships Program (HOME) 448
  III. Office of Fair Housing and Equal Opportunity 448
  IV. Office of Healthy Homes and Lead Hazard Control 449
      A. Lead Safe Housing Rule 450
      B. Lead Disclosure Rule 450
  V. Office of Housing 451
      A. Single-Family Housing 451
      B. Multifamily Housing 452
      C. Mortgagee Review Board 452
      D. Limited Denials of Participation (LDPs) 453
      E. Other Tools 453
  VI. Office of Public and Indian Housing 453
      A. PHAS Designations 453
      B. Declarations of Substantial Default 454
      C. Remedies for Substantial Default 455
  VII. Departmental Enforcement Center 456
      A. Compliance Division 456
      B. Operations Division 457
      C. Satellite Offices 457
      D. Office of Program Enforcement 458
      E. Civil Money Penalties 458
  VIII. Office of Hearings and Appeals 459
      A. Office of Appeals 459
      B. Office of Administrative Law Judges 459
  IX. Office of the Inspector General (OIG) 460
      A. Office of Audit 461
      B. Office of Investigation 461

Chapter 16
Epilogue—Looking to the Future **463**

Index **467**

Preface

> Daedalus built the Labyrinth, famous throughout the world. Once inside, one would go endlessly along its twisting paths without ever finding the exit . . . . There was no possible way to escape. In whatever direction they ran they might be running straight to the monster; if they stood still he [the Minotaur] might at any moment emerge from the maze.
>
> —Edith Hamilton, *Mythology*[1]

The realm of U.S. Department of Housing & Urban Development (HUD) laws and regulations certainly is not as perilous as Daedalus's Labyrinth, but practitioners may still confront uncertainty about how to navigate these requirements in an effective manner. This book is designed to help practitioners identify a clear path for achieving their objectives, and to enable them to overcome the HUD-related challenges they may encounter.

We would like to thank the highly knowledgeable authors who took time from their busy housing practices to write this book. Working with such professionals has been a joy, and we hope you benefit from their expertise in navigating the maze.

—The Editors

---

1. EDITH HAMILTON, MYTHOLOGY (Boston, Toronto & London: Little Brown & Co., 1942) at 212.

About the Editors

Julie S. McGovern is a member of Reno & Cavanaugh, PLLC, whose practice focuses on affordable housing development and operation, with a concentration on public housing authorities and rural lending. Julie provides comprehensive representation in mixed-finance transactions, from negotiation of the development agreement, through multiple phased closings and regulatory and legal issues arising in operation of mixed finance units.

Julie also represents clients on the use public housing funding streams, such Operating, Capital, HOPE VI and Choice Neighborhood Funds, both on their own and used in conjunction with low-income housing tax credits (LIHTC) and bonds, local loan programs, other HUD financing, such as HOME and CDBG Funds, project based-vouchers, and FHA-insured financing, as well as Federal Home Loan Bank's affordable housing program (AHP). She also has extensive experience in advising PHAs on the structuring and use of public housing affiliates, procurement, and conflict of interest.

A member of the Governing Committee of the American Bar Association Forum on Affordable Housing and Community Development Law and a member of the National Association of Housing and Community Development Officials (NAHRO) and the Housing and Development Law Institute (HDLI), Julie regularly speaks and advises clients on the complex issues arising in low-income housing tax credit transactions, the use of affiliates in public housing development, modifying mixed-finance transactions for the operating subsidy and asset-based management requirements, project-based vouchers, and the Neighborhood Stabilization Program (NSP).

Julie is a graduate of the University of Pennsylvania School of Law and the University of Virginia.

George Weidenfeller is a partner in the law firm of Reno & Cavanaugh, PLLC. He represents owners, developers, managers, lenders, and public housing authorities on residential development; FHA transactions; asset management; program, regulatory and fair housing enforcement; Federal procurement; ethics; and personnel law.

George was previously a member of the Goulston and Storrs Real Estate group, with a particular focus on Affordable Housing and Economic Development. He served for more than 16 years as Deputy General Counsel and Acting General Counsel, in the HUD Office of General Counsel in Washington D.C., under six HUD secretaries. During that period, he provided substantive legal advice on all HUD programs, supervised a staff of more than 700 professionals, and managed a budget of more than

$75 million. Before becoming Deputy General Counsel, he was Special Assistant to the Assistant Secretary for Housing and a staff attorney for HUD in Boston and Boston Redevelopment Authority.

George is a member of the ABA Affordable Housing and Community Development Forum Governing Committee and chairs the Forum's HUD Practice Committee; is a member of the ULI Workforce Housing Council; and is on the National Housing Conference Board of Trustees. He holds a BA from the University of Massachusetts, JD from Suffolk Law, MPA from the University of Southern California, and an MLT (tax) from Georgetown Law.

About the Contributors

Charles C. Bissinger, Jr., a partner in the Cincinnati, Ohio, office of Vorys, Sater, Seymour and Pease LLP, has over 30 years of experience in representing lenders, borrowers, developers, investors, and contractors in FHA-insured financings for multifamily and health-care projects. Mr. Bissinger served as co-chair of the FHA Closing Documents Workgroup of the Mortgage Bankers Association, preparing and coordinating industry comments on FHA's new Multifamily Form Closing Documents and related changes in HUD regulations, published in 2011. Mr. Bissinger also played a leading role in the preparation and coordination of comments made by the HUD Practice Group of the American Bar Association's Affordable Housing Forum on FHA's new *Multifamily Closing Guide*, also published in 2011. Mr. Bissinger is a frequent speaker on topics related to FHA mortgage insurance programs.

Harry Carey served in the Office of General Counsel at the Department of Housing and Urban Development (HUD) for more than 36 years, retiring in 2007. Mr. Carey has specialized in civil rights and fair housing laws and their impact on housing and community development programs and activities. He served as the Assistant General Counsel for Fair Housing Enforcement and the Associate General Counsel for Fair Housing. Mr. Carey participated in drafting of the Fair Housing Amendments Act of 1988 and led a team of HUD staff in the development of regulations implementing the Fair Housing Act. Mr. Carey is now working with the National Fair Housing Training Academy and National Association of Housing and Redevelopment Officials (NAHRO).

John Daly served in HUD's Office of General Counsel for 35 years as an attorney-advisor for FHA and Ginnie Mae programs and in-house tax counsel for HUD programs. From 1990 until retirement in July 2011, he was responsible for legal support of all FHA mortgage insurance programs as the Associate General Counsel for Insured Housing.

Michael Decina is a shareholder with Kantor Taylor Nelson Boyd & Evatt PC whose practice emphasizes HUD Programs, including Section 202/811s and Section 202/811 Mixed-Finance transactions, Section 8 matters, and loan closings and mortgage assumptions utilizing HUD and FHA/GNMA loan products. Prior to joining Kantor Taylor, Michael was an attorney at the U.S. Department of Housing and Urban Development (HUD), first as an attorney-advisor in HUD Region III and later as an Associate Regional Counsel in HUD Region X. Further information can be found at www.kantortaylor.com.

Mary Grace Folwell, an associate with Ballard Spahr LLP and a member of the firm's Housing Group, advises clients on HUD regulatory and statutory matters and compliance with HUD programs. She has considerable experience in a variety of HUD programs and requirements, including the Section 8 Housing Choice Voucher Program, the MTW Program, the Uniform Relocation Act, OIG audits, Davis-Bacon, HOME and CDBG Programs, the NSP Program, fair housing compliance, and formation and compliance of nonprofit affiliates.

Elizabeth H. Friedgut is a partner in the Chicago office of DLA Piper. Before joining DLA Piper, Ms. Friedgut was as an attorney with the U.S. Department of Housing and Urban Development in Washington, D.C., for seven years. Ms. Friedgut has been designated an Illinois Super Lawyer as the result of research projects conducted jointly by *Law & Politics* and *Chicago* magazines. The Leading Lawyers Network has named her among the Top 50 Women Real Estate–Related Lawyers in Illinois.

Sharon Wilson Géno is a partner with Ballard Spahr LLP in Washington, D.C. Ms. Géno focuses her practice on affordable housing and real estate transactions, legislative advocacy, general corporate and nonprofit organizations, and administrative law. She has represented housing authorities on HOPE VI and mixed-finance transactions, administrative and regulatory issues, the MTW Program, and the borrowing of private monies secured by a pledge of Public Housing Capital Funds.

Amy M. Glassman represents public housing authorities and other recipients of HUD funds in regulatory, administrative, transactional, and related matters. An associate with Ballard Spahr LLP and a member of the firm's Housing Group, Ms. Glassman has extensive experience assisting housing authorities with HUD regulatory and statutory compliance issues.

N. Linda Goldstein is a partner at the law firm of Reno & Cavanaugh in Washington, D.C. Ms. Goldstein is a past chair of the American Bar Association Forum on Affordable Housing and Community Development Law and is presently co-chair of the National Leased Housing Association, Green/Energy Committee. Ms. Goldstein focuses her practice on affordable housing and economic development, mixed-use real estate transactions, energy efficiency and renewable energy, community development financial institutions and the mandates of the Community Reinvestment Act. Ms. Goldstein began her career with HUD.

Tatiana Gutierrez Abendschein is an associate at Nixon Peabody LLP. Tatiana commenced her career in affordable housing at Georgetown University Law Center's Harrison Institute for Public Law in 2002. For the past eight years, Tatiana has focused her practice on HUD regulatory matters, including Section 8 project-based contract renewals, restrictions, and assignments.

Robert Hazelton is president of the Dominion Due Diligence Group, which is headquartered in Richmond, Virginia, and is a third-party due diligence consultant for the HUD-FHA-MAP mortgage insurance industry. In addition, the firm has a full-service environmental and engineering real estate due diligence team and healthcare group.

Michael Johnson is a vice president at the mortgage banking firm Walker & Dunlop, one of the largest Fannie Mae DUS™, Freddie Mac Program Plus,® and HUD lenders. Walker & Dunlop's multifamily products include market-rate apartments, affordable apartments, manufactured housing developments, seniors housing, and student housing.

Mattye Gouldsby Jones is a partner at the law firm of Coats Rose, PC, in Dallas, Texas. Ms. Gouldsby is a past chair of the American Bar Association Forum on Affordable Housing and Community Development Law. Prior to joining Coats Rose, Ms. Jones served as senior vice president, chief operating officer, and general counsel of the Dallas Housing Authority.

Bob Kenison, upon completing two years as Peace Corps volunteer in Colombia, South America, joined HUD's Office of General Counsel, where he served the last 30 years of his 41-year HUD career heading up the team of legal advisers responsible for assisted housing, including public housing, Section 8, and Section 202, and for the programs discussed in the chapter on community development.

Margarita Maisonet worked at HUD from 1991 to 2006. She joined the Departmental Enforcement Center as the Chicago Satellite Office Director in 2000. In 2003 she was detailed to the Departmental Enforcement Center in HUD Headquarters and in 2004 was appointed to the position of Director. While working in this capacity, she also served as a voting member of the Federal Housing Administration's Mortgagee Review Board and as the Department's Debarring Official. Ms. Maisonet is a partner at Federal Practice Group, LLC.

Amy M. McClain, as a partner at Ballard Spahr LLP and a member of the firm's Housing Group, primarily represents public housing authorities and affordable-housing developers in the context of mixed-finance transactions and is often engaged in matters addressing traditional real estate issues intertwined with low-income housing development.

Kevin McMahan is managing partner of the Federal Practice Group, LLC, which consults with the federal government and state governments concerning low-income multifamily rental housing programs, including energy-efficiency programs.

La Fonte Nesbitt is a partner in the Washington, D.C., office of Holland & Knight LLP. He has more than 23 years of experience with all manners of real estate projects, but his practice emphasizes urban and community development, affordable and multifamily housing, government-related real estate projects and programs, and various types of public-private partnerships and privatization initiatives. Mr. Nesbitt has extensive experience in multifamily housing finance and development, including programs for HUD, Freddie Mac, Fannie Mae, tax-exempt housing bonds, low income housing tax credits, and other affordable housing programs. He serves as counsel to various parties in connection with the acquisition, development, and financing of multifamily housing, retail developments, office buildings, and mixed-use projects, including for-profit and nonprofit developers and owners, investors, lenders, and underwriters, housing authorities, housing finance agencies, and other government and quasi-government agencies. Mr. Nesbitt is a frequent speaker and contributor on affordable housing, military housing, and public-private partnerships, including speaking and moderating many panels at the ABA Forum of Affordable Housing Annual Conference. He currently serves on the District of Columbia, 2012 Comprehensive Housing Strategy Task Force, having been appointed by Mayor Vincent C. Gray.

Stephen ("Steve") Niles joined Klein Hornig LLP as a partner in 2011. Steve has more than 25 years of experience representing for-profit and nonprofit clients in transactional, regulatory, and enforcement matters relating to multifamily housing and community development. Steve assists project owners, sponsors, investors, property management agents, government agencies, and trade associations, among others, with various matters relating to the acquisition, development, financing, and operation of multifamily housing and community development projects. Prior to joining Klein Hornig, Steve was a partner at Holland & Knight and was co-chair of their National Affordable Housing Team. Steve earned an M.S. in real estate from the Johns Hopkins University, a J.D. from the American University, Washington College of Law, and a B.A. from Franklin & Marshall College.

Kristin M. Neun has served as a principal of Hessel, Aluise and Neun, P.C. since 2001. Prior to joining the firm in 1996, Ms. Neun practiced law in the Washington office of Miller, Canfield, Paddock and Stone, P.L.C., and worked at the National Leased Housing Association, the Council for Rural Housing and Development, now known as the Council for Affordable and Rural Housing, respectively. Ms. Neun is active in the ABA Affordable Housing Forum, National Leased Housing Association, and other industry groups.

Joy C. O'Brien's practice focuses on the representation of public housing authorities with respect to mixed-finance real estate transactions, in which she has drafted, negotiated, and prepared the submission of evidentiary and loan documentation to HUD. As an associate with the law firm of Ballard Spahr LLP, she also represents public housing authorities in connection with the disposition and acquisition of their real estate holdings.

Dianne Pickersgill is Of Counsel in the Real Estate Department of Ballard Spahr LLP in Washington, D.C., where she focuses her practice on the representation of public housing authorities and for-profit and nonprofit owners and managers of affordable housing in connection with HUD regulatory compliance matters. She also represents mortgage lenders in a variety of commercial real estate financing transactions, with an emphasis on multifamily project loans.

Andrea R. Ponsor is an associate at Hessel, Aluise and Neun, P.C., where she represents lenders, for-profit and non-profit owners, and developers in a wide range of affordable housing financings and regulatory compliance issues. Ms. Posnor's practice routinely involves negotiating and closing FHA-insured loan financings, advising clients on matters related to Section 8 renewals and modifications, preservation and refinancing of properties financed by HUD and USDA/RD, transfers and ownership restructuring of HUD-assisted properties, and structuring transactions involving public and private sources of green financing. Ms. Posnor was previously an attorney advisor in the HUD Office of Regional Counsel in Atlanta, Georgia, and in the HUD Departmental Enforcement Center Atlanta Satellite Office.

Nydia M. Pouyes represents public housing authorities on a variety of issues, including public housing demolition and disposition and regulatory matters. Ms. Pouyes is an associate with Ballard Spahr LLP's Housing Group. She advises clients on HUD OIG audits and investigations and Section 504 compliance, as well as a variety of other housing-related issues.

Michael H. Reardon is a partner at Nixon Peabody LLP and was previously assistant general counsel for assisted housing at HUD. For more than 20 years, Michael Reardon has concentrated his practice on affordable housing and real estate matters, in particular the public housing and Section 8 housing assistance programs, the Section 202 program for the elderly, the Section 811 program for persons with disabilities, and, most recently, the HOPE VI and mixed-finance public housing development programs. Mr. Reardon provided the legal basis and framework for HUD's implementation of the HOPE VI and mixed-finance public housing development program.

Roberta L. Rubin is Of Counsel at Klein Hornig, LLP in Boston, Massachusetts, and adjunct professor at Tufts University and at Northeastern University School of Law. In her legal practice, she specializes in complex, multifaceted affordable housing and community development transactions, with a particular emphasis on comprehensive neighborhood revitalization, special-needs housing, and neighborhood stabilization activities.

Brianne N. Schwanitz is an associate in the Columbus, Ohio, office of Vorys, Sater, Seymour and Pease LLP, whose practice focuses primarily on representing lenders in FHA-insured financings for multifamily and health-care projects. Ms. Schwanitz worked extensively with the FHA Closing Documents Workgroup of the Mortgage Bankers Association, preparing and coordinating industry comments on FHA's new Multifamily Form Closing Documents and related changes in HUD Regulations, published in 2011. Ms. Schwanitz also assisted in the preparation and coordination of comments made by the HUD Practice Group of the American Bar Association's Affordable Housing Forum on FHA's new *Multifamily Closing Guide*, also published in 2011.

Laura Schwarz is an associate at Reno & Cavanaugh PLLC, in Washington, D.C. Her practice focuses on public housing regulatory issues, mixed-finance transactions, and affordable housing. She has assisted a number of public housing authorities and nonprofit developers in the establishment and operation of their Neighborhood Stabilization programs.

Karen Sherman, principal of ShermanLaw, is an author and frequent lecturer on affordable housing and community development projects financed with low-income housing tax credits, new market tax credits, tax-exempt bonds, HUD 202/811, and public and private debt and grants. She is a former chair of the ABA Forum on Affordable Housing & Community Development Law. Her New York–based firm (www.shermanlaw.net) represents not-for-profit and for-profit developers of affordable housing and community development projects.

Inez Tremain is a partner with the law firm of Tishler & Wald, Ltd., in Chicago, Illinois. She is a past president of the National Leased Housing Association. Prior to practicing law, Ms. Tremain held various managerial positions with HUD.

While at Ballard Spahr, **Margaret H. (Maree) Tucker** represented public housing authorities in various mixed-finance transactions and assisted housing authorities in matters involving the disposition and leasing of their real estate assets. Maree now serves as associate general counsel with Alex Brown Realty, Inc.

Melissa Worden is a partner at Reno & Cavanaugh, PLLC in Washington, D.C., where her practice focuses on affordable housing, mixed finance development, and related regulatory issues. Prior to joining Reno & Cavanaugh, she spent four years in the Detroit Housing Commission's General Counsel's office, where she touched upon many of the issues discussed in this chapter.

William J. Ward, MPA, is currently the Director of Compliance and Capital Improvement at the Detroit Housing Commission. Prior to joining DHC, Mr. Ward spent several years working for or with local units of government in the areas of economic development, governmental affairs, mental health, and airports.

Introduction

The scope of the U.S. Department of Housing & Urban Development (HUD, or the Department) includes a variety of programs, including Federal Housing Administration (FHA) insurance, affordable housing assistance, community development grants, secondary market support, and fair housing oversight. Since its creation in 1965, HUD has been a vehicle for addressing the most important domestic crises, whether they be natural disasters, human-engineered financial instability, or other challenges. Furthering this perception, HUD has been a critical source of financing in times of economic distress as lenders and other funders wait for the restoration of economic stability. Despite this critical function, HUD is one of the smallest cabinet-level departments of the federal government, with a current staff of approximately 9,000 employees, emphasizing the key role that these individuals serve.[1] At the same time, HUD's stated mission is to create strong, sustainable, inclusive communities and quality affordable homes. These dual goals of serving as both a financial institution and an entity with a social mission can create challenges for HUD staff and those who interact with HUD.

This introduction explains HUD's basic structure, including its division into program areas, with a focus on the structure of the Office of General Counsel and how practitioners might interact with this office. The introduction concludes with an overview and guide to the chapters and their interrelationships.

I. DEPARTMENTAL STRUCTURE

HUD's organizational structure forms the basis of the maze and includes headquarters in Washington, D.C., 10 Regional Offices throughout the United States, approximately 70 additional Field Offices,[2] and various "centers" with specialized responsibilities.[3] Staff in the Field Offices report administratively to the Regional

---

   1. For staff size, *see* HUD, FY2013 Budget, Congressional Justifications for Estimates, FTE Summary at B-12, requesting 9,283 full-time employees. This level is considerably lower than, for example, the 13,500 employees in 1992 and the 10,500 employees in 1997. The HUD 2020 Management Reform Plan, 62 Fed. Reg. 43,204, 43,212 (Aug. 12, 1997) [hereinafter the HUD 2020 Plan].

   2. HUD's Local Office Directory, *available at* http://portal.hud.gov/hudportal/HUD?src=/localoffices.

   3. For a general organizational chart, *see* http://www.hud.gov/offices/adm/about/admguide/orgcharts/hud.pdf (last accessed March 5, 2012). For a description of the 10 Regional Offices, *see* http://portal.hud.gov/hudportal/HUD?src=/localoffices/regions (last accessed March 5, 2012). For a list of Field Offices, *see* http://portal.hud.gov/hudportal/HUD?src=/localoffices (last accessed march 5, 2012). The specialized centers include the Departmental Enforcement Center in Washington, D.C., with five satellite offices (New York, Atlanta, Ft. Worth, Chicago, and Los Angeles); the Real

Offices, but substantively to the Assistant Secretary whose programs they are implementing.[4]

Part of this structure is historical artifact. When created in 1965, HUD united a variety of existing governmental entities, including the FHA, the Public Housing Administration, the Urban Renewal Administration, and the Housing and Home Finance Agency.[5] While each entity of the newly created HUD had administered programs relating to housing, community, and economic development, they had not necessarily done so in consultation with the others. For ensuing decades, each Secretary of HUD has placed varying degrees of emphasis on having the agency operate as a cohesive entity that administers all of its programs in a coordinated fashion for the benefit of local communities.[6]

HUD's enabling legislation provides for a Secretary who, as a member of the President's cabinet, is appointed by the President and confirmed by the Senate.[7] HUD's authority is vested in the Secretary, who delegates authority to any of the Assistant Secretaries and other offices and officers.[8] A Deputy Secretary generally has concurrent authority with the Secretary. While all Assistant Secretaries have equivalent levels of authority, four "program" Assistant Secretaries are responsible for the four primary areas of HUD, as further described below.

The FHA Commissioner also serves as the Assistant Secretary for the Office of Housing.[9] The Office of Housing is the largest office in HUD and is responsible for

---

Estate Assessment Center (REAC) in Washington D.C.; the Financial Management Center in St. Louis; four Homeownership Centers (Philadelphia, Atlanta, Denver, Santa Ana); a Single-Family Servicing Center (Oklahoma City); the public housing Special Applications Center in Chicago; and a number of processing centers and program hubs, including two multifamily property disposition HUBs (Atlanta and Ft. Worth).

4. LAWRENCE J. THOMPSON, A HISTORY OF HUD (2006), http://www.hudnlha.com/housing_news/hud_history.pdf, at Figure 3.10 (illustrating current field office structure).

5. Department of Housing and Urban Development Act, Pub. L. No. 89-117, 79 Stat. 451 (Aug. 10, 1965) (codified as amended at 42 U.S.C. § 3531 *et seq.*) [hereinafter, the 1965 Act] at Sec. 5.

6. In one of the most notable examples, Secretary Cuomo's ambitious HUD 2020 Management Reform Plan fundamentally restructured HUD's management. In particular, it consolidated similar functions performed by separate program "cylinders" into functionally oriented centers serving different programs. For example, it created the Real Estate Assessment Center to monitor physical condition of properties in both the Office of Housing and the PIH portfolios. HUD 2020 Management Plan, *supra* note 2 at 43,212.

7. *See* 1965 Act at § 3(a).

8. *See* 1965 Act at § 4(a). In addition, HUD publishes "delegations of authority" establishing the substantive areas of the Assistant Secretaries and their authority to delegate responsibilities to subordinates. In 2010-2011, HUD published a comprehensive overhaul of the delegated authority to various Assistant Secretaries, offices, and officers. A summary web page linking to the delegations, many of which are cited in this introduction, can be found at http://portal.hud.gov/hudportal/HUD?src=/delegations-of-authority.

9. *See* 1965 Act at § 4(b). As of publication of this book, HUD has not yet updated its 2006 delegation of authority. *See* Consolidated Delegation of Authority for the Office of Housing—Federal Housing Administration, 71 Fed. Reg. 60,169 (Oct. 12, 2006).

all FHA programs, including single-family housing as well as multifamily housing, which includes affordable and market-rate rental housing, cooperatives and condominiums, and health care. The Office of Housing's health-care programs include hospitals, nursing homes, and assisted living authorized under the National Housing Act of 1934. The Office of Housing is also responsible for the "project-based" Section 8 program, which provides rental assistance for lower-income housing to participating owners and the Section 202 elderly housing and Section 811 disabled housing programs. This office interacts primarily with lenders, owners, managers, and developers.

The Assistant Secretary for Community Planning and Development (CPD)[10] administers the Office of Community Planning and Development and is responsible for the Community Development Block Grant (CDBG) program, the HOME Investment Partnerships program, the Neighborhood Stabilization Program, homelessness programs, and other community and economic development programs. CPD also oversees relocation compliance and environmental reviews across a variety of HUD funding programs.[11] The CPD office interacts primarily with states, units of local government, and local public agencies.

The Assistant Secretary for Public and Indian Housing (PIH)[12] is responsible for the traditional public housing program authorized under the U.S. Housing Act of 1937 as well as the HOPE VI program, the Choice Neighborhood Initiatives program, and certain existing Section 8 programs along with tenant-based programs and the Indian programs authorized by the Native American Housing Assistance and Self Determination Act of 1996, which reauthorized Indian programs authorized by the 1937 Act. PIH currently oversees the new Rental Assistance Demonstration (RAD) program, which seeks to convert public housing to vouchers or Section 8 programs to leverage private funding in order to refinance and redevelop projects.[13] The Office of PIH interacts primarily with local public housing authorities and Indian housing authorities, as well as with developers, owners, and managers.

The Assistant Secretary for Fair Housing and Equal Opportunity (FHEO)[14] is responsible for the compliance and enforcement of federal civil rights laws, including the Fair Housing Amendments of 1988, and the Section 504 accessibility requirements as they relate to housing. This Assistant Secretary has the authority to

---

10. Consolidated Delegation of Authority for the Office of Community Planning and Development, 76 Fed. Reg. 64,362 (Oct. 18, 2011).

11. *Id.* at 64,363.

12. PIH was authorized by the 1965 Act, *supra* note 6, at Section 4(e)(1)(a). Specific current responsibilities may be found at Delegation of Authority for the Office of Public and Indian Housing, 76 Fed. Reg. 47,224 (Aug. 4, 2011).

13. RAD was created by an appropriations act, Pub. L. 112-55, Nov. 18, 2011, and is not a permanent program. PIH has taken the lead in implementation. *See* HUD, PIH Notice 2012-18, Rental Assistance Demonstration—Partial Assistance and Request for Comments (March 8, 2012).

14. Consolidated Delegation of Authority for the Office of Fair Housing and Equal Opportunity, 76 Fed. Reg. 73,984 (Nov. 29, 2011).

bring charges of discrimination on behalf of a complainant in instances where HUD determines that reasonable cause exists.[15] The Office of FHEO interacts primarily with state fair-housing agencies and individuals who have claims of discrimination.

Other Assistant Secretaries at HUD have portfolios that cut across the four program lines identified above and often provide support to the overall organization. Assistant Secretaries administer the Offices of Policy Development and Research[16] and Congressional and Intergovernmental Relations, among other areas.[17] The Secretary occasionally also appoints an Assistant Secretary for Administration, but at the time of this writing, the primarily internal responsibilities of that position are being discharged by the Chief Operating Officer.[18] Finally, the Chief Financial Officer is responsible for HUD's budget and financial management,[19] the Chief Procurement Officer serves as HUD's contracting officer and oversees all procurement activities,[20] and the Inspector General exercises independent audit authority under the Inspector General Act.[21] Like Assistant Secretaries, the President of GNMA (Ginnie Mae) has programmatic responsibility.[22] As discussed in greater detail below, the Office of the General Counsel addresses all legal matters for HUD.

II. OFFICE OF GENERAL COUNSEL

Unlike many federal departments that include subagencies with their own independent legal departments, such as the Departments of Transportation, Defense, and Health and Human Services, HUD has one Office of General Counsel (OGC) that addresses all legal issues for the entire Department.[23] As the designated ethics offi-

---

15. *Id.*
16. Delegation of Authority for the Office of Policy Development and Research, 76 Fed. Reg. 73,934 (Aug. 30, 2011). This Assistant Secretary is responsible for undertaking and administering programs of research, study, and testing for certain programs assigned by the Secretary.
17. Delegation of Authority for the Office of Congressional and Intergovernmental Relations, 76 Fed. Reg. 62,594 (Oct. 7, 2011). This Secretary manages all relations with Congress except appropriations; maintains a liaison with Congress, the White House, and the Office of Management and Budget on legislative matters; and advises HUD officials on legislation of interest to HUD and recommended legislative strategies.
18. The Deputy Secretary delegated to the COO the responsibility to supervise information technology, human resources, procurement, field office management, disaster preparedness, and strategic planning. *See* Delegation of Authority to the Chief Operating Officer, 76 Fed. Reg. 34,745 (June 15, 2011).
19. Delegation of Authority for the Office of the Chief Financing Officer, 76 Fed. Reg. 73,935 (Aug. 30, 2011).
20. Designation of Chief Acquisition Officer and Senior Procurement Executive and Delegation of Procurement Authority, 76 Fed. Reg. 53,936 (Aug. 19, 2011).
21. Delegation and Redelegation of Authority for the Office of the Inspector General, 75 Fed. Reg. 61,166 (Oct. 4, 2010).
22. Consolidated Delegation of Authority to the President of the Government National Mortgage Association, 76 Fed. Reg. 53,931 (Aug. 30, 2011).
23. Consolidated Delegation of Authority to the General Counsel, 76 Fed. Reg. 42,462 (July 18, 2011) [hereinafter the General Counsel Delegation].

cial, the General Counsel has source-selection authority for outside legal services, has certain delegated enforcement authorities from the program Assistant Secretaries, is responsible for interpreting the authority of the Secretary and whether proposed issuances are consistent with such authority, directs all litigation concerning HUD, and acts upon appeals under the Freedom of Information Act.[24] The Office of the Inspector General has its own counsels, who provide advice to the OIG but not the Department.

As with other appointees at the Assistant Secretary level, the General Counsel is nominated by the President and confirmed by the Senate. The General Counsel is HUD's chief legal officer and is responsible for providing all legal guidance to HUD. All outside legal services procured by and for HUD must go through the General Counsel,[25] who typically is served by several politically appointed Deputy General Counsels and several Special Assistants. The number and allocation of the political appointees are generally left to the discretion of the General Counsel and Secretary. However, the General Counsel's office usually also includes a career Deputy General Counsel at the Senior Executive Service (SES) level. This career executive often becomes the Acting General Counsel during transitions. There are approximately eight Associate General Counsels at the SES level who provide counsel either across program lines or across HUD.[26] Each Associate General Counsel directs an office staffed with attorneys who are experts in their fields of specialization.

All of the approximately 600-person OGC staff,[27] other than the General Counsel and the political Deputies and Special Assistants, are career employees who work either at HUD's Headquarters, Regional Offices, or Field Offices. The 10 Regional Offices are each headed by a politically appointed Regional Administrator. The Regional Administrators report to the Office of Field Policy and Management, but they have no specific program authority.[28] Instead, Regional Administrators coordinate between program areas, supervise Field Offices, raise issues to Headquarters, and serve as a liaison for regional constituents. Each of the 10 Regional Offices includes a Regional Counsel, a Housing HUB Director, a PIH Director, a CPD Director, and a FHEO Director.

---

24. General Counsel Delegation at 42,462–63.
25. General Counsel Delegation at 42,462.
26. For example, the Associate for Insured Housing, the Associate for Fair Housing, and the Associate for Assisted Housing and Community Development provide counsel across program lines, while the Associate for Litigation, the Associate for Legislation, and the Associate for Human Resources provide counsel across HUD. For a good overview of Office of General Counsel responsibilities, *see About OGC*, http://portal.hud.gov/hudportal/HUD?src=/program_offices/general_counsel/aboutogc For specific delegated authority of Associate General Counsels, *see* General Counsel Delegation, *supra* note 24, 42,465–66.
27. This includes the Departmental Enforcement Center, or DEC. *See* http://portal.hud.gov/hudportal/HUD?src=/about/principal_staff/general_counselor_kanovsky.
28. *Field Policy/Management—Overview, at* http://portal.hud.gov/hudportal/HUD?src=/program_offices/field_policy_mgt. *See also* A History of HUD, by Lawrence J. Thompson (2006), at 38, which describes the current field office structure in layperson's terms.

The Regional Counsel Offices generally have responsibility for FHA closings and other transactional work, field litigation, and fair housing enforcement, and are generally staffed with attorneys focused on those matters. The local Field Counsel offices are headed by an Associate Regional Counsel (formerly called Chief Counsel), include one to three attorneys, provide legal advice across program lines, and often spend considerable time on the transactional closing of FHA-insured loans. As noted above, HUD has approximately 80 Field and Regional Offices of varying sizes and responsibilities. Fifty of those offices are considered "full service" and have professionals who address the above-identified programs.[29]

III. ABOUT THE CHAPTERS

The HUD regulatory landscape is complex, with policy formally created by statutes and regulations. Secondary formal guidance is created by handbooks, notices, and other similar publications. While this secondary guidance may carry less weight under the terms of the Administrative Procedure Act and related litigation, it nevertheless provides significant insight into HUD's existing practices and procedures.[30] In addition, HUD informally establishes policies through letters, e-mails, phone calls, or other ad hoc resolutions to specific problems. This book seeks to help practitioners advance through the labyrinth as smoothly as possible and therefor explains and supplements, but does not replace, formal and informal HUD guidance.

A. FHA and Multifamily Programs

We start our journey through the labyrinth with a visit to the Office of Housing. This visit includes three chapters on FHA-insured financing, an overview of the Section 202 elderly housing program, and a meander through the well-known complexity of the 2530 approval process. These chapters, which focus on development, should be read in conjunction with Chapter 12, "Resolution of Troubled or Defaulted HUD-Insured Multifamily and Health-Care Loans."

"FHA Multifamily Programs: General Overview and Recent Developments" (Chapter 1) addresses the range of FHA-financing options and processing methods. Use of FHA financing has increased dramatically in the wake of the credit tightening of the "great recession" of 2008. FHA has increased its underwriting standards and has been asked to insure more loans with sizes much greater than those historically experienced by FHA.[31] The FHA landscape is constantly shifting with modifications

---

29. In 1997, HUD reorganized the field offices as part of the 2020 Management Reform. The HUD 2020 Management Reform Plan; Notice of New HUD Field Structure, 62 Fed. Reg. 62,478 (Nov. 21, 1997) (identifying specific services and programs to be supported at each Field and Regional Office). Staffing, and thus services, have been reduced from that level, but the notice is a good overall guide.

30. *See, e.g.*, 5 U.S.C. § 501 *et seq.* and Chevron U.S.A. Inc. v. Natural Resources Defense Council, Inc., 467 U.S. 837 (1984) and its progeny.

31. HUD, Fed. Housing Comm'r, Notice H 2011-36 (Dec. 29, 2011).

to HUD policy, and recent changes include the first overhaul of multifamily closing documents in a quarter of a century, with related changes to the *Multifamily Accelerated Processing (MAP) Guide* and HUD closing guide.

"Multi-Family Housing Preservation" (Chapter 2) follows the FHA property life cycle by addressing preservation of programs and financing strategies for properties developed with FHA-insured funding. This chapter explains the statutory and regulatory framework authorizing the continued availability of these assets and discusses the variations of each program, including the Flexible Subsidy Program, ELIHPA, LHPRHA, and MAHRA.

"Healthcare and Hospital Financing" (Chapter 3) addresses the complexities of the FHA-insured health-care programs, including the nursing home/assisted-living programs and the hospital program. This chapter also discusses LEAN, the innovative method of processing that HUD introduced for the Section 232 nursing home program.

The Section 202 elderly housing program is one of the most popular and competitive programs available through HUD. "HUD Section 202 and Mixed-Finance Guide for Development and Operation of Supportive Housing for the Elderly" (Chapter 4) provides historical perspective, the evolutionary changes associated with this program, and a discussion of the program's future.

Many HUD programs require an analysis of participants' previous participation in HUD and other federal programs as part of the approval process. The 2530 requirements, procedures, and challenges are discussed in great detail in "The 2530 Previous Participation Approval Process" (Chapter 5). The chapter concludes with suggestions of issues to be addressed in the future, which discussion also serves as a guide to some of the thornier 2530 issues.

B. *Community Planning and Department (CPD)*

"Community Development" (Chapter 6) addresses the CDBG and HOME programs, which distribute block grant funds by formula to over a thousand communities and states throughout the country. This chapter also discusses recurring concerns with these two programs and concludes with a review of CPD homeless programs, including Supportive Housing and ShelterPlus Care.

"Emerging Neighborhood Stabilization Programs" (Chapter 7) narrows its focus to the three (to date) iterations of the Neighborhood Stabilization Program (NSP), a temporary program that originated with the federal stimulus programs that combines CDBG regulations with HOME use restrictions and other NSP-specific requirements. This chapter addresses strategic ways that NSP funds can be used on the project level, emphasizing affordability requirements, program income limitations, and other practical considerations. The chapter also articulates ways in which evolving interpretations of the NSP requirements may affect longstanding policies of the CDBG and HOME programs.

C. Public and Indian Housing

Further into the labyrinth, we find three key areas administered by the Office of Public and Indian Housing, with chapters focused on public housing development, public housing operations, and Section 8 housing.

"Public Housing Development—Mixed-Finance in the Context of Historical Trends" (Chapter 8) begins with a history of the public housing program, including its evolution from a model entirely based on public ownership with federal financing, and focuses on the complex financing and ownership structures used today in public housing development and revitalization projects. The chapter discusses in detail the complexities of mixed-finance development, leveraging of future streams of capital funds through Capital Fund Financing, and financial and operational issues.

"Public Housing Operations" (Chapter 9) identifies the web of regulations affecting virtually all actions of a public housing authority in administering its public housing program, from procurement to HUD funding, admission and occupancy to property standards, and monitoring.

"The Section 8 Rental Assistance Program" (Chapter 10) describes the basics of the project-based and tenant-based Section 8 rental assistance programs, the current funding mechanism for the programs, and the eligibility requirements for tenants. It also discusses the way in which HUD currently renews Section 8 project-based program contracts and the process by which a housing authority can use its Section 8 tenant-based assistance to provide owners, lenders, and investors with Section 8 Project-Based Voucher assistance.

D. Multi-program Issues, Compliance, and Enforcement

We round out our journey with a look at issues and requirements that apply across a number of program areas and funding sources.

"The Heat is On: Trimming HUD's Energy Bill for Public and Privately Owned Assisted Housing" (Chapter 11) focuses on the high cost of providing energy to affordable housing and the efforts under way to reduce those costs in a myriad of program areas. This chapter addresses multiple programs and suggests that some programs are moving faster than others to provide tools to address rising energy costs.

"Resolution of Troubled or Defaulted HUD-Insured Multifamily and Healthcare Loans" (Chapter 12) addresses possible solutions to the challenges associated with asset resolution of troubled or defaulted loans.

"Cross-Cutting Requirements: Federal-Wide Requirements Impacting HUD Programs" (Chapter 13) addresses requirements such as Davis-Bacon, environmental approval, procurement, relocation, and subsidy-layering review, which are imposed by laws and regulations external to HUD program regulations but nevertheless apply to virtually all HUD-funded activities.

"Civil Rights Programs Administered and Enforced by HUD" (Chapter 14) addresses the basic fair housing and civil rights programs governing housing, including the Fair Housing Act, accessible design standards, reasonable accommodations, reasonable modifications, and the HUD fair housing enforcement process. It also addresses the obligation to "affirmatively further fair housing," which has recently been the focus of litigation and about which HUD intends to issue updated regulations.

"Compliance and Enforcement" (Chapter 15) addresses HUD compliance mechanisms in a variety of different programs. This chapter discusses the variety of tools available to HUD to audit, investigate, and take action when HUD either determines or has reason to believe that its requirements have been violated. Finally, this chapter explains the various roles of the Office of the Inspector General and the Department Enforcement Center.

FHA Multifamily Programs: General Overview and Recent Developments[1]

Brianne N. Schwanitz and Charles C. Bissinger, Jr.

I. INTRODUCTION

The Federal Housing Administration (FHA), which became a part of the U.S. Department of Housing and Urban Development (HUD) in 1965,[2] provides mortgage insurance with respect to loans for the construction, substantial rehabilitation, acquisition, and/or refinancing of eligible multifamily housing projects under a number of mortgage insurance programs. HUD has statutory authority to insure such loans under the National Housing Act[3] (the Act), but the upper limit that HUD may commit to insure each fiscal year is established through the appropriations process. As a condition of providing mortgage insurance, HUD requires that the lender pay an initial mortgage insurance premium at the time of the loan closing and annual mortgage insurance premiums each year for as long as the loan is insured by FHA (the initial and annual mortgage insurance premiums are referred to as MIP).[4] Lenders pass on the cost of the MIP to

---

1. The information in this chapter reflects the guidance in effect as of January 1, 2012. It is important to note that HUD's requirements change over time due to changes in statutes, market conditions, HUD's experiences, and numerous other factors. Readers should consult source materials on HUD's website (*available at* www.hud.gov), and current Regulations, *see infra* notes 21 and 26, for current requirements.

2. *See* 42 U.S.C. § 3534 (2009), enacted by Department of Housing and Urban Development Act of 1965, Pub. L. No. 89–174.

3. 12 U.S.C. §§ 1701 *et seq.* (2010). Unless otherwise specified, Section references in this chapter refer to Sections of the National Housing Act.

4. MIP payments are calculated based upon a percentage of the original loan amount or the outstanding principal balance.

borrowers. HUD has the authority to adjust MIP rates annually by publication in the *Federal Register*.[5] Although HUD generally sets MIP rates at a level that is intended to cover anticipated mortgage insurance losses, certain programs are projected to operate at a loss and require a legislative allocation of credit subsidy to cover anticipated losses. Credit subsidy rates are determined annually based on anticipated mortgage insurance losses and are published in the *Federal Register*.[6] Collectively, however, the programs are designed to operate at no cost to the taxpayer, as other programs operate at a surplus.

Although each program is subject to its own specific statutory and regulatory requirements, the general structure of each FHA-insured loan transaction (and, indeed, many of the more detailed requirements) is consistent regardless of the section of the Act under which the loan is insured. In each FHA-insured loan transaction, there will be at least three parties: the FHA-approved lender, the borrower, and HUD. HUD does not make loans to borrowers but instead insures mortgages made by approved lenders. This insurance provides the lender with protection against loss because of a default by the borrower. Provided that the lender complies with the requirements of the claims process,[7] the lender is entitled to receive mortgage insurance benefits from HUD when there is a qualifying event of default.[8] In connection with this insurance, the lender and borrower must adhere to the requirements imposed by HUD in the mortgage insurance contract. HUD regulates the borrower and the project through the terms of the Regulatory Agreement, Form HUD-92466M (the Regulatory Agreement),[9] which is recorded contemporaneously with the Multifamily (Mortgage, Deed of Trust, Deed to Secure Debt, or Other Designation as Appropriate in Jurisdiction), Assignment of Leases and Rents and Security Agreement, Form HUD-94000M (the Security Instrument).[10] The amount of HUD's exposure with respect to a mortgage insurance claim is limited by the amount approved for insurance, as set forth in the endorsement panel to the Note (Multifamily), Form HUD-94001M (the Note).[11] With respect to construction loans, HUD first endorses the Note for insurance to the extent of advances during the construction period approved by HUD (initial endorsement). Following completion of construction and satisfaction of all necessary conditions, HUD then will endorse

---

5. 24 C.F.R. § 207.254 (2011). The annual MIP rate for a loan is established based on the rate in effect on the date that FHA issues a firm commitment to insure the loan and does not change during the life of the loan. For annual MIP rates for fiscal year 2011, *see* Federal Housing Administration (FHA) Mortgage Insurance Premiums for Multifamily Housing Programs, Health Care Facilities and Hospitals and Credit Subsidy Obligations for Fiscal Year (FY) 2011, 76 Fed. Reg. 40,741 (July 17, 2011).

6. The credit subsidy rate and the credit subsidy allocation have the effect of limiting the aggregate amount of loans that FHA can insure each fiscal year under the affected programs.

7. *See* Chapter 12 for a discussion of the claims process.

8. *See* 24 C.F.R. § 207.255 (2011).

9. *See* Section V.C.3 of this chapter for a detailed discussion of the Regulatory Agreement, Form HUD-92466M (Rev. 04/11) [hereinafter *Regulatory Agreement*].

10. *See* Section V.C.1 of this Chapter for a detailed discussion of the Multifamily (Mortgage, Deed of Trust, Deed to Secure Debt, or Other Designation as Appropriate in Jurisdiction), Assignment of Leases and Rents and Security Agreement, Form HUD-94000M (Rev. 04/11) [hereinafter *Security Instrument*].

11. *See* Section V.C.2 of this Chapter for a detailed discussion of the Note (Multifamily), Form HUD-94001M (Rev. 04/11) [hereinafter *Note*].

the Note for insurance in an amount equal to the total sum of advances to the borrower as approved by HUD (final endorsement). For acquisitions or refinancings, the Note is endorsed only once for a total approved sum (initial/final endorsement).

To be eligible for mortgage insurance, the loan must be made by an FHA-approved lender,[12] and the borrower must be an "eligible borrower," possessing the necessary powers to own and operate the project and comply with HUD's requirements.[13] With the borrower's assistance, the lender prepares and submits an application for mortgage insurance to HUD, and, if approved, HUD issues a commitment to insure the loan (the Firm Commitment).[14] HUD currently utilizes two different sets of procedures for processing applications for multifamily mortgage insurance:

(1) The most commonly used procedure is Multifamily Accelerated Processing (MAP) pursuant to the Multifamily Accelerated Processing Guide (the MAP Guide).[15] Under MAP, the lender underwrites the loan and HUD reviews the lender's underwriting to determine whether or not (and the terms under which) HUD will issue a Firm Commitment.

(2) Loans that are not eligible for processing under MAP may be processed pursuant to HUD's Traditional Application Processing (TAP) procedures.[16] Under TAP, rather than underwriting the loan, the lender "packages" the loan for HUD to underwrite

Typically, following receipt of the Firm Commitment, the lender and borrower will enter into a financing commitment or other agreement pursuant to which the lender will agree to make the loan, and the borrower will agree to accept the loan. This agreement (which often is referred to as the rate lock agreement) ordinarily will set forth the interest rate on the loan (which may differ from the rate set forth in the Firm Commitment), prepayment terms, various fees and expenses, and closing deadlines. If the "locked" interest rate differs from the interest rate set forth in the Firm Commitment, an amendment request is processed with HUD to incorporate the "locked" interest rate and any corresponding changes (such as a change in the monthly loan payment) into the Firm Commitment.

---

12. *See* 24 C.F.R. §§ 202 *et seq.* (2011), incorporated by reference at 24 C.F.R. § 200.10 (2011), for lender requirements.

13. *See* Section II.B of this chapter regarding eligible borrowers.

14. *See* Section IV of this chapter for a discussion of the application and approval process.

15. Multifamily Accelerated Processing (MAP) Guide, revised Nov. 23, 2011, Office of the Assistant Secretary for Housing – FHA Commissioner, HUD GUIDEBOOK 4430.G [hereinafter *MAP Guide*], *available at* http://portal.hud.gov/hudportal/HUD?src=/program_offices/administration/hudclips/guidebooks/hsg-GB4430.

16. Pursuant to *MAP Guide* ¶ 1.2, HUD requires that all projects that are eligible for MAP processing be submitted using MAP processing. However, "FHA approved multifamily Lenders who are not approved to submit MAP applications can submit loans for mortgage insurance using TAP." *Id. See also* Question 22 of Questions and Answers Risk Mitigation Housing Notice (H 2010-11) and Mortgagee Letter (ML 2010-21) issued 8/23/10, *available at* http://www.hud.gov/offices/hsg/mfh/map/qnahudnotice201011.pdf, providing that projects that cannot be processed under MAP due to an identity of interest are still eligible to be processed under TAP.

Once HUD's requirements for closing have been satisfied, including any special conditions identified in the Firm Commitment, and the borrower has adequately funded required escrows and reserves, HUD endorses the Note for mortgage insurance and the lender makes the loan to the borrower. The lender typically will fund the loan through the issuance and sale to an institutional investor of mortgage-backed securities guaranteed by the Government National Mortgage Association (Ginnie Mae).[17] Ginnie Mae mortgage-backed securities are securities backed by mortgages that are pooled and used as collateral for the issuance of such securities.[18] Ginnie Mae mortgage-backed securities often are referred to as "pass-through" securities because the principal and interest payments made by the borrower on the underlying loans (net of a Ginnie Mae guaranty fee and a lender's servicing fee) are "passed through" to investors. However, the monthly payments are required to be made to the investors on the 15th day of the month, regardless of whether the mortgage payment has been made by the borrower.[19] Although many lenders service the loans they originate, many other lenders only originate loans and sell them to other lenders to service.[20]

The rights and obligations of the parties to an FHA-insured loan transaction are governed by the mortgage insurance contract, comprising the Firm Commitment together with the exhibits referred to therein, and the applicable HUD regulations (Regulations)[21] in effect as of the date of the Firm Commitment. The Firm Commitment sets forth the basic terms of the loan, including, but not limited to, the amount of the loan, the term of the loan, the underwritten interest rate, required monthly principal and interest payments, escrows and reserves that must be funded at closing, repairs that must be completed, and any special conditions that must be satisfied.

Additional sources of guidance are issued by HUD in the form of Mortgagee Letters, Housing Notices, the MAP Guide, the Multifamily Program Closing Guide[22] (the Closing

---

17. Ginnie Mae is, and always has been, a wholly-owned government agency and part of HUD.

18. Although the use of the term "pooled" suggests that two or more loans are combined into a "pool" to back a Ginnie Mae security, this terminology is a carryover from Ginnie Mae's single-family mortgage program, and almost all multifamily "pools" consist of a single loan.

19. "If a borrower fails to make a timely payment on a mortgage, the Issuer [i.e., the lender] must use its own funds to ensure that the security holders receive timely payment. If an Issuer fails to ensure that the funds necessary to make timely payment are available or otherwise defaults in the discharge of its responsibilities, Ginnie Mae, in accordance with its guaranty, will make payments to security holders." GINNIE MAE MORTGAGE BACKED SECURITY GUIDE, Ginnie Mae 5500.3, Rev. 1, Section 1-1, *available at* http://www.ginniemae.gov/guide/guidtoc.asp.

20. *MAP Guide* ¶ 1.2 ("Some MAP-approved Lenders only originate loans and do not service them. . . . A loan servicer who receives a transferred MAP loan for servicing must be FHA-approved for multifamily housing, but it need not be a MAP-approved Lender.").

21. *E.g.,* 24 C.F.R. §§ 207 *et seq.* for loans insured under Section 207; 24 C.F.R. §§ 220 *et seq.* for loans insured under Section 220; 24 C.F.R. §§ 221 *et seq.* for loans insured under Section 221(d); 24 C.F.R. §§ 231 *et seq.* for loans insured under Section 231; 24 C.F.R. §§ 241 *et seq.* for loans insured under Section 241.

22. Federal Housing Administration Multifamily Program Closing Guide, Sept. 1, 2011 [hereinafter *Closing Guide*], *available at* http://portal.hud.gov/hudportal/HUD?src=/program_offices/general_counsel/mffaqs.

Guide), Handbooks, and form documents.[23] Although a Housing Notice typically contains an expiration date, that date often is extended and, in some instances, HUD may continue to use a Housing Notice as a source of guidance even following the official date of expiration. In many instances, the Handbooks have been superseded by the MAP Guide, which provides guidance for all projects processed using MAP. However, for those projects processed using TAP, the Handbooks remain a primary source of guidance. With respect to applications under MAP, if there is a conflict between the MAP Guide and a Handbook, the MAP Guide takes precedence, but if the MAP Guide is silent on a matter, the lender should consult with HUD.[24] However, from a practical standpoint, if the MAP Guide is silent, HUD generally will follow Handbook requirements. The Closing Guide provides guidance with respect to loan document preparation and closing procedures for all multifamily projects, whether the project was processed under MAP or TAP.[25]

Section II of this chapter discusses overarching requirements that apply to FHA-insured loans for multifamily projects, regardless of the section of the Act under which the loan is insured. Many of these requirements are regulatory in nature,[26] but to the extent other sources of guidance apply across the various programs, they also are discussed in Section II. Section III addresses many of the distinguishing characteristics among HUD's active multifamily insurance programs.[27] Note, however, that HUD's active insurance programs for health-care projects, including nursing homes, assisted-living facilities, and hospitals, are not covered in this chapter, but instead are discussed in Chapter 3. Section IV provides an overview of the approval process for mortgage insurance applications, including how that process differs between loans that involve new construction or substantial rehabilitation and loans that involve refinancing or acquisition. Section V discusses the closing process, including closing documents and requirements of the Closing Guide. Note that the closing requirements and documents discussed in Section V reflect HUD's current requirements, which apply for all multifamily projects receiving a Firm Commitment on or after September 1, 2011. Projects that received Firm Commitments before September 1, 2011, were governed by different closing documents, which imposed different requirements.[28]

---

23. *See* http://portal.hud.gov/hudportal/HUD?src=/program_offices/administration/hudclips for Mortgagee Letters, Housing Notices, Handbooks, and form documents.

24. *MAP Guide, supra* note 15, at ¶ 1.4.A.

25. *Closing Guide, supra* note 22, at ¶ 1.A.

26. *See generally* 24 C.F.R. § 200, Subpart A, the provisions of which are incorporated by cross-reference into the applicable Regulations for loans insured under (i) Section 207 of the Act by 24 C.F.R. § 207.1, (ii) Section 220 of the Act by 24 C.F.R. § 220.51, (iii) Section 221(d) of the Act by 24 C.F.R. § 221.501, (iv) Section 231 of the Act by 24 C.F.R. § 231.1, and (v) Section 241 of the Act by 24 C.F.R. § 241.1.

27. For a general overview of each of HUD's active multifamily insurance programs, *see* Programs of HUD, *available at* http://portal.hud.gov/hudportal/HUD?src=/hudprograms/toc.

28. The form closing documents for loans receiving commitments prior to Sept. 1, 2011, are also *available at* http://portal.hud.gov/hudportal/HUD?src=/program_offices/administration/hudclips.

II. Hallmarks of HUD Programs

A. Eligible Projects

To be eligible for mortgage insurance, the project being financed with loan proceeds must be located within one of the 50 United States, the District of Columbia, or a U.S. territory, including Puerto Rico, Guam, the U.S. Virgin Islands, and the Northern Mariana Islands. The project must constitute "rental housing," which is defined to include "housing, the occupancy of which is permitted by the owner thereof in consideration of the payment of agreed charges, whether or not, by the terms of the agreement, such payment over a period of time will entitle the occupant to the ownership of the premises or a space in the manufactured home court or park properly arranged and equipped to accommodate manufactured homes."[29] Furthermore, the project must be used primarily for residential purposes[30] and cannot be used for hotel or transient purposes.[31] "Rental for transient or hotel purposes shall mean: (a) rental for a period of less than thirty (30) days or (b) any rental, if the occupants of the residential units are provided customary hotel services such as room service for food and beverages, maid service, furnishings or laundering of linens, and bellhop service."[32] HUD's Regulatory Agreement provides that residential leases also must prohibit tenants from entering into subleases for periods of less than 30 days or providing any of the above-listed services.[33]

Although they may be eligible for insurance under HUD's insurance programs for healthcare projects, projects that provide extensive services, such as those that would be available in a nursing home, board-and-care facility, or assisted-living facility, are not eligible for mortgage insurance under HUD's multifamily insurance programs.[34] Therefore, projects with mandatory resident services, including, but not limited to, mandatory meal requirements or continuous protective oversight, would not be eligible for multifamily mortgage insurance, with limited exceptions.[35] Each unit also must have a private bathroom and a full standard kitchen to be eligible for insurance under the multifamily programs.[36]

B. Eligible Borrowers

An eligible project must be owned by an eligible borrower for the financing to qualify for mortgage insurance. The borrower must be a single-asset entity, unless otherwise approved by HUD.[37] Therefore, unless otherwise approved by HUD, the borrower cannot own property other than the project, or engage in any business or activity other than the ownership and

---

29. 12 U.S.C. § 1713 (2010).
30. However, a limited portion of the property may be used for commercial purposes. *See* Section II.O of this chapter for a discussion of commercial space and income limitations.
31. 12 U.S.C. § 1731b (2010).
32. *See Regulatory Agreement, supra* note 9, at ¶ 28. *See also* 12 U.S.C. § 1731b (2010), prohibiting rental for a period of less than 30 days.
33. *Regulatory Agreement, supra* note 9, at ¶ 30.
34. *MAP Guide, supra* note 15, at ¶ 3.4.S.
35. *Id.*
36. *Id.*
37. 24 C.F.R. § 200.5(a)(1) (2011).

operation of the project.[38] Natural person borrowers and tenant-in-common borrowers are prohibited.[39] A borrower and its principals also must obtain previous participation clearance, disclosing to HUD, inter alia, previous projects in which the individual or entity has participated, along with whether the loan for any such previous project is or has been in default, as well as certain other legal or credit issues, during the period beginning 10 years prior to the date of the previous participation certification.[40]

C. First-Lien Requirement

Except for limited exceptions, including loans insured under Section 241 or Section 223(d), to be insured by FHA, the loan must be secured by a mortgage or deed of trust that constitutes a first lien on the property.[41] In addition, under the Regulations and the terms of the Regulatory Agreement and the Security Instrument, the borrower cannot grant any inferior liens on the property or project sources unless such liens are approved by HUD and the lender.[42]

D. Mortgageable Interest

The lien must be a mortgage or deed of trust on (i) real estate in fee simple, and an undivided interest in common elements in the case of condominium projects or projects involving air rights, if applicable, or (ii) a leasehold interest under a lease of adequate duration.[43] A condominium project may be considered for insurance if it is operating as a rental project with all the units being owned by a single borrower entity.[44] HUD may consider a waiver for a condominium project "with a limited number of individually owned units (i.e., 10 percent or less of total units) if all the owned units are located in a separate building or in a separate section of a single building apart from the rental units. HUD will not consider a waiver if any ownership units are interspersed with the rental units."[45] The insured project may constitute one or more condominium units within a condominium that includes non-insured units not owned by the

---

38. *See Regulatory Agreement, supra* note 9, at ¶ 12b.
39. 24 C.F.R. § 200.5(a)(2) (2011). Note that the prohibition on natural person and tenant in common borrowers does not apply to loans receiving commitments prior to September 1, 2011.
40. *See* Section IV.A.1.c of this chapter and Chapter 5 for detailed discussion of previous participation requirements.
41. *See* 24 C.F.R. § 200.80 (2011) ("The mortgage shall be . . . a first lien on the property securing the mortgage."); *see also* 12 U.S.C. § 1713(a) (2010) ("[T]he term 'first mortgage' means such classes of first liens as are commonly given to secure advances (including but not being limited to advances during construction) on, or the unpaid purchase price of, real estate under the laws of the State, in which the real estate is located . . .").
42. *See* 24 C.F.R. § 200.71 (2011); 24 C.F.R. § 200.85 (2011); *Regulatory Agreement, supra* note 9, at ¶ 3; and *Security Instrument, supra* note 10, at ¶ 17. *See also* Section II.N of this chapter for a discussion of subordinate financing.
43. *See e.g.,* 12 U.S.C. § 1707(a) (2010), 12 U.S.C. § 1713(a) (2010); *Closing Guide, supra* note 22, at ¶ 3.2.F.
44. *MAP Guide, supra* note 15, at ¶ 3.2.T. Although outside the scope of this chapter, HUD may insure loans for condominium projects, including loans for the acquisition or purchase of individual units under HUD's Single Family Housing Programs, pursuant to Section 234 of the Act. *See* 12 U.S.C. § 1715y (2010).
45. *MAP Guide, supra* note 15, at ¶ 3.2.T.

mortgagor (for example, a residential apartment unit within a mixed-use condominium development). However, "[t]he insured loan must be secured by a mortgage on the rental apartment portion and any mortgagable commercial space. Joint use and maintenance agreements and easements between the insured portion and any separately demised condominium portion must be defined."[46] Air rights may be owned (and mortgaged) in fee simple, but often are the subject of long-term leases as well.[47] Regardless of whether it is subject to a fee or leasehold interest by the borrower, the mortgaged property must constitute a conveyable parcel, without the need for subdivision or other government approval.[48]

With respect to leasehold mortgages insured under Section 220 or Section 221 of the Act, the lease term must be (i) not less than 99 years and renewable or (ii) for a period of not less than 10 years beyond the maturity date of the mortgage.[49] For leasehold mortgages insured under Section 207, Section 207 pursuant to Section 223(f), or Section 231 of the Act, the lease term must be (i) not less than 99 years and renewable or (ii) for a period of not less than 50 years from the date the mortgage was executed.[50]

For a leasehold mortgage, regardless of the section of the Act under which insurance is provided, the lease must conform to the requirements of the HUD Lease Addendum, Form HUD-92070M (the Lease Addendum). Unless otherwise approved by HUD, the lease must be a ground lease, with all buildings, improvements, and fixtures owned by the tenant.[51] Under the required Lease Addendum, HUD has the right to purchase fee simple title to the real estate in the event HUD acquires title to the leasehold interest[52] (which would occur if HUD acquired the leasehold estate by foreclosure or deed-in-lieu of foreclosure in connection with a mortgage insurance claim). The purchase price is determined at the issuance of the Firm Commitment and is not adjusted over time. HUD may permit the purchase option to be omitted from a ground lease where the landlord is a state or local governmental authority.[53] Additionally, the landlord must give HUD and the lender notice of any event of default prior to terminating the lease.[54] The Lease Addendum provides HUD and the lender six months to cure such default.[55] If the

---

46. *Id.*
47. *See id.* at ¶ 11.5.A regarding Air Rights and Other Shared Interest Projects.
48. *See Closing Guide, supra* note 22, at ¶ 3.2.F.3.
49. *See* 12 U.S.C. § 1707(a) (2010). *See also* 12 U.S.C. § 1715k(c) (2010) and 12 U.S.C. § 1715l(c) (2010), incorporating 12 U.S.C. § 1707(a) by reference. *Accord Closing Guide, supra* note 22, at ¶ 3.2.F.
50. *See* 12 U.S.C. § 1713(a) (2010). *See also* 12 U.S.C. § 1715v(a)(3) (2010), incorporating 12 U.S.C. § 1713(a) by reference. Note that the Regulations applicable to loans insured under Section 241 and Section 223(d) of the Act do not specifically incorporate either 12 U.S.C. § 1707(a) or 12 U.S.C. § 1713(a). With respect to loans insured under those sections, the provisions applicable to the existing loan apply with respect to the subordinate loan.
51. Lease Addendum, Form HUD-92070M (Rev. 04/11) [hereinafter *Lease Addendum*] introductory paragraph.
52. *Id.* at ¶ b.
53. If HUD waives its option right, "Paragraph [b] of the Addendum shall be deleted and the [language] of paragraph [e(i)] following the words 'the total value of the [Property] as established by' [is] to be deleted and there is to be added 'the Federal Housing Commissioner at $_____.'" HANDBOOK 4420.1, § 1-17(b).
54. *Lease Addendum, supra* note 51, at ¶ f.
55. *Id.*

default is not cured and the landlord terminates the lease, HUD and the lender have six months to elect to take a new lease on the property on the same terms as the original lease.[56] The lease cannot be modified without the written consent of HUD and the lender.[57]

E. Maximum Loan Amounts

Generally, the maximum insurable loan amount is the *lowest* of (i) the amount supportable by the applicable loan ratio, (ii) the amount allowed by statutory limits, and (iii) the amount supportable by debt service.[58]

A loan ratio reflects a comparison of either loan to value or loan to cost, depending on the section of the Act under which the loan is insured. Section 207, Section 207 pursuant to Section 223(f), and Section 241 are value-based programs.[59] Section 220 and Section 221(d) are cost-based programs.[60] Section 231 is a cost-based program for new construction projects and a value-based program for substantial rehabilitation projects.[61]

Statutory limits are calculated on a per-unit basis with respect to each program and are published annually in the *Federal Register*.[62] The per-unit limits are higher for elevator projects than they are for non-elevator projects, and they are subject to geographic cost-adjustment factors for projects in high-cost areas.[63] HUD periodically publishes high-cost percentage multipliers in Housing Notices and Mortgagee Letters.[64] In addition, the maximum loan amount under the statutory limit criterion is adjusted by the sum of costs not attributable to dwelling use, multiplied by the applicable loan ratio.[65] Costs not attributable to dwelling use include items such as exterior land improvements (including parking, garages, tennis courts, swimming pools, and other recreational facilities), leasing centers, maintenance space, commercial or community space, non-occupant storage areas,[66] and the cost of the land.[67]

---

56. *Id.* at ¶ g.
57. *Id.* at ¶ k.
58. However, *see* Section III of this chapter for additional limitations based on the section of the Act under which the loan is insured. *See* Supplement to Project Analysis, Form HUD-92264-A for details regarding the calculation of the maximum insurable loan amount, including deductions for the unpaid balance of special assessments and lease costs.
59. *See* 12 U.S.C. § 1713(c)(2) (2010) (but note that for housing projects in Alaska or Guam insured under Section 207, the mortgage may be limited by cost rather than value); Notice H 93-89; *MAP Guide*, *supra* note 15, at ¶ 3.9.I; 12 U.S.C. § 1715z-6(b)(1) (2010).
60. *See* 12 U.S.C. § 1715k(d)(3)(B)(ii) (2010); 12 U.S.C. §§ 1715l(d)(4)(iii)–(iv) (2010); 12 U.S.C. § 1715l(d)(3)(iii) (2010).
61. *See* 12 U.S.C. §§ 1715v(c)(3)–(4) (2010).
62. *See, e.g.*, Annual Indexing of Basic Statutory Mortgage Limits for Multifamily Housing Programs, 76 Fed. Reg. 10,387 (Feb. 24, 2011) for Calendar Year 2011.
63. High-cost areas are those areas in which the replacement cost for multifamily housing exceeds the statutory per-unit limits. HANDBOOK 4425.1, Rev-2.
64. *See e.g.*, Notice H 2011-13 and Mortgagee Letter 2011-24 for high cost percentage multipliers effective as of Jan. 1, 2011.
65. *MAP Guide*, *supra* note 15, at ¶ 8.7.A.1(c).
66. *See, e.g.*, 12 U.S.C. § 1713(c)(3)(A) (2010); 12 U.S.C. § 1715l(d)(3)(ii) (2010); 12 U.S.C. § 1715l(d)(4)(ii) (2010); Multifamily Summary Appraisal Report, Form HUD-92264; *MAP Guide*, *supra* note 15, at ¶ 6.3.C.3(c).
67. *See MAP Guide*, *supra* note 15, at ¶ 8.7.A.1(c).

A debt service coverage ratio (DSCR) is calculated by dividing underwritten net operating income by debt service payments, including MIP. In an effort to mitigate risk, HUD imposed programmatic requirements in 2010 that increased the applicable debt service coverage ratios and decreased the relevant loan ratios, as identified below.[68] Although most programmatic requirements may be waived by the Hub Director,[69] the debt service coverage ratio and loan ratio set forth in the MAP Guide are specifically excepted from this waiver authority.[70]

Debt Service Coverage Ratio (Form HUD-92264-A, Criterion 5) and Loan Ratio (Form HUD-92264-A, Criterion 3) Requirements			
Section of the Act	Criterion 5-DSCR (Programmatic)[71]	Criterion 3-Loan Ratio (Statutory)[72]	Criterion 3-Loan Ratio (Programmatic)[73]
207	None published	90.0%	None published
220, 221(d)(4), or 231, with 90% or greater rental assistance[74]	1.11	90.0%[75]	90%
220, 221(d)(4), or 231, affordable[76]	1.15	90.0%	87.0%
220, 221(d)(4), or 231, market rate	1.20	90.0%	83.3%
221(d)(3) affordable and 221(d)(3) with 90% or greater rental assistance	1.11	100.0%	95.0%
223(a)(7) nonprofit	None published	None set by statute	95.0%
223(a)(7) for profit	None published	None set by statute	90.0%[77]
223(f) refinance of a Section 202 property[78]	1.11	None set by statute	90.0%
223(f) with 90% or greater rental assistance	1.15	None set by statute	87.0%
223(f) affordable	1.18	None set by statute	85.0%
223(f) market rate refinance or acquisition	1.20	None set by statute	83.3%[79]
241	None published	90.0%	90.0%

68. *See* Notice H 2010-11 and Mortgagee Letter 2010-21, the requirements of which are now incorporated into the MAP Guide, *see infra* note 71.

69. HUD currently operates the multifamily insurance program through 17 "Hubs." Each Hub serves a specified geographic area and includes the HUD office where the Hub is located and may include one or more "Program Centers" or "field offices." Each Hub is headed by a Hub Director, which is "the organizational position with delegated authority pursuant to delegations of authority published in the Federal Register and current administrative notices for making administrative policy determinations with respect to insuring an FHA loan for multifamily rental projects, in accordance with Program Obligations." *Closing Guide, supra* note 22, at ¶ 1.3.B.3.

70. *MAP Guide, supra* note 15, at ¶ 11.2.G.

71. *See MAP Guide, supra* note 15, at ¶ 3.7.C with respect to loans insured under Section 220; *id.* at ¶ 3.5 with respect to loans insured under Section 221(d)(4); *id.* at ¶ 3.6.B with respect to loans insured under Section 221(d)(3); *id.* at ¶ 3.9.I with respect to loans insured under Section 223(f); and *id.* at ¶ 3.8.D with respect to loans insured under Section 231. Note that as of the date of this writing,

DSCR requirements had not been published with respect to loans insured under Section 207, Section 223(a)(7), or Section 241. Similarly, programmatic guidance with respect to the applicable loan ratio for loans insured under Section 207 had not been published as of the date of this writing. Additional guidance on the programmatic requirements for Section 223(a)(7) and Section 241 is anticipated in the form of a future MAP Guide release. *Id.* at ¶ 1.2.B.

72. *See* 12 U.S.C. § 1713(c) (2010) with respect to loans insured under Section 207; 12 U.S.C. § 1715k(d)(3)(B)(ii) (2010) with respect to loans insured under Section 220; 12 U.S.C. § § 1715l(d)(4)(iii)–(iv) (2010) with respect to loans insured under Section 221(d)(4); 12 U.S.C. § 1715l(d)(3)(iii) (2010) with respect to loans insured under Section 221(d)(3); 12 U.S.C. §§ 1715v(c)(3)–(4) (2010) with respect to loans insured under Section 231; and 12 U.S.C. § 1715z-6(b)(1) (2010) with respect to loans insured under Section 241.

73. *See supra* note 71. *See also* Notice H 93-89 with respect to loans insured under Section 223(a)(7); HANDBOOK 4585.1 with respect to loans insured under Section 241.

74. *See* Chapter 10 for a discussion of Section 8 project-based rental assistance.

75. For loans insured under Section 231 involving nonprofit borrowers, the statutory loan ratio is 100% of value (or cost for substantial rehabilitation) for affordable projects and projects with 90% or greater rental assistance. 12 U.S.C. § 1715(c)(3) (2010).

76. "Affordable housing is defined as projects meeting *all* of the following requirements: (a) projects that have a recorded regulatory agreement that will be in effect for at least 15 years after [f]inal [e]ndorsement, (b) projects that meet at least the minimum [low income housing tax credit (LIHTC)] restrictions of 20% of units at 50% of area median income (AMI), or 40% of units at 60% of AMI, with economic rents (i.e., the portion paid by the residents) on those units no greater than LIHTC rents; and (c) mixed-income projects if the minimum low-income unit rent and occupancy restrictions and regulatory agreement meet the above criteria. . . . "An 'affordable project' does not need to have actual LIHTCs so long as a recorded Regulatory Agreement is in place for the term specified, that meets or exceeds the rent and income limitations for the LIHTC program." *MAP Guide*, *supra* note 15, at ¶ 3.2.Q (emphasis in original).

77. *See infra* note 377 and accompanying text for additional restrictions on the maximum insurable mortgage for loans insured under Section 223(a)(7).

78. Although now a capital advance program, Section 202 of the Housing Act of 1959 originally authorized direct loans made by HUD to finance the construction or substantial rehabilitation of residential projects for the elderly or the handicapped. Section 811 of the American Homeownership and Economic Opportunity Act of 2000 authorized the prepayment of Section 202 direct loans. *See* Notice H 02-16 regarding the requirements for prepayment of such direct loans.

79. *See infra* notes 342–45 and accompanying text for additional restrictions on the maximum insurable mortgage for loans insured under Section 223(f). For all cash out refinances, the loan to value ratio cannot exceed 80%. *See* Section III.C.3 of this chapter.

F. Large Loan Limits

In a further effort to mitigate risk, HUD has imposed additional programmatic requirements for large loans, defined as those greater than or equal to $25 million in size and/or those that support projects in excess of 150 housing units.[80] These programmatic requirements further increase the applicable debt service coverage ratios and decrease the relevant loan ratios based on the size of the loan, as set forth below.

Large Loan Debt Service Coverage Ratio (Form HUD-92264-A, Criterion 5) and Loan Ratio (Form HUD-92264-A, Criterion 3) Requirements[81]			
Section of the Act	Loan Size (in millions)	Criterion 5- DSCR	Criterion 3- Loan Ratio
220, 221(d), and 231, affordable	Under $40	1.15	87.0%
	$40 - $60	1.20	85.0%
	Over $60	1.25	80.0%
220, 221(d), and 231, market rate	Under $40	1.20	83.3%
	$40 - $60	1.25	80.0%
	Over $60	1.30	75.0%
223(f) affordable	Under $50	1.18	85% without cash out 80.0% with cash out
	$50 - $75	1.20	83.3% without cash out 75.0% with cash out
	Over $75	1.25	80.0% without cash out 70.0% with cash out
223(f) market rate	Under $50	1.20	83.3% without cash out 80.0% with cash out
	$50 - $75	1.25	80.0% without cash out 75.0% with cash out
	Over $75	1.30	75.0% without cash out 70.0% with cash out

For loans of more than $100 million, the above standards apply unless HUD advises within five business days after the required concept meeting[82] that a higher standard will be applied as a result of project-specific risks. Large loans also are subject to increased initial operating deficit reserve requirements,[83] and the principals of large loan borrowers must meet

---

80. *See* Notice H 2011-36; Mortgagee Letter 2011-40. Note that with respect to loans under $25 million, the impact of having over 150 housing units relates primarily to initial operating deficit requirements. The number of housing units does not impact debt service coverage ratio requirements, loan ratio requirements, net worth and liquidity requirements, or experience requirements. *See infra* notes 81–86 and accompanying text.

81. *See* Notice H 2011-36 ¶ III.A; Mortgagee Letter 2011-40 ¶ III.A.

82. *See infra* notes 404–05 and accompanying text.

83. For loans with a loan size under $25 million or a unit count of fewer than 150 units (whichever is the lower controlling criteria), initial operating deficit reserves must be established in an amount equal to the greater of 4–6 months of debt service or 3.0% of the mortgage amount.

certain net worth and liquidity requirements.[84] With respect to properties owned less than three years as of the date of the application, in determining the maximum loan amount, no increase in appraised value may be recognized above the acquisition cost plus direct costs of improvements.[85] Developers and borrowers must demonstrate sufficient experience with other large multifamily projects to qualify for a large loan insured under FHA's insurance programs.[86] The large loan requirements do not apply to loans insured under Section 223(a)(7) or refinancing or substantial rehabilitation loans with rental assistance for 90 percent or more of the units.[87]

G. Mortgage Term

All FHA-insured multifamily loans must have a mortgage term of not less than 10 years,[88] but the maximum mortgage term varies based on the section of the Act under which the loan is insured. For new construction projects, the construction period is excluded from the mortgage term.[89]

The initial operating deficit reserve requirement increases to (i) the greater of 9 months of debt service or 4.50% of the mortgage for loans with a loan size from $25 million to $40 million or a unit count between 150 and 250 units, (ii) the greater of 12 months of debt service or 6.25% of the mortgage for loans with a loan size of more than $40 million up to $60 million or a unit count between 251 and 400 units, and (iii) the greater of 15 months of debt service or 8.0% of the mortgage for loans with a loan size over $60 million or a unit count of 401 units or more. However, certain reductions in initial operating deficit reserve requirements may be permitted for projects that will complete rent-up within 12 months of construction completion. Notice H 2011-36 ¶ III.B; Mortgagee Letter 2011-40 ¶ III.B.

84. Including aggregate net worth of at least 20% of the loan amount and liquidity equal to at least 7.5% of the loan amount. These requirements apply only to loans that are greater than or equal to $25 million in size. Notice H 2011-36 ¶ III.D(i); Mortgagee Letter 2011-40 ¶ III.D(i).

85. Notice H 2011-36 ¶ III.D(ii); Mortgagee Letter 2011-40 ¶ III.D(ii). This requirement applies only to loans that are greater than or equal to $25 million in size, and the Hub Director may issue a waiver to recognize an increase in appraised value of the property in certain limited circumstances.

86. Notice H 2011-36 ¶ III.D(iii); Mortgagee Letter 2011-40 ¶ III.D(iii). These requirements apply only to loans that are greater than or equal to $25 million in size.

87. Notice H 2011-36 ¶ I; Mortgagee Letter 2011-40 ¶ I.

88. 24 C.F.R. § 200.82(b) (2011); *MAP Guide, supra* note 15, at ¶ 8.5.

89. *MAP Guide, supra* note 15, at ¶ 8.5.

Section of the Act	Maximum Mortgage Term
207, 220, 221(d), 231	Lesser of 75% of remaining estimated economic life of improvements or 40 years.[90]
207/223(f)	Lesser of 75% of remaining estimated economic life of improvements or 35 years.[91]
223(a)(7)	With HUD approval, the term may be extended up to 12 years beyond the term of the original insured mortgage, subject to the term limitations of the program under which the original insured mortgage was insured and provided the remaining economic life of the project supports the term. If a project is refinanced more than once using loans insured under Section 223(a)(7), the cumulative extension of the term pursuant to all Section 223(a)(7) loans cannot exceed 12 years.[92]
223(d)	Cannot exceed the remaining term of the existing mortgage.[93]
241	Lesser of 75% of remaining estimated economic life of improvements or 40 years;[94] however, because additions constructed under Section 241 often have a limited impact on the remaining economic life of the project as a whole, loans insured under this Section often are coterminous with (or have only a slightly longer term than) the existing loan.

H. Prepayment Restrictions

If the loan is *not* funded with "bond obligations" or Ginnie Mae mortgage-backed securities, the borrower must be given the right to prepay the loan, in whole or in part, on 30 days' written notice to the lender, and the lender cannot charge a prepayment premium for the prepayment of up to 15 percent of the original principal amount in any one calendar year.[95] Because investors typically demand greater prepayment restrictions, FHA-insured loans almost always are funded with "bond obligations" or Ginnie Mae mortgage-backed securities.

If the loan is funded with "bond obligations" or Ginnie Mae mortgage-backed securities, prepayment restrictions and prepayment premiums may be imposed as long as they comply with HUD's requirements, including allowing HUD to override the restrictions in the event of a default.[96] For loans funded through the issuance of taxable or tax-exempt state or local government bonds, the prepayment lockout period cannot end later than 10 years after commencement of amortization,[97] and the premium for prepayment in the first year following

---

90. 24 C.F.R. § 200.82(a) (2011); *MAP Guide, supra* note 15, at ¶¶ 3.4.D, 8.5.
91. *Id.*
92. 12 U.S.C. § 1715n(a)(7) (2010); *MAP Guide, supra* note 15, at ¶ 11.7.A.3. Provided, however, that a mortgage insured pursuant to Section 223(a)(7) that is subject to a mortgage restructuring and rental assistance sufficiency plan under the Multifamily Assisted Housing Reform and Affordability Act of 1997 (MAHRA) may have a term of not more than 30 years. 12 U.S.C. § 1715n(a)(7)(B) (2010).
93. 12 U.S.C. § 1715n(d)(4) (2010).
94. HANDBOOK 4470.1.
95. 24 C.F.R. § 200.87(a)–(b) (2011).
96. 24 C.F.R. § 200.87(c)–(d) (2011), *see also Note, supra* note 11, at ¶ 9.
97. Although the MAP Guide provides that the lockout period may be tied to either (a) the date of commencement of amortization or (b) the date of completion as stated in the construction contract,

lockout cannot exceed 5 percent, declining on a graduated basis to an amount not to exceed 1 percent at the end of the fifth year following the end of the lockout period.[98] For loans funded with Ginnie Mae mortgage-backed securities or "other bond obligations,"[99] it is permissible to have (a) a lockout period ending not later than 10 years after commencement of amortization,[100] (b) a prepayment premium of 10 percent or less, declining to an amount not to exceed 1 percent at the end of the 10th year following commencement of amortization,[101] or (c) a combination of the lockout and premium charges described in (a) and (b).[102]

I. Cost Certification

Because cost is a factor in calculating the maximum insurable mortgage under several sections of the Act,[103] it is important that HUD be provided with an accurate statement of the actual costs incurred by the borrower and, where applicable, the contractor. This is particularly true in the case of new construction or substantial rehabilitation, for many of the costs to complete the project must be estimated at the time of the initial endorsement. Therefore, to ensure that the insured mortgage amount does not exceed the amount supported by actual costs, borrowers are required to submit a certification of actual cost.[104] Excepted from this requirement are projects insured under Section 223(d) of the Act,[105] projects insured under Section 223(a)(7) of the Act,[106] projects insured under Section 223(f) of the Act with a loan-to-value ratio of 80 percent or less,[107] and projects insured under Section 221(d) or Section 220 involving tax credits "[i]f it is determined at the time of Firm Commitment issuance that the ratio of loan proceeds to the actual cost of the project is less than 80 percent."[108] HUD,

---

from a practical standpoint, commencement of amortization will always occur on a date later than the date of completion as stated in the construction contract. *See MAP Guide, supra* note 15, at ¶ 11.7.B.3.

98. *Id.*

99. "'Other bond obligations' refers to any agreement under which Mortgagee has obtained the mortgage funds from third party investors and has agreed in writing to repay such investors at a stated interest rate and in accordance with a fixed repayment schedule." *Id.* at ¶ 11.7.B.4.

100. The date of completion as stated in the construction contract may be used in lieu of the date of commencement of amortization under the terms of the MAP Guide. *See supra* note 97; *MAP Guide, supra* note 15, at ¶ 11.7.B.4.

101. The date of completion as stated in the construction contract may be used in lieu of the date of commencement of amortization under the terms of the MAP Guide. *See supra* note 97; *MAP Guide, supra* note 15, at ¶ 11.7.B.4.

102. *MAP Guide, supra* note 15, at ¶ 11.7.B.4.

103. *See supra* notes 60–61 and accompanying text.

104. *See* 12 U.S.C. § 1715r (2010); 24 C.F.R. § 200.96 (2011).

105. *See* HANDBOOK 4470.1. Although cost certification requirements with respect to the original loan must have been satisfied in order for the borrower to be eligible for an operating loss loan, a separate cost certification is not required in connection with obtaining a loan insured under Section 223(d).

106. *See* Notice H 93-89; HANDBOOK 4470.2 § 1-2. Additional guidance on the programmatic requirements for Section 223(a)(7) is anticipated in the form of a future MAP Guide release. *MAP Guide, supra* note 15, at ¶ 1.2.B.

107. *See MAP Guide, supra* note 15, at ¶ 13.1.

108. *Id.* at ¶ 13.4.

borrower, lender, and, where applicable, contractor enter into an Agreement and Certification, Form HUD-93305M (the Agreement and Certification),[109] pursuant to which the borrower agrees to provide a certificate of actual cost and to comply with mortgage reduction requirements if actual costs do not support the mortgage amount.[110]

1. New Construction and Substantial Rehabilitation Projects

For loans insured under Section 207, Section 220, Section 221, Section 231, or Section 241,[111] in addition to the borrower, the contractor must certify actual costs if (i) there is an identity of interest between the borrower and the contractor or (ii) the construction contract is designated a cost-plus contract, regardless of whether an identity of interest exists.[112] Furthermore, subcontractors, equipment lessors, and material suppliers must cost-certify if (i) they have an identity of interest either with the borrower or with a contractor that must cost-certify and (ii) the total of the entity's subcontracts, purchases, and leases is more than 0.5 percent of the mortgage amount.[113] "If more than 50 percent of the actual cost of construction is subcontracted with any one contractor or subcontractor, or more than 75 percent with three or fewer contractors or subcontractors (50–75 percent Rule), [builder's and sponsor's profit and risk allowance] shall not be allowed as an actual cost, and Borrower shall be limited to the inclusion on its Certificate of Actual Cost of [sponsor's profit and risk allowance]. Further, in that event, for the purpose of determining actual cost, HUD will not allow any expense for [g]eneral [c]ontractor's general overhead."[114]

The certificates of actual cost must be on HUD-approved forms[115] and audited by an accountant in a manner acceptable to HUD.[116] Cost certifications must be submitted not less

---

109. Agreement and Certification, Form HUD-93305M (Rev 04/11) [hereinafter *Agreement and Certification*]. Only paragraphs 1, 2, and 6 of the Agreement and Certification apply for refinancing projects insured under Section 223(f) or 223(a)(7). *See Agreement and Certification*, page 2, "Finacning or refinancing"option paragraph.

110. 24 C.F.R. § 200.96(a) (2010).

111. Loans insured under Section 241 and substantial rehabilitation loans insured under Section 231 are value based and arguably should not require cost certification, but as of the date of this writing, the available guidance did not specifically address or except loans insured under these programs from cost certification requirements. Additional guidance on the programmatic requirements for Section 241 is anticipated in the form of a future MAP Guide release. *MAP Guide*, *supra* note 15, at ¶ 1.2.B.

112. *Id.* at ¶ 13.6.B.

113. *Id.* at ¶ 13.6.C.

114. *Agreement and Certification*, *supra* note 109, at ¶ 10.c. *See also* Section III.A.1 for a further discussion of builder's and sponsor's profit and risk allowance and sponsor's profit and risk allowance.

115. *See, e.g.,* Mortgagor's Certificate of Actual Cost, Form HUD-92330, Contractor's Certificate of Actual Cost, Form HUD-92330A, and Mortgagor's Certificate of Actual Cost (Section 207 Pursuant to Section 223(f) Form, FHA-2205A. *See also, Agreement and Certification*, *supra* note 109, at ¶ 1.

116. 24 C.F.R. § 200.96(b) (2011); *MAP Guide*, *supra* note 15, at ¶ 13.12.B.6.

than 30 days before the final closing date and within 30 to 45 days after the cutoff date for soft costs as established by the borrower.[117] If the mortgage amount exceeds the applicable statutory percentage of certified actual costs, a mortgage reduction is required under the provisions of the Act.[118]

2. Refinancing Projects

With respect to mortgages insured under Section 207 pursuant to Section 223(f), costs are certified at closing using the "short form" cost certification.[119] This form of certification, which need not be audited, must be submitted after the critical repairs[120] have been completed and at least 15 days prior to closing.[121] For projects with non-critical repairs being completed after closing, a supplemental certification of cost also may be required following completion of the deferred repairs.[122] If the actual costs following completion of the repairs do not support the mortgage amount, a mortgage reduction may be required.[123] In the alternative, however, excess funds as a result of lower actual repair costs may be used to pay for additional repairs approved by the lender and HUD or deposited into the project's reserve for replacements account.[124]

J. Reserve for Replacements, Mortgage Insurance Premiums, and HUD Fees

1. Reserve for Replacements

The Firm Commitment sets forth an annual deposit amount for, and, if applicable, an initial deposit to, the reserve for replacement account. These funds are to be used for replacement of "major structural elements and mechanical equipment of the Project."[125] The amount of the annual deposit is payable in 12 equal monthly payments together with the monthly payment on the Note and may be adjusted every 10 years, or more frequently at HUD's discretion, based on an analysis of the use of reserve for replacement funds in the prior 10 years and projected uses.[126] Borrowers are entitled to earn interest on the amounts deposited in the

---

117. *MAP Guide, supra* note 15, at ¶ 13.10. The cutoff date for inclusion of soft costs in the cost certification cannot be more than 60 days past the date of substantial completion, which is defined as the date the architect certifies on Permission to Occupy Project Mortgages, Form HUD-92485 that the construction work is sufficiently complete and the project can be occupied. *MAP Guide, supra* note 15, at ¶ 13.8.

118. 12 U.S.C. § 1715r (2011).

119. *I.e.,* Mortgagor's Certificate of Actual Cost (Section 207 Pursuant to Section 223(f), Form FHA-2205A).

120. *See infra* notes 354–55 and accompanying text.

121. *MAP Guide, supra* note 15, at ¶ 13.12.C.

122. 24 C.F.R. § 200.96(a) (2011).

123. *MAP Guide, supra* note 15, at ¶ 13.20.B.

124. Escrow for Non-Critical Deferred Repairs, Form HUD-92476.1M (Rev. 04/11) [hereinafter *Repair Escrow*]. *See* Section II.J.1 of this chapter for a discussion of reserve for replacements.

125. *Regulatory Agreement, supra* note 9, at ¶ 10.

126. *Id.*

reserve for replacements. HUD consent is required for disbursements from the reserve for replacements.[127]

2. Mortgage Insurance Premiums (MIP)

HUD collects MIP as part of the consideration for providing mortgage insurance. For loans that involve insurance of advances, the first MIP payment is collected at the initial endorsement,[128] with the second payment of MIP due on the date of the first payment to principal, unless commencement of amortization begins more than one year following the initial endorsement, in which case subsequent annual payments of MIP are due on each anniversary of the initial endorsement of the Note for insurance until the commencement of amortization.[129] Thereafter, annual MIP payments are due on the date of commencement of amortization and each anniversary thereof as long as the loan is insured by HUD.[130] For other projects, the first payment of MIP is due at the initial/final endorsement.[131] Thereafter, annual MIP payments are due on the anniversary of commencement of amortization as long as the loan is insured by HUD.[132] Specific MIP rates for each program, in an amount not less than one-fourth of 1 percent and not more than 1 percent of the principal amount of the mortgage, are published in the *Federal Register* for each fiscal year.[133] The MIP rates are subject to adjustment by HUD based on factors such as defaults and projected losses and recoveries under each program.

Although the lender is responsible for remitting these payments to HUD, the borrower must make sufficient escrow payments under the Security Instrument to cover annual MIP amounts when due,[134] and this amount is included in the calculation of the debt service coverage ratio. When applying mortgage payments, the lender must first apply the amounts received to payment of MIP.[135]

---

127. *Id.*
128. MIP payments are prepaid, and MIP payments are collected prior to final endorsement on an estimated basis and later reconciled based upon the actual outstanding balance.
129. 24 C.F.R. § 207.252 (2011).
130. *Id.*
131. *Id.*
132. *Id.*
133. *See, e.g.,* Federal Housing Administration (FHA) Mortgage Insurance Premiums for Multifamily Housing Programs, Health Care Facilities and Hospitals and Credit Subsidy Obligations for Fiscal Year (FY) 2011, 76 Fed. Reg. 40,741 (July 17, 2011). The MIP rate for the first year of the loan term (for all programs except Section 223(a)(7)) is currently 100 basis points of the outstanding principal balance. The annual MIP rate for (i) projects without low-income housing tax credits insured under Section 221(d)(3) or Section 241 and (ii) projects insured under Section 223(d) is currently 80 basis points. The annual MIP rate for all other FHA-insured multifamily projects is currently between 45 and 50 basis points. *Id. See also infra* notes 301 and 306.
134. 24 C.F.R. § 200.84(b)(2) (2011).
135. 24 C.F.R. § 200.84(c) (2011); *see also Security Instrument, supra* note 10, at ¶ 7(a)(3). MIP may be paid "in cash or in debentures at par plus accrued interest." 24 C.F.R. § 207.252(f) (2011).

3. Escrowing for Taxes/Property Insurance Premiums/Mortgage Insurance Premiums

In addition to principal, interest, the monthly deposits to the reserve for replacements, and the monthly escrow deposit for MIP, the borrower's monthly payment to the lender must include sufficient amounts for the payment of taxes, assessments, and property insurance premiums at least one month prior to the date on which such payments would become delinquent.[136]

All escrows for taxes, insurance premiums and MIP, reserve for replacements deposits, residual receipts deposits, and other escrows must be placed in "accounts insured or guaranteed by a federal agency and in accordance with Program Obligations."[137] The amounts escrowed (other than the reserve for replacements and residual receipts) must equal the amounts reasonably estimated by the lender to be necessary plus one-sixth of such estimate.[138] Lenders are not obligated to pay amounts due for taxes, assessments, or premiums to the extent such bills or invoices exceed the amount of the funds deposited with the lender for such purposes.[139] Escrowed funds are to be used only for the purpose for which they were collected and any excess funds after payment of taxes, assessments, or premiums are credited to "subsequent monthly payments of the same nature."[140]

4. FHA Application Fee

"An application for Firm Commitment must include an application fee equal to $3 per $1,000 (30 basis points) of the requested mortgage amount."[141] For market-rate new construction or substantial rehabilitation projects submitted for two-stage processing,[142] a nonrefundable application fee equal to $1.50 per $1,000 (15 basis points) of the requested mortgage amount is submitted at the pre-application stage, which is credited to the Firm Commitment application fee if an invitation letter is issued and Firm Commitment application is submitted.[143] For affordable housing projects, no application fee is required at the pre-application and the full

---

136. 24 C.F.R. § 200.84(b) (2011); *see also Security Instrument, supra* note 10, at ¶ 7(a)(2).

137. *Security Instrument, supra* note 10, at ¶ 8(b); *see also* HANDBOOK 4350.4 for general requirements for servicing and investment of escrows. "Program Obligations" is defined as: "(1) all applicable statutes and any regulations that apply to the Project, including all amendments to such statutes and regulations, as they become effective, except that changes subject to notice and comment rulemaking become effective upon completion of the rulemaking process, and (2) all current requirements in HUD handbooks and guides, notices, and mortgagee letters that apply to the Project, and all future updates, changes and amendments thereto, as they become effective, except that changes subject to notice and comment rulemaking become effective upon completion of the rulemaking process, and provided that such future updates, changes and amendments shall be applicable to the Project only to the extent that they interpret, clarify and implement terms in [the applicable closing document] rather than add or delete provisions from such document." *Regulatory Agreement, supra* note 9, at ¶ 1(y); *Security Instrument, supra* note 10, at ¶ 1(dd).

138. *Security Instrument, supra* note 10, at ¶ 8(d).

139. *Id.* at ¶ 8(c).

140. *Id.* at ¶ 8(a).

141. *MAP Guide, supra* note 15, at ¶ 3.2.F. *See also* 24 C.F.R. § 200.40 (2011). The application fee is sometimes referred to as the FHA exam fee.

142. *See* Section IV of this chapter for a discussion of application processing.

143. *MAP Guide, supra* note 15, at ¶ 3.2.F.

amount instead is collected with the application for Firm Commitment.[144] For Section 223(a)(7) refinancing projects, the full application fee is collected, but half of this fee is refunded by HUD if the loan is endorsed for insurance.[145]

5. FHA Inspection Fee

HUD collects an inspection fee to cover the cost of inspecting repairs and improvements in an amount not to exceed $5 per $1,000 (50 basis points) of the commitment amount for new construction projects and $5 per $1,000 (50 basis points) of improvement costs for substantial rehabilitation projects.[146] "For loans insured pursuant to Section 207/223(f) or 223(a)(7), the inspection fee is the following:

1. $30 per unit where the repairs/improvements are greater than $100,000 in total but $3,000 or less per unit.
2. $30 per unit or one percent of the cost of repairs, whichever is greater, where the repairs/improvements are more than $3,000 per unit.
3. $1,500 where the repairs/improvements are less than $100,000, which fee may be waived by the Hub/[Program Center]."[147]

K. Defaults

The Regulations and the Security Instrument provide for a two-tiered default structure, composed of monetary and covenant events of default.[148] A monetary event of default is failure to make a monthly payment under the Note or Security Instrument when due.[149] This includes a failure to make necessary deposits to escrows for taxes, assessments, or insurance; reserve for replacement deposits; or deposits to any other required escrows.[150] The date of default is the date of the first failure to make such payment.[151] The lender is not entitled to receive insurance benefits unless the monetary default has continued for a period of 30 days.[152] If a monetary event of default occurs and is continuing, the lender may, without HUD approval, accelerate the debt and exercise other remedies under the Note or Security Instrument.[153]

---

144. *Id.*
145. Mortgagee Letter 2006-03.
146. 24 C.F.R. § 200.40(e) (2011); 24 C.F.R. § 241.515 (2011); *MAP Guide, supra* note 15, at ¶ 3.2.G.
147. *MAP Guide, supra* note 15, at ¶ 3.2.G. *See also* 24 C.F.R. § 200.40(e) ("for a mortgage being insured under section 223(f) of the Act, if the application provides for the completion of repairs, replacements and/or improvements (repairs), the Commissioner will charge an inspection fee equal to one percent (1%) of the cost of the repairs. However, where the Commissioner determines the cost of repairs is minimal, the Commissioner may establish a minimum inspection fee that exceeds one percent of the cost of repairs and can periodically increase or decrease this minimum fee.").
148. 24 C.F.R. § 207.255 (2011). *Security Instrument, supra* note 10, at ¶ 22.
149. 24 C.F.R. § 207.255(a)(1)(i) (2011).
150. *Security Instrument, supra* note 10, at ¶ 22(a).
151. 24 C.F.R. § 207.255(a)(4)(i) (2011).
152. 24 C.F.R. § 207.255(a)(3) (2011).
153. *Security Instrument, supra* note 10, at ¶ 43. This section of the Security Instrument is subject to variation as provided in HUD-approved state-specific addendum forms.

Covenant events of default include (i) fraud or material misrepresentation by the borrower with respect to the loan application, or any financial statement, rent roll, report, or request for lender consent; (ii) commencement of a forfeiture action or proceeding that, in the lender's reasonable judgment, could materially impair the lender's security interest; (iii) material failure to comply with obligations under the Security Instrument that continues for 30 days after notice from the lender of such failure (unless in the lender's judgment, the failure could impair the lender's security interest if action is not immediately taken, in which case notice is not required); or (iv) violations of the Regulatory Agreement, if HUD requests that the lender treat the violation as a default.[154] The date of default is the date of the first uncorrected violation for which the lender accelerated the debt[155] and the lender only may accelerate the debt due to a covenant default with HUD approval.[156] HUD also may request that the lender accelerate the debt to protect HUD's interest on the occurrence of a covenant event of default.[157] If the lender refuses to "comply promptly" with HUD's request to accelerate the debt and later elects to assign the loan, payment of the lender's mortgage insurance claim will be reduced by the difference between (i) the project's market value as of the date HUD requested that the lender accelerate the debt and (ii) the market value as of the date the lender makes the election to assign.

Although the Security Instrument does not provide a cure period to the borrower for a monetary event of default, it does provide that the lender must give principals[158] notice of either a monetary or covenant event of default within five business days after giving notice of such event of default to the borrower to allow the principals an opportunity to cure.[159] However, the lender may not be obligated to notify principals of a default if there is no requirement to provide notice to the borrower.[160]

L. Assumability/Transfer of Physical Assets

FHA-insured mortgages are fully assumable, subject to HUD's transfer of physical assets (TPA) process[161] and compliance with the requirements of the Regulatory Agreement.[162] TPAs

---

154. *Id.* at ¶ 22(b).
155. 24 C.F.R. § 207.255(a)(4)(ii) (2011).
156. *Security Instrument, supra* note 10, at ¶ 43.
157. 24 C.F.R. § 207.257 (2011).
158. *See infra* note 438 for the definition of principals.
159. *Security Instrument, supra* note 10, at ¶ 22(c). Note, however, "The sole purpose of this requirement is to provide notice of the potential default so that if the Principals want to step in and timely cure the default they will have been given notice of the problem. This language does not create any additional rights for the Principals." Multifamily Document Reform Implementation Frequently Asked Questions, Security Instrument, Question 6, *available at* http://portal.hud.gov/hudportal/HUD?src=/program_offices/general_counsel/mffaqs/security#Q6.
160. *See, e.g., Security Instrument, supra* note 10 at ¶ 22(b)(3), providing that the lender need not provide notice to the borrower in the event of a material failure by borrower to perform obligations under the Security Instrument "which could, in Lender's judgment, absent immediate exercise by Lender of a right or remedy under this Security Instrument, result in harm to Lender or impairment of the Note or this Security Instrument."
161. HANDBOOK 4350.1, Ch. 13; Notice H 99-13.
162. *Regulatory Agreement, supra* note 9, at ¶ 36(a), requiring HUD approval for substitution of the borrower.

require either "full" or "modified" HUD review depending on the nature of the interest being transferred. Full review is required for transfer of title to the property to a new entity, transfer of an interest in the mortgagor entity that results in dissolution of the entity, or transfer of the entire beneficial interest in a passive trust resulting in change of control in the project.[163]

Ordinarily, in a full TPA, the purchaser assumes the note, mortgage, and, if applicable, any Housing Assistance Payments contracts and use agreements.[164] The purchaser also must either assume the existing Regulatory Agreement or enter into a new Regulatory Agreement with HUD.[165] TPA applications will be accepted only if the mortgage payments are current or if the TPA will cause the mortgage to be brought current.[166] A full TPA review occurs in two phases. HUD first reviews the TPA application and all exhibits thereto[167] to determine the completeness of the application and the acceptability of the transfer. For TPAs requiring full review, an application fee in the amount of $0.50 per $1,000 (five basis points) of the original face amount of the mortgage is required.[168] If the transfer is approved, HUD will issue a preliminary approval letter, stating the terms and conditions of the approval, including any changes needed to the documents submitted for preliminary approval review. The purchaser then has 45 business days to submit all executed recorded and unrecorded documents, an audited interim financial statement, balance sheet, mortgage statement, original regulatory agreement, attorney's opinion, title policy or endorsement, and rental schedule (Form HUD-92458).[169] If the documentation submitted is acceptable, HUD will issue a final approval letter.

Modified TPA review is required when there is a substitution of a general partner or a single transfer in excess of 50 percent (or a transfer of less than 50 percent if it results in change of control of the borrower) of the interest in a borrower entity that does not cause dissolution of the entity, transfer of all or a portion of the beneficial interest in a passive trust

---

163. HANDBOOK 4350.1 § 13-7.
164. Although it is possible for a TPA to be done on a "subject to" basis, this is rarely if ever done, as the seller would not be released from its obligations under the HUD loan documents.
165. HANDBOOK 4350.1, Chapter 13, Appendix G. For projects that received Firm Commitments prior to September 1, 2011, the "old" form of Regulatory Agreement should be used in connection with the TPA. *See* Multifamily Document Reform Implementation Frequently Asked Questions, General Questions, *available at* http://portal.hud.gov/hudportal/HUD?src=/program_offices/general_counsel/mffaqs/general#Q9 ("All TPAs, whether full or modified, processed for Projects closed under the 'old' documents will use the old documents in closing the transfer of physical assets."). For form closing documents for loans receiving commitments prior to September 1, 2011, *see* http://portal.hud.gov/hudportal/HUD?src=/program_offices/administration/hudclips.
166 HANDBOOK 4350.1 § 13-13.
167. Exhibits include, but are not limited to, the purchaser's letter, previous participation certificates, the purchaser's resume and credit reports, a sources and uses of funds statement, executed but unrecorded copies of the sales contract, deed, Regulatory Agreement and assignment, assumption, and modification agreement, purchaser's financial statements, proposed rental schedule (Form HUD-92458), and executed organizational documents of the purchaser. "The [p]urchaser's letter must describe in detail all financial consideration flowing to the project and the mortgagor/seller as a result of the transfer. This letter must detail all funds allocated to project operations as well as those funds designated for use in correcting the physical needs of the project. The letter should describe the entire transaction. . . ." *Id.* at Chapter 13, Appendix A.
168. 24 C.F.R. § 200.40(h) (2011).
169. HANDBOOK 4350.1 § 3-39.

that does not result in change of control of the project, or any other transaction that results in a change of control of the borrower.[170] Modified TPA review follows the same two-stage approval process, but substantially fewer documents are required for review.[171] In addition, the application fee is not required for substitution of a general partner or assignment of a beneficial interest in a passive trust that does not result in a change in control of the project.[172]

For projects that receive Firm Commitments on or after September 1, 2011, the lender has an obligation under the loan documents to "promptly review any Borrower's request to transfer the Project and not unreasonably withhold Lender's approval of the transfer" and, if HUD approves the transfer, the lender has an obligation to execute documents as needed to incorporate the new Regulatory Agreement into the Security Instrument in connection with the transfer.[173] The lender is permitted to charge a fee in connection with the review of the transfer request and granting approval does not prejudice the lender's rights under the mortgage insurance contract.[174] With respect to projects that received Firm Commitments prior to September 1, 2011, lender approval of a transfer is not required unless secondary financing that will be secured by a lien on the project is requested or the current owner desires a release from the lender, and the lender is not required to consider or approve a transfer request.[175]

M. Prevailing Wage Requirements

Davis Bacon prevailing wage requirements set forth minimum wages and fringe benefits that must be paid to laborers and mechanics under certain construction contracts financed with the assistance of a U.S. agency.[176] The Secretary of Labor sets prevailing wage requirements for various classes of laborers and mechanics based on the type of project and area where the work is performed.[177] Whether Davis Bacon prevailing wage requirements apply depends on the section of the Act under which the loan is insured. Generally, with the exception of certain loans insured under Section 241 as noted below, new construction and substantial rehabilitation projects are subject to prevailing wage requirements, while refinancing and acquisition projects are not.[178]

---

170. *Id.* at § 13-7.

171. Required exhibits include, but are not limited to, previous participation certificates, rental schedule (Form HUD-92458), sources and uses of funds statements, amended organizational documents, and purchaser's letter. *Id.* at Chapter 13, Appendix B.

172. HANDBOOK 4350.1 § 13-6; Application for Transfer of Physical Assets (TPA), Form HUD-92266.

173. Lender's Certificate, Form HUD-92434M (Rev. 04/11) [hereinafter *Lender's Certificate*] ¶ 34; Request for Endorsement, Form HUD-92455M (Rev. 04/11) [hereinafter *RFE*] ¶ I.A.13.

174. *Id.*; *Security Instrument, supra* note 10, at ¶ 21(a).

175. *See* Application for Transfer of Physical Assets (TPA), Form HUD-92266.

176. 29 C.F.R. § 1.1 (2011). *See* Chapter 13 for a more detailed discussion of prevailing wage requirements.

177. 29 C.F.R. § 1.1 (2011). Wage determinations are available online at http://www.wdol.gov/

178. The requirement to pay Davis Bacon prevailing wages under relevant sections of the Act applies regardless of whether the loan is being insured through insurance of advances or insurance upon completion. *See* Sections III.A & III.B of this chapter for a discussion of insurance of advances and insurance upon completion.

Section of the Act	Davis Bacon Prevailing Wages Apply?
Section 220	Yes.[179]
Section 221(d)	Yes.[180]
Section 231	Yes.[181]
Section 207/223(f)	No.[182]
Section 223(a)(7)	No.[183]
Section 241	Yes, if the existing mortgage is insured under a section of the Act that requires the payment of Davis Bacon prevailing wages. No, if the existing mortgage is insured under a section of the Act that does not require the payment of Davis Bacon prevailing wages.[184]

N. Subordinate Financing

Although the project generally must be free and clear of all liens other than the insured mortgage, secondary financing secured by a subordinate lien may be permitted if certain conditions are met.[185] Except for operating loss loans insured by FHA pursuant to Section 223(d)[186] of the Act or supplemental loans insured by FHA pursuant to Section 241[187] of the Act, payments on account of inferior liens may not be made from project sources other than surplus cash[188] or residual receipts[189] as and to the extent permitted under the terms of the

---

179. *See* 24 C.F.R. § 220 (2011), regulations governing Section 220, incorporating by reference 24 C.F.R. § 200.33.

180. See 24 C.F.R. § 221.501 (2011), regulations governing Section 221, incorporating by reference 24 C.F.R. § 200.33.

181. *See* 24 C.F.R. § 231 (2011), regulations governing Section 231, incorporating by reference 24 C.F.R. § 200.33.

182. 24 C.F.R. § 200.33(a)(1) (2011).

183. HANDBOOK 4567.1 § 2-8. Although theoretically it is possible to insure a substantial rehabilitation project under Section 223(a)(7), in which case Davis Bacon Prevailing Wages would apply, this is never done in practice.

184. *See* 12 U.S.C. § 1715z-6(b)(5) (2010) and 24 C.F.R. § 200.33(a)(2) (2011). Therefore, Davis Bacon prevailing wages would not apply to the construction of an addition financed with a loan insured under Section 241 if the existing project was subject to a mortgage insured under Section 207, pursuant to Section 223(f).

185. *See* 24 C.F.R. § 200.71 (2011); *MAP Guide, supra* note 15, at ¶ 8.9; *Closing Guide, supra* note 22, at ¶ 3.3.

186. *See* Section III.E of this chapter.

187. *See* Section III.F of this chapter.

188. "'Surplus Cash' means any cash plus amounts received under Section 8 project-based subsidy payments (earned in the applicable fiscal period) remaining after: (1) The payment of: (i) all sums immediately due or currently required to be paid under the terms of the Note, the Security Instrument and this Agreement on the first day of the month following the end of the fiscal period; including without limitation, all amounts required to be deposited in the Reserve for Replacement or other reserves as may be required by HUD; and (ii) all other obligations of the Project (accounts payable and accrued, unescrowed expenses) unless funds for payment are set aside or deferment of payment has been approved by HUD, and (2) The segregation and recording of: (i) an amount equal to the aggregate of all special funds required to be maintained by Borrower; (ii) the greater of

Regulatory Agreement.[190] HUD consent is required for any such payments made from residual receipts.[191]

If secondary financing is provided by a governmental funding source and is to be secured by a lien on the property, a Subordination Agreement must be entered into among the borrower, the FHA lender, and the subordinate lender that sets forth certain rights of the parties and the relationship between the FHA-insured loan and the subordinate financing.[192] The Subordination Agreement provides that the subordinate note cannot have a maturity date prior to the maturity date of the FHA-insured mortgage and that payments on the subordinate note may be made only from surplus cash or residual receipts or from funds not derived from project sources.[193] The Subordination Agreement expressly recognizes that the subordinate loan is subject and subordinate to the terms of the FHA-insured loan documents and provides reciprocal notice and cure rights to both the subordinate lender and the FHA lender.[194]

When secondary financing is provided by a private entity, the Subordination Agreement does not apply. Instead, if the subordinate loan is to be secured by a lien on the property, a Secondary Financing Rider must be attached to the security instrument with respect to the subordinate loan.[195] Many of the provisions of the Subordination Agreement (such as the prohibition on subordinate loan payments except from surplus cash or residual receipts and the requirement that the term of the subordinate loan last as long as the term of the FHA-

---

Borrower's total liability or the amount held by Borrower for tenant security deposits; and (iii) all accounts and accrued items payable within thirty (30) days after the end of the fiscal period." *Regulatory Agreement*, supra note 9, at ¶ 1(gg).

189. "'Residual Receipts' is a term that applies to certain funds held by Non-Profit, Public Body and Limited Dividend Borrowers whose Notes are insured or held by HUD pursuant to Section 220, Section 221(d)(3) and 231 of the National Housing Act, as amended. After the calculation of Surplus Cash, as described [above], Borrower may make any Distributions permitted by [the Regulatory] Agreement. 'Residual Receipts' shall be the restrictive [sic] cash held by Section 220, Section 221(d)(3) and 231 Non-Profit, Public Body, and Limited Dividend Borrowers remaining after any allowable Distributions. The use of these Residual Receipts is restricted under this Agreement." *Id.* at ¶ 1(ee). After any distributions allowable under the Regulatory Agreement are made, the remaining restricted cash is deposited in a separate account and may disbursed only at the direction of HUD. *Id.* at ¶ 11.

190. 24 C.F.R. § 200.85 (2011); *Regulatory Agreement*, supra note 9, at ¶ 3; *Security Instrument*, supra note 10, at ¶ 17.

191. *Regulatory Agreement*, supra note 9, at ¶ 11.

192. *MAP Guide*, supra note 15, at ¶ 8.9.A; *Closing Guide*, supra note 22, at ¶ 3.3.A.1(a); *see also See* Subordination Agreement, Form HUD-92420M [hereinafter *Subordination Agreement*].

193. Project sources include the mortgaged property, loan proceeds, and any reserve or deposit required by HUD in connection with the FHA-insured loan. *See Subordination Agreement*, supra note 192. Note, that in very rare circumstances, such as a subordinate loan from a public source on a project where the FHA-insured loan is a low-leverage loan, HUD may grant a waiver to allow for a second mortgage payable from project sources.

194. *Id.* at ¶¶ 5–6.

195. *Closing Guide*, supra note 22, at ¶¶ 3.3.A.1(b), 5.1. "Note that liens against the project real estate to secure secondary financing from a private entity are not allowed, except for (1) Section 223(f) transactions; (2) operating loss loans under Section 223(d); (3) supplemental loans under Section 241; or (4) when the HUD-insured loan accounts for less than 50% of the project cost." *Id.* at ¶ 3.3.A.1(b).

insured mortgage) also are contained in the Secondary Financing Rider.[196] Additionally, in the event of a conflict, the terms of the FHA-insured loan documents control and the subordinate loan documents automatically terminate if HUD acquires title to the property by foreclosure or a deed in lieu of foreclosure.[197]

Unsecured promissory notes also may be used to evidence secondary loans.[198] As with the terms of the Subordination Agreement and the Secondary Financing Rider, the HUD prescribed forms of Surplus Cash Note[199] and Residual Receipts Note[200] include provisions limiting the payment to surplus cash/residual receipts or non-project sources and restricting the maturity date of the secondary loan to a date on or after the maturity date of the HUD-insured mortgage.[201]

O. Commercial Space

Although rental income from apartments is the primary source of a project's gross income, income generated by commercial space is also permitted, subject to limitations on the amount of commercial space and income, which vary by program.[202] With respect to loans insured under Section 220, commercial space is limited to 20 percent of the net rentable area and commercial income is limited to 30 percent of the effective gross income.[203] For all loans insured under Section 221(d), commercial space is limited to 10 percent of the net rentable area and commercial income is limited to 15 percent of the effective gross income.[204] Loans insured under Section 207 pursuant to Section 223(f) may have commercial space of up to 20 percent of the net rentable area and commercial income up to 20 percent of the effective gross income.[205] In calculating space and income limitations, space and ancillary income related to project amenities for the use of residents are excluded. Parking spaces for residents and any income derived therefrom are similarly excluded, while income and space for non-residents must be included in the calculation.[206] Waivers of commercial space limits may be issued by the Hub Director in limited circumstances, while waivers of the commercial income limits must receive approval from HUD Headquarters.[207]

---

196. *Id.* at ¶ 5.1.
197. *Id.*
198. *Id.* at ¶ 3.3.B; *MAP Guide*, *supra* note 15, at ¶ 8.9.D.3(h).
199. Surplus Cash Note, Form HUD-92223M.
200. Residual Receipts Note (Nonprofit Borrowers), Form HUD-91710M (when the borrower is a nonprofit entity); Residual Receipts Note (Limited Dividend Borrowers), Form HUD-91712M (when the borrower is a limited dividend entity).
201. *MAP Guide*, *supra* note 15, at ¶ 8.9.D.3(h).
202. *See* 24 C.F.R. § 200.73 (2011).
203. *MAP Guide*, *supra* note 15, at ¶ 3.7.B; Mortgagee Letter 2011-32.
204. Mortgagee Letter 2011-32.
205. *Id. MAP Guide*, *supra* note 15, at ¶ 3.9.M.
206. Mortgagee Letter 2011-32.
207. "Documentation supporting the space limit waiver must include: 1. Demonstration that the additional space will not negatively impact on the use of the project by its residential tenants and will not create a nuisance to the surrounding community; 2. There is ample market support to assure occupancy of the space within the projected absorption period; and 3. Any issues involving easements, liability insurance, parking and zoning must be resolved prior to granting the waiver." *Id.* at ¶ IV.B. Commercial income limitations will be waived only upon a demonstration of clear mitigating circumstances.

For new construction and substantial rehabilitation projects, the initial operating deficit must include funding for operating expenses and debt service during the commercial space lease-up period.[208] Preleasing of commercial space may be required in circumstances in which any vacancy of commercial units would prevent the project from achieving sustaining occupancy.[209] Even if the space is preleased, the commercial space allocation of the initial operating deficit must be funded, but can be released once the pre-leased space is occupied and the first month's revenue is received.

III. HUD'S ACTIVE INSURANCE PROGRAMS

Despite the numerous common requirements that apply to all FHA-insured loans, each program is authorized by a separate section of the Act and subject to its own specific regulatory and administrative requirements.

A. Insurance of Advances (New Construction and Substantial Rehabilitation)

Insurance of advances is the process by which HUD insures loans for both the construction and permanent loan periods, approving periodic releases of mortgage proceeds and other funds for the construction or substantial rehabilitation of the project. New construction and substantial rehabilitation projects may be insured under Section 207, Section 220, Section 221(d)(3), Section 221(d)(4), or Section 231, but of these programs, Section 221(d)(4) is the most commonly utilized.[210] Therefore, the discussion of general requirements with respect to construction and substantial rehabilitation projects that follows is based on the program requirements for loans insured under Section 221(d)(4) but applies to all new construction and substantial programs unless otherwise specified.[211]

1. New Construction versus Substantial Rehabilitation

Projects may qualify for insurance under insurance of advances programs as either new construction (construction of new improvements) or substantial rehabilitation. Substantial rehabilitation means that either "[t]he cost of repairs, replacements, and improvements exceeds the *greater* of 15 percent of the estimated property replacement cost after completion of all repairs, replacements, and improvements or $6,500 per unit in repairs, replacements, and improvements as adjusted by the Hub/[Program Center] high cost percentage for that area, *or*

---

208. *Id.* at ¶ IV.G.
209. "Sustaining occupancy is defined as the project having sufficient residential income and income from the commercial portion of the project to pay its operating expenses, monthly debt service, escrow and reserve for replacement requirements for 3 consecutive months." *Id.* at ¶ IV.H.
210. *See* 12 U.S.C. § 1715l(d)(4) (2010) for program authorization. *See also* 24 C.F.R. § 221 (2011) and 24 C.F.R. § 207, Subpart B (2011) (incorporated by cross-reference at 24 C.F.R. § 221.752) for applicable regulations.
211. *See* Section III.A.10 of this chapter for program variations. *See also* Section III.F of this chapter for a discussion of Section 241. Unless otherwise specified, the general requirements with respect to construction and substantial rehabilitation projects discussed herein apply to loans insured under Section 241.

[t]wo or more major building components are being substantially replaced."[212] If the cost of the repairs, replacements, and improvements is below this threshold, the project instead may qualify for insurance under Section 207 pursuant to Section 223(f) as a refinancing project with repairs.[213] For purposes of determining whether a project qualifies as substantial rehabilitation, the cost of additions is not included, although additions may be constructed as part of a substantial rehabilitation project.[214]

Most new construction loans will be subject to loan-to-cost limitations,[215] and, for purposes of calculating the loan-to-cost ratio, "cost" is HUD's estimate of the replacement cost of the project following completion of the improvements and includes "the land, the proposed physical improvements, utilities within the boundaries of the land, architect's fees, taxes, interest during construction, and other miscellaneous charges incident to construction and approved by [HUD], and shall include an allowance for builder's and sponsor's profit and risk [(BSPRA)] of 10 per centum of all of the foregoing items except for land."[216] The land value is based on appraised value and "any cash out from the excess land or property equity above what is required at initial endorsement [to meet equity requirements] must be deferred . . . until the project is complete and it has demonstrated to the Hub/[Program Center]'s satisfaction that it has achieved six consecutive months of break-even occupancy. This does not prevent applying land value equity to fund operating deficit or working capital escrows, or other cash requirements at initial endorsement."[217] "Other miscellaneous charges" incident to construction include contractor's general overhead, carrying charges, and legal, organizational, and audit expenses.[218]

The borrower's equity contribution is reduced by the amount of BSPRA, provided there is an identity of interest between the borrower and the contractor and no paid builder's profit is included in the mortgage calculation.[219] If there is no such identity of interest, sponsor's profit and risk allowance (SPRA) in an amount of 10 percent of the estimated cost of the architect's fees, carrying and financing charges, and legal, organizational, and audit expenses are included in the replacement cost calculation in lieu of BSPRA.[220] SPRA also is included in

---

212. *MAP Guide, supra* note 15, at ¶ 3.4.C (emphasis in original). Major building components include roof, wall, or floor structures, foundations, plumbing, electrical systems, or heating and air-conditioning systems. *MAP Guide, supra* note 15, at ¶ 5.12.B.
213. See Section III.C of this chapter.
214. *MAP Guide, supra* note 15, at ¶ 3.4.C; *see* also Section III.F of this chapter for a discussion of insurance of loans under Section 241 for purposes of constructing additions.
215. Except for new construction loans insured under Section 207, which is a value-based program. *See supra* note 59.
216. 12 U.S.C. § 1715l(d)(4)(iii) (2010); *see also* 12 U.S.C. § 1715k(d)(3)(B)(ii) (2010); 12 U.S.C. § 1715v(c)(4) (2010). Note that for new construction projects, replacement cost does not include a construction contingency amount.
217. *MAP Guide, supra* note 15, at ¶ 8.13.J. *See also id.* at ¶ 12.15.F. Excess proceeds available from land value can be used for the purposes set forth in the MAP Guide, including, but not limited to, the funding of working capital and operating deficit escrows. *Id.* at Appendix 12A ¶ D.
218. *Id.* at ¶ 3.4.U.
219. *Id.*
220. *Id.*

lieu of BSPRA if the so-called "50–75 percent Rule" is violated.[221] The 50–75 percent Rule provides, "Whether or not there is an identity of interest, *no* general contractor's fee (general overhead and profit) will be allowed when: (1) More than 50 percent of the contract sum in the Construction Contract–Cost Plus, Form HUD-92442M, is subcontracted to one subcontractor, material supplier, or equipment lessor or (2) 75 percent or more [of the contract sum is subcontracted] with three or less subcontractors, material suppliers, and equipment lessors."[222] If the borrower is a nonprofit entity, the calculation of replacement cost may not include BSPRA or SPRA but instead may include a developer's fee in an amount generally not to exceed the lesser of (i) 8 percent of the mortgage amount and (ii) $400,000.[223] The developer's fee may be used to pay for various costs associated with development.[224]

When calculating the loan-to-cost ratio for substantial rehabilitation projects,[225] the calculation of "cost" generally includes the same elements utilized in calculating cost for new construction projects, except that the estimated cost of repair and rehabilitation, including a contingency reserve,[226] is added to the "as is" value of the property prior to repair and rehabilitation.[227] As with new construction loans, cash out from the "as is" value of land and improvements above that are required to meet equity requirements to close must be deferred until the project demonstrates to HUD's satisfaction that it has achieved six months of breakeven occupancy.[228] BSPRA (equal to 10 percent of the estimated costs, excluding, however, the as-is value of the existing structure) or SPRA (equal to 10 percent of the estimated cost of the architect's fees, carrying and financing charges, and legal, organizational, and audit expenses) is included in the replacement cost calculation.[229]

2. Early Start Procedures

For new construction and substantial rehabilitation projects, no work may be done prior to initial endorsement unless the work is done in accordance with HUD-approved early start

---

221. *Id.* at ¶ 13.16.M.3.
222. *Id.*
223. *Id.* at ¶ 7.13.K. The developer's fee cannot be less than $40,000 or more than $400,000. But for mortgages in excess of $5 million the maximum fee may be increased "to provide an additional 2 percent based on that portion of the mortgage that is in excess of $5,000,000."
224. Such as closing costs, staff salaries, working capital or operating deficit escrows, relocation expenses, financing fees over 3.5 percent, and environmental studies. *Id.*
225. Note that substantial rehabilitation loans under Section 207 and Section 231 are value-based. *See supra* notes 59 and 61 and accompanying text.
226. MAP Guide, *supra* note 15, at ¶ 13.16.L.7 ("The contingency reserve may be used for unforeseen costs of necessary change orders approved by HUD and unanticipated soft costs for time extensions approved by HUD.").
227. 12 U.S.C. § 1715l(d)(4)(iv) (2010); 12 U.S.C. § 1715k(d)(3)(B)(ii) (2010). This formula is not used, however, with respect to loans insured under Section 220 if the property has been rehabilitated by a local public agency in accordance with the Housing Act of 1949. In that instance, the mortgage is based upon the appraised value of the property.
228. MAP Guide, *supra* note 15, at ¶¶ 8.13.J, 12.15.F. As with new construction projects, excess proceeds available from land value can be used for the purposes set forth in the MAP Guide. *See id* at Appendix 12A ¶ D.
229. MAP Guide, *supra* note 15, at ¶ 3.4.U.1.

procedures.[230] Any construction[231] done prior to initial endorsement is undertaken at the borrower's own risk, and any mechanic's or materialmen's liens filed in connection with the construction must be released before any advances can be made under the FHA-insured loan.[232] Absent a waiver, HUD will approve an early start only if a firm commitment has been issued, there is a valid and compelling reason to start construction prior to the anticipated closing date, and an immediate closing is not practical.[233]

3. Borrower Equity and Escrow Requirements

The lender's underwriter must analyze and calculate the cash requirements to close the loan. Recognizing that the borrower typically will not have net income during construction and lease-up periods, particularly with respect to new construction projects, insurance of advances typically will be conditioned on the collection of certain escrows at the initial endorsement, including a front-money escrow and escrows for working capital, initial operating deficit, off-site improvements, and demolition. The required escrows and cash requirements (other than the front-money escrow, if any) may be funded by excess mortgage proceeds to the extent that there are excess proceeds available from land value or other equity.[234] Escrowed funds are subject to application to the outstanding indebtedness in the event of a default under the loan.[235]

a. Front-Money Escrow

The Firm Commitment may require a front-money escrow to be established for costs required to complete the project in excess of the loan amount, including on-site construction costs, fees, and carrying charges.[236] The front-money escrow may be provided in the form of cash, a grant/loan from a non-governmental source,[237] and/or a grant/loan from a governmental source.[238] Funds in the front-money escrow generally must be expended prior to advancing

---

230. *MAP Guide*, supra note 15, at ¶ 3.4.B.1. Early start approval requires a pre-construction conference and delivery of the executed Agreement and Certification, executed Construction Contract, evidence of permanent financing, the inspection fee check, and building permits covering the scope of work to be done prior to initial endorsement. *See MAP Guide*, supra note 15, at ¶ 5.7.F; Request for Permission to Commence Construction Prior to Initial Endorsement for Mortgage Insurance, Form HUD-92415.

231. Grading, clearing, or other preliminary work constitutes the start of construction, while demolition, environmental remediation, and off-site work do not. *Closing Guide*, supra note 22, at ¶ 1.7.A; *MAP Guide*, supra note 15, at ¶ 5.7.F.

232. Request for Permission to Commence Construction Prior to Initial Endorsement for Mortgage Insurance, Form HUD-92415.

233. *Closing Guide*, supra note 22, at ¶ 1.7.C.2; *MAP Guide*, supra note 15, at ¶ 5.7.F.3. An inability to undertake construction during certain seasons often is a consideration as to when a borrower might seek to begin construction early.

234. *MAP Guide*, supra note 15, at ¶ 8.13.J.

235. *See, e.g.*, Escrow Agreement for Working Capital, Form HUD-92412M (Rev. 04/11) [hereinafter *Escrow Agreement for Working Capital*] ¶ 6; Escrow Agreement for Operating Deficits, Form HUD-96476a-M (Rev. 04/11) [hereinafter *Escrow Agreement for Operating Deficits*] ¶ 6.

236. *Id.* at Appendix 12A ¶ A.1.a.

237. *See supra* Section II.N regarding secondary financing requirements.

238. *Lender's Certificate*, supra note 173, at ¶ 9(a).

insured loan proceeds, with the exception of funds provided from a governmental source, which may be advanced concurrently and on a pro rata basis with mortgage proceeds.[239] HUD cannot require the escrowing of 100 percent of tax credit equity, but HUD may require an installment of tax credit equity (generally equal to or greater than 20 percent of the total available equity) to be invested in the project at the initial endorsement.[240] In projects where tax credit equity and/or one or more grants/loans from governmental sources will be used to fund all or a portion of the front-money escrow, HUD requires that a disbursement agreement governing disbursements of such funds be executed and delivered at initial endorsement.[241]

b. Working Capital Escrow

HUD requires a working capital escrow for all new construction and substantial rehabilitation projects.[242] For new construction projects, the working capital escrow requirement is 4 percent of the loan amount.[243] This deposit is divided equally between a "Working Capital Amount" and a "Construction Contingency Amount."[244] The Construction Contingency Amount may be used only for cost overruns and HUD-approved change orders.[245] Draws on the Working Capital Amount may be approved by the lender, without prior approval of HUD, for "(i) the cost of furniture, fixtures, and equipment for the Project that are not paid from Loan proceeds; (ii) the cost of marketing and leasing up the Project; (iii) for accruals during the course of construction, for interest, mortgage insurance premiums, taxes, ground rents, property insurance premiums and assessments, when funds available for these purposes under the Building Loan Agreement have been exhausted, and also for allocation to such accruals after completion of construction."[246] With respect to substantial rehabilitation projects, only 2 percent of the mortgage amount is deposited under the Escrow Agreement for Working Capital, the entire amount being used for the purposes set forth above with respect to the Working Capital Amount.[247]

The working capital escrow may be deposited as cash or a letter of credit and is not included in the calculation of the replacement cost.[248] The remaining balance of the Working Capital Amount, if any, may be released to the borrower on the later of 12 months following the final endorsement or when it is demonstrated to HUD's satisfaction that the project has

---

239. *MAP Guide, supra* note 15, at ¶ 8.10.C.2(e); *id.* at Appendix 12A ¶ A.1.c.
240. *Id.* at ¶ 8.13.L.1.
241. *See Closing Guide, supra* note 22, at ¶ 3.9.E.
242. *Id.* at ¶ 8.13.E. *See also Closing Guide, supra* note 22, at ¶¶ 2.7.D, 2.8.G.
243. *Id.* Historically, the working capital escrow deposit was 2% of the mortgage amount, but Mortgagee Letter 2010-21 and Notice H 2010-11 increased the requirement for new construction projects to 4%. This change has been incorporated into the Escrow Agreement for Working Capital. *See MAP Guide, supra* note 15, at ¶ 8.13.E.
244. *Escrow Agreement for Working Capital, supra* note 235, at ¶ 2. The Construction Contingency Amount is required for new construction projects because, unlike substantial rehabilitation projects, there is no construction contingency included in the replacement cost calculation for new construction projects.
245. *Id.* ¶ 3(b).
246. *Id.* ¶ 3(a).
247. *Closing Guide, supra* note 22, at ¶¶ 2.7.D, 2.8.G; *Escrow Agreement for Working Capital, supra* note 235, at ¶ 2.
248. *MAP Guide, supra* note 15, at ¶ 8.13.E.

achieved 1.0 debt service coverage (also referred to as break-even occupancy) each month for six consecutive months, unless a different number of months or debt service coverage ratio is required by the Firm Commitment or Program Obligations.[249] The remaining balance of the Construction Contingency Amount, if any, may be returned to the borrower at the final endorsement with HUD approval.[250] Although interim releases of the Working Capital Amount may be made without HUD consent, the final release is effectively subject to HUD approval for break-even occupancy, which must be demonstrated to HUD's satisfaction.

c. Operating Deficit Escrow

The operating deficit escrow provides funds to cover the shortfall between rents and reasonable operating expenses that occur during the lease-up period.[251] Cash or a letter of credit is deposited with the lender and may be released monthly *with* HUD's written consent.[252] As with the working capital escrow, the operating deficit escrow is not included in the calculation of the replacement cost, and the remaining balance, if any, may be returned to the borrower on the later of 12 months after final endorsement or when the project achieves 1.0 debt service coverage each month for six consecutive months, unless different requirements are specified by the Firm Commitment or Program Obligations, consistent with the release conditions for the Working Capital Amount.[253]

d. Off-site Escrow

Improvements to be constructed outside the boundaries of the project property, such as access drives or utility lines (other than short off-site extensions of on-site facilities) are not included in the Construction Contract, Form HUD-92442M (the Construction Contract) and are not to be funded from loan proceeds.[254] Additional assurance of completion is required for any such off-site work.[255] This assurance of completion can be provided in the form of (i) evidence acceptable to HUD that the off-site improvements will be completed by public authorities or public utility companies, (ii) an off-site bond, and/or (iii) an escrow for off-site facilities.[256] If assurance of completion is provided in the form of an escrow, the amount deposited must equal or exceed HUD's estimate of the cost of off-site improvements and may be in the form of cash, a letter of credit, or excess mortgage proceeds.[257] The off-site work generally must be completed on or before the date of completion specified in the Construction Contract for on-site improvements, and the work must be guaranteed against latent defects for a period of one year following completion of the off-site improvements.[258]

---

249. *Escrow Agreement for Working Capital, supra* note 235, at ¶ 4.
250. *Id.*
251. *Escrow Agreement for Operating Deficits, supra* note 235.
252. *Id.* at ¶¶ 2–3.
253. *Escrow Agreement for Operating Deficits, supra* note 235, at ¶ 4.
254. *MAP Guide, supra* note 15, at ¶ 6.3.C.2.b.
255. *Closing Guide, supra* note 22, at ¶ 3.5.E.
256. *Id.; Lender's Certificate, supra* note 173, at ¶ 10.
257. *See id.; MAP Guide, supra* note 15, at ¶ 12.15.A.4.
258. Escrow Agreement for Offsite Facilities, Form FHA-2446.

e. Demolition Escrow

If the project involves demolition work to remove existing structures, footings, foundations, and utilities, this work cannot be included in the Construction Contract,[259] and assurance of the completion of the demolition work is provided in the form of an escrow agreement, consistent with that used to guaranty the completion of off-site work. The escrow requirements that apply to the completion of off-site facilities, including use of Escrow Agreement for Off-site Facilities, Form FHA-2446 governing release of the escrow, also apply to any escrow established with respect to demolition work.[260]

4. Assurance of Completion

Assurance of the completion of the improvements is provided either (i) in the form of Payment and Performance Bonds, each issued by an approved surety[261] and each in the full amount of the Construction Contract (plus an assumed builder's profit on BSPRA transactions), guaranteeing payment for labor, materials and equipment, and construction of the project in accordance with the terms and conditions of the Construction Contract, free of liens,[262] or (ii) through a Completion Assurance Agreement, Form HUD-92450M, funded by cash or a letter of credit in the amount of 15 percent (25 percent in the event the project is a building with elevator(s) and four or more stories) of the Construction Contract amount (plus an assumed builder's profit on BSPRA transactions) securing against loss or damage because of a default by the contractor under the Construction Contract.[263]

5. Minimum Property Standards

The design for new construction and substantial rehabilitation projects must comply with HUD's Minimum Property Standards for Housing, which incorporate local or national building codes accepted or designated by the local HUD office.[264] The majority of the Minimum Property Standards relate to conditions on the site, including environmental hazards, site grading and topography, parking areas, noise control, and design requirements and materials.[265] The Minimum Property Standards also address some off-site conditions, such as access to streets. Many of the standards apply to all FHA-insured projects, not just new construction and substantial rehabilitation projects.[266]

---

259. *See MAP Guide, supra* note 15, at ¶ 6.3.C.2(a)(3). However, interior demolition within existing structures undergoing substantial rehabilitation may be included in the Construction Contract, Form HUD-92442M (Rev. 04/11) [hereinafter *Construction Contract*]. *Id.* at ¶ 6.3.C.2(a)(4).

260. When completing Escrow Agreement for Offsite Facilities, Form FHA-2446, with respect to demolition, all references to "offsite facilities" should be replaced with references to "demolition."

261. A list of approved sureties may be found at www.fms.treas.gov/c570/index.html.

262. *MAP Guide, supra* note 15, at ¶ 3.4.M; *Closing Guide, supra* note 22, at ¶ 3.5.

263. *Id. See also* Completion Assurance Agreement, Form HUD-92450M.

264. *MAP Guide, supra* note 15, at Appendix 5A ¶ A.

265. HUD HANDBOOK 4910.1 Chapters 3–6.

266. For example, the requirement that the project site, if not a single plot, be grouped in a manner to allow for convenient and efficient management. *Id.* at § 201.

6. Procedures for Advances

Advances are made pursuant to a Building Loan Agreement, Form HUD-92441M, between the lender and borrower (the Building Loan Agreement).[267] The initial and final advances of mortgage proceeds must be approved by HUD, but interim advances generally may be made by the lender without HUD approval, unless the advance requests release of any portion of the contractor's holdback under the Construction Contract.[268] For interim advances to be made, the contractor must prepare and submit a Contractor's Requisition, Form HUD-92448, including on-site work completed in accordance with contract documents, as observed and approved by the architect, along with materials and components stored on-site.[269] The HUD inspector reviews the Contractor's Requisition for acceptability and, if acceptable, approves the amount of the draw requested by the contractor. The draw is based on a percentage of completion of the trade items identified in the processing of the Firm Commitment and is not based on invoiced costs. After HUD approval of the Contractor's Requisition, the lender will prepare and sign the Certificate of Mortgage Insurance, increasing the amount of mortgage insurance by the amount approved for advance less any amounts funded from the front-money escrow.[270] HUD will monitor interim draws, and, if problems are identified, HUD may withdraw the lender's authority to approve advances.[271]

7. Change Orders

Change orders, including changes to the scope of the contract work, contract price, or contract time, must be approved by HUD.[272] Requests for approval must be submitted on the Request for Construction Changes, Form HUD-92437, signed by the mortgagor, architect, lender, and contractor. Change orders will be approved only if they are necessary, betterments, or equivalent changes.[273] For new construction projects, the Construction Contingency Amount under the Escrow Agreement for Working Capital is to be used to fund approved change orders and cost overruns.[274] Once the Construction Contingency Amount of the working capital escrow is exhausted, and if HUD estimates that the change orders will increase the construction contract sum by $5,000 or more, an escrow must be established to fund change orders. This escrow may be funded by excess mortgage proceeds if available.[275] With respect to substantial rehabilitation projects, certain change orders may be funded from the contin-

---

267. *See* Section V.C.5 of this chapter regarding the Building Loan Agreement.
268. *MAP Guide, supra* note 15, at Appendix 12A. *See* Section III.A.9 of this chapter regarding final endorsement with respect to approval of the final draw. *See also* Section V.C.6 of this chapter regarding the Construction Contract.
269. *MAP Guide, supra* note 15, at Appendix 12B.
270. *Id.* at Appendix 12A.
271. *Id.*
272. *Id.* at ¶ 12.8.
273. Necessary changes include those that arise from latent conditions that differ from construction document conditions, state or local code changes after initial endorsement, architect's errors or omissions, and damage to completed construction. Betterment changes must be economically justified because they increase net income or reduce operating expenses. Equivalent changes involve substitution with equivalent or better items. *Id.*
274. *See* Section III.A.3.b of this chapter.
275. *MAP Guide, supra* note 15, at ¶ 12.8.

gency reserve.[276] If assurance of completion was provided in the form of Payment and Performance Bonds, the surety's approval must be obtained in writing before any changes increasing the contract sum by 10 percent or more are approved.[277]

8. Mortgage Increases

HUD will consider requests to increase the amount of the FHA-insured mortgage once the project has been completed and cost certification submitted.[278] Mortgage increases may be approved for necessary changes, betterment changes, other costs resulting from unforeseen conditions, or to correct a substantial HUD processing error.[279] Cost overruns or changes primarily for the convenience or benefit to the borrower or contractor are not bases for a mortgage increase.[280] "Any mortgage increase for an insured project must be more than 2.5 percent of the original mortgage and at least $50,000."[281] If the increase is approved, the closing documents for final endorsement must include a supplemental Note in the amount of the increase, a supplemental Security Instrument, a modification and consolidation agreement, and an endorsement to the title policy increasing the amount of insurance.[282] Borrower's counsel also must provide a supplemental legal opinion regarding the supplemental loan documents.[283]

9. Final Endorsement

Once construction has been completed, certified costs have been approved by HUD, and required final closing exhibits have been submitted and approved,[284] the loan may go to final endorsement. The final advance of mortgage proceeds must be approved by HUD. To obtain such approval, the lender submits the Request for Final Endorsement of Credit Instrument, Form HUD-92023M (Request for Final Endorsement), which must correctly identify the amount of each advance and the total of all advances.[285] The borrower and contractor must identify any unpaid obligations on the Request for Final Endorsement, and evidence must be provided that sufficient cash is available to pay all outstanding obligations in full.[286] In addition, an escrow may be required at the final endorsement if there are incomplete items of on-site construction.[287] The contractor must submit the Contractor's Requisition, Form HUD-

---

276. The changes must be necessary changes or betterment changes, and the amount approved for payment from the contingency reserve cannot exceed the HUD cost estimate for such changes. *Id.* at ¶ 12.8.D.2.
277. *Id.* at ¶ 12.8.A.4.
278. *Id.* at ¶ 13.22.A.
279. Costs resulting from unforeseen conditions could include concealed subsurface conditions, natural disasters, or requirements of local authorities. *Id.* at ¶ 13.22.
280. *Id.* at ¶ 13.23.
281. *Id.*
282. *Closing Guide, supra* note 22, at ¶ 1.13.C.
283. *Id.*
284. Including, but not limited to, an as-built survey and evidence of updated title insurance. *Id.* at ¶ 1.14.A.
285. *Id.* at ¶ 1.15.A.1.
286. *Id.* at ¶ 1.15.A.2.
287. *See* Escrow Agreement for Incomplete Construction, Form HUD-92456M (Rev. 04/11). Incomplete on-site construction must be identified on the Application for Insurance of Advance of Mortgage Proceeds, Form HUD-92403.

92448, identifying the completed work and certifying as to the payment of Davis Bacon prevailing wages, if applicable.[288] Once the conditions for final closing have been met, including the establishment of any required escrows, HUD finally will endorse the Note for the full amount of the maximum insurable mortgage, as the same may have been adjusted as a result of cost certification.[289]

10. Program Variations

a. Section 207

Although insurance of construction and substantial rehabilitation loans is authorized under Section 207,[290] the program is rarely used for this purpose.[291] Section 221(d) and Section 220 are more advantageous to developers and lenders because they are cost-based programs, while Section 207 is a value-based program.[292] The maximum insurable mortgage under Section 220 or Section 221(d) may therefore exceed 90 percent of the value of the property[293] if supported by actual costs (and not otherwise limited by the debt service or statutory limits). Section 207 still is used, albeit rarely, for construction or rehabilitation of manufactured-home parks,[294] as such parks are not eligible for insurance under Section 220 or Section 221(d).[295] Section 207's primary use, however, is as the insurance vehicle for the purchase or refinancing of existing multifamily properties pursuant to Section 223(f) of the Act. Section 223(f) is not a stand-alone insurance program, but instead allows HUD "to insure under any section of [Subchapter II of the Act] a mortgage executed in connection with the purchase or refinancing of an existing multifamily housing project. . . ."[296]

b. Section 220

Section 220 is intended to "aid in the elimination of slums and blighted conditions and the

---

288. *See supra* notes 179–84 and accompanying text.

289. *Closing Guide, supra* note 22, at ¶ 1.15.B. *See* Section II.I of this chapter regarding cost certification. The maximum insurable mortgage may be decreased if costs are not sufficient to support the loan amount. *See also* Section III.A.8 of this chapter regarding mortgage increases.

290. *See* 12 U.S.C. § 1713(b) (2010) for program authorization. *See also* 24 C.F.R. § 200, Subpart A (2011) and 24 C.F.R. § 207 (2011) for applicable Regulations.

291. Of the 12,588 mortgages insured by HUD under the multifamily mortgage insurance programs and Section 232 health-care programs as of September 30, 2011, none were insured under Section 207 to finance construction of new apartments. *See* http://portal.hud.gov/hudportal/HUD?src=/program_offices/housing/comp/rpts/mfh/mf_f47.

292. *See* Section II.E of this chapter.

293. The statutory loan-to-value limit for loans insured under Section 207. 12 U.S.C. § 1713(c) (2010).

294. Of the 12,588 mortgages insured by HUD under the multifamily mortgage insurance programs and Section 232 health-care programs as of September 30, 2011, nine were used to finance construction of mobile-home projects. *See* http://portal.hud.gov/hudportal/HUD?src=/program_offices/housing/comp/rpts/mfh/mf_f47.

295. *See* 12 U.S.C. § 1715l(d)(f) (2010), limiting eligibility to projects with five or more family units.

296. 12 U.S.C. § 1715n(f)(1) (2010).

prevention of deterioration of residential property"[297] by insuring loans for new construction or substantial rehabilitation of multifamily projects located in areas of urban renewal, code enforcement, or revitalization.[298]

Section 220 offers certain advantages over Section 221(d)(4), including (i) higher commercial space and income limitations[299] and (ii) higher statutory mortgage limits.[300] However, Section 220 loans may be subject to higher MIP rates,[301] can be used only for projects in eligible locations,[302] and cannot be age-restricted for seniors.

c. Section 221(d)(3)

While Section 221(d)(4), Section 220, and Section 231 may each be utilized by either nonprofit or for-profit borrowers, insurance under Section 221(d)(3) is limited to loans to nonprofit or limited dividend borrowers.[303] As a result, the calculation of cost for loans insured under Section 221(d)(3) includes a developer's fee rather than an allowance for BSPRA.[304] Loans insured under Section 221(d)(3) are subject to higher statutory limits and higher loan-to-cost ratios than loans insured under Section 221(d)(4).[305] However, Section 221(d)(3) loans also may be subject to higher MIP rates and are subject to the availability of credit subsidy.[306]

---

297. 12 U.S.C. § 1715k(a) (2010).

298. *See* 12 U.S.C. § 1715k(b) (2010) for program authorization. To be eligible for insurance, the property must be located in "[e]xisting slum clearance and urban redevelopment projects covered by a Federal aid contract before the effective date of the Housing Act of 1954, [a]n approved urban renewal area under Title I of the Housing Act of 1949, [d]isaster urban renewal projects assisted under Section III of the Housing Act of 1949 as amended, [a]n area of concentrated code enforcement being carried out under Section 117 of the Housing Act of 1949, [or a] concentrated development area, approved by the Hub/[Program Center], in which concentrated housing, physical development and public service activities are being carried out in a coordinated manner, pursuant to a locally developed strategy for neighborhood improvement, conservation or preservation." *MAP Guide, supra* note 15, at ¶ 3.7.A. *See also* 12 U.S.C. § 1715k(d) (2010).

299. *See* Section II.O of this chapter.

300. *See* Annual Indexing of Basic Statutory Mortgage Limits for Multifamily Housing Programs, 76 Fed. Reg. 10,387 (Feb. 24, 2011).

301. For projects without low-income housing tax credits, the FY 2011 MIP rate for loans insured under Section 220 was 50 basis points, while the rate for loans insured under Section 221(d)(4) was only 45 basis points. For projects with low-income housing tax credits, the MIP rate was 45 basis points for loans insured under either section. Federal Housing Administration (FHA) Mortgage Insurance Premiums for Multifamily Housing Programs, Health Care Facilities and Hospitals and Credit Subsidy Obligations for Fiscal Year (FY) 2011, 76 Fed. Reg. 40,741 (July 17, 2011).

302. *See supra* note 298.

303. *See* 12 U.S.C. § 1715l(d)(3) (2010) for program authorization. *See also* 24 C.F.R. § 221 (2011) and 24 C.F.R. § 207, Subpart B (2011), incorporated by cross-reference at 24 C.F.R. § 221.752, for applicable regulations.

304. *See supra* note 223 and accompanying text.

305. *See supra* note 300. *See also supra* notes 71–73 and accompanying text.

306. For projects without low-income housing tax credits, the FY 2011 MIP rate for loans insured under Section 221(d)(3) was 80 basis points, while the rate for loans insured under Section 221(d)(4) was only 45 basis points. For projects with low-income housing tax credits, the MIP rate was 45 basis points for loans insured under either section. Federal Housing Administration (FHA) Mortgage Insurance Premiums for Multifamily Housing Programs, Health Care Facilities and Hospitals and Credit Subsidy Obligations for Fiscal Year (FY) 2011, 76 Fed. Reg. 40,741 (July 17, 2011).

d. Section 231

Loans insured under Section 231 are intended to "assist in relieving the shortage of housing for elderly persons and to increase the supply of rental housing for elderly persons"[307] and/or handicapped persons.[308] To that end, the Section 231 program sometimes is utilized to insure loans financing the construction or substantial rehabilitation of multifamily projects.[309] Section 231 includes additional design, marketing, and review requirements. This, together with lower statutory mortgage limits than under Section 221(d), results in most housing projects for the elderly that are financed using FHA insurance being insured under Section 221(d) rather than Section 231.[310] To achieve the purpose of providing rental housing to elderly persons, defined as persons age 62 or older, projects financed through loans under Section 231 must contain eight or more units and at least 75 percent of the units must be specially designed for use and occupancy by elderly persons.[311] However, in certain circumstances, HUD may approve a project for insurance under Section 231 that has fewer than 75 percent of the units designed for use and occupancy by elderly persons, provided that at least 50 percent of the units are so designed.[312] With respect to a project financed with a loan insured under Section 231, "other than for units designed for the use and occupancy of handicapped persons and their families, all persons living in a unit must be age 62 or older."[313] Therefore, the borrower must make a bona fide effort to obtain occupancy by elderly persons through advertising and marketing efforts.[314] The restriction to use and occupancy by only elderly residents also means that projects insured under Section 231 are exempt from a provision in the Regulatory Agreement prohibiting discrimination against families with children.[315] Dis-

---

307. 12 U.S.C. § 1715v(a) (2010).

308. A handicapped person is defined as "A person who has a physical impairment which: (a) Is expected to be of a long-continued and indefinite duration; (b) Substantially impedes his/her ability to live independently; and (c) Is of such a nature that his/her ability to live independently could be improved by more suitable housing conditions." *MAP Guide, supra* note 15, at ¶ 3.8.A.1(b).

309. Of the 12,588 mortgages insured by HUD under the multifamily mortgage insurance programs and Section 232 health-care programs as of September 30, 2011, 54 were used to finance construction or substantial rehabilitation of housing for the elderly under Section 231. *See* http://portal.hud.gov/hudportal/HUD?src=/program_offices/housing/comp/rpts/mfh/mf_f47.

310. *See, e.g.,* Annual Indexing of Basic Statutory Mortgage Limits for Multifamily Housing Programs, 76 Fed. Reg. 10,387 (Feb. 24, 2011) setting forth calendar-year 2011 statutory mortgage limits.

311. *MAP Guide, supra* note 15, at ¶ 3.8.A. *See also Regulatory Agreement, supra* note 9, at ¶ 31(c). Particular attention must be given to room layout and design, installation of handrails and grab bars, hallway widths, slip-resistant floor finishes, grade limits for walkways, etc. *See* HANDBOOK 4910.1 § 100.2.

312. 12 U.S.C. § 1715v(a)(1).

313. *MAP Guide, supra* note 15, at ¶ 3.8.A.1.a.

314. *Regulatory Agreement, supra* note 9, at ¶ 31(d).

315. *Id.* at ¶ 31(a). "If the Security Instrument is originally a HUD-held purchase money mortgage, or is originally endorsed for insurance under any Section of the National Housing Act, as amended, *other than Section 231 units specially designed for use and occupancy of Elderly Persons exclusively,* Borrower shall not, in selecting tenants, discriminate against any person or persons by reason of the fact that there are children in the family, unless in accordance with the Fair Housing Act and otherwise approved in writing by HUD." (emphasis added).

crimination against families with children is not permitted with respect to multifamily projects insured under other sections of the Act.[316]

Another primary difference between Section 231 and other new construction and substantial rehabilitation programs is that Section 231 is a cost-based program for new construction, but a value-based program for substantial rehabilitation.[317] This, combined with the requirement that the project be designed for use by the elderly, results in some differences in application processing, particularly with respect to valuation review.[318] Additionally, all Section 231 pre-applications and applications for Firm Commitment must be reviewed by the National Loan Committee.[319] Senior housing projects that permit elderly living with children may be processed under Section 221(d)(4) and also require review by the National Loan Committee.[320]

B. Insurance Upon Completion (New Construction or Substantial Rehabilitation)

Insurance Upon Completion (IUC) is a process by which HUD provides mortgage insurance for a loan used to finance new construction or substantial rehabilitation after construction or rehabilitation of the project is complete and costs have been certified.[321] IUC "is an option for new construction and substantial rehabilitation projects financed under Sections 207, 220, 221(d), and 231."[322] Because HUD is not insuring construction advances, HUD does not monitor advances or assist in resolving construction issues in IUC projects, although any change orders still require the approval of HUD.[323] However, the application and approval process for IUC is the same as for insurance of advances cases, with limited exceptions.[324]

The requirements for IUC vary from the requirements for insurance of advances in a number of respects. The Firm Commitment must be issued prior to commencement of construction, but unlike insurance of advances cases, construction takes place prior to the initial endorsement of the Note, in a time period specified in the Firm Commitment.[325]

---

316. *Id.* With respect to loans insured under Sections of the Act other than Section 231, "[o]wners may neither exclude families with children from their properties, nor may they develop policies or procedures that have the purpose or effect of prohibiting children (e.g., policies in tenant selection plan, occupancy standards, house rules)." HANDBOOK 4350.3 § 3-32.D.2. *See also* The Fair Housing Act, 42 U.S.C. §§ 3601 *et seq.* (2010), prohibiting discrimination based on "familial status," defined as "one or more individuals (who have not attained the age of 18 years) being domiciled with (1) a parent or another person having legal custody of such individual or individuals; or (2) the designee of such parent or other person having such custody, with the written permission of such parent or other person."
317. *See* 12 U.S.C. §§ 1715v(c)(3)–(4) (2010).
318. *See* Section IV.A.1.b and Section IV.A.3.c of this chapter.
319. *MAP Guide, supra* note 15, at ¶ 3.8.A.
320. Additional guidance on senior housing is anticipated to be released by HUD in a future Housing Notice.
321. Cost certification procedures are the same as those required for insurance of advances cases. *See MAP Guide, supra* note 15, at ¶ 12.16.P.
322. *Id.* at ¶ 8.12.
323. *Id.* at ¶ 12.16.
324. *See* Section IV.A of this chapter for a discussion of the approval process.
325. *MAP Guide, supra* note 15, at ¶ 12.16.B.

While many of the same closing documents are required for IUC and insurance of advances closings,[326] the Building Loan Agreement[327] and assurance of completion required for insurance of advances are not applicable for IUC cases.[328] Additionally, the 2 percent Construction Contingency Amount required under the Escrow Agreement for Working Capital for new construction projects does not apply to IUC projects.[329] For IUC projects, an escrow for latent defects must be established in an amount equal to 2-1/2 percent of the total amount of the Construction Contract, in the form of cash, a letter of credit, or a surety bond, to be retained until the later of (i) 15 months following the date of completion as identified in the HUD Representative's Trip Report and (ii) the date that latent defects have been corrected to HUD's satisfaction.[330] Because no assurance of completion is required, surety approval is not required for change orders.[331] In addition, "[a]n escrow is not required for additive change orders, because HUD has no risk exposure until final closing. The mortgagor must be able to provide the additional funds required and must not have any outstanding mortgage obligation in connection with construction other than the insured mortgage at the time the mortgage is presented for insurance."[332]

IUC is rarely used, primarily because there is no active market for forward commitments with fixed interest rates. Therefore, with respect to loans insured through IUC, often the interest rate will not be "locked" until after construction is complete and shortly before HUD is prepared to endorse the Note for mortgage insurance, thus leaving the borrower subject to market fluctuations throughout the period of construction. In the alternative, to lock the interest rate earlier in the process, the borrower typically will have to accept an interest rate that is significantly higher than would be available for a loan with insured advances. In addition, the borrower must obtain separate construction financing and pay the costs associated therewith. Davis Bacon prevailing wage requirements apply despite the fact there is no FHA insurance in effect during the period of construction.[333]

C. Section 223(f) (Acquisition or Refinancing)

Section 223(f) of the Act is used to insure loans under Subchapter II of the Act in connection with the purchase or refinancing of an existing project.[334] It can be used to acquire or refinance existing multifamily housing projects under Section 207, existing hospitals under Section 242, or existing nursing-home, assisted-living, intermediate-care, and/or board-and-care

---

326. These include a Construction Contract; Agreement and Certification, plans and specifications; a title policy acceptable to HUD; and survey and Surveyor's Report. *Id.* at ¶ 12.16.C.
327. See Section V.C.5 of this chapter.
328. *MAP Guide, supra* note 15, at ¶ 12.16.C; *see also Closing Guide, supra* note 22, at ¶ 1.21.D.
329. *MAP Guide, supra* note 15, at ¶¶ 8.12.C, 12.16.C.
330. Escrow Agreement for Latent Defects, Form HUD-92414M (Rev. 04/11).
331. *MAP Guide, supra* note 15, at ¶ 12.16.I.
332. *Id.*
333. *See supra* note 178.
334. *See* 12 U.S.C. § 1715n(f) (2010) for program authorization. *See also* 24 C.F.R. § 207 (2011) for applicable regulations.

facilities under Section 232.³³⁵ Refinancing existing projects pursuant to Section 223(f) generally facilitates preservation of the properties by reducing interest rates and providing financing for the cost of repairs.

1. Eligible Projects

In addition to the general eligibility requirements set forth in Section II.A above, construction or substantial rehabilitation of the project must have been completed at least three years prior to the date of application.³³⁶ The completion of cosmetic and/or minor repairs, not rising to the level of substantial rehabilitation, within the three years preceding an application for insurance does not render the project ineligible for insurance under Section 223(f). Additionally, a project that was constructed or rehabilitated with an FHA-insured loan in the past three years will be eligible for insurance under Section 223(f) if the latent defects guarantee period has expired.³³⁷ Finally, "[p]rojects with additions completed less than three years before the application are eligible for refinancing so long as the size and number of units in the addition are not larger than the size and number of units in the original project."³³⁸ If the repairs required to the project are extensive enough to rise to the level of substantial rehabilitation,³³⁹ the project currently is not eligible for insurance under Section 207, pursuant to Section 223(f), but may be eligible for insurance under one or more of Sections 207, 220, 221(d)(3), 221(d)(4), or 231.³⁴⁰ Although eligible for insurance under Section 207, manufactured home parks are not eligible for acquisition or refinance under Section 223(f).³⁴¹

2. Maximum Insurable Mortgage

When calculating the maximum insurable mortgage, in addition to the statutory limits, debt service ratio limits, and loan ratio limits described in Section II.E above, loans insured under Section 207 pursuant to Section 223(f) are subject to additional limiting criteria. For refi-

---

335. *See* Chapter 3 hereof for a discussion of health-care projects insured under Section 242 and Section 232. Although at the time of this writing Notice H 10-06, by which HUD implemented its authority to provide insurance pursuant to Section 223(f) for existing hospital projects, had expired, Regulations permanently implementing refinancing pursuant to Section 223(f) for hospital projects are anticipated to be issued in 2012.

336. *MAP Guide, supra* note 15, at ¶ 3.9.A. HUD granted temporary authority to waive the three-year rule "for the purpose of providing liquidity to recently constructed or substantially rehabilitated, self-sustaining properties that are unable to secure permanent long-term financing due to the freeze in capital markets." Notice H 10-19, Mortgagee Letter 2010-30. This grant of temporary authority expired February 17, 2012. *See* Mortgagee Letter 2011-13. Completion of construction generally must be evidenced by a certificate of occupancy issued by the local authority, although in some substantial rehabilitation cases a certificate of occupancy may not be applicable. Notice H 10-19, Mortgagee Letter 2010-30.

337. *MAP Guide, supra* note 15, at ¶ 3.9.A.

338. *Id.*

339. See Section III.A.1 of this chapter for the definition of substantial rehabilitation.

340. At the time of this writing, it was anticipated that HUD may raise the limit as to the amount of repairs that may be completed with the proceeds of a loan insured under Section 207, pursuant to Section 223(f).

341. *MAP Guide, supra* note 15, at ¶ 3.9.B.

nancing transactions, if the requested mortgage amount exceeds 80 percent of the value, cost certification is required and the loan amount cannot exceed the cost to refinance.[342] If the requested loan amount amount is 80 percent or less of value, there is no obligation to cost certify,[343] and the borrower is eligible to receive excess cash, if any, from loan proceeds.[344] For acquisition transactions, the maximum insurable mortgage may not exceed the lesser of the appraised value or acquisition cost, each as multiplied by the applicable loan ratio (which is determined based on whether the project is market rate, affordable, or receives rental assistance).[345]

The cost to refinance consists of the amount needed to pay off eligible existing indebtedness plus "the initial deposit to the Reserve Fund for Replacements; [t]he sum of reasonable financing charges, legal and organizational, and title and recording expenses paid by the borrower; [t]he Lender's estimate of repair cost, if any; [e]ligible discounts paid by the borrower; [e]ligible architect's fees, mechanical engineering fees, municipal inspection fees, HUD inspection fees, if applicable, and other fees as may be determined eligible by the Lender including the cost of Lender third-party reports" less "the amount of any [r]eserve escrow for replacement and/or major movable equipment that will be purchased as an asset of the project."[346] Initial operating deficit and debt service escrows also are excluded from the cost to refinance. Acquisition cost is similarly calculated, but with the purchase price included in lieu of the amount needed to pay off existing indebtedness.[347]

3. Cash Out Refinance

For refinancing transactions in which the loan-to-value ratio is 80 percent or less,[348] a cost certification is not required, and if there are excess cash proceeds remaining once the mortgageable costs (including assurance of completion requirements) have been funded, those excess proceeds may be paid to the borrower.[349] However, when applicable, 50 percent of such cash-out proceeds must be held in escrow until any noncritical and owner-elected repairs have been completed to HUD's satisfaction.[350] This amount must be escrowed at initial/final endorsement, using the Escrow Agreement for Non-Critical, Deferred Repairs, Form HUD-92476.1M (the Repair Escrow).[351] The cash-out proceeds may be released once all repairs

---

342. *Id.* at ¶¶ 3.9.I, 8.8.A.2(b), 13.1.
343. Cost certification is required, however, with respect to Section 223(f) refinancings of Section 202 projects, even if the requested loan amount is 80 percent or less of value. *See supra* note 78 regarding Section 202 of the Housing Act of 1959.
344. *See* Section III.C.3 of this chapter.
345. The same ratio applies for loan-to-value and loan-to-acquisition cost, and is (i) 90% for the refinance of a direct loan originally made under Section 202 of the Housing Act of 1959; (ii) 87% for projects with 90% or greater rental assistance; (iii) 85% for affordable projects; and (iv) 83.3% for market-rate projects. *Id.* at ¶¶ 3.9.I, 8.8.A.1(e).
346. *Id.* at ¶ 8.8.A.2(b).
347. *Id.* at ¶ 8.8.A.1(e).
348. Lower loan to value ratios are required in cash out refinancing transactions for large loans. *See* Section II.F of this Chapter.
349. *MAP Guide, supra* note 15, at ¶ 8.8.A.2(c).
350. *Id.* at ¶¶ 3.9.J, 8.13.K; *Repair Escrow, supra* note 124, at ¶ 3.
351. *Repair Escrow, supra* note 124, at ¶ 8.

have been completed to HUD's satisfaction, evidence of clear title has been provided to HUD, and assurance against latent defects has been provided.[352]

4. Reserve for Replacements; Repairs

In connection with the application for mortgage insurance pursuant to Section 223(f),[353] the Lender obtains a Project Capital Needs Assessment (PCNA) Report, which analyzes the project's current physical condition and identifies, among other things, a recommended initial deposit to the reserve for replacements and immediate repair needs.[354] Any identified required repairs must be completed either prior to closing or within a specified period after closing, depending on whether they are deemed "critical" or "noncritical." Critical repairs are "life and safety" repairs, those that "(a) [e]ndanger the safety or well-being of residents, patients, visitors, or passers-by; (b) [e]ndanger the physical security of the property; (c) [a]dversely affect project or unit(s) ingress or egress; or (d) [p]revent the project from reaching sustaining occupancy."[355] These repairs must be completed prior to closing.[356]

Noncritical repairs or owner-elected repairs typically must be completed within 12 months following endorsement or such shorter time period as specified in the Firm Commitment.[357] To ensure post-closing completion of repairs, when applicable, a Repair Escrow must be established at closing in an amount equal to 120 percent of the estimated cost of any deferred repairs.[358] The "Repair Estimate Amount," equal to 100 percent of the estimated cost of deferred repairs, must be deposited in cash withheld from mortgage proceeds.[359] The "Additional Deposit Amount," equal to 20 percent (or 10 percent, as applicable)[360] of the estimated cost of deferred repairs may be deposited in either the form of cash or a letter of credit.[361] With prior written approval of HUD, the Lender may release funds from the Repair Estimate Amount for completed work, but the Additional Deposit Amount must be retained until *all* repair work has been completed to HUD's satisfaction, evidence of clear title has been provided to HUD, and assurance against latent defects has been provided.[362] If the actual cost of the repairs is less than was

---

352. *Id.* at ¶¶ 5, 8.
353. See Section IV below for a discussion of the approval process.
354. *MAP Guide, supra* note 15, at ¶ 5.26 and Appendix 5G. *See also* Section II.J.1 of this Chapter regarding reserve for replacements.
355. *MAP Guide, supra* note 15, at ¶ 12.17.A.1.
356. *Id. See also id.* at ¶ 3.9.C.
357. *Id.* at ¶ 5.26.D.3.
358. *Repair Escrow, supra* note 124, at ¶¶ 1–2. *See also MAP Guide, supra* note 15, at ¶ 5.26.D.2. *See also* Section III.C.3 of this chapter as to additional escrow amounts required for cash-out refinancings. With respect to loans insured pursuant to Section 223(a)(7) that have noncritical deferred repairs, an escrow in an amount equal to *110 percent* of the estimated cost of deferred repairs must be established at closing. Notice H 93-89. With respect to a Section 223(f) refinance of a direct loan originally made under Section 202 of the Housing Act of 1959, the escrow amount is also 110 percent of the estimated cost of deferred repairs. Memorandum from Deputy Assistant Secretary Charles H. Williams, dated April 18, 2006.
359. *Repair Escrow, supra* note 124, at ¶ 1. *See also MAP Guide, supra* note 15, at ¶ 5.26.D.2.
360. *See supra* note 358.
361. *Repair Escrow, supra* note 124, at ¶ 2. *See also MAP Guide, supra* note 15, at ¶ 5.26.D.2.
362. *Repair Escrow, supra* note 124, at ¶¶ 5, 8.

estimated, the remaining balance in the Repair Estimate Amount may be (i) used to pay for additional repairs as approved by the lender and HUD, (ii) applied to reduce the outstanding balance of the loan, or (iii) deposited in the reserve for replacements.[363]

Latent defects assurance, in an amount equal to two and one-half percent of the repair estimate amount, may be provided in the form of cash, a letter of credit, or surety bond.[364] Typically, latent defects assurance is withheld from the Additional Deposit Amount; however, if the entire amount of the Repair Escrow has been exhausted in completing the repairs, the borrower must deposit additional funds for latent defects assurance. The latent defects assurance amount will be released back to the borrower on the later of 15 months following completion of the repairs or when any latent defects have been corrected to HUD's satisfaction.[365]

5. Other Requirements and Restrictions

Under the Act, loans for multifamily projects insured pursuant to Section 223(f) cannot be prepaid in whole or in part for a period of five years from the date of the initial/final endorsement, unless approved by HUD.[366] This prepayment restriction is intended to ensure that the property is used as rental property for at least five years from the date of endorsement, but it may be waived by HUD on one of the following conditions: (1) The borrower enters into a HUD-approved use agreement to maintain the property as rental housing for the remainder of the five-year period;[367] (2) HUD determines that "conversion of the property to a cooperative or condominium form of ownership is sponsored by a bona fide tenants' organization representing a majority of the households in the project;"[368] (3) HUD determines maintenance of the property as rental housing no longer is necessary to ensure adequate rental housing for low- and moderate-income people;[369] or (4) maintenance of the property as rental housing "would have an undesirable and deleterious effect on the surrounding neighborhood."[370]

Projects insured pursuant to Section 223(f) must demonstrate a stable average physical occupancy rate of at least 85 percent for a period lasting from at least six months prior to application for mortgage insurance through endorsement.[371] Stable occupancy must be demonstrated by an updated rent roll dated no more than 30 days prior to closing. If the updated rent roll shows a significant change in occupancy, the Firm Commitment may be cancelled.[372]

---

363. *Id.* at ¶ 9.
364. *Id.* ¶ 8.
365. *Id.*
366. 12 U.S.C. § 1715n(f)(3) (2010); *see also Note, supra* note 11, at ¶ 9(h).
367. *See* Use Agreement, Form HUD-93150, *available at* http://portal.hud.gov/hudportal/HUD?src=/program_offices/administration/hudclips/forms/hud9a.
368. 12 U.S.C. § 1715n(f)(3) (2010).
369. *Id.*
370. *Id.*
371. Mortgagee Letter 2010-21 ¶ 3.B.1; Notice H 2010-11 ¶ 3.B.1. The MAP Guide states, "Section 223(f) has minimum and maximum physical occupancy eligibility and underwriting requirements. See Section 7.6.A.7 for further details." *MAP Guide, supra* note 15, at ¶ 3.9.Q. However, this internal cross-reference appears to be incorrect, and physical occupancy requirements were not addressed in detail by the MAP Guide as of the date of this writing.
372. Mortgagee Letter 2010-21 ¶ 3.B.1; Notice H 2010-11 ¶ 3.B.1.

D. Section 223(a)(7) (Acquisition or Refinancing)

As with loans insured pursuant to Section 223(f), obtaining a loan insured pursuant to Section 223(a)(7) may reduce interest rates and provide funds for minor repairs. However, unlike Section 223(f), insurance under Section 223(a)(7) is available only to refinance existing mortgages currently insured by HUD and also, in the case of the mark-to-market program, existing mortgages currently held by HUD.[373] A mortgage refinanced pursuant to Section 223(a)(7) is insured under the same section of the Act under which the existing mortgage was originally insured, and the mortgage insurance contract is a continuation of the mortgage insurance contract from the original loan.[374] This is evidenced by language appearing in the endorsement panel of the Note.[375] In addition to transferring the mortgage insurance contract to the new loan, existing reserves for replacement funds and residual receipts, if any, are transferred from the existing loan to the accounts established with respect to the new loan. However, despite being a continuation of the existing mortgage insurance contract, the applicable Regulations for loans insured pursuant to Section 223(a)(7) are those in effect as of the date the Firm Commitment was issued for the Section 223(a)(7) loan, as HUD has determined that amendments to the existing insurance contract may encompass subsequent amendments to the Regulations.[376]

When calculating the maximum insurable mortgage for a loan insured pursuant to Section 223(a)(7), in addition to the debt service ratio and loan ratio limits set forth in Section II.E above, the maximum insurable mortgage also cannot exceed the lesser of (i) the original principal amount of the existing insured mortgage and (ii) the unpaid principal balance of the existing insured mortgage plus the cost of improvements, outstanding debt incurred in connection with capital improvements, and loan closing charges.[377] Borrowers may not receive cash out from the proceeds of any loan insured pursuant to Section 223(a)(7).

---

373. 12 U.S.C. § 1715n(a)(7) (2010). The mark-to-market program was authorized by the Multifamily Assisted Housing Reform and Affordability Act of 1997 (42 U.S.C. § 1437(f) note) and is designed to reduce the cost of project-based rental assistance (primarily Section 8) while continuing to preserve low-income affordable housing.

374. *See* 12 U.S.C. § 1715n(a)(7)(A)(iv) (2010) ("[A]ny multifamily mortgage that is refinanced under this paragraph shall be documented through amendments to the existing insurance contract and shall not be structured through the provisions of a new insurance contract.").

375. *Note, supra* note 11, at endorsement panel. "For purposes of compliance with Section 223(a)(7)(A)(iv) of the National Housing Act, as amended, the Contract of Insurance regarding HUD Project No. [*Old Project Number*] is transferred to HUD Project No. [*New Project Number*], and said Contract of Insurance is hereby amended to reflect the terms, conditions and provisions of the National Housing Act, as amended, as evidenced by HUD's endorsement for insurance of this Note."

376. Multifamily Document Reform Implementation Frequently Asked Questions, General Questions, *available at* http://portal.hud.gov/hudportal/HUD?src=/program_offices/general_counsel/mffaqs/general#Q9 ("The existing insurance contract is evidenced on the endorsed Note panel. Amendments to the existing insurance contract can include amendments to the regulations applicable to the insurance contract and can include the regulations published on May 2, 2011.").

377. 12 U.S.C. § 1715n(a)(7)(A) (2010); Notice H 93-89.

E. Section 223(d) (Operating Loss Loan)

Section 223(d) is intended to avoid mortgage insurance claims by providing projects subject to existing FHA-insured mortgages a vehicle to obtain an additional FHA-insured loan to cover operating losses and to reimburse borrowers for funded losses. Although rarely used,[378] a loan insured under Section 223(d) is one of the specifically enumerated exceptions to the general requirement that the FHA-insured mortgage must constitute a first lien on the property.[379] As with loans insured pursuant to Section 223(a)(7), an operating loss loan is insured under the same section as the original mortgage.[380] However, unlike a loan insured pursuant to Section 223(a)(7), an operating loss loan is not a continuation of the existing mortgage insurance contract but is instead a separate, subordinate loan subject to a separate mortgage insurance contract.

If the operating losses occur during the first 24 months after the date of completion of the project, the loan will be insured under Section 223(d)(2).[381] If the loan covers losses experienced during any other consecutive two-year period within the first 10 years after the date of completion, the loan will be insured under Section 223(d)(3).[382] A single project may receive *both* an operating loss loan insured pursuant to Section 223(d)(2) and an operating loss loan insured pursuant to Section 223(d)(3), provided the loans cover two separate loss periods.[383]

"'[O]perating loss' means the amount by which the sum of taxes, interest on the mortgage debt, mortgage insurance premiums, hazard insurance premiums, and expense of maintenance and operation of the project covered by the mortgage exceeds the income of the project."[384] It does not include principal payments, depreciation, reserve for replacements deposits, fees in connection with an operating loss loan application, projected or anticipated losses, expenses that were funded or should have been funded from the working capital escrow, construction cost overruns, officers' salaries, bad debt, or write-offs as a result of an identity-of-interest tenant.[385] To be eligible for an operating loss loan, the borrower entity must have owned the project during the period the operating loss occurred, cost certification requirements must have been satisfied, the loan must have been finally endorsed for mortgage insurance, and all funds in the operating deficit escrow, if any, must have been disbursed.[386]

The maximum insurable mortgage for loans insured under Section 223(d)(2) is limited to the amount of the operating loss.[387] For loans insured under Section 223(d)(3), the maxi-

---

378. Of the 12,588 mortgages insured by HUD under the multifamily mortgage insurance programs and Section 232 health-care programs as of September 30, 2011, 34 were used to cover operating losses, 20 of which related to projects insured under Section 232. *See* http://portal.hud.gov/hudportal/HUD?src=/program_offices/housing/comp/rpts/mfh/mf_f47.
379. *See* 24 C.F.R. § 200.71 (2011).
380. 12 U.S.C. § 1715n(d)(4) (2010).
381. 12 U.S.C. § 1715n(d)(2)(B) (2010).
382. 12 U.S.C. § 1715n(d)(3)(B) (2010). Loans insured under Section 223(f) are not eligible for operating loss loans. Handbook 4470.1 ¶ 17-1.
383. 12 U.S.C. § 1715n(d)(4) (2010).
384. 12 U.S.C. § 1715n(d)(1) (2010).
385. Handbook 4470.1, ¶ 17-1.
386. *Id.* at ¶ 17-3.
387. 12 U.S.C. § 1715n(d)(2)(C) (2010).

mum insurable mortgage is limited to 80 percent of the unreimbursed cash contributions made by the borrower for use by the project during the applicable two-year loss period.[388] Regardless of whether the operating loss loan is insured under Section 223(d)(2) or Section 223(d)(3), it must be coterminous with the original loan.[389] A failure of the borrower to make a payment under either the original loan or the operating loss loan is considered a default under both mortgages and, provided the lender complies with the requirements of the claims process,[390] such a default would entitle the lender to mortgage insurance benefits with respect to both the operating loss loan and the original loan.[391]

F. Section 241 (Supplemental Loan)

Section 241 permits HUD to insure supplemental loans used to finance additions, improvements, renovations, or repairs to existing projects that already are subject to FHA-insured mortgages.[392] A supplemental loan insured under this section of the Act is one of the explicit exceptions to the first lien requirement and restriction on the granting of inferior liens.[393] Although Section 241 is primarily used to finance additions or improvements intended to extend the economic life of the project, increase energy efficiency, or increase occupancy or income, larger projects may take advantage of Section 241 to complete construction in phases.[394] However, completion of construction of larger projects in phases also may be financed through multiple loans insured under Section 221(d), Section 220, or Section 231. This approach generally is more desirable than utilizing Section 241, for loans insured under Section 241 require credit subsidy and are subject to higher MIP rates than loans insured under Section 221(d)(4), Section 220, or Section 231.[395]

When calculating the maximum insurable mortgage for a loan insured under Section 241, in addition to the loan ratio limits set forth in Section II.E above, the total of the amount of the loan or loans insured under Section 241, when added to the outstanding balance of the existing loan, cannot exceed the statutory maximum insurable mortgage applicable to the

---

388. 12 U.S.C. § 1715n(d)(3)(B) (2010).
389. 12 U.S.C. § 1715n(d)(4) (2010).
390. See Chapter 12.
391. 12 U.S.C. § 1715n(d)(4) (2010); 24 C.F.R. § 207.255 (2011). Note, however, that the date of the Firm Commitment for the operating loss loan, rather than the date of the Firm Commitment for the original loan, shall apply in determining the interest rate for debentures representing the portion of the claim allocable to the operating loss loan.
392. See 12 U.S.C. § 1715z-6(a) (2010) for program authorization. See 24 C.F.R. § 241 (2011) for applicable regulations. "The purpose is to provide the HUD-FHA insured or Secretary-held project with means to keep the project competitive, extend its economic life, and provide for financing replacement of obsolescent equipment through the use of HUD-FHA insured loan." HANDBOOK 4585.1.
393. 24 C.F.R. § 200.71 (2011).
394. See MAP Guide, supra note 15, at ¶ 7.14.A.3(b), discussing the restriction of the absorption period to 18 months and noting, "Larger projects may phase additional units under a separate application for mortgage insurance (e.g. under Section 241(a))."
395. See supra note 133. However, Section 221(d)(3) does not offer these same advantages over Section 241.

section under which the original mortgage is insured.[396] Unlike under Section 223(d), a cross-default between the original loan and the loan insured under Section 241 is not mandated by statute. Also unlike Section 223(d), Section 241 is a stand-alone section of the Act, such that the supplemental loan is insured under Section 241 rather than under the same section as the original mortgage.

IV. APPROVAL PROCESS

The vast majority of HUD-insured multifamily loans (other than loans insured under Section 223(a)(7)) are processed using MAP,[397] but the application and approval process varies between new construction/substantial rehabilitation projects and refinancing projects insured under Section 223(f). The approval process under MAP for new construction/substantial rehabilitation projects and Section 223(f) refinancing projects will be discussed in turn herein. As Section 223(d) and IUC are rarely used, the approval process for operating loss loans and IUC is not addressed in this chapter. Furthermore, Section 223(a)(7) and Section 241 are not discussed herein as additional guidance on the programmatic requirements for insurance under these sections of the Act is anticipated in the form of a future MAP Guide release.[398]

Most decisions regarding approval of loans are made by the Hub Director[399] or field office, other than those that require waivers from HUD Headquarters.[400] However, certain loans, including large loans and senior housing projects, must be approved by the National Loan Committee.[401]

A. New Construction/Substantial Rehabilitation

Market-rate new construction and substantial rehabilitation projects generally are processed under a two-stage process that includes a pre-application and subsequent application for Firm Commitment.[402] With respect to affordable new construction and substantial rehabilitation projects, the lender may elect to follow the two-stage process or instead submit the project

---

396. 12 U.S.C. § 1715z-6(a)(b) (2010).
397. *See supra* notes 15–16.
398. *MAP Guide, supra* note 15, at ¶ 1.2.B.
399. *See supra* note 69.
400. *E.g.,* waivers of debt service coverage or loan ratio requirements and commercial income requirements. *See supra* notes 70 & 207 and accompanying text.
401. *See* Notice H 2010-13.
402. *MAP Guide, supra* note 15, at ¶ 4.1.B. "The Hub Director may waive two-stage processing and allow a direct to Firm Commitment application for properties in which the concept meeting yields strong evidences [sic] of the following: (a) Stable markets, capable HUD experienced Lender, mortgagor, general contractor, architect and management agent and that there are not environmental issues, or (b) A stable occupied market rate substantial rehabilitation property that, during the rehabilitation period, will not have: (i) major rehabilitation or unit reconfiguration, (ii) tenant displacement except for short periods during interior rehabilitation of a unit, (iii) a reduction in current occupancy levels, (iv) negative cash flow; (c) A pre-application letter that has recently expired, but delays prevented submission of the Firm Commitment application within the allowed time frames, and the Hub Director agrees that the application, the market data and the due diligence has [sic] not fundamentally changed." *MAP Guide, supra* note 15, at ¶ 11.2.I

directly for Firm Commitment.[403] Regardless of whether the project is market-rate or affordable, the lender must participate in a concept meeting prior to the submission of the application for all new construction and substantial rehabilitation projects.[404] The concept meeting provides HUD with an overview of the project, including discussion of the projected mortgage amount, the proposed site and improvements, potential commercial uses, amenities, general market conditions, environmental issues, potential risks and mitigating factors, development status, green or sustainability issues, anticipated waiver requests, availability of any state or local support, whether the project is market-rate or affordable, and basic information (including previous HUD experience) about the developer, principals, management company, and contractor.[405] Based on this project overview, HUD can assess the overall feasibility of the project and make a recommendation as to whether the lender should submit the application.

Although HUD must approve the lender's underwriter, the lender is responsible for the selection and management of all reviewers, including third-party consultants.[406] The names and résumés, if possible, of the reviewers should be submitted to HUD as soon as they are identified.[407] In addition, HUD approval also must be obtained before submission of the application if one or more of the principals have greater than $250 million in outstanding FHA-insured debt.[408]

1. Pre-application

The pre-application submission includes those exhibits that are most important in assessing the project's feasibility and is accompanied by a narrative prepared by the lender. The pre-application exhibits are composed primarily of architectural/engineering exhibits (A/E Exhibits) and valuation-related exhibits. No detailed cost estimate is done at the pre-application stage.[409] For market-rate projects, one-half of the application fee is remitted at the time of the pre-application. For affordable housing projects, the application fee is collected with the application for Firm Commitment.[410]

---

403. *MAP Guide, supra* note 15, at ¶ 4.1.B. If submitted directly for Firm Commitment, the application must include all the exhibits required at both the pre-application and Firm Commitment stages.

404. *Id.* at ¶ 4.2.A.1.

405. *Id.*

406. *Id.* at ¶ 4.2.B. Although typically third-party consultants, the appraiser, market analyst, architectural and engineering reviewer, and construction cost estimator may be employees of the lender.

407. *Id.; see also MAP Guide, supra* note 15, at Appendix 4 (the submission should include résumés of lender's underwriter, appraiser, and/or market analyst for pre-application review if not submitted prior to pre-application).

408. The amount of outstanding FHA-insured debt is determined based on the principal's Schedule of Real Estate Owned. *MAP Guide, supra* note 15, at ¶ 4.2.A.1(c). The lender must also perform a thorough preliminary mortgage credit review of such principals.

409. *Id.* at ¶ 6.7. For new construction projects, the HUD cost estimator will estimate a cost for structures based on the approximate gross floor area and project type, and for substantial rehabilitation projects, the HUD cost estimator will estimate the cost of rehabilitation work based on the work write-up submitted as an architectural exhibit.

410. *See* Section II.J.4 of this chapter for a discussion of the FHA Application Fee.

a. A/E Review

The architect must visit the site and develop preliminary sketches, including location maps with the property clearly defined, a sketch of the site showing overall building dimensions and major site features, a sketch plan of the main building, and sketch floor plans of the typical dwelling units, which are submitted as part of the pre-application.[411] For substantial rehabilitation projects, the A/E Exhibits also include sketch plans of existing buildings, a basic work write-up of the proposed rehabilitation, and lead-based paint and asbestos test reports.[412] The HUD architectural analyst reviews the A/E Exhibits for conformance with HUD Minimum Property Standards, conformance with energy-efficiency standards, unusual site conditions, and typical features of residential buildings, including whether the proposed apartment sizes are marketable for the proposed rents.[413] Based on this review, the HUD architectural analyst will make a recommendation as to acceptance or rejection of the A/E portion of the pre-application.

b. Valuation Review

Valuation review is intended to assess whether the project is economically viable and capable of supporting the proposed loan amount.[414] To make that determination, the HUD valuation analyst reviews the market study prepared by the lender's market analyst at the pre-application stage to assess the rental demands of the market.[415] The market study "must estimate the number of renter households with sufficient incomes to afford the type of housing at the rents proposed. In addition, the study must estimate the number of units that the market could reasonably absorb over a specified forecast period, which is typically three years, taking into consideration competitive units in the existing inventory, units currently under construction, and units in the planning pipeline, as well as the gross and contract rents of those units."[416] To support these conclusions, the market study must include a description of the project;[417] identification of the housing market area and a discussion of the economic, demographic, and housing market conditions therein;[418] a discussion of other rental projects under construction

---

411. *Id.* at ¶ 5.5.A.
412. *Id.* at ¶ 5.15.A.
413. *Id.* at Appendix 5F.
414. *Id.* at ¶ 7.1.
415. "Market studies are not required for properties with at least 90% of the units covered by a long term (5 years or more) rental assistance contract and with any rent increase confirmed before initial or final endorsement." *Id.* at ¶ 7.4.
416. *Id.* at ¶ 7.5.A.
417. The description of the project should specifically identify any characteristics impacting the desirability and marketability of the proposed site, including amenities, access to schools, shopping, churches, parks, hospitals, and availability of parking. *Id.* at ¶¶ 7.5.C, 7.9.
418. "The Housing Market Area (HMA) is the geographic area in which units with similar characteristics, e.g., number of bedrooms and rents, are in equal competition." *Id.* at ¶ 7.5.D. The discussion of economic and demographic conditions of the HMA should address employment trends, growth sectors in the economy and past and future trends in demographics. *Id.* at ¶ 7.5.E. The analysis of housing market conditions must consider vacancy levels and absorption issues experienced by existing rental projects, along with any recent rent increases or decreases for existing projects. *Id.* at ¶ 7.5.F.

or in the planning pipeline;[419] and an estimate of demand.[420] For projects designed for the elderly,[421] the market study must focus on the number of elderly households, rather than renter households more generally, that would need and could afford the proposed projects.[422] Similarly, for low-income housing tax credit (LIHTC) projects, the market study must focus on demand by income eligible residents (i.e., residents "whose income does not exceed the maximum permitted by the affordability restriction but who [have] sufficient minimum income to pay the LIHTC rent without being overburdened").[423]

Pre-application valuation exhibits also include an estimate of land value and an estimate of market rents prepared by the lender's appraiser based on comparables[424] adjusted for differences in utilities/services provided, project location and project amenities,[425] along with photographs and a location map of the rent comparables used in the analysis.[426] The lender's appraiser also must provide an analysis of operating expenses[427] to determine a net income estimate for the project. For new construction projects, use of comparable projects will be needed to estimate operating expenses, while the estimate for substantial rehabilitation projects is adjusted based on comparable projects but is tested against the existing project.[428] The total estimate of operating expenses is based on the sum of fixed expenses,[429] variable expenses, and the reserve for replacements.[430] As with estimates of market rent, adjustments in expense estimates are made to account for significant differences between the comparables and the proposed project.[431]

A Phase I Environmental Site Assessment (Phase I Report) with narrative environmental report is submitted to establish acceptability of the site.[432] The Phase I Report identifies any

---

419. *Id.* at ¶ 7.5.G.
420. In estimating demand, the market study should consider renter growth, trends in home ownership versus renting, and the loss of existing rentals or current excess rental supply. The market study must specifically address the impact of the proposed project on existing insured projects. *Id.* at ¶ 7.5.G.
421. *See* Section III.A.10.d of this chapter.
422. *MAP Guide*, *supra* note 15, at ¶ 7.5.A. With respect to projects designed for the elderly, the market study should also include a discussion as to additional services available to residents and fees for optional services, as well as proximity of the proposed project to health-care facilities, public transportation, shopping, and other services essential to elderly residents. The amenities and location of existing and pipeline projects in the Housing Market Area should also be considered. *Id.* at ¶¶ 7.5.C.6, 7.5.D.5, 7.5.G.4. *See supra* note 418 for a definition of Housing Market Area. The MAP Guide also sets forth additional assumptions that must be factored in when estimating demand and absorption for project designed for the elderly. *Id.* at ¶ 7.5.I.
423. *Id.* at ¶ 7.5.D.6. In identifying income eligible residents, consideration should be given to other forms of assistance, if any, the project receives that may further reduce rents.
424. Using Estimates of Market Rent By Comparison, Form HUD-92273.
425. *MAP Guide*, *supra* note 15, at ¶ 7.7.
426. *Id.* at ¶ 7.10.A.
427. Using Operating Expense Analysis Worksheet (Multifamily Housing), Form HUD-92274.
428. *MAP Guide*, *supra* note 15, at ¶ 7.8.B.
429. Such as real estate taxes and insurance costs. *Id.* at ¶ 7.8.C.1.
430. *Id.* at ¶ 7.8.C.4.
431. *Id.* at ¶ 7.8.F.
432. *Id.* at ¶ 7.10.A.

site contamination by the presence of hazardous substances,[433] and the environmental report, Environmental Assessment and Compliance Findings for the Related Laws, Form HUD-4128, identifies special environmental hazards that, if serious and unable to be mitigated, may make the project site ineligible for mortgage insurance, such as flooding and wetlands, subsidence or unstable soils, danger from fire and explosion, exposure to low-flying airplanes, airport noise and other noise exposure, proximity to railroads, chemical fumes, or the presence of endangered species on the site.[434] The HUD appraiser will review the valuation exhibits[435] to determine the market demand for rental housing, the acceptability of the proposed site, acceptability of proposed rents and estimated operating expenses, and the land value (or "as is" value of land and existing improvements with respect to substantial rehabilitation projects).[436]

c. Mortgage Credit Review

Mortgage credit analysis is designed to evaluate the suitability, creditworthiness, and experience of the proposed borrower, principals, contractor, and management agent. Pre-application review is relatively limited, with the borrower and development team providing résumés, an organizational chart, and summary financial data.[437] To analyze the acceptability of the borrower, principals, contractor, and management agent, a Previous Participation Certification, Form HUD-2530 (the HUD-2530), must be completed for each principal participant,[438] identifying the Social Security Number or Employer Identification Number of each indi-

---

433. *Id.* at ¶ 9.3.
434. *Id.* at ¶ 9.5.
435. Evidence of site control and Application for Multifamily Housing Project, Form HUD-92013 are also submitted as valuation exhibits in the pre-application stage. *Id.* at ¶ 7.10.A.
436. *Id.* at ¶ 7.10.C.
437. *Id.* at ¶ 8.2. For large loans, the résumés of the borrower and contractors must demonstrate substantial prior experience in developing, constructing, and owning multifamily projects that are similar in size and scope to the proposed project. *See* Notice H 2011-36 ¶ III.D(iii); Mortgagee Letter 2011-40 ¶ III.D(iii).
438. "Principals include all individuals, joint ven-tures, partnerships, corporations, trusts, non-profit organizations, any other public or pri-vate entity, that will participate in the proposed project as a sponsor, owner, prime contractor, turnkey developer, managing agent, nursing home administrator or operator, packager, or consultant. Architects and attorneys who have any interest in the project other than an arms length fee arrangement for professional ser-vices are also considered principals by HUD. In the case of partnerships, all general partners regardless of their percentage inter-est and limited partners having a 25 percent or more interest in the partnership are considered principals. In the case of public or private corporations or governmental entities, princi-pals include the president, vice president, secretary, treasurer and all other executive officers who are directly responsible to the board of directors, or any equivalent govern-ing body, as well as all directors and each stockholder having a 10 percent or more inter-est in the corporation. Affiliates are defined as any person or business concern that directly or indirectly controls the policy of a principal or has the power to do so. A holding or parent corpora-tion would be an example of an affiliate if one of its subsidiaries is a principal." Instructions for Completing Form HUD-2530. *See also* 24 C.F.R. § 200.214(e); *MAP Guide, supra* note 15, at ¶ 8.3.D. An electronic HUD-2530 (E-2530) may be submitted through HUD's Active Partner Performance System (APPS) in lieu of using a paper HUD-2530. *MAP Guide, supra* note 15, at ¶ 8.2.A.4.

vidual or entity,[439] the role the individual or entity will play in the proposed transaction, any previous projects in which the individual or entity has participated, along with any adverse performance indicators, such as whether the loan for any previous project is or has been in default during the previous 10 years, whether there are any unresolved HUD audit issues, and whether the principal has been convicted of a felony.[440] The HUD-2530 *may* be submitted as early as the pre-application stage.[441] HUD processes the HUD-2530, reviewing the information for any adverse indicators and making inquiries to other agencies or HUD field offices as necessary as to the past performance of the sponsor, borrower, principal, or contractor. In addition to reviewing the HUD-2530 if submitted at the pre-application, HUD must approve any nonprofit sponsors and/or borrowers involved in the transaction prior to submission of the firm application if the project is being submitted for nonprofit processing.[442]

2. Letter of Invitation

After completing the pre-application review, HUD either issues an invitation letter or declines to issue an invitation to submit a firm application.[443] A letter of invitation signals that if the exhibits submitted at the firm application stage are consistent with the exhibits submitted for the pre-application, it is anticipated that HUD will issue a commitment to insure a loan with respect to the project.[444] If HUD decides to issue a letter of invitation, but concerns relating to project acceptability were raised during the course of the pre-application review, the invitation letter also may address these issues.[445] When HUD declines to issue a letter of invitation, the application will be returned to the lender. If there are minor deficiencies, the lender may be given five days to correct deficiencies.[446]

---

439. This information is also disclosed in Section K of the Application Multifamily Projects, Form HUD-92013, but on that form, "[p]roviding the [Social Security Number or Employer Identification Number] is mandatory for the sponsor, borrower and their principals; however, this information is voluntary for all other participants." *MAP Guide, supra* note 15, at ¶ 8.3.B.1. With respect to Previous Participation Certification, Form HUD-2530, the Social Security Number or Employer Identification number must be provided for each principal participant in order for HUD to identify the participant's records. Instructions for Completing Form HUD-2530.

440. Previous Participation Certification, Form HUD-2530. *See also* Chapter 5 for further discussion of previous participation requirements.

441. *MAP Guide, supra* note 15, at ¶ 8.2.A.4. But for principals with greater than $250 million in outstanding FHA-insured debt, Previous Participation Certification, Form HUD-2530 should be submitted prior to application. *Id.* at ¶ 8.3.K.

442. *Id.* at ¶ 8.2.A.3. Nonprofit borrowers are eligible to receive loans with higher loan-to-value ratios and/or lower debt service coverage requirements. *See supra* notes 71–75 and accompanying text. However, a nonprofit borrower may elect profit-motivated processing of the loan, in which case the lower loan-to-value ratios and higher debt service coverage requirements would apply.

443. *MAP Guide, supra* note 15, at ¶ 4.2.D.

444. *See id.* at Appendix 4C for sample invitation letter format, providing: "It is important to understand that this letter is not to be construed as a commitment on the part of FHA to insure a mortgage for your proposal. It is intended only to establish general agreement on the basic concept, market, rents and expenses for your proposal."

445. *Id.* at ¶ 4.2.D.1.

446. *Id.* at ¶ 4.2.E.2.

For projects receiving a letter of invitation, the lender has 30 calendar days to advise HUD whether or not it plans to submit an application for Firm Commitment.[447] If a lender fails to notify HUD of its intent within this time frame but wishes to proceed to Firm Commitment, a new pre-application review may be required.[448] The lender has 120 days from the date of the letter of invitation to submit the firm application, although HUD may approve extensions of this time frame in its discretion.[449]

3. Firm Commitment

In preparing the Firm Commitment application, the lender must review the exhibits, perform an underwriting analysis, and prepare a narrative summarizing its recommendations. Changes or updates to information supplied at the pre-application should be clearly identified. For market-rate projects, the balance of the application fee is collected with the application for Firm Commitment. For affordable housing projects, the entire application fee is collected at this time.[450]

a. A/E Review

For purposes of the firm application submission, the lender's architectural analyst must review a number of A/E Exhibits provided by the borrower[451] and prepare a review report as to the completeness of the A/E Exhibits, conformance with local code requirements and HUD standards, accessibility, and acceptability of site design and building design.[452] The borrower's firm application A/E Exhibits and lender's architectural analyst's review report are reviewed by the HUD architectural analyst, who will determine if the underwriting conclusions are supportable, and will recommend approval, modification, or rejection of the A/E portion of the firm application.[453] For LIHTC projects, a streamlined procedure is in place with respect

---

447. *Id.* at ¶ 4.2.D.2.
448. *Id.*
449. "The Hub Director may authorize three 30-day extensions (or one 90-day extension) of the 120-day limit, but there is no requirement that the Lender's request for extensions be approved. The Hub Director will review the circumstances reported by the Lender to justify the extension of time and must determine that the requested delay beyond 120 days is not likely to change the underwriting data on which the invitation was based or to undermine the feasibility of the project due to a change in the market or other factors that were previously determined to be acceptable at pre-application." *Id.* at ¶ 4.2.D.3. The Hub Director may also grant additional extensions on a case-by-case basis and without Headquarters review and approval. *See* Notice H 2010-01.
450. *See* Section II.J.4 of this chapter for a discussion of the FHA Application Fee.
451. Including Application for Project Mortgage Insurance, Form HUD-92013; Owner Architect Agreement, AIA Document B-108 (or AIA Document B-181 for projects receiving a firm commitment prior to Sept. 1, 2011); survey and surveyor's report; engineering reports; utility "will serve" letters; architect certifications regarding site soil limitations and compliance with accessibility laws; plans and specifications and a description of any off-site work. *MAP Guide*, *supra* note 15, at ¶ 5.5.B. For substantial rehabilitation projects, the borrower will also provide a scope of rehabilitation write-up based on the results of a joint inspection conducted by borrower and lender. *Id.* at ¶ 5.14.
452. *Id.* at ¶ 5.6.B.
453. *Id.* at ¶ 5.9. "HUD A/E recommendations will be based on areas of concern in the review report not covered at the Pre-application stage." *Id.* at ¶ 5.9.B.2. This would include factors such as site soils information, accessibility for persons with disabilities, site design, and building design.

to A/E review, which allows for the deferred submission of final drawings and specifications until 30 days prior to the initial endorsement.[454]

b. Cost Review

The lender's cost estimator prepares a detailed cost estimate in accordance with a method generally recognized in the construction industry, including cost estimates for structures and on-site land improvements, costs not attributable to dwelling use, on-site demolition costs, off-site improvement costs, contractor's general requirements, general overhead, builder's profit, architect design and supervision fees, bond premiums, borrower's other fees, and contractor's other fees.[455] Additional cost exhibits include the property insurance schedule, plans, and specifications, and the Contractor's and/or Mortgagor's Cost Breakdown, Form-2328 (the Cost Breakdown).[456] The HUD cost analyst will examine whether the lender's cost estimate is supported by the cost exhibits and recommend acceptance, modification, or rejection of the cost portion of the Firm Commitment application.[457] For LIHTC projects, the lender's cost estimator may provide a preliminary cost estimate at the firm application stage, pending the finalization of the architectural drawings and specifications.

c. Valuation Review

At the firm application stage, the lender's appraiser completes an appraisal that establishes the replacement cost or value of the project, as applicable.[458] Mortgages for new construction projects insured under Section 220, 221(d), or 231 "are replacement cost limited mortgages by mandate of the National Housing Act and require a site valuation, a debt service analysis, and a cost approach to value. An estimate of market value after completion is not required."[459] The appraiser must consider proposed construction costs in establishing the replacement cost, and the appraiser also must determine "warranted price of land."[460] In determining the warranted price of land, the appraiser must value the land for its intended multifamily use rather than for its "highest and best use" and assume that all off-site improvements are completed.[461] For substantial rehabilitation funded by loans insured under Section 220 or 221(d), the ap-

---

454. In the firm commitment application for an LIHTC project, schematic drawings may be submitted in lieu of final drawings and specifications. *Id.* at ¶ 5.28.
455. *Id.* at ¶ 6.3.C.
456. *Id.* at ¶ 6.8.A. For substantial rehabilitation projects, the estimated life of replacement reserve components should also be provided.
457. *Id.* at ¶ 6.8.B.
458. *See supra* notes 59–61 and accompanying text for a discussion of cost-based and value-based programs.
459. *MAP Guide, supra* note 15, at ¶ 7.6.A.6(a). Because Section 207 is a value-limited program, the appraiser must include an "as complete" value conclusion, rather than identifying replacement cost. *See* Mortgagee Letter 2007-05 ("At Firm Commitment, an 'as is' value and a value after the completion . . . are required. The narrative appraisal report must contain both of these value determinations. The Form HUD 92264 shall be prepared to summarize the post [completion] value. A separate Form HUD 92264 is not required for the 'as is' value.").
460. *See MAP Guide, supra* note 15, at ¶¶ 7.6.A.6, 7.11.B.
461. Multifamily Summary Appraisal Report, Form HUD-92264 Note 1.

praisal is similar to that for new construction, but the appraiser must determine the "as is" value of the property, including land and existing improvements, rather than the warranted price of land.[462] The "as is" value is based on income and direct sales comparisons and does not assume completion of off-site improvements, instead reflecting only those improvements (both on-site and off-site) that are present at the time of the appraisal.[463] "Substantial rehabilitation under Section 231 differs from Section 220, 221(d)(3), and 221(d)(4) in that market value based on the completion of the rehabilitation is required."[464] This is because Section 231 is a cost-based program for new construction cases but a value-based program for substantial rehabilitation cases.[465]

In addition to the appraisal, the valuation exhibits for the Firm Commitment application include updates of the estimates of market rents by comparison and the analysis of operating expenses,[466] evidence of permissive zoning, evidence of the last arm's-length transaction and purchase price of the land (and existing improvements, if applicable), environmental exhibits as needed (including evidence that any environmental issues identified at the pre-application stage have been, or will be, resolved),[467] and certain other HUD form documents.[468] If the lender's conclusions as to value differ from those of the lender's appraiser, this inconsistency must be explained in the lender's underwriting summary. The HUD appraiser then will review the valuation exhibits and will recommend approval or rejection based on the completeness of the appraisal and whether the HUD appraiser agrees with the estimated income, total operating expenses, total estimated replacement cost,[469] and warranted price of land or the "as is" value of land and existing improvements, as appropriate, as determined by the lender's appraiser. If appraised land value or "as is" value is contributed to meet financial requirements for closing, any cash out of excess value must be deferred until the project demonstrates to HUD's satisfaction that the project has achieved six consecutive months of break-even occupancy.[470]

d. Mortgage Credit Review

If not previously submitted with the pre-application, the HUD-2530 must be submitted with the Firm Commitment application for each principal participant. In addition, current résumés, credit reports, bank references, and certifications authorizing the release of banking and credit

---

462. *MAP Guide, supra* note 15, at ¶ 7.11.B.
463. *Id.* at ¶ 7.6.A.6(b); Handbook 4465.1 §§ 2–3(a).
464. *MAP Guide, supra* note 15, at ¶ 7.6.A.8.
465. *See supra* note 61.
466. *MAP Guide, supra* note 15, at ¶ 7.11.A.
467. *Id.* at ¶ 7.10.A ("All exhibits for HUD to complete the Environmental Assessment and [Compliance] Findings for the Related Laws (HUD-4128), including any documentation that was required as a result of findings made during Pre-Application Processing"); *see also id.* at ¶ 9.2.C.1.
468. Including Application for Multifamily Housing Project, Form HUD-92013; Multifamily Summary Appraisal Report, Form HUD-92264; and Supplement to Project Analysis; Form HUD-92264A. *Id.* at ¶ 7.11.A.
469. Or value as fully improved for loans insured under Section 207 or substantial rehabilitation cases insured under Section 231.
470. *See supra* notes 217 and 228 and accompanying text.

information must be provided for the sponsor, borrower, key principals, and contractor.[471] The sponsor, borrower, principals,[472] and contractor must submit financial statements, for three years or the length of existence if a newly created entity, including supporting documentation.[473] The financial statements must be dated within three months of the date the Firm Commitment application is submitted, except that audited financial statements may be up to one year old if supplemented by management-prepared year-to-date financial statements.[474]

Based on the mortgage credit exhibits, the lender's underwriter must determine the acceptability of the principal parties and recommended maximum mortgage amount.[475] HUD reviews the HUD-2530, if it was not previously processed during the pre-application or if there have been changes since the pre-application, reviews the lender's underwriter's recommendations, and determines the maximum mortgage amount and financial settlement requirements.[476]

e. Management Review

Management analysis is intended to determine the capability of the management agent, if any, to effectively and efficiently manage the project. A HUD-2530 must be submitted and processed by HUD with respect to any proposed management agent.[477] In addition, a management entity profile, identifying the organization, operation, and experience of the management agent must be submitted, along with a narrative setting forth proposed leasing and management strategies and a Project Owner's/Management Agent's Certification, Form HUD-9839, by which the agent and owner agree to comply with HUD requirements, including execution of an acceptable management agreement.[478] Information regarding proposed staffing, resident complaint resolution procedures, and a copy of the proposed management agreement also are reviewed as part of the management analysis.[479] The lender must review the management agent's past performance and experience and make a recommendation to HUD as to approval of the management agent. If the lender and HUD determine the proposed management agent is capable of effectively

---

471. *MAP Guide, supra* note 15, at ¶ 8.3.B.
472. The requirement to submit current financial statements and supporting schedules "appl[ies] to those principals identified in Section 8.3.D [of the MAP Guide]. These are principals who are actively involved in property operating decisions or are significant financial investors as identified in the borrower entity's organizational structure. The Lender's Underwriter must determine which principals have control of the single asset entity and the property, and must assess their financial stability and how it will impact the risk to FHA, and must review their financial statements along with these schedules." *Id.* at ¶ 8.4.A.5(a).
473. Supporting documents include schedules of Real Estate Owned, aging schedules of accounts receivable and notes receivable, and schedules identifying pledged accounts, marketable securities, accounts payable, notes and mortgages payable, and legal proceedings. *Id.* at ¶ 8.4.B.2(d).
474. *Id.* at ¶ 8.4.C.1.
475. *Id.* at ¶ 8.3.
476. *Id.* at ¶ 8.1.
477. *Id.* at ¶ 10.4. Flags that may result in rejection of a proposed management agent include if the agent or any principals have been suspended, debarred, placed on ineligible status, or placed under a Limited Denial of Participation, or if the HUD field office has raised concerns about the management agent's performance.
478. *Id.* at ¶ 10.2.
479. *Id.*

managing the project, the borrower and management agent may enter into a management agreement, provided it incorporates the provisions required by HUD, including a right of HUD to require the borrower to terminate the agreement.[480]

B. Acquisition or Refinancing under Section 223(f)

For acquisition or refinancing projects, concept meetings are recommended (but not required), there is no pre-application review, and applications are submitted directly for Firm Commitment.[481] Because there is no pre-application, the list of reviewers[482] and their experiences should be submitted to HUD as soon as they are identified. The Firm Commitment application submission includes A/E Exhibits, cost exhibits, valuation exhibits, mortgage credit exhibits, and management analysis exhibits. The application fee is collected with the application for Firm Commitment.[483]

1. A/E Review

A Project Capital Needs Assessment (PCNA) Report prepared by the lender and dated no earlier than 120 days prior to submission of the Firm Commitment application must be included in the A/E Exhibits.[484] The PCNA Report must include a Physical Inspection Report, identifying the current condition, immediate repairs categorized as critical or noncritical, anticipated future repairs over the life of the mortgage, and a Statement of Resources and Needs, setting forth a recommended amount of the initial deposit, if any, and annual deposits required from the borrower for deposit to the reserve for replacements.[485] The lender's review of the PCNA Report is submitted as an A/E Exhibit, along with certificates of occupancy, if available, evidence of building code and zoning compliance, as-built survey, surveyor's report, location map, and, if available, as-built plans.[486] As with the Firm Commitment stage review for new construction or substantial rehabilitation projects, the HUD architectural ana-

---

480. "HUD may require the owner to terminate the agreement (1) Immediately if a default occurs under the Mortgage, Note, Regulatory Agreement, or Rental Assistance Contract that is attributable to the actions of the management agent; (2) Upon 30 days written notice, for failure to comply with the provisions of the Management Certification or other good cause; or (3) When HUD takes over the property as Mortgagee in Possession . . . If HUD terminates the agreement pursuant to its authority under the loan documents, the owner will promptly make all arrangements for providing management satisfactory to HUD . . . [and] [t]he management agent must turn over to the owner all of the project's cash, accounts, deposits, investments, and records immediately, but in no event more than 30 days after the date the management agreement is terminated." *Id.* at ¶ 10.6.B.2. *See also infra* Section V.C.3.d of this chapter for a discussion of provisions in the Regulatory Agreement relating to the management agent.
481. *MAP Guide, supra* note 15, at ¶ 4.1.C.
482. *See supra* notes 406–07.
483. *See* Section II.J.4 of this chapter for a discussion of the FHA Application Fee.
484. *MAP Guide, supra* note 15, at ¶ 5.26.A. "The date of the PCNA is the date that the actual physical inspection of the property was performed . . . In the event that the Lender fails to submit an acceptable application for Firm Commitment within 120 days from the date of the original physical inspection, then the Lender must order an updated PCNA."
485. *Id.* at ¶ 5.26.B and Appendix 5G ¶ IV.C.
486. *Id.* at ¶¶ 5.25.B–D.

lyst will review the A/E Exhibits and recommend acceptance, modification, or rejection of the A/E portion of the application.[487]

2. Cost Review

The cost estimates for critical and noncritical repairs and initial and monthly deposits to the reserve for replacements from the PCNA Report are submitted as a cost review exhibit, along with the lender's review of those costs and the property insurance schedule.[488] HUD's cost analyst reviews the exhibits and recommends approval, modification, or rejection of the cost portion of the Firm Commitment application.[489]

3. Valuation Review

Unlike most new construction or substantial rehabilitation projects, an appraisal is commissioned to determine the value of the property. Market studies typically are not required for loans insured under Section 223(f).[490] However, a market study may be warranted in certain circumstances, including in declining or volatile markets, if the project has high vacancy rates, or if there is a proposed change in the type of occupancy.[491] Aside from the market study, valuation exhibits submitted in the Firm Commitment application for refinancing or purchase transactions include many of the same exhibits submitted at the pre-application and Firm Commitment stage for new construction or substantial rehabilitation projects.[492] The lender also must submit balance sheets, operating statements, and rent rolls for the project.[493] In addition to being reviewed by HUD's architectural analyst and cost analyst, the PCNA Report is submitted as a valuation exhibit for review by the HUD appraiser. The HUD reviewers must consider how the information in the PCNA Report impacts the estimate of the remaining economic life of the project, which is used in determining the maximum mortgage term.[494] Any environmental concerns raised by the Phase I Report must be addressed in the Firm Commitment application, including how those concerns have been resolved or identifying a plan of correction.[495] As with new construction and substantial rehabilitation projects, the HUD appraiser will recommend approval, modification, or rejection based on the acceptability of the proposed site, acceptability of proposed rents and expenses, and the acceptability of the conclusions of the lender's appraiser.[496]

---

487. *Id.* at ¶ 5.27.
488. *Id.* at ¶ 6.9.
489. *Id.* at ¶ 6.11.
490. *Id.* at ¶ 7.4.A.
491. *Id.*; *see also* Mortgagee Letter 2010-21 ¶ III.B.2; Notice H 2010-11 ¶ III.B.2.
492. Including the Application for Multifamily Housing Project, Form HUD-92013; location map; evidence of permissive zoning; evidence of site control; Phase I Report; appraisal; Rental Housing Project Income Analysis and Appraisal, Form HUD-92264; and Supplement to Project Analysis, Form HUD-92264A; Estimates of Market Rent by Comparison, Form HUD-92273; and Operating Expenses Analysis Worksheet, Form HUD-92274. *MAP Guide, supra* note 15, at ¶ 7.12.A.
493. *Id.*
494. *See* Section II.G of this chapter.
495. *Id.* at ¶ 9.2.C.
496. *Id.* at ¶ 7.12.C.

4. Mortgage Credit Review

The mortgage credit analysis for acquisition or refinancing projects generally requires the submission and analysis of the same exhibits as submitted for the pre-application and Firm Commitment application on new construction and substantial rehabilitation projects. The primary difference is that review for acquisition and refinancing projects requires the submission of *audited* financial statements for the past three fiscal years, along with copies of the most recent property tax bills and three years of tax returns for the property borrowing entity and for the key principals.[497] An owner-certified balance sheet and operating statement is required in any instance in which the audited financial statement is more than three months old or if audited financial statements are unavailable for circumstances outside the borrower's control.[498] If audited financial statements are unavailable, the statement for the last full year must be reviewed by a Certified Public Accountant or Independent Public Accountant.[499] Any past-due accounts payable or past-due liabilities for operating expenses must be resolved at or before the initial endorsement.[500]

5. Management Review

The management agent exhibits for acquisition and refinancing projects are the same as those required with the Firm Commitment application for new construction or substantial rehabilitation projects.

C. Issuance of the Firm Commitment

The HUD Team Leader will review the recommendations of each HUD analyst and prepare a memorandum summarizing the individual reviews and providing the Team Leader's overall recommendation. The Hub Director reviews the Team Leader's memorandum, along with a draft Firm Commitment prepared by the Team Leader, and either issues the Firm Commitment, recommends modification, or rejects the application.[501] The Firm Commitment will expire after 60 days, although the Hub Director may grant two 60-day extensions at the lender's request.[502]

V. CLOSING PROCESS

If a Firm Commitment is issued, draft closing documents are prepared, primarily by the lender's counsel, using HUD's required forms[503] and are reviewed by the HUD closing attorney and program staff. Once a complete set of documents has been reviewed and approved, a

---

497. *Id.* at ¶ 8.4.B.3. *See id.* at ¶ 8.4.A.5.a, which applies the requirements of paragraph 8.4.B of the MAP Guide to principals as identified in paragraph 8.3.D of the MAP Guide.
498. *Id.* at ¶ 8.4.B.3.
499. *Id.*
500. *Id.* at ¶ 8.4.B.3(c).
501. *Id.* at ¶ 11.2.D.
502. *Id.* Hub Directors may grant additional extensions "on a case-by-case basis, so long as prolonged extensions of commitments do not occur and any approval is based on updated due diligence." *Id.* at ¶ 4.2.F; *see also* Notice H 2010-01.
503. *See* http://portal.hud.gov/hudportal/HUD?src=/program_offices/administration/hudclips for form documents for loans which received Firm Commitments both prior to or after Sept. 1, 2011.

closing is scheduled in accordance with the Closing Guide. Although historically FHA-insured loan closings have been attended by all parties, at the discretion of the HUD attorney, closings may be conducted by mail.[504] In most instances, recordable documents are recorded on or before the date of closing.[505]

A. Borrower Entity's Organizational Documents

In connection with closing, the borrower must provide copies of all organizational documents, including (a) Secretary of State–certified copies of filed formation documents, (b) good standing or similar status certificates issued by the Secretary of State, (c) foreign qualification certificates, if applicable, (d) authorizing resolutions, and (e) a certificate signed by an officer or designee of the borrower confirming that the organizational documents attached thereto are true and correct copies and setting forth incumbency of the borrower's officers and key principals.[506] HUD prescribes certain provisions that must appear in the borrower's organizational documents, including, but not limited to, limitations on amending certain organizational document provisions without HUD consent, a statement that in the event of conflict the HUD loan documents prevail, and confirmation of the entity's single-asset status.[507] The required provisions also include limits on indemnification of members, partners, officers, or directors; require incoming members to comply with the provisions of the Regulatory Agreement; and state that the key principals identified in the Regulatory Agreement will be liable in their individual capacities as set forth therein.[508]

B. Title and Survey

Multiple duplicate originals of the title policy must be delivered at closing, issued by a title company in a form acceptable to HUD and dated as of the date of endorsement of the Note for insurance.[509] The policy must show the HUD-insured loan as a first lien, except in the case of loans insured under Section 241 or Section 223(d). Any exceptions or liens (such as subordinate secondary financing liens) listed on the title policy must be approved by HUD, and HUD-required endorsements must be included except when unavailable or prohibitively expensive under state or local practice.[510] The legal description contained in the title policy must

---

504. *Closing Guide, supra* note 22, at ¶ 1.3.C. HUD may also approve a "skeleton closing," attended by only some of the parties traditionally required at a HUD closing.

505. *Id.* at ¶ 1.3.B. However in some states, such as New York, documents are typically recorded following endorsement of the Note for mortgage insurance.

506. *Id.* at ¶ 3.1.

507. *Id.* at ¶ 5.2

508. *Id. See also* Section V.C.3 of this chapter. The key principals that are required to sign the Regulatory Agreement are to be identified in the Firm Commitment. *See Regulatory Agreement, supra* note 9, at ¶ 50.

509. *Closing Guide, supra* note 22, at ¶ 3.2.B.

510. *Id.* at ¶ 3.2.C. Required endorsements include, to the extent available under state law, (i) Comprehensive, ALTA Endorsement Form 9-06 (or 9.3-06); (ii) Access, ALTA Endorsement Form 17-06; (iii) Zoning, ALTA Endorsement 3.1-06; (iv) Environmental Protection Lien, ALTA Endorsement Form 8.1-06; (v) Same as Survey, ALTA Endorsement 25-06; (vi) Deletion of arbitration provisions; and (vii) if applicable, pending disbursements, future advances, leasehold, air rights and/or easement endorsements.

match the legal descriptions contained in the loan documents and on the survey. The survey must be prepared in accordance with the 2011 Minimum Standard Detail Requirements for ALTA/ASCM Land Title Surveys[511] and HUD's Survey Instructions, Form HUD-92457A-M (HUD Survey Instructions), including the Table A items listed and certification set forth in the HUD Survey Instructions.[512] The survey must be dated within 120 days of closing, show all easements and encroachments, and be accompanied by the Surveyor's Report, Form HUD-92457M.[513]

C. Closing Documents

Part 4 of the Closing Guide contains Closing Checklists that set forth the form documents that must be used with respect to the various FHA insurance programs. Generally, the HUD form closing documents are not subject to negotiation. Changes to the forms, other than filling in blanks, deleting inapplicable provisions, attaching exhibits or riders, and making those changes permitted by Program Obligations that do not require HUD approval, must be approved by HUD and identified in a memorandum attached to the Lender's Certificate, Form HUD-92434M (the Lender's Certificate) or Request for Endorsement of Credit Instrument, Form HUD-92455M (the RFE), as applicable.[514] The Hub Director may approve administrative changes, while the HUD Closing Attorney may approve legal changes required by local law or custom.[515] All other changes require approval by the Assistant General Counsel for Multifamily Mortgage Insurance.[516] Numerous closing documents are required under FHA insurance programs, but only the key documents are discussed below.

1. Security Instrument

The Security Instrument is used to secure the loan and grant a first lien, or a second lien in the case of loans insured under Section 241 or Section 223(d), on the Mortgaged Property as defined in the Security Instrument.[517] Although there is only a single form of Security Instrument, optional text must be selected depending on whether the jurisdiction utilizes mortgages or deeds of trust, and HUD-approved provisions containing jurisdiction-specific modifica-

---

511. *Available at* http://www.alta.org/forms/index.cfm?archive=0.
512. *Id.* at ¶ 3.2.D. Required Table A items include 1, 2, 3, 4, 6a, 6b, 7a, 8, 9, 10a, 10b, 11b, 12, 13, 16, 17, 18, 19, and 20a.
513. *Id.*
514. *Id.* at ¶ 2.1.B.
515. *Id.*
516. *Id.*
517. Including land, improvements, fixtures (excluding tenant-owned goods and property), personalty, current and future rights (such as zoning, air rights, etc.), awards, payments or compensation by a Governmental Authority; all contracts, options, and other sale agreements; all proceeds from the conversion of the mortgaged property, rents and leases, earnings, royalties, instruments, accounts, accounts receivable, Imposition Deposits (including taxes, special assessments, MIP payments, Reserve for Replacements and all other escrows and deposits), refunds or rebates of Impositions, forfeited tenant security deposits, trademarks, trade names, goodwill, deposits and/or escrows held by or on behalf of the lender; and all awards, payments, or settlements from litigation involving the property. *Security Instrument, supra* note 10, at ¶ 1(w).

tions are to be attached to and incorporated into the Security Instrument.[518] The Security Instrument includes covenants and remedies customarily found in modern multifamily mortgages, including an assignment of rents and leases and provisions granting a security interest under the Uniform Commercial Code.

The Security Instrument obligates the borrower to maintain insurance coverages as required by the lender[519] and to provide the lender with financial statements within 120 days of the end of the fiscal year.[520] The Security Instrument imposes certain requirements with respect to nonresidential leases,[521] addresses borrower's obligations with respect to environmental hazards,[522] and, in addition to providing remedies for covenant or monetary events of default,[523] provides specific remedies in the event the borrower commits waste.[524] The lender must apply payments received under the Note and Security Instrument in the order specified by HUD[525] and collect and maintain records with respect to Imposition Deposits.[526] Imposition Deposits, as

---

518. *See id.* at ¶¶ 43, 49. Jurisdiction-specific addenda are *available at* http://portal.hud.gov/hudportal/HUD?src=/program_offices/administration/hudclips/forms/hud9/riders-addendums. For projects receiving a Firm Commitment prior to September 1, 2011, each state had a separate form of mortgage or deed of trust. In addition, borrower and lender entered into a separate security agreement, the form of which was not prescribed by HUD. The form of Security Instrument eliminates the need for a separate security agreement for loans receiving Firm Commitments on or after September 1, 2011.

519. *Id.* at ¶ 19. Insurance required includes, but is not limited to, "coverage against loss by fire and allied perils, general boiler and machinery coverage, builders all-risk and business income coverage . . . commercial general liability insurance, workers' compensation insurance and such other liability, errors and omissions and fidelity insurance coverage" as required by the Lender or Program Obligations. If warranted, the lender may also require flood insurance, sinkhole insurance, mine subsidence insurance, earthquake insurance, and/or building ordinance or law coverage. *Id.*

520. *Id.* at ¶ 15(d). This requirement can be satisfied by delivering financial statements to the lender concurrently with delivery of the same to HUD as provided in the Regulatory Agreement. *See* Section V.C.3.c of this chapter.

521. *Security Instrument*, *supra* note 10, at ¶ 4. Nonresidential leases must be expressly subordinate to the Security Instrument and include attornment provisions. Note that although paragraph 4(f)(2) of the Security Instrument calls for nonresidential leases to provide that after a foreclosure or deed in lieu of foreclosure, the lender or purchaser may terminate the lease, this is inconsistent with Mortgagee Letter 2011-14 and the form of Subordination, Non-Disturbance and Attornment Agreement attached thereto, which expressly includes non-disturbance provisions.

522. *Id.* at ¶ 48. Including representations and warranties regarding prohibited environmental activities or conditions, notice requirements to lender if any such activities or conditions are discovered, payment by borrower of costs for environmental inspections, and borrower's obligation to indemnify lender and servicers against claims related to environmental hazards.

523. *See* Section II.K of this chapter regarding defaults and remedies.

524. *Security Instrument*, *supra* note 10, at ¶ 45. If borrower commits waste, lender may (i) exercise any remedies for a covenant event of default under Section 43 of the Security Instrument, (ii) obtain an injunction to the extent waste has impaired or threatens to impair the lender's security, and/or (iii) recover damages limited to the amount of waste to the extent that waste impaired the lender's security. Waste is defined in Security Instrument ¶ 1(jj).

525. *Id.* at ¶ 7(a)(3). Payments shall be applied to pay items in the following order: (1) MIP, (2) taxes, assessments, and property insurance premiums, (iii) interest on the Note, and (iv) amortization of principal of the Note. This order of payment application is also required by 24 C.F.R. § 200.84 (2010).

526. *Security Instrument*, *supra* note 10, at ¶ 8.

defined in the Security Instrument, include escrows for taxes, insurance premiums and MIP, along with Reserve for Replacement deposits, Residual Receipts deposits, and all other escrows. The Imposition Deposits, excluding Reserve for Replacements and Residual Receipts, must equal the amount reasonably estimated to be necessary plus one-sixth of such estimate and must be placed in accounts insured or guaranteed by a federal agency in accordance with Program Obligations.[527] The lender must keep a record of how much of the Imposition Deposits are held for purposes of paying taxes, insurance premiums, and each other obligation.[528]

Under the terms of the Security Instrument, if there is an event of default,[529] the lender may take control of the Mortgaged Property and collect rents directly, but if the lender does so and rents are not sufficient to meet the costs of control and management, any advances made by the lender for such purposes shall become an additional part of the indebtedness secured by the Security Instrument only if made with the prior written approval of HUD.[530] Similarly, any advances made by the lender to protect its security interest must either (i) be required by Program Obligations or (ii) approved by HUD in advance for such advances to become an additional part of the secured indebtedness.[531]

2. Note

The loan is evidenced by a Note, the terms of which must be consistent with the Firm Commitment. As with the Security Instrument, there is a single form of Note for use in all jurisdictions, but any HUD-approved jurisdiction-specific provisions may be added as necessary.[532] The Note contains alternative language used to specify whether the loan has (i) a split interest rate (i.e., the construction interest rate and permanent interest rate differ) or (ii) a single interest rate, either because the construction and permanent interest rates are the same or because the loan does not involve insurance of advances.[533] Similarly, the Note contains alternative language for specifying the monthly payment depending on whether the loan is a split-rate construction loan, single-rate construction loan, or a non-construction loan.[534] Alternative prepayment provisions also are included, the selection of which is determined based on how the loan is being funded, consistent with the regulatory requirements.[535] The lender may assess a late charge of 2 percent of the monthly amount due under the Note for payments received after the 10th day of the month.[536]

---

527. *Id.* at ¶¶ 8(b), 8(d).
528. *Id.* at ¶ 8(a).
529. *See* Section II.K of this chapter regarding defaults and remedies.
530. *Security Instrument, supra* note 10, at ¶ 3(f).
531. *Id.* at ¶ 13.
532. For loans receiving Firm Commitments prior to September 1, 2011, each state had its own specific form of note.
533. *Note, supra* note 11, at introductory paragraph.
534. *Id.* at ¶ 3.
535. *Id.* at ¶ 9; *see* Section II.H of this chapter regarding regulatory prepayment restrictions.
536. *Note, supra* note 11, at ¶ 7; *see also Closing Guide, supra* note 22, at ¶ 2.4.D.1; *MAP Guide, supra* note 15, at ¶ 11.7.D.1, but note that the MAP Guide incorrectly states that the payment must be 15 days in arrears (rather than 10 days as required under the Note, Closing Guide, and 24 C.F.R. § 200.88). For loans receiving commitments prior to September 1, 2011, it is required that payment be 15 days in arrears in order for late charges to apply.

FHA-insured loans are nonrecourse and impose no personal liability on the borrower or principals of the borrower for payment of amounts due under the Note.[537] However, the Note does impose liability on the borrower (but not principals of the borrower) for damages arising from certain defaults under the Security Instrument, including (i) failure to pay rents to the lender following an event of default, (ii) failure to appropriately apply insurance or condemnation proceeds, (iii) failure to deliver books and records, (iv) violation of the single-asset-entity requirement, (v) a transfer or the granting of a lien or encumbrance on the project in violation of the Security Instrument, or (vi) fraud or material misrepresentation by the borrower in connection with the loan application, creation of the indebtedness, or any request for any action or consent by lender; but the payment of damages for such defaults is limited to available proceeds from insurance policies, surplus cash, or other escrow accounts.[538] In addition, the borrower (but not the principals of the borrower) is liable for losses and damages related to waste[539] and for indemnification with respect to environmental matters.[540]

For new construction and substantial rehabilitation insurance of advances projects, the Note will be endorsed at the initial endorsement to the extent of advances approved by HUD.[541] At the final endorsement, HUD finally will endorse the Note for the full amount of the maximum insurable mortgage, as the same may have been adjusted as a result of cost certification.[542] For loans that do not include insurance of advances (such as loans insured under Sections 223(a)(7), 223(d), and 223(f) and Insurance Upon Completion cases), there is one initial/final closing at which FHA endorses the Note for the amount of the maximum insurable mortgage.[543]

3. Regulatory Agreement

All borrowers must execute a Regulatory Agreement.[544] The Regulatory Agreement is recorded in the real estate records immediately after the Security Instrument.[545] This document governs the relationship between HUD and the borrower, identifying the rights of HUD and the responsibilities and project operation obligations of the borrower.[546] The Regulatory Agree-

---

537. *Security Instrument, supra* note 10, at ¶ 6; *Note, supra* note 11, at ¶ 8.
538. *Note, supra* note 11, at ¶ 8(b).
539. *Id.* at ¶ 8(c); *Security Instrument, supra* note 10, at ¶ 45(c).
540. *Note, supra* note 11, at ¶ 8(c); *Security Instrument, supra* note 10, at ¶ 48.
541. *Closing Guide, supra* note 22, at ¶ 1.5; *Note, supra* note 11, at endorsement panel.
542. *Closing Guide, supra* note 22, at ¶ 1.15.B.
543. *Id.* at ¶¶ 1.18.B, 1.19.G.6, 1.21.F.
544. Whether the borrower is a for-profit, nonprofit, public body, or limited dividend borrower is indicated on the Regulatory Agreement, along with whether the project was processed MAP or TAP.
545. *MAP Guide, supra* note 15, at ¶ 3.2.A.
546. Including but not limited to the requirement that borrower maintain and repair the project; requirement for HUD approval for the terms of commercial leases; prohibition of the assignment of tenant's leasehold interest without borrower's approval; prohibition of discrimination against families with children (unless insured under Section 231); prohibition of admission fees, key fees or similar payments; prohibition of charging a deposit other than prepayment of the first month's rent and a security deposit in the amount of one month's rent or less. *Regulatory Agreement, supra* note 9, at ¶¶ 1(ll), 29–31, 33–35.

ment includes representations of the borrower, including that the borrower has any permits and approvals necessary to own and operate the property, that the property is free of liens other than those reflected in the title policy, and that there are no outstanding obligations except as approved by HUD.[547] Additionally, the single-asset requirement of 24 C.F.R. 200.5 is incorporated into the Regulatory Agreement, as is the prohibition against use of the property for hotel or transient services.[548]

a. Reserve for Replacements and Residual Receipts

The Regulatory Agreement governs deposits to the reserve for replacements and, if applicable, the residual receipts account.[549] These deposits must be held by the lender or a depository designated by the lender in an interest-bearing account insured or guaranteed by a federal agency.[550] Distributions from the reserve for replacements require written consent of HUD, and HUD may direct application of the reserve for replacements to pay amounts due on the indebtedness if accelerated because of an event of default or for other purposes as solely determined by HUD.[551] Residual receipts are under HUD's control and disbursed only at the direction of HUD.[552]

b. Distributions

The borrower's ability to make distributions from project income is limited by the terms of the Regulatory Agreement to semiannual payments made from surplus cash or residual receipts.[553] Surplus cash generally is defined as cash remaining after (i) payment of amounts due under the Note, Security Instrument, or Regulatory Agreement as of the first day of the month following the fiscal period, (ii) payment or set-aside of funds for all other obligations of the project, and (iii) the segregation of (a) any required special funds, (b) the greater of borrower's total liability or amount held for tenant security deposits, and (c) accounts payable within 30 days at the end of the fiscal period.[554] No distributions can be made during construction or if (i) an event of default has occurred, (ii) HUD has given the borrower notice of a violation under the Regulatory Agreement, (iii) HUD or governmental authorities have identified physical repairs or deficiencies, such as building code violations, or (iv) necessary services are not being provided.[555]

c. Financial Reporting Requirements

Consistent with regulatory requirements, the Regulatory Agreement requires borrowers to submit audited financial statements, prepared in accordance with generally accepted account-

---

547. *Id.* at ¶¶ 3, 7.
548. *Id.* at ¶¶ 12(b), 28, 30.
549. *See supra* note 189.
550. *Regulatory Agreement, supra* note 9, at ¶¶ 10(a), 10(c), 11.
551. *Id.* at ¶ 10(d).
552. *Id.* at ¶ 11.
553. *Id.* at ¶ 14.
554. *Id.* at ¶ 1(gg).
555. *Id.* at ¶ 14.

ing principals and government auditing standards, to HUD and the lender annually, within 90 days after the end of the fiscal year.[556] If the borrower fails to do so, HUD may hire a Certified Public Accountant, at the borrower's expense, to prepare the report.[557] The Certified Public Accountant must be independent, having no business relationship with the borrower outside of preparation of the audit and taxes, unless otherwise approved by HUD.[558]

d. Management

Contracts with management agents must provide that books and records be properly maintained and open to inspection by HUD and that on termination, the books and records remain with the project.[559] Any management agreement must include provisions relating to HUD's right to require termination of the agreement and a prohibition on assigning the management agreement without HUD consent.[560] The management of the property must be acceptable by HUD, and "[a]t HUD's discretion, HUD may require replacement of the management."[561]

e. Actions Requiring HUD Approval

Without prior written approval of HUD, the borrower may not, inter alia, (i) transfer, encumber, or otherwise dispose of any interest in the Mortgaged Property or the borrower (unless permitted by Program Obligations); (ii) enter into any financing arrangement or incur any liability other than for reasonable operating expenses; (iii) pay compensation to any principal, officer, director, stockholder, trustee, beneficiary, partner, member, or manager (or any nominee thereof), except from surplus cash or residual receipts; (iv) enter into any arrangements for supervisory or managerial services or leases for operation of the project, except as permitted by Program Obligations; (v) convey any right to receive rents except as permitted in the Security Instrument; (vi) remodel, add to, subtract from, construct, reconstruct, or demolish any part of the Mortgaged Property, except to restore damaged property or replace deteriorated fixtures and personalty with substitutes of the same or greater quality or value; (vii) amend organizational documents of the borrower in any material way; (viii) except for permitted payments from surplus cash or residual receipts, reimburse any party from the Mortgaged Property for expenses other than reasonable operating expenses; (ix) receive any fees or compensation from the management agent or vendors; (x) initiate or acquiesce in any zoning change that would change the permitted use of the project; (xi) establish a condominium; or (xii) materially change the number or configuration of units in the project.[562]

---

556. 24 C.F.R. § 5.801(c)(2) (2011); *Regulatory Agreement, supra* note 9, at ¶ 18. These financial statements must be submitted electronically.
557. *Regulatory Agreement, supra* note 9, at ¶ 18.
558. *Id.*
559. *Id.* at ¶ 17.
560. *Id.* at ¶¶ 21, 23. *See also supra* note 480.
561. *Regulatory Agreement, supra* note 9, at ¶ 22.
562. *Id.* at ¶ 36.

f. Nonrecourse Provisions

While not personally liable for payments under the Note or Security Instrument, for reserve for replacement deposits, or matters outside their control, each principal identified by HUD in the Firm Commitment must sign a statement in the Regulatory Agreement acknowledging such principal may be held personally liable under the Regulatory Agreement with respect to "(a) funds or property of the Project coming into its hands which, by the provisions [of the Regulatory Agreement], it is not entitled to retain; (b) for authorizing the conveyance, assignment, transfer, pledge, encumbrance, or other disposition of the Mortgaged Property or any interest therein in violation of Section 36(a) of [the Regulatory] Agreement without prior written approval of HUD; and (c) for its own acts and deeds, or acts and deeds of others, which it has authorized in violation of the provisions [of the Regulatory Agreement]."[563] The principals identified in the Firm Commitment as being required to sign the Regulatory Agreement are selected by HUD "based upon their control of the Borrower and their capitalization and assets, in HUD's discretion."[564]

4. Lender's Certificate/Request for Endorsement

The lender must disclose fees and charges and make certain certifications[565] and acknowledgments[566] pursuant to the terms of (i) the Lender's Certificate, for transactions involving insurance of advances or (ii) the RFE, for other transactions. The lender must disclose fees, charges, and escrows collected or to be collected, and must certify as to the acceptability of letters of credit when accepted in lieu of cash to fund escrows.[567] In addition, the Lender's Certificate and RFE require the lender to notify HUD in writing immediately on learning of any violation of the Regulatory Agreement.[568] Memoranda setting forth (i) a list of all closing documents submitted to and accepted by HUD at the closing and (ii) changes to the HUD form documents must be attached to the Lender's Certificate or RFE.

5. Building Loan Agreement

For transactions involving insurance of advances, the Building Loan Agreement sets forth the

---

563. *Id.* at ¶ 50.
564. *MAP Guide, supra* note 15, at ¶ 3.2.C.
565. Including but not limited to the following certifications: (i) that all conditions of the Firm Commitment have been fulfilled, including that the work done prior to endorsement has been approved by HUD in writing; (ii) that the Security Instrument and the UCC financing statement filings establish a perfected first-lien security interest in favor of Lender; (iii) that Lender has made a reasonable inquiry and discovered no liens or encumbrances that are not reflected as exceptions to coverage in the title policy; (iv) that except as disclosed, the Lender has no identity of interest with the borrower, borrower's counsel, principal of the borrower, contractor, or subcontractor. *Lender's Certificate, supra* note 173, at ¶¶ 2, 40, 32, 25–26; *RFE, supra* note 173, at ¶¶ I.A.1, I.D.12, I.D.6–7.
566. Including an acknowledgment that based on reasonable due diligence, all necessary licenses, permits and approvals are in effect. *Lender's Certificate, supra* note 173, at ¶ 30; *RFE, supra* note 173, at ¶ 1.D.10.
567. *See Lender's Certificate, supra* note 173, at ¶¶ 7–12, 23; *RFE, supra* note 173, at ¶¶ I.B, I.C.1–3, I.D.4.
568. *Lender's Certificate, supra* note 173, at ¶ 33; *RFE, supra* note 173, at ¶ I.A.14.

basic agreement of the lender to advance funds to the borrower and for the borrower to complete the project, addition, or improvements in accordance with the HUD-approved plans and specifications.[569] The borrower must make monthly requests for advances with respect to completed construction and materials stored on-site, less a 10 percent holdback, using the Application for Insurance of Advances, Form HUD-92403.[570] In addition, the borrower must keep the loan in balance, obtain lien waivers as needed, provide surveys before the first advance and after completion of construction, and provide worker's compensation and other required insurance.[571] Items and amounts that make up the total maximum advance are listed on an exhibit to the Building Loan Agreement. Failure to complete the construction in the time period specified in the Building Loan Agreement, as the same may be extended with the consent of HUD and the Lender, constitutes a default by the borrower, allowing the lender to terminate its obligation to make any further advances.[572] The lender has the right to take possession of the project and complete construction if the borrower defaults in its obligations under the Building Loan Agreement.[573]

6. Construction Contract

For transactions involving insurance of advances, the Construction Contract is an agreement between the borrower and the contractor setting forth the scope of the contract, the time for completion, and the contract sum. General Conditions (AIA) of the Contract for Construction, Supplementary Conditions of the Contract for Construction, and Cost Breakdown are incorporated as part of the contract. The Construction Contract may be either a cost-plus or lump-sum contract, and the Construction Contract contains alternative language as to the contract sum depending on the form selected.[574] The contractor must make monthly requests for payment from the borrower for the value of work completed in the preceding month along with the value of materials delivered and stored, less a 10 percent holdback, using Contractor's Requisition for Project Mortgages, Form HUD-92448.[575] The values are identified on the Cost Breakdown, attached to the Construction Contract. Payment is advanced as a percentage of the work completed, not on a cost-expended basis. The contractor must furnish lien releases (and obtain lien releases from subcontractors as needed) and furnish assurance of

---

569. Building Loan Agreement, Form HUD-92441M (Rev. 04/11) [hereinafter *Building Loan Agreement*] ¶¶ 1–2.
570. *Id.* at ¶ 4(a). The 10% retainage may be reduced with HUD approval if (i) the contractor has no identity of interest with the borrower greater than a 5% equity interest, (ii) prior written consent has been given by the surety, and (iii) there are no questions regarding the contractor's performance with respect to quality, compliance with the construction contract, and any change orders or work in progress.
571. *Id.* at ¶¶ 6–8, 10.
572. *Id.* at ¶ 9.
573. *Id.* at ¶ 9.
574. Under a cost plus contract, the borrower pays the contractor the actual cost of construction plus builder's profit, but the total amount payable cannot exceed the amount specified. *See Construction Contract*, *supra* note 259, at ¶ 4.A. Under a lump-sum contract, the borrower pays the contractor a single specified sum.
575. *Id.* at ¶ 5.A. The 10% retainage may be reduced if certain conditions are met. *See supra* note 570.

completion for the work running to the borrower, lender, and HUD.[576] Cost certification by the contractor is required for cost-plus contracts or if there is an identity of interest between the borrower and contractor.[577]

7. Opinion of Borrower's Counsel

All transactions, whether they involve insurance of advances, refinancing, or acquisition, require that borrower's counsel deliver an opinion addressed to HUD, the lender, and lender's counsel, using the Guide for Opinion of Borrower's Counsel, Form-91725M (Opinion of Borrower's Counsel). Although certain limited changes, including those required by local law, may be approved by the HUD attorney, the Opinion of Borrower's Counsel generally is not open to negotiation.[578] Borrower's counsel opines, inter alia, as to the valid existence of the borrower entity;[579] that execution of the documents and performance of obligations thereunder were duly authorized by the borrower;[580] that the loan documents are valid and enforceable against the borrower, subject to certain qualifications;[581] and that the Security Instrument is sufficient in form for recording and to create a lien and security interest in the property.[582] In addition, borrower's counsel confirms, inter alia, that borrower's counsel has no financial interest in the project and will not assert a claim or lien against the project; that borrower's counsel does not have any interest in the borrower or its principals and does not represent any lender in connection with the transaction; that, to borrower's counsel's knowledge, there are no liens or encumbrances against the property not reflected as exceptions in the title policy; that, to borrower's counsel's knowledge, there are no undisclosed side deals between the borrower and other parties to the transaction; and that, to borrower's counsel's knowledge, there is no pending litigation against the borrower (or the general partner, managing member, etc.) or the property, except as disclosed in an attachment to the legal opinion.[583]

8. Additional Documents

Additional documents routinely required for new construction and substantial rehabilitation projects include Escrow Agreement for Working Capital,[584] Escrow Agreement for Operating Deficit,[585] Escrow Agreement for Offsites or Demolition, if applicable,[586] Escrow Agreement for Incomplete Construction, if applicable at final endorsement,[587] Payment and Performance

---

576. *Construction Contract*, supra note 259, at ¶¶ 6.D, 8. *See also* Section III.A.4 of this chapter regarding assurance of completion.
577. *Construction Contract*, supra note 259, at ¶ 13. *See also* Section II.I of this chapter regarding cost certification.
578. Instructions to Guide for Opinion of Borrower's Counsel, Form-91725M-Inst (rev. 04/11).
579. Guide for Opinion of Borrower's Counsel, Form-91725M (Rev. 04/11) ¶ 1.
580. *Id.* at ¶ 4.
581. *Id.* at ¶ 5.
582. *Id.* at ¶ 8.
583. *Id.* at confirmation paragraphs (c)–(g).
584. *See* Section III.A.3.b of this chapter.
585. *See* Section III.A.3.c of this chapter.
586. *See* Section III.A.3.d-e of this chapter.
587. *See* Section III.A.9 of this chapter

Bond or Completion Assurance Agreement,[588] and Agreement and Certification.[589] An Agreement and Certification is also required for refinancing and acquisition projects,[590] and an Escrow Agreement for Noncritical Repairs often will also be required for such projects.[591]

D. Construction Period and Final Closing

For transactions involving insurance of advances, construction will begin following initial endorsement (assuming there was no HUD-approved early start).[592] Construction "must be diligently pursued without appreciable delay between activities."[593] The HUD inspector will make at least two job-site visits each month to ensure the construction is progressing and that it is being done in accordance with the contract documents.[594] The HUD inspector completes a Representative's Trip Report, Form HUD-95379 (Trip Report) identifying any noncompliance or deficiencies and reporting the percentage of completion.[595] The Trip Reports are provided to the HUD construction manager for review.[596] The HUD construction manager also will make at least one field review inspection to evaluate the inspector's performance. Once there is safe ingress and egress to the units, as evidenced by a certificate of occupancy from the locality, the inspector completes the FHA Inspection Report portion of the Permission to Occupy, Form HUD-92485.[597] HUD approval is required before units may be occupied. To proceed to final closing, the final Trip Report must be issued indicating the project is complete and the entire project must be approved for occupancy by both HUD and the local authority.

After the borrower (and contractor, if applicable) has submitted the cost certification,[598] HUD will calculate the maximum insurable mortgage based on the eligible actual costs and issue the Maximum Insurable Mortgage, Form HUD-92580 (the Maximum Insurable Mortgage), establishing the final mortgage amount. Once any conditions of final closing have been met and final closing exhibits (including an as-built survey, evidence of updated title insurance, the Request for Final Endorsement, the Contractor's Requisition, and an Application for Insurance of Advances) have been submitted and approved, and provided that the loan is current, HUD finally will endorse the Note for the amount as set forth in the Maximum Insurable Mortgage.[599] There are no minimum-occupancy or debt-service requirements to convert from a construction to a permanent loan.

---

588. *See* Section III.A.4 of this chapter.
589. *See supra* notes 109–110 and accompanying text.
590. *Id.*
591. *See* Section III.C.4 of this chapter.
592. *See* Section III.A.2 of this chapter.
593. *MAP Guide*, *supra* note 15, at ¶ 12.1.A.
594. *Id.* at ¶ 12.3.D. "The inspector is a HUD representative, not a superintendent for the contractor or 'clerk of the works' for the owner or Architect." *Id.*
595. *Id.* at ¶ 12.3.D.13.
596. *Id.* at ¶ 12.3.A.3.
597. *Id.* at ¶ 12.3.D.10.
598. *See* Section II.I of this chapter for a discussion of cost certification requirements.
599. *See* Section III.A.9 of this chapter.

VI. CONCLUSION

Although many of the characteristics of HUD's multifamily insurance programs have remained constant since their inception, the programs are dynamic, evolving over time. The months preceding publication of this chapter were marked by the issuance of new form closing documents and a new Closing Guide, a number of changes to the Regulations, the issuance of an updated MAP Guide, and the issuance of several Mortgagee Letters and Housing Notices imposing significant new requirements and procedures. This represented a major overhaul of the established guidance, the likes of which had not been seen in decades. While it is unlikely that such substantial changes will be undertaken again in the near future, additional revisions to the MAP Guide are anticipated,[600] and HUD routinely issues new Mortgagee Letters and Housing Notices on a variety of topics. Therefore, borrowers, lenders, and others involved in FHA-insured loan transactions should frequently consult the various sources of HUD guidance to determine whether any rules, requirements, or other Program Obligations have changed.

---

600. Including the issuance of additional program guidance with respect to loans insured under Section 223(a)(7) or Section 241. *MAP Guide, supra* note 15, at ¶ 1.3.B.

Multifamily Housing Preservation 2

John Daly

The need for affordable multifamily housing continues, especially when the rate of homeownership is decreasing. Compared to authority enacted for affordable housing programs in the 1960s and 1970s, there are fewer congressionally appropriated federal programs today that facilitate preservation of multifamily housing. This chapter will describe some current programs that are authorized under the National Housing Act.[1]

The Department of Housing and Urban Development (HUD) provides mortgage insurance through the Federal Housing Administration (FHA). FHA insurance is available for loans secured by single-family houses, multifamily projects, health-care facilities (*e.g.*, nursing homes, assisted-living facilities, long-term care facilities, and board and care facilities), and hospitals, as well as for rehabilitation loans and loans for manufactured home parks. This chapter will focus on the FHA multifamily mortgage insurance programs that have been authorized under Title II of the National Housing Act and related statutes.

Some basic concepts about FHA mortgage insurance should be reviewed before applying for FHA mortgage insurance, especially when a project owner is considering whether to refinance a conventional mortgage with FHA-insured support to preserve affordable multifamily housing. After completing review of an application for multifamily mortgage insurance, FHA will issue a Firm Commitment for that insurance. The insurance commitment is a contract between HUD and a mortgage lender stipulating that FHA will provide mortgage insurance if all conditions in the insurance commitment have been satisfied at, or

---

1. 12 U.S.C. § 1701 *et seq.*

before, loan closing. Sometimes a loan closing date may be set on a date after a lapse in HUD appropriations. FHA still can provide a mortgage insurance endorsement after a lapse in HUD appropriations if an FHA commitment had been issued pursuant to insurance commitment authority available prior to the lapse in HUD appropriations.[2]

I. FHA MORTGAGE INSURANCE—INCONTESTABLE?

Can FHA cancel its mortgage insurance after providing its endorsement on a note creating the debt secured by a multifamily project? NHA Section 203(e)[3] states:

> Any contract of insurance heretofore or hereafter executed by the Secretary under this title shall be conclusive evidence of the eligibility of the loan or mortgage for insurance, and the validity of any contract of insurance so executed shall be incontestable in the hands of an approved financial institution or approved mortgagee from the date of the execution of such contract, except for fraud or misrepresentation on the part of such approved financial institution or approved mortgagee.

In other words, the eligibility for mortgage insurance cannot be challenged after FHA endorsement of a note unless there has been fraud or misrepresentation by the mortgagee that originated the loan (or assignee mortgagee of that loan originator if such mortgagee had conspired with the loan originator in the fraud or misrepresentation). Unlike fraud, which involves a knowing submission to FHA of an ineligible mortgage loan for insurance endorsement, misrepresentation can occur even if the mortgage originator is not aware that one or more FHA requirements have not been satisfied when the loan is submitted for FHA insurance endorsement. For example, a mortgagee may receive assurance from a project owner that certain FHA occupancy requirements have been satisfied when, unknown to the mortgagee, the owner has provided an assurance that is not true. Relying on the mortgagor's assurance, the mortgagee then assures HUD that all FHA requirements have been satisfied, and HUD relies upon the mortgagee's assurance when providing the mortgage insurance endorsement. Under Section 203(e), FHA can make a post-endorsement determination that, if the loan still is owned by the loan originator, it is not eligible for FHA insurance due to the originator's misrepresentation, even though the mortgagee was not aware of the misrepresentation at the time of insurance endorsement. Case law on Section 203(e) construes "misrepresentation" to include an unknowing, material misrepresentation to FHA by a mortgagee based on representations to the mortgagee by a project owner and a property marketer that were not true.[4] In other words, had FHA known at the time of initial insurance endorsement what it later found to be false, FHA would have determined at that time that the loan was not eligible for FHA insurance.

---

2. *See* Antideficiency Act at 31 U.S.C. § 1341(a)(1)(B).
3. 12 U.S.C. § 1709(e).
4. Jayson Investments, Inc. v. Kemp, 746 F. Supp. 807 (N.D. Ill. 1990). The court ruled that material misrepresentation gave HUD the right to terminate its contract of coinsurance.

II. FHA MORTGAGE INSURANCE

A. Full Faith and Credit of the United States?

Is FHA mortgage insurance backed by the full faith and credit of the United States? This question arises occasionally, particularly in connection with mortgage funds derived from the proceeds of bond sales. For example, bond proceeds may be used directly to fund a mortgage loan to be insured by FHA or indirectly to purchase one or more Ginnie Mae mortgage-backed securities (MBS), the sale of which provides funds for the mortgage loan to be insured by FHA. The question addresses whether a bond issuer or a Ginnie Mae issuer can rely on the full faith and credit of the United States in connection with payment of an FHA mortgage insurance claim. The answer is that the FHA insurance is not backed by the full faith and credit of the United States. FHA provides mortgage insurance,[5] the payment of which is contingent upon a mortgagee satisfying all prerequisites for payment of its mortgage insurance claim. For example, a mortgagee's claim can be denied by FHA if the mortgagee cannot assign a mortgage to HUD that is a first lien, as commonly given in the jurisdiction in which a multifamily project securing loan repayment is located.[6] For comparison, the Ginnie Mae guarantee is triggered if a holder of a Ginnie Mae MBS does not receive a monthly pass-through payment in the timely manner promised by the MBS issuer.[7] Lack of a timely pass-through payment by a Ginnie Mae issuer would be all that is needed for an MBS holder to be eligible to receive payment from Ginnie Mae. Depending on the FHA program under which an insurance claim is submitted, FHA can pay either in cash or debentures. Note that payment in debentures, which are issued in connection with an eligible FHA mortgage insurance claim, is backed by the full faith and credit of the United States.

B. Funding for FHA Mortgage Insurance Claims

Will FHA have sufficient funds to pay all eligible mortgage insurance claims (*e.g.*, during periods when there is a lapse in appropriations for HUD and FHA)? FHA has permanent, indefinite authority to pay eligible mortgage insurance claims pursuant to NHA Section 1, which states, in part:

---

5. The term "insurance" sometimes is described as a "guarantee." Although the term "guarantee" is used in federal budget documents and appropriations bills, the contractual arrangement between FHA and an approved mortgagee provides for payment of mortgage *insurance* upon loan default, subject to a mortgagee satisfying all prerequisites for such payment by FHA. Note that the insurance is not equivalent to a guarantee of payment by FHA.

6. NHA § 207(a)(1), 12 U.S.C. § 1713(a)(1); NHA § 207(g), 12 U.S.C. § 1713(g), 24 C.F.R. § 207.258a. Mortgagees have the option of conveying project title to HUD or assigning a loan in default to HUD in exchange for FHA mortgage insurance benefits. Although 1% of the unpaid loan amount is deducted from an insurance claim when a project mortgage is assigned to HUD, mortgagees usually elect this option to avoid the delay and expense of possible mortgagor bankruptcy if a loan were to be foreclosed by a mortgagee prior to conveyance of clear title to HUD as part of a mortgage insurance claim.

7. A Ginnie Mae issuer of an MBS also would be the FHA-approved mortgagee that originates the loan insured by FHA.

> The Secretary . . . may make such expenditures . . . as are necessary to carry out the provisions of . . . title . . . II . . . without regard to any other provisions of law governing the expenditure of public funds. All such . . . expenses . . . shall be paid out of funds made available by this Act. . . .[8]

FHA authority for expenditures to pay insurance claims is not subject to the payment ceiling in Section 1 (*i.e.*, 35 percent of income from premiums and fees received by HUD during the previous fiscal year).

The FHA mortgage insurance contract[9] contains the terms and conditions between HUD and a mortgagee in connection with a specific multifamily loan. Conversely, HUD has authority under the NHA[10] to enter into a regulatory agreement with each project owner by which the owner agrees to operate a project in a manner (*i.e.*, "methods of operation") that is satisfactory to HUD.[11] This agreement contains requirements for preserving a project as an affordable housing resource.

The National Housing Act (NHA) was enacted in 1934[12] and included authority for mortgage insurance in connection with multifamily project financing under the terms specified in NHA Section 207. Some NHA provisions are archaic in that they are sometimes difficult to apply to modern forms of real estate finance. Many provisions were enacted years ago (sometimes decades ago), when federal government subsidies were relatively plentiful, but today they are available only in much smaller quantity.

C. NHA Section 223

An important distinction should be kept in mind when considering use of FHA-insured financing to preserve multifamily housing. The words "insured under" and "insured pursuant" have different meanings when distinguishing between NHA provisions that contain their own insuring authority and those that contain prerequisites for FHA insurance but do not contain their own FHA insurance authority. For example, NHA Section 223(a) states, in part:

> Notwithstanding any of the provisions of this Act and without regard to limitations upon eligibility contained in any section or title of this Act, . . . the Secretary is authorized upon application by the mortgagee, to insure or make commitments to insure *under any other section or title of this Act* any mortgage—[13] (Emphasis added).

---

8. 12 U.S.C. § 1702.
9. *See* 24 C.F.R. § 207.251(e), which states:

   The term *contract of insurance* means the agreement evidenced by such endorsement [of the credit instrument] and includes the terms, conditions and provisions of this part [207] and of the National Housing Act.

10. For example, § 207(b)(2), 12 U.S.C. § 1713(b)(2); § 213(a)(3), 12 U.S.C. § 1715e(a)(3); § 220(d)(2), 12 U.S.C. § 1715k(d)(2); § 221(d)(3), (d)(4)(iv), 12 U.S.C. § 1715*l*(d)(3), (d)(4)(iv); § 231(c)(3), (4), 12 U.S.C. § 1715v(c)(3), (4); § 234(d)(2), 12 U.S.C. § 1715y(d)(2); § 241(e)(4), 12 U.S.C. § 1715z-6(e)(4).
11. Form HUD 92466M (Rev. 04/11). *See* a more complete description *supra*.
12. Pub. L. No. 84-345, 48 Stat. 847, 1252 (1934).
13. 12 U.S.C. § 1715n(a). *See* description of this authority *supra*. Note that this authority applies to FHA single-family programs as well as FHA multifamily programs, although the discussion in this chapter will focus on its application to multifamily housing preservation.

The remainder of Section 223(a) describes FHA insurance prerequisites that apply, "notwithstanding" any inconsistent requirements that may appear in another NHA section under which FHA could insure a mortgage. For example, if a proposed loan were to satisfy the prerequisites expressed in Section 223(a)(7), the loan could be insured "under" NHA section 221 even if it would not be eligible for FHA insurance when reviewed only in the context of prerequisites in Section 221. Although Section 223(a)(7) authorizes insurance only on loans that refinance existing loans already insured by FHA, the loan amount nevertheless could be increased up to the original amount of the existing loan, and the remaining amortization period could, under limited circumstances, be increased by up to 12 years. In this example, the note endorsement would state that the FHA insurance is being provided under Section 221 pursuant to Section 223(a)(7). Upon closing, attorneys should remember that a loan insured "pursuant to" Section 223(a)(7) does not create a new mortgage insurance contract. Section 223(a)(7)(A)(iv) states:

> Any multifamily mortgage that is refinanced under this paragraph shall be documented through amendments to the existing insurance contract and shall not be structured through provisions of a new insurance contract. . . .

Closing attorneys should note that the note endorsement by FHA should contain special language in order to comply with this requirement (even if an FHA case number is used for the new loan that differs from the case number for the existing loan being refinanced).[14]

Another option is available, under NHA Section 223(f),[15] to facilitate preservation of multifamily housing, including projects with existing loans that are not insured by FHA. Section 223(f)(1) states, in part:

> Notwithstanding any of the provisions of this Act, the Secretary is authorized, in his discretion, to insure *under any section of this title* [II] a mortgage executed in connection with the purchase or refinancing of an existing multifamily housing project . . . . (Emphasis added).

As in the case of FHA mortgage insurance provided "pursuant to" Section 223(a)(7), the insurance pursuant to Section 223(f) is authorized, "notwithstanding" any inconsistent requirements that may appear in another NHA section under which FHA can insure a mortgage. Note that there is a five-year statutory restriction on prepayment or refinancing of a mortgage secured by rental housing, unless, with some limited exceptions, HUD receives assurance that the project will continue to be used as rental housing for at least five years after the date on which

---

14. The reason for this requirement is that Congress wanted to limit the amount of credit subsidy, which may be needed for FHA insurance, to that amount by which the increased amount of a new loan exceeded the amount owed on the existing loan being refinanced. The amount of credit subsidy on the remaining balance of the existing loan would have been applied at the time an insurance commitment was issued by FHA to insure the existing loan. The point is to make sure that the appropriate language is used in the FHA insurance endorsement on the note for the new loan even if a credit subsidy no longer is a factor in the transaction.

15. 12 U.S.C. § 1715n(f). *See* description of this authority *supra*.

16. *See* Notice H 11-06, Feb. 17, 2011; Mortgagee Letter 2011-13, Feb. 17, 2011. *See* exception in Notice H 2012-1, Feb. 3, 2012.

HUD endorsed the note for FHA insurance. Note also that HUD has adopted what is known as the "Three Year Rule," which applies when a loan is insured pursuant to Section 223(f). The purpose of this administrative requirement is to avoid a situation in which a project, which was recently constructed or substantially rehabilitated with conventional construction financing (possibly with the intent of not paying Davis-Bacon Act wages during the period of construction), serves as security for a permanent loan refinancing with FHA insurance pursuant to Section 223(f). Consequently, HUD imposed the Three Year Rule, which requires that there must be a period of at least three years between project construction or substantial rehabilitation and the date of application for a FHA Firm Commitment. Although some of these projects have become self-sustaining within this three-year period, some projects have not been able to obtain long-term financing because of the lack of liquidity in the capital markets. Consequently, HUD has authorized[16] its multifamily Hub Directors to waive the Three Year Rule if certain conditions are satisfied, including documentation evidencing unsuccessful efforts to obtain conventional financing and, for new construction projects, the receipt of a Certificate of Occupancy for the entire project dated no later than the date of application to FHA for a Firm Commitment. This waiver authority expired on February 29, 2012.

The "pursuant to" insurance authority described above must be used in connection with another NHA multifamily program "under" which the basic FHA insurance authority can be provided. A brief description and comments on these multifamily programs are provided below. Complete descriptions of these programs appear in Chapter 1.

D. NHA Section 207

For many years, Section 207 was the most common mortgage insurance program for multifamily project financing,[17] as NHA Section 203[18] has been for the FHA single-family mortgage programs since 1934. Among the eligibility criteria for determining the maximum insurable mortgage amount under Section 207 (and Section 203) is the value of the project that will secure repayment of the insured project loan. Section 207(c)(2)[19] states, in part:

> To be eligible for insurance under this section a mortgage on any property or project shall involve a principal obligation in an amount . . . (2) not to exceed 90 per centum

---

17. A noteworthy provision in Section 207(c) is that an insurable mortgage loan "shall provide for complete amortization by periodic payments." That concept is familiar today, but such a mortgage provision was rare at the time of the Great Depression in the 1930s and illustrates the invaluable contribution the NHA has provided as a pioneer for the self-amortizing mortgage that is so common today. Another noteworthy provision in Section 207(c) is the requirement that a mortgage "shall bear interest at such rate as may be agreed upon by the mortgagor and the mortgagee." In other words, FHA no longer has authority to regulate the interest rate on multifamily mortgagee loans (and single-family loans under NHA § 203(b)(5)) to be insured by FHA, a practice that was common until the 1980s and often caused delays and confusion in processing applications for FHA mortgage insurance.

18. NHA § 203, 12 U.S.C. § 1709 continues today as authority for the most frequently used FHA single-family mortgage insurance programs.

19. 12 U.S.C. § 1713(c)(2).

of the *estimated value* of the property or project (when the proposed improvements are completed) . . . (Emphasis added).

Exceptions to this value limitation are provided for mortgages on projects in Alaska and Guam, where HUD's estimated project replacement cost is used. In addition, the authority in Section 207(c)(3)[20] limits the amount of mortgage insurance based on dollar amounts per family unit, including separate dollar amounts related to the number of bedrooms per unit. In the past, these dollar amounts created problems because they resulted in limits on the amount of FHA mortgage insurance that increasingly were out of alignment with the amount needed in modern real estate financing. Congress provided relief from this antiquated provision through enactment of NHA Section 206A,[21] which provides a formula for annual adjustment of the dollar amounts based on input that is calculated by the Federal Reserve, with input from the Consumer Price Index for all urban consumers (CPI-U). HUD provides, through the *Federal Register*, an annual revision to these dollar amounts.[22]

Although the "value" limitation on the amount of mortgage insurance has resulted in use of other FHA programs (*e.g.*, the Section 221 program described below with a more advantageous "replacement cost" limitation), there is other authority in Section 207 and related statutes that is useful for preservation of multifamily housing. Section 207(k) contains authority for FHA regarding multifamily loans assigned to HUD, and Section 207(l) has authority in connection with projects conveyed to HUD. These provisions apply to loans assigned, or projects conveyed, through other FHA multifamily programs.[23] Section 207(k) permits HUD to:

> exercise all the rights of a mortgagee under such mortgage, including the right to sell such mortgage, and to take such action and advance such sums as may be necessary to preserve and protect the lien of such mortgage.

This provision is significant for determining what HUD expenditures FHA can make with regard to these assets. Note that, under this authority, FHA can make such expenditures to preserve a project as would be permitted for any other mortgagee to make under the terms of a loan like that assigned to HUD. FHA also can agree to subordinate its HUD-held first lien to new conventional debt to finance necessary project rehabilitation for its preservation, an action not possible while the loan was insured by FHA. In other words, this authority is broader than that available to HUD when FHA insures a multifamily mortgage loan, but narrower than that available when HUD owns title to a project.

Section 207(k) also contains authority for HUD to make expenditures on projects conveyed to HUD, usually as the result of foreclosure of a loan assigned to HUD. Section 207(k) states, in part:

---

20. 12 U.S.C. § 1713(c)(3).
21. 12 U.S.C. § 1712a.
22. Dollar amounts, 76 Fed. Reg. 79,704 (Dec. 22, 2011).
23. For example, *see* NHA § 221(g)(2), (3); 12 U.S.C. § 1715*l*(g)(2), (3).

[t]he Secretary shall also have power, for the protection of the interests of the General Insurance Fund, to pay out of the General Insurance Fund[24] all expenses or charges in connection with, and to deal with, complete, reconstruct, rent, renovate, modernize, insure, make contracts for the management of, . . . , or sell for cash or credit or lease in his discretion, any property acquired by him under this section;[25] . . . .

Although this authority provides a useful source of funds for preservation of multifamily housing, use of this authority is limited to the period of time when HUD owns a project.

E. Statutes "Related" to NHA

There are some "related" statutes with authority that supplements that provided in Section 207(k) and (l). NHA Section 223(c)[26] contains broad authority (*i.e.*, without regard to any limitations or requirements elsewhere in the NHA) for FHA to insure any mortgage assigned to HUD under the NHA or any mortgage in connection with the sale of any property acquired by HUD under the NHA. In addition, Section 203 of the Housing and Community Development Amendments of 1978[27] prescribes many details about the sale of multifamily loans or projects acquired by HUD. For example, Section 203(k)(1) and (2) limit the sale of HUD-held subsidized loans or HUD-owned subsidized projects to those that would, for a fixed period of time, "provide rental housing on terms at least as advantageous as to existing and future tenants as the terms required by the program under which the loan or mortgage was made or insured." In addition, Section 203(f)(4) authorized the alternative use of budget authority for Section 8 project-based assistance to provide up-front grants "for the necessary cost of rehabilitation and other development costs" incurred *after* conveyance of a multifamily project by HUD. However, for many years, Congress has not provided Section 8 budget authority for this purpose. Instead, new flexible authority was enacted in Section 204(a) of the Departments of Veterans Affairs and Housing and Urban Development, and Independent Agencies Appropriations Act, 1997.[28] Section 204(a) states, in part:

[t]he Secretary may manage and dispose of multifamily properties owned by the Secretary, including . . . the provision of grants and loans from the General Insurance Fund (12 U.S.C. § 1725(c)) for the necessary costs of rehabilitation, demolition, or construction on the properties (which shall be eligible whether vacant or occupied) and multifamily mortgages held by the Secretary on such terms and conditions as the Secretary may determine, notwithstanding any other provision of law. . . .[29]

---

24. The General Insurance Fund is separate from the Mutual Mortgage Insurance Fund (MMIF), which applies to nearly all FHA single-family mortgage insurance programs.
25. Congress imposes limits, through annual appropriations acts, on credit sales of HUD-owned projects.
26. 12 U.S.C. § 1715n(c).
27. 12 U.S.C. § 1715z-11.
28. Pub. L. No. 104-204, 110 Stat. 2894 (1996), 12 U.S.C. § 1715z-11a(a), as amended. This authority was made permanent through subsequent amendment. *See* Pub. L. No. 106-377 § 204, 114 Stat. 1441, 1441A-24 (2000).
29. Congress limited funding for this purpose in FY 2006 through FY 2010 to appropriated funds rather than funds from the General Insurance Fund. *See* Deficit Reduction Act of 2005, § 2003(a), Pub. L. No. 109-171, 120 Stat. 4, 20 (2006).

Consequently, HUD now has broad authority to establish terms and conditions for the sale, not only of projects owned by HUD, but also for project mortgage loans acquired by HUD. Section 204 supplements the authority in NHA Section 207(l) for preservation of multifamily housing by authorizing funding for expenditures, *after* project conveyance by HUD. In other words, the project purchaser, not HUD, carries out project rehabilitation and obtains whatever additional funding may be needed for that purpose. The grant agreement between HUD and the project purchaser will contain provisions for HUD to reacquire a project if a purchaser fails to complete project rehabilitation in a timely manner. Although the broad statutory authority in Section 204(a), including its "notwithstanding" language,[30] relieves HUD from compliance with requirements in Section 203 of the Housing and Community Development Amendments of 1978, HUD nevertheless can elect to use the authority in Section 204(a) to include terms in the sale of a project or a mortgage loan that are consistent with those found in Section 203.

F. Preservation of Rental Assistance Payments

Another provision related to the sale of HUD-acquired mortgage loans and HUD-owned projects can be found in Section 217 of the "Department of Housing and Urban Development Appropriations Act, 2012,"[31] HUD's FY 2012 appropriations act.

Section 217 requires that, in FY 2012, rental assistance payments under either Section 8 of the U.S. Housing Act of 1937[32] or other federal programs that are attached to project units must be preserved when HUD disposes of a HUD-acquired mortgage loan or a HUD-owned project, including during the foreclosure process. If a project no longer is feasible for rental assistance payments, HUD may contract for such assistance with an owner or owners of other existing projects after consultation with tenants and the local government. The ability to ensure continuity of rental assistance payments is valuable both to the project tenants and in preparing a disposition plan for a project upon title conveyance or loan sale by HUD.

G. Funding Source Transfers

Section 212 in HUD's FY 2012 appropriations act provides an opportunity to transfer existing funding sources to different projects. Section 212 (a) states, in part, that in FY 2012 and FY 2013, the Secretary may:

> authorize the transfer of some or all project-based assistance, debt and statutorily required low-income and very low-income use restrictions, associated with one or more multifamily housing project [sic] to another multifamily housing project or projects.

---

30. 24 C.F.R. § 290.1, the last sentence of which states: "With respect to the disposition of multifamily projects under subpart A, HUD may follow any other method of disposition, as determined by the Secretary."

31. *See* Consolidated and Further Continuing Appropriations Act, 2012 § 217, Pub. L. No. 112-55, 125 Stat. 552, 698 (2011). This preservation authority has been among administrative provisions in HUD appropriations acts for several years.

32. 42 U.S.C. § 1437f. *See* description of the Section 8 authority *infra*.

The term "multifamily housing project" includes housing subject to a mortgage insured by FHA as well as housing receiving a "Mark-to-Market" debt restructuring. "Project-based assistance" includes Rent Supplement Payments under Section 101 of the Housing and Urban Development Act of 1965[33] as well as Interest Reduction Payments under NHA Section 236,[34] and Section 8 rental assistance payments. Under Section 212(b), the assistance may be transferred in phases to "accommodate the financing and other requirements related to rehabilitating or constructing the project or projects to which the assistance is transferred."

The Section 212 authority applies "notwithstanding any other provision of law," but it is subject to compliance with prerequisites in Subsection 212(c). Some of these requirements include preservation not only of the amount of assistance, but also of the number of low-income and very low-income projects and their configuration (*i.e.*, bedroom size). The transferring project must be either physically obsolete or not economically viable, and the receiving project must meet or exceed HUD physical condition standards. Project owners also must consult with tenants in the transferring project and obtain approval from all appropriate local governmental officials. In addition, HUD must determine that the transfer of the assistance is in the best interests of the tenants.

Section 212 combines flexible authority with funding already available so that a transaction can be structured to meet the financial requirements for a specific project. Experience has shown that the area in which a project is located can change over an extended period of time, so that tenants in a multifamily project would be better served in another project. The ability to draw upon HUD funding that already is available to one or more projects, coupled with the option to transfer that funding to one or more projects, provides new opportunities to preserve multifamily housing. In addition, there is statutory authority in Section 212(c)(7) to waive the NHA "first lien" requirement if HUD determines that "a waiver is necessary to facilitate the financing of acquisition, construction, and/or rehabilitation of the receiving project or projects."

Resuming a review of NHA provisions "under" which FHA insurance authority can be made available "pursuant to" NHA Section 223, the following summaries highlight elements of FHA programs that are available to assist with the preservation of multifamily housing. More complete summaries of these provisions are available *supra*.

H. NHA Section 220

NHA Section 220[35] authorizes FHA insurance on loans secured by projects in areas of slum clearance, urban renewal, concentrated code enforcement, and development. The projects have market rents with no NHA subsidy. The insured financing can include both the construction loan and the permanent loan, upon completion of construction that is satisfactory to HUD. An attractive element of this program is that a relatively large amount of commercial space can be included in the mortgaged property. Commercial space can occupy up to 20 percent of total net rentable area, and commercial income can be up to 30 percent of effective

---

33. 12 U.S.C. § 1701s.
34. 12 U.S.C. § 1715z-1. *See* description of the NHA Section 236 program *infra*.
35. 12 U.S.C. § 1715k.

gross income.[36] The figures are twice the amount permitted for commercial space in NHA Section 221 projects.

I. NHA Section 221

NHA Section 221[37] authorizes several multifamily programs (in addition to an inactive single family program) with a large volume of program activity relative to other FHA multifamily programs. Section 221, under which financing can be insured for moderate income and displaced family[38] housing as well as for elderly housing (head of household or spouse age 62 or over),[39] provides a more attractive option for obtaining FHA insurance on a higher loan amount than what can be obtained through Section 207. In other words, the amount of FHA insurance based on replacement cost (Section 221) can exceed the amount that would be available if project value (Section 207) were used as a limiting factor. The program is authorized for moderate income and displaced families, but there are no NHA statutory rent restrictions. Distributions to project owners may be limited, depending on the form of project ownership (*e.g.*, public body, private nonprofit entity, limited distribution entity, or profit-motivated entity).

The Section 221 insurance authority was enacted in 1961, and it is available for new construction and substantial rehabilitation of properties. "Substantial rehabilitation" is defined as the cost of repairs, replacements, and improvements that exceeds the greater of 15 percent of the estimated cost of a property after repairs, etc. (or $6,500 per unit in repairs, etc.), or the replacement of two or more major building components.[40] The loan limit in Section 221 can be an amount up to 90 percent or 100 percent of either project's replacement cost for new construction, or the sum of the estimated cost of repair and rehabilitation plus HUD's estimate of property value before repair and rehabilitation, depending on the type of mortgagor entity. Preservation of existing but deteriorated multifamily housing is possible through a combination of debt refinancing insured by FHA under Section 221 pursuant to Section 223 together with equity funding obtained through allocation of federal low-income housing tax credits (LIHTC, discussed *infra*) for the cost of project purchase and/or substantial rehabilitation. When considering substantial rehabilitation, note that other federal requirements may apply, such as environmental reviews and labor standards under the Davis-Bacon Act.

Although no longer a program under which new FHA firm commitments are issued, the following information is provided for reference on existing loans still insured under Section 221(d)(3) with a below-market interest rate (BMIR) pursuant to NHA Section 221(d)(5). This

---

36. HUD GUIDEBOOK 4430.G, Multifamily Accelerated Processing (MAP) Guide, rev. (Aug. 18, 2011), [hereinafter *MAP Guide*], at ¶ 3.7 B.

37. 12 U.S.C. § 1715*l*.

38. There is a statutory preference in Section 221(f) for multifamily dwelling units for "displaced families," defined as those displaced from an urban renewal area, or as a result of governmental action, or as a result of a major disaster declaration by the President. 12 U.S.C. § 1715*l*(f).

39. *MAP Guide*, *supra* note 36, at ¶ 3.4 S. If a head of household or a spouse is age 62 or over, other persons under age 62, including children under age 18, can occupy the elderly unit in the Section 221 program.

40. *MAP Guide*, at ¶ 3.4 C.

FHA mortgage insurance was provided on loans with an interest rate generally at 3 percent, and the loans were purchased by HUD, at par, and subsequently sold by HUD, through the Ginnie Mae Tandem Program (NHA Section 305), for whatever discount price a purchaser would bid at periodic sales. Any loss to HUD on loans sold at discount prices was recovered by HUD through appropriated funds. The authority in NHA Section 305 for the Tandem Program has been repealed, but HUD continues to monitor these Section 221(d)(3/(5) (BMIR) projects, including their budgets, through its regulatory agreement with project owners.

J. NHA Section 231

NHA Section 231[41] provides mortgage insurance for loans secured by projects designed to provide housing for "elderly persons" who are age 62 or older. Note that the statutory limits elderly occupancy to only 50 percent of the living units. In addition, the housing may include units designed for use and occupancy by a disabled person or family, defined by HUD as a person who has a physical impairment that:

(1) is expected to be of a long-continued and indefinite duration;
(2) may substantially impede his/her ability to live independently; and
(3) is of such a nature that his/her ability to live independently could be improved by more suitable housing conditions.[42]

In addition to new construction loans, insurance under Section 231 is available for loans to substantially rehabilitate existing projects. Consequently, preservation of existing elderly housing is possible through a combination of debt refinancing insured by FHA under Section 231, pursuant to Section 223, together with equity funding obtained through allocation of federal low-income housing tax credits for the cost of project purchase and/or substantial rehabilitation.

K. NHA Section 236

A familiar FHA multifamily new construction and substantial rehabilitation program, enacted as a successor to the Section 221 program, has received renewed interest because of an amendment that facilitates project loan refinancing. NHA Section 236,[43] which was enacted

---

41. 12 U.S.C. § 1715v.
42. *MAP Guide*, at ¶ 3.8 A. 1.
43. 2 U.S.C. § 1715z-1. Regulations at 24 C.F.R. pt. 236, but note "savings" provision in Section 236.1(c), which states:

> Any mortgage approved by the Commissioner for insurance pursuant to sections 236(j) or 236(n) of the National Housing Act is governed by subpart A of this part *as in effect immediately before May 1, 1996, contained in the April 1, 1995 edition of 24 C.F.R., parts 220 to 499*, and by subparts B through E of this part, except as otherwise provided in this subpart. (emphasis added)

Refer to the 1995 edition of 24 C.F.R. pt. 236 to view regulations that may apply to a specific transaction, including a decoupling transaction.

in 1968, was amended in 2000[44] to authorize continuation of a HUD Interest Reduction Payment (IRP) after a loan refinancing. In other words, the IRP is "decoupled" (a term chosen by HUD) from the original Section 236 mortgage that established the basis upon which the IRP payments were made by HUD. A prerequisite for a decoupling transaction is that an owner must continue to operate a project in accordance with low-income affordability restrictions tied to the project's federal assistance, including assistance from federal agencies other than HUD, for the remaining duration of the IRP payments plus five years. Although new FHA insurance commitments no longer are issued under Section 236 (with limited exceptions described in Section 236(n)), some background on the Section 236 program is provided below since, these program requirements would apply in any decoupling transaction.

The purpose of Section 236 is to reduce the amount of rent paid by eligible tenants. To do so, HUD pays IRP to a mortgagee on behalf of a mortgagor, the project owner. The mortgage loan must be insured, or held, by HUD under Section 236 or be a mortgage financed under a state or local program that provides assistance on behalf of nonprofit entities, limited dividend entities, public entities, or cooperative housing corporations through loans, loan insurance, or tax abatements. The amount of IRP is calculated as the difference between monthly payments for principal, note rate of interest, plus mortgage insurance premium (MIP) that a mortgagor is obligated to pay under the mortgage and the monthly payment for principal plus interest that the mortgagor would be obligated to pay if the note interest rate were 1 percent. Note that this formula calculates only the amount of a monthly IRP payment by HUD, not whether the payment is to be treated as an interest component of the total mortgage payment. In fact, the amount of interest on a mortgage loan during the final years of amortization may be less than the amount of an IRP payment. The Internal Revenue Service (IRS) issued Revenue Ruling 76-75 to describe the IRP as:

> [p]ayments by the Government for the benefit of the tenant of a portion of what otherwise would be fair rental value of the space the tenant occupies. Thus, such payments are treated as if they were received by the taxpayer as rent and subsequently paid to the mortgagee as part of the interest due under the mortgage obligation.[45]

Consequently, a mortgagee is to include the IRP in its gross income while deducting, as an interest expense, the total amount of interest paid on the mortgage, including the IRP component.[46]

A very attractive feature of the Section 236 program is that the IRP paid by HUD needs no annual appropriation from Congress, as the total amount of IRP already is available from an appropriation available at the time HUD previously endorsed the mortgage for FHA insurance or entered into an agreement with a state or local entity to provide IRP on loans without FHA insurance. In addition, the terms "Budget Authority" and "Contract Authority" relate to the amount of IRP payable monthly (and annually) on a specific mortgage. The Budget

---

44. Departments of Veterans Affairs and Housing and Urban Development, Independent Agencies Appropriations Act, 2000 § 532(a), Pub. L. No. 106-74, 113 Stat. 1047, 1116 (2000).
45. 1976-1 C.B. 14.
46. A Section 236 mortgage loan has a note rate of interest comparable to a market rate of interest (e.g., 7%) at the time of loan origination.

Authority refers to the total amount of IRP to be paid by HUD over the amortization period of a specific loan. The Contract Authority is the amount of IRP payable on a specific loan in a given year. The amount of IRP paid by HUD cannot exceed the monthly (or annual) Contract Authority or the overall Budget Authority available over the mortgage term.

Section 236 contains limits on the amount of rent payable and the amount of a tenant's income. "Basic Rent" is the amount owed by a tenant, which is the amount needed for project operations plus payment of principal and interest under a hypothetical mortgage at a 1 percent interest rate. "Market Rent" is the amount needed for project operations plus payment of principal, note rate of interest, and MIP under the project mortgage. The amount needed to operate a project (*i.e.*, budget-based) is monitored and approved by HUD, as an increase in operating budget expenses has a direct effect on the amount of Basic Rent and Market Rent for a specific project.

Tenant income generally cannot exceed 80 percent of area median income (AMI), which is determined by HUD and adjusted for family size. Like Section 221, Section 236 contains authority related to projects for elderly (head of household age 62 or older) and disabled persons. Tenant rent payments cannot exceed 30 percent of a tenant's adjusted income. In some cases, 30 percent of a tenant's income is not sufficient to pay the Basic Rent, but the shortfall can be made up by HUD through a Rental Assistance Payment (RAP) under Section 236(f)(2), a Rent Supplement payment, a Section 8 assistance payment under the U.S. Housing Act of 1937, or an owner subsidy. In other cases, 30 percent of a tenant's income exceeds the amount of Basic Rent, and the amount in excess of the Basic Rent is treated as "Excess Rent" that an owner must return to HUD for deposit into the fund for Flexible Subsidies (discussed *infra*). Excess Rent is calculated on a unit-by-unit basis, and HUD may permit some (or all) of that amount to be retained by a project owner either for project use or, if an owner in good standing with HUD (*e.g.*, has form 2530 clearance) agrees to extend project affordability restrictions for an additional five years, for non-project use.

HUD guidance and application procedures for a "decoupling" transaction under Section 236(e)(2) were issued in 2000.[47] Although the Housing Notice technically expired in 2001, its guidance still provides information available from HUD for use of this loan refinancing tool to preserve multifamily housing. As stated above, a prerequisite for decoupling the IRP assistance from a Section 236 mortgage is that an owner must enter into a new IRP agreement and a use agreement, either with HUD or a HUD-approved state or local agency, to preserve the project as a low-income housing resource for five years beyond the term of the IRP and other federal assistance, if any.

The Section 236 program has complex requirements, but these details merit attention, especially in a "decoupling" transaction in which an owner must agree to enter into a use agreement to continue compliance with them, even if the Section 236 loan is refinanced with a conventional loan. A refinanced loan through a decoupling transaction often reduces the amount of interest owed on a project loan that, in turn, could extend the period during which Budget Authority and Contract Authority remain available for IRP. Planning in advance of such a refinancing should include what source of funds an owner will need to pay the debt service on the loan after the Budget Authority and the Contract Authority have been ex-

---

47. Notice H 00-8, May 16, 2000.

hausted. Use of federal low-income housing tax credits and tax-exempt bond financing for project rehabilitation as part of a decoupling transaction raises additional issues that are described below.

A final point about Section 236 concerns the authority in Section 236(s) for grant and loan funds for the capital cost of project rehabilitation, which, at first glance, may appear attractive for preserving multifamily housing, but a closer look will show why this authority is rarely, if ever, used. The funding would be derived from IRP funds returned to HUD (*e.g.*, recaptured upon prepayment of a Section 236 mortgage). Repayment of a loan would be from recaptured IRP, the amount of which would determine funds available for the loan, which would have a maturity consistent with the remaining term over which the recaptured IRP would have been paid. This statutory requirement causes difficulty both for obtaining adequate notice about the amount of recaptured IRP that would be available and for determining whether that amount is sufficient when added to other funding sources for project rehabilitation. For capital grants, the statute requires HUD to ensure that the recaptured IRP is paid out in the same periodic amounts as if the IRP were being paid in accordance with the schedule for the Section 236 loan from which the IRP was recaptured. Timely preparation of a complete source and use statement would be difficult in light of this statutory limitation on the flow of funds from a Section 236(s) grant.

L. NHA Section 241

FHA insurance is available under NHA Section 241[48] to preserve multifamily housing through supplemental loans (construction and permanent loans), which are designed to finance improvements or additions to existing multifamily projects, including improvements for energy efficiency. Generally, these supplemental loans must be secured by projects that already are security for FHA-insured loans. The exception in Section 241(d) is for projects that "would assist in preserving, expanding, or improving housing opportunities, or in providing protection against fire or other hazards." The option for a Section 241 supplemental loan can be useful when assembling a source of funds in connection with the rehabilitation of projects that are to be purchased or are currently owned.

M. NHA Section 250

Preservation of FHA Subsidized Projects

Preservation of multifamily projects, which are subsidized under the NHA, is the subject of statutory restrictions in NHA Section 250.[49] If terms in these loan documents state that prior HUD approval is needed for prepayment of such loans, that approval under Section 250 (and termination of FHA insurance pursuant to NHA Section 229[50]) will not be given unless:

---

48. 12 U.S.C. 1715z-6. *See* description of this authority *supra*.
49. 12 U.S.C. 1715z-15.
50. 2 U.S.C. 1715t.

(1) the Secretary has determined that such project is no longer meeting a need for rental housing for lower income families in the area;[51]
(2) the Secretary
   (A) has determined that the tenants have been notified of the owner's request for approval of a prepayment;
   (B) has provided the tenants with an opportunity to comment on the owner's request; and
   (C) has taken such comments into consideration; and
(3) the Secretary has ensured that there is a plan for providing relocation assistance for adequate, comparable housing for any lower-income tenant who will be displaced as a result of the prepayment and withdrawal of the project from the program.

The requirement in Section 250(1) has been controversial. Situations arose in the 1980s involving subsidized multifamily projects that needed debt financing for substantial repairs and rehabilitation for project preservation. Lenders providing such new financing desired a first lien position that would require prepayment on the FHA-insured loan, but existing that first lien could not be subordinated to another loan. Prepayment of the insured loan would require a finding by HUD under Section 250(1) that the project no longer was needed for low-income rental housing, but such housing was needed rehabilitation in order to continue providing such housing in its area. HUD determined that preservation of a low-income housing project could be accomplished with HUD approval of a refinancing that would prepay the existing FHA-insured loan (and terminate the regulatory agreement) as long as the project owner entered into a recorded use agreement to continue maintaining the low-income character of the project. HUD issued Notice H 06-11 to provide guidance about the types of project, which need a "significant amount of rehabilitation,"[52] the refinancing of which would be subject to Section 250 as well as sample scenarios and a sample notification letter to tenants. This guidance is an important reference for an issue that may arise in a transaction involving the low-income housing tax credit, tax-exempt bond financing, and grants or a combination of these funding sources.

III. FLEXIBLE SUBSIDY PROGRAM

A program for preserving some multifamily projects is the Flexible Subsidy program, authorized under Section 201 of the "Housing and Community Development Amendments of 1978."[53] This assistance serves to restore or maintain project financial soundness; permit capital im-

---

51. The term "lower income families" is defined, per Section 250(c), by reference to Section 3(b)(2) in the U.S. Housing Act of 1937 as families whose income does not exceed 80% of Area Median Income, adjusted for family size. HUD can adjust the 80% figure up or down based on prevailing levels of construction costs or unusually high or low family incomes. Note that this definition implies that Section 250 is not intended to apply to projects not specifically limited to this type of tenant occupancy.

52. *See* Clarification of Housing Notice H 06-11, Prepayment Subject to Section 250(a) of the National Housing Act, under Multifamily Program Information at HUD.GOV for guidance about what HUD considers a "significant amount of rehabilitation."

53. 12 U.S.C. § 1715z-1a.

provements to maintain decent, safe, and sanitary housing; assist in the improvement of project management through a management improvement operating plan (MIOP); and maintain a project's low- or moderate-income character. The types of projects eligible cover those assisted under the following provisions:

(1) NHA Section 221(d)(3)/(5) (BMIR) or NHA Section 236, and
(2) Section 8 of the U.S. Housing Act of 1937 following conversion to such loan management assistance from assistance under NHA Section 236 (*i.e.*, Section 236 Rental Assistance Payments) or Section 101 of the Housing and Urban Development Act of 1965 (*i.e.*, Rent Supplement assistance).

As previously discussed, "Excess Rents" recaptured by HUD under Section 236 are placed in the Flexible Subsidy Fund together with other funds, such as those repaid on existing Flexible Subsidy loans. Note that the availability of these funds is limited by Section 201(j) to that approved in an annual appropriation act.

Receipt of this assistance under Section 201(d)(1) includes a condition that a project owner must agree to maintain the low- or moderate-income character of a project for at least the remaining term of a project mortgage. Mortgage terms can be up to 40 years, and, many years after receipt of a Flexible Subsidy loan, a property location may no longer compatible with continuing the project. An extreme example would be one in which a Flexible Subsidy project has been demolished in an area converted completely to industrial use. The recorded use agreement still requires the vacant site of the former project to be used for low- or moderate-income rental housing. The problem is that compliance with this statutory requirement cannot be waived by HUD.

HUD has issued guidance[54] containing policies and procedures for deferred repayment of operating assistance loans. Under the regulation at 24 CFR 219.220(b) (1995),[55] a Flexible Subsidy loan must be repaid upon the earliest of the expiration of a mortgage term, termination of FHA mortgage insurance (note a possible NHA Section 250 compliance issue), mortgage prepayment (possibly a Section 236 decoupling transaction), or project sale. When projects need repair and rehabilitation, there may not be adequate funds from a refinance loan to both pay for the rehabilitation and repay a Flexible Subsidy loan that would become due when a refinance loan is closed. This regulatory requirement is not based on a statutory prerequisite, so the regulation could be waived by the Assistant Secretary for Housing-Federal Housing Commissioner[56] and the due date for payment of all, or part, of a Flexible Subsidy loan could be deferred until the another date (*e.g.*, the expiration of the term for a new refinance mortgage).

---

54. Notice H 2011-05, Feb. 14, 2011.
55. The regulations in 24 C.F.R. pt. 219 were "streamlined" in 1996, but note the "savings" provision at Section 219.2. The content of the regulation at 24 C.F.R. § 219.220(b), however, can be found only through a copy of Title 24 of the Code of Federal Regulations issued before 1996 (e.g., 1995, as cited in the text).
56. Under Section 7(q)(2) of the Department of Housing and Urban Development Act, 42 U.S.C. § 3535(q)(2), a regulation can be waived only by "an individual of Assistant Secretary rank or equivalent rank, who is authorized to issue the regulation to be waived."

The Housing Notice provides instructions for completing the process and includes a requirement for execution by the owner of a recorded use agreement to maintain project affordability, which also will involve continued HUD oversight and monitoring.

IV. EMERGENCY LOW INCOME HOUSING PRESERVATION ACT OF 1987

In the late 1980s, multifamily projects with subsidized FHA-insured financing were approaching a point in their amortization period that project owners could prepay loans without HUD's consent. In order to preempt a possible loss of a significant amount of low-income multifamily housing, the Emergency Low Income Housing Preservation Act of 1987 (ELIHPA)[57] was enacted to provide temporary authority (*i.e.*, a two-year moratorium) on certain multifamily project loans. Eligible low-income housing included projects financed by a mortgage that was:

(1) insured or held by HUD under NHA Section 221(d)(3) and receiving Loan Management Set-Aside assistance under Section 8 of the U.S. Housing Act of 1937;
(2) insured or held by HUD under NHA Section 221(d)(3)/(5) (BMIR);
(3) insured, assisted, or held by HUD or a state agency under NHA Section 236; or
(4) a purchase money mortgage held by HUD that, immediately before HUD's acquisition, was classified under (1) through (3) above.

The mortgage also must have had to be eligible for prepayment, without HUD's consent, pursuant to a contract or regulation in effect before November 1, 1987. A project owner needed HUD approval of a Plan of Action, which included HUD incentives authorized by ELIHPA. For example, the NHA was amended to add a new Subsection 241(f) that authorized FHA insurance on a second mortgage for an equity loan so that a project owner could take out a portion of a project's equity. Payments on the debt service for the insured loan were provided by HUD through Section 8 assistance.

V. LOW INCOME HOUSING PRESERVATION AND RESIDENT HOMEOWNERSHIP ACT

ELIHPA was repealed and replaced by the Low Income Housing Preservation and Resident Homeownership Act of 1990[58] (LIHPRHA), but preservation plans established under ELIPHA (and later through LIHPRHA) still remain in place, even if the FHA-insured loan in place at the time of preservation plan closing subsequently was paid in full, in order to preserve affordability restrictions for the remaining useful life of a project (*e.g.*, 50 years). The definition of "eligible low income housing" remained the same under LIHPRHA as under ELIHPA, except that that the date of "February 5, 1988" replaced "November 1, 1987." Financial incentives were included in HUD-approved Plans of Action (*e.g.*, NHA Section 241(f)[59] was amended to include acquisition loans for project purchasers in addition to the previously

---

57. Pub. L. No. 100-242, 101 Stat. 1877 (1988), 12 U.S.C. § 1715*l* note. Regs. at 24 C.F.R. pt. 248, subpt. C.
58. Pub. L. No. 101-625, 104 Stat. 4249 (1990), 12 U.S.C. § 4101 *et seq*. Regs. at 24 C.F.R. pt. 248, subpt. B.
59. The ELIHPA and LIHPRHA authority in Section 241(f) was available only through a HUD-approved Plan of Action.

authorized equity takeout loans for project owners.). Like ELIHPA, an owner either may work with HUD under LIHPRHA to modify a Plan of Action or may terminate low-income affordability restrictions if HUD does not provide the assistance in the HUD-approved Plan of Action. In addition, an owner may work with HUD to modify an existing Plan of Action if continued performance under the plan is no longer possible (*e.g.*, destruction of project by a natural disaster, such as Hurricane Katrina).

The project owner restrictions in ELIHPA and LIHPRHA have been expensive and subject to extensive litigation. Consequently, NHA Section 241(f) was repealed in 1996.[60] In addition, notwithstanding contrary provisions in NHA Sections 229 and 250 (*supra*), Section 219 of the HUD FY 1999 appropriations act[61] prospectively restored authority for owners of these projects to prepay, and mortgagees to accept prepayment of, their mortgages. In addition, a project owner again can request voluntary termination of FHA mortgage insurance (thereby extinguishing the regulatory agreement between HUD and a project owner). These actions must be consistent with terms and conditions of the mortgage and the mortgage insurance contract, and the owner must agree not to increase rents for a 60-day period after a loan prepayment or mortgage insurance termination. An owner also must provide notice of intent to prepay a loan or terminate mortgage insurance to each tenant and to the state or local government in the jurisdiction where a project is located. Note that this notice must be provided not less than 150 days, but not more than 270 days, before the prepayment of the termination. This requirement needs special attention to avoid additional expenses when putting together a transaction, as a date for loan prepayment or mortgage insurance termination may have to be postponed in order to ensure compliance with this timing requirement.[62]

VI. PORTFOLIO REENGINEERING DEMONSTRATIONS AND MULTIFAMILY ASSISTED HOUSING REFORM AND AFFORDABILITY ACT OF 1997

In the mid-1990s, Congress was concerned about the amount of funding needed for assistance under Section 8 of the U.S. Housing Act of 1937, especially when Section 8 rents were in excess of the fair market rent of the locality where a project was located. Congress realized that, if the amount of funding for Section 8 assistance at these projects were to be reduced, project owners might not have sufficient funds to pay operating expenses and debt service, including FHA-insured financing. Two demonstration programs were authorized for FY 1996 through FY 1998 to study options for addressing this situation.[63] These demonstrations were known as Portfolio Reengineering Programs (Pre) and produced adjustments in Section 8 rents for about 200 projects. The lessons learned from them were applied to legislation for a

---

60. Pub L. No. 104-204, 110 Stat. 2874, 2885 (1996).

61. Departments of Veterans Affairs and Housing and Urban Development, and Independent Agencies Appropriations Act, 1999, Pub. L. No. 105-276, 112 Stat. 2461, 2487 (1998). This provision has been referred to as the Wellstone Amendment.

62. *See* sample letter in Attachment 1 to Notice H 06-11, *supra* note 16, for an example.

63. Departments of Veterans Affairs and Housing and Urban Development, and Independent Agencies Appropriations Act, 1996, § 210, Pub. L. No. 104-134, 110 Stat. 1321, 1321-285 (1996). Section 210 was repealed by the Departments of Veterans Affairs and Housing and Urban Development and replaced by the Independent Agencies Appropriations Act, 1997 § 212, Pub. L. No. 104-204, 110 Stat. 2874, 2897 (1996).

temporary Mark-to-Market program, enacted in the Multifamily Assisted Housing Reform and Affordability Act of 1997[64] (MAHRA).

The intent of MAHRA is to reduce the cost of federal assistance; address physical needs of projects; preserve affordable low income rental housing; and reduce the cost of FHA mortgage insurance claims. The initial "sunset" date for the program was October 1, 2001, and it has been amended three times, the latest being October 1, 2015.[65] Although the sunset date has been extended, the basic structure of the Mark-to-Market program remains essentially the same as the four-year program initially enacted (*i.e.*, a four-year program allowing owners a single opportunity to participate in the program). Participation in the Mark-to-Market program is voluntary, unlike the ELIHPA and the LIHPRHA programs.

The Mark-to-Market program presents an opportunity to adjust project rents, enable a moderate amount of project repair and rehabilitation to preserve affordable multifamily housing, and avoid payment of a full FHA mortgage insurance claim when rents are reduced. To be eligible, an owner must be receiving project-based Section 8 assistance or Rent Supplement assistance that is expiring, and the loan secured by the project must be FHA-insured or held by HUD. ELIHPA, LIHPRHA, and Pre projects are excluded from participation, and some bond-financed project are exempt from the program. In addition, project rents must be in excess of comparable rents (*i.e.*, local market rents for non-assisted projects). HUD has entered into Portfolio Restructuring Agreements (PRAs) with Participating Administrative Entities (PREs) to administer the program. The PREs can be state or local housing finance agencies, but the most active PRAs are private entities that also hire private attorneys to close debt restructurings on behalf of HUD, including loans with FHA mortgage insurance.

The PAEs and project owners prepare debt restructuring plans, formally known as Mortgage Restructuring and Rental Assistance Sufficiency Plans, for HUD approval. Expiring Section 8 contracts are extended during this process. A debt-restructuring plan includes a reduction of rents to comparable rents, but there is a limited option for "exception rents" up to 120 percent of the fair market rent based on housing and community needs in the area where a project is located. If necessary, a plan provides for payment by FHA of a non-default mortgage insurance claim in order to reduce the unpaid principal balance of a first mortgage lien. This reduction, combined with modified payment terms on the unpaid balance, results in an amount that can be paid, after operating expenses, with reduced rents. The FHA insurance claim payment is included in a new second, non-recourse mortgage loan, in an amount which a project owner can reasonably be expected to repay, and at an interest rate that is not below the applicable federal rate, as determined by the Department of Treasury. The IRS has indicated that this type of second mortgage will not be subject to a portion of the loan principal being treated as interest for federal income tax purposes.[66] Payment on the second mortgage is deferred, except that surplus funds, if any, are applied to payment of the second mortgage (75 percent) and to the project owner (25 percent) if the owner meets benchmarks for man-

---

64. Departments of Veterans Affairs and Housing and Urban Development and Independent Agencies Appropriations Act, 1998 Title V, Subtitle A, Pub. L. No. 105-65, 111 Stat. 1343, 1384 (1997), 42 U.S.C. § 1437f. Regs. at 24 C.F.R. pt. 401.
65. Consolidated and Further Continuing Appropriations Act, 2012, *supra* note 31, at § 237.
66. Rev. Rul. 98-34, 1998-1 C.B. 983.

agement and housing quality. Payment is due on the second mortgage when the first mortgage is paid in full or terminated. The amount of the FHA insurance claim payment not included in the second mortgage is placed in a third mortgage secured by the project. Each debt-restructuring plan also includes a 30-year affordability and use restriction that is recorded to preserve affordable multifamily housing.

A Section 8 contract is renewed at closing of the debt-restructuring transaction for a specified period of time (*e.g.*, up to 20 years), subject to the availability of appropriated funds. Rent adjustments in subsequent contract renewals generally are based upon an Operating Adjustment Cost Factor (OCAF) published by HUD. Project owners must accept Section 8 contract renewals if their terms and conditions are consistent with the debt-restructuring plan. Rents for ELIHPA, LIHPRHA, and Pre projects are renewed in accordance with plans approved under those statutes.

Requirements for the initial four-year program remain essentially the same as those in the statute that currently has a sunset date of October 1, 2015. The absence of revisions to substantive requirements in a program that now will be in effect through FY 2015 has raised legal issues not contemplated when the temporary program initially was authorized in 1997. For example:

- MAHRA Section 514(h) provides an exemption for projects that have received primary, FHA-insured financing from a state or local government if a debt restructuring plan would "conflict with applicable law or agreements governing such financing." If a Section 8 contract on that project were to expire during the initial four year period of the program, would that project later be exempt from debt restructuring even if a subsequent Section 8 contract were to expire five years later (*i.e.*, after the initial sunset date had been extended for five additional years) when the "conflict" no longer existed due to retirement of the government-issued bonds?
- In another situation, a project had rents that did not exceed comparable market rents during the initial four-year period of the program but did exceed comparable market rents five years later (again, after the first extension of the sunset date). Once a project is initially determined to be ineligible for the Mark-to-Market program, is that project forever ineligible—even in this example, when project rents subsequently exceed comparable market rents?
- A separate issue arises in connection with the second mortgage, which can be modified, assigned, or forgiven (in whole or in part) under certain conditions set forth in the restructuring tools under Section 517(a). When must a second mortgage be assigned to an acquiring organization under authority in Section 517(a)(5), immediately upon closing of a debt restructuring transaction or at another time in the future? HUD has determined administratively that the assignment can take place within three years of the closing of the debt restructuring, which would allow time to close the subsequent assignment of the second mortgage to the acquiring organization. Is the three-year time period too long or too short?

Special attention is needed on these and other issues arising from implementation of a statute that initially was intended to expire on October 1, 2001, but that now has been extended until October 1, 2015.

VII. PROJECT LOAN FUNDING SOURCES

The program descriptions above have concentrated on FHA mortgage insurance programs and related statutes that preserve multifamily housing. What is the source of funding for these loans insured by FHA? The loans are eligible for placement in a pool of mortgages (usually one mortgage per multifamily pool) that back securities (*i.e.*, mortgage-backed securities or MBS) issued by mortgagees that are guaranteed by the Government National Mortgage Association (Ginnie Mae). The MBS are sold to investors by mortgagees that are Ginnie Mae-approved issuers that also are FHA-approved mortgagees. The dollars received from the sale of MBS by Ginnie Mae issuers are used to fund loans insured by FHA. This arrangement is particularly attractive because it allows a borrower flexibility in obtaining funds: when the borrower obtains a construction loan, he can also receive a commitment for financing a permanent loan after completion of construction. The MBS during the construction phase are known as construction loan securities, which are redeemed by permanent loan securities immediately after FHA final endorsement of a project mortgage loan. The Ginnie Mae guaranty on these securities is backed by the full faith and credit of the United States.

VIII. LOW-INCOME HOUSING TAX CREDITS

Total project financing generally includes equity funding as well as debt financing. Equity funding can come from contributions of partners in a limited partnership (LP), from members of a limited liability company (LLC), or from grants from various sources. Equity contributions reduce debt service expenses for a project that can make rents more affordable for tenants. A familiar source for equity is through investor contributions in return for low-income housing tax credits (LIHTCs) authorized under Section 42 of the Internal Revenue Code of 1986 (IRC).[67] A tax credit is a dollar-for-dollar reduction in the tax liability of a taxpayer. Of course, a taxpayer must have taxable income in order to take advantage of a tax credit, and thus investor interest in providing this type of equity contribution for project financing may depend on the overall financial status of the investor.

Section 42 is the longest IRC provision, and it provides a housing program administered by the Treasury Department through the IRS. Its complexity requires the assistance of professionals, such as attorneys and accountants, who have expertise in this subject matter. A complete description of LIHTC requirements is beyond the scope of this chapter, but a brief summary for some of the basic requirements will help determine what FHA-insured financing is most suitable for preserving multifamily housing.

An owner of a newly constructed or substantially rehabilitated building may claim, each year for 10 years, a credit equal to the "applicable percentage" times the "qualified basis" for a building. The applicable percentage[68] generally is 9 percent for new construction or substantial rehabilitation that is not federally subsidized (*e.g.*, not financed with bonds, the interest on which is exempt from taxation under IRC Section 103) and 4 percent for acquisition of

---

67. I.R.C. § 42.
68. The Treasury Department prescribes the applicable percentages each month at approximately 4% and 9%, but the applicable percentage for new construction, without federal subsidy, is fixed at 9% for buildings placed in service after July 30, 2008, and before Dec. 31, 2013.

existing buildings or construction and rehabilitation that is federally subsidized. The qualified basis generally is the cost of project construction, acquisition, and/or rehabilitation times the percentage of low income tenants. The basis cannot include any costs financed with proceeds from a federally funded grant.[69] In addition, at least 10 years must elapse between the date of acquisition by a new owner and the date an existing building previously was placed in service, Under I.R.C. § 42(d)(6)(C), however, the limitation does not apply to:

> any building which is substantially assisted, financed, or operated under section 8 of the United States Housing Act of 1937, section 221(d)(3), 221(d)(4), or 236 of the National Housing Act, . . . or any other housing program administered by the Department of Housing and Urban Development . . . .

There are occupancy and rent restrictions for projects that receive LIHTC funds. An owner must make an irrevocable election that:

(1) 20 percent or more of project residential units are both rent-restricted and occupied by individuals whose income is 50 percent or less of area median gross income, or
(2) 40 percent or more of project residential units are both rent-restricted and occupied by individuals whose income is 60 percent or less of area median gross income.

Unit rents, which do not include the amount of Section 8 assistance, are restricted to 30 percent of the income limit for the unit. The rent and income restrictions remain for 30 years (a 15-year compliance period, in which tax credits can be recaptured by the IRS, plus a 15-year extended-use period) and any additional period that a state housing credit agency may require.[70]

The amount of LIHTC available for investors is determined under a formula in IRC Section 42(h) that limits the amount that state housing credit agencies can allocate each year. This limitation is similar to the allocation for private activity bonds that can be used for financing a "qualified residential rental project," as defined in IRC Section 142(d). The volume limit in IRC Section 42(h), however, does not apply if project financing involves tax-exempt bond financing that is subject to the volume limit in IRC Section 146 (*i.e.*, a project will receive a 4 percent LIHTC). Investors often make their contributions over a period of time, so interim financing may be needed upfront to enable completion of a project purchase, construction, or rehabilitation. HUD formerly required a substantial portion of this equity contribution to be placed in escrow at the time of initial FHA insurance endorsement, thereby placing some mortgagors in the position of having to obtain costly bridge loan financing for this cash deposit.

---

69. In Rev. Rul. 2002-65, 2002-43 I.R.B. 729, the IRS determined that rental assistance payments under the Rent Supplement and RAP programs are not grants, but stated that IRP payments under NHA Section 236 are not included within the scope of this revenue ruling. The ruling stated that the Treasury Department and the IRS are studying the proper treatment of IRP under IRC Section 42.
70. Although a foreclosure (or deed-in-lieu of foreclosure) may terminate an extended-use period, note that, under IRC § 42(h)(6)(E)(ii), the restrictions for existing tenants generally must continue for three years after such termination.

HUD has amended the regulation at 24 CFR 200.54 (2010), as required by NHA Section 228,[71] so that FHA no longer requires the escrowing of equity from the sales of LIHTC. This regulation also provides the same relief for equity contributions derived from the sale of historic and new market tax credits. Upon approval by FHA, funds from the sale of these tax credits do not need to be fully disbursed before the disbursement of mortgage proceeds. In addition, FHA has issued guidance[72] on its policy and procedures regarding the use of a Master Lease structure to maximize the benefits from the use of multiple types of tax credits.

IX. CONCLUSION

Preservation of multifamily housing is a very significant matter, especially when the rate of home ownership is declining. Although no new loans are being insured by FHA under deep subsidy programs, such as the NHA Section 221(d)(3)/)5) (BMIR) and the NHA Section 236 programs, there still are opportunities to use incentives described in this chapter to preserve and improve existing multifamily housing. For example:

- An acquisition of a project currently subject to a conventional loan could be refinanced with FHA mortgage insurance under Section 221(d)(4), pursuant to Section 223(f), in a transaction that also could include equity contributions for a 9 percent LIHTC for substantial rehabilitation of the project. Tax-exempt bond financing could be an option for funding the refinance loan, possibly with bond proceeds providing funds to purchase Ginnie Mae MBS that, in turn, could fund the refinance loan. The 10-year placed-in-service LIHTC rule would not apply, since the refinance loan would be insured under Section 221. The five-year prepayment prohibition, however, would apply pursuant to Section 223(f).
- A similar arrangement would be one in which a loan currently insured by FHA is refinanced with a new loan insured under Section 221(d)(4) pursuant to Section 223(a)(7). In this case, the refinance loan could be increased up to the amount of original loan being refinanced, and there would be no five-year prohibition on prepayment of the refinance loan.
- Section 236 decoupling transactions provide an option to use remaining IRP budget authority and contract authority as a component of financing to purchase and/or rehabilitate projects. Note that, if LIHTCs are used in a Section 236 decoupling transaction, HUD requires that existing tenants be protected. Income and rent limits for LIHTC are below those requirements for a Section 236 project so, if a tenant in a Section 236 project currently has income at 80 percent of AMI and pays 30 percent of that income for Basic Rent, those amounts would not qualify for an LIHTC unit. Careful planning is needed for a transaction in which LIHTC equity will be used to acquire and/or substantially rehabilitate a project occupied by tenants currently receiving HUD assistance. Note that the LIHTC use agreement also may be for longer period than that required for the Section 236 decoupling.

---

71. 12 U.S.C. § 1715s.
72. *MAP Guide*, at ch. 16.

There are many other options and permutations, such as increased Section 8 assistance payments in Mark-Up-to-Market transactions, to be used to motivate project owners to continue providing a resource for affordable multifamily housing. Additional information about the use of Section 8 rental assistance in preservation transactions is provided in the Section 8 chapter.

Planning and executing these transactions may be challenging, but they also will be very rewarding, as an attorney's professional skill is needed to help meet a basic human need for housing. Attorneys in HUD's Office of General Counsel (Headquarters and Field Offices) are available to provide assistance in interpreting the legal requirements in the HUD statutes described in this chapter. Generally, issues involving analysis of provisions in these statutes are provided by Headquarters OGC attorneys in order to ensure consistent interpretations nationwide. OGC Attorneys in HUD Field Offices generally provide assistance in applying the legal requirements in the statutes to specific transactions involving these programs.

Health-Care and Hospital Financing

Kristin M. Neun and Andrea R. Ponsor

I. INTRODUCTION

HUD provides mortgage insurance under Sections 232 and 242 of the National Housing Act of 1934 (the Act), as amended, to private lenders to improve the availability of mortgage credit to finance skilled-nursing, intermediate-care, and assisted-living facilities, as well as hospitals.[1] HUD provides mortgage insurance under Section 232 of the Act for loans financing the creation and operation of skilled-nursing, intermediate-care, and assisted-living facilities. Under Section 242, in furtherance of its community development mission, HUD provides mortgage insurance to hospital facilities to ensure that adequate mortgage capital is available for needed facilities.

Until 2008, applications for mortgage insurance under Section 232 were processed by the Office of Housing multifamily housing staff in HUD field offices in the jurisdiction where the project was located. In 2008, HUD began to transition the processing of Section 232 loans from multifamily housing to HUD employees assigned to the Office of Healthcare Programs (OHP), formerly known as the Office of Insured Healthcare Facilities (OIHCF). OHP is comprised of the Office of Residential Programs (ORP), which is responsible for Section 232 loans, and the Office of Hospital Facilities (OHF), which is responsible for hospital facilities insured under Section 242. ORP and OHF do not have employees in each HUD field office but rather key employees in HUD Headquarters and in a handful of field offices across the country.

---

1. National Housing Act of 1934, §§ 232, 242, 12 U.S.C. § 1715w, 1715z-7 (2010).

Along with transitioning the processing and asset management of 232 loans from multifamily housing to OHP, in 2008, HUD began a continuous improvement program for the Section 232 and 242 programs. Using the LEAN methodology pioneered by Toyota, HUD set out to reduce waste in application processing and loan closings by standardizing work using new Section 232 specific addendums to existing forms and comprehensive punch lists. The LEAN process creates some notable administrative differences between the processing of loans insured under Section 232 and processing under multifamily programs.[2] HUD has applied a similar streamlined approach to Section 242 financings.

II. SECTION 232

A. Authority and Guidance

Statutory authority for the insurance of mortgage loans for skilled-nursing, intermediate-care, and assisted-living facilities is found at Section 232 of the National Housing Act, as amended.[3] The Housing Act of 1959 amended the National Housing Act by adding Section 232, which authorized a mortgage insurance program for the construction and rehabilitation of proprietary nursing homes.[4] The program was expanded to include intermediate-care facilities in 1969 and board-and-care facilities in 1983.[5] The Housing and Community Development Act of 1987 further expanded the program to permit the insurance of mortgages used to purchase or refinance mortgages insured under Section 232 pursuant to Section 223(f) of the National Housing Act.[6] In 1994, HUD issued regulations permitting insurance of loans used to refinance or purchase eligible facilities not previously insured by the FHA.[7]

Regulations governing loans insured under Section 232 (Section 232 Loans) and the facilities that secure them (Section 232 Facilities) are found at 24 CFR Part 232, though, as noted below, statutory and regulatory provisions related to refinancing Section 232 Loans also may apply. As with other HUD mortgage insurance programs, handbooks, notices, and mortgagee letters provide critical policy and administrative information for lenders and borrowers. Since the advent of the LEAN 232 program, the OHP website and LEAN 232 e-mail blasts sent regularly to those on the 232 Mailing List have been HUD's primary vehicles for communicating processing information and form changes.[8] Key handbooks and notices are

---

2. Multifamily mortgage insurance programs are discussed in Chapter 1, *supra*.
3. 12 U.S.C. § 1715w (2010).
4. Housing Act of 1959, Pub. L. No. 86-37, Title I, § 115, 73 Stat. 663 (1959).
5. Housing and Urban Development Act of 1968, Pub. L. 90"448, Title III, § 314, 82 Stat. 511 (1968); Housing and Urban-Rural Recovery Act of 1983, Title IV, Part A, Subpart 3, § 437(a)–(f), 97 Stat. 1222 (1983).
6. Housing and Community Development Act of 1987, Pub. Law 100-242, Title IV, Subtitle A, § 409, 101 Stat. 1904.
7. 24 C.F.R. § 232.902 (2011).
8. U.S. Dep't of Housing and Urban Development, Section 232 LEAN Program, *available at* http://portal.hud.gov/hudportal/HUD?src=/federal_housing_administration/healthcare_facilities/section_232/lean_processing_page (last accessed April 8, 2012). Interested parties may search email blasts or subscribe to the mailing list through a link on the Underwriting Guidance section of the HUD LEAN 232 website.

listed below and important forms and guidance found on the OHP website are referenced throughout this chapter. Updated comprehensive guidance on the underwriting, processing, and closing of Section 232 Loans is being developed by OHP but has not yet been published. Practitioners should regularly check the HUD LEAN 232 website for updates.

Key Guidance for Section 232 Loans

Statute	12 U.S.C. §1715w	
Regulations	24 C.F.R. Part 232	
Handbooks/Guides	Handbook 4600.1 Rev-1	Residential Care Facilities—Nursing Homes (SNF and ICF), Board-and-Care Homes, and Assisted-Living Facilities
	Guide to Multifamily Accelerated Processing (March 15, 2002) ("MAP Guide")	
Notices/Letters	HUD Housing Notice 01-03	Review of Health-Care Facility Portfolios and Changes to the Section 232 Programs
	HUD Housing Notice 04-01	Professional Liability Insurance for Section 232 Programs
	HUD Housing Notice 08-09	Accounts Receivable (AR) Financing
	Mortgagee Letter 2011-15	Revision to Procedures for Partial Payment of Claims of Section 232 Mortgages
Website	HUD LEAN 232 Website	http://portal.hud.gov/hudportal/HUD?src=/Federal_housing_administration/healthcare_facilities/section_232/lean_processing_page

B. General Terms and Requirements

Similar to multifamily mortgage loans insured under the Act, Section 232 Loans are made by HUD-approved lenders and endorsed for mortgage insurance by HUD at closing. While there are some processing differences, the general procedure in which the lender underwrites the loan and presents it to HUD for insurance of the loan is the same.[9] Section 232 Loans may be securitized by the lender with Government National Mortgage Association mortgage-backed securities.

---

9. Processing of multifamily mortgage insurance is described *supra* at Ch. 1.

With the exception of 232/223(a)(7) Loans (defined below), the term of Section 232 Loans ranges from 35 to 40 years.[10] Section 232 Loans are fixed-interest-rate loans.[11] Generally, the mortgagor may be a profit-motivated or nonprofit entity; however, the mortgagor must be a single-asset entity.[12]

C. Eligible Facilities

Mortgage insurance under Section 232 is available to four broad categories of residential health-care facilities, discussed in detail below. In general, HUD will not insure a loan for a facility unless it has a certificate of need, if applicable, and is licensed and regulated by the state or municipality in which it is located. In areas where licenses are not issued, HUD may look for other assurances that the facility complies with all state and local requirements.[13]

1. *Nursing Homes—also known as Skilled Nursing Facilities (SNF)*

The statute defines nursing homes as facilities for convalescents or others who are not acutely ill and do not require hospital care, but who do require skilled medical care and nursing services. In nursing homes, care is provided by and/or under the supervision of medical professionals licensed by the state where the facility is located.[14] Nursing homes may be publically or privately owned by profit-motivated or nonprofit entities.[15] Nursing homes may include additional facilities for nonresidential care for the elderly or others with disabilities.[16] The statute also includes in the definition of nursing home and intermediate-care facility such additional facilities as may be authorized by the Secretary for the nonresident care of elderly individuals and others who are able to live independently but who require care during the day.[17]

2. *Intermediate-Care/Board-and-Care Facilities (IC Facilities)*

IC facilities are designed for residents who because of "incapacitating infirmities" require continuous care but not medical or nursing services.[18] The statute does not authorize insurance of publicly owned IC facilities. Like nursing homes, IC facilities may include additional facilities for nonresident care (e.g., adult day care).[19]

3. *Board-and-Care Facilities*

Board-and-care facilities are a special category of residential facilities that provide room, board, and "continuous protective oversight." By definition, these facilities are regulated by

---

10. *MAP Guide*, Ch. 3 (2002).
11. *Id.*
12. *Id.*
13. 12 U.S.C. § 1715w(d)(4) (2010).
14. 12 U.S.C. § 1715w(b)(1) (2010).
15. *Id.*
16. HUD, HUD HANDBOOK 4600.1, Para. 2-1E.
17. 12 U.S.C. § 1715w(b)(3) (2010).
18. 12 U.S.C. § 1715w(b)(2) (2010).
19. *See supra* note 10.

the state under Section 1616 of the Social Security Act.[20] HUD regulations provide that not less than one bathroom must be provided for every four residents of a board-and-care facility and that access from any bedroom or sleeping area must not pass through a public corridor.[21]

4. Assisted-Living Facilities (ALF)

The statute defines ALFs as licensed facilities that make available to residents supportive services to assist residents in the "activities of daily living," which include, but are not limited to, bathing, dressing, eating, shopping, taking medication, managing money, and housework.[22] ALFs must include separate dwelling units for residents and common areas appropriate for supportive services. Resident units may include separate bathrooms and kitchens. An ALF insured under Section 232 may be publicly or privately owned.[23]

D. Types of 232 Loans

Similar to multifamily mortgage insurance programs, new construction, substantial rehabilitation, supplemental, and refinancing loans may be insured under Section 232. Underwriting criteria for each program vary.

1. 232 New Construction and Substantial Rehabilitation

Loans financing the new construction of eligible facilities are insured under Section 232, as are loans financing the repair of an existing eligible facility where the hard costs of repairs, replacements, improvements, and additions exceed 15 percent of the facility's value after completion or where two or more major building components are being replaced (Substantial Rehabilitation loans). Maximum loan amounts for new construction and substantial rehabilitation Section 232 Loans are set at the lesser of the application amount, a percentage of value, the debt serviceable by a percentage of net operating income (NOI), rehabilitation costs, and replacement cost less the amount of grants and gifts.[24] The applicable percentages and criteria vary by the type of Section 232 Facility and whether the borrower is profit-motivated or nonprofit.

2. 232/223(f)

Loans used to purchase or refinance Section 232 eligible facilities may be insured under Section 232 pursuant to Section 223(f) of the Act. As with multifamily loans insured pursuant to Section 223(f), there is no requirement that the facility have an FHA-insured loan at the time of the application. Facilities requiring repairs above the substantial rehabilitation thresholds cannot be processed pursuant to Section 223(f). Where a 223(f) loan will be used to refinance existing indebtedness, it is important to note that debt-seasoning requirements of up

---

20. 42 U.S.C. § 1382e(e) (2010).
21. 24 C.F.R. § 232.2 (2011).
22. 12 U.S.C. § 1715w (b)(6).
23. *Id.*
24. 12 U.S.C. § 1715w (d)(2), and *MAP Guide*, Ch. 8.8 (March 15, 2002).

to five years may apply when calculating the permitted loan amount.[25] No equity takeout is permitted.[26] Loan amounts are based on the lesser of (i) a percentage of the value (as repaired); (ii) a percentage of acquisition or refinancing costs; and (iii) the debt service supportable by a percentage of NOI. Applicable percentages are determined by the type of borrower and the nature of the transaction (acquisition or refinancing).[27]

3. 232/223(a)(7)

Eligible facilities currently financed with a Section 232 Loan may be eligible to refinance the Section 232 Loan with a new first mortgage loan insured under Section 232 pursuant to Section 223(a)(7) (232/223(a)(7) Loan).[28] These loans are used primarily to lower interest rates on existing FHA properties. The term of a 232/223(a)(7) Loan generally may not exceed the term of the existing 232 Loan; however, maturity may be extended by up to 12 years if required for project feasibility.[29] 232/223(a)(7) Loans are limited to the lesser of (i) 90 percent of the value of the facility; (ii) the total outstanding indebtedness on the existing FHA-insured loan plus the cost of improvements required and the debt incurred to make the necessary improvements; and (iii) loan closing charges, or the amount of debt supported by 90 percent of NOI.[30] The maximum insurable mortgage calculation prevents equity takeouts.

4. 232/241

Section 241 supplemental loans are second mortgage loans available only to mortgagors/properties that currently have FHA-insured first mortgage loans. Section 241 loans may be used to finance repairs, improvements, and additions.[31] The proceeds of the loan also may be used to purchase equipment for the facility.[32] It is worth noting that HUD typically does not permit private second mortgages on properties with Section 232 Loans, so the Section 241 loan is a unique product.[33] The maximum loan amount is 90 percent of the value of the addition or improvements, provided that the Section 241 loan must not exceed an amount that when added to the outstanding balance of the existing FHA insured loan is more than the

---

25. U.S. Dep't of Housing and Urban Development, HUD's LEAN 232 Program Update as of April 10, 2009, *available at* http://portal.hud.gov/hudportal/HUD?src=/federal_housing_administration/healthcare_facilities/section_232/lean_processing_page/underwriting_guidance_home_page (last accessed Dec. 2, 2011).
26. HUD, HUD HANDBOOK 4600.1, para. 14-9; *MAP Guide*, Ch. 3.11 (2002).
27. *MAP Guide*, Ch. 8.9 (2002).
28. 12 U.S.C. § 1715n(a)(7) (2010).
29. HUD, HUD HANDBOOK 4567.1, Ch. 2–4
30. *Id.* at Ch. 2–2.
31. 12 U.S.C. § 1715z-6 (2010).
32. *Id.*
33. *MAP Guide*, revisions to Ch. 8.10. Private secured secondary financing is permitted only for loans insured under Section 232/223(f). Private secondary financing for loans insured under any other section must be unsecured. All private secondary financing is payable only from surplus cash/residual receipts. Secured secondary from a public source is permitted for loans under Section 232, but is also payable only from surplus cash/residual receipts.

maximum insurable mortgage under the section of the National Housing Act pursuant to which the outstanding loan is insured.[34]

E. LEAN Processing for New Section 232 Loans

1. Application

OHP's LEAN approach to processing new loan applications requires a more in-depth submission at the initial loan application. To standardize processing of Section 232 Loans, OHP has developed a standard underwriting narrative and extensive checklists for use in the submission and review of Section 232 applications.[35] Much of the MAP Guide guidance regarding processing no longer applies to Section 232 applications.

Under LEAN, Section 232 applications include super certifications from the lender, the borrower and its principal, the facility operator and its principal, and the management agent that cover many of the certifications historically delivered at closing. Such certifications include: "Byrd Amendment" certifications regarding lobbying, identity of interest certifications, lender certifications regarding due diligence for the Section 232 loan, borrower and operator certifications of compliance with the Fair Housing Act and Equal Employment Opportunity Act, and borrower acknowledgments regarding standard mortgage insurance requirements.[36]

OHP also requires the submission of many legal documents at the application stage. Loan documents are not submitted with the legal package at this stage, but all other documents requiring legal review are submitted at the application stage, including organizational documents, accounts receivable financing documents, and a pro forma title policy. The documents submitted at this stage should include any HUD-required language and provisions, but may be in draft form.[37] Given the shift in the timing of many of the certifications and the submission of the legal documents, both lenders and borrowers should engage counsel early in the application process to ensure smooth processing.

2. Application Processing

The large number of applications that precipitated the transition to LEAN has continued since the transition to LEAN, and while OHP aims to reduce processing time, it continues to experience a heavy pipeline of projects.[38] To expedite processing, OHP has established a

---

34. *Id.*

35. The standard underwriting narrative and checklists are available under the applicable program link at HUD, Underwriting Guidance Home Page, http://portal.hud.gov/hudportal/HUD?src=/federal_housing_administration/healthcare_facilities/section_232/lean_processing_page/underwriting_guidance_home_page (last accessed Dec. 5, 2011).

36. *See id.* for Lender Consolidated Certifications, Mortgagor Consolidated Certifications, Principal of Mortgagor Consolidated Certifications, Operator Consolidated Certifications, Principal of Operator Certifications, and Management Agent Certifications.

37. U.S. Dep't of Housing and Urban Development, HUD's LEAN 232 Program Update as of Sept. 1, 2011, and Feb. 2, 2012, *available at* http://portal.hud.gov/hudportal/documents/huddoc?id=Search EmailBlast2011.doc (last accessed April 8, 2012).

38. *See Our Queues, Information on Projects with New Units, and Statistics,* HUD, Underwriting Guidance Home Page, *supra* at note 35.

queue system for some loans. Complete applications are submitted by the lender to a HUD office designated by HUD and placed in a queue with other Section 232 Loans of the same type.[39] When a project reaches the top of the queue, it is assigned to an underwriter in a HUD field office, which may or may not be in the state where the facility is located. Issues or deficiencies noted during the review must be timely and satisfactorily addressed or the application may be returned to the queue.

Unlike the multifamily loan application process in which legal review begins after issuance of the firm commitment, substantive legal review for Section 232 Loans begins during the application stage by HUD counsel. Generally, minor comments and revisions to documents may be addressed in the draft closing docket submitted after the issuance of the firm commitment; however, more substantive issues may require correction before a firm commitment can be issued.

3. From Commitment to Closing

When application and underwriting review is complete, the underwriter makes a recommendation to OHP's internal loan committee in Washington regarding the issuance of a firm commitment. If the application is approved after review by the OHP loan committee, OHP issues a firm commitment to insure the proposed loan (the "commitment"). After the lender and borrower have reviewed and executed the commitment, a fully executed commitment is returned to the OHP underwriter. The lender also works with the underwriter to address any special conditions to the commitment, such as critical repairs to the property. Once the executed commitment has been returned and all special conditions have been cleared, an OHP closing coordinator is assigned. Generally, a draft closing docket must be submitted to the closing coordinator and HUD counsel within a relatively short period of time following the assignment of the closing coordinator.[40] If the closing submission is untimely or incomplete, the loan may be returned to the closing queue, so it is critical that the parties communicate regarding the status of the application and begin preparation of the closing docket, particularly updates to third-party reports, prior to issuance of the firm commitment.

4. Special Processing—Portfolio Transactions

The Section 232 program has attracted a number of national and regional operators of healthcare facilities. The insurance of multiple Section 232 Loans secured by separate facilities owned or operated by the same parent entity presents additional business risks and considerations for HUD as the insurer of the loan. To evaluate these additional concerns, HUD has established an additional level of review for "portfolio" transactions.

The threshold requirements and criteria for portfolio reviews are outlined in HUD Housing Notice 01-03, "Review of Health Care Facility Portfolios and Changes to the Section 232 Program" (H 01-03). Portfolio review is triggered by the volume of Section 232 Loans that

---

39. *Id.*
40. U.S. Dep't of Housing and Urban Development, HUD's LEAN 232 Program Update as of Jan. 25, 2011, *available at* http://portal.hud.gov/hudportal/HUD?src=/federal_housing_administration/healthcare_facilities/section_232/lean_processing_page/underwriting_guidance_home_page.

an owner processes in an 18-month period. For purposes of H 01-03, HUD has defined the owner as the mortgagor entity or an affiliate.[41] People or entities are defined as affiliates under H 01-03 if, directly or indirectly, either one controls or has the power to control the other, or, a third person controls or has the power to control both.[42]

Criteria for HUD portfolio review are determined by the size of the portfolio: large, midsize, or small.[43] Large portfolios are defined as an owner/operator seeking Section 232 Loans for 50 or more projects in an 18-month period or combined estimated mortgage amounts exceeding $250,000,000.[44] Midsize portfolios are currently defined as an owner/operator seeking Section 232 Loans for 11 to 49 projects in any 18-month period or combined estimated mortgage amounts of $75,000,001 up to $250,000,000. Small portfolios are defined as those where the owner/operator is seeking Section 232 financing for up to 10 facilities within any 18-month period and has combined estimated mortgage amounts of up to $75 million. Applications for portfolios of Section 232 Loans should include a certification disclosing the number, location, and estimated mortgage amount of all actual or potential Section 232 applications or pre-applications to be submitted to HUD within an 18-month period and the owner/operator's level of involvement.

Small portfolios may be processed without HUD Headquarters review. For large and midsize portfolio reviews, HUD Headquarters performs a mortgage credit review before any applications are submitted to the Hub with jurisdiction for processing. Before submitting the portfolio for processing, owners of large and midsize portfolios must purchase a review and analysis from one of the major rating agencies that have developed such products for HUD (e.g., Dun & Bradstreet). Rating agency reports will require the submission of additional documentation to the rating agency by the owner/operator and may include a site visit and additional review. Once approved, midsize and large portfolios of 232/223(f) refinancings must be processed in batches and all applications must be complete for batches to move forward.[45] Loans may be closed concurrently or on a staggered basis, but logistics of closing must be carefully coordinated with HUD closing counsel.

---

41. HUD, Housing Notice 01-03, Appendix 1.
42. Note that under HUD Housing Notice 01-03 indicia of control include, but are not limited to, interlocking management or ownership, identity of interests among family members, shared facilities and equipment, or common use of employees. Additionally, a business entity organized following the suspension or debarment of a person or entity that has the same or similar management, ownership, or principal employees as the suspended, debarred, ineligible, or voluntarily excluded person or entity may also be deemed an affiliate of that person or entity.
43. U.S. Dep't of Housing and Urban Development, Office of Healthcare Programs, *Lender Underwriting Training* (Sept. 13, 2011). In connection with forthcoming guidance, OHP has proposed increased thresholds for small and midsize portfolios.
44. HUD, Housing Notice 01-03.
45. U.S. Dep't of Housing and Urban Development, HUD's LEAN 232 Program Update as of Nov. 2, 2011, *available at* http://portal.hud.gov/hudportal/documents/huddoc?id=Search EmailBlast2010.doc (last accessed Dec. 5, 2011).

F. Special Issues in Underwriting and Closing 232 Loans

1. Owner/Operator/Management Agent Structure

HUD recognizes that many Section 232 Facilities are owned and operated by separate entities for financial and operational reasons. Operating leases and management agreements are both permitted in Section 232 projects, subject to HUD requirements intended to protect HUD's interest in the mortgage security.

a. Permitted Structures

i. Operating Lease

Section 232 Loans are available only to owners of eligible projects. HUD permits the facility to be leased by the owner/mortgagor to an operating lessee that will carry out the daily operations of the project. The operating lessee may be an affiliate of the owner or an unaffiliated entity experienced in the operation of Section 232 Facilities. Regardless of the relationship between the parties, the lessor must be the owner/mortgagor under the HUD insured loan and the operating lease must meet HUD requirements.[46] Both the owner/mortgagor and the operating lessee are reviewed in the Section 232 underwriting and both are subject to HUD's previous participation (2530) review.[47, 48]

A. Operating Lease Requirements

Any operating lease of a Section 232 project must be approved by HUD. HUD requires a written lease that incorporates certain HUD required provisions set out in the HUD Addendum to Operating Lease available on the LEAN website. Key HUD required provisions include subordination of the operating lease to the mortgage, an agreement to comply with HUD requirements, an acknowledgment that amounts due under the operating lease are sufficient to operate the property and enable the mortgagor to meet all expenses associated with the Section 232 Loan, and provisions regarding licensing, insurance, management contracts, and government receivables.

There is no specific requirement for the term of the operating lease; however, HUD must have the ability to terminate the lease in the event of a default and the lease may not be terminated without prior HUD approval. An estoppel from the operator and recorded evidence of the lease will typically be required.

Where the mortgagor and the operator are unaffiliated, HUD may permit a subordina-

---

46. In limited circumstances, HUD may insure a mortgage loan secured by a ground lease interest; however the mortgagor must be the lessee under a ground lease, not merely an operating lease. For additional information on requirements for ground leases, *see MAP Guide*, Ch. 7.16 (2002).

47. For additional information regarding 2530, *see infra* at Ch. 5.

48. *See* Closing Checklists and Legal Punchlists for operator submission requirements, HUD, Sample Closing Documents, *available at* http://portal.hud.gov/hudportal/HUD?src=/federal_housing_administration/healthcare_facilities/section_232/lean_processing_page/underwriting_guidance_home_page/sample_closing_documents (last accessed Dec. 5, 2011).

tion, non-disturbance, and attornment agreement (SNDA). SNDAs are not permitted where the operator is an affiliated entity in order to protect HUD's ability to remove the affiliated operator in the event of default under the mortgage or regulatory agreements.

B. Regulatory Agreements for Operators

In addition to incorporating HUD-required provisions in the operating lease, operating lessees must enter into a Regulatory Agreement (HUD-92466-NHL), as modified for the LEAN program.[49] The Regulatory Agreement establishes a relationship between the operator and HUD and requires the operator's compliance with HUD requirements, including, but not limited to:

- Lease must be subordinate to the mortgage.
- Lease payments must be sufficient to maintain the property and service the loan.
- Project will be used only as a Section 232 Facility.
- HUD may terminate the lease for a violation of the Regulatory Agreement on notice to the owner and operator.
- No early termination is allowed except with HUD approval.
- HUD must approve any change in operator/lessee.
- No change to the bed capacity of the project can be made without prior HUD approval.
- Lessee agrees to grant HUD a first-lien security interest in all of its personal property related to the facility.

If the operator fails to cure a violation of the Regulatory Agreement within 30 days of notice of violation from HUD, the operating lease may be cancelled. The cure period may be extended if additional time is required to cure, provided certain conditions are met.[50]

C. Operator Security Agreement

Where the project is subject to an operating lease, the operating lessee also will be required to enter into a security agreement with the lender, naming HUD as an additional secured party, to ensure that HUD obtains security interests in all licenses and certificates needed to operate the property, as well as any accounts and equipment held by the operator.

ii. Management Agent

Owner-operated projects and projects subject to an operating lease also may have a management agent. The HUD requirements and level of review of the management agent in a Section 232 Facility is determined by the management agent's responsibilities and level of interaction with the facility staff and patients/residents. All management agents are subject to 2530 clear-

---

49. LEAN Rider to Nursing Home Regulatory Agreement, *available at* http://portal.hud.gov/huddoc/LEAN_Rider_NH_Reg_Agree_11.doc (last accessed Dec. 2, 2011).
50. *See* LEAN Rider to Nursing Home Regulatory Agreement for Nursing Homes, para. 10, *supra* at note 48.

ance and review of the management agreement and must submit a modified version of the Project Owner/Management Agent Certification (9839) and a consolidated certification from the management agent.[51] If the management agent will have any interaction with patients or will oversee the facility staff, HUD may also require that the management agent satisfy other requirements. The existing FHA management documents are designed only for multifamily housing properties and may require revision or modification to avoid inaccurate certifications by either party.

2. Security for the Loan

Given the specialized nature of Section 232 Facilities, the security for the loan must be carefully considered. A Section 232 Facility without a license and certificate of need is considerably less valuable, as is a Section 232 Facility without the necessary equipment. Additionally, unlike a multifamily property where rents are received on a monthly basis, many Section 232 Facilities rely heavily on reimbursements from Medicare, Medicaid, and insurance companies, which may lag by several months. Given the considerable expense in operating a Section 232 Facility and the reliance on reimbursements, it is critical that the lender and HUD have a secured interest in the facility's license(s) and accounts.

a. Deposit Account Control Agreements

In the transition to LEAN, HUD reevaluated the legal requirements for perfection of the lender's security interest in the accounts and receivables of Section 232 projects and as a result began requiring a Deposit Account Control Agreement (DACA) and a Government Health-Care Receivables Deposit Account Agreement (DAISA).

The mortgagor and the operator will enter into a security agreement in favor of the lender. The attached collateral description should specifically reference the license, certificate of need, health-care insurance receivables, government receivables, and deposit accounts. The lender's security interest in health insurance receivables (non-governmental) and most other personal property attaches when the security agreement is delivered, provided other requirements for enforcement are met and the security interest is perfected by filing a UCC-1 financing statement in the borrower's state of organization.[52] On the other hand, the lender's security interest in a deposit account, such as the project account, attaches and is perfected only if the lender has "control" of the collateral.[53] In the context of an FHA-insured loan where the facility will continue to be operated by the account holder until an event of default, the most viable means of lender control is through the agreement between the borrower, the bank, and the secured party, also known as the DACA.

---

51. Requirements can be found on the relevant application checklists available on the Underwriting Guidance Home Page, *supra* at note 35.
52. U.C.C. § 9-203, 9-301 (2001).
53. U.C.C. §§ 9-312, 9-314 (2001). Pursuant to UCC § 9-104, a secured party is deemed to have control of a deposit account under the UCC if (1) the secured party is the bank holding the account; (2) the borrower, the bank, and the secured party have agreed that the bank will take instructions from the secured party without further consent from the borrower; or (3) the secured party becomes the bank's customer with respect to the account.

To attach and perfect the security interest in the project's operating accounts, the owner, the bank holding the operating accounts, and the lender enter into a DACA, which typically creates a springing lockbox account. In the event of a default, the lender may give notice to the bank in the form prescribed by the DACA and immediately exercise control over the account.

Perfection of the lender's secured interest is further complicated by Medicare and Medicaid law, which generally prohibits assignment of Medicare and Medicaid receivables or the account into which they are deposited.[54] To comply with this law and ensure that proceeds are available as security for the 232 Loan, a two-account structure has been developed. Under this structure, Medicare and Medicaid payments are deposited into a separate government receivables account subject to a DAISA. The DAISA, which is an agreement between the owner, the bank, and the lender, typically provides that all funds in the government receivables account will be swept on a daily basis into the project's operating account. The instructions in the DAISA are revocable, which avoids violations of Medicare and Medicaid law, but also prevents perfection of the lender's security interest in the government receivables account. To give the lender control of the proceeds of the government receivables account, the funds in the DAISA account are swept into an operating account subject to a DACA. The daily sweep allows the proceeds to remain identifiable while moving them into an account in which the lender can have an attached and perfected security interest.

The party entitled to receive the government receivables and in whose name the project operating account is held must be a party to the DACA and DAISA. In many cases, this will be the operating lessee. Facilities that do not accept government receivables (private-pay facilities) will not have a DAISA; however, the operating account will be subject to a DACA.

Lenders and their counsel should discuss this requirement with prospective borrowers early in the process as some owners/operators may need to establish separate government receivables accounts that may require several months' lead time. Additionally, many banks have their own forms of DACA and DAISA that may need to be negotiated with the bank, account holder, and HUD. HUD has collected forms that have been negotiated with a number of national and regional banks and will provide forms on request. HUD will accept other forms provided that they meet certain requirements. One key requirement is that HUD cannot be obligated to indemnify the bank in the event it accepts an assignment of the loan or otherwise becomes the lender or owner of the project.

b. Collateral Including License/Certificate of Need

As noted above, in most states, licenses and certificates of need (CON) are required to operate a Section 232 Facility. Without this license or certificate of need, the project may not operate

---

54. 42 U.S.C. § 1395g (c), 42 U.S.C. § 1395u(b)(6), 42 U.S.C. § 1396a(a)(32). For a more thorough discussion of the interplay of Medicare and Medicaid anti-assignment law and security interests under the Uniform Commercial Code, *see* Kimberly E. Zirkle, *Not So Perfect: The Disconnect Between Medicare and the Uniform Commercial Code Regarding Health Care Insurance Receivables,* 9 N.C. BANKING INST. 373 (2005), and Andrea C. Barach & Wendy A. Chow, *FHA Insured Loans for Long-Term Healthcare Facilities: Recent Developments as a Popular Product Evolves to Meet Growing Needs,* THE HEALTH LAWYER (an ABA publication), Vol. 23, No. 5 (June 2011).

as a health-care facility. This creates a risk for HUD that in the event of default and assignment of the loan, it would not be able to sell the facility for an amount sufficient to cover the insurance claim. To mitigate this risk, HUD requires that the license and certificate of need be included in the description of collateral for the Section 232 Loan.

3. Accounts Receivable Financing

A majority of Section 232 Facilities rely on reimbursements from Medicare, Medicaid, and private insurance companies for services provided to patients/residents. As noted above, reimbursements, particularly Medicare and Medicaid payments, may not be received for several weeks or months after services are rendered, which has the potential to create short-term cash-flow shortfalls. To address the shortfall and finance operations until reimbursements are received, many Section 232 Facility operators utilize accounts receivable financing (AR Financing) from a private lender. HUD does not provide or insure AR Financing.

AR Financing is typically a working capital loan from a bank or other lending institution to the owner or operator of a Section 232 Facility or its parent. These loans are secured by the receivables of a Section 232 Facility, including Medicare, Medicaid, long-term care insurance, and private-pay receivables. HUD recognizes the need for AR Financing in Section 232 Facilities and values the additional oversight provided by the accounts receivable lender; nonetheless, HUD must review and consent to AR Financing for Section 232 projects to assess the impact of the AR Financing on the overall financial viability of the project and distinguish the security interests of the FHA lender from those of the AR lender.[55]

a. General Program Guidance and Requirements

The requirements for AR Financing are outlined in HUD Housing Notice 08-09. Additional guidance is found on the LEAN 232 website.

HUD's primary concern when reviewing requests for consent to AR Financing is the financial viability of the project.[56] HUD typically recommends that the owner, operator, AR lender, and mortgagee meet with HUD before the request is submitted. HUD accepts for review AR Financing that is based on a percentage of receivables consistent with prudent business practice. Typically, the loan to receivable ratio does not exceed 85 percent and the AR should not be aged more than 120 days.[57]

HUD consent to AR Financing is based on a holistic assessment of the impact of AR Financing on the financial viability of the project, but the following criteria and safeguards should be met:

- Funds must be used as provided under the HUD Rider to Intercreditor Agreement.
- Cross-collateralization should be permitted only for those facilities subject to FHA-insured mortgages.
- Regulatory Agreements and Riders should be executed.

---

55. HUD Housing Notice 08-09.
56. *Id.* at p.2.
57. *Id.* at p.3.

- AR lender should have a first priority interest in the operator's AR and the FHA Mortgagee should have a second priority interest until the AR Financing is repaid.
- AR Lender must have sufficient experience to monitor the mortgagor.

Requests for consent to AR Financing should be included in the application and typically include a narrative and financial analysis of the terms, description of the security, and schedule of proposed fees. Additional documentation will include the draft loan agreement, draft DAISA and DACA, a narrative describing the mortgagor's and operator's legal structure, and a draft flow of funds.[58] Conflicts or identities of interest between any of the parties must be disclosed. A legal opinion from the operator's counsel also may be required to demonstrate that the operator has the authority to carry out the AR Financing transaction and that the mortgagee's, HUD's, and the AR lender's security interests have attached and been perfected. Additional submissions may be required to allow HUD to fully evaluate the impact of the proposed AR Financing on the financial viability of the Section 232 Facility.

The AR lender will require a security interest in the health-care receivables and deposit accounts of the Section 232 Facility, which typically requires the two-account DACA and DAISA structure described earlier in this chapter. HUD also requires a security interest in the health-care receivables and deposits as security for the Section 232 Loan, but if it consents to the AR Financing, it will permit the AR lender to have the first priority security interest in the AR Financing. The parties must execute an intercreditor agreement to clarify these interests. HUD has produced form intercreditor agreements and requires the use of a form HUD Rider to the Intercreditor Agreement that addresses the HUD requirements set forth above.[59]

Additionally, given that AR Financing is generally provided to the parent or sponsor, AR Financing documents often provide for cross-collateralization of receivables from affiliated facilities. AR Collateral for a Section 232 property may not be used to collateralize AR Financing on a non-FHA insured property. If the AR Collateral of a property proposed for Section 232 financing has been cross-collateralized with non-FHA insured property, the AR Lender must agree to terminate its interest and any contractual agreements between the mortgagor/operator and the AR Lender with respect to AR Financing on non-FHA insured properties.[60]

4. Master Leases/Portfolio Transactions

As discussed in this chapter, insurance of multiple Section 232 Loans secured by several distinct facilities owned or operated by the same parent entity or affiliated entities creates additional considerations and risks for HUD. To mitigate this risk, HUD requires the use of a

---

58. *Id.*
59. HUD, Rider to Intercreditor Agreement, *available at* http://portal.hud.gov/hudportal/documents/huddoc? id=RidertoIntercreditor.doc (last accessed December 7, 2011).
60. Koren McKenzie-John, U.S. Dep't of Housing and Urban Development, Office of Healthcare Programs, Lender Underwriting Training (Sept. 14, 2011).

master lease structure for all portfolio transactions.[61] Under the master lease structure, each mortgagor is a lessor under the master lease. The master tenant, a special purpose entity created for this purpose, is the only lessee under the lease. The master tenant then subleases each facility to the respective operator. The master tenant collects from the subleases rents totaling at least the "Base Rent," which is the aggregate amount of money needed to service the debt and cover the expenses associated with all mortgaged properties. The master tenant may reallocate each project's contribution to the base rent if necessary to maintain the financial health of the facilities.

HUD must approve all master leases and can provide sample forms. HUD requires that the master lease be renewed through the mortgage term and release from the master lease is not automatic on prepayment/maturity.[62] HUD will require a standard cross-default provision providing that a default under any of the subleases will result in a default under all subleases. These cross-default provisions guard against the risk that the master tenant/sponsor will cherry-pick the profitable facilities in a bankruptcy and leave the lender/FHA with failing facilities while retaining profitable affiliated facilities.[63] The master lease structure raises a number of issues of liability that should be carefully reviewed by the prospective borrower and their counsel.[64] Furthermore, given the cross-default provisions, it is critical that the owner and lender have tools to remediate defaults and other issues.

The master lease also must be subordinate to the mortgage through a subordination agreement. Where the owner and operator are unaffiliated, a subordination, non-disturbance, and attornment agreement (SNDA) may be permitted to evidence the parties' agreement that in the event of a default, the operator will attorn to a new landlord and the landlord will not disturb the operator's lease.

G. Asset Management Issues

OHP handles all asset management responsibilities for Section 232 Facilities. OHP asset managers are currently assigned based on the facility's mortgagor. All properties financed by a mortgagor should be managed by the same asset manager or group of asset managers. OHP stresses the relationship between the lender and HUD, and, more so than in multifamily asset matters, the lender and its counsel may take the lead in communications with HUD. While any number of issues may arise over the life of a loan and the facility that secures it, a few common issues are addressed below.

---

61. HUD has required a master lease for groups of as few as three facilities. Guidance on master leases has been provided primarily through checklists and LEAN email blasts, and at Underwriting Trainings. Additional formal guidance is anticipated. The information in this section reflects HUD's current policies and presentations made at U.S. Dep't of Housing and Urban Development, Office of Healthcare Programs, Lender Underwriting Training (Sept. 14, 2011).

62. U.S. Dep't of Housing and Urban Development, Office of Healthcare Programs, Lender Underwriting Training (Sept. 14, 2011).

63. *Id.*

64. *See* Andrea C. Barach & Wendy A. Chow. *FHA Insured Loans for Long Term Healthcare Facilities: Recent Developments as a Popular Product Evolves to Meet Growing Needs*, THE HEALTH LAWYER (an ABA publication), June 2001, at 9, for a summary discussion of market risks addressed by master lease structure and the legal issues it raises.

1. REAC

Section 232 Facilities are subject to regular physical inspection by HUD's Real Estate Assessment Center.[65] These inspections, commonly known as REAC inspections, include an inspection of a portion of the property for compliance with Housing Quality Standards. The frequency of inspection is determined by the facility's most recent inspection score.[66] REAC inspections have proved problematic for many Section 232 Facilities as the Housing Quality Standards on which inspection criteria are based are created for multifamily housing projects and not well suited to a long-term care facility. There has been some discussion of eliminating this requirement for Section 232 Facilities, given that such facilities are typically heavily regulated and regularly inspected by state authorities.

2. Transfers of Physical Assets

Transfers of ownership of the Section 232 Facility and transfers of ownership interests in the mortgagor are considered transfers of physical assets (TPA) and subject to review by OHP. Transfers of the ownership of the project or a 100 percent ownership interest in the mortgagor are considered a full TPA and require a thorough review. Transfers of smaller interests in the mortgagor may be considered a modified TPA and require a more streamlined review.[67] The general TPA criteria apply to Section 232 Loans, but OHP has added additional healthcare-specific requirements.[68] A detailed checklist for all TPAs can be found on the LEAN website. Changes in the management agent or operator/lessee also require HUD approval and are addressed in the same checklist. TPA applications are first reviewed by the lender and then submitted to the OHP asset manager for further review.

3. Distressed Assets

While HUD and the lender make every effort to underwrite a performing loan, even the best owners and operators can experience economic conditions or operating challenges that put the Section 232 Facility in distress. OHP prides itself in active management of its assets. Where a facility is unable to meet its financial obligations, the mortgagor should communicate with the lender and HUD to explore options. Before accepting an assignment of the Section 232 mortgage from the lender, OHP typically explores a 232/223(a)(7) to reduce the interest rate and debt service on the FHA-insured loan and improve the facility's financial position.

OHP also has begun processing partial payments of claims (PPC) on the mortgage insurance. Guidance for PPCs of Section 232 Loans is found in HUD Mortgagee Letter 2011-15, which complements Mortgagee Letter 87-9. Under a PPC, HUD works with the lender to modify the existing mortgage to an amount and level of debt service reasonably supportable by the facility's operations. The difference between the outstanding indebtedness and the modified loan becomes soft debt. PPCs require evidence of a significant contribution by the owner and considerable analysis and supporting documents. The requirements for and pro-

---

65. 24 C.F.R. § 200.853 (2011).
66. 24 C.F.R. §§ 200.855, 200.857 (2011).
67. *See* HUD, HUD Handbook 4350.1, Chapter 13.
68. *See id.*

cessing of a PPC on a Section 232 Loan differ from the requirements and processing for a multifamily PPC.[69]

******

In conclusion, Section 232 offers a unique financing vehicle for nursing homes, intermediate-care facilities, board-and-care homes, and assisted-living facilities. Given the unique nature of the program and HUD's recent attempts to streamline processing, special issues arise that are not encountered in other FHA insurance programs and program requirements are continually changing. The LEAN website is an excellent resource and LEAN e-mail blasts are an essential resource for practitioners working regularly in this area.

II. SECTION 242

A. Authority and Guidance

The Federal Housing Administration's involvement in mortgage insurance for hospital financings was first authorized in 1968 under a newly added Section 242 of the Act.[70] The overarching policy intent was to expand HUD's community development mission and permit HUD to facilitate the construction, rehabilitation, and renovation of facilities[71] that would provide acute care normally furnished by a hospital without regard to the level of public or private support.[72] Congress determined that while there were many financing resources for hospitals that were investment-grade, numerous below–investment grade yet financially feasible hospital facilities were unable to obtain affordable capital.[73] The addition of Section 242 to the Act along with subsequent amendments[74] allowed HUD to expand the playing field for hospitals across the country and provide access to capital that many facilities had previously lacked the ability to secure.

Though historically the 242 Program was overseen by HUD and the Department of Health and Human Services (formerly Health, Education, and Welfare),[75] the OHF under OHP over-

---

69. HUD Handboook 4350.1, Chapter 14 is the primary source of guidance on PPCs and provides that Section 232 Loans are ineligible for processing under Chapter 14.

70. 12 U.S.C. § 1715z-7 (2010).

71. Section 311(a) of the Housing and Community Development Act of 1974 (12 U.S.C. § 1715n(f)) authorized refinancing as well.

72. *See supra*, note 69.

73. HUD.Gov/Federal Housing Administration/Healthcare Programs/Why Choose FHA Mortgage Insurance for Hospitals, *available at* http://portal.hud.gov/hudportal/HUD?src=/federal_housing_administration/healthcare_facilities/mortgage_insurance/why_choose_fha_mortgage_insurance_for_hospitals.

74. Amendments include: Section 110 of HUD Act of 1970 (Pub. L. 91-609) (added for-profit entities as eligible mortgagors under Section 242); Section 315 of the Housing and Community Development Amendments of 1979 (Pub. L. 96-153) (prohibits the use of Ginnie Mae securities with tax-exempt bonds); Hospital Mortgage Insurance Act of 2003 (Pub. L. 108-91) (exempts critical access hospitals from 50% patient day rule); and the Rural Health Care Capital Access Act of 2006 (Pub. L. 109-240) (extended critical access hospital exemption until July 31, 2011).

75. United States Dep't of Housing and Urban Development, Section 242 Hospital Mortgage Insurance Program, *available at* http://portal.hud.gov:80/hudportal/HUD?src=/federal_housing_administration/healthcare_facilities/section_242/additional_resources (last accessed December 6, 2011).

sees the program today.[76] In an effort to increase the viability and transparency of the program, in 2007 the Commissioner issued comprehensive regulations that consolidated most hospital regulations under 24 CFR 200 and 242.[77] As with the Section 232 and other HUD mortgage insurance programs, the Department also had relied on a host of handbooks, notices, and mortgagee letters to supplement and expand the Department's regulatory policies and procedures. While HUD's Handbook, *Mortgage Insurance for Hospitals*, was initially issued in 1973[78] and an updated version has yet to be published, OHP and its predecessors have been issuing updated guidance through Mortgagee Letters, Housing Notices, the OHP program website, and 242 e-mail blasts. Furthermore, HUD has indicated that until such time as a more modern handbook has been cleared for publication, it will provide waivers as needed to conform to current standards.[79] Key HUD resources are listed below.

Key Guidance for Section 242 Loans

Statute	12 U.S.C. § 1715z-7	
Handbook	Handbook 4615.1	*Mortgage Insurance for Hospitals Handbook*
Notices/Letters	Mortgagee Letter 04-08	*Implementation of the Hospital Mortgage Insurance Act of 2003*
	Mortgagee Letter 08-42	*Implementation of 24 CFR Parts 200 and 242, Revisions to the Hospital Mortgage Insurance Program; Final Rule*
	H Notice 09-05 H 10-06	"Hospital Mortgage Insurance: Section 223(f) Refinancing in Conjunction with Section 242 Financing."
Website	*http://portal.hud.gov:80/ hudportal/rc=/federal_housing _administration/healthcare_ facilities/section_242*	HUD 242 OHF Website[80]

---

76. U.S. DEP'T OF HOUSING AND URBAN DEVELOPMENT, SECTION 242 HOSPITAL MORTGAGE INSURANCE PROGRAM, *available at* http://portal.hud.gov:80/hudportal/HUD?src=/federal_housing_administration/healthcare_facilities/section_242 (last accessed Dec. 6, 2011).
77. 72 Fed. Reg. 62,546, Nov. 28, 2007.
78. *See* HUD HANDBOOK 4615.1 and 4615.2 (Supplement to Mortgage Insurance for Hospitals, 242).
79. U.S. DEP'T OF HOUSING AND URBAN DEVELOPMENT, SECTION 242 HOSPITAL MORTGAGE INSURANCE PROGRAM, *available at* http://portal.hud.gov:80/hudportal/HUD?src=/federal_housing_administration/healthcare_facilities/section_242/additional_resources/Helpful Tools, 2011 Lender Training Materials "NEW."
80. *See supra*, note 73.

B. General Terms and Requirements

As with Section 232 and multifamily mortgage loans insured under the Act, loans insured under Section 242 of the Act (Section 242 Loans) are made by HUD-approved lenders and endorsed for mortgage insurance by HUD at closing. Given the uniqueness of hospital transactions, the underwriting and application process is somewhat distinct from its multifamily and Section 232 counterparts.

With the exception of the 242/223(a)(7) Loan (defined below), the term of a Section 242 Loan is 25 years from the start of amortization.[81] Section 242 Loans are fixed-interest-rate loans, though such rates may be different during construction versus on conversion to permanent loan status.[82] Eligible mortgagors include public entities, profit-motivated entities that meet the definition of hospital or nonprofit corporations or associations;[83] however, regardless of organizational type, the mortgagor must be a single-asset entity.[84] The source of funding for Section 242 Loans includes taxable or tax-exempt bonds and Government National Mortgage Association mortgage-backed securities.[85]

1. Eligible Facilities

The National Housing Act requires that a hospital meet three basic criteria:[86]

   a. 50 percent or more of the total patient days must be acute[87] care (i.e., not sub-acute chronic convalescent, nursing-home-type stays);[88]
   b. It must provide community services for inpatient care of injured and sick; and
   c. Facility must be regulated by the state and/or local government bodies.[89]

2. Standard Types of Facilities

The 242 Program has facilitated the development and equipment of a broad array of hospital facilities as outlined below.

   a. *Urban Hospitals.* Traditional urban hospital centers have been the largest recognized users of 242 FHA-insured financing. Several years ago, the Department and others raised concerns about the high concentrations of usage of the 242 Program for such urban hospitals, given that the bulk of them were located in the Northeast, with the

---

81. 24 C.F.R. § 242.27 (2011).
82. *See* 24 C.F.R. § 242.26 (2011).
83. 24 C.F.R. § 242.10 (2011).
84. 24 C.F.R. § 242 *et seq.* (2011).
85. *See supra*, note 74.
86. *See supra*, note 1.
87. Such acute care is deemed inpatient medical care that excludes categories of "chronic convaelescent and rest, drug and alcoholic, epileptic, mentally deficient, mental, nervous and mental, and tuberculosis." 24 C.F.R. § 242.1 (2011). *See also supra*, note 79.
88. Excludes Critical-Access Hospitals (those facilities designated as such under the Medicare Rural Hospital Flexibility Program, 7/31/2011. *See* Hospital Mortgage Insurance Act of 2003, Pub. L. 108-91 as codified and amended.
89. Such regulation can be in the form of a Certificate of Need (CON) and/or licensing issued by the state, or if not the state, the local municipality. 24 C.F.R. § 242.8 (2011).

heaviest concentrations in New York state.[90] To ensure there was a greater range of hospitals accessing the 242 Program, certain statutory provisions were altered that broadened the appeal to those facilities previously disqualified from participation.[91]

b. *Rural Hospitals, Critical-Access Hospitals (CAHs).* Long having been excluded from FHA financing because of the statutory requirement that 50 percent of the beds be used for acute rather than sub-acute care, rural and CAHs were provided relief in amendments to the Act passed in 2003.[92] Under such statutory modifications, any hospital meeting the definition of critical-access hospital (as designated under the Medicare Rural Hospital Flexibility Program) would be exempted from the 50 percent requirement.[93] Often these are smaller hospitals with 25 beds or less.[94]

c. *Start-Up Hospitals.* While currently within its authority, HUD will review start-up hospitals carefully, given that there is little track record on which to do a risk analysis.[95] Such review includes a look at projected cash flows, evidence of operating cash, review of the need for such a hospital facility, hospital management's prior experience with start-up hospitals, and the amount of reliance on a limited number of individuals for management and recruitment. Threshold issues for start-up hospital viability are failure of existing hospital facilities in the area and an ability to meet market demand/need.[96]

d. Physician Owned/Investor Owned. While not prohibited, HUD targets a special focus on physician or other professional ownership of a hospital given the insurance risk that such facilities have had historically. As part of its overall review, HUD will perform an intensive risk assessment of all federal, state, and local regulatory practices regarding self-dealing, kickbacks, and related issues that could increase FHA risk.[97]

e. Design-Build Facilities. Although limited to loans of $60 million or less, such hospitals have a single team that will handle design and construction, thus theoretically reducing costs and providing a resource for dealing with the up-front cost of development.[98]

f. Leased Hospital. HUD generally prohibits transactions that involve a complete lease of the hospital facility. Exceptions are considered where leasing is a result of state

---

90. *See* GAO Report, *Hospital Mortgage Insurance Program: Program and Risk Management Could Be Enhanced,* February 2006.

91. Hospital Mortgage Insurance Act of 2003, Pub. L. 108-91, as codified and amended.

92. *Id.*

93. 24 C.F.R. § 242.1 (2011).

94. *See supra,* note 74. Note that the authority for such exemption expired in July 2011. A bipartisan proposal to extend the deadline has been introduced. *See* S. 1431, 112 Cong., 1st Session (2011) and H.R. 2573, 112 Cong., 1st Session (2011).

95. Hospital Mortgage Insurance Program, Section 242 of the National Housing Act, Applicant's Guide Pre-Application, Office of Hospital Facilities, Summer 2011, last revised August 2011, Start-Up Supplement.

96. *Id.*

97. *See* 24 C.F.R. 242.9 (2011).

98. *See* discussion, Mike Mazer, Rod Owens & Noreen Quereshi, *FHA Hospital Mortgage Insurance: An Affordable Source of Construction Capital in a Turbulent Market,* Bloomberg Law Reports, HEALTH LAW, Vol. 1, No. 7 (August 2008).

law prohibitions on mortgaging state-owned projects as well as instances where leases would result in protection against a claim on the FHA insurance fund.[99]

3. Types of FHA-Insured Hospital Loan Products

The Department has the authority to provide insured loans for new construction, substantial rehabilitation/modernization, and refinancing, as listed below.

a. *Section 242 New Construction/Substantial Rehabilitation.* HUD will insure loans that involve construction of a new hospital facility or the substantial rehabilitation (and, as necessary, replacement) of an existing hospital facility.[100]

b. *Section 242/223(f) Refinancing of Hospitals.* Historically, a new construction program, the 242 Program, was expanded via authority contained in the Housing and Community Development Act of 1987 to permit the insurance of mortgages used to purchase or refinance mortgages under Section 242 pursuant to Section 223(f) of the National Housing Act.[101] Despite long-standing authority, unlike Section 232 refinancings, the Department delayed implementation of its refinancing authority until only just recently.[102] As the market tightened in 2007 and 2008, the Department realized that sources of refinancing loans long thought to be prevalent had dried up, leaving hospital facilities at risk.[103] While regulations are pending that would permanently implement such a refinancing program; in the interim, the Department has implemented the program through Housing Notices.[104]

- Though there are no criteria requiring hard construction under a Section 223(f) refinancing, should there be hard costs, 20 percent of the loan amount must be allocated for hard construction costs and equipment (including construction manager fees and construction-related fees.)[105]
- Candidates must make a showing of (1) need in the community, (2) the existence of a credit crisis, and (3) evidence of the savings that will result from the refinancing, including, but not limited to, reduction in overall expenses and the interest rate.[106]

c. *Section 242/223(a)(7).* Like with the multifamily insurance programs, Section 223(a)(7) is used to minimize risk to the FHA insurance fund by dropping the interest rate on those hospital facilities that already are subject to a Section 242 insured loan.[107] Standard Section 223(a)(7) restrictions apply; the mortgage term must equal the balance of the existing 242 mortgage loan term or, if deemed beneficial for the long-term well-being of the facility, the existing mortgage term plus 12 years; the

---

99. 24 C.F.R. § 242.72 (2011).
100. 24 C.F.R. § 242.4 (2011).
101. Pub. L. 100-242, Section 409, codified at 12 U.S.C. 1715n(f) (2010).
102. H 09-05, Hospital Mortgage Insurance: Section 223(f) Refinancing in Conjunction with Section 242 Financing.
103. *Id.* at p.2.
104. H 09-05, as amended and restated in H 10-06.
105. *See* H 10-06, *supra.*
106. *Id.*
107. 12 U.S.C. § 1715(n)(a)(7) (2010).

debt service payment must be less than or equal to the existing 242 loan debt service payments; and the principal amount of the loan must be limited to the lesser of Section 242 original principal loan balance or the unpaid principal amount with certain closing and improvement costs.[108]

d. *Section 241.* Section 242 may be used in combination with the Section 241 mortgage insurance program,[109] which authorizes the Secretary to insure secondary financing to permit the construction of additional improvements. Such loans are governed by regulations promulgated by the Secretary for standard Section 241 loans as modified for 242.[110]

C. Processing/Underwriting Issues

Long deemed a cumbersome process, OHP and its predecessors have worked aggressively since 2005 to create a more predictable and efficient process for Section 242 financings. To that end, it has put into place certain preliminary threshold inquiries designed to "weed out" candidates that will not or cannot meet HUD criteria. The process has also been modified to review potential risk factors earlier in the pre-application and application stages.[111] Below is a brief summary of the process.

1. Preliminary Meeting/Inquiry

To save costs and time for all concerned parties, the initial inquiry to HUD OHF (or if already an existing 242 asset, to the Account Executive having jurisdiction over the project) is designed to lay out the most basic facts about the financing plan: type of facility, confirmation of 50 percent acute care bed criteria, type of financing desired, rehabilitation/construction plan, 20 percent hard construction cost, identity of mortgagee, existence of issues with granting complete first lien to HUD, and other basic threshold questions.[112]

2. Preliminary Review

On learning of the proposed hospital financing thumbnail and determining that it is not automatically disqualified for failure to meet certain basic threshold tests noted above, OHF will require the applicant to complete a preliminary review template and a list of attachments designed to provide OHF a basis on which to evaluate, without cost to the applicant, whether an application process should be pursued.[113] The preliminary review includes the following:

a. *Ownership Structure.* Understanding the organizational structure of the borrower entity, the sponsor and all affiliate relationships are critical. OHF will review to ensure

---

108. 24 C.F.R. § 242.91.
109. 12 U.S.C. § 1715z-6 (2010).
110. 24 C.F.R. § 242.89 (2011).
111. See supra note 79.
112. *See* U.S. Dep't of Housing and Urban Development, Program Offices, Chief Human Capital Officer, HUDclips, Form Resources, HUD-9 Forms, *available at* http://portal.hud.gov/hudportal/documents/huddoc?id=DOC_20610.pdf.
113. *See supra* note 95, Applicants Guide, Pre-Application, OHF Summer 2011. *See also* 24 C.F.R. § 242 *et seq.*

that there is a single-asset entity structure in place and review the assets and relationships to sponsor, parent, and affiliates to understand asset ownership, financial wherewithal, and ability to pledge assets. Ultimately, HUD will review and/or require affiliation agreements, management agreements, and other agreements regarding transfer properties to ensure that it is aware of all instances where any pledge of assets excludes assets segregated for the benefit of an affiliate or where any obligation is permitted to remain outstanding.[114] Any ownership changes to occur in connection with the new financing need to be outlined for HUD and steps taken to ensure such changes are in place at closing.[115]

b. *Statutory Criteria.* To confirm that the project is not automatically disqualified, OHF will review information to ensure that all statutory criteria described above are met.[116]

c. *90 Percent LTV (Loan to Value).* LTV must be calculated on HUD's Form 92103-HOSP (*i.e.*, total mortgage divided by total estimated replacement cost, including net cost of equipment to be used on installation completion). Note that mortgage values will be lower in cases of leasehold mortgages versus mortgages granted on property owned in fee simple.[117]

d. *Sources of Additional Funds.* Sources of equity and working capital needed to supplement loan and to otherwise provide for the operations of the property must be identified.[118]

e. *Legal Compliance.* The hospital must be in substantial compliance with all local, state, and federal laws. Disclosure of investigations, findings, or violations must be disclosed for evaluation and cleared by OHF. Serious violations and findings can be expected to result in a rejection at this stage.

f. *Existing Loan Refinancing.* HUD will evaluate terms of existing financing, including bond terms. It will further ensure that the hospital has not been completed less than two years prior to applicant's intent to submit applications to HUD. Finally, it will ensure the 20 percent hard construction threshold is met as evidenced on the draft HUD Form 92013.[119]

g. *First-Lien Interest.* Mortgagor must grant a first-lien interest in all property including land, fixtures, equipment, accounts, and receivables. Evaluation of how the Mortgagor holds title to the land, equipment, and facility are all essential for determining the extent to which those can be pledged as security for the 242 Loan. Title review becomes critical to determine whether there are any reversionary interests that would prohibit expansion or construction of the facility contemplated.[120] Furthermore, a complete list of assets needed to operate the hospital should be included for evaluation; should assets be excluded from the list, explanations should be provided sup-

---

114. *Id.*
115. *Id.*
116. *Id.*
117. 24 C.F.R. § 242.23(b) (2011).
118. *See supra* note 111.
119. *See supra* note 111.
120. *See supra* note 79.

porting and explaining such exclusions. Accounts receivable financing programs either existing or planned must be disclosed and reviewed. Ultimately, the final review and approval of any exclusions will need to be reflected in the Security Agreement and related collateral lists.[121] As with Section 232 financing, the deposit control agreement becomes a key component in ensuring that the Department retains a perfected security interest in the project.

h. *Status of CON Application (if applicable).* While not needed at the pre-application stage, the CON process must be under way; it must be completed by the application stage.[122]

i. *Type of Project.* HUD will review the type of project (e.g., physician-owned, design-build project, leased facilities) to ensure that any basic thresholds are met (*e.g.*, $60 million loan limitation on design-build).[123]

j. *Commencement of Construction.* HUD will need to understand the construction schedule and determine whether work has begun or otherwise create issues under the site plan.[124]

k. *Lender Selection.* HUD will request information on the lender selected (if applicable) or will otherwise provide information on lenders experienced with the Department's 242 financings.[125]

3. Resolve Issues or Schedule Pre-application Meeting[126]

HUD reserves 10 days to review the preliminary review template submissions and attachments. Should the applicant fail to submit a complete package or submit information that requires further clarification, HUD will contact the applicant to address such deficiencies. If, on submission, HUD determines that the project does not qualify, it will so advise the applicant. If, based on the preliminary review, the project looks promising, HUD will invite the applicant in for a preliminary meeting to review any open issues and materials and to review basic issues covered by the template. Should HUD determine that the project is worthy of pursuing a full-blown application, it will inform the applicant within 24 hours of the applicant's preliminary meeting.

4. Application Process[127]

The HUD application process includes extensive review by numerous divisions of HUD, including not only OHF, but also the Multifamily HUB for environmental review and the Office of General Counsel who will close the loan. OHF has attempted to create a more transparent and fluid process through issuance of its Application Process Checklist, which is

---

121. *See supra* note 113.
122. *Id.*
123. *Id.*
124. *Id.*
125. *Id.*
126. *Id.*
127. Hospital Mortgage Insurance Program, Section 242 of the National Housing Act, Applicant's Guide, Office of Hospital Facilities, Summer 2011.

updated throughout the process.[128] Such process includes not only submission of a written application and review of such but also includes a site visit by HUD, environmental review, and legal review. The application itself will have three major components: (1) programmatic documentation, including organizational documents and authority, 2530s, and executed covenants; (2) financial documentation that includes all manner of audit history, pro formas, and a financial feasibility study; and (3) A&E documentation that includes title, survey, construction plans, and environmental plans. Should OHF approve the application, it will issue a Firm Commitment setting forth all conditions to closing. Closing will be held over a period of two or three days, overseen by the Office of General Counsel.[129] Some integral issues and components are highlighted below.

a. *Underwriting/Financing Issues*

i. Mortgage Reserve Fund

All hospital financings must establish as a condition of HUD's Firm Commitment a Mortgage Reserve Fund (the Fund). Such fund is designed to provide sufficient cash resources (through a combination of up-front deposits and earnings) that will cover the following key costs: (1) cost of a management consultant should Mortgagor's operations start to decline and a business plan is needed to secure the project's performance; (2) delinquent mortgage payments; (3) and on assignment of the loan to HUD, the use of such proceeds to cover HUD's insurance claim exposure. HUD requires mortgagors to make quarterly payments into the Fund in accordance with a schedule established at closing. Should the Fund fail to achieve the minimum thresholds, (i.e., one year's worth of debt service by year 5 of the Project and two years' worth of debt service by year 10), the Mortgagor will be required to remit out of investment income or find sources of funds to fill the gap within a 60-day period of the required deposit. Such terms typically are set forth in a Mortgage Reserve Fund Agreement between the mortgagor and HUD. HUD also traditionally requires a three-way agreement between HUD, the mortgagor, and the lender/trustee that will hold the Mortgage Reserve Fund (MRF) monies in a trust fund for the benefit of HUD. The Mortgage Reserve Trust Fund Agreement sets forth terms regarding investment and withdrawal of such MRF monies, trustee rights, and obligations, as well as HUD's rights to determine the usage of such funds.

ii. CON/Financial Feasibility Study

The guts of the hospital financial review starts with a CON and/or Feasibility Study. In those states where it is applicable, a hospital must have a CON issued prior to submission of the application. Regardless of the CON status of a particular state, each facility will undergo a distinct feasibility review. Such review will be performed by an independent Certified Public Accountant in accordance with the American Institute of CPAs (AICPA). Such report will provide an in-depth analysis of market need and financial feasibility and is one of the most critical tools for providing a comprehensive determination as to the viability of the project.

---

128. *Id.*
129. *See supra,* note 79.

The experience of such CPA with hospitals and HUD financing may render the success or failure of such feasibility study. Such study will evaluate trends in population growth, demographics, use rate, and demand for the proposed new services or facilities, and market share. The report also will contain extensive data on financial accounting assumptions, including the manner of payment, the changes in reimbursements, assumptions as to expenses, including staff and physician salaries, and outpatient versus inpatient revenue comparisons. HUD will use this study as a starting point for its own verification of such components. For HUD, "[T]he Path from Historical to Forecast Should be Clear."[130] Should the report be flawed, HUD will either request corrections or reject the application altogether.[131]

b. Regulatory and Operational Requirements

i. Covenants

To ensure that its security interests are covered, HUD will require owners to enter into a set of covenants. Such covenants will cover a wide range of matters and include collateral covenants assuring HUD a first-lien interest in all personalty, including tangibles and intangibles. While there is a standard set of covenants that must be executed and submitted as part of the application, HUD also will approve and establish special conditions that may be warranted for the transaction.[132] Special conditions can include cost-savings covenants, requirements regarding cash payment of insurance benefits, and covenants stipulating non-interference by the parent in the hospital. In some cases, the covenants will need to be reviewed carefully and adjusted to fit the transaction. Covenants are set forth in the Firm Commitment but should be reviewed during the application process to ensure the hospital's governing board does not have an issue with signing them. Most often incorporated by a rider to the Regulatory Agreement the form of which varies depending on whether the borrower is a for-profit or nonprofit borrower,[133] the covenants may become a ground for mortgage default if violated.[134]

ii. Insurance Requirements

Even more so than for its multifamily counterparts, HUD has extensive insurance requirements for hospital facilities. Liability, vehicle, malpractice, and related forms of insurance must be usual and customary for the health-care industry and must be adequate to cover mortgagee, HUD, and owner interests.[135] Such insurance must include fire and hazard insurance in an amount at least equal to the mortgage amount.[136]

---

130. *See supra*, note 79.
131. HUD, Mortgagee Letter, 04-08 p. 3.
132. *See supra* note 79.
133. *See supra* note 95.
134. *See id*. Applicant Checklist; examples of covenants include requirements to file interim financial statements and business plans in event of loss of cash flow and operating loss thresholds.
135. Mortgagee Letter 08-42; 24 C.F.R. § 242.33 (2011).
136. *Id*.

iii. Financial Reporting[137]

Considered crucial to the long-term success of the program, HUD imposes financial reporting requirements on the borrower and loan servicer. Such reporting requirements entail not only the annual audited financial statement due 120 days after the end of the fiscal year (rather than the more typical 90 days for multifamily and 232), but also quarterly interim financial statements, an annual budget, and monthly unaudited balance sheet information during construction.

iv. Affiliate Relationships[138]

While the affiliate relationships, asset ownership, and lien issues are reviewed during the pre-application stage, such review is continued in the application stage to ensure that documentation and conditions set forth in the Firm Commitment are as needed to protect HUD's interests. As mentioned above, these are key.

5. Construction[139] and Construction Completion/Final Endorsement

Like its multifamily counterparts, Davis-Bacon wages, HUD approval to initiate an "early start" of construction after Firm Commitment issuance but before Initial Endorsement and draw processes will apply. That said, there is more room in the Section 242 world for obtaining HUD authorization to start early site work prior to Firm Commitment issuance but after HUD receipt of the Firm Commitment application.[140] Threshold submissions for such approval include 2530, environmental review completion, review of the work to be performed, and an assertion of a compelling reason to do so.[141] All such construction starts prior to Initial Endorsement are done with no commitment or obligation for HUD to endorse the note and therefore are done at the mortgagor's risk.

For hospital construction, generally a lump-sum contract is used and can only be awarded after the mortgagor solicits competitive bids from at least three sources. Similar bidding requirements apply to the construction manager, which is required. Contractors excluded from participation in federal programs may not bid. On completion of construction, HUD will require a cost certification to be submitted.[142] After review and approval of such certification, HUD will undertake standard steps to finally endorse the note for mortgage insurance.[143]

G. Asset Management Issues

Asset managers in OHF are integrally involved in both the processing of new loans, refinances, and the post-closing oversight of the Section 242 Loan. Asset management team members, as led by the facility's appointed account executive, will review the HUD Form

---

137. *See* 24 C.F.R. § 242 Subpart D (2011).
138. *Id.*
139. *See* 24 C.F.R. § 242 Subpart E (2011).
140. 24 C.F.R. § 242.45 (2011).
141. *Id.*
142. 24 C.F.R. § 242 Subpart D (2011).
143. *Id.*

92013 and perform risk assessment functions as part of the loan processing.[144] On completion of the project, Asset Management's oversight will include the following key matters impacting hospital facilities:

1. TPA

As stipulated in the HUD Regulatory Agreement and related regulations, all transfers must be approved by HUD, whether mortgagor- or management-related.[145] Mergers may not be accomplished without careful review by HUD as to the implications for the HUD-insured loan.[146] Any transfer or creation of an affiliate subsidiary or acquisition that requires disclosure under audit rules must receive prior approval from HUD.[147]

2. Operating Difficulties/Business Plan

HUD has taken very seriously the issue of risk mitigation in the hospital world. To that end, it requires far more interim reporting and certifications as to operating losses than is required for other insurable programs. In addition to quarterly unaudited financial reports and, if required, monthly financial reports, HUD will hold the hospital governing board (the board) responsible for biannual reviews and, should the hospital fail to meet certain thresholds, including, but not limited to, operation losses greater than 1 percent, net income that is less than 0.0, and/or failure to fund the Mortgage Reserve Fund, submission of a written report to HUD regarding the health of the hospital.[148] On review of the board's report, should HUD believe it warranted, it will require the hospital to submit a business plan that will provide (1) a thorough analysis of the reasons for financial results; (2) a proposed plan to turn around the facility; (3) key areas that need to be addressed; (4) a time line for implementation; and (5) financial forecasts and projected savings measures.[149]

3. Risk Mitigation/Priority Watch List Default

So as to continue its long history of low-default rates[150] and to ensure the health of the FHA mortgage insurance fund, for those projects that start to show signs of problems, the department has established a priority watch list.[151] Thresholds for projects being placed on such a watch list include danger of default in the next 12 months, failure to make a mortgage payment by the 15th day of the month, and violations of the Regulatory Agreement that put at risk HUD's collateral or HUD's ability to protect the asset.[152]

---

144. *See supra*, note 79.
145. 24 C.F.R. § 242.67 (2011).
146. *Id.*
147. *Id.*
148. *See supra*, note 79.
149. *Id.*
150. *Id.*
151. *Id.*
152. *Id.*

4. Problem Solving

The account executive in consultation with a risk-mitigation team and asset-management and senior OHF staff will explore several key solutions with the hospital to reverse both the hospital and HUD's exposure.[153] In certain cases, a consultant will be hired to develop a strategic plan that will provide an analysis of possible solutions and their viability in addressing the circumstances. Chief among these possible solutions is working with the board to identify other assets that may be tapped, both property held by affiliates and charitable donations or available accounts receivable.[154] Should further deterioration occur, the Mortgage Reserve Fund will be evaluated to determine its sufficiency to prevent a claim during the evaluation period, and, as a last resort, the asset manager will determine if Section 223(a)(7) can be used to remedy the situation.[155] The hope is that, through an early-detection system and a comprehensive review of all possible solutions, the Department can work with the hospital to successfully restore the health of the hospital facility, thus benefiting the hospital and its patients and avoiding a claim on the insurance fund.

******

In conclusion, the OHF, through streamlining efforts and a proactive review policy, both during the application process as well as postclosing, has enabled the 242 Program to become a viable tool for hospital financing. The preapplication review, the postclosing financial reviews, and the priority watch list system allow HUD to eliminate inefficiencies and target the critical issues sooner in the process. This saves applicants and participants significant costs, increases the likelihood of success, and ensures the 242 Program will succeed in its mission to facilitate hospital financing throughout the country.

---

153. *Id.*
154. *Id.*
155. *Id. See also* 24 C.F.R. § 242.14 (2011).

HUD Section 202 and Mixed Finance Guide for Development and Operation of Supportive Housing for the Elderly

Karen Sherman and Michael Decina

I. INTRODUCTION

The United States Department of Housing and Urban Development (HUD) Section 202 Supportive Housing for the Elderly program is the primary federal financing program for the development and operation of housing for low-income elderly persons (Section 202 Program or Section 202). The financing structures for development and operation of the 202 Program have changed since its inception. This chapter provides a brief history of the 202 Program, an exploration on how transactions are currently structured, and the lawyers' role in assisting their clients in developing housing affordable for low income seniors with these funds.

Specific consideration is given to Section 202 "Mixed Finance" transactions, whereby Section 202 funding is combined with federal low-income housing tax credits (LIHTCs) to leverage resources and provide affordable housing, especially in areas where the costs to develop and construct affordable and sustainable housing requires multiple sources of funding. Consideration is also given to combining Section 202 funding with other subordinate financing.

Further, this chapter provides a brief survey of the predecessor to the current Section 202 Program, the Section 202 Direct Loan Program (Section 202 Direct Loans), and the manner in which nonprofit owners of projects with Section 202 Direct Loans can refinance and rehabilitate their housing projects.

Given that the Section 202 program is in the midst of change and reform, the practitioner is advised to verify its current rules, policies, and requirements prior to representing a client on a matter that involves Section 202 funds.

II. STATUTORY, REGULATORY, AND PROGRAMMATIC AUTHORITY

A. *Statutory Authority*

From its inception by the Housing Act of 1959 and extending through 1974, the 202 Program provided low-cost loans and operating rental subsidies to build housing for moderate-income seniors.[1] After 1974 and through 1990, the 202 Program added project-based section 8 rental assistance.

In 1990, the Cranston-Gonzales National Affordable Housing Act[2] restructured the 202 Program as a 202 capital advance (202 Capital Advance) secured by a HUD mortgage;[3] repayment is required only if the owner fails to comply with HUD's regulatory requirements, which include that the housing remain affordable to low-income elderly persons for 40 years. The 202 Capital Advance is based on each 202 project's development costs, such as prevailing cost of construction, rehabilitation and acquisition of property, as designed for the elderly with congregate facilities. A typical development has between 42 and 50 one-bedroom units.[4]

To be eligible for the housing, the occupant must be a household of one or more persons, with at least one person being age 62 or older at the time of initial occupancy, and earn less than 50 percent of the Area Median Income (AMI).[5] To subsidize operations, HUD enters into a Project Rental Assistance Contract (PRAC) with the owner for a period of years, subject to extension. As discussed herein, the term of the PRAC may be as short as three years. Although the PRAC is generally renewed, the uncertain length of its term has been an obstacle in obtaining other sources of financing for these projects because it creates an uncertain operating revenue stream.

Throughout most of the country, the 202 Capital Advance is not sufficient to build affordable housing for low-income elderly. Developers explored obtaining equity from the sale of Low Income Housing Tax Credits (LIHTC) to develop their projects. The LIHTC program was enacted as part of the Tax Reform Act of 1986[6] and provides LIHTC to states based on their population. The states then allocate those credits to developers to obtain equity for the development of affordable rental housing. (A discussion of the LIHTC and the application process is beyond the scope of this chapter, but is addressed in other publications of the ABA Forum on Affordable Housing and Community Development, including *The Legal Guide to Affordable Housing Development*.) However, because the 202 Program required that the housing be owned by a nonprofit corporation (recognized by the Internal Revenue Service (IRS) as a charitable corporation under Section 501(c)(3) of the Internal Revenue Code of 1986 as it may be amended (Code)[7]), it was incompatible with the LIHTC program. Specifically, HUD's required 202 ownership structure did not allow for an organizational

---

1. Pub. L. 86-372.
2. Pub. L. 99-514.
3. 12 U.S.C. § 1704 (2010).
4. *Section 202 Supportive Housing for the Elderly: Program Status and Performance Measurements*, p. 20.
5. 12 U.S.C. § 1701q(k)(1).
6. Pub. L. 99-514.
7. 24 C.F.R. § 891.805 (2010).

structure that permitted an equity investment from the sale of tax credits under the LIHTC program.

In 2000, Congress passed the American Homeownership and Economic Opportunity Act (AHEO),[8] which paved the way for use of the equity from LIHTC with the 202 Program by permitting ownership of 202 housing by for-profit limited partnerships. In addition, AHEO permitted the nonprofit developer to structure the 202 Capital Advance as a loan that was not to be treated as federal grant for tax purposes, thereby avoiding reduction of tax credit equity otherwise required for federal grants under the LIHTC program. However, there were other obstacles to combining the Section 202 Program with LIHTCs.

Under the LIHTC program, developers may qualify for tax credits that are either 9 percent or about 4 percent of certain qualified costs. Prior to 2008, the 9 percent credit could be used only for new construction that was not federally subsidized; the 4 percent credit could be used for either federally subsidized new construction or existing buildings. The definition of federal subsidy included below-market federal loans, which is how nonprofit 202 developers lend the 202 Capital Advance to their projects. With only the 4 percent LIHTC available for the sale, and the substantial costs associated with structuring such a transaction, the value of the LIHTC was diminished.

In 2008, Congress passed the Housing and Economic Recovery Act of 2008[9] (HERA), which removed the phrase "below market federal loans" from the LIHTC definition of federal subsidy. This permitted the housing to be developed with equity from the sale of 9 percent LIHTC and 202 Capital Advance.

In 2010, with the enactment of the amendment to Section 202 of the Housing Act of 1959, known as the Section 202 Supportive Housing and Elderly Act of 2010 (2010 Act), some of the legal structuring problems were resolved. This amendment permits the *sole* general partner of a for-profit limited partnership to be a nonprofit corporation, a for-profit corporation, or a limited liability company. Each of these potential partners has to meet certain requirements, as discussed herein.

B. Regulatory Authority

The regulations implementing the Section 202 Program are found at 24 C.F.R. Part 891. 24 C.F.R. Part 891, Subpart F (Subpart F), sets forth the regulatory requirements for the Section 202 Mixed-Finance program. For regulatory background, the practitioner would be well-served to also review the preamble in the Federal Register under which the Subpart F was issued, which provides commentary and analysis to the Subpart F regulations.[10] Of note, in the commentary and analysis, HUD asserts that it will seek to be flexible in its review of proposed structures for closing Section 202 Mixed Finance transaction.[11] This concept of requiring flexibility in order to structure and close a Section 202 Mixed-Finance transaction

---

8. Pub. L. 106-569.
9. Pub. L. 110-289.
10. 70 Fed. Reg. 54,210, Sept. 13, 2005.
11. *Id.* at 54,202 (For example, HUD states "The parties are free, subject to compliance with legal requirements and HUD review, to structure this transaction in the way most appropriate for the development." *Id.*).

has been a guiding principle both in structuring such transactions and as a preliminary justification for the various regulatory waivers that are needed to facilitate the closing of these transactions.

C. Programmatic Guidance and Authorities

As with many federal programs, the bulk of the requirements that apply to the Section 202 program are described in such guidance as Housing Notices and Housing Handbooks. Currently, the seminal programmatic guidance for the Section 202 program is set forth in Housing Notice 2011-18, published August 15, 2011. Other guidance is included in Housing Notice 96-102 and in Handbooks 4571.2 and 4571.4. The publication of Housing Notice 2011-18 clarifies certain important aspects of the Section 202 Mixed Finance program, including required funding of operating reserves related thereto, specifically as to projects with additional units not funded by PRAC, which previously had not been set forth in official guidance by HUD.

As to relative priorities of various regulatory and extended-use agreements, HUD clarifies in Notice 2011-18 that its regulatory and use agreement can be subordinate to the LIHTC regulatory agreement required to be recorded against the project in LIHTC transactions.

Additionally, Notice 2011-18 explicitly allows for for-profit "joint-venture" parties in Section 202 Mixed Finance projects. While it is not clear how such a for-profit party could be involved in the ownership of a Section 202 project, given current HUD requirements discussed herein, Notice 2011-18 clearly indicates that some level of involvement is possible in a Section 202 project, perhaps as a co-developer and provider of guaranties to tax credit investors or other debt providers to the transaction. LIHTC investors require the sponsor to deliver guaranties of timely construction completion, payment of cost overruns, timely lease-up, and delivery of tax credits. Some sponsors are not experienced with the requirements of developing and operating a project funded with LIHTCs. To provide LIHTC development expertise and satisfy LIHTC investors that the guaranties are meaningful—i.e., there is substantial net worth to pay for these guaranties, the sponsor often enlists the private developer or construction contractor to act as co-developer and to provide the guaranties and indemnifications to the sponsor in exchange for a part of the development fee.

D. The Process from NOFA to Closing

This section will overview the process whereby an owner applies for Section 202 funds, receives an award of such funds, closes on such award, and begins development of the Section 202 project. First, a sponsor applies for Section 202 funds (both 202 Capital Advance funds to develop and construct the project and PRAC operating subsidy to support the operating cost of the project) pursuant to a competitive process set forth in a Notice of Funding Availability (NOFA), published by HUD in the *Federal Register* each fiscal year. The amount of funds available pursuant to the NOFA is based on appropriations. Each HUD regional office (of which there are currently 10) receives an allocation of Section 202 funds to award. Each applicant sponsor is rated and ranked based on its application for 202 funds. The applicant first must pass certain threshold tests for eligibility of an award, such as adequate site control of the proposed project site and the qualification and eligibility of the sponsor.[12] The application process is extremely competitive; the number of applicants for Section 202 funding awards almost always far exceed the funds available. HUD rates and ranks the proposed projects and offers the highest-scoring sponsor Fund Reservations, which allocate the 202 funds for the specific project and outline certain conditions of receipt. As set forth in the Fund Reservation, the 202 Capital Advance must be initially spent within 24 months or a regulatory waiver is required.[13]

After receipt and execution of the Fund Reservation by the sponsor, the sponsor either forms a separate 501(c)(3) owner corporation to own the Section 202 project or, with Mixed Finance transactions, a for-profit limited partnership entity, in which the sponsor, either in its own name (through a single-member limited liability company of which it is the sole member) or a special purpose corporation formed by the sponsor, is the general partner of the for-profit limited partnership entity. (Examples of ownership structures for 202 projects are provided elsewhere in this chapter.)

With acceptance of the Fund Reservation, the sponsor begins to complete the due diligence and underwriting required by the next stage of the Section 202 process—the stage in which the sponsor applies to HUD for a "Firm Commitment," which will set forth various closing requirements and the process by which HUD verifies and ensures that the project meets certain underwriting and programmatic requirements. Upon issuance of a Firm Commitment, the "Initial Closing" on the transaction occurs. After Initial Closing, construction of the project can commence. After construction is complete and the required audited cost certification and other requirements are met, "Final Closing" can occur and the above described two-stage closing process is complete.

A diagram of the process outlined above is provided as Appendix A. The time that it takes to consummate the process from Fund Reservation to Initial Closing, which is the time frame most sponsors are concerned about, typically is between 12 and 18 months, but it can be substantially longer depending on the complexity of the transaction and the experience of the sponsor and professionals assisting the sponsor in connection with the transaction.

III. MIXED FINANCE

A. Ownership Structure

With the passage of the AHEO, sponsors of Section 202 projects could combine LIHTC equity with Section 202 funds. Given the dearth of single funding sources to provide adequate affordable housing, many sponsors turned to the Section 202 Mixed Finance program as a way to leverage resources and develop larger or more marketable projects. As described above, the Section 202 Mixed Finance program combines LIHTC equity with 202 Capital Advance, in addition to, in many cases, secondary financing, as also described in this chapter. Some examples of ownership structures of the Section 202 Mixed Finance program are included in Appendix B.

---

12. 24 C.F.R. § 891.105 and 24 C.F.R. § 891.805.
13. 24 C.F.R. § 891.165.

One of the more common structures to accommodate Mixed Finance involves the sponsor, which is a 501(c)(3) nonprofit corporation, forming a limited liability company or corporation of which it is the sole member or shareholder, to be the general partner of a limited partnership in which the LIHTC investor is the limited partner. As required by AHEO, the owner entity of the Section 202 Mixed Finance project must be a limited partnership.[14]

Prior to the 2010 Act, having the sponsor act as general partner through the sole member general partner LLC or corporation required a regulatory waiver from HUD, but the 2010 Act specifies that such a structure is permissible without need for a regulatory waiver. However, the Act requires that the general partner entity be organized so that (i) no part of the net earnings of the entity inure to the benefit of any person, and (ii) the governing board of the entity (aa) has a membership selected to ensure that there is significant representation of the views of the community in which the housing is located and (bb) is responsible for the operation of the housing. In the case of a nonprofit organization that is the sponsoring organization of multiple 202 housing projects, HUD may determine the criteria or conditions under which financial, compliance, and other administrative responsibilities exercised by a single-entity nonprofit owner corporation responsible for the operation of the project may be shared or transferred to the governing board of such sponsoring organization.

B. Structure of Loan to Partnership

In most transactions, the 202 Capital Advance is structured as a loan from the sponsor or general partner formed by the sponsor to the limited partnership which will own beneficial interest in the project (the Mixed Finance Owner). The Mixed Finance Owner executes a note (secured by mortgage) that the sponsor assigns for security purposes back to HUD for the 40-year term of the 202 Capital Advance and affordability period required pursuant to the Section 202 program. In instances where, for tax credit or other underwriting purposes, the loan must be for longer than the statutorily required 40-year minimum, HUD has been flexible in allowing such term to exceed the statutory minimum with adequate justification. HUD has to issue formal guidance on whether the affordability restrictions must also continue past 40 years if the note exceeds 40 years.

After the maturity of the 202 Capital Advance loan, assuming all Section 202 rules and requirements have been met by the Mixed Finance Owner for the 40-year Section 202 compliance period, the note and mortgage are reassigned by the sponsor or general partner who lent the 202 Capital Advance to the Mixed Finance Owner at closing. A diagram describing this loan structure of the Section 202 Capital Advance is provided in Appendix C.

C. Timing of the 202 Capital Advance

Typically, Section 202 Capital Advance funds are closed on immediately prior to construction so they can be used for construction of the project. However, in certain instances, such as with tax-exempt financing and so-called four (4%) percent tax credit transactions, the specifics of the transaction may require that the Section 202 Capital Advance be used as permanent take-

---

14. In states where limited liability limited partnerships are provided for pursuant to such states' limited partnership statutes, HUD has provided guidance that limited liability limited partnerships are an acceptable form of ownership entity.

out financing for a construction loan funded with tax-exempt bond proceeds.[15] In this scenario, upon completion of the project, the Section 202 Capital Advance is closed upon and the initial and final closing models described earlier in this chapter are replaced by one initial/final closing. HUD aptly calls this process the 202 Capital Advance Upon Completion (CAUC) model. Previously, the authority for CAUC closings was informal, and such transactions were closed on a case-by-case basis under such informal guidance, but the issuance of Housing Notice 2011-13 explicitly authorizes CAUC transactions. To close a CAUC transaction where the Section 202 Capital Advance funds will be used to repay the construction loan funded by the proceeds of the tax-exempt bonds, a regulatory waiver[16] is necessary. HUD has typically, but not always, granted such waivers; therefore, sponsors should discuss this waiver very early in the process with their local HUD office.

D. Additional Unit Projects

Projects funded by a Section 202 Capital Advance pursuant to the sponsor's Fund Reservation are given operating subsidy pursuant to PRAC as previously described in this chapter. However, HUD allows additional or non-PRAC units to be constructed in a Section 202 project, which HUD calls "Additional Units." Additional Units allow sponsors to leverage the 202 Capital Advance and PRAC to build more scalable and economically feasible affordable housing.[17]

Under Section 202 rules, PRAC cannot be used to pay for, among other items, development fees, required investor or general partner asset management fees, or permanent debt. However, HUD has no restrictions on the uses of Additional Unit cash flow. Therefore, many Section 202 Mixed Finance projects have Additional Units to create cash flow to pay for typical uses in a standard LIHTC development. In instances where there are no Additional Units and a need to provide a source of funds for such standard fees and uses, reserves may be capitalized at closing for such purposes as permitted by HUD.

HUD, by regulation, requires a three-month operating reserve,[18] which Notice 2011-13 clarifies as applying only to Additional Units. This policy clarification reflects HUD's concern about operating revenue shortfalls derived from Additional Units that do not receive PRAC, which prevent operating shortfalls in PRAC units. Further, Notice 2011-18 clarifies that the HUD regulatory agreement and use agreement pertain only to the units assisted by HUD under PRAC and not to Additional Units. Among other things, this policy clarification means that HUD's reserve for replacement requirements, which typically is far in excess of other lenders and investors, does not apply to Additional Units.

---

15. Primarily, the reason the 202 Capital Advance is used to pay off a construction loan funded by bond proceeds is the 50% test under Section 42 H4 Internal Revenue Code whereby at least 50% of the bond proceeds must be used to pay for eligible items included in tax basis, and the bonds must stay outstanding until at least "placed in service" pursuant to IRS regulations.
16. 24 C.F.R. § 891.830C4.
17. To that end, although the subject of changing policy, HUD has awarded additional points to Additional Unit proposals during the NOFA stage of the Section 202 process.
18. 24 C.F.R. § 891.860.

E. Structural Issues to Be Addressed to Maximize Tax Credit Equity

Gaps in financing 202 projects are often filled by the nonprofit developer lending the 202 Capital Advance and funds from other grants (collectively Sponsor Loan) to the beneficial owner of the project, which is the recipient of LIHTC equity. In certain instances, due to prevailing-wage requirements, high-cost locations of the Project, and high depreciation,[19] the limited partner's capital account may quickly erode, which could result in the investor limited partner's capital account going negative during the LIHTC period. If this occurs, the investor limited partner would not be able to claim the depreciation or other passive losses inuring from the property unless there is an offset of minimum gain, i.e., if the nonrecourse debt is greater than the property's basis. Such a reallocation of losses to the general partner would jeopardize the ability to monetize the LIHTC, because the limited partner investor will lose the benefits of those losses and the LIHTC generated for such year.[20]

To address this undesirable tax consequence in Section 202 Mixed Finance projects, HUD has allowed the sponsor to form an unrelated (for tax purposes) for-profit entity, *i.e.*, an entity with less than 80 percent overlap in ownership interest, to facilitate the flow of Section 202 Capital Advance funds into the ownership entity. Caution should be taken with this structure to ensure that there are no unfunded tax consequences resulting from the unrelated new lender's recognition of accrued interest on its loan to the partnership as income.

F. Secondary Financing

Because Section 202 Capital Advance is often insufficient to construct decent, safe, and sanitary affordable senior housing in most cases, even prior to the changes in law that allowed for Section 202 Mixed Finance projects, sponsors utilized secondary sources of subordinate financing (Secondary Financing) to bridge the funding gap to complete their projects. This utilization of Secondary Financing to close development funding gaps remains prevalent. Secondary Financing sources include HUD programs such as CDBG and HOME, Federal Home Loan Bank's Affordable Housing Program, and other state or local funding programs.

Generally, HUD prohibits secondary financing to pay for the owner's minimum capital investment required under the 202 Program for what HUD considers "excess amenities" (e.g., swimming pools, balconies, and other items that increase operating costs), except in specific circumstances where an owner can prove that it can pay for such excess amenities outside of the 202 Capital Advance or PRAC funds. This could be accomplished through the capitalizing of an adequate excess amenity reserve at closing from non-HUD sources or by providing

---

19. I.R.C. § 168(h)(1)(D) provides that when a tax-exempt entity is engaged in a business venture that generates unrelated business taxable income, then the property shall not be treated as a tax-exempt use property and shall be depreciated in accordance with a standard schedule of depreciation, which in this case is straight-line over 27.5 years.

20. Specifically, the requirement that losses flow to the party that economically financed such losses is called the doctrine of "substantial economic effect," which is contained in Section 704(b) of the Internal Revenue Code of 1986 (the Code). Code Section 704(b) provides that an allocation of profits and losses to a partner will *not* be respected if such allocation lacks substantial economic effect. This concept is fleshed out in the Treasury Regulations, but the intent is that a party that economically funds a loss is the party that should be allocated the tax impacts of that loss.

evidence to HUD that the cash flow deriving from the non-PRAC units in an additional unit Section 202 Mixed Finance can support such excess amenities.

Pursuant to Section 202 rules, virtually any public source can be a source of Secondary Financing on a 202 Project provided the source is from a public body and certain specific HUD requirements are met. Because the 202 statute and regulations are silent about Secondary Financing, HUD's requirements are set through notice and other program guidance. Guidance regarding secondary financing by public bodies is set forth in Housing Notice 95-18. Pursuant to Housing Notice 95-18, Secondary Financing documents can be approved by the local HUD field office if:

(1) The issuer of the funds is a public body;
(2) The secondary financing does not become due and payable in whole or in part until the Section 202 is paid in full except that payments on the secondary financing can be made from residual receipts as defined in the HUD 202 regulatory agreement with HUD prior approval and payments can be made from the sponsor out of non-project funds;
(3) Compliance with HUD 202 requirements satisfies the requirements of the provider of secondary financing;
(4) The provider of secondary financing does not have any requirements which interfere or conflict with HUD's requirements concerning the project's development or operation or in any way jeopardize the continued operation of the project on terms at least as favorable to existing as well as future tenants;
(5) Default under the secondary financing documents cannot be declared without HUD approval; and
(6) HUD approval of a transfer of physical assets (TPA) constitutes approval of the TPA by the second mortgage holder.

Typically in a transaction, the secondary finance requirements are manifested in a rider to the secondary financing loan documents. Most HUD field offices require that such rider is attached to every loan document associated with the secondary financing.

Guidance regarding secondary financing pursuant to the Federal Home Loan Bank's Affordable Housing Program (AHP) is set forth in Housing Notice 99-7. An exhibit to this Housing Notice is a memorandum of understanding (MOU) between HUD and the FHLB setting forth the parties agreement to allow AHP funds in Section 202 projects. Of note, Housing Notice 99-7 and the MOU prohibits use of AHP funds for the minimum capital investment required under the Section 202 program or for what HUD considers excess amenities. Pursuant to Housing Notice 99-7 and the MOU, to ensure that FHLB's regulations are being met, HUD has agreed to provide notice to the FHLB if a 202 project fails to meet Section 202 rent or income requirements or if the project fails to meet certain basic health and safety standards. Included with the MOU is a form of rider to be utilized when AHP funds are utilized in Section 202 project. This form of rider is provided in Appendix D.

Subordinate or secondary financing by other than a public body or the FHLB can be authorized by HUD on a case-by-case basis and, pursuant to Housing Notice 95-30, requires the approval of HUD Headquarters.

Notwithstanding the aforementioned notices, HUD's Secondary Financing requirements can be applied differently depending on the specific facts of the transaction and in which HUD field office the Section 202 project is located. Appendixes E and F are attached as samples of riders used in various HUD field offices.

IV. REFINANCE AND PRESERVATION OF PROJECTS WITH SECTION 202 DIRECT LOANS

Pursuant to the Housing Act of 1959, as amended, from 1959 to 1990, HUD provided direct loans to nonprofit owners to develop and own elderly and disabled housing for moderate-, low-, or very low-income elderly individuals and families. The Section 202 Direct Loan program was replaced with the Section 202 and Section 811 Capital Advance programs[21] under the Cranston-Gonzalez National Affordable Housing Act of 1990.

Except for projects receiving Section 202 Direct Loans in the late 1970s and early 1980s, nonprofit owners of projects with Section 202 Direct Loans could not prepay these loans, with terms lasting up to 40 years, without receiving prior approval of HUD. Not until passage of the American Homeownership and Economic Opportunity Act of 2000[22] (AHEO) did prepayment of these loans and subsequent refinancing and preservation of this aging housing stock become more widespread.

Under the Section 811 of the AHEO, nonprofit owners can prepay their loans if the owner agrees (1) to operate the project, until the maturity date of the Section 202 Direct Loan being prepaid, on the same or better terms to the project's existing or future tenants as required by the Section 202 Direct Loan or HUD Section 8 or other HUD subsidy requirements applicable to the project, and (2) the refinanced loan that will occur because of the prepayment must result in a reduction of interest and debt service paid by the project owner.

In connection with the prepayment of Section 202 Direct Loans under Section 811 of the AHEO, HUD enforces the requirement of equivalent terms for the benefit of tenants by requiring the owner to execute a use agreement at closing that takes precedence over all other liens against the project. The use agreement terminates on the date that the Section 202 Direct Loan would have matured. Section 201 of SHEA, referenced below, increases the term of the use agreement to 20 years beyond the scheduled date of maturity. A form of use agreement is provided by HUD in Housing Notice 2002-16.

Section 811 of the AHEO also required specific uses of the debt service savings, including a ceiling of 15 percent of such savings for supportive services. Because of Section 811 of the AHEO, many HUD field offices required a debt service savings escrow agreement at closing of a refinance of the Section 202 Direct Loan. This escrow agreement sets forth the authorized uses of debt service savings from the refinanced loan. HUD's programmatic policy and requirements for prepayment of Section 202 Direct Loans with the subsequent use of

---

21. While this chapter does not specifically consider the Section 811 Capital Advance program, most of the rules applicable to the Section 202 program apply equally to the Section 811 program except that the Section 811 program applies to very low-income disabled individuals and families. The regulatory authority for the Section 811 program is, as with the Section 202 program, 24 C.F.R. pt. 891.

22. Pub. L. 106-569.

FHA-insured debt are set forth in Housing Notice 2002-16, Housing Notice 2004-20, and a clarification memorandum to Housing Notice 2004 issued by HUD, dated April 18, 2006. However, as Section 811 of the AHEO makes clear, so long as the statutory requirements are met, Section 202 Direct Loans may be refinanced through any source and is not limited to only FHA-insured debt.[23]

Section 811 of the AHEO limited the universe of Section 202 Direct Loans that could be prepaid and refinanced by requiring a reduction of interest and debt service savings. The requirement of debt service savings constrained the ability of certain nonprofit owners to refinance their Section 202 Direct Loans to rehabilitate and preserve aging projects. Section 202 of the Supportive Housing for the Elderly Act of 2010[24] (SHEA) alleviates many of these shortcomings by revising Section 811 of the AHEO to allow for prepayment and refinance of Section 202 Direct Loans, even where there is an increase in debt service if the transaction whereby the Section 202 Direct Loan will be prepaid addresses the physical needs of the project and the Section 202 Direct Loan being prepaid has an interest rate of 6 percent or lower.[25] Further, if there is to be an increase in debt service, the rent charged to tenants for units unassisted with Section 8 or other subsidy cannot be increased unless the tenant receives senior project rental assistance. For assisted tenants, the Section 8 rents cannot be increased except in certain circumstances involving rent increases under Section 524(a)(3) and (4) of the Multifamily Assisted Housing Reform and Affordability Act.[26]

Further, under Section 204 of SHEA, HUD may approve the subordination or assumption of the Section 202 Direct Loan in lieu of prepayment.[27]

Section 202 of SHEA also expands the uses of excess funds as the result of the Section 202 Direct Loan refinance, including allowing for more than 15 percent of excess funds to be used for supportive services upon receiving prior written approval of HUD.

Finally, Section 204 of SHEA authorizes a potential new source of subsidy for nonprofit owners who are prepaying their Section 202 Direct Loans in instances where tenants of the project do not currently receive rental subsidy. Under Section 204, nonprofit owners may be eligible for project-based senior preservation rental assistance that will operate pursuant to the same rules governing the project-based Section 8 program. Such project-based subsidy contracts will be for a term of 20 years, subject to appropriation. As of the writing of this chapter, HUD has not issued any program guidance or implementation about the senior project–

---

23. *Id.*, § 811(b).
24. S. 118-3. Previous appropriations law and Housing Notice 2010-14 issued before SHEA attempt to resolve these and other obstacles to refinancing Section 202 Direct Loans, but SHEA is the first permanent authorizing legislation addressing these matters.
25. *Id.*, § 201.
26. *Id.*
27. While HUD has issued guidance on the subordination of Section 202 Direct Loans in lieu of prepayment in the form of Housing Notice 2010-16, SHEA was passed subsequent to such notice. Further, Housing Notice 2010-16 limits the possibility of such subordination to Section 202 Direct Loans issued after 1974 where prepayment of the Section 202 Direct Loan is not possible under current Section 202 Direct Loan prepayment procedures. Such requirements are not present in Section 204. However, HUD has issued Housing Notice 2011-34, which reaffirms Housing Notice 2010-16, so it is unclear if HUD has determined not to exercise such wider discretion.

based rental assistance program. However, such guidance is forthcoming, as Congress has appropriated funds for the program pursuant to the FY 2012 appropriations for HUD signed into law on November 18, 2011.

V. THE FUTURE AND NEW TRENDS

The focus of HUD's recent proposal appears to reduce dependence on the 202 Capital Program and HUD for the development of housing for seniors and introduce into such housing a skilled-nursing element that had heretofore not existed or been prohibited. The very fabric of the 202 Program in this economic climate is changing in an attempt to reduce dependence on this financing to build senior housing, while redefining "eligible tenant" to include more frail elderly. HUD's appropriation for FY 2012, signed into law on November 18, 2011, includes no funds for Section 202 Capital Advances for FY 2012.

HUD's 202 program appears to be attempting to streamline the administrative processing and change the 202 Program from primary financing to predevelopment and planning and gap financing. Previously, HUD proposed legislation that would prioritize projects whose sponsors set aside a number of units in each project for frail elderly relying on PACE or Medicare/Medicaid Home.

HUD is considering soliciting additional qualified tax-exempt entities, such as local governments and public housing authorities, to participate in the program. This legislation would clarify that HUD may allocate funds over larger geographies (such as the 10 federal regions) and, as warranted by actual housing need (e.g., removing the 15 percent non-metropolitan allocation in favor of a percentage that is set every year based on non-metropolitan low-income elderly with worst-case housing needs), would ensure that projects of an adequate size and scope go to the communities and households that most need this housing.

Further, as of the date of the writing of this article, HUD has proposed new regulations that would be intended to streamline HUD's requirements as to Section 202 projects with additional units not funded with Section 202 Capital Advance of PRAC. Comments to such regulation are due by May 29, 2012. (See *Federal Register*, vol. 77, No. 60.)

Appendix A
Diagram of NOFA Process

202/811 Development Process

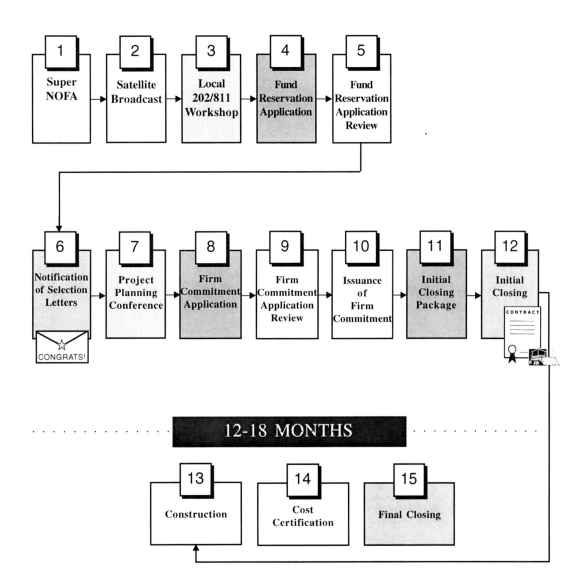

Appendix B
Example of Ownership Structure for Mixed Finance Program

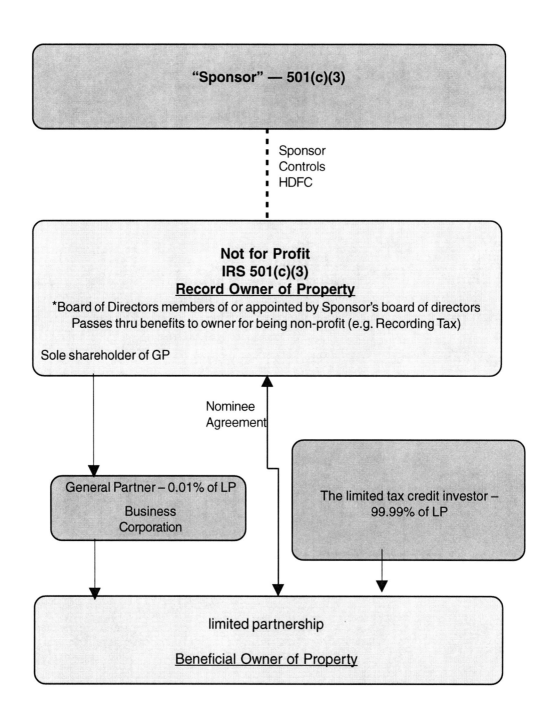

Appendix C
Diagram of Loan Structure

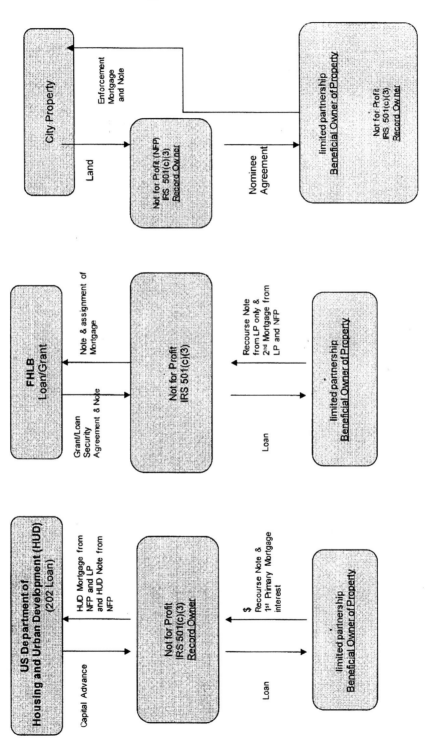

144 Chapter Four

Appendix C
Diagram of Loan Structure (continued)

Example HUD Capital Advance General Partner Loan Structure

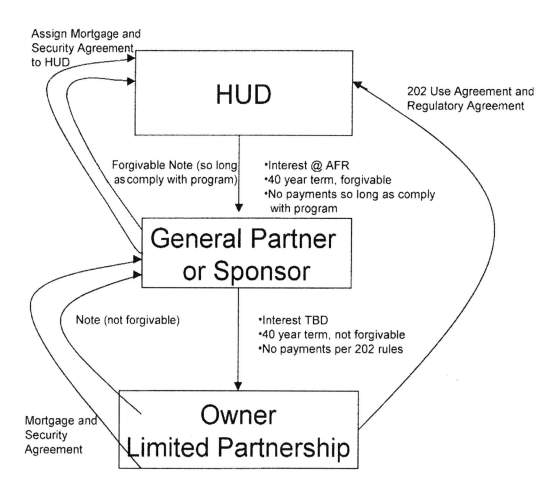

Appendix C
Diagram of Loan Structure (continued)

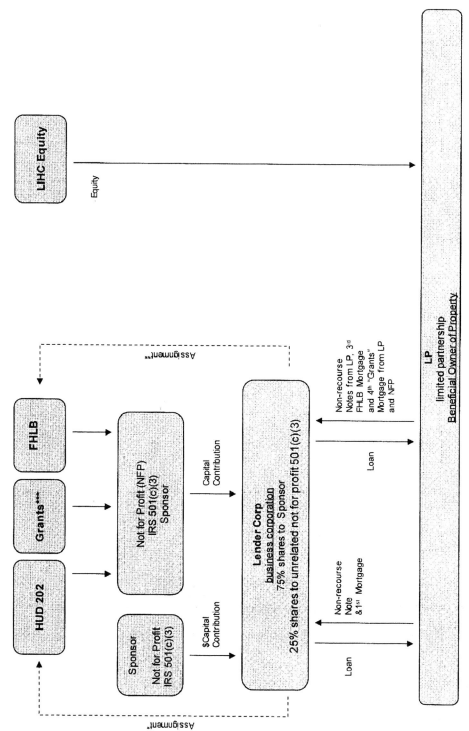

Appendix D
Rider to Be Utilized When Using AHP and 202 Funds

Loan No. _____

RIDER TO LENDER'S DEED OF TRUST [or MORTGAGE]

For value received, the undersigned all agree that the following provisions shall be incorporated into that certain deed of trust [or mortgage] ("Deed of Trust" [or "Mortgage"]) of even date executed by _____ ("Borrower"), in favor of _____ ("Lender" or "Beneficiary"), as Beneficiary, to which Deed of Trust [or Mortgage] this Rider is attached, as well as the promissory note which said Deed of Trust [or Mortgage] secures (the "Note"). In addition, and to the extent that this Rider, and, consequently the Deed of Trust [or Mortgage], affect the rights and responsibilities of the United States Department of Housing and Urban Development ("HUD") under the HUD Section 202 Supportive Housing for the Elderly program (12 U.S.C. § 1701q) ("Section 202 program"), or the HUD Section 811 Supportive Housing for Persons with Disabilities program (42 U.S.C. § 8013) ("Section 811 program"), HUD agrees to have a duly authorized official approve this document by execution on the signature line set forth below. To the extent that the provisions of this Rider are inconsistent with the provisions of the Note, Deed of Trust [or Mortgage], or any other HUD capital advance documentation, including but not limited to Paragraph 21 of the HUD Capital Advance Program Regulatory Agreement ("HUD Regulatory Agreement"), required to be executed pursuant to the HUD Section 202 or Section 811 programs, the provisions of this Rider shall prevail and shall supersede any such inconsistent provisions of the Note, Deed of Trust [or Mortgage], or HUD capital advance documentation.

1. **Transfer of the Property or a Beneficial Interest in Borrower.** With respect to [insert: number of Paragraph in this Deed of Trust [or Mortgage] pertaining to the acceleration of payment in the event of the sale or transfer of all or any part of the Property, or any interest therein] of this Deed of Trust [or Mortgage], such Paragraph is amended as follows:

   a. Excluded from the provisions of this Paragraph shall be a transfer to HUD or to a transferee of HUD, provided that in the event of such transfer by Borrower (other than in the event of foreclosure), HUD or such transferee notifies Lender of its intent to acquire Borrower's interest in the subject Property, and HUD or such transferee expressly agrees to assume Borrower's obligations under the Loan documents, including compliance with the Affordable Housing Program ("AHP") Covenants.

   b. This Deed of Trust [or Mortgage] is subordinate to a first Deed of Trust made by Trustor in favor of the Secretary of HUD ("Secretary") to be recorded securing a Capital Advance made by the Secretary pursuant to [Insert: the Section 202 program, or Insert: the Section 811 program, as applicable,] ("HUD Deed of Trust"), and to a HUD Regulatory Agreement and HUD Capital Advance Program Use Agreement ("HUD Use Agreement") between Trustor and the Secretary, and to [Insert any other agreements applicable to, or required by, other priority lienholders] with respect to the Property referred to herein.

c. During the period the HUD Deed of Trust, HUD Regulatory Agreement and HUD Use Agreement are in effect, except as otherwise provided in this Rider, no default under this Deed of Trust [or Mortgage] may be declared without prior written approval of the Secretary, as applicable including, but not limited to, Lender's rights in the event of Borrower's default set forth in [Insert number(s) of Paragraph(s) in this Deed of Trust [or Mortgage] pertaining to acceleration of payment in the event of Borrower's default] of this Deed of Trust [or Mortgage] (which approval shall not be unreasonably withheld).

d. In the event that during the period the HUD Deed of Trust, HUD Regulatory Agreement and HUD Use Agreement are in effect, the Secretary acquires title to the Property by foreclosure, the lien of this Deed of Trust [or Mortgage] shall automatically terminate.

e. In the event Borrower defaults under the HUD Deed of Trust, HUD Regulatory Agreement or HUD Use Agreement, HUD shall give written notice thereof to Lender at the following address: [Insert Lender's address]. The notice shall specify the nature of the violation and the agreement violated.

f. This Deed of Trust [or Mortgage] shall not be modified during the period the HUD Deed of Trust, HUD Regulatory Agreement, HUD Use Agreement, or [Insert applicable agreements of other subordinate financing sources, including the Federal Home Loan Bank of ___] are in effect without the prior written approval of the Secretary, and the [Insert any other subordinate sources other than the Federal Home Loan Bank of _____] or the Federal Home Loan Bank of ____, as applicable.

g. During the period the HUD Deed of Trust, HUD Regulatory Agreement and HUD Use Agreement are in effect, in the event of any conflict between any provisions of this Deed of Trust [or Mortgage] and [Insert: 12 U.S.C. § 1701q (if a Section 202 program); or Insert: 42 U.S.C. § 8013 (if a Section 811 program)], HUD regulations, or the HUD Regulatory Agreement, this Deed of Trust [or Mortgage] shall be deemed amended to comply with said statute, HUD regulations and HUD Regulatory Agreement, except as follows:

(i) Notwithstanding any term or condition to the contrary in this Rider, neither Lender nor Trustee shall declare a default hereunder, or foreclose this Deed of Trust [or Mortgage], either by judicial action or under the power of sale herein granted, without the prior written approval of the Secretary (which approval shall not be unreasonably withheld) for so long as the HUD Capital Advance evidenced by a first deed of trust remains outstanding; **provided, however,** that in the event the Loan secured hereby is not used in compliance with the AHP Application or the AHP Covenants, due to an action or omission of Borrower, which Borrower has failed to cure, then Lender may, after ten (10) days prior written notice to HUD and Borrower, declare all amounts due hereunder due and payable. In such event, and pursuant to Paragraph 5(c) of the HUD Regulatory Agreement by and between HUD and Borrower, dated _____, HUD shall approve payments to be made by Borrower to Lender from Residual Receipts (as such term is defined in Paragraph 17(g) of the HUD Regulatory Agreement) of the Project, if and to the extent Residual Receipts are available as determined by the HUD Multifamily Hub or Multifamily Program Center Director. As used in Paragraph 17(g)(1)(ii) of the HUD Regulatory Agreement, the term "obligations" shall not include any non-HUD sources of financing.

(ii) Borrower shall comply with the AHP Covenants and all other requirements of the Federal Home Loan Bank of ___ and the Federal Housing Finance Board relating to the AHP, and shall also comply with the requirements of HUD with respect to the development and operation of the Project. Notwithstanding Borrower's compliance with the requirements of HUD, in the event that Borrower's acts or omissions result in noncompliance with the AHP Application or the AHP Covenants, then Borrower shall, to the extent possible, eliminate the circumstances of noncompliance by requesting a modification of the terms of the AHP Application pursuant to 12 C.F.R. §§ 960.7 or 960.9, as applicable. If the circumstances of any noncompliance by Borrower with the AHP Application or the AHP Covenants cannot be, or are not, eliminated by a modification or cured within a reasonable period of time, then the provisions hereof, including notice of noncompliance and repayment of the Loan secured by this Deed of Trust [or Mortgage], shall apply. All capitalized terms used in this Paragraph ___ and not defined in this Rider or the Note shall be as defined in the [Insert name of Federal Home Loan Bank of ___ Subsidy Agreement] by and among the Federal Home Loan Bank of ___, Lender and Borrower, dated ___.

h. Approval by the Secretary of a Transfer of Physical Assets ("TPA") of the Project referred to in the Note secured by this Deed of Trust [or Mortgage] shall constitute approval of the TPA by Lender, provided that prior written notice of the TPA is given to Lender and the transferee expressly assumes all of Borrower's obligations under the Loan documents and AHP Covenants.

2. Retention Agreement. Borrower agrees as follows:

(i) The Property's rental units, or applicable portion thereof, must remain occupied by and affordable for households with incomes at or below the levels committed to be served in the AHP Application for the duration of the retention period (as defined in the AHP Covenants).

(ii) Lender will be given notice of any transfer or refinancing of the Property occurring prior to the end of the retention period.

(iii) In the case of a transfer or refinancing of the Property prior to the end of the retention period, an amount equal to the Loan Amount shall be repaid to the Federal Home Loan Bank of ___, unless the Property continues to be subject to a deed restriction or other legally enforceable retention agreement or mechanism incorporating the income-eligibility and affordability restrictions committed to in the AHP Application for the duration of the retention period.

(iv) The income-eligibility and affordability restrictions applicable to the Property pursuant to the AHP Covenants terminate after any foreclosure.

IN WITNESS WHEREOF, Borrower and Lender (and HUD by indicating its approval) have executed this Rider as follows:

[Insert: NAME OF BORROWER]

By: _____

Its: _____

Date: _____

[Insert: NAME OF LENDER]

By: _____

Its: _____

Date: _____

Approved: UNITED STATES DEPARTMENT OF HOUSING AND URBAN DEVELOPMENT

By: _____

Its: _____

Date: _____

Appendix E
Refinance Sample Riders Used in Various HUD Field Offices

HUD ADDENDUM TO [INSERT LOAN DOCUMENT NAME]

SECONDARY FINANCING OF HUD CAPITAL ADVANCE PROJECTS

Project Name: _____

HUD Project Number: _____

1. Any payments under this [_____] may not become due and payable in whole or in part until the term of the 202 Capital Advance has matured, except as permitted under item 2, below.

2. The only payments allowable under the [_____] prior to release of the HUD 202 documents will be from Residual Receipts, to the extent available, and any such payments will require approval of the local HUD office, in advance. The only exception to this rule would be where the sponsor agrees in advance to make the payments from its own funds, and such funds clearly do not come from the subject project.

3. Compliance by the Borrower with HUD 202 requirements will satisfy the requirements of this [_____] No requirements by the [_____] will be permitted which interfere with or conflict with HUD 202 requirements concerning the development or operation of the project or in any way jeopardize continued operation of the project on terms at least as favorable to existing and future tenants.

4. No foreclosure/default under this [_____] may occur without HUD approval.

5. HUD approval of a Transfer of Physical Assets (TPA) will constitute approval of the TPA by the [_____].

[The balance of this page is intentionally left blank.]

Appendix F
HUD-Required Provision Rider

This HUD-Required Provisions Rider (the "Rider") is dated as of _____, and is attached to and made a part of that certain Loan Agreement (the "Loan Agreement") by and between [_____] (the "Borrower"), and the [_____](the "Junior Lender"), a Promissory Note (the "Junior Lender Note") from Borrower to Junior Lender in the amount of [_____](the "Junior Lender Loan"), a Regulatory Agreement and Declaration of Restrictive Covenants executed by Borrower in favor of the Junior Lender (the "Junior Lender Regulatory Agreement"), a Deed of Trust by Borrower to the Junior Lender (the "Junior Lender Deed of Trust"), and any other document executed by the Borrower in favor of the Junior Lender in connection with the Loan (collectively, the "Junior Lender Documents"), relating to the property commonly known as [_____] (the "Development"). In the event of any conflict, inconsistency or ambiguity between the provisions of this Rider and the provisions of the Junior Lender Documents, the provisions of this Rider shall control. All capitalized terms used herein and not otherwise defined herein shall have the meaning given to such terms in the Junior Lender Documents. As used in this Rider, the term "HUD Documents" shall mean the following documents relating to the HUD Section 202 Capital Advance for the Development, HUD Project [_____]:

A. Deed of Trust from Borrower in favor of the general partner of the Borrower (the "General Partner"), which will be assigned by the General Partner to HUD, and which will be recorded against the Property (the "HUD Deed of Trust");

B. Regulatory Agreement between Borrower and HUD to be recorded against the Property ("HUD Regulatory Agreement");

C. Capital Advance Program Use Agreement between Borrower and HUD to be recorded against the Property (the "HUD Use Agreement");

D. HUD Security Agreement between Borrower in favor of the General Partner, which will be assigned by the General Partner to HUD (the "HUD Security Agreement");

E. HUD Project Rental Assistance Contract (the "PRAC");

F. Other HUD Capital Advance documents.

1. <u>Term of Rider</u>. Notwithstanding anything else in this Rider to the contrary, the provisions of this Rider shall be and remain in effect only so long as the HUD Documents, or any of them, are in effect; thereafter, this Rider and its requirements shall be deemed no longer in effect.

2. Subordination. The covenants contained in the Junior Lender Documents shall be subordinate to the rights of HUD under the HUD Documents, and to the HUD rules and regulations pertaining thereto; and furthermore, the Junior Lender Documents shall not be enforceable against the HUD Secretary, his or her successors and assigns, should the HUD Secretary acquire title to the Property by power of sale, foreclosure, or by deed in lieu of foreclosure. In addition, so long as the HUD Documents are in effect, in the event that there are any conflicts between the terms and conditions in the Junior Lender Documents and the terms and conditions of the HUD Documents and HUD rules and regulations pertaining thereto, the HUD Documents and HUD rules and regulations shall prevail. No default may be declared under the Junior Lender Documents without HUD prior written consent.

3. HUD Rules. During the time period in which Section 202 or the PRAC regulations apply to the Development, rents approved by HUD pursuant to the Section 202 program and the PRAC shall be deemed to be in compliance with the Junior Lender Regulatory Agreement, and compliance by the Borrower with the Section 202 Regulations and the PRAC with respect to continued occupancy by households whose incomes exceed the eligible income limitations of the Junior Lender Regulatory Agreement, or other matters set forth in the Junior Lender Regulatory Agreement, shall be deemed to be compliance with the requirements of the Junior Lender Documents. Nothing in the Junior Lender Documents shall in any way limit, interfere or conflict with the rights of HUD with respect to the development, operation and management of the Development; nor can the Junior Lender Documents in any way jeopardize the continued operation of the Development on terms at least as favorable to existing as well as future tenants.

4. Maturity Date. The Junior Lender Note may not mature, and may not bear a maturity date, prior to the date on which the HUD Note matures. The term of the Junior Loan Documents shall be extended if the Junior Note matures, there are no residual receipts or non-Project funds available for repayment and the HUD Mortgage has not been retired in full or if HUD grants a deferment of amortization or forbearance that results in an extended maturity of the Loan Documents.

5. Residual Receipts. As long as HUD, its successors or assigns, is the insurer or holder of the HUD Documents, any payments due from Project income from the Section 202 units under the Junior Lender Documents, or any prepayments made with Project Income from the Section 202 units, shall be made only from Residual Receipts (as defined in the HUD Documents) of the Development, and subject to the availability of the Residual Receipts in accordance with the HUD Documents. No payments or prepayments using Residual Receipts can be made without HUD approval. Borrower may make payments or prepayments at any time without HUD approval using funds that do not come from Project income from the Section 202 units. The restrictions on payment imposed by this paragraph shall not excuse any default cause by the failure of the makers to pay the indebtedness evidenced by the Junior Lender Note.

6. Indemnification. Enforcement by the Junior Lender of any indemnification provisions in the Junior Lender Documents will not and shall not result in any monetary claim against

the Development, the HUD Capital Advance proceeds, any reserve or deposit required by HUD in connection with the HUD Capital Advance, or the rents or other income from the Development other than Residual Receipts authorized for release by HUD, without the prior written consent of HUD, but Junior Lender shall have the right to add any amounts due the Junior Lender pursuant to indemnification provisions in the Junior Lender Documents to the principal amount of the Junior Lender Loan and the Junior Lender Note, and interest shall accrue thereon commencing on the date indemnification payments are due. In addition, any indemnification provisions shall not be enforceable against the HUD Secretary, his or her successors and assigns, should the HUD Secretary acquire title to the Project by power of sale, foreclosure, or by deed-in-lieu of foreclosure.

7. Transfer. Approval by HUD of a Transfer of Physical Assets (as defined in Handbook 4350-1 Rev-1) ("TPA") shall constitute approval of the transfer by the Junior Lender and the Borrower shall deliver to the Junior Lender, at the same time as its delivery to HUD, any application for HUD's approval of a proposed transfer. Also, the Borrower shall require the transferee to expressly assume the Borrower's obligations under the Junior Lender Documents; provided, however, HUD shall not be required to enforce the requirements of this sentence and if Borrower and any transferee fail to include such assumption in transfer documents, such failure shall not affect the validity of the transfer. The Junior Lender shall have the right to specifically enforce the requirement that any transferee assume the Borrower's obligations under the Junior Lender Documents. In the absence of such written assumption, no transfer shall be deemed to relieve the transferor from any obligations under the Junior Lender Documents.

8. Default under Junior Lender Documents. The Junior Lender shall not declare a default under the Junior Lender Documents unless it has received the prior written approval of HUD, and the Junior Lender's right to accelerate the Junior Lender Note during the term of the HUD Documents shall be enforceable only with the prior written approval of HUD.

9. Receiver. The Junior Lender, for itself, its successors and assigns further covenants and agrees that in the event of the appointment of a receiver in any action by the Junior Lender, its successors or assigns, to foreclose the Junior Lender Deed of Trust, no rents, revenue or other income of the Development collected by the receiver or by the mortgagee-in-possession shall be utilized for the payment of interest, principal, or any other charges due and payable under the Junior Lender Deed of Trust, except from Residual Receipts, if any. The appointment of a receiver shall require approval by the Secretary of HUD, and pursuant to HUD regulations, as long as the Junior Lender is the beneficiary under the Junior Lender Deed of Trust, the Junior Lender cannot be a mortgagee-in-possession. In the event of the appointment, by any court, of any person, other than HUD or the Junior Lender, as a receiver or a mortgagee or party in possession, or in the event of any enforcement of any assignment of leases, rents, issues, profits, or contracts contained in the Junior Lender Documents, with or without court action, no rents, revenue or other income of the Development collected by the receiver, person in possession or person pursuing enforcement as aforesaid, shall be utilized for the payment of interest, principal or any other amount due and payable under the provisions of the Junior Lender Documents, except from Residual Receipts in accordance with the HUD

Regulatory Agreement. The receiver, person in possession or person pursuing enforcement shall operate the Development in accordance with all provisions of the HUD Documents.

10. Deed-in-Lieu of Foreclosure. In the event that HUD acquires title to the Property by deed-in-lieu of foreclosure, the lien of the Junior Lender Deed of Trust will automatically terminate subject to the conditions as hereinafter described. The Junior Lender may cure a default under the HUD Deed of Trust prior to conveyance by deed-in-lieu of foreclosure. HUD shall give written notice to the Borrower of a proposed tender of title in the event HUD decides to accept a deed-in-lieu of foreclosure. HUD will only give such written notice if, at the time of the placing of the Junior Lender Deed of Trust against the Property, HUD receives a copy of an endorsement to the title policy of the Borrower or the Junior Lender which indicates that (a) the Junior Lender Deed of Trust has been recorded and (b) HUD is required to give notice of any proposed election or tender of a deed-in-lieu of foreclosure. Such notice shall be given at the address stated in the Junior Lender Deed of Trust or such other address as may subsequently, upon written notice to HUD, be designated by the Junior Lender as its legal business address. The Junior Lender shall have thirty (30) days to cure the default after notice of intent to accept a deed-in-lieu of foreclosure is mailed.

11. Borrower's Notice to the Junior Lender. Notwithstanding the requirements set forth in Paragraph 10 above, in the event that Borrower contemplates executing a deed-in-lieu of foreclosure, Borrower shall first give the Junior Lender thirty (30) days' prior written notice; provided, however, that the failure of the Borrower to give said notice shall have no effect on the right of HUD to accept a deed-in-lieu of foreclosure.

12. Sale, Transfer or Assignment of the Junior Lender Note. The Junior Lender Note is non-negotiable and may not be sold, transferred, assigned, or pledged by the Junior Lender except with the prior written approval of HUD.

13. Amendment. No amendment to the Junior Lender Documents made after the date of this Rider shall have any force or effect until and unless such amendment is approved in writing by HUD.

Navigating HUD Programs: The 2530 Previous Participation Approval Process

Elizabeth H. Friedgut and Dianne S. Pickersgill*

I. GENERAL OVERVIEW

A. Purpose of Process

The approval of the U.S. Department of Housing and Urban Development (HUD or the Department, as the context may require) is required for particular individuals and legal entities to participate in certain HUD-financed and/or HUD-subsidized multifamily projects and health-care facilities. This approval process, which was instituted in 1966,[1] is called the 2530 Previous Participation Certification and Approval Process (the 2530 Process).

HUD's decisions to approve or disapprove prospective participants are intended to be made on the basis of certain risk factors that are employed to assess the likelihood that a particular applicant will honor its legal, financial, and contractual obligations to the Department in a timely and satisfactory manner.[2] Among the risk factors that HUD considers are (a) the financial stability of the applicant, (b) the applicant's history of compliance with HUD programmatic requirements, (c) the applicant's general business practices, including its per-

---

* The authors also wish to thank the following individuals for their assistance in producing this article: Denise Murphy of Murphy Consulting and Arthur Hessel of Hessel, Aluise and Neun, P.C.
 1. § 1-1 of HUD Handbook 4065-1 REV-1.
 2. 24 C.F.R. § 200.210; Sec. 1-2 of HUD Handbook 4065-1 Rev.-1; Sec. 1.1 of *APPS Users' Guide*—Industry.

formance record with other non-HUD properties, and (d) any other factors that the Department deems relevant to its assessment of whether the applicant can be expected to participate in a particular HUD-financed or HUD-subsidized project in a manner that will further the Department's objective of supporting and providing decent, safe, and affordable housing.[3]

The 2530 Process is intended to supplement the reviews performed by HUD as to such matters as project viability and participant credit capacity and relevant experience in the context of its consideration and analysis of potential new mortgage loans, project transfers, changes in organizational structures of project owners, and selection of project construction and management personnel.

Under the 2530 Process, an application for 2530 approval may be submitted either on HUD Form 2530, Previous Participation Certification (Paper 2530), or via the Internet using HUD's electronic Active Partners Performance System (APPS).

B. Legal Authority

Legal authority for the 2530 Process is set forth in Subpart H of Part 200 of Volume 24 of the Code of Federal Regulations, which was amended on April 13, 2005, at 70 Fed. Reg. 19,660 (the 2530 Amendments). The applicable regulations, as so amended, are collectively referred to herein as the 2530 Regulations. HUD also has issued certain administrative guidances for the 2530 Process as a supplement to the 2530 Regulations, the principal ones of which are contained in:

1. HUD Handbook 4065.1 Rev.-1, "Previous Participation (HUD-2530) Handbook" (the 2530 Handbook);
2. HUD Memorandum, dated July 16, 2004, from Beverly J. Miller, Director of Office of Asset Management, HTG, titled "Reiteration and Reminder—Participation Process and Decisions; Existing Policy," as amended by HUD Memorandum, dated November 23, 2004, from Beverly J. Miller, Director of Office of Asset Management, HTG, titled "Revision #1 to 'Reiteration and Reminder—Participation Process and Decisions; Existing Policy'" (collectively, the November 2004 Miller Memorandum);
3. HUD Memorandum, dated January 17, 2007, from Beverly J. Miller, Director, Office of Asset Management, HTG, titled "Critical Findings—Modification to Previous Participation Review and Approval Process" (the Critical Findings Memorandum);
4. HUD Memorandum, dated March 26, 2007, from Beverly J. Miller, Office of Asset Management, titled "Active Partner Performance System (APPS)—Passive Investor Previous Participation and Certification" (the Passive Investor Memorandum);
5. HUD Memorandum, dated June 21, 2007, from Charles H. Williams, Deputy Assistant Secretary for Multifamily Housing Programs, HT, titled "Previous Participation Certificate (PPC) Operating Procedures Submission Reviews and Controls" (the Williams Memorandum);

---

3. 24 C.F.R. § 200.215(h). Curiously, among the risk factors that HUD does not consider is the lack of any previous participation. In such a situation, HUD 2530 approval can be assumed on the basis of the theory of "benefit of the doubt."

6. HUD Memorandum, dated July 11, 2007, from John L. Garvin, Senior Advisor to FHA Commissioner/Acting Deputy Assistant Secretary for Multifamily Housing Programs, HT, titled "Previous Participation Certificate (PPC) Operating Procedures Limited Liability Corporate Investor" (the LLCI Memorandum); and
7. the APPS Users' Guide—Industry (the User Guide).[4]

In regard thereto, it is important to note that in certain instances the requirements and procedures set forth in the 2530 Regulations (which were last updated in 2005) and the 2530 Handbook (which was last updated in 1994) do not conform to current HUD policies and practices, which are most accurately, although not completely, expressed in the User Guide.

II. TRIGGERS OF THE 2530 PROCESS

Whether any potential participation in a particular HUD-financed and/or HUD-subsidized project triggers the 2530 Process depends on the HUD program involved, the nature of the transaction, and the role that the prospective participant intends to assume in the organizational structure of the 2530 applicant.

A. Covered Projects

The 2530 Process is generally applicable to multifamily projects[5] that fall under the following HUD multifamily programs administered under the jurisdiction of the Assistant Secretary for Housing–Federal Housing Commissioner (Covered Projects):

1. Multifamily projects financed or that are proposed to be financed with a mortgage insured or held by HUD under the multifamily housing programs contained in Title II of the National Housing Act;
2. Health-care facilities and residential-care facilities financed or that are proposed to be financed with a mortgage insured or held by HUD under the Section 232 nursing-home programs contained in Title II of the National Housing Act or with a hospital mortgage insured or held by HUD under Section 242 of the National Housing Act;[6]
3. Multifamily projects financed with direct loans or capital advances from HUD under Section 202 of the Housing Act of 1959 (Housing for the Elderly and Handicapped);
4. Multifamily projects financed with direct loans or capital advances from HUD under Section 811 of the Cranston-Gonzalez National Affordable Housing Act (Supportive Housing for Persons With Disabilities);

---

4. The version of the *User Guide* referenced herein is dated April 2011.
5. For purposes of the 2530 Process, HUD defines a project to mean "(1) [f]ive or more residential units covered by a single mortgage, loan or contract of assistance; (2) a hospital, group practice facility or nursing home; (3) cooperative and condominium developments; and (4) a subdivision being developed and financed with a mortgage under Title X of the National Housing Act." 24 C.F.R. § 200.215(f).
6. Hospitals are included in the 2530 Regulations under the definition of projects, but the Section 242 program is not specifically included in the applicability section of the regulations. In practice, HUD requires 2530 approval for participation in this program.

5. Multifamily projects in which at least 20 percent of the project units are receiving or will receive subsidy from HUD under the following programs (a Subsidy Contract), whether or not the project has a mortgage insured or held by HUD:
   - Interest Reduction Payments (IRP) under Section 236 of the National Housing Act;
   - Rent Supplement Payments under Section 101 of the Housing and Urban Development Act of 1965;
   - Rental Assistance Payments under Section 236 of the National Housing Act;
   - Section 8 Housing Assistance payments under Section 8 of the U.S. Housing Act of 1937, other than Section 8 tenant-based programs such as the Housing Choice Voucher Program, the Project-Based Voucher Program, the Mod Rehab Program, and the McKinney Act Shelter Plus Care Program;[7]
6. Multifamily projects financed or that are proposed to be financed with a risk-share mortgage loan under Section 542(c) of the Housing and Community Development Act of 1992;[8]
7. Multifamily projects subject to a HUD-prescribed use agreement;
8. Multifamily projects and health-care facilities owned and to be sold by HUD or subject to HUD-held mortgage debt that HUD is seeking to foreclose with respect to which HUD reserves the right to approve or disapprove a prospective bidder; and
9. Multifamily projects subject to a Subsidy Contract seeking to participate in HUD's Mark-to-Market program.[9]

At this time, multifamily projects financed with assistance from HUD under its public housing programs, including HOPE VI, capital grants, and/or operating subsidy assistance, are not subject to the 2530 Process. Also excluded are HUD's HOME and Community Development Block Grant programs.

B. Property Submissions

The 2530 Process is applicable to certain types of transactions involving Covered Projects. The purpose of the requisite 2530 submission for these transactions is for the prospective participant to assume a specific new role in connection with a Covered Project and the subject transaction or to assume additional financial responsibilities with respect to a Covered Project in which the applicant currently plays a role.[10] These types of submissions are hereinafter referred to as a "Property Submission." The subject transactions are as follows:

1. New applications for mortgage insurance under the National Housing Act;

---

7. The citations to various exempt Section 8 tenant-based programs contained in the 2530 Regulations are not accurate and/or refer to provisions of the HUD regulations that have been superseded.

8. This program is not referenced in the 2530 Regulations, but it is listed in Appendix 3 to the 2530 HANDBOOK, and, in practice, 2530 approval from HUD is required for participation in the program.

9. 24 C.F.R. §§ 200.213 & 200.217(a); § 1.2 of *User Guide*; Appendix 3 of 2530 HANDBOOK.

10. § 8.0 of *User Guide*.

2. Refinance applications for mortgage insurance under the National Housing Act;
3. New applications for direct loans or capital advances under Section 202 of the Housing Act of 1959 or Section 811 or the Cranston-Gonzales National Affordable Housing Act;
4. Assignment/assumption of a Subsidy Contract;
5. IRP decouplings;
6. Full Transfer of Physical Assets (TPA) applications;[11]
7. Changes in ownership of a project subject to a HUD-prescribed use agreement;
8. The appointment of or change in management agent for a Covered Project;
9. The appointment of or change in lessee or administrator of any nursing-home, assisted-living, or skilled-care facility Covered Project;
10. The purchase of a project pursuant to a foreclosure sale conducted by HUD or on HUD's behalf by a foreclosure commissioner in which HUD reserves the right to approve or disapprove the bidder concurrent with the submission of the foreclosure bid;
11. The purchase of any HUD-owned project;
12. The purchase of a HUD-held note; and
13. The appointment of or change in general contractor or turnkey developer of a Covered Project.[12]

C. Organization Structure Changes

In addition to Property Submissions, certain changes in the organizational structure of an approved Principal (as defined below) of a Covered Project also may trigger the 2530 Process. According to HUD directives set forth in the 2530 Regulations, the 2530 Handbook, the User Guide, and certain other HUD administrative guidance hereinafter described, the relevant changes in organizational structure for 2530 purposes include the direct transfer of significant ownership interests and any other changes that effect a change in control of the Principal or otherwise will have what HUD deems to be a significant impact on the organization in question through the assumption of a new role or the expansion or contraction of an existing role, as well as various ministerial and corrective changes.

Specifically, the 2530 Process is applicable to the following types of Covered Project organizational changes (Organization Change Submissions), even if any of these changes would not otherwise trigger HUD's Full TPA review procedures. The Organization Change Submissions recognized by HUD are as follows:

1. "Major Organization Change," which includes the addition of a Principal or any change in an existing individual or entity Principal's role or percentage of ownership

---

11. HUD's TPA review procedures are applicable to any transfer of title to a Project subject to any multifamily mortgage loan insured or held by HUD (including the transfer of 100% of the beneficial interest in a land or other passive trust that holds title to any such Project) or change in organizational structure that causes the dissolution of the legal status of a Project owner under applicable state (as opposed to federal) law, *i.e.*, a "Full TPA" in HUD parlance. Chapter 13 of HUD HANDBOOK 4350.1 Rev.-1, *Multifamily Asset Management and Project Servicing*.

12. 24 C.F.R. pt. 200, subpt. H; § 8.0 of *User Guide*.

in a Covered Project pursuant to which the individual or entity is deemed to assume or otherwise acquires a controlling interest or aggregate interest of at least 25 percent with respect to any partnership interest or limited liability company membership interest or 10 percent with respect to any corporate stock interest;[13]

2. "Modified TPA," which includes any change in the general partner or managing member (or presumably any other controlling party) in the first tier of the ownership structure of a particular Chief Principal (as defined below) as well as any changes in ownership percentages of five percent or more of any such controlling Principal;[14]

3. "Corporate Buyout," which involves the purchase of one company by another company as a result of which the purchased company ceases to exist, i.e., a so-called forward merger;[15]

4. "Minor Organization Change," which includes removal of a Principal and changing the following information for a Principal: (a) the starting date in the organization; (b) the role in organization (except for changes to limited partner, general partner, managing member, or managing general partner); (c) ownership interest pursuant to which the individual or entity involved will own any partnership interest of less than

---

13. 24 C.F.R. §§ 200.217(a)(12) & (13); Sec. 11.1 of *User Guide*; November 2004 Miller Memorandum.

14. §§ 12.0 & 12.1 of *User Guide*. In this regard, the *User Guide* appears to take a different view of what HUD traditionally has regarded to be a Modified TPA, which, as defined in Chapter 13 of HUD HANDBOOK 4350.1 Rev.-1, includes (a) a single transfer of more than 50% of the interest of a partnership Project owner which does not cause a dissolution of the entity under applicable state law; (b) the substitution of one or more of the general partners; (c) the single transfer of more than 50% of the corporate stock of a corporate Project owner or a single transfer of less than 50% of the total corporate stock of the corporate mortgagor where such transfer results in a change in control of the corporate Project owner; (d) an assignment/transfer of a portion of or all of the beneficial interest in a passive trust when there is no change in control of the Project; (e) a single transfer of more than 50% of the corporate stock of a corporate general partner or a single transfer of an amount less than 50% of the corporate stock of a corporate general partner where such transfer results in a change in control of the corporate general partner; and (f) any other transaction which does not fall within any of the other categories but which, nevertheless, results in a change of control of the owner of any Project *subject to a multifamily mortgage loan insured or held by HUD*. In contrast, the *User Guide* appears to apply the concept of Modified TPA to include any change in the controlling party of any Chief Principal (as defined below), as well as any change in the ownership structure of any such controlling party of five percent (5%) or more in any Covered Project, and not just Covered Projects that are subject to multifamily mortgage loans insured or held by HUD.

As such, it is unclear from the *User Guide* what HUD intends to be the difference between a Major Organizational Change and a Modified TPA. The *User Guide* states that APPS will identify whether a particular submission is a Major Organization Change or a Modified TPA; however, that is not the case. Therefore, if, after reviewing HUD's guidelines on Modified TPAs, an applicant remains unclear as to whether the proposed organization change qualifies as a Major Organization Change or a Modified TPA, the applicant is encouraged to request clarification in writing from HUD.

15. Chapter 13 of User Guide.

25 percent (other than a general partner partnership or managing member interest) and any nonpartnership interest of less than 10 percent;[16] and

5. "Court Order/Inheritance," which involves the acquisition of an interest by a Principal pursuant to court order or inheritance.[17]

The 2530 Regulations require that Organization Change Submissions for Major Organization Changes, Modified TPAs, Corporate Buyouts, and Minor Organization Changes be sent to HUD at least 30 days prior to implementation of the subject changes.[18] Pursuant to the 2530 Regulations, Organization Change Submissions necessitated by Court Order/Inheritance must be submitted within 30 days after implementation of the required change.[19] HUD approval of Organization Change Submissions relating to Major Organization Changes, Modified TPAs, and Corporate Buyouts is required; HUD approval of Organizational Change Submissions relating to Minor Organizational Changes and Organizational Change Submissions necessitated by Court Order/Inheritance is not required.[20]

III. DEFINITION OF PRINCIPAL FOR WHOM HUD APPROVAL IS REQUIRED

2530 approval is required only for those proposed participants who qualify as a Principal. Under Section 200.215(e)(1) of the 2530 Regulations, a "Principal" is defined as any individual or legal entity that proposes to participate or is participating in a Covered Project in any of the following roles in either a particular direct or indirect ownership or control capacity:

1. as a sponsor,
2. as an owner,
3. as a management agent,
4. as a general contractor or turnkey developer,
5. as a nursing-home administrator or operator (including any lessee),
6. as a consultant/packager, or
7. as an attorney or architect who has other than an arm's-length fee arrangement for the provision of professional services.

For purposes of this chapter, any of the foregoing categories of Principal that have direct relationships with HUD (as opposed to those Principals having an indirect ownership or controlling interest in any such Principal) shall hereinafter be referred to as a "Chief Principal."

---

16. Chapter 14 of User Guide. Changes in participant information such as any changes in a participant's name, address, contact person, or type of ownership do not require HUD approval and can be effectuated in APPS by the editing of what is described as the Participant Detail. Chapter 6 of User Guide. Any change in a participant's social security number or employer identification number requires the submission to HUD of documentary evidence of the correct identification number and the manual input into APPS of the change by HUD staff.
17. Chapter 15 of User Guide.
18. 24 C.F.R. §§ 200.217(a)(12) & (13).
19. 24 C.F.R. § 200.217(a)(14).
20. 24 C.F.R. § 200.217(b); *User Guide*, Chapters 14 and 15.

Section 200.215(e)(2) of the 2530 Regulations also includes the following derivative categories within the definition of Principal, which are intended to include entities and natural persons who have a particular indirect ownership or controlling interest in a Chief Principal, as described below:

1. any affiliate of any Principal, i.e., any person or entity that directly or indirectly controls or has the power to control the policy of a Principal;[21]
2. for any partnership Principal, all general partners and any limited partners with a 25 percent or more limited-partner partnership interest in the Principal;
3. for any public or privately held corporation or for any entity included within the definition of Principal, the President, Vice-President, Secretary, Treasurer, and any other executive officers who are directly responsible to the Board of Directors or the equivalent thereof, all members of the Board of Directors, and each stockholder with a 10 percent or more stock ownership interest in the corporation.

To date, the 2530 Regulations have not been revised to include within the definition of Principal the controlling or ownership interests in any limited liability company. However, the November Miller Memorandum recognizes "[t]he regulations are not specific regarding members in a [l]imited [l]iability [c]ompany" and provides that applicants should "treat a limited liablity company as if it were a limited partnership."[22]

Section 200.215(e)(3) of the 2530 Regulations specifically excludes from the definition of Principal (a) any owner or purchaser of less than five individual unit(s) in the same condominium or cooperative development, (b) persons whose sole interest in any Covered Project is that of a tenant, and (c) public housing agencies.

For purposes of this chapter, each such aforementioned Chief Principal and derivative Principal shall hereinafter be referred to as a Principal.

At present, Section 1-3(C) of the 2530 Handbook requires the disclosure and approval as part of the 2530 Process of Principals through the third tier of the ownership structure of any Chief Principal, or such lesser tier in which the Principals are all individuals (the "Three-Tier Rule"). However, the preamble to the 2530 Amendments contains an explicit statement that HUD intends to make the 2530 Process applicable to all tiers of ownership of any Chief Principal, thus eliminating the Three-Tier Rule. As such, current HUD practice now requires the disclosure of the identity and participation histories (with some exceptions, discussed in Section 5 below) of all Chief Principals and all of their derivative Principals until ownership is identified and demonstrated to exist at the individual level.

A view held by certain members of the industry is that the 2530 Process is applicable only to Principals (at whatever ownership tier) that have an equity interest directly or indirectly *in any Chief Principal* of any general partner partnership interest, any limited-liability company managing member interest, any 25 percent or greater limited-partner partnership interest, any 25 percent or greater limited liability company membership interest, or any 10

---

21. 24 C.F.R. § 215(a).
22. *See also* § 8.3(D)(1)(a)(2) of the Multifamily Accelerated Processing Guide, revised as of November 2011 (the *MAP Guide*), which defines as principals of a limited liability company all managing members and all members with a 25% or greater interest.

percent or greater corporate stock interest. However, a strict interpretation of the 2530 Regulations, as amended by the 2530 Amendments, the 2530 Handbook, and the User Guide, does not support that assumption, nor is this interpretation encouraged by the Policy and Participation Standards Division (PPSD) in HUD Headquarters. Accordingly, the interpretation on which practitioners should rely is that the Principal percentage thresholds of the 2530 Process prescribed by the 2530 Regulations apply to *every* defined Principal regardless of their actual deemed percentage interest in the applicable Chief Principal.

IV. DISCLOSURE OF PRINCIPAL PARTICIPATION HISTORY, CERTIFICATION, AND SIGNATURE

Under the 2530 Process, with a few exceptions hereinafter described, all Principals are required to disclose their complete previous participation history as a Principal—without time limitation—not only in any Covered Project but also in any multifamily property financed or subsidized by the Rural Housing Service (RHS) (previously referred to as the Farmer's Home Administration, or FmHA) or any state or local housing finance agency.[23] The previous participation that must be disclosed for any individual or entity Principal includes not only the participation of the particular individual or entity through the Chief Principal for whom HUD 2530 approval for Covered Project participation is requested, but also any separate and discrete previous participation of the individual or entity in any other capacity or context as a Principal.

For example, in the case of an individual who is currently employed as a corporate officer of any Chief Principal or other Principal for whom 2530 approval is required and who was previously employed as a Principal by another entity unrelated to such Chief Principal or other Principal and through his or her previous employer, such individual acquired any HUD-recognized previous participation history, that individual must disclose his or her separate previous participation record to HUD. In addition, the decision by HUD to approve the participation of that individual and his or her current employer in a particular Covered Project will depend, in part, on the acceptability of the previous participation record of the former employer during the individual's period of employment as a Principal with the former employer, regardless of the nature or extent of involvement of the individual with respect to his or her prior employer's previous participation history.

With respect to all projects in which a Principal applicant has any previous participation, the following information is required:

1. Name of property;
2. Property location;
3. Property Identification Number;
4. Name of government agency involved if other than HUD;

---

23. According to PPSD staff in HUD Headquarters, such reportable participation does not need to include participation in any multifamily project that receives, as its sole source of government assistance, any type of tax credits. Also, as a practical matter, in many cases, HUD field office staff have not required that non-HUD-related state or local government agency participation be listed on a 2530 application, although that position is contrary to official HUD guidance.

5. Description of Principal role, including commencement and termination dates, as applicable;
6. Status of project debt during Principal period of participation (whether current, defaulted, assigned, or foreclosed);
7. Confirmation of whether any project default occurred during the Principal's participation, and if so, a written explanation as to how the default was resolved and contact information for a third-party individual or entity that can verify the applicant's explanation;
8. Most current management review score (MOR) and/or physical inspection rating during the Principal applicant's period of participation, including any HUD Real Estate Assessment Center (REAC) physical inspection scores,[24] and in the event of any failing REAC score, documentation indicating the corrective measures taken to correct the physical deficiencies in question.[25]

If a Principal applicant has no HUD-recognized previous participation, the applicant is required to note that fact in the 2530 application.

Under the 2530 Process, pursuant to Section 200.219 of the 2530 Regulations, each Principal in its individual capacity is also required to certify not only as to the completeness and accuracy of the organizational and property-specific information contained in the 2530 application, but also as to the following matters with respect to the preceding 10-year period:

1. No mortgage on any project listed by the Principal applicant has ever been in default, assigned to the government, or foreclosed, nor has any mortgage relief by the mortgagee been given;[26]
2. The Principal applicant has not experienced any defaults or noncompliances under any conventional contract or turnkey contract of sale involving a public housing project;
3. To the best knowledge of the Principal applicant, there are no unresolved audit findings raised as a result of any HUD audits, management reviews, or other governmental reviews involving the Principal applicant or any of its projects;[27]

---

24. HUD's REAC physical inspection system is applicable to all multifamily projects subject to mortgage loans insured or held by HUD or any project-based subsidy contract, as well as public housing projects, including mixed-finance projects. Under REAC, any score below 60 is considered to be failing.

When entering this information in APPS, applicants should take care when updating previous participation to only accept HUD's retrieved scores that apply during the Principal's period of participation and to update scores on the Principal's previous participation list any time they are submitting a new 2530 to HUD for approval, as the scores do not auto-populate into the previous participation list. The *User Guide* puts the onus of updating this information on the applicant. *See* Chapter 10 of *User Guide*.

25. There is sometimes confusion over the meaning of the "and/or" language contained on the form. If the property receives both MORs and REAC inspections, *both* scores must be reported.

26. This would presumably not cover a foreclosure on a single-family HUD-insured property owned on a personal basis by a Principal, as only HUD multifamily insured properties are required to be disclosed.

27. This might be read to include an individual Principal's personal IRS audit, as it applies to "the Principal applicant" broadly, not just as it relates to the Principal's properties.

4. There has not been a suspension or termination of any Section 8 Housing Assistance Payments under any Section 8 Housing Assistance Payments Contract in which the Principal applicant has a legal or beneficial interest;
5. The Principal applicant has not been convicted of a felony and is not presently, to the applicant's knowledge, the subject of a complaint or indictment charging a felony;
6. The Principal applicant has not been suspended, debarred, or otherwise restricted by any department or agency of the federal or any state government from doing business with that particular department or agency; and
7. The Principal applicant has not defaulted on an obligation covered by a surety or performance bond and has not been the subject of a claim under an employee fidelity bond.[28]

Each Principal must also make the following certifications as to its current status:

1. The Principal applicant is not an employee of HUD or FmHA (RHS) or a member of the immediate household of any HUD or FmHA (RHS) employee;
2. The Principal applicant is not currently the Principal in any HUD-assisted or FmHA (RHS)–assisted or -insured project on which construction has stopped for a period in excess of 20 days or which has been substantially complete for more than 90 days, and documents for closing, including any required final cost certification, have not been filed;
3. To its knowledge, the Principal applicant has not been found by HUD or FmHA (RHS) to be in noncompliance with any applicable civil rights laws; and
4. The Principal applicant is not a Member of Congress or a Resident Commissioner nor otherwise prohibited or limited by law from contracting with the federal government.

If a particular Principal applicant is unable to certify as to the accuracy of any of the aforementioned statements, the Paper 2530 requires the applicant to note as deleted in the 2530 application the certifications that cannot be made and to provide a written explanation of the relevant facts and circumstances that prevent the Principal applicant from making the particular certification and any other relevant information that otherwise demonstrates the qualification of the Principal applicant for the Covered Project participation in question. In APPS, the submission for each Principal requires a response to each certification as being true or false, with the requisite explanation to be provided for any "false" response. For purposes hereof, each of the foregoing certifications shall hereinafter be referred to as a "Qualified Certification."

The 2530 Process permits a Principal entity applicant to designate a limited number of individuals to sign and file a 2530 application (including the requisite certifications) on behalf of the entity and its individual and other entity Principals, provided that the application includes specific statements as to the signatory's designated authority and clearly indicates which, if any, of such individual and other entity Principals do or do not have separate

---

28. *See also* Form HUD-2530 p.1.

participation. If any individual or entity Principal of an applicant has any separate previous participation that must be disclosed to HUD under the 2530 Process, each such individual or entity Principal must sign the 2530 application for the applicant separately, as well as list its discrete previous participation records in the applicable submission.

V. SPECIAL SITUATIONS

There are currently two categories of Principals whom HUD has determined to exempt from the 2530 filing process entirely or has decided to restrict the scope of the 2530 filing requirements with respect thereto. There is a third category of Principal for whom HUD has yet to determine the appropriate methodology for making a 2530 filing.

The first such category of Principal is defined by HUD as a "Limited Liability Corporate Investor," or LLCI. The second category of Principal is defined by HUD as a "Passive Investor." The status of both such categories of Principal depends on the degree of HUD perceived and Principal claimed operational and policy control that the Principal in question will have over the Covered Project in which the Principal seeks to participate.

The third category of Principals is foreign national natural persons and entities that serve as direct or indirect Principals in entities seeking to participate in a Covered Project that do not possess either a Social Security Number (SSN) or an Employer Identification Number (EIN). As such, these Principals are unable to make a complete 2530 submission, which requires the inclusion of either an SSN or an EIN, as applicable, depending on the nature of the applicant, to allow for the review of Principal applicants in various federal government databases.

A. Limited Liability Corporate Investors

Among the requirements proposed by HUD in the 2530 Amendments (but then negated by statute) were that all prospective Principal participants make their requisite 2530 submissions in HUD's electronic APPS system by a HUD-prescribed date and that thereafter no Paper 2530s would be accepted by the Department. Because at the time APPS was not well understood by the multifamily industry, and because the system itself at the time was not as functional or secure as it is today, these pronouncements by HUD provoked strong opposition from the multifamily industry, particularly those entities acting as investors in programs such as the federal low-income housing tax credit program.

In response to the concerns about APPS expressed by the affordable housing investment community, in June of 2007, Congress passed the Preservation Approval Process Improvement Act of 2007. This statute required HUD to suspend all mandatory APPS submissions pending submission to Congress of proposed revisions to the 2530 Regulations and to suspend the requirement of 2530 submissions by "limited liability corporate investors who own or expect to own an interest in entities which are allowed or are expected to be allowed low-income housing tax credits under section 42 of the Internal Revenue Code of 1986."[29]

In lieu of making a 2530 submission for Covered Projects, Limited Liability Corporate Investors now may submit a certification of LLCI eligibility to HUD. This certification, which was promulgated in a July 2007 directive from HUD Headquarters to HUD field office

---

29. H.R. 1675, Pub. L. 110-35.

staff, herein defined as the "LLCI Memorandum," contains the following description of what HUD regards as a qualified Limited Liability Corporate Investor:

> An investor with limited or no control over routine property operations or HUD regulatory and/or contract compliance, even if the investor may take control (albeit not routine or repetitive control) of the ownership entity or assume the operating responsibilities in the event of the default of the operating partner or upon specific events all defined under the investment contract/agreement.

Although certain members of the multifamily industry, at least initially, sought to claim LLCI status for the direct Principals in a Chief Principal entity, such as the syndicating limited partner of the low-income housing tax credits, more recently it has become common practice for only investors in the syndicators to claim LLCI status.

The LLCI Memorandum requires the HUD field office with jurisdiction over the Covered Project in question to review the aforementioned certification, as well as the requisite organizational chart to be provided for the Chief Principal involved, which notes the relationship of the LLCI to the Chief Principal and the Covered Project, and then to make the determination as to whether the entity providing the certification qualifies as a LLCI. If that determination is made, the LLCI Memorandum then requires the field office to countersign the LLCI certification and return it with a letter confirming the approval to the applicant. In the alternative, if the field office determines that a particular applicant does not qualify as a LLCI, the LLCI Memorandum requires the field office to send a letter to the applicant setting forth HUD's bases for its decision to deny LLCI status to the applicant. Although in theory, therefore, HUD has the power to deny a particular applicant LLCI status, in practice, that power is rarely exercised. It should also be noted that unless a specific request is made to a field office for verification of LLCI status for a particular applicant by receipt of HUD's countersignature to the LLCI certification, many HUD field offices simply will accept the LLCI certification without further action, i.e., without countersignature and return of the countersigned document to the applicant.

B. Passive Investors

Prior to enactment by Congress of the Preservation Approval Process Improvement Act of 2007, HUD itself sought to alleviate at least some of the burden of compliance with the previous participation reporting and certification requirements of the 2530 Process for the multifamily investment community as a whole, not just those investing in Covered Projects funded with federal low-income housing tax credits. In a March 2007 directive from HUD Headquarters to HUD field office staff, herein defined as the "Passive Investor Memorandum," HUD created a new category of Principal called a "Passive Investor," which it defined as being "[i]nvestment participants [that] do not have operational or policy control or influence but only a passive financial interest in the participant organization."

Although it was generally initially assumed that the Passive Investor Memorandum was superseded by the LLCI Memorandum because the Passive Investor Memorandum required the registration of a Passive Investor in APPS, which HUD could no longer mandate as a result of the enactment of the Preservation Approval Process Improvement Act of 2007, more recently PPSD staff in HUD Headquarters have advised industry representatives orally that

Passive Investor status is available to Principals wishing to file Paper 2530s as well as APPS submissions.

In such instances, pursuant to the Passive Investor Memorandum, a Principal claiming Passive Investor status is required to make a 2530 submission that includes its name, address, EIN/SSN, and signature, as well as that of one individual whom it deems to be its Key Principal, i.e., "a natural person that [is] a principal of the company and/or affiliate and who has authority to legally bind the company in contracts and normal business dealings including dealings with HUD."[30] Neither the Passive Investor Principal nor its Key Principal is required to disclose or certify its respective previous participation in the 2530 submissions. Because the Passive Investor Memorandum does not restrict Passive Investor status to LLCIs, limited Passive Investor 2530 filings are now available to the multifamily investment community as a whole, not just to LLCIs. This will facilitate the involvement in Covered Projects by many investment participants that had never before participated in HUD programs or had elected to discontinue participation because of what they deemed to be HUD's onerous 2530 requirements.

C. Foreign Nationals

The 2530 Regulations and associated administrative guidance are silent as to what type of identification number a foreign national applicant must provide to file a 2530 application if the applicant does not have an EIN or SSN, as is sometimes the case.

In some cases, where a foreign national entity does not or cannot obtain an EIN because it is not considered to be doing business in the United States or is not required to pay federal income taxes, PPSD staff in HUD Headquarters have orally taken the position that the entity is ineligible to participate in HUD programs.

In the case of foreign national natural persons, PPSD staff have orally taken the position that to participate in a Covered Project, the foreign national is required to obtain an Individual Taxpayer Identification Number (ITIN) from the Internal Revenue Service (IRS). The principal purpose of an ITIN is to facilitate the required filing by foreign nationals of federal income tax returns; and, indeed, the inclusion of an income tax return is required with an application for an ITIN.[31] Although the IRS guidance does recognize certain exceptions from the stated IRS income tax return filing purposes and related requirements of the ITIN procedure, none of these exceptions is applicable to the 2530 Process.

As such, even if a particular foreign national prospective HUD participant was not otherwise required to file any income tax returns with the IRS, the applicant would still be required to do so, thus subjecting himself or herself to potential federal income tax liability to obtain the ITIN needed, according to HUD, to make a 2530 submission.

It is unclear why PPSD staff has taken either of the aforementioned positions, particularly because neither takes into account our global economy and the cross-border nature of current investments in real estate in the United States. We note that the standards for participation by foreign nationals set forth in the MAP Guide state that "[g]enerally, foreign nationals and corporate entities may participate as principals, however, the single asset borrower entity must

---

30. Passive Investor Mem., note 4.
31. IRS Form W-7 and Instructions for Form W-7.

be registered in the United States in the State where their corporate office is located. At least one principal with operational decision-making authority must be a United States Citizen."[32]

VI. DUE DILIGENCE AND FLAGS

Prior to making a 2530 submission, all prospective participants with previous participation histories with HUD would be well advised to perform due diligence regarding the status of compliance of their properties with applicable HUD requirements. Not only is this due diligence needed for an applicant to be able to make the required certifications to HUD described in Section 4 of this chapter, but it also can do much to facilitate the processing, and, ultimately, the approval by HUD of 2530 submissions.

HUD's primary analysis of any 2530 submission is whether there are any critical findings associated with a particular applicant. Critical findings are defined by HUD to include "(1) all events of noncompliance and/or performance issues shown in HUD's systems and (2) those elements within a participant's Previous Participation Certificate (PPC) disclosure and certification that indicate noncompliance or performance below established norms."[33]

A subset of the HUD universe of critical findings are those findings that generate so-called "flags" against participants. "Flags" are HUD's method of recording incidents of possible noncompliance or failure to meet HUD standards for review and consideration by all Departmental personnel, not just those in the field office with jurisdiction over a particular problematic asset. Most flags are placed in APPS by HUD personnel, including Headquarters and field office staff; some flags are generated automatically by the system. Flags are associated with a participant's individual SSN or EIN. A flag may be either direct or indirect. A direct flag results from the person's or entity's participation in a Covered Project. An indirect flag is attributed to a participant because of an affiliation or relationship with a person or entity who participated in a Covered Project that has a direct flag.

Because flags are considered by HUD to be indicators of potential risk, the existence of a flag is a factor that HUD will consider in evaluating a 2530 application for a Principal's participation in a new transaction with respect to a Covered Project, and, in certain circumstances, the issues that caused the flag(s) may also result in referral to the HUD Departmental Enforcement Center (DEC), which may impose administrative sanctions against the participant.

The following are the key "Critical Findings" that may result in a flag:

1. An unacceptable physical assessment (i.e., REAC inspection score);[34]

---

32. § 8.3(C)(2) of the *MAP Guide*.
33. Attachment 1 to Critical Findings Mem.
34. Pursuant to recent HUD directives, a HUD field office is no longer required to place a flag against a project or Principal when the property receives, for the first time, a REAC score below 60 but above 30 on its physical inspection. If the property receives a score below 30 on any inspection or receives a score below 60 on subsequent inspections, the field office is required to place a flag against the project and each Principal. HUD Notice H2010-4, dated January 22, 2010, titled "Revised Protocol for Placing a Flag in the Active Partners Performance System (APPS) When a Property Receives a Physical Inspection Score Below 60 but Above 30," as reissued by HUD Notice H2011-24, dated Sept. 13, 2011, titled "Reisssuance of Revised Protocol for Placing a Flag in the Active Partners Performance System (APPS) When a Property Receives a Physical Inspection Score Below 60 but Above 30" (the Revised REAC Protocol Memorandum).

2. A below-average or unsatisfactory management review rating;[35]
3. A financial (mortgage/direct loan) default;[36]
4. A mortgage assignment;
5. A foreclosure;
6. A General Services Administration Excluded Party Listing name match;
7. A notice of contract or regulatory violation issued by HUD;
8. A notice of civil money penalties;
9. Any regulatory agreement violation or breach;
10. A felony indictment or conviction;
11. A debarment, suspension, or temporary denial to participate;
12. Any HAP contract violation, breach, or default;
13. Financial Assessment Subsystem findings that relate to regulatory performance and compliance;
14. Any "no" answer on a previous participation certification;
15. A conditional participation approval or a participation denial;
16. Failure to file financial statements;[37] and
17. "Other significant event of noncompliance or nonperformance."[38]

---

35. HUD's current policy with respect to MOR flags is as follows:

    HUD staff should also consider placing a flag in APPS for ongoing deficiencies. In addition, an owner/agent who receives an overall Below Average or Unsatisfactory rating would normally be flagged in APPS. However, the Multifamily Hub Director has discretion with recording and resolving flags. In the event the Multifamily Hub Director determines the APPS flag should be delayed (or not placed at all), the Hub Director must document the decision in the iREMS Problem Statement screen and notify Headquarters. DEC enforcement action could result in suspension, debarment, limited denial of participation, civil money penalties, and/or other appropriate sanctions.

Section 6.15 of HUD HANDBOOK 4350.1 Rev.-1, Chg-2, *Multifamily Asset Management and Project Servicing*.

36. Under the current 2530 Process, HUD field offices have been instructed by PPSD staff in HUD Headquarters to flag all Principals in any project in default of its HUD-insured or HUD-held mortgage loan as posing a potentially unacceptable risk of participation to the Department. HUD Memorandum, dated Dec. 23, 2003, from Beverly J. Miller titled "Risk Alert—Placing APPS Risk Flags and Reporting Requirements Related to Mortgage Default and Financial Relief." In the event any Principal applicant is flagged, HUD will expect the applicant, regardless of its status in the ownership or management structure of the defaulted Project, to provide some form of corrective or exculpatory response to the flag as a condition of 2530 approval for a new application. If a 2530 application notes the existence of a default among any of a Principal applicant's participation, including any non-HUD projects, HUD field offices have been instructed to send the 2530 application in question to PPSD for further investigation and risk analysis. If the investigation of any defaulted project proves reasonably satisfactory, PPSD will then direct the HUD field office recipient of the 2530 application to issue the requested approval. If not, the application may be referred to the Multifamily Participation Review Committee for disposition. Depending on its severity, a flag may result in a denial of the applicant's 2530 application.

37. Flags for failure to file annual financial statements (AFS) electronically in HUD's Financial Assessment System (FASSUB) are generated automatically by HUD's system 10 days after the filing deadline has passed with no AFS submission completed in FASSUB. The system does not automatically resolve the flag when the required AFS submission is transmitted.

38. Critical Findings Mem.

A Coordinator/User who has activated access to a participant's TIN or SSN in APPS has the ability to view all flags pertaining to the participant by performing what is known as an "Entity Flag Report."[39] In many cases, those participants who do not have access to the APPS system learn of flags only when notified of the flag by HUD (which does not occur with regularity) and/or in the course of applying for new participation.

Once a flag has been placed, HUD may "resolve" or "absolve" the flag, or it may elect to have the flag remain on the participant's record. The flag may be "resolved" by HUD when the condition that gave rise to the flag has been corrected. Typically, REAC and MOR flags will remain in place until the next inspection/review. HUD must take affirmative action to resolve the flag; it will not be resolved automatically. Who at HUD is authorized to perform this action depends on who placed the flag and the reason for the flag. The HUD official who placed the flag is responsible for resolving the flag. If that individual is no longer with HUD, then the Field Office Supervisor where the project is located must research the issue and make the determination regarding whether or not to resolve the flag. Flags that are generated automatically by the system (presently only flags for failure to file an AFS) may be resolved by the HUD Project Manager assigned to the project. In these cases, resolution of the flag must be specifically requested by the owner or its designee after the condition has been corrected (in this case, the AFS filing has occurred).

Once HUD approves an entity for a specific property role (e.g., management agent), flags that the entity had up to that point are deemed to be "absolved" with respect to that particular property role, meaning that if the entity is subsequently part of a 2530 submission for the same type of property role, APPS will not show these flags to the reviewer.[40] Absolution of a flag assures that HUD reviewers will not waste time unnecessarily, considering the same issues over and over again for approval of a previously approved role. However, if the subsequent 2530 submission is for a different property role and the entity's flag for the different role has not been absolved, that flag will be displayed in APPS for the reviewer and will require further analysis by HUD, thus potentially delaying the approval of the submission.

In light of the above, HUD participants should take appropriate precautionary measures to avoid the placement of flags against their Principals by HUD and to resolve the placement of any and all flags that do result against their Principals, at the same time and as quickly as possible, to avoid any delay or potential denial of 2530 clearance for any new Covered Project, change in role, or Principal.

VII. 2530 APPLICATION SUBMISSION FORM—PAPER OR APPS

As noted above, HUD currently accepts both Paper 2530 applications and applications via APPS.

Traditionally, 2530 submissions were made to HUD using the HUD Form 2530, Previous Participation Certification, herein referred to as a "Paper 2530." In a Paper 2530 submis-

---

39. APPS can also be used to determine whether an applicant is on the General Service Administration's Excluded Party List and/or is subject to a limited denial of participation by HUD. *User Guide*, Chapter 18.

40. APPS Online Glossary of Terms, *available at* www.hud.gov.

sion, the applicant completes and executes the HUD Form 2530 and submits the hard copy to the HUD field office with oversight over the Covered Project for which HUD participation approval is being sought. The HUD Form 2530 must include for each Principal: the requested role in the Covered Project, contact information, SSN or EIN, previous participation history, the requisite certifications and explanations, as applicable, and original signatures.[41] Each Principal in the submission is then reviewed by the HUD Project Manager assigned to the particular Covered Project for its history of compliance with HUD programmatic and other federal governmental requirements and the existence of any outstanding critical findings and/or flags. This review is done manually by the HUD Project Manager by running the Principal applicants' names and SSNs/EINs through HUD's databases. Written approval of the Paper 2530 may be provided to the applicant by HUD, and the Paper 2530 is placed in the Covered Project file.

An APPS submission is done entirely via the Internet, through the HUD Web Access Secure System, also known as WASS (the HUD System), except that hard copies of the signature pages must be forwarded to HUD Headquarters or the HUD field office with jurisdiction over the submission in question. APPS was developed by HUD to automate and standardize the 2530 submission and review process and reduce the paperwork burden imposed on both HUD and the industry by the maintenance of Paper 2530s through the use of computerized recordkeeping. APPS was first launched on a limited basis in 2000 and on a wider basis in 2005 as a result of cooperative efforts undertaken by HUD and the multifamily industry to improve 2530 procedures. The first users of the system experienced certain difficulties with the new computerized system; in recent years, APPS has become more accepted and utilized by the multifamily industry. Today, APPS is HUD's preferred form of 2530 submission.

An APPS submission for a new user or participant requires the completion of five steps in HUD's electronic system: first, the registration of participants and Principals in HUD's Business Partners Registration System; second, the procurement of access to the system by the party designated by the applicant as its Coordinator/User in APPS; third, the Coordinator/User's connection in the HUD System to each participant and Principal via their respective TINs and/or SSNs; fourth, the creation of a "Baseline" for the application, which consists of the entry into APPS of the organizational structure and the previous participation record for each Principal in the organizational structure of the applicant;[42] and fifth, the request for HUD approval of the proposed role of the applicant in the transaction involving the Covered Project in question via a Property Submission or an Organization Change Submission. This step includes the completion of the requisite certifications as True or False for each Principal listed and the inclusion in the available comment sections in APPS of any required explana-

---

41. HUD Form-2530; *see also* Williams Mem.
42. In this regard, Baseline Submissions under APPS are intended, in part, to replace the so-called master 2530 lists authorized by Section 200.222 of the 2530 Regulations and Section 2-8 of the 2530 Handbook for Principals with numerous Projects and a complex and extensive previous participation record with HUD. Baselines do not require HUD review or approval and are not, technically, "submitted" to HUD, so the term is somewhat of a misnomer. For more information regarding Baseline Submission requirements, see Chapter 5 of *User Guide*.

tions as to why the Principal has responded "False" for any certification. Thereafter, the applicant is required to print out the 2530 submission package and arrange for the original signatures of the appropriate Principals and send the signed 2530 submission package to the HUD field office with jurisdiction over the subject Covered Project or PPSD in HUD Headquarters, as applicable.

Once the aforementioned steps one through four for each Principal are completed, any new Property Submission or Organizational Change Submission involving the Principal in APPS requires only updating of the previous participation record for each Principal, completion of step five, and the transmittal of the signed 2530 submission package to HUD.

VIII. 2530 REVIEW BY HUD FIELD OFFICES AND HUD HEADQUARTERS

HUD's current procedures for the processing of 2530 applications are not completely or accurately described in the 2530 Regulations or the applicable administrative guidance and can depend on whether the application is a Paper 2530 or filed in APPS.

For Paper 2530 applications, the HUD field office with jurisdiction over the Covered Project for which a 2530 submission is made has the authority to approve applications for both Property Submissions and Organization Change Submissions[43] if the applicant (a) has no previous participation, no unresolved flags, or the only unresolved flags were placed by that field office; and (b) has not made a Qualified Certification. A HUD field office does not have authority to disapprove a 2530 application because of the existence of flags and critical findings (other than certain instances involving a failed physical inspection report) with respect to a particular applicant.[44] Accordingly, if a HUD field office does not have the authority to approve a 2530 application for the foregoing reasons, or otherwise has concerns regarding the suitability of an applicant for participation in HUD programs, it can forward it to PPSD with a recommendation for approval or disapproval as it deems appropriate.[45]

For APPS filings, HUD field offices have the authority to approve Property Submissions under the same circumstances described in the preceding paragraph. All APPS submissions for approval of any Major Organization Change, Modified TPA, or Corporate Buyout require the approval of HUD Headquarters,[46] although HUD Headquarters staff will solicit input from any affected HUD field offices regarding a particular Organization Change Submission.

Where HUD Headquarters approval of a 2530 submission is required, either because there are critical findings or flags associated with the applicant or the field office is otherwise unwilling to issue 2530 approval, or because the submission involves a Major Organization Change, Modified TPA, or Corporate Buyout, the current process is that in the first instance, the application goes to the HUD Headquarters contact in PPSD that is responsible for the

---

43. As previously noted, Minor Organization Changes and changes in Principal status resulting from a court decree or inheritance do not require any formal HUD approval, although submission of the requisite disclosure documentation, *i.e.*, the 2350 application materials, is required.

44. November 2004 Miller Memorandum; Critical Findings Memorandum; and Revised REAC Protocol Memorandum.

45. The 2530 Process for a Covered Project is sometimes used as leverage over applicants with regard to their other projects.

46. §§ 11.1 and 12.1 of *User Guide*.

HUD region in which the Covered Project is located or to the staff person who is otherwise assigned to a particular Organization Change Submission (the Review Official). Information regarding the identity of, and contact information for, these Review Officials is available on HUD's website. The Review Official will request input from the affected field office(s) when the submission impacts existing Covered Projects. The field office may recommend approval, not recommend approval, or remain silent. As a general policy, PPSD will not approve a submission if any of the affected field offices state they do not recommend approval. The Review Officials have some unspecified amount of authority to approve an application and also have the authority to disapprove an application in the case of applicants who are suspended or disbarred or otherwise restricted by HUD under 2 C.F.R. Part 2424 or by any other federal government agency.

In the case of 2530 submissions involving what the Review Officials regard to be a particularly problematic prospective participant, or in cases where one or more affected field offices state they do not recommend approval, PPSD may refer the application to the Multifamily Participation Review Committee (the Review Committee) for consideration. This is a body composed of the senior staff of the Office of Multifamily Housing Management and Development at HUD Headquarters, as well as their legal representatives, and it meets on an as-needed basis.[47] Typically, the applicant will have the opportunity to submit written explanatory and/or exculpatory information for the Review Committee to consider in making its decision; however, the applicant does not have the right to make a presentation to the Review Committee or to be present at the meeting where its application is evaluated. Pursuant to the 2530 Regulations, the Review Committee is authorized to take the following actions with respect to any pending 2530 submission under its consideration: (a) approve the application; (b) conditionally approve the application; (c) withhold approval of the application; and (d) disapprove the application.[48]

Pursuant to Section 200.233 of the 2530 Regulations, HUD 2530 approval constitutes approval for a particular applicant for a specific role in a specific Covered Project. Once granted, Section 200.236 of the 2530 Regulations states that "[a]pprovals will not be modified or withdrawn, except in cases where the [P]rincipal is subsequently suspended or debarred from further participation in any HUD programs . . . or is found by the [Multifamily Participation] Review Committee to have obtained approval based upon submission to HUD of a false, fraudulent, or incomplete report or certificate." HUD's administrative guidance includes as additional grounds for the modification of a previous 2530 approval the assumption by a Principal of a participation role not originally proposed and disclosed to HUD on any 2530 application, as well as any change in the nature of a Principal's participation such as a new application for mortgage insurance or a change in its organizational structure.[49]

Pursuant to Section 200.230 of the 2530 Regulations, the Review Committee has the authority to disapprove a 2530 application, whether or not the proposed Principal was actively involved in a particular project for which its previous participation is required to be

---

47. Note that the 2530 Regulations' discussion of the particulars of the composition of this body is not necessarily accurate. 24 C.F.R. § 200.227.
48. 24 C.F.R. §§ 200.228 & 200.229.
49. Sec. 1-3(J) of the 2530 HANDBOOK.

disclosed on the 2530, because of (a) the inability of a Principal applicant to make the requisite certifications or to demonstrate that the negative circumstances that preclude the Principal applicant's ability to make the necessary certifications were beyond the applicant's control, (b) the failure of the Principal applicant to comply with any of its programmatic obligations to HUD in the context of its prior participation, (c) the submission of a false or materially incomplete 2530 application, (d) any significant violation by the Principal applicant of any other programmatic requirements of HUD, RHS, or any state or local government housing agency in connection with any insured or assisted project, (e) any serious and significant violation by a management agent of its management agreement that required, prior to the execution thereof, the approval of HUD or any other governmental agency, or (f) any method of doing business with respect to any project that would make the Principal applicant an unacceptable risk from the underwriting standpoint of an insurer, lender, or government agency. In addition, the submission of any false information or certifications under the 2530 Process could subject any Principal applicant to prosecution for civil and criminal penalties by the federal government.

IX. APPEAL PROCESS

A party may request review of any decision by the Review Official or by the Review Committee where an application is not approved (i.e., conditional approvals, withholding of approvals, and denials). There are essentially two types of appeal procedures. First, the party may request consideration by the Review Committee of an adverse decision by a Review Official or reconsideration of an adverse decision by the Review Committee within 30 days of the receipt of notice of the decision.[50] Alternatively, the party may request a hearing before a hearing officer.[51] This request also must be made in writing within 30 days.

If a party requests reconsideration by the Review Committee under the process described above and does not obtain an approval, the party may then seek a hearing before a hearing officer.[52] The hearing officer reports his or her decision back to the Review Committee, which is bound by the hearing officer's findings of facts and law and will make a final decision.[53] The Review Committee's final decision constitutes final agency action; further appeals must be filed in federal court.[54]

In practice, the official appeals process is seldom used because of the time and expense involved in undertaking an appeal.

X. CONTINUING TROUBLE POINTS FOR PRACTITIONERS

The 2530 Process continues to pose many challenges to the practitioner. The following are some of the most problematic areas:

---

50. 24 C.F.R. § 200.241(a).
51. 24 C.F.R. § 200.243.
52. 24 C.F.R. § 200.243(a).
53. 24 C.F.R. § 200.245.
54. § 4-3(F) of the 2530 HANDBOOK.

- The 2530 Process was originally designed for "Mom and Pop" operators and is not always workable for entities with complex organizational and governance structures and large institutional investors because of the extensive disclosure requirements.
- The governing regulations and administrative guidelines are not always aligned with actual practice and do not address key issues, such as the application of the rules to trusts.
- The rules are not always interpreted consistently by field offices and Headquarters officials.
- Requirements for foreign nationals are not clear.
- The requirements for disclosure of participation in other than HUD-financed and/or HUD-subsidized projects (i.e., RHS and state or local housing finance agency programs) are not clear.
- The time period for disclosure of participation does not conform with the 10-year time frame for providing certifications.
- The 2530 Regulations require 2530 clearance in connection with a "bid to purchase a mortgage note held by the Commissioner,"[55] which is inconsistent with the fact that 2530 clearance is not required for any HUD lender.
- The 2530 Regulations require 2530 approval of any prospective purchaser of a Covered Project being sold at foreclosure by HUD as well as any other Covered Project owned by HUD,[56] even where there is not expected to be continued HUD assistance or other type of continuing relationship between HUD and the project owner/operator.
- Although the situation is much improved since APPS was first instituted, and more applicants are now using APPS and experiencing fewer problems, continued refinement of the system is needed to make it more manageable and user-friendly: for example, making it easier to receive the required activation keys, clearer instructions regarding the role of baselines, providing for automatic updates to previous participation records, clarifying certain naming selections that are misnomers and misleading, and permitting electronic signatures.

Despite these challenges, the objectives of the 2530 Process, i.e., participant disclosure and risk assessment, are consistent with current lending practices.

---

55. 24 C.F.R. § 200.217(a)(11).
56. 24 C.F.R. § 200.217(a)(9) & (10).

Community Development   6

Robert S. Kenison

We in America today are nearer to the final triumph over poverty than ever before in the history of any land. . . . We shall soon with the help of God be in sight of the day when poverty will be banished from this nation.

Herbert Hoover[1]
1928 Acceptance Address

*Time present and time past
Are both perhaps present in time future.*

T. S. Eliot
"Four Quartets (Burnt Norton)," I, ls. 1-2[2]

I. SCOPE

HUD's Office of Community Planning and Development (CPD) administers many programs that may be characterized under several rubrics.[3] Included are

---

1. Acceptance address for Republican party nomination for President, at Stanford University (Aug. 11, 1928).
2. Eliot, The Complete Poems and Plays, 1909–1950, Harcourt Brace Jovanovich (1971).
3. Extensive discussion of HUD's community development programs can be found at the Department's website at http://portal.hud.gov/hudportal/HUD?src=/program_offices/comm_planning/communitydevelopment.

two formula grant programs (CDBG, HOME), which evince the characteristics of block grants. In another sense, all CPD programs may be classified under the increasingly broad framework known as "community development," a reading that includes affordable housing, particularly for low- and moderate-income families.[4] This rationale extends to the service-rich, non-permanent housing programs for the homeless.

We begin with the original, core block grant program, CDBG.

II. COMMUNITY DEVELOPMENT BLOCK GRANTS (CDBG)

A. From "Categoritis" to Block Grants

For 25 years, HUD and its predecessor agencies, under the umbrella Housing and Home Finance Agency,[5] administered several programs to assist localities in urban planning and development, with different infrastructure assistance mechanisms. The oldest and largest of these was urban renewal, created by title I of the Housing Act of 1949.[6] Under this program, the U.S. government made grants to local public agencies to pay for most of the cost of land clearance, public infrastructure, and the ultimate disposition of properties for private redevelopment, in accordance with a locally adopted urban renewal plan meeting federal requirements. The program had some shortcomings—projects often took years to complete, and its uprooting of families without relocation follow-through sometimes prompted criticism as "Negro removal."[7] However, urban renewal was the lodestar for non-housing development assistance.

An interesting approach of sorts to the more comprehensive block grant intention was the Model Cities Program enacted in 1966.[8] Here, grants were made to the mayors rather than to local agencies specializing in urban renewal or specific public facilities like parks or sewers. The menu of eligible activities was broad, but the program design was limited to a select number of cities. Despite its comparative breadth, it was still a categorical grant program. Not until the enactment of CDBG was a broad-scale block grant created.

---

4. Even the CDBG program, HUD's non-housing block grant, saw $1.3 billion of grant funds, 30% of grantee allocations, used for housing in 2010. *CDBG Expenditures Reports*, U.S. Dept. of Housing and Urban Dev., http://portal.hud.gov.hudportal/HUD?src=program_offices/comm_planning/communitydevelopment/budget/disbursementreports. *See also* the analogous formulation in the definition of "community development" in the lending test under the Community Reinvestment Act as expressly including "[a]ffordable housing (including multifamily rental housing) for low- or moderate-income individuals." 12 C.F.R. § 228.12(g)(1)(2010). Note too that community development corporations or "CDCs constitute the largest segment of the nonprofit housing sector." SCHWARTZ, HOUSING POLICY IN THE UNITED STATES 233 (2d ed. 2010). (Emphasis added.)

5. Absorbed into the new cabinet role for HUD under the Department of Housing and Urban Development Act of 1965, 42 U.S.C. § 3531 *et seq.*, Pub. L. 89-174 (1965).

6. 42 U.S.C. § 1441 *et seq.*, Pub. L. 81-171 (1949).

7. "Where Did They Go?" was a question already begun to be asked in the 1950s; *see* "Greater Pittsburgh. 39" (October 1957), CPL Exchange Bibliography # 714. The Uniform Relocation Assistance and Real Property Acquisition Policies Act of 1970 was not enacted until near the end of the urban renewal program. 42 U.S.C. 1441, Pub. L. 91-646 (1971).

8. Demonstration Cities and Metropolitan Development Act of 1966, Pub. L. 89-754 (1966).

B. Indicia of a Block Grant

There are four essential indicia of a block grant. The first is that it authorizes in a single program a "block" of eligible activities, often formerly funded under several previously existing categorical grant (or loan) programs. Second, it allocates and distributes funds according to a formula on which recipients can rely annually.[9] Third, the funds are typically allocated to general purpose governments, responsible for coordinating activities and responsive to local voters. Last, there is a minimal reliance on application submission and review, and a shift to federally decentralized operation of the program by local officials subject only to conducting post-audit review and enforcing sanctions for statutory and regulatory non-compliance.

C. The Community Development Block Grant Profile

The CDBG program was enacted under title I of the Housing and Community Development Act of 1974.[10] CDBG meets all the characteristics of a true block grant program, described above. It effectively blocked six categorical programs previously administered by HUD,[11] effectively making almost[12] all previously eligible activities permissible under this block grant. Second, it allocates funds to "entitlement" recipients consisting of metropolitan cities with a population over 50,000, to very large "urban counties" with a population generally exceeding 200,000 (not counting metropolitan cities therein) or meeting other requirements, and to States for the funding of smaller communities.[13] These allocations are pursuant to a statutory formula created in 1974 and amended only once, in 1977.[14] Unlike previous categorical programs, the grant is made to general purpose governments. Utilization of specialist local agencies is exclusively up to the general purpose government. Last, from a fairly basic application submission that was required at the program's outset, CDBG has evolved into an even further, generally decentralized operation, with emphasis on how the recipient has spent its funds rather than a probing federal agency look at how it intends to spend them.

D. Activity Eligibility

Virtually all of the activities eligible under the prior categorical programs are eligible under CDBG.[15] This broad range includes land acquisition,[16] land disposition,[17] public facilities and

---

    9. Of course, the enabling legislation and formula thereunder cannot guarantee appropriations in the future, but they can and do establish a reliable mechanism for funding whatever is appropriated.

   10. 42 U.S.C. § 5301 *et seq.*; Pub. L. 93-383 (1974).

   11. 42 U.S.C. § 5316. The predecessor programs were model cities and urban renewal, and also water and sewer facilities grants, public facilities loans, open space grants, and rehabilitation loans.

   12. *See* discussion of new housing construction at notes 22–25 and accompanying text.

   13. All of these terms for different entitlement units of general local government are defined at 24 C.F.R. § 570.3 (2010). All subsequent citations to 24 CODE FED. REGS. are as of April 1, 2010.

   14. A dual, alternative formula was fashioned in 1977 for midwestern and northeastern "rust belt" community needs.

   15. 42 U.S.C. § 5305; § 570.200–210.

   16. § 570.201(a).

   17. § 570.201(b).

improvements[18] (excluding buildings for the general conduct of government[19]), clearance and remediation activities,[20] and public services.[21] Use of CDBG for the construction of housing was not permissible when the program began, but over time some particularized approaches have been authorized. While the "Eligible Activities" portion of the regulations[22] contains only one express reference to new housing construction, pursuant to CDBG funds being utilized with Housing Development Grant program moneys under section 17 of the United States Housing Act of 1937 (now repealed),[23] other new construction inroads are available for specific purposes, such as the "last resort" housing provisions of the Uniform Relocation Assistance and Real Property Acquisition Policies Act of 1970,[24] and, where Community Based Development Organizations (CBDOs) are utilized by the grantee, "activities not otherwise listed as eligible under" the provisions of the regulations governing activity eligibility.[25] Other eligible activities include relocation assistance,[26] direct homeownership assistance to low- or moderate-income households,[27] and technical assistance to private nonprofit entities to increase their capacity to carry out eligible neighborhood revitalization or economic development activities.[28]

A subprogram within CDBG is the section 108 loan guarantee program, named for the section in the block grant legislation where it is authorized.[29] CDBG grantees pledge future grants, should they become necessary, to repay loan obligations incurred for many activities eligible under CDBG.[30] There are also "special purpose" grants"[31] authorized under title I, including funding for technical assistance, insular areas, some university programs, and other special needs. None of these small programs is in the nature of a block grant.

E.   Programmatic Eligibility

In addition to the above broad but specifically identified span of eligible activities, a different requirement, here called "programmatic eligibility," is contained in the CDBG program. This flows from the "primary objective" of the Act[32] where the focus is on low- and moderate-

---

18. § 570.201(c).
19. § 570.207(a).
20. § 570.201(d).
21. § 570.201(e). CDBG funds for public services are limited in relative amounts and may not be used to supplant, or substitute for, public services previously funded by the locality or received from the state, unless the "decrease in the level of service was not within the control of the unit of general local government." *Id.*
22. § 570.201.
23. § 570.201(m).
24. 42 U.S.C. §§ 4601–4655; 24 C.F.R. pt. 42.
25. § 570.204(a).
26. § 570.201(i).
27. § 570.201(n).
28. § 570.201(p).
29. 42 U.S.C. 5308.
30. Pt. 570, subpt. M.
31. Pt. 570, subpt. E.
32. 42 U.S.C. § 5301(c).

income[33] benefit and is formally integrated into the first of two key statutory requirements,[34] namely, that the grantee certify that its "projected use of funds has been developed so as to give maximum feasible priority to activities which will benefit low- and moderate-income families or aid in the prevention of slums or blight," or meet other particularly urgent needs.[35] This is sometimes called the "three-pronged test" under which each funded activity must meet one of the three statutory criteria.

Of these three prongs of national objectives, the most important is low- and moderate-income benefit, and its dominance constitutes the second key requirement.[36] Grantees must "ensure that, over a period of time, specified in their certification not to exceed three years, not less than 70 percent of the aggregate of CDBG fund expenditures shall be for activities" benefiting low- and moderate-income persons.[37] There are certain narrow exclusions,[38] but the low/mod benefit test effectively governs the program.

Low/mod benefit is made realistically feasible by virtue of two important typologies for such activities. The first kind of calculated benefit relates to "area benefit activities," where benefits are deemed available to all the residents of a given primary residential area when 51 percent or more of those residents are low- and-moderate income persons.[39] An important exception permits activities in areas serving less than 51 percent low- and moderate-income persons when the proportion of such persons is within the highest quartile of all areas within the recipient's jurisdiction.[40]

The second vehicle for low/mod counting is "limited clientele activities," where at least 51 percent of the eligible participants are low- or moderate-income persons.[41] Expressly excluded are benefits available to all residents of the area; housing-related activities; and certain job creation.[42] Limited clientele presumptions exist for battered spouses, elderly persons, persons with AIDS, migrant farm workers, or when there are income eligibility requirements effectively limiting the range of benefit.[43]

The other two national objective prongs have considerably less regulatory oversight, the "elimination of slums and blight" prong, with a largely urban renewal orientation,[44] and the "particularly urgent community development needs" prong, frequently focused on recent disasters.[45]

---

33. In the CDBG program, the definition of low- and moderate-income persons is pegged at 80% of median income for the area, with adjustments for smaller and larger families. 42 U.S.C. § 5302(a)(20).
34. 42 U.S.C. 5304(b)(3).
35. *Id.*; § 570.200(a)(2).
36. *Id.*
37. § 570.200(a)(3).
38. § 570.200(a)((3)(i)–(v).
39. § 570.208(a)(1)(i).
40. § 570.208(a)(1)(ii).
41. § 570.208(a)(2).
42. *Id.*
43. § 570.208(a)(2)(A), (C).
44. § 570.208(b).
45. § 570.208(c).

F. Program Administration

"Entitlement" cities and urban counties administer their own grants, utilizing public and private entities. The former application submission requirements are now simplified primarily in a regulatory designed "Consolidated Plan" (or ConPlan)[46] including citizen participation,[47] submission of information satisfying the statutory requirement of a statement of projected use of funds, and annual action plans.[48] The ConPlan is also used for the HOME and Emergency Shelter Grants programs, described *infra*, and several other HUD programs.

Similar requirements attend administration of the State's Program.[49] Although states do not expend their grants on program activities, but fund their included units of general local government for this purpose, the program administration requirements are comparable to those for metropolitan cities and urban counties.[50]

HUD performance reviews of entitlement local governmental grantees include compliance with primary and national objectives and other program requirements,[51] the timely manner of CDBG-funded activities,[52] Consolidated Plan responsibilities,[53] equal opportunity and fair housing,[54] and the grantee's continuing capacity to carry out its CDBG-funded activities in a timely manner.[55] The rather detailed statutory sanctions available to HUD are closely tracked in the program regulations.[56] Comparable but somewhat stripped down performance review provisions also govern the state's program.[57]

G. Program Requirements

Besides the numerous requirements peculiar to program activities described above, CDBG recipients are also required to comply with requirements under the operative provisions of the Civil Rights Acts of 1964[58] and 1968,[59] as well as a requirement to carry out their programs in a manner to affirmatively further fair housing[60] and the specific nondiscrimination provisions at section 109 of the CDBG legislation.[61] Other applicable laws include the labor standards provisions of the Davis-Bacon Act,[62] environmental requirements,[63] and the Uniform Reloca-

---

46. *See* 24 C.F.R. pt. 91 generally.
47. 24 C.F.R. pt. 91, subpt. B.
48. § 91.220 (§ 91.320 for states).
49. Pt. 570, subpt. I.
50. §§ 91.115, 91.320.
51. § 570.901.
52. § 570.902.
53. § 570.903.
54. § 570.904.
55. § 570.905.
56. §§ 570.910–913.
57. §§ 570.490–496.
58. § 570.601(a)(1).
59. § 570.601(a)(2).
60. *Id.*
61. § 570.602.
62. § 570.603.
63. § 570.604.

tion Assistance and Real Property Acquisition Policies Act of 1970.[64]

Apart from these statutory mandates, important controls consisting of uniform administrative requirements for all federal grantees are imposed administratively by the Federal Office of Management and Budget.[65] Last, increased clarity and detail have been articulated by HUD with respect to permissible expenditures by CDBG-funded faith-based entities.[66] All of these requirements in this paragraph also apply to public grantees in our next reviewed program, HOME.

III. HOME, A "COMMUNITY DEVELOPMENT" HOUSING PROGRAM

The Home Investment Partnerships Program (hereafter HOME or HOME program) was enacted at title II of the Cranston-Gonzalez National Affordable Housing Act in 1990.[67] The purpose of the program is to extend the supply of decent, safe, sanitary, and affordable housing, with primary attention to rental housing, for low-income and very low-income families.[68] While located organizationally in HUD's Office of Community Planning and Development, the program is strictly limited to housing activities, unlike the broader swath of CDBG. However, it is properly identifiable as a "community development" program both under the contemporary characterization[69] meshing housing and other community development activities and in terms of its block grant–like functions.

Although the HOME enabling legislation did not "block" previously existing categorical programs, the list of eligible activities thereunder is sufficiently broad that it may be, and is, viewed as HUD's block grant for low- and moderate-income housing. Here too, the funding is meted out by an annually reliable formula, again with general purpose governments, identified as "participating jurisdictions," or "PJs," as grantees. Finally, the HOME program follows the characteristic structure of decentralized block grants, with substantial reliance on the performance of governmental PJs and relatively minimal oversight[70] by HUD.

A. Fund Allocation

Like CDBG, HOME utilizes a formula method of fund allocation for its PJs. But unlike CDBG, the HOME legislation[71] does not contain the formula, rather, a requirement that one be implemented by regulation according to fairly prescriptively specified formula factors.[72]

---

64. § 570.606. A separate requirement under section 104(d) of the Housing and Community Development Act of 1974 imposes upon CDBG and HOME grantees the "one-for-one" requirement, under which an additional obligation to replace all occupied and unoccupied and vacant occupiable lower-income dwelling units that are demolished or converted to another use, in connection with a program-assisted activity, with comparable lower-income dwelling units. *See* § 42.375.

65. The OMB Circulars A-87 (Cost Principles for State, Local, and Indian Tribal Governments) and A-95 (Uniform Administrative Requirements for Grants and Cooperative Agreements to State and Local Governments) are prescribed at § 570.502.

66. § 570.200(j).
67. 42 U.S.C. § 12701 *et seq.*, Pub. L. 101-625.
68. § 92.1.
69. *See* note 4.
70. *But see* discussion at note 164, *infra*.
71. 42 U.S.C. § 12747.
72. 42 U.S.C. § 12747(b).

That regulation allocates about 60 percent of the funds to CDBG-type "metropolitan cities" and "urban counties," as well as HUD-approved consortia, and 40 percent to the states.[73] The formula factors concentrate on low-income rental units and other poverty indicia.[74]

B. Eligible Activities, Costs

Participating jurisdictions may use funds to provide incentives to develop and support affordable rental housing and homeownership affordability through acquisition, new construction, reconstruction, or rehabilitation.[75] Tenant-based rental assistance (TBA) is also permitted; the PJ must certify in its ConPlan if it is including this type of assistance, must specify local market conditions supporting this programmatic option, and can make such assistance available only to very low-income and low-income families.[76] Administrative and planning costs[77] are eligible as is payment of operating costs of CHDOS,[78] discussed *infra*.

To achieve all these objectives, PJs can pay for eligible project costs consisting of development hard costs, refinancing costs, acquisition costs, related soft costs, relocation costs, and costs relating to payment of loans when the HOME assistance was part of the original financing for an eligible project.[79]

C. Community Housing Development Organizations (CHDOs)

Every year the grantee must reserve at least 15 percent of its formula allocation for investment only in housing to be developed, sponsored, or owned by Community Housing Development Organizations, or CHDOs.[80] CHDOs[81] are private nonprofit entities; organized under state or local law; having no part of net earnings inuring to the benefit of any member, founder, contributor, or individual; are not controlled by those seeking profit from the CHDO; with tax exemption under section 501(c)(3) or (4) of the Internal Revenue Code of 1986;[82] and do not include a public body (including the PJ).

Each PJ must make reasonable efforts to identify CHDOs capable of carrying out elements of the jurisdiction's approved Consolidated Plan and to "encourage [them] to do so."[83] Apart from the grantee's mandatory 15 percent suballocation to CHDOs, the PJ can use up to

---

73. § 92.50.
74. § 92.50(c).
75. § 92.205(a).
76. § 92.209(b) and (c).
77. § 92.207. The breadth and length of this list of matching contributions may bring back to the minds of older readers the non-cash grants-in-aid that characterized the urban renewal program in the 1950s, 1960s, and 1970s, . . . and were one of the occasions of extensive federal review that prompted the switch to a community development block grant approach.
78. § 92.208.
79. § 92.206.
80. § 92.300(a)(1).
81. § 92.1.
82. 26 C.F.R. § 1.501(c)(3-1)(2011).
83. § 92.300(b).

5 percent of its annual formula allocation for CHDOs' operating expenses (but not CHDOs acting as subrecipients or contractors in the HOME program).[84]

D. Program Administration

Receipt of the Participating Jurisdiction's HOME allocation is tied to submission of the ConPlan.[85] The grantee must make all reasonable efforts to maximize private sector participation.[86] Its HOME grant is not to be used inconsistently with ConPlan objectives, and must be used within its own boundaries or in joint projects with contiguous boundaries.[87] As in CDBG, state PJs distribute their funds throughout the state, consistent with ConPlan identification of housing need.[88] Operative site and neighborhood standards suitable from the standpoint of nondiscrimination requirements apply.[89]

The HOME program prescribes income targeting. For rental housing and TBA, at least 90 percent of benefiting families cannot have annual incomes exceeding 60 percent of area median income, with some adjustments for family size, *or* at least 90 percent of assisted units must be occupied by families meeting these income limits, and the remainder of (1) such families qualify as low-income families (i.e., below 80 percent of area median income) or (2) the assisted units are occupied by such households.[90] For home ownership, discussed at greater length *infra*, 100 percent of the units must be invested in dwelling units that are occupied by households that qualify as low-income families.[91]

There is a 25 percent matching requirement[92] for all PJs with respect to qualifying affordable housing[93] with some exceptions (administrative and planning costs; CHDO operating expenses; capacity building of CHDOs).[94] The match may be made with respect to assisted tenants;[95] HOME-assisted units;[96] non-HOME-assisted portions of projects where at least half of the units are HOME-assisted;[97] or commercial space where at least 50 percent of floor space is residential and at least 50 percent of the units are HOME-assisted.[98] The match

---

84. § 92.208(a). *See also* § 92.300(e) and (f).
85. *See* note 46. These elements of the ConPlan—content, process of development, citizen participation, submission date, HUD approval, and amendments—all constitute HOME submission requirements. § 92.150.
86. § 92.200.
87. § 92.201(a).
88. § 92.201(b).
89. § 92.202.
90. § 92.216.
91. § 92.217.
92. § 92.218(a).
93. The breadth and length of the list of matching contributions may bring back to the minds of older readers the non-cash grants-in-aid that characterized the urban renewal program in the 1950s, 1960s, and 1970s, . . . and were one of the occasions of extensive Federal review that prompted the switch to a community development block grant approach.
94. § 92.218(c).
95. § 92.219(a)(1).
96. § 92.219(a)(2).
97. § 92.219(a)(3).
98. § 92.219(a)(4).

cannot be made from federal funds. It may be in cash;[99] in State or local tax, fee, or charge forbearance;[100] donated real property;[101] required on-site or off-site infrastructure;[102] State or local housing project bond financing proceeds;[103] the reasonable value of donated site preparation and construction materials and equipment, and of sweat equity provided to a homeownership project;[104] and the direct cost of supportive services and homebuyer counseling services provided to assisted families.[105]

Among the limitations in the program is a maximum per-unit subsidy amount[106] that may not exceed the per-dollar limitation established under section 221(d)(3)(ii) of the National Housing Act for elevator-type projects[107] for the area where the HOME project is located. The PJ must undertake a "subsidy layering" analysis under its own adopted guidelines to ensure that no more HOME funds than are necessary are invested in the housing.[108] HOME-assisted housing must meet applicable local codes, rehabilitation standards, and zoning ordinances.[109]

The maximum rent for rental housing is the lesser of the Fair Market Rent for the Section 8 Existing Housing program[110] or a rent not to exceed 30 percent of the adjusted income of a family whose annual income equals 65 percent of the median income for the area, as determined by HUD, with adjustments for the number of bedrooms in the unit.[111] Additional rent limitations attend rental-assisted units.[112]

Further, the program posits affordability period requirements, gauged according to the depth of assistance undertaken as measured by cost. Thus, $15,000 of rehabilitation would call for a five-year period; from $15,000 to $40,000, 10 years; and costs higher than that, 75 years. Any new construction or acquisition for construction would carry a minimum period of 20 years.[113]

E. Home Ownership

For many years, HUD and other providers of housing, as well as political figures of all stripes, have pointed to home ownership as the "American Dream." Few, if any, foresaw the

---

99. § 92.220(a)(1).
100. § 92.220(a)(2).
101. § 92.220(a)(3).
102. § 92.220(a)(4).
103. § 92.220(a)(5).
104. § 92.220(a)(6)–(9).
105. § 92.220(a)(10)–(11).
106. § 92.250(a). Increases of up to 240% programwide are permissible upon HUD approval.
107. 12 U.S.C. § 17151(d)(3)(ii).
108. § 92.250(b). A comparable requirement is imposed on HUD for its own approval of directly funded housing projects, pursuant to section 102(d) of the Department of Housing and Urban Development Reform Act of 1989, 42 U.S.C. § 35345(d)(2), Pub. L. 101-235. *See, e.g.*, Administrative Guidelines for Subsidy Layering for Section 8 Project-Based Housing Assistance Contracts, July 9, 2010, Fed. Reg. 39,561–73.
109. § 92.251(a).
110. *See* 24 C.F.R. § 888.111, § 92.252(a)(1).
111. § 92.252(a)(2).
112. § 92.252(b).
113. § 92.252(e).

morphing of the dream into the nightmare in recent years for some families, a nightmare resulting in part from questionable marketing approaches, including derivatives floating in a transactional fog, with families now confronted by difficult choices ahead.[114]

In the HOME program, HUD has been a measured steed in the homeownership program stable. As indicated earlier,[115] the HOME program limits all homeownership opportunities to low-income families. It is further limited to single-family housing.[116] Moreover, it is to be "modest," as detailed in the regulation,[117] with required periods of affordability ranging from 5 to 15 years, depending on the amount of HOME assistance per unit.[118] To ensure[119] such affordability, the PJ must impose, at its option, resale or recapture requirements, which HUD must determine are appropriate.[120]

While the foregoing sets out programmatic standards for when HOME moneys are actually used for home ownership, it should be noted that the American Dream Downpayment Initiative (ADDI)[121] was authorized as a special set-aside of up to $200 million annually for home ownership by first-time homebuyers. This initiative was first funded for almost $75 million in FY 2003, but it has not received any appropriations since 2008.

IV. HOMELESS PROGRAMS

A. More Community Development Programs

Early in the 1980s a confluence of forces laid bare the increase of homelessness in the United States. The deinstitutionalization of patients from mental hospitals, the continuing difficulty of reacclimatization of some veterans who had returned from their service in Vietnam,[122] and the basic economic problems some families were having all exposed to the country the growing incidence of homelessness.

An early response by the Congress was to include special homeless funding provisions in the appropriations Act for HUD, but in short time, temporary appropriations action took on the more permanent shape of authorization legislation in 1987.[123] From an appropriations set-

---

114. For clear-sighted capture of the history and content of this less than successful public policy, *see generally* EDWARD M. GRAMLICH, SUBPRIME MORTGAGES: AMERICA'S LATEST BOOM OR BUST, Urban Inst. Press (2007).
115. *See supra* note 91 and accompanying text.
116. § 92.254(a)(1).
117. § 92.254(a)(2).
118. § 92.254(a)(4).
119. § 92.254(a)(5).
120. *Id.*
121. American Dream Downpayment Act, title I, Pub. L. 108-186 (2003).
122. Today's more publicized analogue is the many instances of post-traumatic stress experienced by veterans of Iraq and Afghanistan tours of duty. CLINT VAN WINKLE, SOFT SPOTS: A MARINE'S MEMOIR OF POST TRAUMATIC STRESS DISORDER, St. Martin's Press (2009); EDWARD TICK, WAR AND THE SOUL: HEALING OUR NATION'S VETERANS FROM POST-TRAUMATIC STRESS DISORDER, Quest Books (2005).
123. Stewart B. McKinney Homeless Assistance Act, 42 U.S.C. § 11301 note, Pub. L. 100-77 (1987), named for Rep. McKinney (R-Conn.), who spearheaded enactment of such assistance, and subsequently renamed the McKinney-Vento Homeless Assistance Act to honor Rep. Bruce Vento (D-Minn.), who also supported such actions.

aside, homeless grants are now the single largest competitive grant program in CPD and in HUD.

As has been described previously in this chapter,[124] there are entire aspects of HUD's "community development" programs that are composed largely of housing assistance. That is also the case with the homeless programs. By its nature, homeless assistance is generally temporary, which differentiates it from other HUD housing programs. Further, only one program in the homeless assistance arsenal approaches the rudiments of a block grant. That is the Emergency Shelter Grant Program (ESG).[125]

B. Program Typologies

As can often be said of government programs, one person's program count may differ from another's. For CPD's homeless initiatives, there are at least four principal programs: ESG; the use of federal real property to assist the homeless;[126] Shelter Plus Care;[127] and the Supportive Housing Program.[128]

As noted, ESG is in the nature of a block grant. It does not "block" a series of previously existing categorical programs, *a la* CDBG. (Neither does HOME.) However, ESG is a formula grant program, in which general purpose governments (states, metropolitan cities, urban counties, and Indian tribes) are allocated grants pursuant to an annually reliable formula. That formula is calibrated to the same percentage that cities, counties, and states receive under the CDBG formula.[129] The slate of eligible activities is limited, as the program's title suggests, to "emergency shelter" activities, but within that sphere broadly encompasses renovations, rehabilitation, essential services, and homeless prevention activities.[130]

HUD's role in the *use of federal property to assist the homeless* is a coordinative function among federal agencies, all of which are to advise HUD of any surplus, excess, unutilized, or underutilized federal real property. Next, HUD determines which properties are suitable for the homeless.[131] The other, owner agencies then determine which properties will be made available for the homeless.

Shelter Plus Care links rental housing assistance to supportive services for hard-to-serve homeless persons with disabilities.[132] Eligible grantees are states, units of general local government, and public housing agencies.[133]

Last (but most) is the *Supportive Housing Program,* which provides grants to promote the development of supportive housing and supportive services. The funds can be used for (a) transitional housing to facilitate movement to permanent housing; (b) permanent housing for persons with disabilities; (c) particularly innovative housing for homeless persons; and (d)

---

124. *See especially* the discussion of the HOME program, *supra*.
125. 24 C.F.R. pt. 576.
126. 24 C.F.R. pt. 581.
127. 24 C.F.R. pt. 582.
128. 24 C.F.R. pt. 583.
129. 42 U.S.C. § 11373; § 576.5(b).
130. § 576.21.
131. § 581.4(a).
132. § 582.1.
133. § 582.5.

supportive services to homeless persons that are not provided in conjunction with supportive housing.[134] Within these objectives, grants can be made for acquisition and rehabilitation,[135] new construction,[136] leasing,[137] supportive services,[138] and operating costs.[139] The grantee must match dollar-for-dollar the funds provided by HUD for acquisition, rehabilitation, and new construction.[140]

C. Some Recurring Issues, Legal and Policy

The Supportive Housing Program, with over $1 billion available every year, has become the largest competitive grant program in all of HUD. The program is competed annually, pursuant to a Notice of Fund Availability (NOFA) published in the *Federal Register*, pursuant to section 102 of the Department of Housing and Urban Development Reform Act of 1989 (the Reform Act).[141] The process is detailed and prescriptive but scandal-free and written clearly for applicants.

However, the scale of this more than $1 billion program is in one sense practically diminished by the reality of "renewal grants." The regulations provide that grants "may be renewed on a non-competitive basis to continue ongoing leasing, operations, and supportive services for additional years beyond the initial funding period."[142] While this approach is consistent with the Reform Act, such discretionary authority is rarely needed. Rather, it is the continuing need of formerly funded entities and, consequently, their participation in the overall competition that place a strain on that competition. In any year the increased demand for renewal grants, typically including requests from nonprofit entities with few other sources of funding, ultimately means that new access for others to the enormous over-$1 billion competitive program is effectively lessened.[143] But HUD is—for homes for the homeless, at least—the biggest, if not the only significant, game in town. Accordingly, in 2010 the Department was still able to award more than $216 million for almost 700 new homeless programs.[144]

Another phenomenon with legal implications is the prominent role played in homeless assistance by faith-based entities, which have long dedicated their efforts to this subcategory of housing need, as well as to those benefiting from the anti-poverty thrust of CDBG. Consequently, HUD has continually refined its community development regulations[145] to maximize

---

134. § 583.1(b).
135. § 583.105.
136. § 583.110.
137. § 583.115.
138. § 583.120.
139. § 583.125.
140. § 583.145(a).
141. 42 U.S.C. 3537a; *see* 24 C.F.R. § 4.5.
142. § 583.235(a).
143. In January 2010, HUD awarded over $1.4 billion in Continuum of Care grants to renew funding to 7,000 existing local homeless programs. http://portal.hud/gov/hudportal/HUD?src=/press/press_releases_med. The Continuum of Care competition also includes Shelter Plus Care grants and a small single-room occupancy program.
144. *Id.*
145. § 583.150(b); § 570.200(j).

participation by such entities, but always within the permissible ambit of the separation of church and state, as required by the First Amendment of the U.S. Constitution.

V. OTHER COMMUNITY DEVELOPMENT PROGRAMS, OTHER BLOCK GRANTS

In navigating community development in HUD programs, one must note that the Office of Community Planning and Development administers many other programs, ranging all the way from a loan guarantee fund for church arson recovery[146] to Housing Opportunities for Persons with AIDS (HOPWA)[147] to Urban Empowerment Zones and Enterprise Communities.[148] However, the CDBG, HOME, and homeless assistance programs described above may be viewed as the bedrock of community development, with two of them representing the block grant approach and all three aimed at benefiting low- and moderate-income persons and families.

HUD has another block grant program, which is funded under NAHASDA, or the Native American Housing Assistance and Self-Determination Act.[149] This program, run by HUD's Office of Public and Indian Housing, blocks several previous housing categorical programs and uses a formula allocation of funds to Indian tribes (i.e., the general purpose governments, and not Indian housing authorities or other special purpose governments) in a mode that delegates functions to the grantee with "post-audit" monitoring by HUD. Perhaps the decentralist thrust is strongest in this program inasmuch as HUD is funding nations, not municipal or state governments.

VI. "NOW VEE MAY PERHAPS TO BEGIN. YES?"[150]

Reading, understanding, delving into, and otherwise grappling with the foregoing statutory and regulatory provisions, the practitioner will often still require additional assistance in seeking, obtaining, and administering program funds or a program advisory role. Unlike HUD's housing programs, there is a dearth of handbooks for the CPD programs. Only the CPD Monitoring Handbook, 6509.2 Rev-6, discusses HOME and not many more cover CDBG,[151] once again reflecting the decentralized, post-audit nature of these programs. Nevertheless, there is a wealth of material besides handbooks that is available to practitioners and to the general public, and it comes in two fundamental types.

---

146. 24 C.F.R. pt. 573.
147. 24 C.F.R. pt. 574.
148. 24 C.F.R. pts. 597 and 598.
149. 25 U.S.C. § 4101 *et seq.*; 24 C.F.R. pt. 1000.
150. The last line of the novel, and the first line by the psychiatrist spoken to Alexander Portnoy. PHILIP ROTH, PORTNOY'S COMPLAINT, Random House (1969).
151. This handbook governs HUD's monitoring of its grantees. Chapters 3–6 cover CDBG; chapter 7, HOME; and chapters 9–13, the homeless programs. It is designed to (a) ensure that programs and technical areas are carried out efficiently, effectively, and in compliance with laws and regulations; (b) assist program participants in improving their performance, developing or increasing capacity, and augmenting their management and technical skills; and (c) stay abreast of the efficacy of CPD-administered programs and technical areas within the communities these programs serve. Ch. 1, ¶ 1–2. *See* http://portal.hud.gov/hudportal/HUD?src=/program_offices/comm_planning/library/monitoring/handbook.

First, to the extent one may want to speak with or write to those officials administering a program, HUD's website at www.hud.gov offers two basic, extensive resources. First, of course, recourse to HUD Field Offices provides the paramount expertise of those administering the federal program. The HUD website provides access to all field offices with program responsibilities. Simply navigate from the "Contact Us" key to HUD's Local Office Directory. A common incident of navigating HUD's community development programs is the need to recognize and use correctly the Department's field office structure, broken out into 10 intermediate regional offices and more than 70 field offices.[152] Any grantees, applicants, practitioners, and others interested in the program are encouraged to start with field offices. For the two block grant programs, Headquarters is the locale for devising important policy changes, proposing legislation, drafting regulations, *etc.* But unless a case problem requires something for which the field has not been delegated authority (such as waiver of non-statutorily required regulations), invariably the soundest—and fastest—approach is to approach the field. Even with the homeless programs, where the Continuum of Care competition is administered nationally out of Headquarters, conventional questions, including the application process, are best handled by the field offices.

In addition, the practitioner can have immediate access to the state or local governmental entity carrying out the program at the local level. Recall that the first two programs, CDBG and HOME, involve grants to the general purpose government. In any case, access to all three programs and the state and local officials carrying them out is available at http://www.comcon.org/programs/contact_cdbg.html for the CDBG program, http://www.hud.gov/offices/cpd/affordablehousing/programs/home/contacts for HOME, and http://www.hudhre.info/index.cfm?do=viewCocContacts for the homeless programs.

Beyond establishing contact with federal and local officials, the HUD website is rich in access to procedures, programmatic advice, and an accessible entry to how and why the programs operate. Using the *hudclips* tool on the website opens literally thousands of doors to HUD programs. So, notwithstanding the general absence of applicable "handbooks" to assist the CDBG/HOME/homeless practitioner, there are notices, letters, "HOMEfires" (this last is limited to the HOME program), and other guidance pointed to representative topics such as:

- "Using LIHTC with HOME Funds" (with focus on receiving the nine percent credit; four ways to add HOME funds to an LIHTC project; gap financing; and monitoring);
- the urban county qualification notice for CDBG entitlement funding;
- homeowner rehabilitation program guidance in the HOME program, with seven links to notices, mortgagee letters, and HOMEfires;
- the one-for-one replacement housing requirement;[153]
- "Using CDBG and HOME Funding for Disaster Recovery" (including the use of program income); and
- "Guide for Review of Community Housing Development Organization (CHDO)."

---

152. Some field offices are limited to Federal Housing Administration matters; others also handle the community development programs. *See generally* http://portal.hud.gov/hudportal/HUD?src=localoffices.

153. *See* note 64.

Be advised that the shelf life for notice and other non-handbook guidance is typically only one year, although the document may frequently be updated and re-released in a following year.

VII. COMMONALITIES

Readers will have noted to this point the absence of *case law* citations in the description of these three core programs. Perhaps this absence is because of the decentralist thrust of program administration to grantees themselves; in any case, the programs have not been marked by programwide litigation. In the beginning of the CDBG program, entitlement grantees had to submit an application, which included a Housing Assistance Plan (HAP), designed to provide a link between the grantee's funded program (which did not cover new construction) and the housing assistance made available under title II of the landmark 1974 legislation.[154] Early litigation in Connecticut challenged HUD's responsibilities in terms of how actively grantees must posit goals and how thoroughly HUD must review them, particularly with regard to those families "expected to reside" in communities where they then worked but did not live.[155]

But with even greater deference to decentralization upon statutory changes (1) substituting a final statement and projected use of funds in lieu of an application in 1981[156] and (2) ultimately deleting the HAP in 1990,[157] attendant litigation also dropped off. It remains to be seen what import a recent *qui tam* action under the False Claims Act will hold for CDBG, or other programs, where the grantee is responsible for "affirmatively furthering fair housing," an obligation of broad import for the Secretary of HUD under the Civil Rights Act of 1968,[158] but passed on to CDBG grantees regulatorily and later[159] statutorily; the same certification is required for all ConPlan participants,[160] which include HOME program grantees and more than a dozen smaller programs.[161] The instant case brought by a nonprofit organization led to a consent decree with Westchester County, New York.[162]

Our survey is intended to illustrate the generally successful design of HUD's major community development programs. Some questions do lurk, however, and may continue to do so. Among them is how comprehensively and specifically can/should lower income benefit be measured? As indicated earlier, there need not be a dollar-for-dollar benefit to poor persons to be eligible for CDBG activities. See discussion of area benefit activities and limited clientele

---

154. The Section 8 housing assistance program was created under Title II.
155. Hartford v. Hills, 408 F. Supp. 889 (1976); City of Hartford v. Town of Glastonbury, 561 F.2d 1032 (1976).
156. § 302 of the Housing and Community Development Amendments of 1981, 42 U.S.C. 5304, Pub. L. 97-35 (1981).
157. § 905 of the Cranston-Gonzales National Affordable Housing Act, 42 U.S.C. 1441 *et seq.*, Pub. L. 101-625 (1990).
158. Title VIII of the Civil Rights Act of 1968, 42 U.S.C. § 3608(e)(5), Pub. L. 90-284 (1968).
159. § 104(c)(1) of the Housing and Urban-Rural Recovery Act of 1983, Pub. L. 98-181 (1983).
160. § 91.225(a)(1).
161. § 91.2(a).
162. *See* Hayes, *Enforcing Civil Rights Obligations Through the False Claims Act,* 1 Colum. J. Race & Law 29 (2011).

activities.[163] These mechanisms date back to early implementation of the program and have never been challenged legally. They are realistic, serviceable, and workable.

Another question endemic to block grants may be asked: At what point is the decentralized oversight of block grants by the federal grantor to be revised or altered? Absent multipage submission applications and with reliance on performance review, how deeply should the grantor's performance review cut? The HUD record has been largely successful.[164]

In the final analysis, these two block grant programs and the McKinney-Vento Act are well accepted by local program users and by federal legislators. It is likely that not a small amount of such support comes from the recognition that these program dollars are intended to benefit, and do benefit, low- and moderate-income persons and families, as planned for and carried out by local officials asking the perhaps always-to-be-asked question posed by lawyer/poet Wallace Stevens:

> Who can think of the sun costuming clouds
> When all people are shaken
> Or of night, endazzled, proud,
> When people awaken
> And cry and cry for help?[165]

---

163. Notes 39–43, *supra*.

164. *But see* the 2011 articles on HOME in *The Washington Post* captioned "Million-Dollar Wasteland" (May 15, 2011). The *Post* claimed "a trail of failed [HOME] developments in every corner of the country" (p.1). The Obama Administration shortly thereafter advised Congress that it "would work to tighten rules and requirements for" this program. *HUD to tighten rules for HOME program*, WASH. POST, June 4, 2011, p.2. HUD Secretary Shaun Donovan took issue with the *Post*'s findings and conclusions, stating that "more than half of the 797 projects that could have been flagged as 'stalled' based on the *Post*'s criteria are finished" and further pointing out that "less than 4 percent of the projects in the *Post*'s sample of more than 5,000 HOME projects are currently delayed or canceled." *The HOME Program I know*, WASH. POST, June 9, 2011, *available at* http://www.washingtonpost.com/opinions/the-home-program-i-know. As for *Post* charges of HUD "trusting local agencies to police projects," Secretary Donovan observed that "[i]n other words, it's a block grant. HOME, which was signed into law by President George H. W. Bush in 1992, provides funds directly to state and local governments to meet local needs for affordable housing." *Id.* Patrick B. Pexton, the *Post*'s ombudsman, subsequently wrote that there were arguments on both sides but, as here pertinent, noted that "HUD is correct to point out that HOME was designed to let local jurisdictions handle monitoring and oversight. Congress didn't want an army of bureaucrats looking over the shoulders of local agencies." *The Post vs. HUD on the HOME story*, WASH. POST (July 15, 2011), http://www.washingtonpost.com/opinions/the-post-vs-hud-on-the-home-story. As is the case from time to time, such problems can result in a funding cutback, and that has occurred here. The Congress proposed an almost 38 percent reduction in funding for the HOME program. *Congress cuts HUD fund for the poor*, *available at* http://www.washingtonpost.com/politics/congress-slqshes-huds-cobstruction-fund-for-the-poor/2011/11/17/gIQAYOf4VN_story.html. One month later HUD published a proposed rule in the *Federal Register:* Improving Performance and Accountability; and Updating Property Standards in the HOME program. 76 Fed. Reg. 78,344 (Dec. 16, 2011).

165. *A Fading of the Sun*, THE COLLECTED POEMS OF WALLACE STEVENS, Alfred A. Knopf (1993 ed.).

7 Community Planning and Development: Emerging Neighborhood Stabilization Programs

Laura Schwarz

Since June 2008, Congress has appropriated more than $6.92 billion for the Neighborhood Stabilization Program (NSP) for the redevelopment of blighted structures and abandoned, vacant, and foreclosed homes and residential properties. Implemented by the Office of Community Planning and Development (CPD) in the U.S. Department of Housing and Urban Development (HUD), the NSP program has provided significant funding for acquisitions, rehabilitation, new construction, and land banking throughout the country. Preliminary studies suggest that when funds are used effectively, the program can be instrumental in stabilizing vulnerable neighborhoods and in generating further private investment.[1]

Despite popular references to a single NSP program, Congress actually authorized three distinct but related programs. The first program, now known as NSP1, was authorized under Title III of Division B of the Housing and Economic Recovery Act of 2008 (HERA) and received approximately $3.92

---

1. *See, e.g.,* Carolina Reid, *The Neighborhood Stabilization Program: Strategically Targeting Public Investments*, 23 COMMUNITY INVESTMENTS, Spring 2011 at 27; Ira Goldstein, *Maximizing the Impact of Federal NSP Investments through the Strategic Use of Local Market Data, in* REO AND VACANT PROPERTIES: STRATEGIES FOR NEIGHBORHOOD STABILIZATION 65, 73 (Federal Reserve Banks of Boston and Cleveland and the Federal Reserve Board, 2010); and Robin Newberger, *Pre-implementation findings from the Neighborhood Stabilization Program: Milwaukee, Wisconsin, Lafayette, Indiana, and Cook County Suburbs*, PROFITWISE NEWS AND VIEWS at 10 (Federal Reserve Bank of Chicago) (Nov. 2010).

billion.[2] Congress appropriated approximately $2 billion in additional funds for the NSP2 program under Title XII of Division A of the American Recovery and Reinvestment Act of 2009 (the Recovery Act).[3] Finally, Section 1497 of the Wall Street Reform and Consumer Protection Act of 2010 (the Dodd-Frank Act) authorized the last round of NSP funding (NSP3) and approved approximately $1 billion in corresponding funds.[4] While each of these three NSP programs (collectively, the NSP program) has characteristics that distinguish it from the others, the similarities between the programs often permit broader generalizations, particularly with respect to eligible activities and other programmatic requirements.

While CPD has made significant efforts to release NSP guidance in a timely manner, the fragmented nature of this guidance has been confusing to many recipients and practitioners attempting to understand the applicable requirements. Although many of the underlying NSP requirements are derived from the Community Development Block Grant (CDBG) program, the NSP program includes key distinctions, particularly with respect to eligible activities, participants, and income targeting. Furthermore, because the NSP program also incorporates provisions from CDP's HOME Investment Partnership program (HOME), participants and practitioners must be aware when different programmatic requirements apply. In addition, as the NSP guidance on developer fees for public entities and conditional contracts demonstrates, CPD has also used the NSP program to revise guidance applicable to these other programs. Because CPD often issues NSP guidance informally, recipients of HOME or CDBG funds are often unaware of the effect that the NSP requirements will have on other programs.

Even as CPD continues to release guidance clarifying applicable NSP requirements, because the NSP programs involve federal stimulus funds, HUD has intensified its oversight of these programs. For example, in addition to routine program audits, HUD's Office of the Inspector General (OIG) also conducts special audits for Recovery Act NSP2 funds, reviewing compliance in areas as diverse as undue enrichment of developers, compliance

---

2. Pub. L. No. 110–289 (July 30, 2008) (partially codified as a note to 42 U.S.C. § 5301) [hereinafter HERA], with implementing requirements at the Notice of Allocations, Application Procedures, Regulatory Waivers Granted to and Alternative Requirements for Emergency Assistance for Redevelopment of Abandoned and Foreclosed Homes Grantees under HERA, 73 Fed. Reg. 58,330 (Oct. 6, 2008) [hereinafter the NSP1 Allocation Notice], with corrections issued in 74 Fed. Reg. 29,223 (June 19, 2009), 75 Fed. Reg. 18,228 (April 9, 2011), and 75 Fed. Reg. 52,772 (Aug. 27, 2010). Additional modifications were issued pursuant to the Notice of Formula Allocations and Program Requirements for Neighborhood Stabilization Program Formula Grants, 75 Fed. Reg. 64,322 (Oct. 19, 2010) [hereinafter, the Combined Notice].

3. *See, e.g.*, second undesignated paragraph under the heading Community Planning and Development, Community Development Fund, Pub. L. 111-005 (Feb. 17, 2009) (partially codified as a note to 42 U.S.C. § 5301) (hereinafter the Recovery Act), with a Notice of Availability: Notice of Funding Availability (NOFA) for the Neighborhood Stabilization Program 2 Under the American Recovery and Reinvestment Act, 2009 [hereinafter, the NOFA] issued on May 4, 2009, pursuant to 74 Fed. Reg. 21,377 (May 7, 2009), with corrections issued by 74 Fed. Reg. 29,715 (June 17, 2009), 74 Fed. Reg. 58,973 (Nov. 16, 2009), and 75 Fed. Reg. 4410 (Jan. 27, 2010). Additional modifications were issued pursuant to the Combined Notice, *supra* note 2.

4. Pub. L. No. 111-203 (July 21, 2010) (partially codified as a note to 42 U.S.C. § 5301) [hereinafter the Dodd-Frank Act], with implementing requirements in the Combined Notice, *supra* note 2.

with Title VIII of the Civil Rights Act of 1968, and documentation of purchase price limitations.[5] The combination of rapid expenditure deadlines, extensive but unconsolidated guidance, and heightened scrutiny of programmatic compliance underscores the importance of identifying and understanding the applicable requirements. In response to these concerns, this chapter attempts to provide a comprehensive overview of the NSP program while also indicating unresolved issues or guidance that departs from generally accepted interpretations of the CDBG and HOME programs.

By expanding the types of developers and recipients that may use NSP funds, CPD has also created widespread support that may allow the NSP framework to be used in other contexts. For example, unlike the CDBG program, NSP allows both private and public developers to receive funds, and the NSP2 program also allows non-governmental entities to apply directly to HUD for the funds. Likewise, by working with the Federal Housing Administration (FHA) to give qualified NSP participants exclusive access to review and purchase newly conveyed FHA real estate owned (REO) properties, CPD has helped develop the interest and capacity of publicly focused entities in acquiring or developing such properties. As the Federal Housing Finance Agency (FHFA) Request for Information on REO disposition indicates, the economic instability motivating the creation of the NSP programs remain, and federal and quasi-federal entities remain eager to leverage the capacities of entities with experience in neighborhood stabilization.[6] Similarly, congressional proposals have been introduced that resemble the NSP programs, again indicating the possibility of funding successor NSP programs and the importance of understanding the existing NSP programs.[7]

This chapter is intended as a reference guide for the NSP programs, where Part 1 provides an overview of the three NSP programs and discusses the applicable obligation and expenditure deadlines for each program.[8] Part 2 describes eligible participants, properties, and uses of NSP funds, and Part 3 discusses the affordability restrictions that apply to rental and homeownership developments. Part 4 summarizes the ways in which common cross-cutting federal requirements apply to the NSP program and outlines some of the challenges associated with CPD's interpretations of these requirements. Part 5 concludes with a brief discussion of some of the effects of the NSP program on local markets and on other funding programs. Finally, Appendix A provides a summary of basic NSP-eligible activities.

I. PROGRAM OVERVIEW

A. Neighborhood Stabilization Program 1

As noted above, the NSP program consists of three separately authorized programs that share a similar regulatory framework. Signed into law on July 30, 2008, HERA appropriated approximately $3.92 billion for NSP1, to be used for the redevelopment of blighted structures

---

5. *See generally* CPD, GRANTEE MONITORING HANDBOOK 6509.2, Rev. 6, Chapter 8: Economic Recovery Programs.

6. Federal Housing Finance Agency, Request for Information: Enterprise/FHA REO Asset Disposition (Aug. 10, 2011).

7. *See, e.g.,* American Jobs Act of 2011, Subtitle G, H.R. 12, 112th Congress and Project Rebuild Act of 2011, H.R. 3502, 112th Congress (2011).

8. This article is not intended to serve as legal advice, or as advice for specific situations. Readers are advised to consult legal counsel familiar with the details of their transactions.

and vacant, abandoned, and foreclosed homes and residential properties.[9] Most significant for future program administration, HERA provided that NSP1 funds were to be treated as supplemental CDBG funds unless otherwise indicated.[10] Unlike the later NSP2 program, NSP1 did not competitively award the funds but allocated them through a grant formula devised by HUD.[11] Under this formula, HUD distributed NSP1 funds to both states and eligible entitlement communities as well as to other traditional CDBG recipients.[12] States also could distribute funds to any jurisdiction within the state, regardless of whether the jurisdiction had received a direct NSP grant from HUD.[13] The HUD allocation was based on a formula that considered a number of factors, including (a) the number and percentage of home foreclosures, (b) the number and percentage of homes financed by a subprime mortgage loan, and (c) the number and percentage of homes delinquent or in default.[14] HUD announced the awards on October 6, 2008, and began signing grant agreements several months thereafter.[15]

After signing their agreements with HUD, NSP1 grantees were required to satisfy a number of administrative requirements that reflected the tension between the need for rapid disbursement and a need for public participation in the process. As a prior recipient of CDBG funds, each grantee already had a Consolidated Plan and an annual Action Plan.[16] NSP1 required grantees to publish a "Substantial Amendment" to their Consolidated Plans and annual Action Plans by December 1, 2008, although guarantees could follow an abbreviated public comment period to expedite adoption of the revised plan.[17] Upon completion of the comment period, HUD required grantees to publicize the substantial amendment and notify HUD that the amendment had been adopted.[18] At the conclusion of this process, each grantee then could begin awarding and disbursing the funds.[19] As many observers noted, the protracted approval process and the difficulties of developing an entirely new program led to numerous delays in expending the funds.[20]

Under NSP1, grantees had 18 months to obligate the funds after executing their grant agreements with HUD.[21] HUD interpreted this requirement to mean that orders were placed

---

9. See HERA, Pub. L. No. 110–289 (July 30, 2008) at § 2301(a) and § 2305 for funding amounts and § 2301(c)(3) for eligible uses.
10. HERA § 2301(e).
11. HERA § 2301(b).
12. For general allocation requirements, see HERA § 2301(a). For allocation methodology, see NSP1 Allocation Notice, *supra* note 2, at 58,332 and 58,344–45.
13. NSP1 Allocation Notice, *supra* note 2, at 58336 and 58344.
14. HERA § 2301(b)(3). *See also* NSP1 Allocation Notice, *supra* note 2, at 58344-5.
15. NSP1 Allocation Notice, *supra* note 2, at 58,345.
16. *See id.* at 58,331 for premise that each jurisdiction already had a consolidated plan; *see* 24 C.F.R. Part 91 for required components of the plans.
17. For submission deadline, *see* NSP1 Allocation Notice, *supra* note 2, at 58,332. For waiver of citizen participation requirements in preparation of substantial amendment, *see* NSP1 Allocation Notice, *supra* note 2, at 58,333. For Consolidated Plan requirements, *see* 24 C.F.R. § 91.505.
18. NSP1 Allocation Notice, *supra* note 2, at 58,333.
19. *Id.*
20. *See generally supra* note 1.
21. HERA, Pub. L. No. 110–289 (July 30, 2008) at § 2301(c)(1) and NSP1 Allocation Notice, *supra* note 2, at 58,340. Grantees receiving reallocated NSP1 funds will have separate obligation and expenditure deadlines. CPD, NSP Policy Alert: Guidance on the NSP1 Recapture and Reallocation Notice (Aug. 26, 2010).

or contracts were awarded or similar transactions occurred that required payment by the grantee.[22] Significantly, funds were not obligated if the grantee merely made an award to a subrecipient.[23] Finally, HUD suggested that if a grantee or sub-recipient awarded funds to a developer, the obligation of NSP1 funds for property acquisition could be recorded only after the developer identified specific properties to be acquired or rehabilitated and after the developer agreement was executed.[24] With respect to other costs, the developer had to provide the grantee with documented cost estimates such as rehabilitation and construction costs for each identified property.[25] Accordingly, HUD implemented provisions to recapture the unobligated funds of grantees that failed to meet the 18-month obligation.[26]

In addition to the 18-month obligation deadline, HUD requires NSP1 grantees to demonstrate that they have expended an amount equal to or greater than their initial NSP allocation funds within four years of receipt of the funds.[27] Failure to meet this deadline may result in the recapture of any unexpended funds.[28] As discussed in greater detail below, the funds expended to satisfy this requirement may include funds from the initial NSP1 award as well as program income funds generated by the initial award.[29]

B. Neighborhood Stabilization Program 2

On February 17, 2009, Congress authorized the creation of the NSP2 program as part of the Recovery Act.[30] While broadly similar to NSP1, the authorization for NSP2 included several key differences. Most significant, NSP2 funds were competitively awarded through a Notice of Funding Availability (NOFA) to a variety of applicants, including states, units of local government, nonprofit organizations, and consortia that included these entities.[31] Such consortia could also include for-profit partner organizations.[32] HUD required applicants to commit to activities within defined census tracts, neighborhoods, or other areas that exhibited

---

22. NSP1 Allocation Notice, *supra* note 2, at 58,332; for corresponding definition of "obligation" in HUD procurement guidance, *see* 24 C.F.R. § 85.3. *See also* CPD, NSP Policy Alert: Guidance on Tracking and Reporting the Use of NSP Funds: Obligations for Specific Activities (April 23, 2010) at 2–3 [hereinafter, Policy Alert: Guidance for Tracking and Reporting the Use of NSP Funds].

23. NSP1 Allocation Notice, *supra* note 2, at 58,332.

24. Policy Alert: Guidance for Tracking and Reporting the Use of NSP Funds, *supra* note 22, at 2–3.

25. *Id.*

26. *See, e.g.*, Notice of Neighborhood Stabilization Program Reallocation Process Changes, 75 Fed. Reg. 52,772 (Aug. 27, 2010). *See also* CPD, NSP Policy Alert: Guidance on the NSP1 Recapture and Reallocation Notice (Aug. 26, 2010).

27. Notice of Neighborhood Stabilization Program Reallocation Process Changes, 75 Fed. Reg. 52,772 (Aug. 27, 2010) at 52,773.

28. *Id.*

29. NSP1 Allocation Notice, *supra* note 2, at 58,340.

30. Recovery Act, Pub. L. 111-005 (Feb. 17, 2009), Title XII of Division A, Community Planning and Development, Community Development Fund.

31. NOFA, *supra* note 2, at 2–3.

32. *Id.*

heightened foreclosure scores and other risk factors.[33] These commitments could be modified only in limited circumstances, with a strict review process for proposed amendments.[34]

After HUD's execution of the NSP2 grant awards, grantees had two years to spend 50 percent of their award funds and three years to spend the entirety of their awards.[35] Grantees usually had until February 2012 to meet the first deadline and typically have until February 2013 to spend their full allocation.[36] Unlike the NSP1 program, NSP2 does not impose an "obligation" deadline for the awarded funds. However, as under NSP1, grantees in the NSP2 program may satisfy their expenditure deadlines by spending an amount equal to or greater than their initial NSP allocations.[37] Effectively, this permits grantees to include both the original NSP2 allocation and program income funds when calculating the amount of expended funds.

C. Neighborhood Stabilization Program 3

With the passage of the Dodd-Frank Act, Congress provided an additional $1 billion in NSP funding. While the Dodd-Frank Act retained some NSP2 expenditure requirements, in many ways the NSP3 program more closely resembles NSP1. As with NSP1, the NSP3 program provides a formula-based funding allocation, and only states, entitlement jurisdictions, and certain other areas with significant need could apply.[38] Grantees entitled to receive NSP3 awards under the formula were required to submit applications to HUD, identifying proposed uses for the funds, and were required to use a mapping tool provided by HUD to identify their targeted geographic areas.[39] As in the NSP2 program, grantees have two years to spend 50 percent of their award funds and they have three years to spend the entirety of their awards.[40] Likewise, NSP3 grantees must spend an amount equal to or greater than their initial NSP allocations.[41] Based on HUD's estimated schedule for award-

---

33. *Id.* at 14–15.

34. *See generally* CPD, NSP Policy Alert: Guidance on Substantial Amendment Procedures (March 28, 2011) at 2–4 [hereinafter Policy Alert: Guidance on Substantial Amendment Procedures].

35. Recovery Act, Title XII of Division A, Community Planning and Development, Community Development Fund, 2d para. *See also* NOFA, *supra* note 2, at 68.

36. NSP2 funding applications were due on July 17, 2009, and HUD announced funding awards on Jan. 14, 2010. Press Release, HUD Secretary Donovan Announces $2 Billion in Recovery Act Grants to Stabilize Neighborhoods, Rebuild Local Economies (Jan. 14, 2010) (HUD No. 10-012). Grantees had 30 days to return their executed grant agreements to HUD. NOFA, *supra* note 2, at 32.

37. Combined Notice, *supra* note 2, at 64,336 (addressing NSP2 requirements even though the notice applies to NSP1 and NSP3). *See also* CPD, NSP Policy Alert: Guidance on Calculating Expenditures for NSP2 and NSP3 (Sept. 3, 2010) at 1.

38. Dodd-Frank Act, Pub. L. No. 111-203 (July 21, 2010), § 1497(a)(3). *See also* Combined Notice, *supra* note 2, at 64,340–41.

39. HUD permitted an expedited public participation process but still required grantees to complete and submit a Substantial Amendment to their Consolidated Plan and annual Action Plan for these uses. *See* Combined Notice, *supra* note 2, at 64326–27.

40. Dodd-Frank Act § 1497(a) incorporates the expenditure requirements applicable to NSP2 funds under the Recovery Act. *See also* Combined Notice, *supra* note 2, at 64,336.

41. Combined Notice, *supra* note 2, at 64,336.

ing the funds, these deadlines will probably occur in March 2013 and March 2014, respectively.[42]

D. General Sources of Guidance

As noted above, the NSP program is administered through the Office of Community Planning and Development (CPD) within HUD. In addition to administering the CDBG program, which provides the underlying regulatory framework for NSP, CPD also administers HOME and a variety of other community and economic development programs.[43] To supplement the authorizing legislation and applicable Federal Register notices, CPD has devised an informal system for promulgating guidance relating to the NSP program. Most of this guidance can be found on HUD's Neighborhood Stabilization Program Resource Exchange at http://hudnsphelp.info/ (the Resource Exchange). While this guidance has been issued without rulemaking or the benefit of public notice and comment, it nevertheless provides insight into CPD's views of the applicable NSP requirements.

CPD issues its more extensive guidance in NSP Policy Alerts, which typically address a single topic such as administrative fees, program income, Davis Bacon wage rates, or other regulatory issues.[44] In addition to Policy Alerts, CPD has also assembled a collection of Frequently Asked Questions (FAQs) to answer questions about particular factual situations. FAQs provide advice in response to questions ranging from concerns about combining NSP funds with other funds to queries about to the term of the NSP affordability period. With more than 500 FAQs, this resource often indicates CPD's current interpretation of the requirements applicable to a specific situation.[45] The Resource Exchange also includes a number of NSP Toolkits, which are form documents that grantees and sub-recipients may adapt to facilitate implementation of their own programs. As with the other CPD guidance, these form documents often reflect CPD's view of best practices rather than mandatory procedures, although the distinction is not always apparent.[46] While this informal guidance provides insight into CPD's interpretations of the requirements applicable to the NSP program, the occasionally opaque nature of CPD's recommendations has created some uncertainty for NSP

---

42. The Combined Notice requires that grantees submit their substantial amendments to HUD by March 1, 2011. Combined Notice, *supra* note 2, at 64,326. However, recognizing that many grantees experienced difficulties using the new HUD mapping tool, HUD permitted grantees to simply provide HUD with information about how the grantees would select developers and sub-recipients, but HUD was unable to modify the statutory expenditure requirements. *See* CPD, NSP Policy Alert: Guidance on Mapping and Data Needs for State NSP3 Action Plans (Dec. 29, 2010).

43. *See, e.g.,* CPD, About CPD, *available at* http://www.hud.gov/offices/cpd/about/ (last accessed Jan. 9, 2012). Chapter 6 of this book provides additional information about these other CPD programs.

44. It is advisable to review these Policy Alerts in reverse chronological order because newer alerts sometimes conflict with prior publications.

45. As with the Policy Alerts, it is helpful to review the more current FAQs first. Additionally, the number of these FAQs varies because CPD periodically deletes some FAQs and adds others.

46. For example, the Sample NSP Single-Family Developer Agreement is part of the "Homeownership Toolkit" and contains a disclaimer that "[t]his document is not an official HUD document and has not been reviewed by HUD counsel. It is provided for informational purposes only."

participants, particularly because this guidance may change without notice.[47] As a result, NSP participants may want to consider retaining their own copies of any guidance that they have relied on as part of their compliance documentation. As HUD's OIG website indicates, frequent audits routinely require NSP participants to justify their actions.[48]

In contrast to the practices of many other HUD offices, CPD does not require grantees or subgrantees to submit their projects to CPD for approval before NSP funds may be expended and typically declines to conduct such reviews. Public housing authorities, FHA lenders and borrowers, and other entities accustomed to dealing with different HUD offices should be aware that because CPD is separate from PIH, FHA, and other HUD offices, another office's approval of a transaction does not necessarily indicate that CPD has sanctioned the proposed use of NSP funds. As a result, CPD encourages grantees to review the guidance described above and contact their field offices or NSP technical assistance providers with questions relating to eligible uses of funds or other issues.

II. ELIGIBLE PARTNERS, PROPERTIES, AND USES

A. Eligible Partners

While the CDBG program provides the general framework for the NSP program, the CDBG program itself generally restricts participation to grantees, sub-recipients, and organizations that have been certified as Community Based Development Organizations (CBDOs).[49] In accordance with the NSP implementing legislation, CPD has expanded the types of entities that may participate in the NSP program. Generally, these changes have proven beneficial to a variety of participants, which NSP categorizes as grantees, subrecipients, consortium members, developers, or contractors (collectively "NSP participants"). As discussed in greater detail below, this categorization determines the applicability of various other requirements, including those related to procurement and compensation.

1. Grantees

In its programwide definition of "grantee," HUD describes a grantee as a government to which a grant is awarded and the entity that is accountable for the use of the funds.[50] Because the NSP2 program also permitted nonprofits to apply for grants, and the for-profit partners of any eligible entity could also apply directly for NSP2 funds, the term "grantee" also refers to these direct recipients of NSP2 funds as well.[51] Grantees that qualify as "public nonprofit" entities are subject to the regulatory requirements applicable to public entities, including the

---

47. *See, e.g., infra* note 245. For example, CPD issued FAQs with respect to program income, and then deleted the guidance from the Resource Exchange without an announcement when CPD's interpretation of the underlying requirements changed

48. For OIG's Recovery Act audits, *see* http://www.hud.gov/offices/oig/recovery/ARRAaudits.html.

49. 24 C.F.R. § 570.204.

50. 24 C.F.R. § 85.3. This section is applicable to the CDBG program through 24 C.F.R. § 570.502(a) (government entities).

51. For eligibility of nonprofits, consortia, and for-profit partners, *see* NOFA, *supra* note 2, at 2–3.

administrative and procurement requirements at 24 C.F.R. Part 85 and the environmental requirements at 24 C.F.R. Parts 50 or 58.[52] If a grantee is a private nonprofit, it instead will be subject to similar administrative provisions at 24 C.F.R. Part 84 and the environmental review requirements at 24 C.F.R. Part 50.[53]

In accordance with NSP guidance that CDP suggests is consistent with CDBG guidance, grantees serving as developers may not charge developer fees on the portion of the transaction funded with NSP funds and may instead claim administrative fees to cover that portion of their expenses.[54] However, CPD now allows most grantees to collect reasonable developer fees on the portion of any project not funded with NSP funds.[55] For example, if a grantee typically receives a 10 percent developer fee for its services as a developer, then it generally would receive a fee of $10,000 on a project with $100,000 in development costs. However, if the project was funded with $40,000 in NSP funds and $60,000 with other funds, then the NSP guidance allows the grantee to receive a developer fee calculated as 10 percent of $60,000 (i.e., a fee of $6,000 rather than $10,000). CPD has cautioned that the grantee may not simply charge the full $10,000 to the non-NSP funding. This limitation on developer fees likewise applies to subrecipients and consortium members.[56]

Because grantees cannot fully cover their costs through developer fees, CPD permits recovery of additional costs through direct and indirect administrative fees.[57] In contrast to activity delivery costs that are charged to a specific NSP project, administrative costs include staff salaries, outreach costs, and other reasonable administrative costs that benefit the grantee's NSP activities but cannot be easily identified with a particular project.[58] However, because grantees may not use more than 10 percent of their total award on administrative fees,[59] many have begun reviewing the costs that may be characterized as direct program delivery that can be charged to the NSP grant.

2. Consortium Members

To accommodate the structure of the NSP2 program, CPD has clarified the status of consortium members. In guidance issued several months after the NSP2 grants were awarded, CPD announced that it considered consortium members to be part of the grantee and thus subject to

---

52. *See, e.g.,* NOFA, *supra* note 2, at 7–8.
53. NOFA, *supra* note 2, at 7–8.
54. CPD, NSP Policy Alert: Guidance on Allocating Real Estate Development Costs in the Neighborhood Stabilization Program (Jan. 12, 2011) at 3–4 [hereinafter Policy Alert: Allocating Development Costs]. This is one example of NSP guidance that may have significant consequences for other programs.
55. Policy Alert: Allocating Development Costs, *supra* note 54 at 4, and FAQ 943 (Dec. 7, 2010).
56. Policy Alert: Allocating Development Costs, *supra* note 54, at 4.
57. *Id.* at 2–3.
58. *Id.* Some indirect costs may also be reimbursed as administrative costs if the subrecipient has an indirect cost allocation plan that has been approved by HUD; grantees may impose additional restrictions. *Id.*
59. NSP1 Allocation Notice, *supra* note 2, at 58,337; NOFA, *supra* note 2, at 56–57; Combined Notice, *supra* note 2, at 64,324.

the administrative requirements applicable to grantees and sub-recipients.[60] Despite the fact that many NSP2 applications described some consortium members as housing developers, CPD continues to suggest that consortium members may receive developer fees only to the extent that grantees and subrecipients may charge these fees.[61] As discussed above with respect to grantees, this means that consortium members may charge developer fees only against the portion of the project not developed with NSP funds, and NSP funds cannot be used to pay the fees.[62] In addition to these fee-based requirements, consortium members are subject to the procurement[63] and environmental[64] review requirements applicable to government entities or nonprofit organizations. Some consortium members have responded by requesting that HUD consider a substantial amendment to their NSP2 applications to remove them as consortium members.[65]

3. Subrecipients

Most NSP participants are not grantees or consortium members but will be categorized as subrecipients, developers, or contractors. Typically, grantees characterize their partners as either "subrecipients" or "developers," and these entities then may engage contractors. A subrecipient is an entity that assists a grantee or another subrecipient in administering the NSP program, while a developer receives NSP assistance to acquire and redevelop foreclosed, abandoned, or vacant properties.[66] While the difference between these definitions is somewhat ambiguous, a subrecipient's duties generally are more administrative, while a developer maintains site control and manages the development of the project.[67] Most important, each role imposes different compensation structures and regulatory requirements, although many NSP participants have found that status as a developer offers significantly greater flexibility.

As noted above, subrecipients may not receive full developer fees in the NSP program, but they are partially compensated through reimbursements for eligible "activity delivery costs" and "administrative costs." Like consortium members, subrecipients may claim a reasonable developer fee on the portion of a project that is not NSP-funded but must recover their remaining costs as either activity delivery or administrative costs.[68] Activity delivery

---

60. CPD, Policy Alert: Guidance on Charging Administrative Costs Incurred by NSP2 Grantees (March 24, 2010) at 1.
61. FAQ 943 (Dec. 7, 2010).
62. Policy Alert: Allocating Development Costs, *supra* note 54, at 4.
63. *See, e.g.,* 24 C.F.R. § 570.610, which requires that procurements be conducted in compliance with 24 C.F.R. pt. 84 or pt. 85, as applicable. *See also* CPD, Cross-Cutting Regulations Overview Series: Procurement (July 2010) at 2, *available at* http://hudnsphelp.info/media/resources/CrosscuttingRegs_Procurement.pdf [hereinafter, *Cross-Cutting Regulations Overview*].
64. *See, e.g.,* 24 C.F.R. § 570.604 (environmental review requirements of 24 C.F.R. part 50 or part 58 apply).
65. For a discussion of substantial amendment procedures, *see generally* Policy Alert: Guidance on Substantial Amendment Procedures, *supra* note 34.
66. CPD, NSP Policy Alert: Guidance on Developers, Subrecipients, and Contractors (Aug. 27, 2010) at 1 [hereinafter Policy Alert: Guidance on Developers, Subrecipients, and Contractors].
67. *Id.*
68. Policy Alert: Allocating Development Costs, *supra* note 54 at 4, and FAQ 943 (Dec. 7, 2010).

costs must be related to a specific NSP project and include the costs of acquiring a property, certain due diligence expenses, and the costs of rehabilitation, redevelopment, or new construction. Administrative costs include staff salaries, outreach costs, and other reasonable administrative costs that benefit the subrecipient's NSP activities but cannot be easily identified with a particular project.[69] Additionally, subrecipients generally are subject to federal procurement requirements,[70] which may increase the time and cost of making purchases. However, grantees are not required to procure their subrecipients, and, as discussed below, subrecipients are not required to procure developers.[71] Finally, as discussed in Part 4 of this chapter, if subrecipients receive income that has been directly generated from the NSP program, they are required to treat these funds as program income that is subject to the full requirements of the NSP program, including procurement and environmental review.[72] As a result, while subrecipient status may be appropriate for an entity that does not intend to directly develop a project, many participants should review whether this role is best suited to their intended activities.

As part of its guidance relating to grantees, consortium members, and subrecipients, CPD has released interpretations relating to public housing authorities (PHAs) that further restrict the abilities of these entities to participate in the NSP program. Most significant, CPD announced that PHAs may not serve as developers because the CDBG regulations require developers to be "private entities."[73] CPD has also indicated that public entities with an "identity of interest" with the grantee may carry out NSP development activities only under a subrecipient agreement and not under a developer agreement.[74] However, because CDP has been willing to relax this prohibition for some PHAs as long as the developer fee is paid with non-NSP funds, PHAs seeking to charge a developer fee may wish to consult their HUD representatives for additional information.[75]

4. Developers

In contrast to its guidance for grantees, consortium members, and subrecipients, CPD permits developers to receive full developer fees on NSP projects and subjects developers to fewer regulatory restrictions.[76] While CPD has not issued specific guidance about the appropriate amount of developer fees, grantees may permit developer fees that are reasonable and customary for similar projects in their communities.[77] CPD has also noted that fees often range

---

69. Certain indirect costs may also be reimbursed as administrative costs where the subrecipient has an indirect cost-allocation plan that has been approved by HUD; grantees may impose additional restrictions.
70. Cross-Cutting Regulations Overview, *supra* note 63 and FAQ 486 (Sept. 8, 2010).
71. FAQ 486 (Sept. 8, 2010).
72. *See, e.g.*, CPD, NSP Policy Alert: Program Income in the Neighborhood Stabilization Program (July 13, 2011) at 2 [hereinafter, Policy Alert: Program Income].
73. Policy Alert: Guidance on Developers, Subrecipients, and Contractors, *supra* note 66, at 2.
74. *Id.*
75. *Id.*
76. Policy Alert: Allocating Development Costs, *supra* note 54 at 3-4.
77. CPD, FAQ 332 (Sept. 8, 2010).

from 1 percent to more than 10 percent of the total development costs, indicating that grantees have considerable flexibility in establishing these percentages.[78] Furthermore, developers also may receive reimbursements for NSP-eligible costs,[79] although many grantees require developers to execute promissory notes and deeds of trust or mortgages for these amounts to avoid violating CPD's prohibition on undue enrichment of third parties. CPD also permits developers to retain sales proceeds, cash flow, and other income from their projects and does not require that developers return such funds to the grantee as program income.[80] Additionally, CPD does not require developers to follow federal procurements standards, and so neither grantees nor subrecipients are required to procure developers, and developers, in turn, need not procure their contractors.[81] However, developers' expenses still must be eligible, necessary, and reasonable.[82] As a result, many organizations find that designation as a developer rather than as a subrecipient is a desirable way to gain greater control over their own projects.

5. Contractors

CPD has issued the least guidance on contractors, which is the final category of common NSP participants. Contractors are entities that supply goods or services, including construction services on a property owned by the grantee or subrecipient, and they also may provide housing counseling services.[83] As noted above, grantees and subrecipients must procure contractors, but developers are not subject to this restriction.[84] Having been procured or otherwise hired by a developer, contractors are not subject to federal procurement requirements, although their fees must be eligible, necessary, and reasonable.[85]

B. Eligible Properties

The authorizing legislation for all three NSP programs requires that NSP funds be used for one of five approved uses. As a threshold matter, the underlying property must qualify as foreclosed, abandoned, or vacant at the time of acquisition, or must contain blighted structures. Once a grantee determines that a property is eligible, NSP funds may be spent on

---

78. CPD, FAQ 535 (July 18, 2010).
79. For additional guidance on what costs may be included in the calculation of developer fees, see Policy Alert: Allocating Development Costs, *supra* note 54.
80. Policy Alert: Program Income, *supra* note 72, at 3 and Policy Alert: Guidance on Developers, Subrecipients, and Contractors, *supra* note 66, at 3.
81. *See* Policy Alert: Guidance on Developers, Subrecipients, and Contractors, *supra* note 66, at 3 (federal procurement process does not apply); Cross-Cutting Regulations Overview, *supra* note 63; FAQ 330 (July 1, 2010) (developers not subject to procurement requirements with respect to contractors). CPD has stated that developers are "different than grantees or subrecipients because they are considered "end users" of the NSP funds, similar to the way that a homeowner receiving a rehab grant is an end use," and CPD appears to suggest that this is sufficient to assure that developers are exempt from procurement. FAQs 705 (Sept. 30, 2010) and 486 (Sept. 8, 2010). However, if other public funds are used, this procurement-related flexibility may be less relevant.
82. *See e.g., supra* note 81 and FAQ 534 (July 18, 2010).
83. Policy Alert: Guidance on Developers, Subrecipients, and Contractors, *supra* note 66, at 2.
84. *Supra* note 81.
85. *Id.* at 2 and CPD, FAQ 534 (July 18, 2010).

property acquisition, construction or rehabilitation costs, demolition, or land banking. Additionally, the owner of the property must also agree to various long-term affordability requirements as a condition to receiving the NSP funds. While many of these requirements have evolved since the inception of the NSP program, these conditions generally remain consistent across the NSP1, NSP2, and NSP3 programs. As discussed in greater detail below, CPD has developed extensive eligibility criteria for properties and uses under the NSP program, and program participants may benefit from periodic review of these requirements to ensure compliance with any modifications.

1. Foreclosed Properties

Once a grantee has determined that a property is located in an eligible area, the property must also qualify as foreclosed, abandoned, vacant, or blighted to be eligible for NSP funding.[86] Initially more restrictive, foreclosed properties may now describe the greatest number of NSP-eligible properties because in April 2010, HUD expanded the definition of "foreclosed" with respect to the NSP1 and NSP2 programs, and incorporated this definition into the NSP3 program as well.[87] The current definition of "foreclosed" states:

> Properties now qualify as foreclosed *if any of the following conditions apply*: (a) the property's current delinquency status is at least 60 days delinquent under the Mortgage Bankers of America delinquency calculation and the owner has been notified; (b) the property owner is 90 days or more delinquent on tax payments; (c) under state, local, or tribal law, foreclosure proceedings have been initiated or completed; or (d) foreclosure proceedings have been completed and title has been transferred to an intermediary aggregator or servicer that is not an NSP grantee, subrecipient, developer, contractor, or end-user.[88]

In contrast to the prior standard,[89] the new definition simply requires that foreclosure proceedings be initiated by the time the grantee, subrecipient, or developer acquires the property. The revised language likewise permits properties to qualify if they have a delinquency status of at least 60 days and implicitly permits the use of short sales as well.[90] While this revision expands the number of properties that may qualify to receive NSP funds, CPD suggests that this change also imposes additional restrictions on properties that would have qualified under a different eligibility category. For example, CPD indicates that the revised language *requires* properties to be deemed foreclosed if they would qualify under this defini-

---

86. *See generally* Combined Notice, *supra* note 2, at 64,333.
87. For expansion of NSP1 definition, *see* 75 Fed. Reg. 18,228 at 18,230 (April 9, 2010); for limited retroactive applicability to NSP1 program, *see* CPD, NSP Policy Alert: Guidance on the Impact of New Definitions for NSP-Eligible Properties (April 2, 2010) at 4 [hereinafter Policy Alert: New Definitions]; for application to NSP2 program, *see* HUD Notice 5321-N-04 (published to HUD website April 2, 2010), with additional guidance at Policy Alert: New Definitions, *supra*; for application to NSP3 program, *see* Combined Notice, *supra* note 2, at 64,325.
88. Combined Notice, *supra* note 2, at 64,325.
89. *See, e.g.,* NSP1 Allocation Notice, *supra* note 2, at 58,331 for prior NSP1 definition; *see* NOFA, *supra* note 2, at 42 for prior NSP2 definition.
90. *See also* Policy Alert: New Definitions, *supra* note 87, at 3.

tion, and that grantees therefore lack the discretion to deem the properties abandoned, vacant, or blighted instead.[91]

This requirement that properties be deemed to be foreclosed even if they would also be eligible for an alternative classification is particularly significant because foreclosed properties are subject to greater restrictions than are other categories of property. In contrast to abandoned, vacant, or blighted properties, foreclosed properties must be purchased at a discount of at least one percent from the current market-appraised value of the property.[92] Furthermore, unless the purchase price is below $25,000, all foreclosed properties must be appraised in compliance with the appraisal standards of the Uniform Relocation Act.[93] Similarly, certain tenant protection requirements (discussed in greater detail in Part 4 below) apply to foreclosed properties but not to abandoned or vacant properties.[94] Finally, if a foreclosed-on home or residential property is sold to an individual as a primary residence, then the sales price to that individual cannot exceed the cost of acquiring and redeveloping the property to a decent, safe, and habitable condition.[95] While this requirement also applies to abandoned properties, it is not applicable to properties that qualify solely as vacant or blighted

---

91. *Id.* at 2.

92. HUD originally set the NSP1 discount requirement at 15%, but reduced it to 1% pursuant to 74 Fed. Reg. 29,223, 29,225 (June 19, 2009). This 1% discount requirement applies to the NSP2 program under the NOFA, *supra* note 2, at 73; NSP3 incorporates this requirement through the Combined Notice, *supra* note 2, at 64,338. *See* FAQs 226 (June 15, 2010), 320 (June 10, 2010), 533 (July 18, 2010), and 715 (Feb. 24, 2011) for contrast to abandoned, vacant, or blighted properties. It appears that all foreclosed properties probably must receive the discount. Policy Alert: New Definitions, *supra* note 87, at 3. However, CPD has issued conflicting guidance for situations in which non-NSP funds are used to purchase the property. *See, e.g.,* FAQ 361 (June 29, 2010) (discount requirement applies regardless of funding source) and 715 (Feb. 24, 2011) (non-NSP funds were not used for acquisition and so purchase price discount did not apply) and FAQ 199 (June 29, 2009) (cannot use other funding sources to pay full fair market value).

93. For general appraisal requirements, *see* HERA, Pub. L. No. 110–289 (July 30, 2008), at § 2301(d) (requiring that properties be acquired at a discount from the appraised market value) and 24 C.F.R. § 570.606(e) (applicability of Uniform Relocation Act (URA) requirements to CDBG acquisitions, as the URA is implemented at 49 C.F.R. pt. 24); for URA appraisal requirement for NSP1 and NSP3, *see* Combined Notice, *supra* note 2, at 64,338; for NSP2 requirement, *see* NOFA, *supra* note 2, at 62. *See also* CPD, NSP Policy Alert: Guidance on NSP Appraisals (Nov. 5, 2009). For acquisitions where the anticipated value of the acquisition is less than $25,000, *see* 49 C.F.R. § 24.102(c)(2)(ii)(C) (allowing HUD to create exemption for properties up to $25,000), and 74 Fed. Reg. 29,223, 29,225–26 (June 19, 2009) and Combined Notice, *supra* note 2, at 64,325.

94. Recovery Act, Pub. L. 111-005 (Feb. 17, 2009), second undesignated paragraph under the heading "Community Planning and Development, Community Development Fund" (describing NSP-specific tenant protections and explaining applicability to future NSP1 expenditures), with additional guidance at CPD, NSP Policy Alert: Guidance on NSP Tenant Protection Requirements Under the Recovery Act (Aug. 12, 2010) [hereinafter Policy Alert: Tenant Protections]. For additional protections for tenants of foreclosed properties, *see* Helping Families Save Their Homes Act of 2009, Pub. L. 111-22, § 701 *et seq.* (May 20, 2009), with implementing guidance at 74 Fed. Reg. 30,106 (June 24, 2009). *See also* Part 4 of this chapter.

95. HERA, Pub. L. No. 110-289 (July 30, 2008), at § 2301(d)(3); *see also* NOFA, *supra* note 2, at 60–61 (for NSP2 requirements) and Combined Notice, *supra* note 2, at 64,334 (for NSP1 and NSP3 requirements).

or that are not sold to individuals as primary residences.[96] Given these distinctions, recipients of NSP funding should be careful in ensuring that they have chosen the correct eligibility categories for their properties.

As part of the determination that a property qualifies as foreclosed, CPD requires NSP participants to document the property's eligibility. For example, HUD requires that grantees maintain sufficient documentation about the purchase and sale amounts of each property to allow HUD to ensure that the requirements applicable to foreclosed properties have been met.[97] While grantees are generally subject to the recordkeeping requirements of the CDBG program, HUD does not otherwise require a particular type of documentation to demonstrate that a property qualified as foreclosed.[98] In the CPD Monitoring Handbook, for example, CPD's field staff are directed to review whether the grantee's properties met the discount requirements but are not instructed to look for a specific type of evidence.[99] To address this ambiguity, some grantees require their partners to submit executed purchase agreements that include recitals demonstrating that the purchase price is at least 1 percent below the appraised value and that the seller has complied with the tenant protection requirements. Grantees typically also require evidence that the property qualified as foreclosed, either through a certification from the seller that the prior owner's mortgage payments were at least 90 days delinquent or through other legal documentation.[100] Grantees that are also public entities should be aware that some of this information may be subject to public inspection.[101]

2. Abandoned Properties

In addition to amending the definition of foreclosed properties, HUD also has expanded the definition of abandoned properties.[102] As with the changes to foreclosure, this modification increased the types of properties that may qualify for NSP funding, although the more minimal restrictions on abandoned property may make this categorization slightly more advantageous. The revised definition allows properties to qualify as abandoned if any of the following factors are met: (a) the mortgage, tribal leasehold, or tax payments are at least 90 days

---

96. *Id.* For inapplicability of price limitation to vacant properties, *see* FAQ 759 (Sept. 30, 2010).

97. NOFA, *supra* note 2, at 61 and Combined Notice, *supra* note 2, at 64,334.

98. For general requirements relating to records for foreclosed properties, see NOFA, *supra* note 2, at 73 and Combined Notice, *supra* note 2, at 64,338. For CDBG requirements relating to recordkeeping, *see* 24 C.F.R. § 570.506.

99. CPD, GRANTEE MONITORING HANDBOOK 6509.2, Rev. 6, Chapter 8, Exhibit 8-10 at page 8-4.

100. For a sample property acquisition checklist that includes these requirements, *see* CPD, NSP Toolkit, Sample NSP Property Acquisition File Checklist.

101. While primarily an issue of state or local public records requirements, some grantees' Consolidated Plans and annual Action Plans may provide for greater public access to some of these records in accordance with 24 C.F.R. § 91.105(h) for local governments and 24 C.F.R. § 91.115(g) for state governments.

102. For expansion of NSP1 definition, *see* 75 Fed. Reg. 18,228 at 18,230 (April 9, 2010), and for limited retroactive applicability to NSP1 program, *see* Policy Alert: New Definitions, *supra* note 87, at 4; for application to NSP2 program, *see* HUD Notice 5321-N-04 (published to HUD website April 2, 2010), with additional guidance at Policy Alert: New Definitions, *supra* note 87. For applicability to NSP3 program, *see* Combined Notice, *supra* note 2, at 64,325.

delinquent; (b) a code enforcement inspection has determined that the property is not habitable and the owner has taken no corrective actions within 90 days of notification of the deficiencies; or (c) the property is subject to a court-ordered receivership or nuisance abatement related to abandonment pursuant to state or local law or otherwise meets a state definition of an abandoned home or residential property.[103] Among other changes, this revised definition removes a more generic requirement that the property be "vacant" for 90 days and clarifies the criteria for code enforcement action, court-ordered receiverships, and nuisance abatement. As with other eligibility categories, grantees are required to document the abandoned property's eligibility,[104] and many do so by requiring sellers to make representations in the purchase agreement that survive transfer of the property to the NSP buyer.

3. Vacant Properties

Unlike its changes to the definitions of foreclosed and abandoned properties, CPD has declined to clarify the definition of vacant property, except to note that raw land and other properties that have never been developed are ineligible to receive NSP funding.[105] Eligible prior development includes residential, commercial, industrial, or other development, and also may be evidenced by infrastructure such as roads, water, sewer, or power lines.[106] CPD has not imposed specific standards for how long a property must have been vacant to qualify under this category but has noted that grantees should exercise reasonable judgment.[107]

As with other property types, NSP grantees are required to document the vacant property's eligibility.[108] Given the lack of clarity regarding the definition of vacant properties, CPD has issued informal guidance suggesting that participants verify that property is vacant and that there are no personal possessions on the site.[109] CPD suggests that documentation include a signed and dated inspection report, photographs, and notes from interviews with neighbors indicating the approximate last date of occupancy. If information from neighbors is unavailable, CPD recommends including data from a utility company or the local post office indicating the date that service was terminated.[110] These documentary standards suggest that a property must be entirely uninhabited to be eligible to receive NSP funding for vacant properties, although this requirement does not appear to be imposed through any Federal Register notices, Policy Alerts, or FAQs.

---

103. *Supra* note 87. For prior definitions, *see* NSP1 Allocation Notice, *supra* note 2, at 58,331 and NOFA, *supra* note 2, at 41.

104. *See generally* NOFA, *supra* note 2, at 57 and Combined Notice, *supra* note 2, at 64,332–33.

105. For formal lack of definition and examples of eligible properties, *see* FAQ 210 (Nov. 18, 2011). *See also* CPD, NSP TOOLKIT, CREATING A NSP-ELIGIBLE RENTAL PROJECT, at 3.

106. For examples of eligible prior development, *see* CPD, NSP Policy Alert: Guidance on Property Types Under Each Eligible Use (Dec. 3, 2009) at 4 [hereinafter Policy Alert: Guidance on Property Types]. For infrastructure requirements, *see* FAQ 210 (Nov. 18, 2011).

107. FAQ 210 (Nov. 18, 2011).

108. *See generally* NOFA, *supra* note 2, at 57 and Combined Notice, *supra* note 2, at 64,332–33.

109. CPD, NSP TOOLKIT, GUIDE TO PROPERTY ACQUISITION at 11 and 15–16. *See also* CPD, NSP TOOLKIT, SAMPLE NSP PROPERTY ACQUISITION FILE CHECKLIST.

110. CPD, NSP TOOLKIT, GUIDE TO PROPERTY ACQUISITION at 11 and 15–16. *See also* CPD, NSP TOOLKIT, SAMPLE NSP PROPERTY ACQUISITION FILE CHECKLIST.

Acknowledging a key component of many redevelopment strategies, NSP also permits the demolition of blighted structures and allows significant local discretion in determining which structures are blighted. The structure simply must exhibit "objectively determinable signs of deterioration" that represent a threat to human health, safety, and public welfare.[111] Unlike many of the other NSP-eligible uses, CPD permits NSP participants to demolish any type of blighted structures, regardless of whether they originally served residential, commercial, or industrial purposes.[112] However, NSP2 and NSP3 funds may not be used to demolish public housing.[113] Because grantees may not spend more than 10 percent of their total NSP awards on the demolition of blighted structures without a waiver from HUD,[114] grantees often are less interested in identifying properties that qualify under this category.

4. Timing Considerations

In addition to determining that the property qualifies as foreclosed, abandoned, vacant, or blighted, grantees must ensure that the property was NSP-eligible at the time of acquisition. Most significantly, NSP participants who purchase vacant properties before the execution of an NSP agreement with HUD may still be able to use NSP funds at the property, although NSP funds may not be used to reimburse the cost of acquisition.[115] CPD has issued conflicting guidance with respect to properties that were abandoned or foreclosed, although it seems that participants may purchase such properties only after the execution of a written agreement with the NSP funder, even if the acquisition is not made with NSP funds.[116] This restriction may stem from CPD's conclusion that the property no longer qualifies as foreclosed if the property has changed ownership since foreclosure.[117] However, participants can sometimes benefit from this restriction because CPD appears to view the property classification as fluid. For example, if an NSP grantee acquires a foreclosed property that is also vacant, the grantee then may be able to transfer the property to an NSP participant, which can then treat the property as vacant rather than as foreclosed, and so the property will be subject to the less-

---

111. NOFA, *supra* note 2, at 42 and Combined Notice, *supra* note 2, at 64,325.

112. Policy Alert: Guidance on Property Types, *supra* note 106, at 3; FAQ 545 (July 18, 2010).

113. Recovery Act, Pub. L. 111-005 (Feb. 17, 2009), second undesignated paragraph under the heading "Community Planning and Development, Community Development Fund." *See also* NOFA, *supra* note 2, at 20 and Combined Notice, *supra* note 2, at 64,333.

114. Recovery Act, Pub. L. 111-005 (Feb. 17, 2009), second undesignated paragraph under the heading "Community Planning and Development, Community Development Fund." *See also* NOFA, *supra* note 2, at 20 and Combined Notice, *supra* note 2, at 64,333.

115. FAQs 290 (Sept. 8, 2010) and 489 (Sept. 8, 2010). *See also* CPD, NSP Policy Alert: Environmental Review and Option Contracts (Sept. 16, 2011) at 1 [hereinafter, Policy Alert: Environmental Review].

116. FAQs 290 (Sept. 8, 2010) (grantees may use pre-NSP properties) and 489 (Sept. 8, 2010) (pre-NSP acquisitions are not acceptable) and 426 (July 18, 2010) (abandoned or foreclosed properties must be acquired after execution of the grant agreement). *See also* Policy Alert: Environmental Review, *supra* note 115 at 1 (indicating that pre-NSP acquisitions are acceptable) and CPD, NSP Policy Alert: Guidance on NSP-Eligible Acquisition and Rehabilitation Activities (Dec. 11, 2009) at 1 and Policy Alert: New Definitions, *supra* note 87 at 4.

117. CPD, NSP Policy Alert: Guidance on NSP-Eligible Acquisition and Rehabilitation Activities (Dec. 11, 2009) at 1 and FAQ 548 (July 18, 2010).

rigorous requirements applicable to foreclosed properties.[118] Finally, in addition to these NSP-specific restrictions, participants also must document that acquisition occurred after the applicable environmental review requirements were satisfied.[119] Among other limitations, participants who intend to use NSP funds may not acquire property or take other "choice-limiting" actions before completion of an environmental review,[120] thus limiting the ability to use many properties acquired before receipt of NSP funds.

In addition to the timing restrictions discussed above, if a grantee or subgrantee owns or acquires an NSP-eligible property, the grantee or subgrantee may not transfer the property to another NSP participant and then provide NSP funds to itself or the other parties to compensate for the acquisition price of the property.[121] To avoid violating the applicable conflict of interest requirements, the grantee or subgrantee may instead donate or sell the property to the subrecipient, developer, or individual where NSP funds are not a financing source for sale.[122] However, neither the NSP guidance nor the underlying CDBG regulations appear to prohibit the purchaser from using other funds to compensate the grantee or subgrantee for the cost of the property.[123] As a result, some grantees and subgrantees have considered using low-income housing tax credit (LIHTC) equity or other private funds to reimburse such acquisition costs.

C. Eligible Uses

After determining that a property is NSP-eligible, the grantee or another party will need to ensure that the proposed activity also qualifies. The authorizing legislation provides five basic activities that may be funded with NSP funds. Often referred to as Eligible Uses (A) through (E), these include:

(A) Establish *financing mechanisms* for purchase and redevelopment of foreclosed-on homes and residential properties, including such mechanisms as soft seconds, loan loss reserves, and shared-equity loans for low-income and moderate-income homebuyers.

(B) *Purchase and rehabilitate* homes and residential properties that have been abandoned or foreclosed on in order to sell, rent, or redevelop such homes and properties.

(C) Establish and operate *land banks* for homes and residential properties that have been foreclosed on.

(D) Demolish *blighted structures.*

(E) *Redevelop* demolished or vacant properties as housing.

Despite the similarities between these eligible uses, HUD has issued guidance indicating that each use should be viewed separately unless the project's circumstances suggest that the

---

118. FAQ 207 (Nov. 7, 2008).
119. *See, e.g.,* 24 C.F.R. § 58.22 and Policy Alert: Environmental Review, *supra* note 115, at 1.
120. 24 C.F.R. § 58.22 (a) and (c). *See also infra* Part 4.
121. NOFA, *supra* note 2, at 73; Combined Notice, *supra* note 2, at 64,338. For underlying CDBG conflict of interest requirement, *see* 24 C.F.R. § 570.611(a)(2).
122. Combined Notice, *supra* note 2, at 64,338 and FAQ 290 (Sept. 8, 2010).
123. While this may be difficult to accomplish in a transaction funded exclusively with NSP funds, projects involving low-income housing tax credits or other private funds may have more ability to compensate the grantee or subrecipient.

project qualifies under multiple approved uses.[124] While it is possible that simple projects may qualify only under a single use, more complex undertakings may require more significant review to ensure that the appropriate combination of uses is documented. The remainder of this section will discuss each of these possible uses, and Appendix A provides a chart showing the relationship between types of eligible properties and eligible uses.

1. Eligible Use (A): Financing Mechanisms

CPD has indicated that financing mechanisms will be among the less common eligible uses, in part because the activities allowed by Eligible Uses (B) and (E) may address many financing mechanisms more directly.[125] Additionally, the authorizing legislation suggests that financing mechanisms may be used only with respect to foreclosed properties, further limiting this Eligible Use.[126] While some ambiguity remains about the permissibility of the more complex financing mechanisms discussed below, CPD has clearly stated that NSP funds may not be used under Eligible Use A or any other use to refinance existing mortgages and prevent foreclosure[127] although new homebuyers may receive direct financial assistance under Eligible Uses (A), (B), or (E).[128] However, limited number of strategies may require the use of financing mechanisms as independent activities under Eligible Use (A). For example, CPD has indicated that loan loss reserves, revolving loan funds, and certain tax-exempt bond financing may need to be conducted as financing mechanisms under Eligible Use (A),[129] although other readings of the authorizing legislation suggest that these activities might also qualify as part of other Eligible Uses. Most significant, if NSP funds are used with respect to loans or financing made available under this eligible use, CPD has suggested that the proceeds of that loan must be used in accordance with the requirements that would apply if NSP funds had been used directly.[130]

CPD's interpretation of some requirements associated with Eligible Use (A) has created difficulties for projects involving complex, multisource funding. For example, CPD has indicated that NSP funds cannot be used to "purchase" tax-exempt bonds because it would be

---

124. FAQ 290 (Sept. 8, 2010).
125. Policy Alert: Guidance on Property Types, *supra* note 106, at 2–3.
126. For description of financing mechanisms applicable to all three programs, *see* Combined Notice, *supra* note 2, at 64,333. *See also* Policy Alert: Guidance on Property Types, *supra* note 106, at 7.
127. FAQ 40 (June 15, 2010).
128. Combined Notice, *supra* note 2, at 64,333; FAQ 32 (June 15, 2010).
129. For general guidance about criteria for financing mechanisms, *see* FAQ 212 (June 17, 2009). For guidance on loan loss reserves, *see* CPD, Policy Alert: Guidance on Loan Loss Reserves (Dec. 7, 2010) [hereinafter, Policy Alert: Guidance on Loan Loss Reserves] and Policy Alert: Guidance on Property Types, *supra* note 106, at 2–3. For guidance on revolving loan funds, *see* Policy Alert: Guidance on Property Types, *supra* note 106, at 3, and FAQs 109 (Sept. 9, 2009), 128 (Apr. 14, 2010), 1141 (May 31, 2011), 1142 (May 31, 2011), and 1143 (May 31, 2011). For guidance on tax-exempt bond financing, *see* Policy Alert: Guidance on Property Types, *supra* note 106, at 3 and FAQs 109 (Sept. 9, 2009), 112 (Jan. 23, 2009), and 352 (Oct. 26, 2010).
130. *See, e.g.*, Policy Alert: Guidance on Loan Loss Reserves, *supra* note 129, at 2 and FAQ 112 (Jan. 23, 2009).

more cost-effective to simply use the NSP funds to cover the eligible costs directly.[131] While this reasoning might be accurate in a transaction funded solely with bonds collateralized with NSP funds, this analysis disregards some aspects of the financing leveraged by more sophisticated NSP participants. For example, some grantees and their partners have begun to develop NSP properties as part of 4 percent LIHTC deals, and these projects can leverage their private LIHTC equity only if the transaction also includes tax-exempt private activity bonds.[132] Often, NSP funds are the least expensive source of collateral for such bonds. Furthermore, without the bond financing, these projects will not qualify for the 4 percent LIHTC credits, which means that the investor will be unwilling to participate, the project will be unable to leverage the anticipated private equity, and the project will be unable to proceed as contemplated. As with other aspects of the NSP program, CPD's written guidance and ability to waive such guidance suggests both the dangers and benefits of implementing a program without formal guidance or public notice and comment, and grantees or other participants may benefit from working directly with CPD to remove such barriers to the development of their projects.[133]

2. Eligible Use (B): Purchase and Rehabilitation of Foreclosed and Abandoned Properties

Under Eligible Use (B), NSP participants may purchase and rehabilitate abandoned or foreclosed properties, but CPD has indicated that Eligible Use (B) permits rehabilitation but not new construction.[134] As a result, NSP participants conducting activities under Eligible Use (B) must ensure that (1) the property is either foreclosed or abandoned and (2) the activities qualify as "rehabilitation." CPD has not provided significant new definitions of rehabilitation but has relied instead on the guidance issued for the CDBG program.[135] Generally, to qualify as rehabilitation, the number of dwelling units on the site may not be increased but the number of rooms per unit may be increased or decreased.[136] CPD permits deviations from the original design for reasons of safety or if it would be impractical to retain the prior design. In addition, rehabilitation includes the rebuilding of a structure on the same site in substantially

---

131. FAQ 352 (Oct. 26, 2010).

132. For general Internal Revenue Code (IRC) requirements relating to such 4% Low Income Housing Tax Credits, *see* IRC 42(h)(4)(a).

133. CPD's interpretation of the requirements relating to the use of NSP funds for reserves further illustrates the complexities of justifying activities under Eligible Use (A). Typically, grantees are required to minimize the time elapsing between the transfer of funds and disbursement by the grantee or subgrantee in accordance with the Treasury regulations at 31 C.F.R. pt. 205 pursuant to 24 C.F.R. 85.21(b). However, CPD has also released guidance indicating that NSP funds may be used to fund such reserves as long as such reserves are of a reasonable size and are required by the investor. FAQs 33 (Apr. 28, 2010), 352 (Oct. 26, 2010), and 485 (Sept. 8, 2010). As a result, grantees may want to request written CPD approval in situations where NSP funds are not disbursed within approximately three days.

134. NOFA, *supra* note 2, at 59; Combined Notice, *supra* note 2, at 64,333; Policy Alert: Guidance on Property Types, *supra* note 106, at 5; FAQ 463 (July 18, 2010).

135. *See, e.g.,* FAQ 90 (Apr. 27, 2010), 93 (May 5, 2010) and 337 (July 17, 2010).

136. CPD, CPD Notice 07-08: Use of Community Development Block Grant (CDBG) Program Funds in Support of Housing (Nov. 21, 2007) at 6 [hereinafter CPD Notice 07-08].

the same manner as the prior structure.[137] In contrast, new construction involves the addition of dwelling units, significant expansion of the size of units without justification, or changes to the tenure type of the unit.[138] As with activities under Eligible Uses (A) and (E), NSP participants also may provide down-payment and closing-cost assistance to homebuyers purchasing homes rehabilitated under this eligible use, although any down-payment assistance may not exceed 50 percent of the amount of the down-payment costs required to close the transaction.[139] NSP participants also may make soft second loans or offer purchase price discounts without violating the limit on down-payment assistance.[140] Finally, because Eligible Use (E) does not allow the use of NSP funds for acquisition of non-vacant or demolished properties, some grantees acquire foreclosed or abandoned property under Eligible Use (B), demolish the structure in accordance with Eligible Use (D) or use private funds to do so, and then engage in new construction under Eligible Use (E).[141]

As with many Recovery Act–funded programs, NSP also imposes requirements with respect to energy-efficiency and construction standards for rehabilitation. While only the NSP3 program explicitly requires compliance with Energy Star standards for new single-family homes and multifamily buildings, HUD strongly encourages such compliance in the NSP1 and NSP2 programs as well.[142] Additionally, NSP2 funds may be spent on a public building or public work only if all the iron, steel, and manufactured goods used in the project are produced in the United States (the "Buy American" requirements).[143] While these requirements typically do not apply where the grantee merely serves as a lender, if the grantee or its instrumentality serves as a developer or exercises significant functions within the project's ownership structure, then the Buy American requirements may apply.[144] Significantly, these requirements apply to all NSP-funded construction and not simply to activities funded under Eligible Use (B).

3. Eligible Uses (C) and (D): Land Banking and Demolition

While the NSP program authorizes both land banking and demolition, CPD views both of these activities as intermediate actions and so requires grantees to also demonstrate that the end use qualifies under another NSP-eligible use.[145] However, both land banking and demolition may serve as additional mechanisms to stabilize communities without immediately redeveloping the property. For example, Eligible Use (C) authorizes the use of NSP funds to

---

137. *Id.*
138. FAQ 337 (July 17, 2010).
139. FAQ 32 (June 15, 2010); Housing and Community Development Act of 1974, § 105(a)(24(D).
140. FAQ 57 (April 28, 2010).
141. FAQ 207 (Nov. 7, 2008).
142. For NSP3 requirements, *see* Combined Notice, *supra* note 2, at 64,334 and 64,347-48. For NSP2 requirements, *see* NOFA, *supra* note 2, at 13 and 80–83. For NSP1, *see* NSP1 Allocation Notice, *supra* note 2, at 58,338.
143. NOFA, *supra* note 2, at 35–36. For inapplicability to NSP3, *see* CPD, NSP Open Forum Webinar Transcript (Dec. 21, 2010) at 68.
144. CPD, CPD Notice 09-05: CPD Implementation Guidance for the Buy American Requirement of the American Recovery and Reinvestment Act of 2009 Including the Exception process (Oct. 7, 2009) at 29.
145. Policy Alert: Guidance on Property Types, *supra* note 106, at 4.

purchase foreclosed properties and to establish and operate land banks using these properties.[146] Under NSP, a land bank is a governmental or nongovernmental nonprofit entity that assembles, temporarily manages, and disposes of unused land.[147] Land banks must operate in a defined geographic area, facilitate redevelopment of the property, and market and dispose of the property in accordance with an established plan.[148] If the land bank is a governmental entity, it also may maintain foreclosed property that it does not own as long as the governmental entity charges the property owner the full cost of the service or places a lien on the property for the full cost of the service.[149] Unlike other properties that must be used in accordance with an Eligible Use by the expenditure deadline, grantees must reuse land purchased under Eligible Use(s) within 10 years, in accordance with the grantee's documented plan for such activities. However, CPD requires that the final use of the property also qualify as an NSP-eligible use.[150] Because public land banks are often highly regulated by state and local law, participants should also ensure compliance with additional requirements as well.

As with land banking, CPD views demolition of blighted structures under Eligible Use (D) as an intermediary use and requires grantees to ensure that the end use also qualifies as an NSP-eligible use.[151] As discussed above, NSP permits the demolition of a variety of structures, including those that served industrial, commercial, or residential purposes, but such structures must qualify as blighted. If a structure has been foreclosed, abandoned, or vacant but is not blighted, then NSP funds may not be used for demolition.[152] Furthermore, NSP2 and NSP3 funds may not be used to demolish federally financed public housing.[153] Because NSP2 and NSP3 grantees may not spend more than 10 percent of their total NSP awards on demolition of blighted structures without a waiver from HUD, grantees are often less interested in identifying properties that qualify under this category.[154] As a result, many choose to acquire property using NSP funds and then use private resources to accomplish any necessary demolition.

4. Eligible Use (E): Redevelopment of Demolished or Vacant Property

Perhaps the most useful of the activities permitted under the NSP program, Eligible Use (E) allows the redevelopment of demolished or vacant properties.[155] Under this use, NSP partici-

---

146. NOFA, *supra* note 2, at 49–,50 and Combined Notice, *supra* note 2, at 64,333.
147. *See, e.g.,* NOFA, *supra* note 2, at 42 and Combined Notice, *supra* note 2, at 64,325.
148. FAQ 545 (July 18, 2010).
149. *See, e.g.,* NOFA, *supra* note 2, at 43 and Combined Notice, *supra* note 2, at 64,325.
150. *See* NOFA, *supra* note 2, at 50 for NSP2 requirements and Combined Notice, *supra* note 2, at 64,330 for NSP1 and NSP3 requirements.
151. Policy Alert: Guidance on Property Types, *supra* note 106, at 3–4; FAQ 545 (July 18, 2010).
152. *Id. See also* CPD, Program Overview for New NSP3 Grantees (webinar transcript) (Jan. 26, 2011) at 6.
153. Combined Notice, *supra* note 2, at 64,333.
154. *Id.*
155. NOFA, *supra* note 2, at 58; Combined Notice, *supra* note 2, at 64,333; Policy Alert: Guidance on Property Types, *supra* note 106, at 5. Under NSP1, these funds may be used for nonresidential purposes, while NSP2 and NSP3 funds must be used for housing. Combined Notice, *supra* note 2, at 64,333.

pants may use NSP funds to acquire any kind of demolished or vacant property, regardless of whether the property had served an industrial, commercial, or residential use.[156] Most important, Eligible Use (E) is the only use that permits new construction.[157] As discussed above, CPD defines new construction as the addition of dwelling units, significant expansion of the size of units, or changes to the tenure type of the unit.[158] Furthermore, with the passage of the Dodd-Frank Act, expenditures undertaken under Eligible Use (E) may now be included when determining whether a grantee has satisfied the 25 percent set-aside requirement for persons at or below 50 percent of the area median income (AMI).[159] As with Eligible Uses (A) and (B), NSP participants may make down payment and closing cost assistance available to purchasers of properties developed under Eligible Use (E) and may also make soft second loans and purchase-price discounts available as well.[160]

III. AFFORDABILITY RESTRICTIONS

Recognizing the significant federal investment in properties funded under the NSP program, Congress imposed additional requirements to ensure that these properties remain affordable to certain lower-income groups for a sufficient period of time. Generally, all NSP-funded units must be occupied by households that qualify as low-income, moderate-income, or middle-income households.[161] In accordance with these requirements, NSP units must be rented or purchased and occupied by households with annual incomes that do not exceed 120 percent of the area median income (AMI) as adjusted.[162] In addition, at least 25 percent of each grantee's funds must be spent on behalf of households whose incomes do not exceed 50 percent of AMI.[163] With the passage of the Dodd-Frank Act, this requirement may be met by expenditures relating to any of the Eligible Uses.[164] The income limits for households at or below 120 percent and 50 percent of the AMI are calculated with respect to the Section 8 income limits and are published

---

156. Policy Alert: Guidance on Property Types, *supra* note 106, at 4.
157. *Id.* at 5.
158. CPD Notice 07-08, *supra* note 136; FAQ 337 (July 19, 2010) and FAQ 90 (Apr. 27, 2010).
159. *See, e.g.*, Dodd-Frank Act, Pub. L. No. 111-203 (July 21, 2010), § 1497(b)(1)(A) and CPD, Policy Alert: Guidance on Amendments to the Twenty-Five Percent Set-Aside Requirement (July 23, 2010) at 2 [hereinafter Policy Alert: Amendments to the Twenty-Five Percent Set-Aside Requirement].
160. *See, e.g.*, FAQ 57 (Apr. 28, 2011).
161. For NSP1, *see* HERA, Pub. L. No. 110–289 (July 30, 2008) at § 2301(f)(3) and NSP1 Allocation Notice, *supra* note 2, at 58,335–36. For NSP2, *see* Recovery Act, Pub. L. 111-005 (Feb. 17, 2009), Title XII of Division A, Community Planning and Development, Community Development Fund, second paragraph (noting that HERA applies unless otherwise specified) and NOFA, *supra* note 2, at 48. For NSP3, *see* Dodd-Frank Act, Pub. L. No. 111-203 (July 21, 2010), § 1497(a) (noting that provisions of the Recovery Act apply unless otherwise specified) and Combined Notice, *supra* note 2, at 64,328–31.
162. *Id.*
163. *Id.* This 25% expenditure requirement is commonly known as the "25% set-aside."
164. *See* Dodd-Frank Act, Pub. L. No. 111-203 (July 21, 2010), § 1497(b)(1)(A) and Combined Notice, *supra* note 2, at 64,330. However, NSP1 and NSP2 funds already obligated or expended before July 21, 2010, may not automatically satisfy this requirement. *Id. See also* Policy Alert: Amendments to the Twenty-Five Percent Set-Aside Requirement, *supra* note 159.

by HUD for each applicable area.[165] When new participants are selected, the grantee or another party must verify each participant's income information using the procedures applicable to the Section 8 program or in accordance with one of several other approved methods.[166] This verification usually includes an examination of Social Security Numbers, wage statements, interest statements, unemployment statements, or other documentation.[167]

As discussed in greater detail below, NSP participants must also ensure that properties satisfy certain long-term affordability requirements in both the rental and homeownership contexts. While the CDBG program provides the regulatory framework for most of the NSP program, the HOME program's affordability standards are the safe-harbor requirements for NSP units.[168] However, CPD has allowed participants to adapt these standards to reflect the more expansive requirements of the NSP program.[169] Unlike the HOME program, NSP also limits the sales price of foreclosed or abandoned properties that are purchased, redeveloped, or otherwise sold to individuals as primary residences.[170] Under NSP, the sales price for such dwellings cannot exceed the cost to acquire and redevelop or rehabilitate the home or property up to a decent, safe, and habitable condition.[171] This maximum price is determined by aggregating all the costs of acquisition, rehabilitation, and redevelopment, and this limitation may also have a significant impact on how grantees choose to structure their programs.[172]

A. Rental Housing

In the context of rental housing, CPD permits NSP participants to use fair-market rents as the maximum rent for households earning up to 120 percent of the AMI.[173] While the HOME program generally provides the safe-harbor affordability standards for NSP, the HOME standard applies to households whose incomes do not exceed 80 percent of AMI and so is inapplicable to households earning up to 120 percent of AMI, leading CPD to allow use of the fair-

---

165. For CDBG regulations that apply Section 8 limits, *see* 24 C.F.R. § 570.3 (definitions) and 24 C.F.R. § 570.208(b) (relating to national objectives). *See also* Combined Notice, *supra* note 2, at 64,331 and NOFA, *supra* note 2, at 51–52. For current income limits, *see* http://www.huduser.org/portal/datasets/NSP.html.
166. *See generally* 24 C.F.R. 570.3 (definition of "income"), including the definition of income under 24 C.F.R. Part 813, which has been replaced by the definitions at 24 C.F.R. Part 5.
167. 24 C.F.R. Part 5, Subpart B.
168. For CDBG requirements, *see* 24 C.F.R. § 570.208(b). For HOME safe harbor standards, *see* NSP1 Allocation Notice, *supra* note 2, at 58,334; NOFA, *supra* note 2, at 45 and Combined Notice, *supra* note 2, at 64,328.
169. For ability to use other reasonable standards, *see* FAQ 65 (June 15, 2010).
170. HERA, Pub. L. No. 110–289 (July 30, 2008) at § 2301(d)(3) and NSP1 Allocation Notice, *supra* note 2, at 58338; NOFA, *supra* note 2, at 60–61; Combined Notice, *supra* note 2, at 64,334. Significantly, this restriction only applies to abandoned and foreclosed properties and does not apply to vacant properties. HERA, § 2301(d)(3). However, if a vacant property also qualifies as abandoned or foreclosed, it is deemed to be subject to the requirements of abandoned or foreclosed property. Policy Alert: New Definitions, *supra* note 87, at 3 and FAQ 759 (Sept. 30, 2010). Further references to the maximum sales price should be read as incorporating this distinction.
171. *Id.*
172. *Id.*
173. FAQ 723 (Sept. 30, 2010).

market rents described above.[174] Participants may develop other methods as well, as long as these methods are reasonable.[175] With respect to units intended to satisfy the very-low-income set-aside requirement, the HOME safe-harbor standard remains unmodified. Rents for these units may not exceed 30 percent of the annual income of a family whose income equals 50 percent of AMI, as determined by HUD.[176] Alternatively, NSP participants may limit rents so that they do not exceed 30 percent of the very low-income household's adjusted income.[177]

In addition to restricting tenant incomes and rents, NSP participants must also ensure that the property remains affordable for an appropriate period of time. This means that while maximum rents may be recalculated based on revised rent limits published by HUD, the grantee, subrecipient, or project's owner must ensure that rents at the project comply with these standards for the entire affordability period.[178] Typically accomplished through a use restriction or declaration of restrictive covenants, the affordability period is generally based on the amount of NSP funds used in a transaction.[179] In addition, while the maximum affordability period for rehabilitated units depends on the amount of funding per unit but generally does not exceed 15 years, newly constructed rental dwellings must remain affordable for at least 20 years, regardless of the amount of NSP funds invested in the project.[180] Unless terminated by foreclosure, the affordability restrictions must remain in place for the entire period, regardless of the repayment of any NSP loan.[181]

B. Homeownership Units

Unlike the HOME program, NSP also limits the sales price of foreclosed or abandoned properties that are purchased, redeveloped, or otherwise sold to individuals as primary residences.[182] Under NSP, the sales price for such dwellings cannot exceed the cost to acquire and redevelop or rehabilitate the home or property up to a decent, safe, and habitable

---

174. *See* FAQ 723 (Sept. 30, 2010) for ability to charge fair market rents. The HOME standard at 24 C.F.R. § 92.252(a) provides that rents for households earning no more than 80% of AMI may not exceed the lesser of (1) fair market rent for comparable units, or (2) 30% of the income of a family whose annual income equals 65% of the area median income.

175. FAQ 65 (June 15, 2010). Grantees should also ensure that any alternative standards are in accordance with their NSP applications and Substantial Amendments, as applicable.

176. *Supra* note 161; *see* 24 C.F.R. § 92.252(b) for HOME standards.

177. 24 C.F.R. § 92.252(b)(2).

178. For general long-term affordability requirement, *see* HERA, Pub. L. No. 110–289 (July 30, 2008) at § 2301(f)(3)(B). *See also supra* note 161. For ability to revise rents based on revised HUD limits, *see* 24 C.F.R. § 92.252(f).

179. *See generally* 24 C.F.R. § 92.252(e). However, grantees have also committed to longer periods in their NSP applications or Substantial Amendments.

180. 24 C.F.R. § 92.252(e).

181. *Id.*

182. HERA, § 2301(d)(3) and NSP1 Allocation Notice, *supra* note 2, at 58,338; NOFA, *supra* note 2, at 60–61; Combined Notice, *supra* note 2, at 64,334. Significantly, this restriction only applies to abandoned and foreclosed properties, and does not apply to vacant properties. HERA § 2301(d)(3). However, if a vacant property also qualifies as abandoned or foreclosed, it is deemed to be subject to the requirements of abandoned or foreclosed property. Policy Alert: New Definitions, *supra* note 87, at 3 and FAQ 759 (Sept. 30, 2010). Further references to the maximum sales price should be read as incorporating this distinction.

condition.[183] This maximum price is determined by aggregating all of the costs of acquisition, rehabilitation, and redevelopment.[184] However, once the homeowner has purchased the property, the HOME program's safe-harbor standards generally apply and limit the situations in which homeowners may sell the property or retain equity from the sale.[185] In accordance with the HOME requirements, NSP participants must impose either "resale" or "recapture" restrictions on such homebuyers and their properties.[186] Within certain limits, participants may choose which type of restriction to impose, although the maximum affordability period under either approach will generally be 15 years.[187] While the distinctions between resale and recapture methods may seem esoteric, a recent OIG audit of 40 HOME projects suggests that CPD attaches particular importance to these differences.[188] Finally, to accommodate the NSP program's endorsement of financing mechanisms involving shared equity, CPD allows NSP participants to develop shared-equity programs using either resale or recapture provisions.[189]

If an NSP participant imposes resale requirements, the unit must be the homebuyer's principal residence for the entire affordability period.[190] If the homebuyer wishes to sell the dwelling before the end of the affordability period, the unit must be sold to another income-eligible household.[191] The affordability period under the resale approach is based on the total amount of program funds invested in the housing, regardless of whether the funds were used as a purchase price write down, development subsidy, or other funding.[192] However, if NSP funds are used only as a development subsidy, NSP participants must impose resale restrictions and cannot impose recapture restrictions.[193] In addition to ensuring long-term affordability, the resale price must provide the original homebuyer with a fair return on the original homebuyer's investment, which includes both the homeowner's initial purchase and any capital improvements.[194]

These affordability requirements endure until the end of the affordability period described above. If the homeowner violates the resale requirements, repayment of any NSP2 investment depends on the terms of any applicable loan documents.[195] Additionally, the grantee

---

183. *Supra* note 170.
184. *Id.*
185. *Supra* note 161. However, for ability to select alternative requirements, *see* FAQ 65 (June 15, 2010). Such election would typically be made in the NSP2 application or in the NSP1 or NSP3 Substantial Amendment.
186. 24 C.F.R. § 92.254(a)(5).
187. *See* 24 C.F.R. § 92.254(a)(5)(ii)(A)(5), last sentence, for limit on ability to select recapture restrictions. For affordability periods, *see* 24 C.F.R. § 92.254(a)(4).
188. HUD, OIG Audit Report 2010-CH-002: The Office of Affordable Housing Programs' Oversight of Resale and Recapture for HOME Investment Partnerships Program-Assisted Homeownership Projects Was Inadequate (April 13, 2010).
189. FAQ 381 (July 8, 2010).
190. 24 C.F.R. § 92.254(a)(5)(i),
191. *Id.*
192. *Id.* For numerical examples illustrating this concept *see* CPD, HOME, and NSP: Creating Affordable Housing, Revitalizing Neighborhoods (undated) at page 32.
193. 24 C.F.R. § 92.254(a)(5)(ii)(A)(5), last sentence.
194. 24 C.F.R. § 92.254(a)(5)(i).
195. 24 C.F.R. § 92.254(a)(5)(i)(A).

will be obligated to repay the funds to HUD if it fails to enforce the affordability requirements.[196] HUD has noted that the affordability restrictions do not preclude having a mortgage on the home that is repaid on the sale of the home, and many grantees and subgrantees have therefore chosen to require the homebuyer to execute a promissory note and mortgage as additional security for the homebuyer's obligation to comply with the affordability requirements.[197] Additionally, while it appears that NSP participants may use soft second loans without violating the sales price limitation, the associated loan documents must clearly demonstrate that the loans are intended to ensure affordability and that they are not additional consideration for the sale.[198]

In contrast to resale restrictions, recapture provisions ensure that the NSP participant recovers all or a portion of the NSP assistance if the homebuyer sells the home during the affordability period.[199] The period of affordability is based on the amount of NSP assistance that enabled the homebuyer to purchase the unit.[200] This amount includes any NSP assistance that reduced the purchase price from fair-market value to an affordable price, but excludes any development subsidy paid to the developer.[201] As a practical matter, this means that the affordability period for a property using recapture provisions can be designed to be much shorter than the affordability period for a property not using recapture provisions. As noted above, if the NSP funds are used only as a development subsidy, they are not subject to recapture, and so resale restrictions must be used.[202] Given this limitation, CPD has informally suggested that NSP participants provide a small amount of direct homebuyer assistance if participants wish to avoid resale restrictions.[203]

Unlike resale restrictions, recapture provisions allow the original homebuyer to sell the home to any willing and able buyer during the affordability period, but the NSP funder must recapture all or a portion of the NSP funds subject to recapture at the point of sale.[204] HUD provides a number of different options for structuring recapture provisions and allows NSP participants to (a) recapture the entire amount subject to recapture, (b) reduce the amount subject to recapture on a pro rata basis to account for the time the homeowner has occupied the housing, (c) share the net proceeds with the homeowner, or (d) allow the homeowner to fully recover the owner's investment in the home before the NSP participant recaptures any of the funds.[205] However, the recaptured amount may not exceed the "net proceeds" of the

---

196. 24 C.F.R. § 92.504(b).
197. CPD, HOME, and NSP: Creating Affordable Housing, Revitalizing Neighborhoods (undated) at page 31.
198. FAQ 530 (July 18, 2010). While CDP provided this response to a question about recapture provisions, it appears that a similar argument could be made to support soft second loans made in the resale context as well.
199. 24 C.F.R. § 92.254(a)(5)(ii).
200. *Id.*
201. 24 C.F.R. § 92.254(a)(5)(ii)(A)(5). For a numerical illustration of this concept, *see* CPD, HOME and NSP: Creating Affordable Housing, Revitalizing Neighborhoods (undated) at p.30.
202. 24 C.F.R. § 92.254(a)(5)(ii)(A)(5).
203. CPD, NSP Open Forum Webinar Transcript (May 20, 2010) at 105 and CPD, NSP Continued Affordability and Addressing Technical Issues with Recapture and Resale Transcript (July 8, 2010) at 25.
204. 24 C.F.R. § 92.254(a)(5)(ii).
205. 24 C.F.R. § 92.254(a)(5)(ii)(A)(1)–(4).

sale, where net proceeds are defined as the sales price minus the repayment of any superior, non-NSP loans.[206] As noted above, CPD has confirmed that soft second mortgages may be used in the recapture context without violating the NSP sales price limitation.[207] However, the loan agreement must clearly demonstrate that the soft second is not additional consideration for the sale but is instead an enforcement mechanism to preserve the long-term use of the NSP funds for affordable housing.[208]

In addition to ensuring long-term affordability, NSP participants must require each NSP-assisted homebuyer to receive and complete at least eight hours of homebuyer counseling from a HUD-approved housing counseling agency before the homebuyer obtains a mortgage loan.[209] If the NSP subrecipient or grantee is able to show good cause for failure to satisfy this requirement, the grantee may request that HUD approve an exception.[210] Furthermore, developers that also offer HUD-approved counseling programs may do so under a separate contract with the NSP grantee, although the applicable conflict of interest requirements will still apply.[211] Furthermore, grantees must ensure that the homebuyer obtains an appropriate mortgage loan that does not reflect predatory lending practices and must document compliance with this requirement.[212] This requirement has caused difficulties for some grantees who have been unable to locate lenders willing to make the disclosures necessary for the grantee to document compliance with this requirement.

C. Combining NSP Funds with Other Funding Sources

By allowing NSP participants to use NSP funds with other sources, CPD has significantly improved participants' ability to leverage these funds. Among other combinations, NSP funds may be used in conjunction with HOME and CDBG funds, public housing and Section 8 funds, and various FHA programs.[213] In addition, many NSP participants have found that NSP funds are beneficial in LIHTC transactions and other privately financed deals. However, when combining NSP funds with other sources, participants must still ensure that they have

---

206. 24 C.F.R. § 92.254(a)(5)(ii)(A).
207. FAQ 530 (July 18, 2010).
208. *Id.*
209. NSP1 Allocation Notice, *supra* note 2, at 58,334; NOFA, *supra* note 2, at 45–46; Combined Notice, *supra* note 2, at 64,328. *See also* Policy Alert: Guidance on Developers, Subrecipients, and Contractors, *supra* note 66, at 1 and 3.
210. FAQ 157 (Apr. 27, 2010).
211. For ability to provide counseling, *see* Policy Alert: Guidance on Developers, Subrecipients, and Contractors, *supra* note 66 at 3. For conflict of interest requirements, *see* 24 C.F.R. § 570.611(b).
212. *Supra* note 209.
213. For HOME, *see* FAQ 53 (June 15, 2010) and CPD, HOME, and NSP: A Guide for Successfully and Effectively Combining Funding Sources (undated). For CDBG, *see* FAQ 53 (June 15, 2010). For public housing, *see* FAQ 198 (Oct. 31, 2008). For Section 8, *see* FAQ 439 (Sept. 8, 2010). For FHA financing under Section 236, *see* FAQ 675 (Oct. 28, 2010). In addition to allowing FHA participation, CPD and the FHA have developed a streamlined program, First Look, that allows registered NSP participants to have exclusive access to purchase newly conveyed FHA real estate–owned properties. *See, e.g.,* CPD, NSP Policy Alert, Guidance on FHA First Look Sales Method (April 1, 2011).

provided at least a minimum number of NSP units and also a minimum number of units for households earning less than 50 percent of the AMI.[214]

When combining NSP funds with other funds, NSP participants are required to calculate the ratio of NSP funds to non-NSP funds to determine the required number of NSP units. Generally, the proportion of the total development cost borne by NSP assistance cannot exceed the proportion of units in the project that will be designated as NSP units.[215] For example, if all the units in a development are of comparable size and have similar amenities and NSP funds represent 30 percent of the total development costs for a project, then at least 30 percent of the units must be occupied by low-income, moderate-income, and middle-income persons on completion.[216] Despite this guidance, if an NSP participant can demonstrate that the NSP funds only assisted a specific unit in a multi-unit structure and not the structure as a whole, then only the assisted unit must meet the income eligibility requirements.[217] Additionally, predevelopment activities such as property acquisition, demolition, and installation of infrastructure may be included in these calculations.[218] Similar standards apply when calculating the percent of units that must satisfy the 25 percent very low income set-aside requirement.[219]

IV. CROSS-CUTTING FEDERAL REQUIREMENTS

As with many programs administered by CPD, NSP funds trigger a variety of cross-cutting federal requirements. While many of these requirements are discussed elsewhere in this book, CPD has interpreted several in a way that appears to be unique to the NSP program. In particular, environmental review, tenant protections, and program income requirements have emerged as issues requiring careful review by NSP participants.

As the implementing regulations explain, all NSP assistance is subject to the National Environmental Policy Act of 1969 and related federal environmental authorities and regulations at 24 C.F.R. Part 58 or Part 50.[220] Among other issues, these regulations generally require that an environmental review be conducted before property is acquired for a HUD-funded project.[221] Government entities with jurisdiction over their own environmental reviews typically review property acquisitions under 24 C.F.R. Part 58, while nonprofit entities and other governmental entities without jurisdiction generally must request that HUD or

---

214. Combined Notice, *supra* note 2, at 64,330–31. *See also* FAQs 194 (Nov. 19, 2009), 195 (Apr. 30, 2009), and 430 (June 23, 2010).

215. Combined Notice, *supra* note 2, at 64,330–31.

216. FAQ 194 (Nov. 19, 2009). The grantee or NSP participant may need to develop an alternative method for making this calculation if the units are not of similar sizes or if they lack comparable amenities. FAQ 430 (June 23, 2010).

217. For example, down-payment assistance for a homebuyer to purchase a condominium unit qualifies for this exception. FAQ 194 (Nov. 19, 2009).

218. FAQ 194 (Nov. 19, 2009).

219. FAQ 194 (Nov. 19, 2009) and 195 (Apr. 30, 2009).

220. For requirements applicable to CDBG funds, *see* 24 C.F.R. § 570.604. For NSP guidance incorporating these requirements, *see* NSP1 Allocation Notice, *supra* note 2, at 58,333; NOFA, *supra* note 2, at 8; Combined Notice, *supra* note 2, at 64,327. *See also* Policy Alert: Environmental Review, *supra* note 115.

221. 24 C.F.R. § 58.22(a).

another agency review the property under 24 C.F.R. Part 50.[222] Under these regulations, NSP participants may not commit NSP funds to acquire property until HUD has approved the participant's Request for the Release of Funds (RROF) or until the responsible entity has documented its decision that the project is exempt or excluded from such requirements.[223] Additionally, participants generally may not commit non-HUD funds at the property until the participant receives the approved RROF.[224] However, the regulations permit the execution of option agreements before the RROF has been received as long as the option agreement is conditioned on receipt of environmental approval and the cost of the option is a "nominal" portion of the purchase price.[225]

Despite these regulatory requirements, which apply to a variety of HUD programs, CPD has issued supplemental NSP guidance that distinguishes between "option contracts" and "conditional contracts" and imposes different requirements on each category of contract.[226] For example, any type of property may be acquired using an option contract as long as the contract complies with the requirements described above, and CPD permits a flexible definition of a "nominal" option price.[227] While not explicitly described by the regulations at Part 58, however, CPD also permits NSP participants to execute conditional contracts before the environmental review is complete. NSP participants may use conditional contracts for acquisitions or rehabilitations of existing single-family and multifamily residential units but may not use conditional contracts to acquire multifamily properties in special flood-hazard areas or properties whose development will require significant density changes.[228] Most significant, purchasers may not pay earnest money or make other nonrefundable deposits that exceed $1,000 for single-family properties.[229] Likewise, participants may not make a nonrefundable deposit that exceeds three percent of the purchase price.[230] Given these increased restrictions on conditional contracts, NSP participants may wish to clearly document that their contracts qualify as standard option contracts under 24 C.F.R. § 58.22(d).

---

222. For ease of reference, this chapter will discuss only 24 C.F.R. Part 58, but the requirements of 24 C.F.R. Part 50 are generally similar. For a description of when Part 50 applies, *see* 24 C.F.R. § 50.1(d). For a description of when Part 58 applies, *see* 24 C.F.R. § 58.1(b). For additional information on reviews conducted under Part 50, *see* CPD, Environmental Review Guide for Private Nonprofit Recipients of NSP2 Grants—24 C.F.R. Part 50 (undated).

223. 24 C.F.R. § 58.22(a) and (b).

224. *Id.* For limits on actions of prospective recipients of NSP funds, *see* 24 C.F.R. § 58.22(c).

225. 24 C.F.R. § 58.22(d). When releasing the final rule for 24 C.F.R. § 58.22(d), HUD declined to define this term and noted that "any reasonable interpretation is acceptable." Environmental Review Procedures for Entities Assuming HUD's Environmental Responsibilities, 68 Fed. Reg. 56,116, 56,122 (Sept. 29, 2003).

226. *See generally* Policy Alert: Environmental Review, *supra* note 115. *See also* CPD, NSP Policy Alert: Using Option and Conditional Contracts for Purchase of Real Property (Sept. 1, 2011) [hereinafter Policy Alert: Option and Conditional Contracts (Sept. 1, 2011)] and CPD, NSP Policy Alert: Guidance on Conditional Purchase Agreements for NSP-Assisted Acquisition and Rehabilitation of Single-Family Properties (1–4 units) (Feb. 1, 2010).

227. 24 C.F.R. § 58.22(d) and Policy Alert: Environmental Review, *supra* note 115 at 1 and Policy Alert: Option and Conditional Contracts, *supra* note 226 at 2.

228. *Id.* at 3.

229. *Id.* at 3.

230. *Id.*

Like environmental review procedures, the mandatory NSP tenant protections have caused some confusion among NSP participants and require careful documentation of compliance. Unlike many HUD programs, NSP funds are subject to three separate tenant protection requirements.[231] The first, known as the Uniform Relocation Assistance and Real Property Acquisition Policies Act of 1970 (URA), as amended, is familiar to many recipients of HUD funds and is discussed in Chapter 13 of this book.[232] The second requirement, however, is unique to the NSP programs. First described in the Recovery Act and made retroactive to NSP1, the NSP programs require that if foreclosed-upon properties are acquired with NSP funds, the initial successor in interest must provide bona fide tenants with at least 90 days' notice before requiring such tenants to vacate the property.[233] An initial successor in interest is often the successful purchaser at a foreclosure and typically includes the lender or trustee for holders of obligations secured by mortgage liens.[234] A bona fide tenancy is created if (i) the tenant was not the former mortgagor of the property, (ii) the lease or tenancy was the result of an arm's-length transaction, and (iii) the lease or tenancy requires the receipt of rent that is not substantially less than fair-market rent for the property.[235] Additionally, unless the initial successor in interest will occupy the unit as a primary residence, the initial successor in interest may not require bona fide tenants to move before their leases expire.[236] The third of these tenant protection requirements, known as the Protecting Tenants at Foreclosure Act of 2009 (PTFA),[237] requires that similar tenant protections be extended when a foreclosure occurs.[238] However, PTFA is not governed by the NSP program's definitions of "foreclosed," "bona fide tenant," or "initial successor in interest" but instead is the subject of other guid-

---

231. For the separate nature of these requirements, *see* Policy Alert: Tenant Protections, *supra* note 94.

232. As in other programs, NSP participants are also required to provide various URA notices to sellers of properties purchase with NSP funds; these URA requirements are discussed elsewhere in this book.

233. Recovery Act, Pub. L. 111-005 (Feb. 17, 2009), Title XII of Division A, Community Planning and Development, Community Development Fund, last "Provided further" on page 104. However, this requirement applies only to foreclosed properties purchased after Feb. 17, 2009. *See also* Policy Alert: Tenant Protections, *supra* note 94 at 3. For definitions of bona fide tenants and initial successors in interest (which may include NSP participants who purchase property directly from the defaulting owner at a short sale), *see* Policy Alert: Tenant Protections, *supra* note 94, at 2–3. For requirement that tenants who have materially violated a lease term be evicted only after 90 days' notice, *see* FAQ 887 (Nov. 22, 2010).

234. Policy Alert: Tenant Protections, *supra* note 94, at 2.

235. *Id.* at 3.

236. Recovery Act, Pub. L. 111-005 (Feb. 17, 2009), Title XII of Division A, Community Planning and Development, Community Development Fund, last "Provided further" on p. 104.

237. Pub. L. 111-22, Helping Families Save Their Homes Act of 2009 Title VII, §§ 701–704, as amended by § 1484 of Pub. L. 111-203 (July 21, 2010).

238. PTFA requires compliance where a foreclosure has occurred on a federally related mortgage loan "or on any dwelling or residential real property." While some commentators have expressed the belief that PTFA applies only to foreclosures on properties with federally related mortgages, PIH has indicated its belief that PTFA applies to all successors in interest of residential property, regardless of whether a federally related mortgage is present. Protecting Tenants at Foreclosure: Notice of Responsibilities Placed on Immediate Successors in Interest Pursuant to Foreclosure of Residential Property, 74 Fed. Reg. 30,106–07 (June 24, 2009).

ance, and NSP participants should separately review those requirements as well.[239]

While environmental reviews and tenant protections relate more directly to property acquisition and development, the questions surrounding program income remain key administrative issues for NSP participants, many of whom have not encountered the concept in their prior dealings with HUD. Basically, program income is defined as gross income that is generated directly from the use of NSP funds and that is received by grantees, consortium members, and subrecipients; developers and contractors are not subject to these requirements.[240] Loan repayments, proceeds from the sale of properties, and rental income are common sources of program income for grantees, consortium members, and subrecipients.[241] Under NSP, program income must be used for an NSP-eligible purpose and is likewise subject to Davis-Bacon requirements, environmental review, and all the other cross-cutting federal requirements that apply to the NSP program.[242] As noted above, revenue received by developers and contractors is not considered program income, and CPD instead encourages grantees to avoid undue enrichment of developers.[243] As a practical matter, this may be accomplished by lending the NSP funds to a developer and then requiring repayment on the achievement of certain conditions.[244]

While tracking program income can be challenging from an administrative perspective, the greatest difficulty for many grantees appears to be determining how the 25 percent set-aside requirement for very low-income persons applies to program income funds. This difficulty stems from the fact that CPD has issued conflicting guidance on this issue and appears to require different actions from recipients of NSP funds from different funding rounds. For example, CPD initially determined that the 25 percent set-aside requirement applied only to the initial NSP1 or NSP2 allocation, and program income was not independently subject to the set-aside requirements.[245] In later guidance applicable only to NSP1 and NSP3 grantees,

---

239. *See, e.g.,* Protecting Tenants at Foreclosure Act: Guidance on Notification Responsibilities Under the Act With Respect to Occupied Conveyance, 75 Fed. Reg. 66,385 (Oct. 28, 2010) and Protecting Tenants at Foreclosure: Notice of Responsibilities Placed on Immediate Successors in Interest Pursuant to Foreclosure of Residential Property, 74 Fed. Reg. 30,106 (June 24, 2009).

240. For general definition of program income, *see* 24 C.F.R. § 570.500(a). For applicability to NSP program, *see* NOFA, *supra* note 2, at 68-69, and Combined Notice, *supra* note 2, at 64,337. *See also* Policy Alert: Program Income, *supra* note 72, at 9–10.

241. Policy Alert: Program Income, *supra* note 72, at 1. While CPD notes that proceeds from the sale of properties acquired with NSP funds may also constitute program income, the applicable CDBG regulations at 24 C.F.R. § 570.503(b)(7) and 24 C.F.R. § 570.506 suggest that this requirement applies only until five years after grant closeout. Additionally, as of the time of writing, CPD has not provided guidance on program income earned after grant closeout.

242. Policy Alert: Program Income, *supra* note 72, at 2–3 and FAQ 450 (July 18, 2010). For CDBG requirements, *see* 24 C.F.R. § 570.504.

243. Policy Alert: Program Income, *supra* note 72, at 3 and Policy Alert: Guidance on Developers, Subrecipients, and Contractors, *supra* note 66, at 3. While at least one OIG audit of a NSP grantee cited the grantee for failure to require a subrecipient to return program income to the grantee, the regulations and NSP guidance do not appear to support such findings. For one such audit, *see* HUD, OIG Audit Report 2010-AT-1014: Polk County, FL, Did Not Comply with Procurement and Contract Requirements in Its NSP and HOME Program (Sept. 28, 2010) at 17.

244. Policy Alert: Program Income, *supra* note 72 at 3.

245. FAQs 324 (Sept. 8, 2010) and 587 (Nov. 24, 2010). Interestingly, these FAQs have been removed from HUD's website.

however, CPD changed its approach and explained that NSP1 and NSP3 grantees also must demonstrate that 25 percent of their program income expenditures also serve very low-income persons.[246] Recognizing that it has not issued similar guidance for the NSP2 program, CPD noted that it will address the relationship between NSP2 program income expenditures and the low income set-aside requirements in a future publication.[247] While such guidance might provide useful insight into CPD's current analysis of the implementing legislation, the frequent changes in these interpretations and the inconsistent application of these requirements in different NSP programs create challenges for NSP participants seeking to develop multi-year programs and budgets.

As with many other programs, NSP funds are subject to a variety of other cross-cutting federal requirements, many of which are discussed in Chapters 13 and 14 of this book. For example, NSP funds may trigger accessibility requirements relating to Section 504 of the Rehabilitation Act of 1973 and Title VIII of the Civil Rights Act of 1968 (the Fair Housing Act),[248] recordkeeping and audit requirements,[249] Davis-Bacon wage requirements,[250] Section 3 requirements relating to low-income workers,[251] and federal requirements for the timing of disbursements.[252] Because these regulations apply to a broad array of HUD programs, however, NSP participants may find that these restrictions are more familiar than others imposed by the NSP program.

V. CONCLUSIONS

As a program that has provided more than $6.92 billion for the redevelopment of blighted structures and abandoned, vacant, and foreclosed properties, the NSP program has served as a vital tool for communities struggling to respond to significant disinvestment. While the lack of public notice and comment can be challenging, and while conflicting guidance and the lack of a formal review process can make practitioners uneasy, the informality of this system also offers advocates the opportunity to interact directly with CPD and secure affirmative approvals of proposed activities. Likewise, as OIG continues to audit NSP participants, careful documentation of compliance with existing NSP requirements may offer participants a way of demonstrating that their actions complied with the guidance that existed at the time. Furthermore, the volume of this guidance suggests that CPD continues to strive to build an efficient, accessible program that can serve a wide range of participants.

---

246. Combined Notice, *supra* note 2, at 64,330. This guidance contradicts FAQs 324 (Sept. 8, 2010) and 587 (Nov. 24, 2010), which were addressed to NSP1 and NSP2 grantees.

247. Policy Alert: Program Income, *supra* note 72, at 2.

248. *See, e.g.,* 24 C.F.R. § 570.602, 24 C.F.R. § 6.1, and 24 C.F.R. Part 8; NOFA, *supra* note 2, at 75 and Combined Notice, *supra* note 2, at 6433. *See also* FAQ 346 (June 29, 2010).

249. *See, e.g.,* 24 C.F.R. § 570.502, 24 C.F.R. § 85.20, and 24 C.F.R. § 85.23; NOFA, *supra* note 2, at 75; and Combined Notice, *supra* note 2, at 64,323.

250. *See e.g.,* 24 C.F.R. § 570.603. *See also* CPD, Policy Alert: Guidance on Applying Davis-Bacon to NSP-Funded Activities (June 16, 2011).

251. *See e.g.,* 24 C.F.R. § 570.607(b) and 24 C.F.R. § 135. *See also* FAQ 588 (Oct. 10, 2010) and CPD, The Applicability of Section 3 of the Housing and Urban Development Act of 1968 to Neighborhood Stabilization Program Funding (undated).

252. *See, e.g.,* 24 C.F.R. § 80.21(b) and *supra* note 133.

The creation of the NSP program has also required CPD and many users of CDBG and HOME funds to reevaluate and clarify how these other programs work. While sometimes this review has been beneficial to program participants, these reinterpretations of existing programs also complicate their administration. Among other issues, this revised guidance raises questions about the applicability of CDBG or HOME guidance issued in the context of the NSP program. For example, by authorizing conditional purchase contracts as valid instruments under the environmental review requirements of 24 C.F.R. Part 58, CPD creates potential confusion for participants in other CPD programs. Without an explanation of the regulatory authority for this guidance, it is not clear whether these types of contracts are valid only in the NSP context or whether CPD has approved them for other CPD programs.

Additionally, the time-sensitive nature of the NSP program may produce CDBG or HOME guidance that has not been carefully reviewed in the context of that program. For example, many observers believed that the CDBG program allows public entities and their affiliates to serve as developers and receive developer fees in some contexts, but CPD's NSP-related guidance suggests that this is not CPD's view of the issue. By issuing this guidance in a NSP Policy Alert dedicated to other issues, CPD limits the ability of non-NSP participants to seek clarification because such non-NSP participants are unlikely to be aware of this guidance.

Despite these ambiguities, the NSP program has offered many participants the opportunity and resources to redevelop properties that have been abandoned, vacated, blighted, or foreclosed on. Furthermore, by permitting nonprofit organizations and other recipients to have a more active role than they would have in the CDBG program, the NSP program has enabled numerous organizations to significantly expand their capacities to successfully develop properties using federal funds. Finally, the block-grant nature of the program and the lack of extensive formal guidance have allowed participants to adapt their programs to meet local needs. In some areas, this has resulted in significant land banking, while other jurisdictions have focused on home ownership or rental development. The intense demand for these funds, however, suggests that the need for such community reinvestment continues.

Appendix A*

Type of property: Eligible Use:	Foreclosed Homes and Residential Properties	Abandoned Homes and Residential Properties	Blighted Structures	Vacant/ Demolished Properties
A. Financing Mechanisms	Yes	No (unless also qualifying as a foreclosed home or residential property)	No (unless also qualifying as a foreclosed home or residential property)	No (unless also qualifying as a foreclosed home or residential property)
B. Purchase and Rehabilitate	Yes	Yes	No (unless also qualifying as an abandoned or foreclosed home or residential property)	No (unless also qualifying as an abandoned or foreclosed home or residential property)
C. Land Bank	Yes (only foreclosed homes and residential properties)	No (unless also a foreclosed home or residential property)	No (unless also a foreclosed home or residential property)	No (unless also a foreclosed home or residential property)
D. Demolition	Yes (if blighted)	Yes (if blighted)	Yes	N/A
E. Redevelopment (New Construction)	No (unless also qualifying as vacant or demolished)	No (unless also qualifying as vacant or demolished)	No (unless also qualifying as vacant or demolished)	Yes

* This chart has been adapted from CPD's Explanation of Property Types Under Each Eligible Use (Dec. 3, 2009).

Public Housing Development— Mixed Finance in the Context of Historical Trends

8

Roberta L. Rubin

I. INTRODUCTION

The public housing program, initially created to stimulate employment, eliminate slums and related public health problems, and improve the quality of housing available to low-income working households, has evolved over the past 75 years to serve as a safety net for millions of extremely poor households. Innovations since the 1990s have permitted the revitalization of troubled urban public housing projects as attractive mixed-income communities, developed through public-private partnerships with a wide range of funding sources.

This chapter describes the evolution of public housing, including major statutory and policy shifts over time, before discussing in detail the "mixed-finance" program of public housing redevelopment. Practitioners primarily interested in "nuts and bolts" information will find that material in Parts III and IV, beginning on pages 253 and 273, respectively.

II. THE PUBLIC HOUSING PROGRAM

A. A False Start: The National Industrial Recovery Act

The National Industrial Recovery Act (NIRA)[1] of June 16, 1933, intended to stimulate the economy by supporting an ambitious public works program,[2] es-

---

1. Act of June 16, 1933, Ch. 90, 48 Stat. 195, formerly codified at 15 U.S.C. § 703.
2. *Id.,* Title I, Declaration of Policy, § 1 (citing "a national emergency productive of widespread unemployment and disorganization of industry").

tablished the Federal Emergency Administration of Public Works (later renamed the Public Works Administration) and endowed that agency with the power of eminent domain in order to carry out federally funded public works projects, including "low-cost housing and slum clearance projects."[3] The Housing Division of the Public Works Administration began efforts to acquire sites for development in late 1933 and early 1934, primarily in slum areas, and undertook a total of 51 projects to house more than 21,000 households.[4] Site assembly became impractical for the Housing Division, however, when the Sixth Circuit Court of Appeals ruled that the federal government could not exercise the right of eminent domain to carry out public housing projects.[5] In the wake of this decision, the Housing Division shifted its focus to funding public housing development by state or locally chartered public housing agencies, setting the stage for subsequent public housing legislation.[6]

B. A New Beginning: The United States Housing Act of 1937

The United States Housing Act of 1937[7] (the 1937 Act), also called the Wagner-Steagall Act, created the foundation for the modern public housing program. Originally a scant 10 pages of text focusing on the mechanism by which the federal government would finance the construction of locally owned public housing, the 1937 Act has grown in both volume and substance. It now serves as the basis for both the Section 8 rental subsidy program[8] and a heavily regulated[9] public housing program that has evolved and changed considerably since the 1930s.

1. Original Goals—Slum Clearance and Economic Stimulus

It is no accident that the 1937 Act was codified under Title 42 of the U.S. Code (Public Health). Activists such as Jacob Riis and Catherine Bauer brought to national attention the conditions then prevalent in densely packed tenement housing, including poor (or nonexistent) sanitation and severe overcrowding that contributed to the spread of such contagious

---

3. NIRA, Title II, Public Works and Construction Projects, Federal Emergency Administration of Public Works, § 202(d).

4. *See* PUBLIC WORKS ADMINISTRATION, AMERICA BUILDS: THE RECORD OF PWA (Washington, D.C. 1939), 207–17, 264. Some of these projects ultimately were compleped by local housing authorities. *See* G. Cam, *U.S. Government Activity in Low-Cost Housing, 1932-38*, 47 J. POLITICAL ECON. 3547, No. 3 (June 1939).

5. *See* United States v. Certain Lands in the City of Louisville, Jefferson County, 78 F.2d 684 (6th Cir. 1935) (holding that the right of eminent domain was reserved to state and local government); *see also* United States v. Certain Lands in the City of Detroit, 12 F. Supp. 345 (B.D. Mich. 1935); *see also* PUBLIC WORKS ADMINISTRATION, AMERICA BUILDS, *supra* n. 4. Construction efforts were also impeded by the transfer of funding to other public agencies in 1934 and 1935. *See* R. FISHER, 20 YEARS OF PUBLIC HOUSING: ECONOMIC ASPECTS OF THE FEDERAL PROGRAM (Westport, Conn.: Greenwood Press, 1959), at 85.

6. *See* G. Cam, *supra* n. 4, at 362–63.

7. United States Housing Act of 1937 (1937 Act), 88 Stat. 653, Pub. L. 98-383, enacted Sept. 1, 1937, codified as amended at 42 U.S.C. § 1437 *et seq.*

8. 42 U.S.C. § 1437f(o); *see also* 24 C.F.R. pt. 982 (Tenant-Based Voucher Program) and pt. 983 (Project-Based Voucher Program).

9. *See generally* 24 C.F.R. pt. 900.

diseases as typhoid and cholera.[10] The public housing program was not seen as a means of increasing the quantity of affordable housing, but as a way of improving the urban housing stock by replacing slums with higher quality housing developments.[11]

At the same time, continued high unemployment, particularly in the construction industry, created the impetus for a program focusing on new housing development. The construction industry, battered by the banking crisis of the 1930s, strongly supported any federally funded construction program that would bring new economic opportunities. In a statement delivered by Harry Hopkins, the Federal Emergency Relief Administrator, in hearings before Congress prior to the adoption of the 1934 National Housing Act (which created the mortgage insurance programs), Hopkins decalred:

> Somewhere between one-third and one-fourth of all the families on relief represent workers in the building trades. . . . My interest in this program at the moment is as a recovery measure.[12]

While the U.S. economy had been slowly recovering from the Great Depression during the early 1930s, in 1937 it took a turn for the worse. Unemployment among the civilian private nonfarm labor force was on the rise: after falling to slightly below 10 percent in 1936, unemployment rates rose to about 12.5 percent in 1938.[13] By late summer in 1937, there was considerable pressure to take additional measures to stimulate the faltering economy.

The twin motivations of slum clearance and economic stimulus are clearly apparent in the 1937 Act's declaration of policy, which reads:

> It is hereby declared to be the policy of the United States to promote the general welfare of the Nation by employing its funds and credit, as provided in this Act, to assist the several States and their political subdivisions to alleviate present and recurring unemployment and to remedy the unsafe and insanitary [sic] housing conditions and the acute shortage of decent safe and sanitary dwellings for families of low-income, in rural or urban communities, that are injurious to the health, safety and morals of the citizens of the Nation."[14]

---

10. *See, e.g.*, JACOB RIIS, HOW THE OTHER HALF LIVES (New York: Charles Scribner's Sons, 1890); CATHERINE BAUER WURSTER, MODERN HOUSING (Boston and New York: Houghton Mifflin, 1934).

11. The preliminary paragraphs of the original Wagner-Steagall bill as introduced in the House of Representatives and the Senate on Feb. 24, 1937, emphasized the threat to the "general welfare of the Nation" (and corresponding public costs) arising from slum conditions, including the threat of contagious disease, fire hazards, and bad influences on moral standards. *See* R. Fisher, *supra* n. 5, at 8–10.

12. National Housing Act Hearing before the U.S. Congress, Senate Committee on Banking and Currency, May 26-24, 1934, Statement of Harry L. Hopkins, Federal Emergency Relief Administrator (Washington, D.C.: U.S. Gov't Printing Office, 1934) at 178–79.

13. *See* Historical Statistics of the United States (Millennial Ed. Online), Susan B. Carter et al., eds., Table Ba470-477—Labor force, employment and unemployment: 890–1990 (Cambridge Univ. Press), http://hsus.cambridge.org/HSUSWeb/; *see also* Sumner H. Slichter, *The Downturn of 1937*, REVIEW OF ECONOMIC STATISTICS 20 (1938) 97–100 (describing an even greater increase in unemployment).

14. 1937 Act, *supra* n. 1, §1.

Strikingly, while the *availability* of decent, safe, and sanitary dwellings for families of low-income was identified as a critical problem, *affordability* was not. In the years since the creation of the public housing program, successive waves of reform have shifted the vision underlying the creation of new public housing. The basic structure, however—as a program in which the federal government finances development and ownership of housing by state and local agencies—remained largely constant from the 1930s through the early 1990s.

2. Federal Financing—Local Development and Operation

The 1937 Act authorized the federal government to provide financial assistance to local housing authorities to develop, own, and operate housing. The legislation contemplated the creation of "public housing agencies" (PHAs), which were authorized to engage in slum clearance as well as to develop or administer "low-rent housing," pursuant to state and/or local authorizing legislation.[15] Because the 1937 Act did not mandate the powers or method of governance of such PHAs, states and localities had the flexibility to establish PHAs' authority (and limits) pursuant to local rules.[16]

Under the 1937 Act, these local PHAs could look to the federal government to provide the lion's share of the funding for housing development. The United States Housing Authority (USHA), predecessor to the modern-day Department of Housing and Urban Development, was authorized to provide capital grants of up to 25 percent of a project's acquisition or development cost and/or 60-year loans of up to 90 percent of development and acquisition cost (less any capital grants), with interest at the "going federal rate" plus one-half of 1 percent.[17] The legislation also authorized the federal government to make additional payments to the PHA on an annual basis for a term of up to 60 years, in an amount sufficient to cover interest on the total development and acquisition cost at the going federal rate plus 1 percent.[18] These additional annual contributions—required to be applied first to principal and interest on the PHA's debt[19]—effectively shifted the cost of the "loans" to the federal government, relieving PHAs of the debt burden affecting many private landlords and thus allowing PHAs to make housing units available at a rent somewhat below market levels for comparable housing.[20] However, the rent from public housing tenants was expected to cover ordinary operating costs.[21]

---

15. 1937 Act, § 2(9) and (11). In 1957, in his seminal study of the first 20 years of the public housing program, Robert Moore Fisher observed that public housing authorities had never chosen the capital-grant alternative because of the relatively onerous local contribution requirements associated with that alternative. *See* Fisher, *supra* n. 5, at 120–23.

16. *Id.*
17. 1937 Act, § 9.
18. 1937 Act, § 10(b).
19. *Id.*

20. During the early years of the program, while some public housing tenants paid more in rent than average urban renters (including occupants of substandard tenement housing), they generally paid "lower rents than occupants of private quarters of *comparable size and quality*." Fisher, *supra* n. 5, at 7–8.

21. *See* Fisher, *supra* n. 5, at 121–22 (providing detailed examples of the relationship between annual contributions, capital grants, operating expenses and rents).

3. Slum Clearance and Public Housing

In keeping with its origins as a mechanism for eliminating unhealthful slum-housing conditions, the 1937 Act required demolition or rehabilitation of one unit of tenement housing for each new unit of public housing created.[22] While rehabilitation was an option, in practice most PHAs opted to demolish slum housing to make way for new public housing developments.[23] Consequently, public housing development generally did not result in a net increase in the number of housing units in an area.[24]

4. Desirable Housing for the Working Poor

The original 1937 Act was intended to benefit persons in the "lowest income group."[25] In the absence of rent restrictions, however, and with no operating subsidy other than annual contributions required to be applied to the PHAs' federal debt,[26] for the first 30 years of the program, public housing units were affordable only to working-class households.[27] Although the statute imposed income ceilings capping most residents' household income at five times the rent,[28] PHAs had a strong incentive to retain stable tenants, and many did not consistently evict residents whose income exceeded the statutory limit.[29] Formal selection policies rarely existed; in practice, PHAs favored war workers, veterans, and those with ties to City Hall.[30]

---

22. A PHA was required to demonstrate that the one-for-one demolition or rehabilitation requirement had been met in order to receive funding under an annual contributions contract. 1937 Act, § 10(a).

23. Ironically, many progressive public housing supporters in the 1930s and 1940s argued against rehabilitating slum neighborhoods, even going so far as to manipulate cost comparison data in favor of demolition and new public housing construction. *See* D. Hunt, Blueprint for Disaster: The Unraveling of Chicago Public Housing (Chicago: Univ. of Chicago Press, 2009), at 72–75.

24. *See, e.g.*, C. Hartman, *Relocation: Illusory Promises and No Relief*, 57 Va. L. Rev. No. 5 (June 1971), 804–05 (estimating that urban renewal and other slum clearance efforts resulted in a net loss of approximately 500,000 dwelling units through 1967, even after taking into account construction of new public housing). African-Americans in particular suffered from displacement as a result of urban renewal programs, dubbed "Negro removal" by author James Baldwin in an on-air interview on Friday, May 24, 1963. *See* K. Clark, The Negro Protest: James Baldwin, Malcolm X., Martin Luther King talk with Kenneth B. Clark (Boston: Beacon Press (1963)), at 9. For description of the effects of urban renewal on displaced black families in Philadelphia, *see* J. Bauman, Public Housing, Race and Renewal: Urban Planning in Philadelphia, 1920–1974 (Philadelphia: Temple Univ. Press, 1987).

25. 1937 Act, § 2(2).

26. *See supra* nn.17–21 and accompanying text.

27. For a discussion of the affordability of the earliest public housing constructed under NIRA by the PWA, *see* Public Works Administration, America Builds, *supra* n. 4, at 216.

28. Income was permitted to be six times the rent for large households. *See* 1937 Act, § 2(1).

29. *See, e.g.*, L. Vale, From the Puritans to the Projects: Public Housing and Public Neighbors (Cambridge, Mass.: Harvard Univ. Press, 2000), pp. 180–82 ("Public housing, in Boston as elsewhere, had been launched at the precise moment in American history when poverty extended far enough into the core of society to permit creation of a mainstream program, yet, precisely because the poverty was so widespread, policymakers had the luxury to choose tenants entirely from within the broad category of 'deserving poor.'").

30. *Id.*

The 1937 Act established development cost limits that were relatively generous, given average construction costs at the time.[31] The newly created United States Housing Agency, however, quickly established fixed per-room cost limits, and many local officials aggressively reduced development costs below the cap, often resulting in extremely small units and loss of such amenities as closet doors (or closets).[32] Still, compared with the appalling conditions in many tenements, in the 1940s these newly constructed dwellings with full bath and kitchen facilities were highly desirable for low-income working households. Early developments were often perceived as enclaves of relative prosperity, serving the most deserving low-income households in the poor neighborhoods where they were sited.[33] Ironically, some design features now condemned for isolating public housing from surrounding neighborhoods—such as the creation of "superblocks" cut off from the surrounding street grids—were intended to emphasize and safeguard the special status of those fortunate enough to gain access to these model urban communities.[34]

Although the 1937 Act did not designate public housing as an *urban* program, two factors weighed heavily against suburban[35] development of public housing. First, the requirement of

---

31. The original 1937 Act permitted public housing development costs (excluding land, demolition, and non-dwelling facilities) of up to $4,000 per family dwelling unit or $1,000 per room in most cases; in high-cost cities, the limits were $5,000 per family dwelling unit or $1,250 per unit. *See* 1937 Act, § 11. By comparison, average per-unit construction expenditures declined during the 1930s, rebounding in the early 1940s and then rising sharply by 1950. In 1935, per-unit construction expenditure for new multi-family structures averaged about $3,075. *See* Leo Grebler, David M. Blank and Louis Winnick, Capital Formation in Residential Real Estate (Nat'l Bureau of Economic Research, 1956) at 112, *citing* Housing and Home Finance Agency, Housing Statistics Handbook, 1948, pp. 15–16).

32. *See* N. Bloom, Public Housing That Worked: New York in the 20th Century (Philadelphia: Univ. of Pa. Press, 2008) (citing stringent cost-cutting measures in New York); Hunt, *supra* n. 23, at 44–47 (quoting Nathan Strauss, first USHA administrator).

33. *See, e.g.,* Vale, From the Puritans to the Projects, *supra* n. 29, at 165 (describing public housing developed in Boston between 1938 and 1954 as "selective collectives."

34. *See* Vale, *supra* n. 29, at 218–20 (describing attempts of public housing designers and planners to reproduce the "ideal of the New England village" and create 'places of enhanced public safety'"). Elizabeth Wood, the first Executive Secretary of the Chicago Housing Authority, insisted that planning for public housing must be "bold and comprehensive. . . . On the basis of experience with large urban redevelopment, we know that if blighted areas are not rebuilt in these protected superblocks, all expenditures will be wasted; the project will decay." E. Wood, Address before the American Public Works Association printed in *The Journal of Housing,* Vol. 3, No. 1, December 1945–January 1946, pp. 12–14, *as quoted in* Martin Meyerson & Edward C. Banfield, Politics, Planning and the Public Interest: The Case of Public Housing in Chicago (Glencoe, Ill.: The Free Press, 1955). Chairman Rheinstein of the New York City Housing Authority cited the importance of superblocks in easing congestion and traffic flow and creating more open space for recreation. *See* Bloom, *supra* n. 32, at 57.

35. Rural housing development has been sponsored by separate federal agencies since the Great Depression, beginning with the Resettlement Administration established by President Franklin D. Roosevelt in 1935 (see Exec. Order 7027) to build relief camps for migrant workers, continuing with the establishment of the Farm Security Administration pursuant to the Bankhead-Jones Farm Tenancy Act of 1937 (P.L. 75-210, July 22, 1937), which in turn was replaced by the Farmers Home Administration (FmHA) in 1946. *See* U.S. Dept. of Agric., A Brief History of the Farmers Home

one-for-one demolition or rehabilitation reduced the likelihood that new public housing would be developed in communities not afflicted with blighted tenement housing. In addition, the statute conditioned federal annual contributions on a 20 percent annual local or state match, either through tax relief or financial support for the project.[36] A community reluctant to accept public housing could simply refuse to provide the local contribution and thereby block new public housing development. As a result, the vast majority of public housing was developed in urban areas.[37]

C. Evolution of the Public Housing Program—Decline in the Urban Core

1. Statutory and Regulatory Changes

a. 1940s and 1950s: Slum Clearance and Urban Redevelopment

Over time, statutory and regulatory changes to the public housing program put a severe financial strain on PHAs, making it difficult for many to pay for basic management and maintenance of their properties. The Housing Act of 1949[38] imposed both an increased burden on localities and an additional element of local control, requiring a written cooperation agreement[39] and making local real estate tax exemption (or an equivalent cash payment) a condition of annual federal contributions.[40] At this time, in response to private developers' outcries over unfair competition by government agencies in housing markets,[41] the 1949 Act required PHAs to demonstrate that the need for new housing was not currently being met by private enterprise[42] and that the housing would be built economically, without "elaborate or

---

ADMINISTRATION (1989). While federal rural housing programs initially focused on helping tenant farmers purchase their own lands, FmHA later operated programs supporting rural multifamily rental housing development utilizing federal mortgage insurance, targeted rental assistance, and other programs similar to, but separate from, those operated by HUD. *Id.*

36. 1937 Act, § 10(a) ("No part of such annual contributions by the Authority shall be made available for any project unless and until the State, city, county, or other political subdivision in which such project is situated shall contribute, in the form of cash or tax remissions, general or special, or tax exemptions, at least 20 per centum of the annual contributions herein provided.").

37. According to HUD, as of 2003, out of a total of approximately 1,094,000 occupied public housing units, 963,000 were located within metropolitan areas; of these, 731,000 were located in central cities, and nearly half were sited in locales with populations of 100,000 or more. *See* HUD, *Characteristics of HUD-Assisted Renters and Their Units in 2003* (May 2008), Appendix C, Table 2–Public Housing Tenants, *available at* http://www.huduser.org/portal/publications/pubasst/hud_asst_rent.html (last accessed Sept. 13, 2011).

38. Housing Act of 1949, 63 Stat. 413, Pub. L. 81-338 (1949 Act).

39. *Id.*, § 301 (added to 1937 Act as new subsection 15(7)(b)). Federal courts later held that a city could not renege on a cooperation agreement once it was approved. *See* Cuyahoga Metro. Housing Auth. v. City of Cleveland, 342 F. Supp. 250 (N.D. Ohio).

40. 1949 Act, *supra* n. 38, § 302(b) (added to 1937 Act as new subsection 10(h)).

41. *See* Alexander von Hoffman, *Why They Built the Pruitt-Igoe Project*, http://www.soc.iastate.edu/sapp/PruittIgoe.html; P. Dreier, *Labor's Love Lost? Rebuilding Unions' Involvement in Federal Housing Policy*, 11 HOUSING POLICY DEBATE, Issue 2, at 334, 349, 341–42 (Fannie Mae Found. 2000).

42. 1949 Act, *supra* n. 38, § 301 (adding a new subsection 7 to § 15 of the 1937 Act).

extravagant design or materials."[43] The new legislation also required PHAs to charge rents at least 20 percent below the lowest rents prevailing in privately owned, unsubsidized housing;[44] imposed new maximum income limits for households newly admitted to public housing;[45] limited most[46] new admissions to households that were about to be evicted, involuntarily displaced by another project, or living in unsafe, unsanitary, or overcrowded dwellings;[47] and established an admissions preference for families that had the most urgent needs as a result of displacement by public housing development or slum clearance.[48] These statutory changes marked the beginning of a series of shifts away from the vision of public housing as model communities for low-income workers, as PHAs, bound by statutory rent restrictions, began struggling to meet operating costs while housing increasingly poor households.

Five years later, the Housing Act of 1954[49] made "urban redevelopment" synonymous with "slum clearance," limiting new expenditures for public housing to areas in which slum clearance and urban redevelopment projects were being carried out,[50] and requiring the local governing body to make a certification that the redevelopment was part of a "workable program" of urban redevelopment,[51] while increasing the mandatory local contribution.[52] The net result of these changes was to virtually ensure that public housing would be built only in low-income communities that desperately needed new housing because of "slum clearance" that destroyed existing tenement housing. At the same time, the 1954 Act imposed new financial constraints on PHAs, limiting their ability to retain revenues in excess of current operating needs[53] while prohibiting them from incurring debt secured by their public housing developments.[54] Denied permission either to save for a rainy day or to borrow to pay for repairs or improvements, and restricted to below-market rents, many PHAs began to experience severe financial difficulties.[55]

b.   1961–1983: Brooke Amendment, Federal Preferences and "the Projects"

Fundamental shifts in public housing policies during the 1960s and 1970s profoundly impacted both the operation of the public housing program and the finances of PHAs. In the late 1960s, Massachusetts Senator Edward Brooke, the first African-American to be elected by

---

43.   *Id.*, § 303 (amending § 15(5) of the 1937 Act).
44.   *Id.*, § 301 (added to 1937 Act as new subsection 15(7)(b)).
45.   *Id.*, § 301 (added to 1937 Act as new subsection 15(8)).
46.   An exception was made for veterans and families of deceased veterans during the five years immediately following the adoption of the 1949 Act. *Id.*, § 301 (added to 1937 Act as new subsection 15(8)(b)).
47.   *Id.*
48.   *Id.*
49.   Housing Act of 1954 (68 Stat. 590), Pub. L. 83-560 (1954 Act).
50.   1954 Act, § 401 (adding a new § 10(i) to the 1937 Act).
51.   1954 Act, § 303 (amending § 101 of the National Housing Act of 1934, but by its terms limiting assistance under the 1937 Act in addition to the mortgage insurance programs operated under the National Housing Act).
52.   1954 Act, § 402 (amending §10(h) of the 1937 Act). The 1954 Act also limited the total number of new public housing dwellings to those needed to relocate families displaced as a result of government action in the community. 1954 Act, § 401.
53.   1954 Act, § 403 (adding new §10(j) to the 1937 Act).
54.   *Id.*
55.   *See* Hunt, *supra* n. 23, at 200.

popular vote to the U.S. Senate, became concerned about the inability of African-American constituents to gain access to public housing.[56] At Senator Brooke's behest, in the wake of civil unrest following the assassination of Dr. Martin Luther King, Jr., Congress adopted the so-called "Brooke Amendment" as part of the Housing and Urban Development Act of 1969 (the 1969 Act)[57] This amendment to the 1937 Act capped the rent that could be charged to any tenant household at a fixed percentage of household income, resulting in extremely low rents for extremely poor households,[58] while increasing rent for households with higher incomes.[59]

The 1969 Act authorized PHAs to utilize annual contributions for purposes other than debt service, paving the way for annual contributions to partially subsidize PHA operations.[60] Many PHAs, however, have contended that the subsidy calculated by HUD is inadequate to cover PHA expenses.[61] Moreover, the amount of subsidy actually made available by HUD is subject to Congressional appropriation, and since 2003, the amount actually appropriated by Congress for PHA operating subsidy often has fallen well below the amount requested by HUD.[62] By the 1960s, even before the Brooke Amendment, PHAs were experiencing severe financial difficulties in the face of relatively high inflation and declining tenant-paid rent.[63]

---

56. *See* 114 CONG. REC. 2281 (1968) (statement of Sen. Brooke).

57. Housing and Urban Development Act of 1969, pulp. 91-152, 83 Stat. 379 (Dec. 24, 1969).

58. *Id.*, § 213 (amending § 2(1) of the 1937 Act to limit tenant-paid rent to one-fourth of income). Subsequently, this percentage was raised to 30% of income. *See infra* n. 328 and accompanying text. HUD has interpreted this statutory limit to mean that a household cannot be required to pay more than the designated percentage of income for rent plus tenant-paid utilities, an interpretation later upheld by the Supreme Court. *See* Wright v. Roanoke, 479 U.S. 418. 107 S. Ct. 766. 93 L. Ed. 2d 781 (1987) (upholding HUD's interpretation and recognizing a private right of action on the part of tenants under 42 U.S.C. §§ 1983).

59. *See, e.g.,* Hunt, *supra* n. 23, at 204 (noting that, in Chicago, income-based rent "meant skyrocketing rents for the small fraction of remaining working-class families. Few stayed.").

60. 1969 Act, § 212(a) (amending § 10(b) of the 1937 Act). Beginning in 1975, under pressure from both Congress and the Office of Management and Budget, HUD implemented the "Performance Funding System" for disbursing operating subsidies, in which subsidy was based on a calculation of past costs incurred by well-managed housing authorities (not including maintenance costs). *See* R. STRUYK, A NEW SYSTEM FOR PUBLIC HOUSING: SALVAGING A NATIONAL RESOURCE (Washington, D.C.: The Urban Inst., 1980) at 79–91; R. BRATT, REBUILDING A LOW-INCOME HOUSING POLICY (Philadelphia: Temple Univ. Press, 1989) at 59.

61. *See, e.g.,* Council of Large Public Housing Authorities, "HUD Announces Eligibility Change to Operating Fund Formula," Dec. 1, 2009, *available at* http://www.clpha.org/articledetail/?aid=48&nid=11 ("[W]e are concerned that HUD's change to the inflation methodology may underfund housing authorities.").

62. *See* A. SCHWARTZ, HOUSING POLICY IN THE UNITED STATES (New York: Routledge, 2d ed., 2010) at 139 (noting that the shortfall between HUD's budget for operating subsidy and the amount appropriated by Congress increased from a pre-2003 average of 2% to a shortfall of 11% in 2008).

63. *See* Vale, *supra* n. 29, at 337 (noting that in 1968, "according to a HUD survey, half of the nation's eighty major housing authorities were operating at a deficit, and seven of the ten largest ones were near bankruptcy." Tenant incomes plummeted in the wake of the Brooke Amendment. "Nationally, between 1961 and 1970, the median family income of nonelderly public housing tenants declined from 47.1 percent to 37.6 percent of the U.S. median family income, and continued to plummet thereafter." *Id.* By 1999, the median household income for public housing tenants had declined to 22% of area median. *See* U.S. Dept. of Housing and Urban Dev., New Facts about Households Assisted by HUD's Programs, *Recent Research Results* (October 2000), http://www.huduser.org/periodicals/rrr/rrr_10_2000/1000_6.html, last accessed Aug. 3, 2011.

Without the ability to borrow or set aside any excess income to cover future deficits,[64] PHAs cut back on essential maintenance and services.[65]

The second major change in the public housing program—the adoption of federal admissions preferences—occurred in part as a response to widespread discrimination in admissions and leasing practices.[66] In the Housing and Community Development Act of 1979, Congress

---

64. See supra nn. 53–54 and accompanying text.

65. See Schwartz, supra n. 62, at 139 (describing a backlog of "billions of dollars worth of unmet capital needs, in part because of deferred maintenance due to insufficient operating revenue").

66. Jordan Luttrell, analyzing data published by the Public Housing Administration (successor to the United States Housing Authority and predecessor to HUD) in the mid-1960s, found that "nearly three-fourths of the housing projects in [public housing] . . . are either all-white or all-Negro." Luttrell further noted that these statistics understated the extent of segregation in public housing, as the PHA then defined a predominantly white public housing development as "integrated" if a single unit was occupied by a family of color (or vice versa). See J. Luttrell, *The Public Housing Administration and Discrimination in Federally-Assisted Low-Rent Housing*, 64 MICH. L. REV. 871 (Issue No. 5, 1966). During the late 1960s, public housing residents took to the courts in numerous lawsuits challenging discriminatory admissions and evictions practices as well as site selection practices that resulted in high concentration of public housing in low-income communities of color. See, e.g., Thorpe v. Housing Auth. of City of Durham, 393 U.S. 268, 89 S. Ct. 518 (1969), citing HUD circular 2-7-67 ("Within the past year increasing dissatisfaction has been expressed with eviction practices in public low-rent housing projects. During that period a number of suits have been filed throughout the United States generally challenging the right of a Local Authority to evict a tenant without advising him of the reasons for such eviction."); Holmes v. New York City Housing Auth., 398 F.2d 262 (2d Cir. 1968) (upholding the ability of public housing applicants to state a federal claim under the 14th Amendment Due Process Clause based on deficiencies in the housing authority's admissions practices). The 1969 Act sought to combat discriminatory admission practices by requiring a PHA to provide notice of its eligibility determination and an informal hearing to applicants deemed ineligible. 1969 Act, § 214 (amending § 10(g) of the 1937 Act). These changes, however, proved insufficient to prevent discrimination practices. See generally DOUGLAS S. MASSEY & NANCY A. DENTON, AMERICAN APARTHEID: SEGREGATION AND THE MAKING OF THE UNDERCLASS (1993); see also Hunt, supra n. 23, at 202–05; F. Roisman, *Long Overdue: Desegregation Litigation and Next Steps to End Discrimination and Segregation in the Public Housing and § 8 Existing Housing Programs*, 4 CITYSCAPE: A JOURNAL OF POLICY DEVELOPMENT AND RESEARCH 171 (Issue No. 3, 1999).

Perhaps the most famous lawsuit challenging discriminatory PHA practices is the case of *Gautreaux v. Chicago Housing Authority*. In two companion cases, the federal district court for the Northern District of Illinois upheld resident challenges to the tenant assignment and site selection practices of the Chicago Housing Authority as well as HUD's assistance in "the carrying on . . . of a racially discriminatory public housing system within the City of Chicago." 296 F. Supp. 907 (N.D. Ill. 1969) and 304 F. Supp. 736 (N.D. Ill. 1969). These decisions (later consolidated into a single case), and subsequent decisions of the district court attempting to fashion remedies to redress the effects of discriminatory practices, were the subject of numerous appellate court decisions, including a 1976 Supreme Court decision upholding the plaintiffs' claim that HUD had violated the Fifth Amendment and the Civil Rights Act of 1964. See, e.g., Gautreaux v. Chicago Housing Auth., 436 F.2d 306 (7th 1970); Gautreaux v. Romney, 448 F.2d 731 (7th Cir. 1971); Gautreaux v. Chicago Housing Auth., 503 F.2d 930 (7th Cir. 1974); Hills v. Gautreaux, 425 U.S. 284 (1976). Despite numerous attempts by the federal courts to force development of public housing outside communities

imposed federal preferences in favor of households that were either occupying substandard housing or involuntarily displaced at the time they were applying for public housing.[67] Subsequently, the Housing and Urban-Rural Recovery Act of 1983 expanded federally imposed admissions standards obligating PHAs to make units available on a priority basis to households paying more than 50 percent of their income for rent.[68] HUD responded to these Congressional enactments and continuing litigation by, or on behalf of, residents by adopting detailed regulations governing PHA admission and occupancy practices[69] as well as lease and grievance procedures.[70] These changes[71] obligated PHAs to shift from their past practice of selecting residents deemed financially stable to selecting those having the greatest need for housing assistance—generally, households with much lower incomes.[72]

Notwithstanding the 1949 Act's ambitious goal of constructing 810,000 new public housing units, Congressional cutbacks severely limited the amount of new public housing developed from 1951 to 1965.[73] In 1968, however, a new Housing and Urban Development Act[74] reaffirmed the national housing goal of "a decent home and suitable living environment for every American family," first declared by Congress in the 1949 Housing Act, and set a numerical goal of establishing 26 million newly constructed or substantially rehabilitated housing units over

---

of color, local opposition to siting of public housing in predominantly white neighborhoods prevented the effective implementation of desegregative remedies. In 1987, the district court placed the Chicago Housing Authority (CHA) in receivership, appointing developer Daniel Levin and The Habitat Company (of which he was founder and chair) to develop and manage scattered-site public housing in Chicago. Gautreaux v. Pierce, Order of Aug. 14, 1987. This receivership order remained in place until May 2010, more than 30 years after the initial lawsuit was filed, and provided for a gradual transition of control back to CHA over a three-year period. *See* Dahleen Glanton, *CHA Again Takes Charge of Public Housing*, CHICAGO TRIBUNE, May 20, 2010. Alexander Polikoff, the plaintiffs' lawyer, has written a book providing a detailed description of the *Gautreaux* litigation and its aftermath. *See* A. POLIKOFF, WAITING FOR GAUTREAUX (Chicago: Northwestern Univ. Press 2006).

67. Housing Act of 1979, Pub. L. 93-383.
68. Housing and Urban-Rural Recovery Act of 1983, Pub. L. 98-181.
69. 24 C.F.R. pt. 960.
70. 24 C.F.R. pt. 966.
71. Some of these changes—notably federal admissions preferences—have since been amended or repealed pursuant to the Quality Housing and Work Responsibility Act of 1998. *See infra* nn. 110–11 and accompanying text.
72. Between 1981 and 1991, the percentage of the public housing population having incomes below 10 percent of area median increased from 2.5% to 20%. *See* B. Katz, *The Origins of HOPE VI*, in FROM DESPAIR TO HOPE: HOPE VI AND THE NEW PROMISE OF PUBLIC HOUSING IN AMERICA'S CITIES, H. Cisneros & L. Engdahl eds. (Washington, D.C.: Brookings Inst. Press 2009). As of 2008, average household income in public housing remained extremely low. While household income averaged roughly $13,600, approximately 18% of public housing households had income below $5,000 per year, another 35% had incomes between $5,000 and $10,000 per year, and 19% had incomes between $10,000 and $15,000 per year. *See* HUD, A Picture of Subsidized Households 2008, *available at* http://www.huduser.org/portal/picture2008/index.html, last accessed Sept. 17, 2011.
73. *See* Hunt, *supra* n. 23, at 129–30.
74. Housing and Urban Development Act of 1968, Pub. L. 90-448, 82 Stat. 476, S. 3497, enacted Aug. 1, 1968 (the 1968 Housing Act).

the next decade, including 6 million for low and moderate families.[75] Between 1968 and 1973, PHAs developed approximately 375,000 units, with construction funded by HUD.[76]

While the majority of public housing residents today still express a high degree of satisfaction with their housing,[77] and most federally assisted public housing units today remain in good condition,[78] many urban high-rise developments fell rapidly into disrepair,[79] resulting in a widespread perception of public housing as housing of last resort for the poorest of the poor.[80] Perhaps the most striking example of this downward spiral was the 33-building Pruitt-Igoe development in St. Louis, demolished less than 20 years after its initial occupancy after the St. Louis Housing Authority declared it "unsalvageable" due to high crime rates, vandalism, poor maintenance, and large numbers of vacancies.[81] By the early 1990s, many public

---

75. 1968 Housing Act, § 1601, 63 Stat. 413, 42 U.S.C. § 1441 note. The terms "low income" and "moderate income" have been defined in different ways for various "federally-assisted housing" programs (including public housing, § 8 rental assistance, subsidized mortgage insurance programs under §§ 221(d)(3) and 236 of the National Housing Act (12 U.S.C. § 1715z–1), and housing for elderly persons and persons with disabilities, respectively, under §§ 202 and 811 of the National Affordable Housing Act (42 U.S.C. § 8013 *et seq.*). See 24 C.F.R. § 5.100). For most federally assisted housing programs, including public housing and § 8, HUD eligibility is limited to "low-income families" having annual income at or below 80% of area median, as adjusted for family size. *See* 24 C.F.R. § 5.603 (defining "low income" for purposes of public housing and Section 8); *see also* HUD HANDBOOK 4350.3 Rev-1, *Occupancy Requirements of Subsidized Multifamily Housing Programs* (Handbook 4350.3), Ch. 3, § 1; for a definition of "annual income, *see* 24 C.F.R. § 5.609. "Moderate income" does not have a consistent definition, but for purposes of the § 221(d)(3) below-market interest rate mortgage program, designed to serve "low and moderate income" households, the maximum allowable household income is 95% of area median. *See* HANDBOOK 4350.3, Ch. 3, § 1.

76. *See* P. Dreier, *Federal Housing Subsidies: Who Benefits and Why?*, in A RIGHT TO HOUSING: FOUNDATION FOR A NEW SOCIAL AGENDA, Rachel G. Bratt, Michael E. Stone & Chester E. Hartman eds. (Philadelphia: Temple Univ. Press 2006).

77. *See* Schwartz, *supra* n. 61, at 142 (citing the results of a 1999 survey of public housing residents commissioned by HUD).

78. A HUD study of the results of a comprehensive Public Housing Assessment Survey (PHAS) of Real Estate Assessment Center (REAC) scores from more than 3,000 PHAs in 1999 found 12.8% of the PHAs surveyed to have a PHAS designation of "substandard" based on physical indicators. Results of the most recent (2011) PHA physical inspection scores are *available at* http://www.huduser.org/portal/datasets/pis.html. HUD has recently issued an interim rule implementing changes to the PHAS. *See* HUD, 24 C.F.R. pts. 901, 902 and 907, Public Housing Evaluation and Oversight: Changes to the Public Housing Assessment System (PHAS) and Determining and Remedying Substantial Default; Interim Rule, 76 Fed. Reg. 36, Feb. 23, 2011. However, the results of the new PHAS are not yet available as of this writing.

79. *See, e.g.*, Hunt, *supra* n. 23; A. Schwartz, *supra* n. 62, at 134–35.

80. *See* Nat'l Comm'n on Severely Distressed Public Housing, *The Final Report of the National Commission on Severely Distressed Public Housing* (1992) (Nat'l Comm'n Report). In the interest of cost-cutting, many high-rise developments boasted elevators that stopped only at every other floor, access to incinerators and trash chutes also only on every other floor, and units without closets. *See* Struyk, *supra* n. 61, at 29–37; E.J. MEEHAN, THE QUALITY OF FEDERAL POLICYMAKING (Columbus, Mo.: Univ. of Missouri Press 1979) at 71–73; Bloom, *supra* n. 32, at 56–57.

81. *See* Hoffman, *infra* n. 41, at 303; Meehan, *supra* n. 80, at 71–73 (describing "construction inadequacies" at Pruitt-Igoe ranging from tiny living space, poor materials, inadequate hot water

housing developments, particularly in urban areas, clearly were "severely distressed," suffering from physical obsolescence, extreme concentration of poverty, low levels of employment among residents, and significant crime and drug problems.[82]

D. A New World of Public Housing Redevelopment: HOPE VI, QHWRA, and Mixed Finance

Throughout most of the history of the public housing program, PHA developments consisted exclusively of low-rent public housing units, occupied by public housing eligible households; with few exceptions, PHAs managed their own portfolios of housing. Beginning in the mid-1990s, however, new models of public housing development emerged, with the advent of the HOPE VI[83] program and the rise of mixed-finance, mixed-income developments created through public-private partnerships.

1. Traditional Public Housing Development

From the enactment of the 1937 Act until the mid-1990s, public housing development was undertaken by PHAs contracting directly with general contractors to build the housing. While public housing built before World War II generally consisted of low-rise apartment blocks having a density of 25 to 60 families per acre,[84] much of the urban public housing constructed

---

pipe shielding, lack of basement waterproofing, and a grossly inadequate elevator system, despite construction costs approximately 60 percent above the national average).

82. *See* Nat'l Comm'n Report, *supra* n. 80. As of 2005, researchers Margery Austin Turner, Susan J. Popkin, and G. Thomas Kingsley estimated that between 47,000 and 82,000 severely distressed units remained in the public housing inventory but were not yet scheduled for demolition and replacement. *See* M. Turner, S. Popkin & G. Kingsley, *Distressed Public Housing: What It Costs to Do Nothing* (Urban Inst., 2005), *available at* http://www.urban.org/UploadedPDF/411159_Costs_of_Inaction.pdf. Even in developments not designated "severely distressed," chronic shortage of funds has resulted in considerable deferred maintenance, prompting resident complaints. *See, e.g., A Report Card for the New York City Housing Authority (NYCHA): Residents' Evaluation of NYCHA and Recommendations for Improvement* (August 2011), *available at* http://cdp-ny.org/report/nychareportcard.pdf; in response to resident complaints, a spokesperson for NYCHA cited under-funding and aging buildings in need of repair. *See* R. Yeh, "Public Housing Residents Give NYCHA a Failing Score," *WNYC News Blog,* Aug. 8, 2011, *available at* http://www.wnyc.org/blogs/wnyc-news-blog/2011/aug/08/tenants-give-nycha-failing-report-card/.

83. During the 1990s, HUD Secretary Jack Kemp promoted a series of programs dubbed HOPE (Homeownership and Opportunity for People Everywhere), the focus of which was the sale of public housing to residents. The first several HOPE initiatives, funded by Congress in successive appropriations bills as "urban demonstration programs," focused exclusively on home ownership, contrasting with the HOPE VI program's focus on revitalization of distressed public housing. For a general description of the early HOPE initiatives, *see* White House Fact Sheet on the HOPE Initiative: Homeownership and Opportunity for People Everywhere, Nov. 10, 1989, *available at* http://bushlibrary.tamu.edu/research/public_papers.php?id=1177&year=1989&month=all, last accessed Sept. 20, 2011.

84. *See* Vale, *supra* n. 29, at 218. For example, in Philadelphia, nine out of ten projects designed and built between 1949 and 1955 either consisted entirely of low-rise structures or contained a mix of row houses and high-rise elevator buildings, with emphasis on community space. *See also* J. Bauman, *supra* n. 24.

in the late 1940s and subsequent decades took the form of large high-rise developments.[85] PHAs, mindful of the legislative mandate to develop modest dwellings without "elaborate" design features, frequently used standardized plans[86] that were approved by HUD and its predecessor agencies without adequate consideration for whether these developments would meet residents' basic needs or how they would fit within the fabric of the surrounding communities.[87] The federal government, in turn, placed intense pressure on PHAs to reduce development costs, fearing that the political fallout from high costs could imperil the survival of the program.[88] These new high-rise properties proved difficult and expensive to maintain.

2. Origins of the HOPE VI Program

In response to the recommendations in the National Commission on Severely Distressed Public Housing's final report to Congress, beginning in 1992, Congress approved a series of "Homeownership and Opportunity for People Everywhere" (HOPE) demonstration grants to carry out "an urban revitalization demonstration program."[89] The initial grant, authorized in October, 1992, under the FY 1993 Appropriation Act, made available a total of $300 million, to be allocated to as many as 15 cities, through grants as high as $50,000 million apiece. These grants were allocated for demonstration programs "involving major reconstruction of severely distressed or obsolete public housing projects, to be administered by local PHAs."[90] While the bulk of the funds (80 percent) were to be used for physical redevelopment, up to 20 percent of the initial grant could be used for services. Contrary to the general rules applicable to public housing,[91] this redevelopment program did *not* require one-for-one replacement of units slated

---

85. Both federal and local officials promoted high-rise development. In part this stemmed from a belief that high-rise structures were more economical, based on a per-apartment basis. *See* Hunt, *supra* n. 23, at 124; Meehan, *supra* n. 81, at 67. Moreover, some planners expressed concern that public housing not be "overwhelmed" by the surrounding neighborhood. *See* Struyk, *supra* n. 60, at 27.

86. For example, the Chicago Housing Authority relied on the low-cost design for one high-rise development as a prototype for numerous later projects. *See* Hunt, *supra* n. 23, at 124.

87. For a blistering attack on public housing design, *see* Catherine Bauer, *The Dreary Deadlock of Public Housing*, Architectural Forum, May 1957. Problems included "false space economy," achieving modest cost savings at a high cost in resident comfort; lack of closet and cupboard doors; and shoddy construction. *See also* Meehan, *supra* n. 80, at 70–73.

88. *See* Hunt, *supra* n. 23, at 125–31. Hunt describes the impetus for the federal Public Housing Administration's issuance of a lengthy policy bulletin, *Low-Rent Public Housing: Planning, Design and Construction for Economy*, demanding cost-containment measures including reduction of already-small room sizes and imposing a new density standard of 50 units per acre for high-cost slum land, "implicitly mandat[ing] the use of multistory designs." *Id.* at 131.

89. FY 1993 Appropriation Act, H.R. 5679, Pub. L. 102-389, approved on Oct. 6, 1992— Title II (FY 1993 Appropriation Act).

90. *Id.*

91. At the time, Section 18 of the 1937 Act (42 U.S.C. § 1437p) required one-for-one replacement of public housing dwelling units as a condition of HUD approval of demolition or disposition. This requirement was repealed by Section 1002(a) of Public Law 104-19, approved July 27, 1995. Section 1002(f) of Public Law 104-19 further provided: "Notwithstanding any other provision of law, replacement housing units for public housing units demolished may be built on the original public housing site or in the same neighborhood if the number of replacement units is significantly fewer than the number of units demolished."

for demolition or disposition; indeed, the FY 1993 Appropriation Act contemplated that up to one-third of the residents at "distressed" sites would relocate with Section 8 vouchers, and the replacement housing would consist of a mix of conventional public housing, home ownership, and other assisted housing.[92] This demonstration grant program, which became known as the HOPE VI program,[93] continued to be authorized solely through appropriations bills[94] until the enactment of comprehensive public housing reform legislation in 1998.[95]

In the early days of the HOPE VI program, PHAs receiving demonstration grants embarked on renovation and modernization programs without the aid of private developers. The first funding applications submitted to HUD focused on renovation of existing developments rather than wholesale demolition and rebuilding.[96] Many PHAs had negotiated a program of renovations in cooperation with resident groups; their focus was on creating a better living environment for existing residents, through a combination of physical improvements and supportive services.[97] Beginning in fiscal year 1996, however, appropriations legislation required public housing demolition as a condition of grant funding,[98] and the HUD Notice of Funding Availability issued in 1996 reflected this policy shift toward comprehensive redesign and redevelopment of "obsolete" public housing.[99]

3. "Mixed Finance" and HOPE VI

As PHAs approached the daunting task of revitalizing "severely distressed" public housing, it became clear that additional resources and capacity were needed to carry out these complex redesign, infrastructure, environmental remediation, and construction projects. This required a fundamental change in the traditional public housing paradigm. In 1992, HUD's General Counsel, Nelson Diaz, issued a memorandum opining that projects owned by private entities should be assisted with public housing funds in conjunction with private capital such as investor equity generated by the Low Income Housing Tax Credit (LIHTC) program or private debt, provided that certain key public housing requirements were met in terms of development and operation of the housing.[100] This memorandum, which became known as the "Diaz Opinion," opened the door to this new method of developing public housing: the "mixed-finance" program.[101]

Initially, the movement within HUD to embrace mixed-finance development was driven by HUD's then-Assistant Secretary for Housing Nicholas Retsinas and Special Assistant Mindy

---

92. FY 1993 Appropriation Act; Interview with C. Hornig, former HUD Deputy Assistant Secretary for Public Housing Investments, April 13, 2011.
93. See supra n. 83.
94. See, e.g., FY 1993 Appropriation Act.
95. See infra n. 107–15 and accompanying text.
96. Interview with C. Hornig, supra n. 92.
97. Id.
98. Omnibus Consolidated Rescissions and Appropriation Act of 1996, P.L. 104-134 (April 26, 1995) (FY 1996 Appropriation Act).
99. See Notice of Funding Availability (NOFA) for Public Housing Demolition, Site Revitalization and Replacement Housing Grants (HOPE VI); Fiscal Year 1996; Notice of Proposed Information Collection for Public Comment, Docket No. FR-4076-N- (FY 1996 HOPE VI NOFA), http://portal.hud.gov/hudportal/documents/huddoc?id=DOC_10000.pdf, last accessed Aug. 8, 2011.
100. Memorandum from Nelson A. Diaz, General Counsel, HUD, to Joseph Shuldiner, Assistant Secretary for Public and Indian Housing, HUD (April 8, 1994) (Diaz Opinion).
101. Interview with C. Hornig, supra n. 92.

Turbov, without the involvement of the newly formed Office of Public Housing Investments (responsible for overseeing the fledgling HOPE VI program).[102] Ultimately, however, the Office of Public Housing Investments took responsibility for implementation of the mixed-finance program, which at that time lacked any explicit statutory or regulatory guidance.[103] This was initially achieved through regulatory waivers; subsequently, HUD issued regulatory guidance in the form of a new Subpart F to the public housing capital regulations at 24 C.F.R. Part 941 (the "Mixed Finance Regulations").[104]

The mixed-finance approach to public housing—most often used in conjunction with, but not restricted to, the HOPE VI program—permitted not only greater flexibility in financing and ownership, but also development of mixed-income communities, including both public housing and non-public housing units. In turn, HUD viewed this as increasing opportunities for "ending the social and economic isolation of public housing residents," epitomized by the stigma associated with "the projects"[105] However, for several years, debate continued within the HOPE VI program as to whether public housing revitalization should occur exclusively through the mixed finance program, or whether PHAs with in-house capacity should focus on solid renovation of their existing housing stock.[106]

Finally, with the adoption of the Quality Housing and Work Responsibility Act of 1998 (QHWRA),[107] Congress codified the HOPE VI program (previously authorized solely through appropriations bills) by substantially rewriting Section 24 of the 1937 Act to explicitly authorize grants for demolition, rehabilitation, reconfiguration of obsolete public housing, site revitalization, deconcentration of poverty through housing, and building sustainable communities, as well as tenant-based assistance for displaced households.[108] At the same time, QHWRA introduced significant changes to generally applicable public housing policies, including the permanent abolition of federal admissions preferences (which had been suspended on a temporary basis since 1996[109]) and the addition of explicit permission for PHAs to establish a system of local preferences within HUD- regulated parameters.[110] QHWRA also introduced

---

102. Interview with C. Hornig, *supra* n. 92.

103. *Id.*

104. HUD has issued a proposed rule amending the mixed finance regulations, but has yet to issue a final rule adopting these changes. See HUD, 24 C.F.R. pt. 941: Streamlined Application Process in Public/Private Partnerships for the Mixed-Finance Development of Public Housing Units; Proposed Rule, 71 Fed. Reg. 78,013 (No. 248, Dec. 27, 2006). More recently, HUD has proposed eliminating 24 C.F.R. pt. 941 and folding all development requirements into 24 C.F.R. pt. 905. See Public Housing Capital Program Proposed Rule, 24 C.F.R. pts. 903, 905, 941, 968, 969, Fed. Reg. Vol. 76, No. 25 pp. 6654–82, Feb. 7, 2011 (PH Capital Program Proposed Rule).

105. *See* FY 1996 HOPE VI NOFA, *supra* n. 100.

106. Interview with C. Hornig, *supra* n. 92.

107. Quality Housing and Work Responsibility Act of 1998, 112 Stat. 2461, P.L. 105-276, Title V, approved Oct. 21, 1998 (QHWRA).

108. *Id.*, § 535 (amending Section 24 of the 1937 Act, codified at 42 U.S.C. § 1437v).

109. *See* Balanced Budget Downpayment Act, I, Pub. L. 104-99 (Jan. 26, 1996).

110. QHWRA, § 514 (amending Section 6(c)(4)(A) of the 1937 Act, codified at 42 U.S.C. § 1437d(c)(5)(a)). These may include local residency preferences (although both residency requirements and residency preferences based on duration of residency are prohibited) as well as preferences for working families (so long as elderly and disabled households receive the benefit of the working family preference). *See* 24 C.F.R. § 960.206(b).

earned-income disregards during the first two years following a resident's shift from public assistance to employment, reducing the disincentive to work resulting from increases in income-based rent,[111] as well as substantial changes in the statutory provisions governing public housing capital and operating funds. These included changes in the formulae to be used by HUD in allocating capital and operating funds to PHAs[112] and the introduction of limited fungibility between capital and operating funds.[113]

QHWRA added a new Section 35 to the 1937 Act, allowing PHAs to own, operate, assist, or otherwise participate in the development of "mixed-finance projects."[114] Under the 1937 Act, as amended by QHWRA, the term "mixed-finance" refers to projects assisted by private resources, which may include low income housing tax credits, in addition to public housing funds, and providing for development:

(a) By a PHA or PHA affiliate; or
(b) By a partnership, limited liability company or other entity in which a PHA or PHA affiliate is the general partner or managing member or otherwise "participates"; or
(c) By any entity that grants a right of first refusal and purchase option to a PHA or PHA affiliate, in accordance with Section 42(i)(7) of the Internal Revenue Code, as amended; or
(d) In accordance with such other terms as the Secretary may prescribe by regulation.[115]

4. Future Funding: HOPE VI and Choice Neighborhoods

Section 24 of the 1937 Act, as amended by QHWRA, contained a sunset provision that prohibited the advance of any capital grants under that section after September 30, 2002.[116] This provision has been amended several times, most recently (as of this writing) pursuant to the Consolidated Appropriations Act, 2010, which authorized up to $200 million in capital grants to be made until September 30, 2011.[117] In May, 2011, HUD awarded approximately $153 million in FY 2010 and FY 2011 HOPE VI grants to PHAs in eight cities nationwide.[118]

---

111. QHWRA, §§ 508(b)(1)(B) and 545 (amending § 3(d) of the 1937 Act, codified at 42 U.S.C. § 1437a(d)).
112. QHWRA, § 519 (amending Section 9 of the 1937 Act, codified at 42 U.S.C. § 1437g) (calling for the public housing capital and operating fund formulae to be determined by negotiated rulemaking); *see also* 24 C.F.R. pts. 905 and 990.
113. QHWRA, § 513(a) (amending Section 16 of the 1937 Act, codified at 42 U.S.C. § 1437n).
114. QHWRA, § 539 (adding new Section 35 to the 1937 Act, codified at 42 U.S.C. § 1437z-7).
115. QHWRA, § 539(d)(2) (codified at 42 U.S.C. § 1437z-7(d)(2)). For a discussion of HUD guidance regarding development by a PHA affiliate or other entity in which a PHA participates, *see infra* § III.G.
116. QHWRA, § 535 (inserting sunset provision as Section 24(n) of the 1937 Act, codified at 42 U.S.C. § 1437v(n)).
117. Consolidated Appropriations Act, 2010 (Pub. L. 111-117), approved Dec. 16, 2009.
118. *See* HUD Press Release No. 11-097, HUD Awards $153 Million to Revitalize Severely Distressed Public Housing in Eight Communities, May 23, 2011, *available at* http://portal.hud.gov/hudportal/HUD?src=/press/press_releases_media_advisories/2011/HUDNo.11-097, last accessed Sept. 21, 2011.

The Consolidated Appropriations Act, 2010 authorized HUD to allocate up to $65 million of the total $200 million in HOPE VI appropriations for a demonstration of the Obama administration's proposed "Choice Neighborhoods" initiative. Subsequently, HUD elected to apply a portion of HOPE VI funding that it received in FY 2011 to Choice Neighborhoods.[119] In late August 2011, HUD awarded an aggregate $122 million in Choice Neighborhoods implementation grant awards to support multifamily assisting housing redevelopment in five cities. A centerpiece of the Obama administration's housing policy, Choice Neighborhoods seeks an even more comprehensive approach to neighborhood revitalization than did HOPE VI, targeting distressed, privately owned HUD-assisted housing as well as public housing, and focusing on educational improvements, local community planning, and coordination with other federal agencies.[120]

In an era of economic crisis and looming budget cuts, the future of the HOPE VI and Choice Neighborhoods grant programs is uncertain. As of early 2012, absent future extensions of the statutory sunset provisions (and additional appropriations), no new grant funds will be available. However, as HOPE VI redevelopment often takes place in multiple phases, many PHAs will continue work on projects funded by previously funded grants for several years to come. Regardless, PHAs have the authority to enjoy the flexibility, under Section 35 of the 1937 Act, to apply the concept of "mixed-finance" to redevelopment, using public housing operating subsidy, accumulated capital funding, and other funds to leverage private resources.

5. Capital and RHF Funds: Additional and Continuing Sources

The 1937 Act, as amended by QHWRA, requires HUD to establish a capital fund to assist PHAs in carrying out capital and management activities, including the development and modernization of public housing.[121] Under HUD regulations governing the Public Housing Capital Fund Program,[122] each PHA is entitled to a formula-based allocation of capital funds, appropriated by Congress to fund current and future PHA modernization and accrual needs. After reserving certain amounts for emergencies, settlement of litigation and other special purposes,[123] HUD is required to allocate 50 percent of the remaining capital funds in accordance with the Capital Fund Formula (CFF) established in the regulations, based on existing PHA modernization needs.[124] The remaining capital funds must be allocated based on the relative accrual needs of PHAs, determined by a series of objective factors such as the age and

---

119. Appropriations legislation for FY 2011 authorized $100 million in HOPE VI funding. See Dep't of Defense and Full-Year Continuing Appropriations Act, 2011 (Pub. L. 112-10), April 15, 2011, § 2237. HUD has allocated a portion of those funds to the Choice Neighborhoods Initiative.

120. See generally http://portal.hud.gov/hudportal/HUD?src=/program_offices/public_indian_housing/programs/ph/cn, last accessed Aug. 9, 2011.

121. See 42 U.S.C. § 1437g.

122. 24 C.F.R. pt. 905. In February 2011, HUD issued the PH Capital Program Proposed Rule, which, if adopted in final form, would make some changes to the CFF; however, this rule has not been issued in final form. See PH Capital Program Proposed Rule, supra n. 104.

123. See 24 C.F.R. § 905.10(b).

124. See 24 C.F.R. § 905.10(c), (d). Newly acquired and/or constructed developments are deemed to have no current modernization needs. Id. By statute, HUD is required to incorporate in the CFF a mechanism to reward performance. See 42 U.S.C. § 1437g(d)(2).

type of units.[125] In general, each public housing unit or section 23 bond-financed unit that is subject to an ACC counts as one unit for purposes of the CFF, subject to certain exclusions (for example, operating subsidy-only units do not receive any CFF allocation).[126]

Permitted uses of capital funds under Section 9(d) of the 1937 Act include "the development, financing, and modernization of public housing projects, including the redesign, reconstruction, and reconfiguration of public housing sites and buildings (including accessibility improvements) and the development of mixed-finance projects," as well as deferred maintenance, planned code compliance activities, replacement of obsolete building systems and dwelling equipment, and other capital expenditures.[127] Funds may also be used to collateralize or provide credit enhancement for bonds issued by a PHA to finance development activities.[128]

Section 9(g)(3) of the 1937 Act generally prohibits a PHA from utilizing amounts allocated to it from the Capital Fund for new construction that would result in a net increase in the number of public housing units owned, assisted, or operated by the PHA on October 1, 1998.[129] The statute permits certain exceptions from this limit (known as the Faircloth Limit), including a specific exception for developments that are part of a mixed-finance project, or otherwise leverage significant additional private or public investments, when the estimated cost of the useful life of the project is less than the estimated cost of providing tenant-based Section 8 assistance for the same period.[130] However, in December 2011, HUD published a notice indicating that, with certain very narrow exceptions (including units funded solely with monies made available under the American Reinvestment and Recovery Act of 2009 (ARRA)), as a matter of policy, HUD will not approve proposals for use of capital funds to develop new units in excess of the Faircloth Limit.[131]

In addition, PHAs that have a reduction in the number of units taken into account in the CFF due to demolition or disposition occurring after October 1, 1998, are entitled to additional funds, known as "replacement housing factor" or "RHF" funds" (1) for the first five years after the reduction in units, and (2) for an additional five years if the PHA meets certain planning, leverage, obligation, and expenditure requirements, including receipt of a firm commitment for additional, non-public housing funds to help finance the cost of the replacement housing.[132] RHF funds are to be used solely for replacement of public housing units lost

---

125. *See* 24 C.F.R. § 905.10(c), (d).
126. *See* 24 C.F.R. § 905.10(e) and 905.10(f).
127. 42 U.S.C. § 1437g(d)(1)(A); *see also* 24 C.F.R. § 905.10(k).
128. *See* 24 C.F.R. § 905.10(k)(2).
129. *See* 42 U.S.C. § 1437g(g)(3).
130. *Id.*
131. *See* PIH Notice 2011-69, Dec. 27, 2011. In addition to the exception for units funded exclusively through ARRA, this Notice permits, *inter alia*, exceptions for mixed-finance units developed before the date of the Notice, reconfiguration of units after October 1, 1998 (so long as the aggregate number of bedrooms is not increased), and units for which approval was given prior to October 1, 1998, for which DOFA occurred after that date. *Id.*, § V.
132. *See* 24 C.F.R. § 905.10(i). In the PH Capital Program Proposed Rule, HUD has proposed reducing the number of years of RHF funding from 10 to 5. *See* PH Capital Program Proposed Rule, *supra* n. 104. A PHA is not eligible for RHF funds if it receives funding under programs that otherwise provide for public housing development, such as HOPE VI, Major Reconstruction of Obsolete Public Housing, or public housing development funds. An agency designated as troubled

to the PHA's portfolio due to demolition or disposition, in accordance with the PHA agency plan.[133] With limited exceptions, funds must be obligated within 24 months following the date the funds become available to the PHA (or, with specific HUD approval, 24 months following the date that the PHA accumulates adequate funds to develop replacement housing).[134] If a PHA fails to timely obligate RHF funds allocated for the first five years following unit disposition or demolition, or fails to expend the funds within a reasonable time thereafter, HUD may reduce the amount of RHF funding for the second five-year period.[135]

HUD has proposed regulatory changes that would combine and streamline "legacy" modernization programs (the Comprehensive Grant Program for large housing authorities, and the Comprehensive Improvement Assistance Program for small housing authorities) and the Public Housing Development Program (including mixed-finance development) into a single "Capital Fund Program."[136] As of this writing, this proposal has not taken effect.

6. Basics of "Mixed Finance"

As it has evolved since the mid-1990s, the mixed-finance program has at its heart four elements: leverage, income-mixing, proportionality of costs, and imposition of both public housing restrictions and private-sector oversight on "public housing" rental developments owned by entities other than PHAs.[137]

a. Leverage

While the initial impetus for mixed-finance development came from PHAs seeking permission to place public housing in private ownership and to utilize non-public housing resources,[138] more recently, HUD has actively encouraged PHAs to use public housing capital to leverage

---

by HUD and not already under the direction of HUD or a court-appointed receiver must utilize an Alternate Management Entity as described in 24 C.F.R. pt. 902. *Id.* High-performing PHAs may receive a performance bonus above the base formula amount. *See* 24 C.F.R. § 905.10(i)(7). For a good general discussion of RHF eligibility and requirements, *see* HUD web page, "Replacement Housing Factor Funding," http://portal.hud.gov/hudportal/HUD?src=/program_offices/public_indian_housing/programs/ph/capfund/rhf, last accessed Jan. 12, 2012.

133. *See* 24 C.F.R. § 905.10(i)(5).
134. *See* 24 C.F.R. § 905.10(i)(7)). Similar obligation deadlines apply to CFF funding generally. *See* 24 C.F.R. § 905.120(a). A PHA may request HUD approval for an extension of the obligation deadline by up to 12 months, based on factors including the size of the PHA, the complexity of its development program, and any limitations imposed by state or local law that affect the PHA's ability to timely obligate the funds. *See* 24 C.F.R. § 905.120(b).
135. *Id.*
136. *See* PH Capital Program Proposed Rule, *supra* n. 104.
137. Public Housing restrictions relating to leasing and occupancy of rental units apply only to new *rental* units designated as public housing; home-ownership units are subject to a more limited set of restrictions. For a discussion of public housing home-ownership programs, *see infra* § III.H.
138. *See* Diaz Opinion, *supra* n. 100 (responding to proposals on behalf of the Fairfax County Redevelopment and Housing Authority and the St. Louis Housing Authority).

other funds.[139] Indeed, in competitive funding rounds for HOPE VI and Choice Neighborhoods grants, HUD has made leverage a key element in evaluating proposals.[140]

b. Income Mixing, Reduced Density, and Deconcentration of Poverty

One of the key findings of the National Commission on Severely Distressed Public Housing in its 1992 Final Report was that residents of severely distressed public housing tended to have extremely high rates of unemployment and reliance on public assistance.[141] The National Commission Report stated that severely distressed public housing was "not simply a matter of deteriorating physical conditions, it is more importantly one of a deteriorating severely distressed population in need of services and immediate attention."[142] Appropriations and rescissions legislation in 1995 amended the 1937 Act to permit development of new public housing units to replace demolished units either on the original site or in the same neighborhood "if the number of such replacement units is significantly fewer than the number of units demol-

---

139. *See, e.g.,* U.S. Dept. of Housing and Urban Redevelopment, "Mixed Finance Public Housing Development," *HOPE VI Guidance,* March 2001, http://portal.hud.gov/hudportal/documents/huddoc?id=DOC_10114.pdf (last accessed Aug. 8, 2011) (citing leverage as a key benefit of mixed-finance development).

140. *See, e.g.,* HUD's Fiscal Year (FY) 2010 NOFA for the HOPE VI Revitalization Grants Program (Docket No. FR-5415-N-07) (HOPE VI 2010 NOFA), http://portal.hud.gov/hudportal/documents/huddoc?id=DOC_9989.pdf (last accessed Sept. 21, 2011, at 35) ("You must actively enlist other stakeholders who are vested in and can provide significant financial assistance to your revitalization effort, both for match and leverage. . . . HUD seeks to fund mixed-finance developments that use HOPE VI funds to match funds requested and leverage the maximum amount of other funds, particularly from private sources . . ."; *see also HOPE VI Guidance, supra* n. 139. In scoring applications, the 2010 HOPE VI NOFA allocated as many points to leveraging as to need (based on severe physical distress of housing project, surrounding neighborhood, and need for HOPE VI funding), and only one point less than that awarded based on the capacity of development team. *See* 2010 HOPE VI NOFA at 50–65. Similarly, under the 2010 Choice Neighborhoods Round 2 Implementation Grant NOFA, leverage counted for a total of 23 points (including leverage of housing dollars, supportive service dollars, CDBG, and other community resources) out of a maximum possible 120 points, and represented 10 out of a possible 31 points under the "Housing" component of the transformation plan; by contrast, long-term affordability represented only two points. *See* HUD's Fiscal Year (FY) 2010 NOFA for the Choice Neighborhoods Initiative—Round 2 NOFA (for Implementation Grant Finalists Only) (Docket No. FR-5473-N-01). http://portal.hud.gov/hudportal/documents/huddoc?id=cnround2nofa.pdf (last accessed Sept. 21, 2011, at 23–24).

141. *See* Nat'l Comm'n Report, *supra* n. 80. Similarly, the HOPE VI Panel Study commissioned by Congress in 1999 to examine the effects of HOPE VI redevelopment efforts, examining baseline conditions at five representative HOPE VI sites, documented poor physical condition of housing units, serious drug and crime problems in the surrounding neighborhoods, inadequate public services and access to retail stores, high rates of mental and physical health problems among both children and adults, low-performing schools and high rates of serious educational problems, low levels of employment, and high rates of reliance on public assistance. *See* Susan J. Popkin et al., *HOPE VI Panel Study Baseline Report: Final Report* (Sept. 1, 2002), http://www.urban.org/url.cfm?ID=410590 (last accessed Aug. 8, 2011).

142. Nat'l Comm'n Report, *supra* at n. 80.

ished."[143] By regulation, HUD imposes less-stringent site selection requirements for public housing projects rebuilt on or near the site of a demolished public housing project, so long as density is reduced by 50 percent.[144] Subsequently, beginning with the FY 1996 NOFA, HUD has placed considerable weight in its funding decisions on the extent to which proposals would decrease the concentration of low-income residents at HOPE VI sites, either by placing public housing in non-poverty neighborhoods or by creating a mixed-income community at the original public housing site.[145]

c. Proportionality

Since the inception of the mixed-finance program, HUD has taken the position that public housing funding should not pay more than PH units' proportionate share of project costs.[146] QHWRA codified this proportionality requirement in Section 35 of the 1937 Act, which requires that each mixed-finance project must be developed in such a manner as to ensure that:

> the number of public housing units bears approximately the same proportion to the total number of units in the mixed-finance project as the value of the total financial commitment provided by the public housing agency bears to the value of the total financial commitment in the project, or shall not be less than the number of units that could have been developed under the conventional public housing program with the assistance, or as may otherwise be approved by the Secretary.[147]

Thus, if a mixed-finance project has a total development cost of $10 million, comprising $3 million in public housing capital funds and $7 million in other funding, 30 percent of the units must be designated as public housing units.[148]

---

143. Emergency Supplemental Appropriations for Additional Disaster Assistance, for Anti-Terrorism Initiatives, for Assurance in the Recovery from the Tragedy that Occurred at Oklahoma City, and Rescissions Act 1995, Pub. L. 104-19, 109 Stat. 236, July 27, 1995 (amending Section 18 of the 1937 Act, 42 U.S.C. § 1437p).
144. 24 C.F.R. § 941.202(c)(2).
145. *See* FY 1996 HOPE VI NOFA, *supra* n. 99, at 1,7, 15, 20; for a more detailed discussion of HOPE VI and the evolution of public housing policy in the 1990s, *see* Susan J. Popkin et al., *A Decade of HOPE VI: Research Findings and Policy Challenges* (The Urban Institute and The Brookings Institution, May 2004), http://www.urban.org/url.cfm?ID=411002 (last accessed Aug. 8, 2011).
146. Interview with C. Hornig, *supra* n. 92. HUD's approval ultimately is based on a combination of total development cost (TDC) limits and proportionality of expenditures for common areas. *See* 24 C.F.R. § 941.608(b). If public housing funds will pay for more than the public housing units' proportionate share of common area costs, the proposal must demonstrate that, on a per-unit basis, the amount of PHA funding will not exceed TDC limits and that any such common areas will benefit all residents of the development. *Id.*
147. 42 U.S.C. § 1437z-7(e)(2).
148. *See also* 24 C.F.R. § 941.612(b)(1)("The PHA and its partner shall certify, in a form prescribed by HUD, prior to the initial drawdown of public housing development funds that the PHA will not draw down and the partner will not request more public housing grant funds than necessary to meet the PHA's pro rata share of the development costs.")

In the case of mixed-finance rental development, the concept of proportionality also applies to ongoing costs. Thus, in developments involving both public housing and non-public housing units, Mixed-Finance Regulations require that the PHA and the owner entity allocate expenses and risks associated with both development and operation "based upon a ratio that reflects the proposed bedroom mix of the public housing units as compared to the bedroom mix and unit count of the non-public housing units in the development, or as otherwise approved by HUD."[149]

d. Applicability of Public Housing Requirements to Mixed-Finance Developments

Since the earliest days of the mixed-finance program, HUD has maintained that key public housing restrictions must apply to a development, regardless of its ownership, in order for the project to receive public housing capital or operating funds.[150] This requirement has been codified in Section 35 of the 1937 Act, which provides: "The units assisted with capital or operating assistance in a mixed-finance project shall be developed, operated, and maintained in accordance with the requirements of this chapter relating to public housing during the period required by under [sic] this chapter, unless otherwise specified in this section."[151] Thus, to understand the mechanics of mixed-finance development, it is essential to understand the body of law governing public housing development and operation generally, and the relationship of this body of law to mixed-finance requirements under Section 35 of the 1937 Act, as discussed in Section III, below.

III. MECHANICS OF PUBLIC HOUSING REDEVELOPMENT IN THE TWENTY-FIRST CENTURY

A. Statutory Underpinnings

The 1937 Act, codified at 42 U.S.C. § 1437 *et seq.*, governs both the public housing program and the rental assistance program commonly known as Section 8.[152] Section 9 of the 1937 Act consolidates authority for public housing operating funds as well as capital funds to cover ongoing capital needs of existing housing.[153] Other key provisions of the 1937 Act, in addition to those previously mentioned, include definitions,[154] rent and occupancy restrictions,[155] PHA annual and five-year plan requirements,[156] provisions governing designated housing for

---

149. 24 C.F.R. § 941.610(a)(2)(iv). A similar proportionality standard applies to the cooperation agreement required to be entered into with the applicable locality governing exemption of local real estate taxes, payments in lieu of taxes, and government services. *See* 24 C.F.R. § 941.610(a)(2)(vi).
150. *See Diaz* Opinion, *supra* n. 100; 24 C.F.R. pt. 941, subpt. F.
151. 42 U.S.C. § 1437z-7(c)
152. This nomenclature refers to Section 8 of the 1937 Act itself, which provides funding authorization for such rental assistance. *See* 42 U.S.C. § 1437f.
153. *See* 42 U.S.C. § 1437g.
154. 1937 Act, § 3(b), codified at 42 U.S.C. § 1437a(b).
155. 1937 Act, § 3(a), codified at 42 U.S.C. § 1437a(a).
156. 1937 Act, § 5A, codified at 42 U.S.C. § 1437c-1.

elderly and disabled families,[157] community service requirements imposed on public housing residents,[158] income targeting and deconcentration of poverty requirements,[159] limitations on PHA demolition or disposition of property (including but not limited to dwellings),[160] authority to convert public housing to vouchers,[161] family self-sufficiency program requirements,[162] authorization for PHAs to borrow money and mortgage or grant a security interest in their properties,[163] pet ownership in public housing,[164] resident homeownership programs,[165] required conversion of distressed public housing to tenant-based assistance (if the ongoing cost of assuring long-term viability would exceed the cost of conversion),[166] and provisions governing grants for supportive services.[167] Many of these are discussed in detail in Chapter 9, on public housing operations.

B. Regulatory and Sub-regulatory Guidance

HUD regulations governing the public housing program are found at Title 24, Chapter 9 of the Code of Federal Regulations.[168] In addition to the Mixed-Finance Regulations,[169] key regulatory guidance is found in Part 5 (general HUD program requirements, including key definitions),[170] Part 966 (requirements for public housing leases and grievance procedures),[171] Part 960 (admissions and occupancy requirements applicable to all public housing),[172] Part 906 (public housing home-ownership program),[173] Part 945 (designated housing for elderly and disabled families),[174] Part 970 (demolition and disposition),[175] Part 971 (assessment of the revitalization potential of distressed public housing),[176] Part 972 (conversion to vouchers),[177] Part 990 (public housing operating fund program),[178] and Part 905 (public housing capital fund program).[179]

In addition to formal regulatory guidance, HUD issues frequent Public and Indian Housing (PIH) notices as part of its implementation guidance, particularly for demolition and

---

157. 1937 Act, § 7, codified at 42 U.S.C. § 1437e.
158. 1937 Act, § 12(c), codified at 42 U.S.C. § 1437j.
159. 1937 Act, § 16, codified at 42 U.S.C. § 1437n.
160. 1937 Act, § 18, codified at 42 U.S.C. § 1437p.
161. 1937 Act, § 22, codified at 42 U.S.C. § 1437t.
162. 1937 Act, § 23, codified at 42 U.S.C. § 1437u.
163. 1937 Act, § 30, codified at 42 U.S.C. § 1437z-2.
164. 1937 Act, § 31, codified at 42 U.S.C. § 1437z-3.
165. 1937 Act, § 32, codified at 42 U.S.C. § 1437z-4.
166. 1937 Act, § 33, codified at 42 U.S.C. § 1437z-5.
167. 1937 Act, § 34, codified at 42 U.S.C. § 1437z-6.
168. 24 C.F.R. § 901 *et seq.*
169. 24 C.F.R. pt. 941, subpt. F.
170. 24 C.F.R. pt. 5.
171. 24 C.F.R. pt. 966.
172. 24 C.F.R. pt. 960.
173. 24 C.F.R. pt. 906.
174. 24 C.F.R. pt. 945.
175. 24 C.F.R. pt. 970.
176. 24 C.F.R. pt. 971.
177. 24 C.F.R. pt. 972.
178. 24 C.F.R. pt. 990.
179. 24 C.F.R. pt. 905.

disposition processing[180] and capital funds.[181] Sub-regulatory guidance has been particularly important in driving the mixed-finance program, which has been implemented through a combination of notices, alerts, model documents,[182] and standards informally imposed by HUD's reviewing staff, none of which have been subjected to formal notice and comment. In the late 1990s, HUD went so far as to publish a *Mixed Finance Guidebook*,[183] but more recently HUD has opted to post notices on the Internet on specific topics as policies evolve.[184] In the absence of updated mixed-finance guidance reflecting the accounting and financial overhaul of the public housing program that began in 2005,[185] some of the posted guidance is inconsistent with regulation and /or practice.[186]

---

180. *See, e.g.*, Notice PIH 2003-9 (Demolition/Disposition Processing Requirements under the 1998 Act), www.hud.gov/offices/pih/publications/notices/03/pih2003-9.pdf (last accessed Aug. 9, 2011).

181. *See, e.g.*, Notice PIH 2011-24 (Capital Fund Awards), portal.hud.gov/hudportal/documents/huddoc?id=11-24pihn.doc (last accessed Aug. 9, 2011); PIH Notice 2009-33 (Capital Fund Awards), www.hud.gov/offices/pih/publications/notices/09/pih2009-33.pdf (last accessed Aug. 9, 2011).

182. *See* http://portal.hud.gov/hudportal/HUD?src=/program_offices/public_indian_housing/programs/ph/hope6/mfph/mf_modeldocs (Mixed-Finance Model Documents). HUD's model documents for the mixed-finance program in particular have become a key source of information for substantive program requirements, often through the wording of key definitions. For example, the Model Regulatory and Operating Agreement (mixed-income) precludes the use of operating subsidy to pay real estate taxes or debt service by excluding those costs from the definition of "allowed development expenses," notwithstanding the fact that PHAs themselves are expressly permitted under the 1937 Act to incur debt secured by their public housing projects. *Id.*, Model Regulatory and Operating Agreement (mixed-income) § 4.1(a)(i). The Model Regulatory and Operating Agreement also mandates rebuilding following a condemnation or casualty unless it is infeasible to do so—a provision much appreciated by developers, but of concern to some project lenders. *Id.*, § 8.2.

183. U.S. HUD & ABT ASSOCIATES, MIXED-FINANCE GUIDEBOOK (Cambridge, Mass., 1998).

184. *See, e.g.*, HOPE VI Demolition Grant Monitoring and Management for Field Offices, March 2007, http://portal.hud.gov/hudportal/documents/huddoc?id=DOC_9891.pdf (last accessed Sept. 21, 2011) ("This guidance supersedes any related chapters in any HOPE VI Guidebook (which has now been discontinued in favor of posting on the web) as well as relevant guidance in Notice HUD 95-10, which has expired."); HOPE VI Revitalization Grant Management and Monitoring, rev. March 2004, http://portal.hud.gov/hudportal/documents/huddoc?id=DOC_10017.pdf (last accessed Sept. 21, 2011). ("This guidance supersedes previous chapters in any HOPE VI Guidebook as well as relevant guidance in Notice HUD 95-10, which has expired.")

185. This culminated in a new regulation governing provision of operating subsidy at 24 C.F.R. § 990, which required PHAs to track income and expenses separately for different properties and explicitly authorized PHAs to charge fees for services. Detailed implementation requirements are found in "Changes in Financial Management and Reporting Requirements," issued September 2006 by PIH Notice 2006-33, supplementing the expired HUD Handbook 7475.1 Rev., CHG-1, FINANCIAL MANAGEMENT HANDBOOK. Asset management changes are discussed in more detail in Chapter 9, on public housing operations.

186. For example, the Model Regulatory and Operating Agreement and a 2001 "Policy Alert" on DOFA/EIOP, still available on HUD's website, address the flow of operating subsidy from HUD based on a specific combination of occupancy and quarter's end, while the current regulation at 24 C.F.R. § 990.120(b) and 990.125(a) provides that a unit is eligible for subsidy once it is occupied. Practically, the PHA may receive that subsidy retroactively after a lengthy wait, or, depending on timing, lose a portion of the subsidy. *See* HUD Guidance on Funding of New Projects/Units, *available*

Many substantive policy shifts in the HOPE VI Program, which may or may not be imported informally into mixed-finance development more generally, have been implemented by means of requirements found only in notices of funding availability, varying year to year.[187] Informal guidance on eligible and ineligible uses of HOPE VI funds, going beyond the limitations included in HUD regulations, is found in a number of sources, including individual notices of funding availability,[188] HOPE VI budget guidance posted on HUD's web page,[189] PIH notices imposing cost controls and safe harbor standards,[190] HUD's HOPE VI total development cost policy, first published in 2000[191] and subsequently modified by means of an informal "Policy Alert,"[192] and close-out procedures governing HOPE VI revitalization grants revised as of November 2009.[193] As noted above, practitioners often face the challenge of determining which guidance actually applies at any point in time, particularly because some outdated materials remain available on HUD's website even when superseded by later informal guidance.[194]

---

at http://portal.hud.gov/hudportal/documents/huddoc?id=DOC_9667.pdf. Similarly, the 2003 Cost Controls and Safe Harbor Standards set maximum levels for management fees at 6 percent of imputed tax credit rents, though the more recent asset management guidance sets separate (and typically higher) levels for management fees that a PHA may charge to a project, which are themselves cited on the mixed-finance web page. *See* http://portal.hud.gov/hudportal/HUD?src=/program_offices/public_indian_housing/programs/ph/hope6/mfph.

187. *See* 2010 HOPE VI NOFA, *supra* n. 140, §§ III.C.2 and III.C.3.

188. *See, e.g.,* 2010 HOPE VI NOFA, *supra* n. 140, § III.C.1 and III.C.3(v) ("Your projected soft costs must be reasonable and comparable to industry standards. Upon award, soft costs will be subject to HUD's 'Safe Harbor' cost control standards. For rental units, these safe harbors provide specific limitations on such costs as developer's fees (between 9 and 12 percent), PHA administration/consultant cost (no more than 3 to 6 percent of the total project budget), contractor's fee (6 percent), overhead (2 percent), and general conditions (6 percent). HUD's Cost Control and Safe Harbor Standards can be found on HUD's HOPE VI website.").

189. *See* HOPE VI budget guidance at http://portal.hud.gov/hudportal/documents/huddoc?id=DOC_9877.pdf (last accessed Sept. 21 2011).

190. *See* Notice PIH 2008-47, http://portal.hud.gov/hudportal/documents/huddoc?id=DOC_8092.pdf (last accessed Sept. 21, 2011). In the case of home-ownership development, HUD home-ownership cost controls and safe harbor standards "will apply only to home-ownership plans that call for fee-simple sale of newly constructed or rehabilitated units receiving the benefit of public housing funds or public housing land." http://www.hud.gov/offices/pih/programs/ph/hope6/mfph/ho_safeharbor.pdf.

191. HOPE VI TDC Policy, http://portal.hud.gov/hudportal/documents/huddoc?id=DOC_9878.pdf (last accessed Sept. 21, 2011).

192. Policy Alert—Frequently Asked Questions on HUD Total Development Cost (TDC) and Housing Cost Cap (HCC) Limit, published as PIH Notice 2001-22 (1/2/2002), *available at* http://www.hud.gov/offices/pih/programs/ph/hope6/mfph/policy_alerts/tdc-2002.pdf (last accessed Sept. 21, 2011).

193. Close-Out Procedures, HOPE VI Revitalization Grants Revised as of November, 2009, http://portal.hud.gov/hudportal/documents/huddoc?id=DOC_9882.pdf (last accessed Aug. 8, 2011).

194. For example, HUD's Cost Control and Safe Harbor Standards for Rental Mixed-Finance Development Revised April 9, 2003, remain available on the Internet at http://www.hud.gov/offices/pih/programs/ph/hope6/grants/admin/safe_harbor.pdf, despite the later publication of cost control and safe harbor standards in Notice PIH 2008-47, *supra* n. 190.

Other key areas in which significant guidance has been made available informally include capitalization and use of reserves,[195] transactions involving PHA affiliates and instrumentalities,[196] "operating subsidy-only" development (in which a mixed-finance development receives public housing operating subsidy but is developed entirely with non-public housing sources),[197] general guidance and monitoring requirements for demolition grants,[198] applicability of Davis-Bacon Wage Rates,[199] and general guidance on community and resident involvement in HOPE VI.[200] While HUD has indicated that a new, revised *Mixed Finance Guidebook* is "under construction,"[201] it appears that informal guidance is likely to remain an important source of information, at least for the time being.

C. HUD Processing in Mixed-Finance Projects

1. HUD Review Process—Disposition, Mixed-Finance Proposal, and Project Review Panel

The proposed sale or ground lease of property owned by a PHA to a separate legal entity and the proposed demolition of all or any portion of a public housing development trigger both HUD approval requirements under Section 18 of the 1937 Act and the implementing regulations at 24 C.F.R. part 970.[202] A PHA seeking disposition and/or demolition approval must submit a disposition/demolition application to the HUD Special Application Center located in Chicago, Illinois.[203] While gaining such approval is an integral part of the HUD process, the application process is almost entirely separate from the general HUD mixed-finance approval

---

195. *See* Policy Alert—Use of Operating Subsidy for Mixed-Finance Project Reserves, revised Apr. 21, 2004, http://portal.hud.gov/hudportal/documents/huddoc?id=DOC_10119.pdf (last accessed Sept. 21, 2011).

196. *See* PIH Notice 2007-15, Applicability of Public Housing Development Requirements to Transactions Between Public Housing Agencies and Their Related Affiliates and Instrumentalities, June 20, 2007, http://portal.hud.gov/hudportal/documents/huddoc?id=DOC_9278.pdf (last accessed Jan. 12, 2012), as extended by PIH Notice 2011-47, Aug. 17, 2011 (HUD Affiliate Notice).

197. *See* PIH Notice 2004-5, HUD PIH Notice for Mixed-Finance Development of Operating Subsidy-Only Projects, April 9, 2004, http://portal.hud.gov/hudportal/documents/huddoc?id=DOC_10118.pdf.

198. HOPE VI Demolition Grant Monitoring and Management for Field Offices, March 2007, http://portal.hud.gov/hudportal/documents/huddoc?id=DOC_9891.pdf (last accessed Jan. 13, 2012).

199. *See* Policy Alert—Applicability of Davis-Bacon Wage Rates for HOPE VI Homeownership and Rental Development (Sept. 24, 2001), *available at* http://portal.hud.gov/hudportal/HUD?src=/program_offices/public_indian_housing/programs/ph/hope6/mfph/policy_alerts/davis_bacon (Davis-Bacon Policy Alert).

200. General Guidance on Community & Resident Involvement, http://www.nhl.gov/offices/pih/programs/ph/hope6/css/guidance.cfm (last accessed Jan. 13, 2012).

201. *See* HUD, Mixed Finance Public Housing, at http://portal.hud.gov/hudportal/HUD?src=/program_offices/public_indian_housing/programs/ph/hope6/mfph (last accessed Sept. 17, 2011).

202. 42 U.S.C. § 1437p.

203. *Id.*

process. Ideally, a PHA should apply for demolition/disposition approval as early as possible, so as not to risk delays at the time of mixed-finance closing.

As the first step in the *mixed-finance* approval process (as distinct from demolition or disposition approval), the Mixed-Finance Regulations require submission of a "proposal" presenting information as to the participating parties; their proposed activities and their relationship(s) with the PHA;[204] a detailed description of the financing needed for implementation, including a 10-year operating pro forma for the development;[205] a description of the methodology for distribution of public housing operating subsidy;[206] a detailed description of the proposed development, including the split between public housing and non-public housing units;[207] site and neighborhood information;[208] market analysis;[209] development cost estimates and schedule;[210] and information regarding any required displacement and temporary or permanent relocation of residents.[211] Creating the mixed-finance proposal frequently is a collaborative effort by PHAs and their developer partners, with responsibilities allocated based on an agreement negotiated between the parties. In addition, PHAs are required to provide various certifications and assurances regarding PHA legal authority; compliance with federal, state, and local procurement requirements; conflict of interest requirements; previous participation; and all applicable public housing requirements.[212]

In the early days of the HOPE VI program, the "mixed-finance proposal" stage of a transaction was quite onerous, involving a voluminous submission and lengthy review process. In 2003, however, HUD established a streamlined Project Review Panel Protocol (the Mixed-Finance Protocol)[213] that has both standardized and simplified the process considerably. Previously, developers needed to prepare a detailed proposal using only the Mixed-Finance Regulations as guidance for the required content. Under the Mixed-Finance Protocol, basic project information is presented primarily through the completion of prescribed HUD templates in the form, respectively, of a Mixed-Finance Rental Term Sheet and a Mixed-

---

204. 24 C.F.R. § 941.606(a).
205. 24 C.F.R. § 941.606(b); *see also* 24 C.F.R. § 941.606(j) (requiring a demonstration of operating feasibility). If the proposal involves new construction, the PHA must submit information sufficient to comply with § 6(h) of the 1937 Act (42 U.S.C. § 1437d), either demonstrating that the cost of new construction is less than or equal to the cost of acquisition of existing housing (with or without rehabilitation) or certifying that there is insufficient existing housing in the neighborhood to develop public housing through acquisition. 24 C.F.R. § 941.606(m).
206. 24 C.F.R. § 941.606(c).
207. 24 C.F.R. § 941.606(d). An analysis of the adequacy of proposed facilities and a life-cycle analysis are also required. 24 C.F.R. § 941.606(h), 24 C.F.R. § 941.606(k).
208. 24 C.F.R. § 941.606(e).
209. 24 C.F.R. § 941.606(f).
210. 24 C.F.R. § 941.606(g).
211. 24 C.F.R. § 941.606(i).
212. 24 C.F.R. § 941.606(n). To expedite processing, PHAs also may solicit comments from the chief executive of the unit of general local government or his or her designee to satisfy HUD "§ 213 clearance" requirements. *See* 24 C.F.R. § 941.606(l); *see generally* 24 C.F.R. pt. 791, subpt. C.
213. *See* HUD, Project Review Panel Protocol, revised April 9, 2003, at http://www.hud.gov/offices/pih/programs/ph/hope6/mfph/project_review_panel.pdf.

Finance Homeownership Term Sheet (collectively, the Mixed-Finance Term Sheets).[214] While PHAs and developers still must submit additional documentation beyond the Mixed-Finance Term Sheet in order to satisfy Mixed-Finance Regulations requirements,[215] these templates have created a more consistent framework for submitting the proposal.

Practitioners should be aware that HUD frequently introduces new forms and templates to use in mixed-finance submissions, not all of which are prominently displayed on HUD's mixed-finance web page; many of these tools have not been formalized by inclusion in regulations, handbooks, guidebooks, or other formal HUD guidance but nevertheless will be required by HUD as a condition of approval. For example, the Project Expense Level (PEL) Estimator[216] is a tool used to estimate the costs to operate a project, excluding utilities, taxes, and certain add-ons; the PEL ultimately is used in calculating the operating subsidy that a PHA may receive under the Public Housing Operating Fund formula.[217] Other forms and templates include budget formats for both rental and home-ownership projects,[218] a developer fee spreadsheet, and a working family addendum to the Mixed-Finance Term Sheet.[219] As HUD guidelines are always evolving, practitioners are advised to check frequently with HUD grant managers to make sure they understand current submission requirements.

The Mixed-Finance Protocol also has established greater consistency in the HUD review process by creating a single panel of reviewers, consisting of four senior staff from the Office of Public and Indian Housing, who meet regularly to review submissions relating to mixed-finance projects.[220] Initially, the Mixed-Finance Term Sheet and accompanying documentation are reviewed by the HUD Grant Manager (typically, but not always, located at HUD headquarters in Washington) who is assigned to the particular mixed-finance project. When the Grant Manager determines that the submission is complete and internally consistent, he or she is responsible for placing discussion of the Term Sheet on the Review Panel's schedule.

---

214. The Rental Term Sheet is Form HUD 50030 (4/2005) and the Homeownership Term Sheet is Form HUD 50029 (4/2005). Both term sheets, as well as model documents and other materials relating to the mixed-finance program, are available on HUD's website at http://portal.hud.gov/hudportal/HUD?src=/program_offices/public_indian_housing/programs/ph/hope6/mfph, last accessed Sept. 21, 2011. *See also* http://www.hud.gov/offices/pih/programs/ph/hope6/mfph/ho_termsheet.doc and http://www.hud.gov/offices/pih/programs/ph/hope6/mfph/ho_budget.xls and on the HUD forms website.

215. For a detailed description of the additional submissions required, *see* HUD, Mixed Finance Protocol, *supra* n. 213.

216. *See* HUD web page, "Project Expense Levels," at http://portal.hud.gov/hudportal/HUD?src=/program_offices/public_indian_housing/programs/ph/am/pels; for HUD regulations describing how to calculate PEL, *see* 24 C.F.R. § 990.165.

217. *See* 24 C.F.R. § 990.110.

218. *See* HUD web page, "Mixed-Finance Public Housing," at http://portal.hud.gov/hudportal/HUD?src=/program_offices/public_indian_housing/programs/ph/hope6/mfph (last accessed Jan.12, 2012) (Excel spreadsheets "Budgets and Unit Mix" and "Homeownership Budgets and Unit Mix").

219. These forms are available on request from HUD.

220. *See* "Mixed-Finance Public Housing." *supra* n. 218.

The Mixed-Finance Protocol sets out clear time frames for Grant Manager review of PHA submissions,[221] Review Panel consideration,[222] communication of the Review Panel's decision to the PHA,[223] and PHA appeal of an adverse decision.[224] HUD advises PHAs that Mixed-Finance Term Sheets and additional required documentation must be submitted at least 90 days prior to closing. In practice, however, HUD review can take considerably longer, particularly if approval is sought during the summer months, near the end of the calendar year, or near the end of HUD's fiscal year (September 30).

2. Mixed-Finance Evidentiary Review and Funding

Approval of a Mixed-Finance Term Sheet is a critical milestone, but it is by no means the final stage in HUD review. In order to proceed to closing, a PHA (and, if any, its developer partner)[225] must have "Evidentiary Materials" for each phase of a mixed-finance development and submit this information to HUD for its approval. These Evidentiary Materials consist of drafts of the key transaction, organizational and management documents, legal opinions, evidence of title, and other documentation required by HUD, as described on HUD's Mixed-Finance Evidentiary Checklist.[226] This process also has been streamlined considerably since the early mixed-finance projects, as HUD has worked with practitioners to identify the language it deems essential to include in the transaction documents and the business terms it considers to be non-negotiable, as discussed in Section III.D below.[227] Nevertheless, while the

---

221. According to the Mixed-Finance Protocol, the Grant Manager must review the Mixed-Finance Term Sheet and provide comments to the PHA within 14 calendar days from receipt. *Id.* In practice, however, HUD review frequently takes considerably longer.

222. According to the Mixed-Finance Protocol, the Review Panel must meet to discuss the Mixed-Finance Term Sheet within 14 calendar days following a determination by the Grant Manager that the submission is complete. *Id.* This timetable, however, is dependent on the Review Panel's meeting schedule, and in practice it often takes considerably longer to obtain Review Panel consideration of a submission.

223. The Grant Manager must attempt to communicate the Review Panel's decision by telephone within two working days and must document the decision formally in writing via e-mail within seven calendar days of the Review Panel's meeting. *Id.*

224. A PHA choosing to appeal an adverse decision must do so within 14 calendar days following receipt of the letter from the Assistant Secretary of Public and Indian Housing documenting the decision. *Id.* In practice, the PHA and Grant Manager conduct an iterative submission process to resolve confusion, address noncompliance, and otherwise produce an approvable mixed-finance proposal.

225. To assist PHAs in identifying all of the tasks and submissions involved in a mixed-finance development and in allocating responsibility for those tasks between the PHA and its developer partner, HUD has developed a Mixed-Finance Responsibility Checklist at http://portal.hud.gov/hudportal/documents/huddoc?id=DOC_10007.pdf (last accessed Jan. 12, 2012).

226. *See* HUD, HOPE VI Guidance—Mixed-Finance Evidentiary Materials, January 2001, at http://portal.hud.gov/hudportal/documents/huddoc?id=DOC_10113.pdf (last accessed Jan. 13, 2012).

227. The model documents published by HUD (*see supra* n. 182 and accompanying text) contain a number of provisions that low-income housing tax credit investors in particular find objectionable. Over the years since HUD's initial publication of these documents, practitioners active in this field have developed alternative provisions that have proven acceptable to HUD on key areas such as investor transfers requiring HUD approval.

Mixed-Finance Protocol recommends submission of Evidentiary Materials at least 45 days prior to closing,[228] in practice it is advisable to allow a longer time period. In part, delays may be due to a multiparty review process: some documents are reviewed by HUD's Office of General Counsel, and others are reviewed at the local HUD field office, while plans and specifications are subject to a separate architectural review for compliance with Section 504 accessibility requirements. Coordinating review by multiple parties can complicate the review process for HUD and for PHAs and their developer partners.

After HUD approves the Evidentiary Materials, one final stage of review remains before HUD will advance public housing funds for a PHA to carry out a mixed-finance transaction. Following closing with the developer and any third-party funding sources (including equity investors and lenders), HUD's Office of General Counsel (OGC) reviews the executed and recorded transaction documents, executed legal opinions, and final title insurance policy to confirm consistency with the submitted Evidentiary Materials. This final review process typically takes two to three weeks, depending on the time of year and the number of other projects under review concurrently by OGC.

In response to comments by PHAs, developers, and their counsel, HUD issued proposed regulations in 2006 (the Proposed Regulations)[229] presenting an even more streamlined process for review and approval of mixed-finance transactions. Under the Proposed Regulations, PHAs would no longer be required to submit a full package of Evidentiary Materials. Instead, in addition to the Mixed-Finance Term Sheet, a PHA would submit certifications assuring HUD that the PHA has reviewed the closing documents for the transaction and confirmed that they are consistent with public housing requirements, and that all described funding is irrevocably committed.[230] HUD's legal review would be limited to the mixed-finance proposal (including the Mixed-Finance Term Sheet and related submissions), a draft Declaration of Restrictive Covenants,[231] a draft Mixed-Finance Amendment to HUD's Annual Contribution Contract with the PHA,[232] and the required PHA certifications.[233] As of the date of this writing, the proposed rule has yet to be adopted in final form, and HUD continues to require the standard evidentiary package for most closings. As a practical matter, the proposed rule would still require PHAs to gather all required evidentiary documentation and certify to HUD as to compliance with public housing requirements; moreover, in order for PHAs to certify compliance to HUD requirements without risking audit findings of noncompliance, HUD would have to formalize the regulatory "requirements" now contained in informal guidance.[234]

---

228. *See* Mixed-Finance Protocol, *supra* n. 213.
229. HUD, Streamlined Application Process in Public/Private Partnerships for the Mixed-Finance Development of Public Housing Units; Proposed Rule, 71 Fed. Reg. 248, Dec. 27, 2006, *available at* http://edocket.access.gpo.gov/2006/pdf/E6-22165.pdf.
230. *Id.*
231. *See infra* § III.D.2.
232. *See infra* § III.D.3.
233. *See* Proposed Regulations, *supra* n. 229.
234. For a discussion of sub-regulatory guidance, *see supra* pt. III.B.

D. Mixed-Finance Documentation: Key HUD Regulatory Documents

Mixed-finance transactions vary considerably in the type of ownership interest(s) held by private owner entities, the level of control over decision-making exercised by PHAs or their affiliates,[235] financing arrangements, the mix of public housing and non-public housing units, the mix of rental and home-ownership units, and the amount of operating subsidy to be provided by PHAs to development owners. To ensure that mixed-finance developments will comply with applicable public housing requirements, HUD requires several regulatory documents that, collectively, address development, operating, and management requirements of the public housing program.

1. Regulatory and Operating Agreement (Rental Developments)

For all rental developments, the PHA must enter into a Regulatory and Operating Agreement that provides "binding assurances that the operation of the public housing units will be in accordance with all applicable public housing requirements," and sets forth the agreement of the PHA and the owner entity with respect to the provision of public housing operating subsidy to the development.[236] Of all of the documents that HUD scrutinizes as part of the Evidentiary Materials for a project, this one is often the most heavily negotiated.

HUD's model form of Regulatory and Operating Agreement[237] requires the owner of the housing to commit to a specified number of public housing units based on the amount of public housing capital funding for the project,[238] in return for which the PHA commits to provide operating subsidy according to an agreed-upon formula. The parties have considerable flexibility in negotiating the operating subsidy formula. Some PHAs have committed only to pass along some or all of whatever they receive from HUD, while in the past others have agreed to provide somewhat greater assurances as to the availability of operating subsidy to the project (although, with the advent of HUD regulations calling on PHAs to introduce project-based asset management, it seems unlikely that PHAs will do this in the future). In all mixed-finance developments, the project owner must explicitly assume the PHA's obligations to maintain the public housing rental units in accordance with HUD housing quality standards. The project owner also must acknowledge that these units are governed by the legal protections and restrictions generally applicable to public housing, although the developer may be entitled to relief from otherwise applicable public housing restrictions if subsidy is reduced due to reductions in appropriations or changes in law.[239]

---

235. For a discussion of additional HUD requirements applicable to transactions in which a PHA affiliate instrumentality or affiliate materially participates, *see* HUD Affiliate Notice, *supra* n. 196.
236. 24 C.F.R. § 941.610(a)(2)(ii) and (iii).
237. *See* Mixed-Finance Model Documents, *supra* n. 182.
238. 24 C.F.R. § 941.610(a)(8)(ii)(B).
239. 24 C.F.R. § 941.602(a); § 941.610(a)(8)(ii)(B)(iii). For many years, the availability of this "transformation" remedy, authorized by § 35 of the 1937 Act as amended by QHWRA (42 U.S.C. § 1437z-7(h)), was subject to debate in the absence of specific HUD implementing regulations. The PH Capital Program Proposed Rule, if adopted in final form, would govern the implementation of transformation remedies following a change in law or decline in appropriations adversely affecting a mixed-finance development. *See* PH Capital Program Proposed Rule, *supra* n. 104. As of the date of this writing, however, HUD has yet to issue this rule in final form.

2. Declaration of Restrictive Covenants (All Mixed-Finance Projects)

As noted earlier, the Mixed-Finance Regulations require a PHA to assure to HUD's satisfaction that the public housing units will be available for use by eligible low-income families for the maximum period required by law, and that public housing tenants' rights be legally enforceable.[240] In traditional, PHA-owned public housing developments, each PHA entered into a Declaration of Trust in favor of HUD, to evidence and secure the PHA's obligation to comply with all applicable public housing requirements.[241] In the mixed-finance context, where housing is owned by an entity other than a PHA and may contain non-public housing units, this restriction takes the form of a Declaration of Restrictive Covenants (forms are available on HUD's website).[242] This Declaration must take priority over all other liens and property rights[243] and must be executed in the form prescribed by HUD. If the mixed-finance development takes place on a site previously used as public housing, it is likely that the site is already encumbered by a HUD Declaration of Trust. However, because that document contains terms that are inconsistent with the mixed-finance program, HUD will release the prior Declaration of Trust and accept the new Declaration of Restrictive Covenants. Even in the case of units being developed as public housing replacement units, to be sold to income-eligible households, HUD will require that a Declaration of Restrictive Covenants be recorded at closing; HUD will partially release individual for-sale units from this Declaration as they are sold, so long as appropriate restrictions are recorded against the units as part of the sale transaction.[244] Typically, the local HUD field office will review both the new Declaration of Restrictive Covenants in the context of its title and survey review and the proposed release of any prior Declaration of Trust.

3. Mixed-Finance ACC Amendment (Rental) and Mixed-Finance Addendum to Grant Agreement (Home Ownership)

Each PHA developing public housing rental units must enter into an Annual Contributions Contract (ACC) with HUD.[245] Because the basic form of contract contemplates a public housing portfolio owned and operated by the PHA, in a mixed-finance transaction involving public housing rental units, HUD requires that the PHA enter into a Mixed-Finance ACC Amendment, modifying the PHA's ACC with HUD to address property-specific issues.[246] The

---

240. *See* 24 C.F.R. § 941.610(a)(2)(i) and 24 C.F.R. § 941.610(a)(5). HUD has taken the position that it has the right to enforce these rights independent of PHAs or residents.
241. *See* 24 C.F.R. § 941.401(c); Form HUD 52190-A, http://www.hud.gov/offices/pih/programs/ph/phari/struct/hud52190-a.pdf.
242. *See* Mixed-Finance Model Documents, *supra* n. 182; *see also* HUD, HOPE VI Guidance, Mixed-Finance Evidentiary Materials, January 2001, at http://portal.hud.gov/hudportal/documents/huddoc?id=DOC_10113.pdf (Evidentiary Guidance).
243. 24 C.F.R. § 941.610(a)(8)(vii).
244. *See infra* § III.H.
245. *See* 24 C.F.R. § 941.302.
246. *See* 24 C.F.R. § 941.609(c), 24 C.F.R. § 941.610(a)(2)(iv). Note that these regulatory requirements can also be satisfied in part by other transaction documents, particularly a development agreement or ground lease (used if the PHA or an affiliate of the PHA retains ownership of the land and grants only a ground lease interest to the developer or its affiliate).

Mixed-Finance ACC Amendment[247] identifies in detail all project funding, transaction documents, and use restrictions, and specifies the public housing units' proportionate share of project costs, as required by HUD regulations.[248] The basic boilerplate form cannot be modified, but HUD will generally accept some limited changes (in the form of a rider) relating to permitted transfers of ownership interests to facilitate both investment patterns of limited-partner investors and investor replacement of the general partner.[249]

In a mixed-finance home-ownership development, because the housing will not receive annual contributions from HUD, the property will not be subject to an ACC. Accordingly, in lieu of a Mixed-Finance ACC Amendment, HUD will require the execution of a Mixed-Finance Addendum to the Grant Agreement by which HUD makes available capital funds to the PHA for the project.[250] Similar to the Mixed-Finance ACC Amendment, the Mixed-Finance Addendum to Grant Agreement [251] identifies in detail all project funding, transaction documents, and use restrictions, and specifies the proportionate share of project costs attributed to the for-sale units designated as replacement public housing units, as required by HUD regulations.[252]

4. *Evidence of Cooperation Agreement (Rental)*

In the traditional public housing program, PHAs were required to enter into a "co-operation agreement" with the localities in which their housing was located, providing for property tax exemption and local commitment to provide public services to the housing.[253] In mixed-finance transactions, the public housing units often constitute only a portion of the overall property; accordingly, for mixed-finance projects, HUD regulations require a demonstration of property tax exemption as to the public housing units only.[254] As amended by QHWRA, however, Section 35(f) of the 1937 Act permits a PHA to exempt mixed-finance public housing units from otherwise applicable requirements for property tax exemption and (if the development of the units is not inconsistent with the local jurisdiction's comprehensive housing affordability strategy) finding of need and cooperation agreement.[255] In practice, cooperation agreements typically are already in place, and the HUD evidentiary process permits PHAs to satisfy 1937 Act requirements regarding property taxes and cooperation of local authorities by means of a PHA certificate or letter from the City Attorney.[256] However, PHAs seeking support from local officials may find it necessary to subject mixed-finance public housing units to local property taxes, and the HUD process alone may not be sufficient to ensure that the local tax assessor(s) exempt the property from real property and other taxes.

---

247. *See* Mixed-Finance Model Documents, *supra* n. 182.
248. 24 C.F.R. § 610(a)(2)(iv).
249. Interview with C. Hornig, *supra* n. 92.
250. *See* form of Grant Agreement Addendum for Homeownership at HUD web page, Mixed Finance Public Housing, at http://portal.hud.gov/hudportal/HUD?src=/program_offices/public_indian_housing/programs/ph/hope6/mfph.
251. *See* Mixed-Finance Model Documents, *supra* n. 182.
252. 24 C.F.R. § 610(a)(2)(iv).
253. *See supra* n. 39 and accompanying text.
254. 24 C.F.R. § 941.610(a)(v).
255. *See* 1937 Act § 35(f), 42 U.S.C. § 1437z-7.
256. 24 C.F.R. § 941.610(a)(2)(vi).

E. Mixed-Finance Evidentiaries

A detailed list of the documents required as part of a mixed-finance evidentiary submission is set forth in HUD's evidentiary checklist.[257] The following merit particular attention:

1. Opinion of Counsel

HUD regulations require an opinion of counsel that not only addresses authority and enforceability, but also attests that: "counsel has examined the availability of the participating party(ies)'s financing, and the amount and source of financing committed to the proposal by the participating party(ies), and has determined that such financing has been irrevocably committed by the participating party(ies) for use in carrying out the proposal, and that such commitment is in the amount required under the terms of the proposal."[258] While the regulations require that this opinion be rendered by the PHA's counsel,[259] the Mixed-Finance ACC Amendment requires opinion from both PHA counsel and owner's counsel.[260] HUD has posted the required form of opinion on its website, together with other model mixed-finance documents,[261] and has accepted modifications and qualifications deemed necessary by counsel to consider the many caveats and conditions to advances found in loan and equity documents, as well as the changes required to comply with state and local law.[262]

2. Management and Occupancy Documents

As part of the evidentiary submission, HUD will review the form of management agreement,[263] as well as the forms of tenant lease and written grievance procedure[264] and the proposed admissions and occupancy policy[265] to be adopted with respect to the public housing units in the mixed-finance development. The management agreement must acknowledge the PHA's right to require that the project owner terminate the agreement for cause,[266] and must

---

257. http://portal.hud.gov/hudportal/documents/huddoc?id=DOC_10113.pdf.
258. 24 C.F.R. § 941.610(a)(3).
259. *Id.*
260. *See* Mixed-Finance Model Documents, *supra* n. 182.
261. *Id.*
262. Typically, a construction loan agreement will condition advances on satisfaction of a variety of conditions ranging from submission of requisitions and backup documentation to satisfaction of financial covenants and compliance with use restrictions. In some jurisdictions, the existence of conditions to disbursement in the loan documents may be sufficient to cause advances to be treated as "optional" or "voluntary," potentially affecting the priority of such advances over liens arising subsequent to the original closing date but prior to the date on which such "optional" advances are made. *See, e.g.,* J. I. Kislak Mtg. Corp. of Delaware v. William Matthews Builder, Inc., et al., 287 A.2d. 686 (Del. Super. Ct. 1972), *aff'd,* 303 A.2d 648 (1973).
263. 24 C.F.R. § 941.610(a)(2)(v). In practice, HUD often also reviews the management plan. Management and leasing document review typically occurs at the HUD field office.
264. *See* 24 C.F.R. pt. 960 for HUD requirements with respect to public housing leases and grievance procedures.
265. *See* 24 C.F.R. pt. 966 for HUD requirements with respect to public housing admissions and occupancy policies.
266. *See* Mixed-Finance Model Documents, Required Provisions, *supra* n.182, Management Agreement, at 5.

contain a series of additional required provisions posted on HUD's website. HUD will review the agreement to assure that management fees are not excessive, although HUD has approved a fee structure where the percentage of rents received from public housing units is higher than typical percentage fees in the market where the housing is located, in circumstances where the relatively low public housing rents would otherwise generate an unreasonably low fee. Admissions and occupancy policies must be consistent with fair housing requirements applicable to public housing,[267] but may provide for site-based waiting lists so long as tenant selection is performed in a nondiscriminatory manner.[268]

Developers' counsel would be well advised to familiarize themselves with public housing leasing and grievance procedure requirements as early as possible in a transaction, including, *inter alia,* provisions dictating specific lease provisions that may (and may not) be included in a public housing unit lease,[269] prohibiting termination of tenancy other than for serious or repeated violation of material lease terms,[270] requiring that tenants receive written notice of any adverse action (including not only for eviction, but also for fines and penalties),[271] and obligating the owner of a public housing unit to hold a formal grievance hearing, pursuant to a written grievance procedure, before taking adverse action against a tenant.[272]

3. Organizational and Financing Documents

While HUD is not generally interested in all the terms and conditions of an owner entity's organizational and financing documents, the mixed-finance regulations require HUD to review these documents "to ensure that they do not provide equity investors, creditors, and any other parties, with rights that would be inconsistent with, or that could interfere with, HUD's interest in the proposed development."[273] HUD reviewers typically also require the partnership agreement provisions provided in the model documents to be included almost verbatim.[274]

4. Site Control and Zoning

The mixed-finance regulations also require a PHA and its development partner, when seeking HUD approval, to demonstrate site control[275] as well as evidence of zoning compliance.[276] Site

---

267. *See* 24 C.F.R. § 960.103. These include, inter alia, the Federal Fair Housing Act, Title VIII of the Civil Rights Act of 1968, as amended, 42 U.S.C. § 3601 *et seq.*, Title VI of the Federal Civil Rights Act of 1964, 42 U.S.C. § 200d–200d-7, and § 504 of the Rehabilitation Act of 1973, 29 U.S.C. § 794. A comprehensive list of applicable equal opportunity and non-discrimination requirements appears at 24 C.F.R. § 5.105(a).
268. *See* 24 C.F.R. § 960.206.
269. *See* 24 C.F.R. §§ 966.1, 966.4, and 966.6.
270. 24 C.F.R. § 966.4(l)(2).
271. 24 C.F.R. § 966.4(d)(8)(i).
272. *See* 24 C.F.R. pt. 966, subpt. B.
273. 24 C.F.R. § 941.610(a)(4).
274. *See* Model Form Limited Partnership [Owner] Provisions, http://portal.hud.gov/hudportal/HUD?src=/program_offices/public_indian_housing/programs/ph/hope6/mfph/mf_modeldocs.
275. 24 C.F.R. § 941.610(a)(6).
276. 24 C.F.R. § 941.610(a)(7). Although the regulations permit a PHA to satisfy this requirement by demonstrating that any needed zoning relief is likely and will not delay construction, in practice HUD seeks to ascertain that a project already has all the zoning relief required to proceed with construction.

control typically takes the form of either a fee conveyance or long-term ground lease. While HUD has posted on its website a model form of ground lease,[277] in practice PHAs and developers may use whatever form they choose, so long as the ground lease clearly states that the provisions of the ACC (as modified by the Mixed-Finance ACC Amendment) and Regulatory and Operating provisions requiring rebuilding in the event of a casualty or condemnation will control, and that any mortgagee's rights shall remain subject to the Declaration of Restrictive Covenants and the Regulatory and Operating Agreement.

5. PHA Certifications

As part of the final evidentiary submission for a mixed-finance rental development, PHAs must certify that public housing use restrictions will last for at least a 40-year period (which may be extended for 10 years after the end of the period in which the public housing units receive operating subsidy from the PHA, or as may be otherwise required by law).[278] To satisfy the proportionality requirement, PHAs must also certify that the number of public housing units remains the same as in the previously submitted proposal. If public housing funding will be paying a disproportionate share of common area costs, the PHA must further certify that the common areas will benefit all residents, including the public housing residents. Finally, if the public housing units are "floating"—that is, if the units that are designated as public housing units may change over time—PHA must certify that the public housing units will continually represent a fixed percentage of the total number of units and that the number of bedrooms in the public housing units will continually represent a fixed percentage of the total number of bedrooms in the rental units in the development.[279]

F. Cross-Cutting Legal Requirements

Mixed-finance public housing development is subject to numerous additional federal requirements. These include[280] labor standards under the Davis-Bacon Act;[281] environmental review under the National Environmental Policy Act;[282] Buy American requirements imposed on

---

277. *See* Mixed-Finance Model Documents, *supra* n. 182.
278. 24 C.F.R. § 941.610(a)(8)(i)(B).
279. 24 C.F.R. § 941.610(a)(8)(ii)(B).
280. A more comprehensive discussion of cross-cutting legal requirements is found in Chapter 13.
281. Davis-Bacon Act of 1931, Pub. L. 71-798, 46 Stat. 1494, March 3, 1931. For applicability to HOPE VI home ownership and rental development, *see* Davis-Bacon Policy Alert, *supra* n.199.
282. National Environmental Policy Act of 1969, Pub. L. 91-190, 42 U.S.C. § 4321-4347, Jan. 1, 1970, as amended (NEPA); for implementing regulations, *see* 24 C.F.R. pt. 58. One issue that often perplexes developers is the NEPA prohibition against engaging in "choice-limiting activities" pending completion of the environmental review mandated by NEPA. In various contexts, HUD has determined that property acquisition and the execution of a binding purchase agreement constitute "choice-limiting activities" prohibited prior to NEPA clearance. *See, e.g.,* HUD, OFFICE OF BLOCK GRANT ASSISTANCE, BASICALLY CDBG (November 2007) at 15-3, § 15.1.4 (Actions Triggering Environmental Review and Limitations Pending Clearance), *available at* http://portal.hud.gov/hudportal/documents/huddoc?id=cdbgchapter15.pdf.

funds appropriated by the American Recovery and Reinvestment Act of 2009;[283] Executive Orders promoting utilization of businesses owned by minorities, women, and "disadvantaged" persons;[284] Section 3 of the Housing and Development Act of 1968 (requiring that economic opportunities generated by construction activity be made available, to the maximum extent feasible, to low-income community residents and businesses;[285] and the Uniform Relocation Assistance and Real Property Acquisition Policies Act of 1970 (URA) (pre-QHWRA projects only).[286] These cross-cutting requirements are detailed in Chapter 13 of this book.

Generally, so long as a PHA procures its developer partner in compliance with HUD procurement requirements at 24 C.F.R. Part 85 (Part 85),[287] the developer and owner entity are not subject to Part 85 requirements in their selection of team members such as the architect and contractor. However, the owner entity will be required to comply with Part 85 if HUD determines that the PHA or a PHA instrumentality exercises significant functions within the owner entity with respect to managing the development of the proposed units.[288] Subsidy

---

283. *See* American Recovery and Reinvestment Act of 2009, Pub. L. 111-5, § 1605.

284. *See* Exec. Order 11,625 of Oct. 13, 1971; Exec. Order 13,157 of May 23, 2000. In the wake of lawsuits calling into question the constitutionality of race-based preferences, the Dept. of Commerce has issued regulations expanding eligibility for MBDA assistance to businesses owned by "socially or economically disadvantaged persons." *See* 15 C.F.R. pt. 1400.

285. 12 U.S.C. § 1701u; 42 U.S.C. § 3535(d); *see also* 24 C.F.R. pt. 135.

286. *See* Uniform Relocation Assistance and Real Property Acquisition Policies Act of 1970, Pub. L. 91-646, codified at 42 U.S.C. § Chapter 61, implementing regulations at 49 C.F.R. pt. 24, and HUD HANDBOOK 1378 (providing guidance on the URA and accompanying regulations in HUD programs). For the applicability of the URA in mixed-finance projects, *see* 24 C.F.R. §§ 941.602, 941.208, and CPD Notice 02-08, "Guidance on the Application of the Uniform Relocation Assistance and Real Property Acquisition Policies Act of 1970 (URA), as Amended, in HOPE VI Projects," as modified by CPD 04-02, "Revision to Guidance on the Application of the Uniform Relocation Assistance and Real Property Acquisition Policies Act of 1970 (URA), as Amended, in HOPE VI Projects," http://portal.hud.gov/hudportal/documents/huddoc?id=DOC_11808.pdf, as modified by http://portal.hud.gov/hudportal/documents/huddoc?id=DOC_11807.pdf. HOPE VI projects approved for disposition after the enactment of QHWRA (Oct. 21 1998) pursuant to a revitalization plan are not subject to the URA; instead, such projects are subject to tenant relocation protections found in § 18 of the 1937 Act, 42 U.S.C. § 1437p. In projects where the URA does apply, the requirement to give tenant notices is triggered by "initiation of negotiations" for acquisition of the property. *See* 49 C.F.R. § 24.2. According to CPD Notice 04-02, *supra*, the initial "Initiation of Negotiations" date is the date HUD approves the PHA's "revitalization plan" embodied in its Proposal; however, "When PIH determines that there are circumstances under which a planned HOPE VI project is either so large, or is located in a community with such limited housing resources to absorb large numbers of residents who will be displaced by the project, that a single ION would be impracticable and/or detrimental to the smooth relocation of residents, demolition of the existing units, and reconstruction of the project, PIH may approve multiple ION dates based on phased demolition as proposed by a PHA in its Revitalization Plan."

287. *See* 24 C.F.R. pt. 85. The PHA may follow qualifications-based procurement practices, rather than basing its decision primarily on cost, so long as its procurement of the developer partner is subject to negotiation of fair and reasonable compensation and applicable cost limitations. *See* 24 C.F.R. § 941.603(d)(1), 24 C.F.R. § 85.36(d)(3)(v).

288. HUD may, on a case-by-case basis, exempt such an owner entity from the need to comply with 24 C.F.R. pt. 85 if it determines that the owner entity has developed an acceptable alternative procurement plan. 24 C.F.R. § 941.603(d)(2). *See also* Financing Transactions and 24 C.F.R. Part 85

layering analysis must be carried out by HUD after its review of the mixed-finance proposal and evidentiary material submissions, and before funding.[289] In addition to complying with cross-cutting requirements applicable to the public housing program, PHAs and developers carrying out mixed-finance projects need to consider carefully whether issues may arise from the combination of public housing with the other public and private sources of financing, such as the HOME and LIHTC programs.[290]

G. Public Housing Authorities as Principals of Mixed-Finance Owners

HUD has encouraged PHAs to explore innovative approaches to mixed-finance development, including the use of "affiliates" or "instrumentalities" as owner entities (or partners, members, or managers of owner entities) to provide stronger PHA control over public housing assets.[291] Practitioners should be aware, however, that use of instrumentalities (as carefully distinguished from affiliates in PIH Notice 2007-15) may trigger requirements that would not otherwise apply to a mixed-finance developer, including those relating to cost allocation and/or fee limitations, accounting and reporting, and conflict of interest and procurement rules.[292]

Under PIH Notice 2007-15, an "instrumentality" is defined as "an entity related to the PHA whose assets, operations, and management are legally and effectively controlled by the PHA, through which PHA functions or policies are implemented and that utilize public housing funds or public housing assets for the purpose of carrying out public housing development functions of the PHA." A PHA "affiliate" or "affiliated entity" is defined as "an entity, other than an instrumentality, formed by the PHA under state law in which a PHA has a financial or ownership interest or participates in their governance. The PHA as an institution has some measure of control over the assets, operations, or management of the Affiliate, but such control does not rise to the level of control to qualify the entity as an Instrumentality."[293] The distinction between an instrumentality and an affiliate, therefore, in many cases is a matter of degree, depending on two factors: the degree of control exercised by the PHA over the entity's assets, operations, and management; and the extent to which the entity uses PHA funds or assets to carry out "functions of the PHA."[294]

If a PHA holds title to a mixed-finance property through a division within its existing governing structure, not surprisingly, such division will be assumed to be an "instrumentality" of the PHA, subject to all legal requirements that would ordinarily apply to the PHA.

---

and 2 C.F.R. Part 225, Capital Fund Finance, Operating Fund Finance and Mixed Finance Programs, *available on* HUD's website at http://portal.hud.gov/hudportal/HUD?src=/program_offices/public_indian_housing/programs/ph/capfund/fintrns Note that HUD has determined that a financial transaction in which a PHA is seeking financing from lenders, syndicators, or other parties is *not* subject to Part 85. *Id.*

289. *See* 24 C.F.R. § 941.611(b).
290. For example, these three programs have different approaches to the issues of "over-income tenants." *See generally* HUD, *Mixed-Income Housing and the Home Program* (2003), *available at* http://www.hud.gov/offices/cpd/affordablehousing/library/modelguides/2004/200315.pdf, at 23.
291. *See* HUD Affiliate Notice, *supra* n. 196, at 3.
292. *Id.*; *see also* 24 C.F.R. pt. 85.
293. HUD Affiliate Notice, *supra* n. 196.
294. *Id.*

When a separate legal entity is created to own, develop, and operate the property, indicia of control include the extent of direction or management by PHA directors and/or staff, PHA rights to appoint directors (both initially and on turnover), or provisions in the organization's governing documents that require return of assets to the PHA in the event of a change in the organization's controlling interest.[295] Generally, to avoid "instrumentality" status, a PHA should refrain from establishing a system of governance for an owner equity that allows the PHA to effectively control that equity's decision-making. For example, while it would be acceptable to have some PHA representation on the owner's board or staff, having a majority of board or officer positions filled by PHA staff (or individuals appointed by the PHA) may rise to the level of control, triggering "instrumentality" status.

While both instrumentalities and affiliates are subject to a variety of public housing requirements, instrumentalities are viewed as an extension of the PHA itself and therefore are subject to a broader range of legal requirements than affiliates. For example, while both are subject to certain conflict of interest requirements under 24 C.F.R. Part 85, the requirements applicable to an instrumentality are more stringent.[296] In addition, when procuring third-party contractors to provide goods or services to the project, an instrumentality is subject to federal procurement requirements under 24 C.F.R. §85.36 that do not apply to unrelated private developers or to PHA affiliates.[297] On the other hand, a PHA is not required to follow Part 85 procurement requirements when selecting an instrumentality to carry out a project, but must do so when procuring an affiliate for that purpose.[298]

If the owner entity is a limited partnership or limited liability company having a PHA-sponsored entity as its general partner or managing member, the nature of the general partner or managing member will determine whether the owner entity is subject to federal procurement requirements. For example, if either the PHA or a PHA instrumentality serves as general partner, then the partnership will be subject to federal procurement requirements; if a PHA affiliate selected by the PHA through a competitive procurement process serves as general partner, federal procurement requirements will not apply to the partnership's procurement of goods and services.[299]

Whether serving as developer, general partner or manager itself, or utilizing an affiliate or instrumentality to carry out development activities, a PHA must bear in mind that public housing funds may be used only for mixed finance development of properties containing at least some public housing units (including home-ownership units developed with public housing funds prior to transfer of title to a homeowner).[300] Similarly, public housing funds may be used to cover costs associated with the creation of an affiliate or instrumentality for the purpose of carrying out a development project, or costs associated with the preparation and submission of an application for low income housing tax credits, only if the project will include some public housing units.[301]

---

295. *Id.* at 5.
296. *Id.* at 9.
297. *Id.* at 11.
298. *Id.* at 12.
299. *Id.* at 13.
300. *Id.* at 4–5, 17.
301. *Id.*

H. Mixed-Finance Home-Ownership Development

While early HOPE VI projects did include some home-ownership units, the legal authority to do so was murky, as the 1937 Act did not generally permit public housing capital funds to be used for home-ownership development. For HOPE VI Grants from FY 1993 through FY 1999, HUD permitted developers to carry out a "middle-income" home-ownership program based loosely on the Nehemiah Housing Opportunity Grants Program (NHOP) established by Title VI of the Housing and Community Development Act of 1987,[302] later repealed by Section 289(b) of the Cranston-Gonzalez National Affordable Housing Act.[303] QHWRA, in amending the 1937 Act, explicitly authorized HUD to utilize public housing capital funds for "appropriate homeownership replacement activities" using authority under Sections 24 and 9 of USHA, and it is this authority that forms the basis for most mixed-finance home-ownership development today.[304] Under the so-called "24/9" mixed-finance home-ownership program (available only for FY 2000 or later grants), public housing funds may be used to finance new construction or rehabilitation of the housing units sold to purchasers with incomes at or below 80 percent of area median (the limit for public housing eligibility)[305] and/or to provide direct financing to eligible purchasers in the form of down payment assistance or "soft" subordinate mortgage loans.[306] Where development costs are so high as to make it infeasible to sell units to income-eligible purchasers at an affordable price, repayment of public housing funds may be forgiven or deferred, effectively "writing down" the cost of construction by allowing units to be sold at a price lower than their actual development cost.[307]

If a PHA plans to use public housing funds for a construction write-down, HUD requires the PHA to establish a shared appreciation policy that will determine whether any portion of the write-down will be recaptured upon resale. PHAs have great flexibility, however, as HUD permits policies ranging from zero recapture to gradual forgiveness, based on the length of

---

302. Housing and Community Development Act of 1987, Pub. L.100-242, codified at 12 U.S.C. § 1715l. While the FY 1993 Appropriations Act authorized home-ownership development that met NHOP requirements, in reviewing these "middle income" mixed-finance home-ownership projects, HUD required that they be "Nehemiah-like," with minimum down payment requirements and maximum income limits loosely based on NHOP requirements; for example, while NHOP required a minimum down payment equal to 10 percent of the cost of the home, this reduced the minimum down payment to 5 percent in middle-income projects. *See* Some Homeownership Guidelines for Public Housing Authorities, http://portal.hud.gov/hudportal/HUD?src=/program_offices/public_indian_housing/programs/ph/hope6/mfph (PH Homeownership Guidelines).

303. Cranston-Gonzalez National Affordable Housing Act, Pub. L. 101-625, 104 Stat. 4079 (Nov. 28, 1990), codified at 42 U.S.C. § 12839. For more information on NHOP, *see* regulations governing existing NHOP grants at 24 C.F.R. pt. 280.

304. *See* PH Homeownership Guidelines, *supra* n. 302.

305. QHWRA, § 535(a) (amending § 24 of the 1937 Act), 42 U.S.C. § 1437v(d)(1)(J). Eligible costs also include "related" costs such as demolition, environmental remediation, site improvements, homeowner counseling, relocation, marketing, and administrative and legal costs, and purchasers must also meet other eligibility requirements. *See* PH Homeownership Guidelines, *supra* n. 302, at 5–6.

306. *Id.*

307. *Id.*

time the initial purchaser owns the home, to recapture of 100 percent of the amount of the construction write-down.[308] Similarly, HUD requires PHAs to establish a policy regarding repayment of direct assistance to homebuyers, such as down-payment assistance or "soft" subordinate mortgage loans, but has accepted policies ranging from total debt forgiveness to 100 percent repayment obligations.[309]

The 24/9 program also permits grant proceeds to be used to assist acquisition of existing units not owned by the PHA.[310] To be eligible to purchase a home assisted under the 24/9 program, a homebuyer must not have owned a home within the prior 18 months, and must have income no greater than 80 percent of area median income at the time the contract to purchase is executed.[311] Homebuyers must make a minimum down payment using their own resources (as opposed to gifts from family members or down payment assistance) in an amount at least equal to the greater of 1 percent of the purchase price or $500.[312]

Regardless of whether units are developed under the "middle income" program (for pre-FY2000 grants only) or the "24/9 program" (for FY 2000 and subsequent grants), certain HUD requirements will apply to all public housing home-ownership developments. All purchasers must commit to occupying their units as their principal residence, and no home-ownership units may be leased or subleased, even if the inability to lease their unit would cause a hardship for the homebuyer.[313] If the PHA operates a Section 8(y) home-ownership program (under which Section 8 rental voucher payments may be used to subsidize the homebuyer's first mortgage loan payment), this program may be used to assist the purchaser of a public housing home-ownership unit.[314] Development under the 24/9 program is also subject to Davis-Bacon prevailing wage requirements.[315]

If the PHA owns the site during construction or rehabilitation, additional requirements apply under Section 32 of the 1937 Act and implementing regulations at 24 CFR 906,[316] which allow PHAs to sell existing public housing units or units acquired by the PHA for

---

308. *See* PH Homeownership Guidelines, *supra* n. 302, at 5, 13.
309. *See id.* at 5, 7. Note that amounts received by a PHA through recapture of proceeds on resale or recapture of appreciation will constitute program income. 24 C.F.R. § 906.5.
310. HUD defines "substantial rehabilitation" as rehabilitation involving costs equal to or greater than 60% of the maximum sales price. *See* PH Homeownership Guidelines, *supra* n. 302, at 21.
311. *See* PH Homeownership Guidelines, *supra* n.302, at 5.
312. *Id.* A PHA may impose a greater down payment requirement and may provide public housing capital or HOPE VI funding in the form of a loan or grant to help meet the greater requirement. *Id.* In contrast, under the "middle income" home-ownership program, HUD requires a minimum down payment at least equal to 5% of purchase price, of which at least 1% of the purchase price must be paid from homeowner's own funds, unless the homebuyer's first mortgage loan is originated or held by a state or local government agency under a program permitting a lower down payment; the balance of the minimum 5% down payment may come from other sources, including HOPE VI funds.
313. *Id.*
314. *Id.*
315. Davis-Bacon Policy Alert, *supra* n. 199. Such requirements did not apply to development under the "middle-income" program for home ownership using FY 1999 and earlier grants. *See* PH Homeownership Guidelines at __.
316. 42 U.S.C. § 1437z4; 24 C.F.R. § 906.

resale to public housing tenants or to enter into lease-purchase arrangements for existing public housing units.[317] If HUD deems a property to be subject to Section 32 of the 1937 Act, the PHA must incorporate its plans for sale of units in its PHA agency plan and must obtain HUD approval of a Section 32 home-ownership program[318] providing for sale of units either directly to public housing-eligible households or to a "purchase and resale entity" for resale within five years.[319] Purchasers must meet public housing income eligibility limits, utilize the home as their principal residence, demonstrate financial capacity based on income/cost ratios and the ability to pay a minimum down payment, and meet other eligibility requirements established by the PHA.[320] Section 32 home-ownership development and sale are managed by the Special Applications Center and are not treated as mixed-finance transactions.[321]

IV. FINANCIAL AND OPERATIONAL ISSUES FOR MIXED-FINANCE PROJECTS

A. Financial Impact of Public Housing Program Limitations

1. Tenant[322]-Paid Rent and Utility Allowances

Since the enactment of the Brooke Amendment in 1969, the maximum amount that a PHA may charge public housing residents for rent, including an allowance for utility costs[323] (collectively, the total tenant payment), has been limited to a percentage of household income.[324] Since 1981,[325] the total tenant payment has been capped at the highest of (A) 30 percent of monthly adjusted income, (B) 10 percent of monthly gross income, or (C) the portion, if any,

---

317. *See generally* HUD regulations implementing § 32 of the 1937 Act at 24 C.F.R. pt. 906.

318. However, HUD disposition requirements generally applicable under § 18 of the 1937 Act (42 U.S.C. § 1437p) do not apply to sale of home-ownership units under a HUD-approved home-ownership plan. *See* 24 C.F.R. § 906.35.

319. *See* 42 U.S.C. § 1437z4(c); 24 C.F.R. §§ 906.1, 906.11.

320. *See* 42 U.S.C. § 1437z4(c)(3); 24 C.F.R. § 906.15. For more information regarding § 32 home-ownership programs, *see* HUD, *Guidance for PHAs Developing a Section 32 Homeownership Plan*, at http://www.hud.gov/offices/pih/centers/sac/homeownership/§32deskguide.pdf.

321. *See* http://portal.hud.gov/hudportal/HUD?src=/program_offices/public_indian_housing/centers/sac/homeownership

322. The limitations on total tenant payments described in this section apply only to tenants who are citizens or legal permanent residents. A "mixed family"—i.e., a family having at least one household member who is a citizen or legal permanent resident—may be eligible for prorated assistance. *See* 24 C.F.R. pt. 5, subpt. E.

323. While the 1937 Act refers only to rent, even before enactment of the Brooke Amendment, HUD had consistently interpreted "rent" to include "a reasonable amount for the use of utilities," an interpretation upheld by the U.S. Supreme Court in 1987. *See* Wright v. City of Roanoke Redevelopment and Housing Auth., 479 U.S. 418, 107 S. Ct. 766, 93 L. Ed. 2d 781, 55 U.S.L.W. 4119 (1987).

324. *See supra* n.58 and accompanying text.

325. *See* Housing and Community Development Amendments Act of 1981, which increased the maximum percentage of adjusted income from 25% to 30%.

of the family's public assistance payments designated for housing costs.[326] In addition, since the enactment of QHWRA, if the earned income of a family increases because of either participation in job training or self-sufficiency programs or increases in earnings of a family member previously unemployed for a year or more or reliant on welfare, the incremental increase in earnings must be disregarded entirely for a period of one year, and half of the incremental increase must be disregarded for an additional year, in calculating the total tenant payment.[327]

The 1937 Act also now requires each PHA to offer each tenant household annually the choice between paying income-based rent or a PHA-established "flat rent" based on the market charges for comparable housing in the private unassisted rental market,[328] and must allow any family who had previously chosen to pay a flat rent to switch to an income-based rent if the family can demonstrate financial hardship.[329] While PHAs are required by statute to establish a minimum rent of up to $50,[330] because PHAs may elect to set the minimum rent at $0[331] and must offer a household relief from the minimum rent upon demonstration of financial hardship,[332] in practice the minimum rent requirement has had relatively little impact on public housing rent collections. On February 13, 2012, President Obama issued a budget proposal for fiscal year 2013 that would, if adopted, require an increase in the minimum rent to $75 across the board for all households receiving assistance under the public housing and Section 8 programs (subject to a hardship exemption);[333] as of the date of this writing, it remains to be seen whether this increase will be implemented.

The income-based rent payable by a tenant household to the owner of a public housing development (whether that owner is a PHA or a mixed-finance owner entity) equals the total tenant payment less an allowance for any utilities that are not included in the rent, calculated

---

326. See 42 U.S.C. § 1437a(a)(1). Adjusted income is calculated by deducting from monthly gross income a series of mandatory exclusions as well as certain permitted exclusions established in the discretion of the PHA. Mandatory exclusions include a $400 exclusion for elderly or disabled families, certain unreimbursed medical expenses in excess of 3% of household income, reasonable child-care expenses necessary for the head of household to pursue education or employment, child support payments of up to $480 per child (to the extent approved in appropriations acts), certain spousal support expenditures, and earned income of minor other than the head of household or his or her spouse. See 42 U.S.C. § 1437a(b)(5)(A). Permissive exclusions may include excessive travel expenses associated with education or employment, earned income (over and above the earned income disregard described below), and other exclusions at the discretion of the PHA. See 42 U.S.C. § 1437a(b)(5)(B); see also 24 C.F.R. pt. 5 for detailed instructions on how to calculate annual income, adjusted income, and total tenant payment.
327. See 42 U.S.C. § 1437a(d); see also 24 C.F.R. § 5.628 and discussion *supra* n.111 and accompanying text.
328. See 42 U.S.C. § 1437a(a)(2)(B)(i); 24 C.F.R. § 960.253(d).
329. See 42 U.S.C. § 1437a(a)(2)(C); 24 C.F.R. § 960.253(f).
330. See 42 U.S.C. § 1437a(a)(3)(A).
331. See 42 U.S.C. § 1437a(a)(3)(B).
332. See 24 C.F.R. § 5.630.
333. See Budget of the U.S. Gov't, Fiscal Year 2013, Department of Housing and Urban Dev., *available at* http://www.whitehouse.gov/sites/default/files/omb/budget/fy2013/assets/housing.pdf, last accessed Feb. 17, 2012.

by the PHA in accordance with HUD regulations.[334] If utilities are separately metered, the tenant is responsible for payment of the amounts owed to the utility companies based on actual utility usage; if the PHA furnishes utilities as part of the rent, but provides meters to measure individual usage, the tenant will be responsible for payment of a surcharge for excess usage of utility costs.[335] If the income-based total tenant payment is less than the utility allowance, then the PHA (or mixed-finance owner) must pay the difference to the tenant in the form of a utility reimbursement (sometimes referred to as "negative rent").[336]

2. Operating Subsidy and Calculation of Project Expense Level and Utility Expense Level

In addition to tenant-paid rent, PHAs receive an operating subsidy from HUD[337] in an amount intended to equal the difference between the actual cost of operating public housing and the amount the PHA is entitled to collect from its residents in the form of tenant-paid rent.[338] Under HUD regulations, a PHA's "formula expense"—the estimate of its operating expenses—is equal to the sum of three components: the Project Expense Level (PEL), the Utility Expense Level (UEL), and other formula expenses (add-ons).[339] PEL and UEL are expressed in terms of per-unit per-month (PUM) costs, multiplied by the number of units eligible to receive subsidy.[340] The PEL is intended to cover basic costs of operation exclusive of utilities and permitted add-ons.[341] Under the Operating Fund Rule, HUD calculates the PEL for each PHA using regression analysis and benchmarking for actual costs of FHA projects, taking into account a series of variables including project size and age, building type and location, bedroom mix and occupancy type (family or senior), location (geographic and neighborhood type), poverty rates and the percentage of households assisted.[342] Calculation of the UEL takes into account consumption levels for each utility and applicable local utility rates; PHAs are entitled to retain 75 percent of decreases in consumption, providing an incentive for

---

334. *See* 24 C.F.R. pt. 965, subpt. E. If a household opts to pay a flat rent, however, the household will pay the full amount of the flat rent without any allowance for utilities. *See* 24 C.F.R. § 960.253(d).

335. A PHA may also impose a surcharge if a tenant is operating major tenant-owned appliances or "optional functions of PHA-furnished equipment," based on published schedules of estimated excess consumption. *See* 24 C.F.R. § 965.506.

336. *See* 24 C.F.R. § 5.632. A PHA may elect to pay the utility reimbursement directly to the utility on behalf of the tenant. *See* 24 C.F.R. § 5.632(b)(2).

337. *See generally* 24 C.F.R. pt. 990.

338. *See* 24 C.F.R. § 990.110.

339. *Id.* Permitted "add-ons" include program coordination costs for family self-sufficiency programs, principal and interest costs incurred in connection with energy conservation measures, payments in lieu of taxes, the cost of independent audits, $25 per occupied unit per year for resident participation activities, limited asset management and information technology fees, limited asset repositioning fees for units being removed from a PHA's inventory, and, at HUD's discretion, costs attributable to changes in federal law, regulation, or the economy. *See* 24 C.F.R. § 990.190.

340. *See* 24 C.F.R. § 990.110.

341. *See* 24 C.F.R. § 990.165.

342. *Id.*

PHAs to achieve energy savings through energy conservation measures.[343] Both PEL and UEL are adjusted by a HUD inflation factor.[344]

The final Operating Fund Rule issued by HUD in 2005 incorporated the findings of a congressionally funded study by the Harvard University Graduate School of Design on the cost of operating well-run public housing.[345] This study has come under attack by public housing authorities for arbitrarily reducing the benchmarks for public housing, failing to take into account the impact of public housing regulations and the unique operating environment of public housing, and omitting asset management fees adequate to cover PHA administrative costs.[346] In mixed-finance development, moreover, the inclusion of market-rate units may require owners to maintain a higher standard of maintenance and property management than might be required to satisfy HUD inspection. While owners controlled by private entities often seek additional subsidy over and above the sum of PEL and UEL to cover these increased costs, PHAs have a vested interest in limiting payment of excess operating subsidy to mixed-finance owners, thereby preserving the subsidy needed to support the remainder of their portfolio and cover their administrative costs. Consequently, many owners provide an internal cross-subsidy from LIHTC-only or market-rate units if actual per-unit cost exceeds the sum of PEL, UEL, and any permitted add-ons.

3. Commencement of Operating Subsidy

For several years after the commencement of the mixed-finance program, in order for newly constructed or substantially rehabilitated public housing to begin to receive operating subsidy, a project was required to demonstrate both that at least 95 percent of the units were ready for occupancy, as evidenced by certificates of occupancy (the Date of Full Availability, or DOFA), and that there was 95 percent occupancy following the expiration of the last day of the calendar quarter after the quarter in which DOFA occurred (the End of Initial Operating Period, or EIOP).[347] While the concepts of DOFA and EIOP remain relevant to the calculation of future eligibility for capital funds,[348] a public housing unit is now eligible to receive operating subsidy on the date it is both placed in service and occupied.[349]

---

343. *See* 24 C.F.R. §§ 990.170, 990.175, 990.180, and 990.185. Consumption calculations take into account variations in consumption over time by comparing current consumption levels (for the 12-month period ending on the June 30th that is six months prior to the first day of the applicable funding period) to a "rolling base" for the 36-month period ending on the June 30th that is 18 months prior to the first day of the applicable funding period. *Id.*

344. *See* 24 C.F.R. §§ 990.165, 990.170.

345. *See* HUD, Revisions to the Public Housing Operating Fund Program; Final Rule, Sept. 19, 2005, 79 Fed. Reg. 54,984, No. 180; Harvard Univ. Graduate School of Design, *Public Housing Operating Cost Study: Final Report*, June 6, 2003, *available at* http://www.hud.gov/offices/pih/programs/ph/am/docs/harvcs-finrptnoapp.pdf.

346. *See, e.g.,* Public Housing Auth. Directors' Ass'n, *PHADA Grades Harvard's Study*, http://www.phada.org/pdf/1813hcs.pdf.

347. *See* Policy Alert—Administration of DOFA/EIOP for Mixed-Finance Developments, Sept. 24, 2001, http://portal.hud.gov/hudportal/HUD?src=/program_offices/public_indian_housing/programs/ph/hope6/mfph/policy_alerts/dofa_eiop, last accessed Aug. 2, 2011. This Policy Alert was superseded by the adoption of the current operating fund rule, 24 C.F.R. pt. 990.

348. *See* 24 C.F.R. § 905.10.

349. *See* 24 C.F.R. § 990.120.

Depending on the period between initial lease-up and submission of annual reporting to HUD, however, there may still be an extensive delay in HUD funding of project operating subsidy—in some cases, as much as 17 months.[350] This hold-up may surprise developers (and their funders), who may well expect that operating funds will begin to flow as soon as the housing is occupied, particularly if they are counting on operating subsidy to achieve break-even operations (in many cases, a condition to the release of equity contributions and/or permanent loan closing). To avoid deficit operations, developers need to include enough funds in their development budgets to cover anticipated operating costs (less anticipated tenant-paid rent) for an extended period after the expected lease-up date.

B. Using Public Housing Capital to Collateralize Bonds

Section 35(b)(1) of the 1937 Act, as amended by QHWRA,[351] provides statutory authorization for a PHA to provide public housing capital funds to a mixed-finance project in the form of collateral or credit enhancement for bond financing; the bond proceeds, rather than the public housing funds, are then used to fund the construction or rehabilitation of the development. This structure may be particularly advantageous for a project seeking to utilize low-income housing tax credits (LIHTCs) in a jurisdiction where the state allocation of LIHTCs is insufficient to fund most or all of the projects seeking LIHTCs. This is because a project receiving tax-exempt bond financing may apply for low-income housing tax credits (LIHTCs) at the reduced level generally available for acquisition costs[352] on a non-competitive basis provided the bond issuance is subject to the state volume cap on tax-exempt bonds.[353]

C. Capital Fund Financings

HUD has issued regulations establishing a "capital fund financing program" (CFF Program), under which, with HUD's written approval,[354] a PHA may pledge a future stream of capital funds as collateral for borrowings, including borrowing as part of a mixed-finance develop-

---

350. *See* HUD Guidance on Funding of New Projects/Units, *supra* n.186.
351. Codified as 42 U.S.C. § 1437z-7.
352. The low income housing tax credit program authorized under 26 U.S.C. § 42 permits eligible projects to receive a credit annually for 10 years based on the developer's "qualified basis"—that is, the developer's eligible cost basis in the portion of the property used for low-income housing—multiplied by the "applicable percentage." *See* 26 U.S.C. § 42(a). The statute requires the Internal Revenue Service to calculate the "applicable percentage" as the percentage which, over the 10-year credit period, will yield an aggregate credit the present value of which is equal to (a) 70 percent of the qualified basis, in the case of new construction or substantial rehabilitation of property not funded with tax-exempt bonds (subject to a floor of 9% for projects placed in service by Dec. 31, 2013) or (b) 30% of the qualified basis, in the case of either acquisition costs or tax-exempt bond-financed development costs. This "30% present value" credit, which over the last several years has floated between 3% and 4%, is frequently referred to by practitioners as the "4 percent credit," harking back to the first year of the LIHTC program, in which the credit percentages were fixed respectively at 9% and 4%.
353. *See* 26 U.S.C. § 42(h)(4), 26 U.S.C. § 146.
354. Submission requirements are detailed at 24 C.F.R. § 905.510.

ment project.[355] PHAs may pledge up to 100 percent of RHF funds, so long as that amount represents no more than 50 percent of the PHA's combined future capital funds (including both RHF funds and formula funding).[356] In general, PHAs may pledge up to 33 percent of existing and projected future Capital Grant funds; however, on a case-by-case basis, HUD may permit a PHA to pledge more than 33 percent of Capital Grant funds that it has already received from HUD, subject to a reasonableness test.[357]

Generally, in order to participate in the CFF Program, a PHA must be designated either a "high performer" or a "standard performer" under the Public Housing Assessment System (PHAS).[358] However, HUD will consider an application from a PHA designated as "troubled" under PHAS if the PHA is able to demonstrate that it has developed the management and financial capability needed to successfully undertake a CFF Program proposal.[359] If a PHA has received a letter of findings, charge, or lawsuit alleging systemic noncompliance with applicable Fair Housing requirements, and such allegations have not been resolved to HUD's satisfaction, then the PHA will be ineligible for CFF Program approval, unless its CFF Program proposal is part of a plan to address such findings and HUD deems the plan to be adequate.[360]

Under the CFF Program regulations, the proceeds of a CFF Program transaction may be used for development of new public housing (subject to a 40-year use restriction) or for modernization of existing public housing (subject to a 20-year use restriction).[361] While the proceeds may be allocated to one or more individual projects, the PHA pledge is not limited to capital funds allocated to specific projects, but rather consists of a pledge of a specified

---

355. *See generally* 24 C.F.R. pt. 905, subpt. E. These regulations have been criticized by practitioners expressing concerns about the adequacy of the pledged funds as collateral, given that funding remains subject to appropriations. *See* HUD, 24 C.F.R. pt. 905, Use of Public Housing Capital Funds for Financing Activities; Final Rule (Oct. 21, 2010), 75 Fed. Reg. 203, at http://www.gpo.gov/fdsys/pkg/FR-2010-10-21/html/2010-26404.htm (CFF Program Final Rule), § III, Summary of Public Comments. Public comment also highlighted some aspects of the HUD review process as unduly cumbersome and criticized submission and reporting requirements for the program as a whole. HUD responded, in its final rulemaking, by reducing reporting requirements for mixed-finance transactions and by eliminating particularly burdensome closing requirements *Id.*

For guidance on other HUD programs designed to facilitate PHA borrowing, *see* HUD, 24 C.F.R. pt.s 905 and 990: Use of Public Housing Capital and Operating Funds for Financing Activities: Proposed Rule, 72 Fed. Reg. 39,545 (July 18, 2007) (Doc. No. FR-4843-P-01) (the only guidance issued as of the date of this writing for the proposed operating fund financing program) and Notice on the Public Housing Mortgage Program, at http://hud.gov/offices/pih/programs/ph/capfund/prop-phmp-notice.pdf (involving the mortgage of public housing assets for financing that will be repaid with resources other than public housing capital or operating funds). HUD has not issued regulations elaborating on the statutory authorization to use a HOPE VI or other one-time capital grant proceeds to establish a bond reserve or otherwise collateralize bonds or other debt obligations.

356. *See* 24 C.F.R. § 905.505(i)(2).
357. *See* 24 C.F.R. § 905.505(i)(1), (3).
358. *See* 24 C.F.R. § 905.505(d).
359. *Id.*
360. *Id.*
361. *See* 24 C.F.R. § 905.505(c).

percentage of the PHA's overall formula and/or RHF allocation of capital funds.[362] The proceeds of a CFF Program transaction may not be used for PHA central office center costs.[363] However, such proceeds may be used for non-dwelling costs[364] and to reimburse predevelopment costs, subject to the limitations generally applicable to predevelopment costs in public housing transactions under 24 C.F.R. Part 941.[365]

While the CFF Program regulations do not specifically negate existing statutory authority for PHAs to pledge real estate assets as collateral for debt, HUD has clearly indicated in its response to public comments that the CFF Program is intended to offer lenders a future stream of appropriations, rather than real estate, as their basic collateral.[366] For any rental property financed with CFF Program proceeds, a Declaration of Trust in favor of HUD, subjecting the property to the applicable use restriction, must be recorded in first position.[367] All CFF Program transactions must provide for mandatory debt service and be fully amortizing over the term of the underlying loan,[368] and, unless otherwise approved by HUD, the financing documents must provide for HUD approval before the lender may accelerate the debt secured with a pledge of PHA capital funds.[369] All variable-interest-rate transactions must include an interest cap.[370]

In general, HUD approval of CFF transactions is conditioned on receipt of a "fairness opinion" from a qualified, independent, third-party financial advisor attesting that the terms and conditions of the proposed financing transaction are reasonable under current market conditions with respect to such matters as interest rate, fees, costs of issuance, call provisions, and reserve fund requirements.[371] This fairness opinion requirement is waived for mixed-finance transactions and for certain standard- and high-performing PHAs.[372]

As a condition of HUD approval, a PHA also must demonstrate that the financing will not negatively impact the PHA's ability to meet the ongoing needs of its public housing portfolio over the term of the financing, based on a projection of both future funding and the PHA's capital needs.[373] Except in the context of a mixed finance project, a PHA seeking approval of a CFF Program transaction involving a pledge of non-RHF capital funding must

---

362. *See* 24 C.F.R. §§ 905.500, 905.505.
363. *See* 24 C.F.R. § 905.505.
364. *See* 24 C.F.R. § 905.505(h)(5).
365. *Id.*
366. *See* CFF Program Final Rule, *supra* n.355.
367. *See* 24 C.F.R. § 905.505(c)(4).
368. *See* 24 C.F.R. § 905.705(j)(1).
369. *See* 24 C.F.R. § 905.505(j)(2).
370. *See* 24 C.F.R. § 905.505(j)(4).
371. *See* 24 C.F.R. § 905.505(k).
372. *See* 24 C.F.R. § 905.507 (waiving the "fairness opinion" as well as the requirement of an independent management assessment for most transactions involving high-performing PHAs undertaking a CFF program of under $20 million cumulatively, high- or standard-performing PHAs undertaking a CFF program of under $2 million cumulatively, or CFF programs undertaken in the context of a mixed-finance transaction). However, HUD has retained discretion to impose such requirements. *Id.*
373. *See* 24 C.F.R. § 905.505(g)(2).

conduct a physical needs assessment of its entire portfolio, and the improvements to be financed with CFF Program proceeds must be based on the physical needs assessment.[374]

D. Using Project-Based Vouchers to Enhance Project Feasibility

Although a particular housing unit cannot receive both public housing operating subsidy under Section 9 of the 1937 Act and project-based assistance under Section 8 of the 1937 Act,[375] a mixed-finance development may include both public housing units assisted with Section 9 funds and non-public housing units assisted with Section 8 funds.[376] The revenue stream from project-based voucher units may enhance project financial stability by reducing market risk, particularly if the project includes a substantial number of LIHTC-only or market-rate units with rents at or below the PBV rent limits approved by HUD for the applicable jurisdiction.[377] A PHA seeking to attach project-based vouchers assistance to non-public housing units in a mixed-finance development must comply with all requirements of the project-based voucher program under 24 C.F.R. Part 983, including, without limitation, requirements governing the process by which a PHA must select projects to receive PBV assistance.[378] This process is discussed further in Chapter 10, which covers vouchers and other Section 8 programs.

E. Educating Funders

Even for lenders and investors with extensive experience in financing affordable housing transactions, the mixed finance program adds a new layer of complexity and, at times, requirements that run contrary to traditional underwriting practices. Developers and PHAs would be well advised to provide as much information as they can, and as early as possible, so their funders can familiarize themselves with the public housing program requirements; the

---

374. *See* 24 C.F.R. § 905.505(g).
375. *See* 24 C.F.R. § 983.51(e).
376. *See* HUD, 24 C.F.R. pt. 983, Project-Based Voucher Program; Final Rule, 70 Fed. Reg. 59,891 (Oct. 13, 2005) (Doc. No. FR-4636-F-02) at 59,900. However, vouchers obtained in connection with the HOPE VI program and used as project-based § 8 assistance will not be considered replacement units in determining whether a development satisfies either the standard of replacement units or the minimum public housing requirement established under the 2010 NOFA. *See, e.g.,* HOPE VI 2010 NOFA, *supra* n.140, at 17.
377. *See* 24 C.F.R. § 983.301. For LIHTC units, so long as the maximum rents permitted under the LIHTC program are "reasonable" (as determined under 24 C.F.R. § 983.303), the owner may receive housing assistance payments equal to the LIHTC rent charged for comparable units in the same building that do not receive PBV assistance, less a reasonable allowance for utilities and any rent paid by the tenants. 24 C.F.R. § 983.301(c). For all non-LIHTC units, the housing assistance payment is capped at 110% of HUD fair market rent (or any exception rent approved by HUD). For all units, rent cannot exceed either the "reasonable" rent, or the rent actually charged by the owner for comparable unassisted units. *See* 24 C.F.R. § 983.301(b).
378. Under 24 C.F.R. § 983.51, a PHA may award PBV assistance to a project without issuing a request for proposals only if (a) its agency plan so permits, (b) the project was awarded assistance under another federal or state program through a competitive process within the three years preceding the award of PBV assistance, and (c) the earlier competitive selection did not involve consideration that the project would receive PBV assistance.

HUD approval process and corresponding timing issues; and the resulting impact on project financing, development, and operations.

V. CONCLUSION

In the face of continuing financial and programmatic challenges, the federal public housing program serves approximately 1.2 million households nationwide.[379] Using the mixed-finance program, PHAs and private developers are continuing to redevelop distressed public housing, utilizing public housing funds to leverage additional resources. Given the complex and sometimes conflicting requirements applicable to the many public and private funding sources involved in these redevelopment efforts, attorneys play a particularly vital role in this process.

---

379. *See* Fact Sheet, HUD's Public Housing Program, available at http://portal.hud.gov/hudportal/HUD?src=/topics/rental_assistance/phprog, last accessed Sept. 7, 2011.

Public Housing Operations 9

Melissa K. Worden and William J. Ward

I. INTRODUCTION

This chapter is intended to provide an overview of the history, structure, regulatory framework, funding methods, operating requirements, and compliance mechanisms of public housing. There are more than 3,300 public housing authorities operating in the United States, Puerto Rico, the U.S. Virgin Islands, and Guam that provide housing to approximately 1.2 million households.[1] Housing authorities are funded in large part by, and are responsible to, the Department of Housing and Urban Development (HUD) and must ensure that their programs, operations, structures, and finances comply with all applicable HUD requirements. Public housing is an extremely regulated program, with regulations governing almost every aspect of a housing authority's activities. The regulatory framework is established in Title 24, Chapter IX (and specifically the public housing regulations contained in Parts 901–990), along with the cross-cutting requirements contained in other regulations, such as those in Part 5 and Part 85. Regulatory interpretation and implementation guidance is provided in the public housing realm through handbooks, guidebooks, forms, notices, and other informal public housing guidance.[2] Note that this chapter does

---

1. U.S. Dep't Hous. & Urban Dev., Public Housing, http://portal.hud.gov/hudportal/HUD?src=/program_offices/public_indian_housing/programs/ph (last visited Jan. 2, 2012).

2. HUD maintains its catalog of handbooks, guidebooks, forms, letters, bulletins, notices, and related guidance through its Client Information and Policy System (HUDCLIPS) online at www.hud.gov/hudclips. Each type of guidance is organized by the various HUD programs, making it possible to search for specific public housing handbooks, guidebooks, and notices on the site.

not cover the Section 8 housing choice voucher program[3] or public housing development programs; those activities are covered in Chapters 8 and 10, respectively, of this book.

II. HISTORY OF THE PUBLIC HOUSING PROGRAM

The federal government's first involvement in public housing occurred as part of an effort to spur the economy and eradicate the tenements and slums spawned by the harsh economic times of the Great Depression. As part of Franklin D. Roosevelt's New Deal legislation, the National Industrial Recovery Act of 1933[4] was enacted that appropriated approximately $3.3 billion to establish the Federal Emergency Administration of Public Works, commonly known as the Public Works Administration (PWA), to fund public building projects, including housing projects developed by the PWA, state and local governments, and limited dividend corporations.[5] From 1933 to 1935, the PWA underwrote the financing for seven major public housing projects throughout the country. Although the housing developments funded by PWA were of high quality, the rents charged were not affordable to many poor families.

The federal government continued its commitment to providing housing for the poor and spurring the economy when it passed the U.S. Housing Act of 1937 (the 1937 Act).[6] The preamble of the 1937 Act sums up the congressional intent of the law:

> An Act to provide assistance to the States and political subdivisions thereof for the elimination of unsafe and insanitary housing conditions, for the eradication of slums, for the provision of decent, safe, and sanitary dwelling for families of low income, and for the reduction of unemployment and the stimulation of business activity, to create a United States Housing Authority and for other purposes.[7]

Scholars may disagree about the success or failure of the policies put forth by the 1937 Act; however, no one disputes the effect the 1937 Act has had on public housing. It established the foundation for subsidized housing in the United States and those roots are still the bedrock of modern public housing policy. While the creation of decent, safe, and affordable housing was an enduring by-product of the 1937 Act, its main intent was actually to create jobs and spur the economy.[8] The 1937 Act, combined with other federally sponsored economic stimuli, served as major catalysts for reducing unemployment from 25 percent to 17 percent between 1930 and 1939.[9] The 1937 Act established the U.S. Housing Authority (USHA), which provided for the creation of local authorities that would receive program

---

3. The Section 8 housing choice voucher program is authorized under Section 8 of the U.S. Housing Act of 1937, 42 U.S.C. § 1437 (2006).
4. National Industrial Recovery Act of 1933, Pub. L. No. 73-67, 48 Stat. 195–211 (1933), *invalidated by* A.L.A. Schechter Poultry Corp. v. United States, 295 U.S. 495 (1935).
5. Paul R. Lusignan, *Public Housing in the United States, 1933–1949*, 25 Cultural Res. Mgmt. 36 (2002), *available at* http://crm.cr.nps.gov/archive/25-01/25-01-16.pdf.
6. U.S. Housing Act of 1937, 42 U.S.C. § 1437 (2006).
7. *Id.*
8. Jennifer A. Stoloff, HUD Office of Policy Dev. & Research, A Brief History of Public Housing. (2004).
9. William H. Chase, The Unfinished Journey: America Since WWII 7 (3d ed. 1995).

direction, financial support, and technical assistance from the USHA.[10] Unfortunately, the USHA's efforts were halted after a few years when, in the run-up to World War II, federal housing funding and policy shifted from affordable housing to defense housing.[11] It should be noted, however, that many of the developments built to house soldiers during the war were converted to public housing once the war ended.[12]

President Truman's 1949 State of the Union address laid out an ambitious domestic reform plan known as the "Fair Deal." At that time, Congress was in a pitched battle with the Administration, so most of the President's reforms did not pass; however, the President was able to get the Federal Housing Act of 1949, which made major changes to federal affordable housing policy and funding, through Congress.[13] In addition to funding urban-renewal projects, reforming the Federal Housing Administration (FHA), and establishing rural home-ownership programs, the Federal Housing Act of 1949 authorized the construction of 800,000 new public housing units, which dramatically increased the number of public housing units across the country.[14]

The Department of Housing and Urban Development was created in 1965 as a cabinet-level agency.[15] In the late 1960s and early 1970s, Congress introduced additional public housing reforms. Most notable was the establishment of the Annual Contributions Contract that created a binding agreement between HUD and local housing authorities governing the funding and operations of housing authorities. During the same period, Congress established an annual operating subsidy that, in theory, provided the difference between tenant-paid rent[16] and the cost to operate the property.[17] In addition, to ensure that the right types of people were being served by this program, Congress also established requirements and standards for admission and continued occupancy of public housing. At the same time, Congress introduced new programs to encourage private developers and landlords to participate in the affordable housing markets. Since the early 1980s, there has been little large-scale funding of public housing programs. Recently, programs such as HOPE VI, Choice Neighborhoods, and Replacement Housing Factor funds have been used to redevelop public housing stock, often through a mixed-finance approach. Because the funding associated with these programs is so limited, many public housing sites are sorely in need of redevelopment that cannot be revitalized because of lack of funding.

---

10. Paul R. Lusignan, *Public Housing in the United States, 1933–1949*, 25 CULTURAL RES. MGMT. 36, 37 (2002), *available at* http://crm.cr.nps.gov/archive/25-01/25-01-16.pdf.

11. *Id.* at 36, 37.

12. *Id.* at 36, 36.

13. Housing Act of 1949, Pub. L. No. 81-171, 63 Stat. 413 (codified as amended in scattered sections of 42 U.S.C.).

14. Jennifer A. Stoloff, *supra* note 8, at 10.

15. Dep't of Housing and Urban Development Act of 1965, Pub. L. No. 89-117, 79 Stat. 451 (codified as amended in scattered sections of 42 U.S.C.).

16. Under the HUD Act of 1969, Pub. L. No. 91-152, 83 Stat. 379 (Dec. 24, 1969), tenants were required to pay 25% of their income as rent. The percentage of income increased to 30% in 1981. *See* 42 U.S.C. § 1437a(a)(1)(A) (2006).

17. HUD Act of 1969, Pub. L. No. 91-152, 213, 83 Stat. 379 (codified as amended in scattered sections of 42 U.S.C.).

In 1998, President Clinton signed the Quality Housing and Work Responsibility Act (QHWRA) into law.[18] QHWRA represented the single largest public housing reform since public housing was established in 1937. QHWRA's reforms included deregulation of various aspects of public housing administration, facilitating mixed-income communities, decreasing concentrations of poverty, providing funding for severely dilapidated public housing, increasing housing authority accountability, consolidating the Section 8 certificate and voucher programs, and creating opportunities and incentives for resident self-sufficiency.[19] QHWRA gave housing authorities greater flexibility in use of federal assistance and encouraged housing authorities to implement reforms by authorizing previously withheld powers. According to a Government Accountability Office (GAO) report that analyzed housing authority views on QHWRA's reforms, most housing authorities found the increased fungibility between various public housing funds very helpful in increasing efficiency in operations and management, and many respondents felt that the reforms did little to aid or hinder public housing operations.[20]

QHWRA included provisions that required HUD to establish a formula for determining the amount of operating assistance that housing authorities would receive to subsidize the cost of operating public housing units.[21] At Congress's urging, HUD engaged Harvard University's Graduate School of Design to study the costs and processes associated with operating well-run public housing.[22] The results, known as the "Harvard cost study," recommended that HUD establish funding criteria similar to those of the FHA's cost and underwriting standards and that it switch to an asset-based management model of operating public housing projects, which, in short, means that each project must be self-sustaining and evaluated and funded separately from other projects.[23]

Recent legislative measures suggest that the public housing program may be substantially transformed in the future. As part of the fiscal year 2012 federal appropriations act, Congress authorized the conversion of up to 60,000 units of public housing and other multifamily units to Section 8 funded units.[24] The program, called the Rental Assistance Demonstration, will select properties for conversion through a competitive process. Projects selected for conversion will be subject to a project-based Section 8 contract through which they will receive the capital and operating funds that would have been available if the units remained in the public

---

18. Quality Housing and Work Responsibility Act of 1998, Pub. L. No. 105-276, 112 Stat. 2461 (codified as amended in scattered sections of 42 U.S.C.).

19. Louise Hunt, Mary Shulhof & Stephen Holmquist, *Summary of the Quality Housing and Work Responsibility Act of 1998* (December 1998), *available at* http://portal.hud.gov/hudportal/documents/huddoc?id=titlev.pdf.

20. *Public Housing, Small and Large Agencies Have Similar Views on Many Recent Housing Reforms,* GAO Report to Ranking Minority Member, Subcommittee on Housing and Transportation, Committee on Banking, Housing and Urban Affairs, U.S. Senate, October 2003.

21. U.S. Dep't Hous. & Urban Dev., *Asset Management Overview*, PUBLIC HOUSING, http://portal.hud.gov/hudportal/HUD?src=/program_offices/public_indian_housing/programs/ph/am/overview (last visited Dec. 29, 2011).

22. *Id.*

23. *Id.*

24. Consolidated Appropriations Act of 2012, Pub. L. 112-074 (Dec. 23, 2011).

housing program.[25] One big benefit of this approach is that Section 8 properties can incur debt that may be used to finance additional capital improvements, in contrast to public housing properties, which must be operated on a break-even basis, leaving no revenue available to repay debt. As of early 2012, HUD is in the initial stages of structuring the demonstration program that will be implemented in the coming months and years. Even more recently, Congress has introduced legislation that would amend and extend the Rental Assistance Demonstration.[26]

III. STRUCTURE OF PUBLIC HOUSING AUTHORITIES AND HUD'S ROLE IN THEIR FUNDING AND REGULATION

As mentioned earlier, the concept of "public housing" was introduced officially at the federal level as part of the 1937 Act that authorized the establishment of local "public housing agencies"[27] with primary responsibility for initiating, designing buildings, and operating housing for low-income families, the elderly, and the disabled. Today, there are approximately 3,300 housing authorities across the United States, Puerto Rico, the Virgin Islands, and Guam that house more than 1.2 million households.[28] Housing authorities are regulated by federal, state, and local law.

A. General Structure, Powers, and Duties of Housing Authorities

Housing authorities are established pursuant to each state's housing authority enabling legislation[29] that sets forth the framework within with each housing authority operates and often establishes various operating standards, such as the housing authority's general powers and duties, its tax status, its relationship with the municipality or governing jurisdiction within which it operates, and the process for appointment and constitution of its board.[30] In addition, many localities have established local laws, in accordance with federal and state statutes, which regulate housing authorities and provide additional, more localized requirements.[31]

While it is hard to make broad generalizations about the rights and responsibilities of all housing authorities, there are some requirements, structures, and characteristics that apply to most. For example, the 1937 Act requires that at least one housing authority board member be a resident of a housing authority site.[32] In addition, most housing authorities are separate legal

---

25. Reno & Cavanaugh, PLLC, *Client Alert: Congress Authorizes Rental Assistance Demonstration for Public Housing Preservation* (Dec. 5, 2011), http://media.redclaycms.com/sites/189/documents/D0226881.pdf

26. *Id.*; Affordable Housing and Self-Sufficiency Improvement Act of 2012.

27. U.S. Housing Act of 1937, 42 U.S.C. § 1437 (2006).

28. U.S. Dep't Hous. & Urban Dev., PUBLIC HOUSING, http://portal.hud.gov/hudportal/HUD?src=/program_offices/public_indian_housing/programs/ph (last visited Jan. 2, 2012).

29. *See, e.g.*, the Michigan Housing Facilities Act 18 of 1933 (Ex. Sess.), MICH. COMP. LAWS § 125.653(a) (2009).

30. *See, e.g.*, MICH. COMP. LAWS § 125.651 *et seq.* (2009).

31. *See, e.g.*, DETROIT (Mich.) CITY CODE § 14-5-1 *et seq.* (2010).

32. *See* U.S. Housing Act of 1937, 42 U.S.C.§ 1437 note (b)(1), and, e.g., MICH. COMP. LAWS § 125.654(2) (2009) and CAL. HEALTH & SAFETY CODE § 34246.5 (2011).

entities from the jurisdictions they serve.[33] Housing authority board meetings generally are subject to the applicable state's open meetings act.[34] In addition, many state statutes authorize housing authorities to do the following: sue and be sued; form and maintain affiliates and instrumentalities; sell, purchase, transfer, construct, mortgage, lease property and improvements, which generally is subject to HUD approval; set rents, admit, manage, and evict tenants; issue bonds; and condemn property. One additional common element of most state and local housing authority laws relates to the payment of taxes. Because federal housing law exempts housing authority property from taxation, state and local jurisdictions require a payment in lieu of taxes (PILOT) and execution of a Cooperation Agreement that provides for the PILOT, as described below.[35]

B. Annual Contributions Contracts

The HUD-established standards and requirements with which housing authorities must comply are outlined in the Annual Contributions Contract the (ACC) entered into between HUD and each housing authority[36] and pursuant to which HUD provides funding for development, maintenance, and operation of the public housing units.[37] The ACC is a standard document that outlines requirements related to housing authority administration, finance, and operation of housing authority–owned units.[38] The ACC incorporates the federal regulations applicable to public housing development,[39] modernization, and operations, and it is updated periodically to reflect changes in legislation or policy. The ACC is organized into two parts. Part I is applicable to all housing authorities and Part II contains more particularized provisions that may or may not be applicable, depending on the specific programs and the scope of the housing authority, to a housing authority's operations.[40] Some notable provisions of the ACC are listed below.[41]

- The housing authority and the local governing body must enter into a Cooperation Agreement that ensures that public housing sites receive the same services as other areas of the jurisdiction, it exempts public housing property and income from taxa-

---

33. *See, e.g.*, MICH. COMP. LAWS § 125.654(1) (2009).
34. *See, e.g.*, MICH. COMP. LAWS § 125.655 (2009).
35. *See, e.g.*, MICH. COMP. LAWS § 125.657 (2009).
36. 42 U.S.C. § 1437c (2010).
37. 42 U.S.C. § 1437c(a)(1) (2010).
38. E.g., units that receive assistance through the Housing Choice Voucher Program are subject to an Annual Contributions Contract for Section 8 assistance as described in Chapter 10.
39. Units developed through the mixed-finance approach, that is, privately owned but with funding from the housing authority, are governed by a Mixed Finance Amendment to the ACC.
40. U.S. Dep't Hous. & Urban Dev. Notice PIH 95-44 (HA): Consolidated Annual Contributions Contract, Form 53012A and Form HUD-53012B (June 23, 1995), *available at* http://www.hud.gov/offices/adm/hudclips/notices/pih/95pihnotices.cfm.
41. U.S. Dep't Hous. & Urban Dev., Form 53012A (1995): Terms and Conditions Constituting Part A of a Consolidated Annual Contributions Contract Between Housing Authority and the United States of America (1995).

tion, and it establishes a 10 percent payment in lieu of taxes for all public housing units.[42]

- HUD will record a deed restriction, called a Declaration of Trust, against all housing authority–owned property, which prohibits conveyance or other encumbrance of the sites and requires the encumbered sites to be operated as public housing for at least 40 years.[43]
- It requires that federal funds received by the housing authority be held pursuant to a General Depository Agreement with a financial institution that, on housing authority default, allows HUD to freeze the account.[44]
- Its conflict-of-interest provisions prohibit the housing authority, its contractors, and its subcontractors from entering into a contract with any of the following: a current or former member of the housing authority's governing body, a housing authority employee, a public official, or with any member of those individuals' immediate families, unless the conflict is disclosed to the housing authority and waived.[45]
- It requires that HUD provide operating subsidy for the housing authority to help support the costs of operating the public housing units in an amount based on annual calculations.[46]
- It allows HUD to call a substantial default for any of the following infractions: conveyance or disposal of the projects without HUD approval, failure to comply with civil-rights requirements, or termination of payment in lieu of taxes by the authorizing jurisdiction.[47]

The ACC gives HUD far-reaching powers of enforcement against housing authorities as described in the "Monitoring and Oversight of Public Housing" section of this chapter.

---

42. U.S. Dep't Hous. & Urban Dev., Form 53012A: Terms and Conditions Constituting Part A of a Consolidated Annual Contributions Contract Between Housing Authority and the United States of America § 6 (1995).

43. U.S. Dep't Hous. & Urban Dev., Form 53012A: Terms and Conditions Constituting Part A of a Consolidated Annual Contributions Contract Between Housing Authority and the United States of America § 8 (1995).

44. U.S. Dep't Hous. & Urban Dev., Form 53012A: Terms and Conditions Constituting Part A of a Consolidated Annual Contributions Contract Between Housing Authority and the United States of American § 9 (1995); U.S. Dep't Hous. & Urban Dev., Form 51999: General Depository Agreement (1991).

45. U.S. Dep't Hous. & Urban Dev., Form 53012A: Terms and Conditions Constituting Part A of a Consolidated Annual Contributions Contract Between Housing Authority and the United States of America § 19 (1995).

46. U.S. Dep't Hous. & Urban Dev., Form 53012A: Terms and Conditions Constituting Part A of a Consolidated Annual Contributions Contract Between Housing Authority and the United States of America § 11 (1995).

47. U.S. Dep't Hous. & Urban Dev., Form 53012A: Terms and Conditions Constituting Part A of a Consolidated Annual Contributions Contract Between Housing Authority and the United States of America § 17 (1995).

III. PROCUREMENT REQUIREMENTS FOR HOUSING AUTHORITIES

When purchasing goods and services in connection with the development, modernization, or operation of public housing, housing authorities must follow 24 CFR 85.36(b), the federal regulations that establish the procurement standards and processes intended to promote full and open competition in procurement actions for activities funded with HUD funds.[48] The federal regulations governing housing authority procurement also govern procurements for many other HUD programs.[49] Chapter 13, "Cross-Cutting Requirements: Federal-Wide Requirements Impacting HUD Programs," provides a detailed overview of the methods of solicitation applicable to various types of public housing procurements.[50] Because Chapter 13 interprets regulations applicable to many HUD programs, it uses more general terms that cover various recipients of HUD grant funds. When reviewing Chapter 13 for applicability to housing authority procurements, recognize that housing authorities are considered grantees. Entities and individuals with whom housing authorities contract are considered subgrantees.

A useful tool for navigating the procurement regulations and applying them to the public housing context is HUD Handbook 7460.8 Rev. 2, *Procurement Handbook for Public Housing Agencies* (the Procurement Handbook).[51] The Procurement Handbook provides technical guidance on a number of public housing procurement standards, including procedural requirements for various types of solicitations; contractual requirements; contract administration standards; cooperative business relationships; Section 3 and small, minority-owned, and women-owned business opportunities; mixed-finance development; and energy-efficiency and utility-related contracting.[52] The Procurement Handbook provides useful guidance to housing authorities and those with which they contract regarding the processes and procedures for selecting and contracting for goods and services.

IV. FORM OF HOUSING AUTHORITY CONTRACTS AND REQUIRED PROVISIONS

HUD prescribes a number of contractual requirements and standards for contracts funded with HUD public housing funds. The types of contracts frequently used in the public housing context and the requirements for such are described below.

---

48. U.S. Dep't Hous. & Urban Dev., Procurement Handbook for Public Housing Agencies No. 7460.8, § 1.3 (2d rev. 2007).

49. 24 C.F.R. § 85, Administrative Requirements for Grants and Cooperative Agreements to State, Local and Federally Recognized Indian Tribal Governments, outlines the procurement requirements applicable to public entities utilizing HUD programs and is HUD's adaptation of the overall federal requirements for public administration of grants and use of federal program grant funds. *See* U.S. Dep't Hous. & Urban Dev., Procurement Handbook for Public Housing Agencies No. 7460.8 (2d rev. 2007).

50. *See* "Procurement by HUD Grantees and Subgrantees" section of Cross-Cutting Requirements chapter.

51. U.S. Dep't Hous. & Urban Dev., Procurement Handbook for Public Housing Agencies No. 7460.8, § 1.3 (2d rev. 2007).

52. *Id.* at i–v.

A. Form of Contracts

HUD provides some degree of flexibility on the form and substance of contracts for goods and services between housing authorities and contractors. This flexibility allows housing authorities to choose the best form of contract given the specifics of the transaction.[53] The following summary provides a brief overview of the various forms of public housing contracts.

B. Fixed-Price Contracts

The most common form of housing authority contract, and HUD's preferred form, is a fixed-price contract.[54] Fixed-price contracts are often used for construction work and for other contracts resulting from sealed bids.[55] The firm fixed-price contract provides the greatest certainty of cost as it sets the cost up-front. In cases where the cost of goods to be used or services to be performed under the contract are subject to substantial increases or decreases because of economic conditions, a fixed-price contract with an economic price adjustment can be used, but the conditions that give rise to price adjustments should be clearly outlined in the contract and limited to contingencies that are beyond the contractor's control.[56]

C. Cost-Reimbursement Contracts

A few types of cost-reimbursement contracts are used in the public housing context. A cost plus fixed fee type of contract establishes a fixed fee for the contractor but allows the costs paid under the contract to be adjusted as a result of changes in the work to be performed, such as by a change order.[57] The disadvantage of this form of contract is that it lowers the incentive of contractors to control costs and it allows for the potential that contractors will attempt to win contracts by submitting low bids then increasing the costs post-award. Cost contracts are cost-reimbursement contracts that reimburse costs but pay no fee. These contracts are often used by nonprofit organizations or in situations where no fees are involved.[58]

D. Indefinite Delivery Contracts

Indefinite delivery contracts should be used only when the exact times or exact quantities of future supplies or services cannot be determined with particularity at the time of the contract award.[59] There are three types of indefinite delivery contracts: definite quantity contracts, requirements contracts, and indefinite quantity contracts.[60] Definite quantity contracts pro-

---

53. *Id.* at § 10.1(A).
54. *Id.* § 10.1(A). The most common form of fixed price contract is a *firm* fixed price contract, but in instances in which market conditions for the particular product
55. U.S. Dep't Hous. & Urban Dev., Procurement Handbook for Public Housing Agencies No. 7460.8, § 10.1(A) (2d rev. 2007).
56. U.S. Dep't Hous. & Urban Dev., Procurement Handbook for Public Housing Agencies No. 7460.8, § 10.1(C) (2d rev. 2007).
57. *Id.* § 10.1(C)(2).
58. *Id.*
59. *Id.* § 10.1(C)(3).
60. *Id.*

vide for a specific amount of supplies or services for a fixed amount of time.[61] Requirements contracts cover all needs of a particular supply or service for a certain amount of time, although the exact quantity or amount may not be determined at the time of the contract.[62] Indefinite quantity contracts provide for delivery of an uncertain amount of services or supplies (minimum and maximum amounts must be stated) at a fixed price per unit or service for a specified period of time.[63] Indefinite delivery contracts should be used only for recurring needs that do not occur at times and in amounts that can be predetermined.

E. Time and Materials and Labor-Hour Contracts

Time and materials contracts or labor-hour contracts can be used only if it is not possible at the time of the contract award to estimate the extent or duration of the work or to anticipate the costs with any degree of confidence[64] and always should include a ceiling price for the services.[65] Time and materials contracts are those that provide for labor hours to be paid at fixed hourly rates and materials to be reimbursed at cost.[66] Labor-hour contracts pay a fixed price per hour for labor performed. They do not provide for materials.[67]

F. Letter Contracts

Letter contracts are preliminary agreements that authorize the contractor to begin performing services while contract terms are being negotiated.[68] They allow contractors to begin performing services before a fully negotiated agreement can be finalized. They should be used primarily in cases where emergency services need to be performed prior to contract negotiation. These types of agreements should provide as much specificity as possible regarding the scope of services, price, time for performance, and other significant terms as this is a binding contract, unlike a letter of intent or notice of intent to award.[69]

G. Prohibited Contracts

HUD prohibits the use of two types of contracts because of their lack of cost controls: cost plus percentage of cost contracts and cost plus percentage of construction cost contracts.[70] Cost plus percentage of cost contracts require payment of all costs incurred as well as payment of a fee based on all costs, no matter how much the costs rise.[71] Cost plus percentage of

---

61. *Id.*
62. *Id.*
63. *Id.*
64. 24 C.F.R. § 85.36(b)(10) (2011).
65. U.S. Dep't Hous. & Urban Dev., Procurement Handbook for Public Housing Agencies No. 7460.8, § 10.1(C)(4) (2d rev. 2007).
66. U.S. Dep't Hous. & Urban Dev., Procurement Handbook for Public Housing Agencies No. 7460.8, § 10.1(C)(4) (2d rev. 2007).
67. *Id.*
68. *Id.* § 10.1(C)(5).
69. *Id.*
70. *See* 24 C.F.R. § 85.36(f)(4) (2011) and U.S. Dep't Hous. & Urban Dev., Procurement Handbook for Public Housing Agencies No. 7460.8, § 10.1(A)(5) (2d rev. 2007).
71. U.S. Dep't Hous. & Urban Dev., Procurement Handbook for Public Housing Agencies No. 7460.8, § 10.1(C)(5) (2d rev. 2007).

construction cost contracts base fees for another service, such as architectural services, on the total cost of construction. This structure could result in increased costs, as architects may be motivated to design high-cost buildings or other improvements so that their fees will be increased.[72] Thus, the HUD form contract for architects requires a fixed fee rather than the AIA standard that establishes fees based on a percentage of the cost.[73]

H. Mandatory Contract Clauses

As outlined in Chapter 13, "Cross-Cutting Requirements: Federal-Wide Requirements Impacting HUD Programs," HUD requires certain clauses and provisions to be included in all contracts utilizing HUD funds.[74] HUD's Office of Public and Indian Housing has adapted the general HUD requirements for application in the public housing context and has issued standard provisions for construction and scaled-down provisions for nonconstruction contracts that must be included in each applicable contract.[75] Form HUD 5370, titled "General Conditions for Construction Contracts—Public Housing Programs," must be included in all construction contracts in excess of $100,000 issued by housing authorities.[76] It covers processes and procedures for undertaking the construction, various construction standards, as well as the regulatory requirements outlined in the HUD procurement regulations at 24 CFR 85.36, including environmental laws, labor laws found in Section 3 of the Housing and Urban Development Act of 1968, and Section 12 of the U.S. Housing Act of 1937, as amended.[77] HUD has adapted the General Conditions for Construction Contracts for contracts that do not involve construction activities. HUD published Form HUD 5370C, "General Conditions for Non-Construction Contracts," that must be included in all non-construction contracts in excess of $100,000 issued by housing authorities.[78]

V. PUBLIC HOUSING FUNDING

HUD provides funds to housing authorities for the development, capital improvements, and operation of public housing units. Both types of funding are authorized by Section 9 of the 1937 Act.[79] The funding, Capital Funds[80] and Operating Funds,[81] is provided annually by formula to each housing authority participating in the respective programs. The funding formulas, requirements, and documentation required to receive such funds are described below.

---

72. *Id.*
73. *See* Form HUD 51915 (Model Form of Agreement Between Owner and Design Professional) (Exp. 01/31/2014).
74. 24 C.F.R. § 85.36(i) (2011).
75. U.S. Dep't Hous. & Urban Dev., Procurement Handbook for Public Housing Agencies No. 7460.8, § 10.5(C)(4) (2d rev. 2007).
76. U.S. Dep't Hous. & Urban Dev., Form 5370: General Conditions for Construction Contracts-Public Housing (2006).
77. *Id.*
78. *Id.* § C (2006). Part I is used for non-construction contracts and Parts I and II are used for maintenance contracts.
79. U.S. Housing Act of 1937, 42 U.S.C. § 1437g.
80. U.S. Housing Act of 1937, 42 U.S.C. § 1437d.
81. U.S. Housing Act of 1937, 42 U.S.C. § 1437e.

A. Capital Funds

QHWRA consolidated the funding previously provided through three public housing capital programs, the Comprehensive Grant Program, the Comprehensive Improvement Assistance Program, and the Public Housing Development Program, into the Capital Fund Program.[82]

Capital Funds are provided annually by formula to housing authorities for the development (including mixed-finance), modernization, deferred maintenance, management improvements, demolition, resident relocation, and capital safety improvements of public housing units.[83] Essentially, it covers non-routine maintenance and capital expenses of public housing and can also be used for development.

After setting aside a small portion for Replacement Housing Factor Funds,[84] HUD allocates half of the annual formula allocation based on the existing modernization needs (formerly referred to as backlog need)[85] and half based on the accrued capital needs of housing authorities.[86]

The formula that allocates funds for existing modernization needs uses the following factors to determine the amount:[87]

- Average number of bedrooms in the development,
- Total number of units in the development,
- Percentage of units that lie in buildings built in 1978 or earlier,
- Cost index of rehabilitating property in the area,
- Nature of the development—urban or non-urban, and
- Region of the country in which the development lies.

The resulting figure is the housing authority's per-unit existing modernization need. However, public housing units that have a date of full availability[88] after October 1, 1991, are considered to have a "zero" existing modernization need.[89]

---

82. Public Housing Capital Fund Program, 76 Fed. Reg. 6654 (proposed Feb. 7, 2011) (to be codified at 24 C.F.R. pts. 903, 905, 941, 968, 969).

83. U.S. Dep't Hous. & Urban Dev., Public Housing, Office of Capital Improvements—Office of Public Housing Investments, *available at* http://portal.hud.gov/hudportal/HUD?src=/program_offices/public_indian_housing/programs/ph/capfund/aboutus (last visited Dec. 27, 2011).

84. These RHF funds are allocated to housing authorities that remove public housing units from their inventory due to demolition or conveyance of units and must be used for construction of new units. 24 C.F.R. § 905.10i (2001). Each year, HUD issues notices governing accrual, documentation, and expenditure of RHF funds, as, *e.g.*, in Notice (PIH 2011-24).

85. 76 Fed. Reg. 49,924 (Sept. 14, 1999).

86. 24 C.F.R. § 905.10(e) (2011).

87. 24 C.F.R. § 905.10(d)(1) (2011). Note that housing authorities with fewer than 250 public housing units are subject to the factors outlined in 24 C.F.R. § 905.10(d)(3), and the New York City Housing Authority and the Chicago Housing Authority are subject to the factors outlined in 24 C.F.R. § 905.10(d)(2).

88. Date of full availability, or DOFA, means the date on which at least 95% of the units in a development are suitable for occupancy. 24 C.F.R. § 970.5 (2011).

89. 24 C.F.R. § 905.10d-1ii (2001).

The remaining 50 percent of the annual Capital Fund appropriation is allocated to cover a housing authority's accrual needs[90] and is allocated based on factors similar to those used to determine the existing modernization needs.[91]

Once the per-unit existing modernization and accrual needs are determined, a housing authority's total Capital Fund eligibility is calculated by multiplying, per development, its total public housing units[92] by its existing modernization need and its accrual need and then dividing each respective sum by the total modernization and accrual needs for all housing authorities. In addition to the standard Capital Fund award, housing authorities designated as "high performers" under HUD's Public Housing Assessment System (PHAS) may receive a performance bonus that awards high performers an additional 5 percent above their base amount of formula Capital Funds.[93]

Two examples of how the formula reflects characteristics of a housing authority's housing stock follow.

- In 2010, a housing authority in the suburban Southeast with approximately 300 public housing units and aging housing stock received approximately $525,000 in formula Capital Funds or approximately $1,750 per public housing unit.
- In 2010, a housing authority in the urban Midwest with approximately 4,000 public housing units and fairly stable housing stock received approximately $9,200,000 in Capital Funds or approximately $2,300 per public housing unit.

B. Use of Capital Funds

As described later in this chapter, housing authorities annually, as well as in five-year increments, prepare PHA Plans describing all aspects of public housing operations. A major component of this planning process involves descriptions of the use of Capital Funds. HUD requires housing authorities to clearly outline the upcoming year's capital budget plan as part of the annual PHA Plan process.[94] Additionally, HUD requires housing authorities to develop five-year action plans[95] that project upcoming capital projects over a five-year period. Housing authorities generally look at recent housing inspections, physical-needs assessments, property

---

90. "Accrued modernization needs" are projected and future repair needs. *See* Capital Needs in the Public Housing Program, Revised Final Report, November 2010, prepared by Abt Associates for the U.S. Department of Housing and Urban Development (Nov. 24, 2010).

91. *See* 24 C.F.R. § 905.10(e)(1) for housing authorities with units in excess of 250 besides New York City and Chicago; *see* 24 C.F.R. § 905.10(e)(2) for New York City and Chicago and 24 C.F.R. § 905.10(e)(3) for housing authorities with fewer than 250 units.

92. 24 C.F.R. § 905.10f (2001). Note that HUD does not include in its Capital Fund allocation units that receive operating subsidy but were not developed using public housing development funds. In addition, units removed from a housing authority's inventory due to demolition or disposition are eligible to receive Capital Funds as described in the Replacement Housing Factor fund section herein.

93. 24 C.F.R. § 905.10j (2001).

94. U.S. Dep't Hous. & Urban Dev., Form 50075.1: Annual Statement/Performance and Evaluation Report (2008).

95. U.S. Dep't Hous. & Urban Dev., Form 50075.2: Capital Fund Program—Five Year Action Plan (2008).

maintenance and repair reports, and input from the residents and property management staff to determine capital needs and priorities when crafting their budgets and PHA Plans.

Currently, there are 17 allowable budget line items (BLI), or allowable expenditures, with the Capital Funds.[96] A number of the BLIs and allowable expenses are outlined below.

- BLI 1406: Operations: Transfer of up to 20 percent of its annual CF to the Operating Fund. Once the transfer occurs, the funds are subject to the requirements of 24 CFR 990.
- BLI 1408: Management Improvements: Allocate up to 20 percent of its annual CFP to enhance the management capacity of the housing authority. Such funds must be attributable to specific projects, not the central office cost center or administrative level.
- BLI 1410: Administration: Allocate up to 10 percent of the annual CF budget for administrative expenses.
- BLI 1440: Site Acquisition: Costs of acquisition of improved or vacant land for the purposes of development of new units.
- BLI 1450: Site Improvements: Costs to maintain and improve nondwelling and exterior common areas of an existing project (e.g., paving, concrete, landscaping, exterior site lighting).
- BLI 1460: Dwelling Structures: Comprehensive rehabilitation activities and single-item life-cycle replacement, including, but not limited to, bathroom and kitchen upgrades, painting, heating, ventilation and air-conditioning (HVAC) replacement, and unit renovation.
- BLI 1465: Dwelling Equipment: Replacement of stoves and refrigerators. System upgrades, such as hot-water tank replacement, are not included in this BLI, but instead in BLI 1460.
- BLI 1470: Non-dwelling Structures: Modernization and construction of administrative buildings, community spaces, on-site management offices, and other types of non-dwelling housing authority buildings.
- BLI 1475: Non-dwelling Equipment: Purchase of non-dwelling equipment for a project site. This line item does not include items used in the central office.
- BLI 1485: Demolition: Demolition of housing authority property in accordance with 24 CFR 970.
- BLI 1495: Moving to Work: Funding the Moving to Work program of an approved Moving to Work agency.
- BLI 1495: Relocation: A housing authority is permitted to allocate resources to relocation services as long as the housing authority is following the Uniform Relocation Act and/or in limited instances providing temporary housing allowances.
- BLI 1499: Development Activities: Development of new public housing projects or mixed.

---

96. U.S. Dep't Hous. & Urban Dev., Form 50075.1: Annual Statement/Performance and Evaluation Report (2008) and U.S. Dep't Hous. & Urban Dev., Form 50075.2: Capital Fund Program—Five Year Action Plan (2008).

- BLI 1501: Collateralization or Debt Service: Retiring existing housing authority debt.
- BLI 9000: Direct Payment of Collateralization or Debt Service: Retiring housing authority debt that is directly processed by HUD. This line item would be used when housing authorities collateralize their future CF payments and use those future payments to repay the debt.
- BLI 1502: Contingency: Up to 8 percent of a housing authority's annual CF budget may be allocated as a contingency to cover any unforeseen conditions such as change orders or emergencies.

Once a housing authority has an approved five-year capital plan and budget, HUD allows the housing authority to have fungibility in moving activities between the five-year and annual budgets to accommodate the changing priorities and needs of the housing authority.[97] After a housing authority has an approved annual PHA Plan, has executed the Capital Fund Program Amendment to the Consolidated Annual Contributions Contract amending the ACC to reflect the Capital Funds, secured the necessary environmental review,[98] and complied with all other applicable housing authority requirements, then the housing authority may begin to undertake the Capital Fund projects outlined in its annual plan.

C. Replacement Housing Factor Funds

In addition to the Capital Funds provided to housing authorities for their existing public housing units, HUD also provides funding to housing authorities for the development or acquisition of new units to replace units removed from inventory because of demolition or conveyance.[99] Capital Funds provided for this purpose are referred to as Replacement Housing Factor (RHF) funds[100] and are provided to the housing authority in the same amount as it would have received if those units had remained in the housing authority's inventory.[101] A housing authority may utilize RHF funds only for the development or acquisition of new public housing rental units, including those developed in accordance with HUD mixed-finance regulations,[102] and may not be used for rehabilitation or modernization of existing public housing units.[103] The eligible housing authorities receive, on request, five years of RHF funds as a matter of right, and an additional five years of funding on evidence of sufficient leveraging of the RHF funds.[104] RHF funds must be obligated within two years and expended within four years of receipt unless the housing authority has an approved RHF Plan that provides for "accumulation" of multiple years of RHF funds, which allows the housing

---

97. 24 C.F.R. § 968.305(1993).
98. See Chapter 13, "Cross-Cutting Requirements: Federal-Wide Requirements Impacting HUD Programs," for a detailed discussion on the environmental review process and requirements.
99. 24 C.F.R. § 905.10i (2001).
100. Id.
101. 24 C.F.R. § 905.10i-3 (2001).
102. 24 C.F.R. § 94f (2001).
103. 24 C.F.R. § 905.10i-5 (2001).
104. 24 C.F.R. § 905.10i-2 (2001).

authority to aggregate years of funding before using those funds for development.[105] Housing authorities that accumulate RHF funds must obligate the funds within two years of reaching the necessary accumulation level and expend those funds within four years of that date.[106] RHF funds must be used in accordance with the HUD requirements for public housing development contained in 24 CFR Part 941.

D. Leveraging Capital Funds

HUD's Capital Fund Financing Program (CFFP) allows housing authorities to pledge a portion of their projected future Capital Fund allocation toward repayment of private debt incurred to develop or modernize public housing units.[107] A housing authority may seek approval from HUD's Office of Capital Improvements to use up to 33 percent of the housing authority's Capital Fund grant allocation for use in making future debt service payments.[108] HUD has imposed a number of requirements on these types of transactions, including standards such as: the term of a loan or bond issuance repaid with CFFP funds can be no longer than 20 years, the housing authority submitting the CFFP proposal must be at least a standard performer under HUD's Public Housing Assessment System, the transaction must meet certain underwriting standards and financial requirements, and the transaction must include certain documents and provisions to ensure that all applicable HUD requirements are enforced.[109] HUD has approved CFFP transactions involving modernization of existing public housing units, rehabilitation of non-dwelling structures, development of new housing authority-owned public housing units, and development of privately owned mixed-finance public housing units.[110]

E. Time Line for Use of Capital Funds

Similar to the time lines for RHF fund expenditure, a housing authority has 24 months from the date of the Capital Fund Program Amendment to the Consolidated Annual Contributions Contract to obligate 90 percent of the funds and an additional 24 months to expend 100 percent of the grant funds.[111] As described above, a housing authority may not expend Capital Funds until it has documented the planned use of those funds in its annual PHA Plan; however, lack of an annual plan will not toll the obligation clock. Except in limited instances, if a housing authority's Capital Funds are not obligated and expended within the requisite time frames, HUD can undertake a number of remedies, including withholding future Capital Funds.[112]

---

105. 24 C.F.R. § 905.10i-7B (2001).
106. 24 C.F.R. § 905.10i-7 (2001).
107. *See* Section 9(d)(1)(A) of the U.S. Housing Act, 42 U.S.C. § 1437 and 24 C.F.R. § 905.500.
108. See U.S. Dep't Hous. & Urban Dev., Public Housing, *Capital Fund Financing Program*, http://portal.hud.gov/hudportal/HUD?src=/program_offices/public_indian_housing/programs/ph/capfund/cffp (last visited Dec. 29, 2011).
109. *See id.*
110. Reno & Cavanaugh, PLLC has represented housing authorities in closing the types of transactions lsted.
111. 24 C.F.R. §§ 905.120a, 120d (2001).
112. 24 C.F.R. §§ 905.120c-e (2001).

F. Operating Funds

HUD provides funding through its Operating Fund[113] to assist housing authorities in covering the cost of operating public housing units covered by a housing authority's ACC.[114] The 1937 Act required HUD to establish a formula for distributing the Operating Fund among all public housing units.[115] In 1998, as part of QHWRA,[116] Congress directed HUD to establish a new formula for allocating the Operating Fund to housing authorities.[117] As part of the negotiated rulemaking process, Congress directed HUD to contract with Harvard University's Graduate School of Design to conduct a cost study analyzing effective methods of operating public housing.[118] The Harvard cost study, completed in 2003, recommended that public housing standards and funding be structured similar to the operating standards established for HUD's multifamily portfolio, which requires that each project be a separate asset with project-based budgeting, accounting, and management.[119] HUD's asset-management reforms require that each project stand on its own, with separate funding, budgets, operations, and oversight specifically geared to each project.[120] It is intended to create greater efficiencies and greater accountability for each project. HUD's public housing monitoring and assessment system has recently been overhauled to measure housing authority performance on a project-by-project basis as opposed to authority-wide.[121] This asset-management approach is reflected in the current Operating Fund Rule.[122]

G. Operating Subsidy

The Operating Fund provides operating subsidies to housing authorities to cover the cost of operating public housing for low-income and very low-income persons.[123] Operating subsidy is the major source of funding for operating public housing units. Operating subsidies cover

---

113. The Operating Fund is authorized under Section 9(e)(1)of the U.S. Housing Act of 1937, as amended, and appropriated annually by Congress. The funds provided to housing authorities through the Operating Fund to subsidize the cost of operation are referred to as operating subsidies. 42 U.S.C. § 1437g (1998).

114. 42 U.S.C. § 1437g (1998).

115. 42 U.S.C. § 1437g (1998).

116. Quality Housing and Work Responsibility Act of 1998, Pub. L. No. 105-276, 112 Stat. 2518 (1998).

117. Quality Housing and Work Responsibility Act Of 1998, Pub. L. No. 105-276, § 519, 112 Stat. 2518 (1998).

118. *See* U.S. Dep't Hous. & Urban Dev., Public and Indian Housing, http://portal.hud.gov/hudportal/HUD?src=/program_offices/public_indian_housing (last visited Dec. 29, 2011).

119. *See* U.S. Dep't Hous. & Urban Dev., Public and Indian Housing, http://portal.hud.gov/hudportal/HUD?src=/program_offices/public_indian_housing (last visited Dec. 29, 2011).

120. *See* U.S. Dep't Hous. & Urban Dev., Public Housing, *Asset Management*, http://portal.hud.gov/hudportal/HUD?src=/program_offices/public_indian_housing/programs/ph/am/overview (last visited Dec. 29, 2011).

121. Public Housing Evaluation and Oversight: Changes to the Public Housing Assessment System (PHAS) and Determining and Remedying Substantial Default, HUD, 24 C.F.R. pts. 901, 902, and 907, Fed. Reg. No. 73, No. 163, Docket No. FR-5094-P-01, p. 49,544 (Aug. 21, 2008).

122. *See* portal.hud.gov/hudportal/HUD?src=/program_offices/public_indian_housing.

123. 24 C.F.R. § 990.100 (2005).

the difference between the cost of operating each unit and the amount tenants pay as rent.[124] To determine the annual amount of funding that will be provided to each project, HUD requires housing authorities to complete HUD Form 52723 and HUD Form 52722 each year for every project.[125] Much of the information included in the 52723 and 52722 forms is prepopulated by HUD into the electronic spreadsheets housing authorities complete for the operating subsidy funding.[126] HUD's Operating Fund Formula is based on the following elements: project expense level, utility expense level, add-ons, and formula income.[127] The project expense level, utility expense level, and add-ons constitute the formula expenses. The difference between the formula expenses and formula income is the amount of operating subsidy the housing authority is eligible to receive.[128] Each aspect of the aforementioned calculation is described below.

A major factor in determining a project's operating subsidy is driven by its project expense level. Each project's project expense level is determined by a regression analysis of various project characteristics, similar to that used by the FHA to underwrite HUD's multifamily portfolio.[129] The project characteristics of the project expense level include: number of units in the project, age of the project, bedroom distribution, building type, location, and area poverty rate.[130] The variables are entered into the regression analysis to produce a project expense level that is adjusted annually for inflation and that is subject to various limits and adjustments.[131]

Another factor used to determine a project's operating subsidy is the project's utility expense level. HUD reimburses housing authorities for the utilities used at each site. The utilities expense level is calculated by multiplying utility consumption by the utility rate by the applicable inflation factor.[132] HUD provides an incentive for housing authorities that decrease utility consumption by allowing those authorities to retain 75 percent of any de-

---

124. 24 C.F.R. § 990.110a-2 (2005).
125. U.S. Dep't of Hous. & Urban Dev., Instructions for Form 52723 (2007). Note that small housing authorities, those with less than 250 units, and Moving to Work agencies with agreements that use an alternative Operating Fund formula, submit one Form 52723 for the entire housing authority portfolio.
126. See HUD PHA User Guide CY 2012 PHA HUD-52723 PHA Excel Tool and PHA User Guide CY 2012 HUD 52722 UEL Excel Tool.
127. 24 C.F.R. § 990.165a (2005).
128. Id. Note that as part of Congress's annual appropriations process, it will fund the operating subsidy at a percentage of need. The 10-year average proration is approximately 93% based on 2011 Council of Large Public Housing Authorities analysis. FFY 2012 Appropriations Act provides for a reduction in the amount of operating subsidy to reflect excess operating reserves held by the housing authority. HUD's Subsidy Allocation Adjustment reduces a housing authority's operating subsidy by those funds it holds in its operating reserve above four months of operations (six months for housing authorities with 250 units or less). Certain exceptions apply, such as allowing housing authorities with prior commitments for those funds to request a waiver of the subsidy allocation adjustment. See HUD Notice PIH 2011-55 Public Housing Operating Subsidy Calculations for Calendar Year 2012.
129. 24 C.F.R. § 990.165a (2005).
130. 24 C.F.R. § 990.990.165b (2005).
131. 24 C.F.R. §§ 990.165c, 165d (2005).
132. 24 C.F.R. § 990.170a (2005).

crease in utility consumption.[133] Conversely, housing authorities that experience increased utility consumption must bear 75 percent of the cost of that increase from sources other than the Operating Fund.[134]

A third factor in determining a project's subsidy is a project's add-ons. HUD reimburses housing authorities for various project expenses and allowances, referred to as add-ons, not included in the project expense level that can include the following: payments in lieu of taxes, audit costs, asset-management fees, resident-participation activities, information technology costs, and asset-repositioning fees.[135] Many of the add-ons are based on either a set amount or the actual costs incurred. One of the add-ons, the asset-repositioning fee, is available only to housing authorities who are removing public housing units from their inventory, either through demolition or conveyance to an entity other than the housing authority.[136] Housing authorities that demolish or dispose of a public housing project or building are eligible to receive a prorated amount of subsidy referred to as an "asset repositioning fee," following the removal of the units from the public housing inventory.[137] Housing authorities that demolish a project or building are eligible to receive 75 percent of the project expense level for the first year following the removal of the units, 50 percent for the second year, and 25 percent for the third year.[138] Housing authorities that transfer ownership or dispose of a project or building but do not demolish the structures are entitled to receive 75 percent of the project expense level for the first year following the removal of the units and 50 percent for the second year.[139]

The final factor in determining a project's operating subsidy is its formula income. Formula income is the rental income a housing authority receives from its tenants.[140] Generally speaking, tenants pay 30 percent of their monthly adjusted income in rent.[141] The factors involved in determining tenant rental payments are discussed in more detail in the "Operation of Public Housing" section that follows.

Based on the Operating Fund Formula, housing authorities should receive, by project, the sum of the project expense level, add-ons, and utility expense level less formula income.[142] But because HUD's budget request for Operating Fund appropriations is often less than housing authorities' demonstrated need, and, in addition, Congress often prorates the amount of operating subsidy it will fund, housing authorities have experienced shortfalls in operating subsidy.[143] In addition, for fiscal year 2012, HUD is requiring that housing authori-

---

133. 24 C.F.R. § 990.170cs (2005).
134. Id.
135. 24 C.F.R. § 990.190 (2005).
136. 24 C.F.R. § 990.190h (2005).
137. See HUD Notice PIH 2011-18, Guidance on the Asset Repositioning Fee Under 24 C.F.R. § 990.190(h) and Guidance on Re-occupying Public Housing Units Proposed or Approved for Demolition, Disposition or Transition to Homeownership.
138. Office of Public and Indian Housing, U.S. Dep't of Hous. & Urban Dev., Notice PIH 2011-18, 2 (2011).
139. Id.
140. 24 C.F.R. § 990.195a (2005).
141. 42 U.S.C. § 1437a (1998).
142. 24 C.F.R. § 990.110b-1 (2005).
143. Note that as part of Congress's annual appropriations process, it will fund the operating subsidy at a percentage of need. The 10-year average proration is approximately 93% based upon a 2011 Council of Large Public Housing Authorities analysis.

ties offset the amount of operating subsidy requested by the excess reserves in current public housing operating reserve.[144]

H. Moving to Work Agencies

Moving to Work (MTW) is a demonstration or pilot program that gives housing authorities flexibility in the way they use their federal funds.[145] MTW was authorized by the Department of Veterans Affairs and Housing and Urban Development and the Independent Agencies Appropriations Act of 1996 (MTW Act).[146] The intent of the MTW Act was to provide housing authorities with fungibility in use of their various sources such that, with certain limitations, Capital Funds, Operating Funds, and housing choice vouchers provided pursuant to Section 8 of the 1937 Act can be combined and used interchangeably to cover various housing authority expenses.[147] Other purposes include promoting housing choice for residents and developing policies to use federal funds more efficiently.[148] Originally, 30 housing authorities were selected to participate in the MTW program, including 15 that would receive technical assistance as well as detailed evaluations to attempt to identify practices that can be replicated on a wider scale.[149] Housing authorities with strong performance under the Public Housing Assessment System, described later in this chapter, received greater consideration in the selection process for MTW agencies.[150] PHAs participating in MTW have used their funds and flexibility in a variety of ways. Many have used the ability to combine funding streams to preserve low-income units that have significant capital needs for which the PHA has no other funding source. Others have used their flexibility to develop new affordable replacement units that are outside of the existing public housing and Section 8 programs. New forms of housing assistance also have been developed, including what is referred to as "sponsor-based" housing, in which a PHA provides housing subsidy dollars to a service provider, who then offers a package of housing and social services to eligible families or individuals. Participating agencies are also experimenting with a wider range of rent policies beyond what is permitted by the 1937 Act. These include policies to streamline rent calculations and others designed to reward and incentivize work by residents.[151] Since the MTW Act was passed in 1996, there have been a number of legislative efforts to expand participation in MTW. Several housing authorities have been added to the program through specific provisions of law. Currently, another effort is under way through legislation to reform the Section 8 program. In the 111th Congress, this was part of the Section 8 Voucher Reform Act (SEVRA). In the 112th Congress, it is included in a successor bill, titled the Affordable Housing and Self-Sufficiency Improvement Act of 2012.

---

144. *See* HUD Notice PIH 2011-55, Public Housing Operating Subsidy Calculations for Calendar Year 2012, Issued Sept. 26, 2011.
145. http://portal.hud.gov/programoffices/public_indian_housing/mtw (last visited Jan. 4, 2012).
146. Pub. L. 104-134; 110 Stat. 1321-281; 42 U.S.C. § 1437(f) note.
147. 42 U.S.C. § 1437f note, Section 204(c)(1).
148. *Id.*
149. 42 U.S.C. § 1437f note, Section 204(b).
150. 42 U.S.C. § 1437f note, Section 204(d).
151. Our firm has advised housing authorities on all of the aforementioned uses.

VI. OPERATION OF PUBLIC HOUSING

Housing authorities must establish requirements and standards for admission to and occupancy of public housing units in accordance with applicable public housing requirements.[152] Such admissions and occupancy policies must be duly adopted by the housing authority, following applicable notice and comment requirements, and must be included in the housing authority's annual PHA Plan.[153]

A. Admissions and Tenant Selection Policies

Housing authorities are subject to federal civil rights laws and fair-housing requirements, many of which apply to the admissions and occupancy of public housing.[154] Please refer to the fair-housing requirements chapter for a discussion of the federal civil-rights laws and requirements applicable to HUD programs.

A housing authority's tenant admissions and selection policies must reflect the following regulatory requirements and limitations:[155]

- Only applicants whose family[156] income is at or below 80 percent of the area median income are eligible to reside in public housing.[157]
- At least 40 percent of the housing authority's tenants must be at or below 30 percent of the area median income.[158]
- At least one family member must be a U.S. citizen or an eligible immigrant.[159]
- Social Security numbers must be provided for all family members age six or older, or certifications are needed evidencing that applicable family members do not possess Social Security numbers.[160]
- Families who include a member possessing any of the following characteristics cannot be admitted:
  - evicted from public housing because of drug-related criminal activity unless the family member completed a housing authority–approved rehabilitation program.[161]
  - currently engaged in drug use.[162]
  - convicted of methamphetamine production on the premises of federally assisted housing.[163]

---

152. 24 C.F.R. § 960 (2001).
153. *See* Section 5(A)(b) of the U.S. Housing Act of 1937 as codified in 42 U.S.C § 1437 (1998) and 24 C.F.R. § 960.202c (2001).
154. 24 C.F.R. § 960.103 (2001).
155. 24 C.F.R. § 960 subpt. B (2001).
156. Families include individuals. *See* 24 C.F.R. § 5.400.
157. 24 C.F.R. § 5.609 and 24 C.F.R. § 960.201 (2001).
158. *See* Section 16 of the U.S. Housing Act of 1937 as codified at 42 U.S.C § 1437(1998), as amended, and 24 C.F.R. § 960.202b (2001).
159. 24 C.F.R. pt. 5 (2001).
160. *Id.*
161. 24 C.F.R. § 960.204a-1 (2001). Note that this prohibition is applicable for three years following the eviction.
162. 24 C.F.R. § 960.204a-2 (2001).
163. 24 C.F.R. § 960.204a-3 (2001)

- subjected to lifetime registration on a sex-offender registry.[164]
- currently abuse alcohol such that it poses a health or safety concern to other residents.[165]

To determine whether any of the aforementioned conditions exist, a housing authority may secure information from law-enforcement agencies and drug-treatment facilities, following notice to the applicant, in the case of criminal records, and consent from the applicant, in the case of drug-treatment records.[166]

As part of a housing authority's admissions policies, it must establish a waiting list or lists that organize and order applicants for admission to public housing units and sites. Such list must set forth policies and standards for determining priorities for admission to public housing and must follow all applicable fair-housing requirements. Housing authorities can determine whether to have central waiting lists, which allow applicants to apply for all applicable housing authority sites, site-based waiting lists, which are located at each site and allow applicants to apply for that site, or site-designated lists, which are centrally administered but allow applicants to designate the site or sites to which they wish to be admitted.[167] If a housing authority chooses to use multiple types of lists, all such lists must be available to all applicants.[168] Before a housing authority may utilize site-based or site-designated waiting lists, it must include its site-based admissions procedures in its annual plan and receive HUD approval for such procedures. Thereafter, the housing authority must take steps to monitor the site-based plan to ensure it is administered fairly.[169]

In organizing the waiting list, housing authorities often choose to rank or prioritize applicants based on local preferences and housing needs.[170] Preferences that housing authorities may establish include:

- Residency in a city or county, but note that residency cannot be used as a requirement for admission.[171]
- Working family, but note that if this preference is utilized, equal preference must be provided to the elderly and disabled who cannot or do not work.[172]
- Disabled, but note that a particular disability cannot be singled out for the preference.[173]
- Victims of domestic violence and their families.[174]
- Single persons who are elderly or disabled.[175]

---

164. 24 C.F.R. § 960.204a-4 (2001).
165. 24 C.F.R. § 960.204b (2001).
166. 24 C.F.R. §§ 960.204c, 205c (2001).
167. 42 U.S.C. § 6(s).
168. *Id.*
169. 24 C.F.R. § 903.7b-2 (2010).
170. 24 C.F.R. § 960.206a-1 (2001).
171. 24 C.F.R. § 960.206b-1ii (2001).
172. 24 C.F.R. § 960.206b-2 (2001).
173. 24 C.F.R. § 960.206b-3 (2001).
174. 24 C.F.R. § 960.206b-4 (2001).
175. 24 C.F.R. § 960.206b-5 (2001).

Housing authorities may decide to rank preferences such that some are given higher priority than others. If housing authorities choose to rank preferences, they must disclose the ranking system in their annual plan.[176] Before applying preferences to an applicant, housing authorities will first match the type of unit, e.g., family or Uniform Federal Accessibility Standard, and the size of the unit, i.e., number of bedrooms, to eligible applicants.[177]

B. Designated Housing

In certain cases, housing authorities may determine it is important to limit occupancy of a site, or portion of a site, to particular populations. Housing authorities may designate projects or buildings within a project for occupancy by elderly families,[178] disabled families, or disabled and elderly combined.[179] To designate housing as elderly only or disabled only, a housing authority must include in its annual PHA Plan the intent to designate housing in such fashion; then it must complete a designated housing plan, also known as an allocation plan,[180] which demonstrates, inter alia, the need for such designation and the mechanism and resources for rehousing current residents of the site who do not meet the designation criteria.[181] The designated housing plan must be approved by HUD before a housing authority may begin to classify units under such designation. A housing authority wishing to house both elderly and disabled families in a project, referred to as "mixed-population" projects,[182] need not seek a designation, but must meet the requirements for mixed-population projects contained in 24 CFR Part 960 Subpart D. Note, however, should a housing authority decide to operate a mixed-population project, it must provide equal priority and preference to both elderly and disabled applicants in its admissions criteria and process.[183]

C. Determining Tenant Rent and Calculating Tenant Income

Once a housing authority selects a tenant for admission, it then must determine the amount of rent that tenant will be charged. Historically, public housing tenants have paid tenant rent payments equal to 30 percent of the household's annual adjusted income.[184] QHWRA[185] provided additional flexibility for determining the manner in which rent is calculated. QHWRA

---

176. OFFICE OF PUBLIC AND INDIAN HOUSING AND OFFICE OF PUBLIC HOUSING AND VOUCHER PROGRAMS, U.S. DEP'T OF HOUSING AND URBAN DEVELOPMENT, PUBLIC HOUSING OCCUPANCY GUIDEBOOK § 3 (2003) (hereinafter PUBLIC HOUSING OCCUPANCY GUIDEBOOK).
177. *Id.*
178. Head of household must be 62 or older. 24 C.F.R. § 5.100 (2001).
179. Head of household must be disabled (receives Social Security Income or has long-term physical, mental, or emotional impairments that impede their ability to live independently. 24 C.F.R. § 5.403 (2001) & 24 C.F.R. § 945.101 (1994).
180. 24 C.F.R. § 945.203 (1994).
181. U.S. Dep't of Hous. & Urban Dev., Notice PIH 97-12 (1997).
182. 24 C.F.R. § 945.105 (1994).
183. 24 C.F.R. § 960.407a (2001).
184. 24 C.F.R. § 5.609 (2001). PUBLIC HOUSING OCCUPANCY GUIDEBOOK § 10 (2003).
185. Title II of the Departments of Veterans Affairs, Housing and Urban Development and Independent Agencies Appropriations Act of 1999, Pub. L. 105-276 (Oct. 21, 1998).

authorized rent to be set based on either a tenant's income or the market rate.[186] QHWRA also provided flexibility in determining which types of income would be included in the income-based rent calculation.[187]

D. Determining Income-Based Rent

If a tenant's rent is calculated based on income, all income except the following types of funds must be included in the calculation:[188]

- Income from children's employment,
- Income from the care of foster children or adults,
- Income received to pay medical expenses,
- Income from a live-in aide,
- Student financial assistance,
- Income receive under various training and supportive-services programs,
- Income in excess of $480 for each full-time adult student,
- Food stamps, and
- Funds provided under various federal grants and programs.

Once a family's annual income is determined, various mandatory statutory income deductions must be applied to yield the family's annual adjusted income.[189] The statutorily prescribed deductions from income include the following:[190]

- $480 for each dependent;
- $400 for an elderly or disabled family; and
- To the extent it exceeds 3 percent of annual income, the sum of reasonable child-care expenses necessary to allow a family member to be employed, seek employment, or further his or her education; medical expenses of an elderly or disabled family; and attendant care for a disabled family member.[191]

QHWRA authorized housing authorities to allow exclusion of various other income from the amount used to calculate tenant rent.[192] Should housing authorities elect to adopt the additional permissive deductions, those deductions must be included in the housing authority's admissions and occupancy policies. In addition, the housing authority should ensure that the

---

186. PUBLIC HOUSING OCCUPANCY GUIDEBOOK § 10 (2003).
187. *Id.*
188. 24 C.F.R. § 5.609c (2001).
189. 24 C.F.R. § 5.611 (2001).
190. 24 C.F.R. § 5.611 (2001).
191. 24 C.F.R. § 5.611 (2011).
192. Examples of the types of income that housing authorities may consider excluding include various medical expenses, the wages of a secondary wage earner, or the cost of looking for work. PUBLIC HOUSING OCCUPANCY GUIDEBOOK § 10.3 (2003) & 24 C.F.R. § 5.611 (2001).

reduction in income received because of the permissive deductions will not result in operating shortfalls for the housing authority.[193]

E. Flat, Market-Based Rent

QHWRA gave tenants the option of having rent set at flat rents, i.e., the rental rate of comparable unassisted units, or utilizing the more common income-based calculation.[194] For tenants whose incomes increase above that necessary to pay market-based rent, flat rents are an attractive alternative to limit the amount of income that a tenant must expend on rent.[195] To set flat rents, housing authorities must analyze various geographic, site, and unit-specific factors to determine the rental payment amounts, much like the criteria applied in the Housing Choice Voucher Program's rent reasonableness standard.[196]

At least once a year, tenants must be given the choice of having income-based or flat rent.[197] In addition, housing authority policies must allow a family that suffers a financial hardship resulting in reduced income to immediately switch from flat rent to income-based rent.[198]

With the introduction of flat rents, ceiling rents, which cap income-based rents, have become somewhat unnecessary.[199] If housing authorities choose to use ceiling rents, they should set the ceiling rents at the flat rent or market-based rent level.[200]

F. Tenant Utility Expenses

If a tenant has opted for an income-based rent calculation, the tenant's utility expenses will factor into the amount of rent a tenant is charged such that a tenant's utility allowance is offset against the tenant's rent payment.[201] While historically utilities were centrally metered, current public housing regulations require housing authorities to convert centrally metered utilities to individually metered units unless it is impractical or would not achieve appreciable cost savings by doing so.[202] Under an individually metered system, residents pay the cost of applicable utilities directly to the utility supplier.[203] Utility allowances are set at the cost of moderate utility usage based on family size, type of unit, and geographic location.[204] When a tenant's rent payment is larger than its utility allowance, the tenant will receive the difference

---

193. 24 C.F.R. § 5.611 (2001). Note that the amount of operating subsidy a housing authority receives will not be increased to offset the decrease in rent received due to the permissive deductions. In addition, rents paid by tenants will still be limited by the minimum rent limits established by the housing authority. 24 C.F.R. § 5.630a (2001) & 24 C.F.R. § 960.253a-2 (2001).
194. PUBLIC HOUSING OCCUPANCY GUIDEBOOK §10 (2003).
195. 24 C.F.R. § 960.253b (2001).
196. 24 C.F.R. § 960.253b (2001) & PUBLIC HOUSING OCCUPANCY GUIDEBOOK § 10.6 (2003).
197. 24 C.F.R. § 960.253a (2001).
198. 24 C.F.R. § 960.253f (2001).
199. PUBLIC HOUSING OCCUPANCY GUIDEBOOK § 10.6 (2003).
200. *Id.* § 10.7 (2003).
201. *Id.* § 10.7 (2003).
202. 24 C.F.R. § 965.401 (2001).
203. PUBLIC HOUSING OCCUPANCY GUIDEBOOK § 14.1 (2003).
204. 24 C.F.R. §§ 965.505a, 505d (2001).

as a monthly utility reimbursement.[205] Because the utility offset is, in effect, rent, public housing tenant leases must include non-payment of utilities as grounds for eviction.[206]

G. Occupancy Standards and Requirements

1. Public Housing Tenant Leases

All tenants admitted to public housing must take occupancy pursuant to a written dwelling lease. HUD rules establish required and prohibited provisions for public housing leases. Such leases must also follow applicable state and local laws.[207] The following types of provisions must be included in any public housing dwelling lease:[208]

- Composition of tenant household, unit number, and tenant's housing authority account number.
- Lease term, which is initially for one year and is automatically renewed for successive one-year terms unless the tenant family violates the community-service and family self-sufficiency requirements.[209]
- Payments due under the lease, including tenant rent, utility allowances and reimbursements, security deposits, late payment charges, repair and maintenance fees.
- Mechanism for annual redetermination of income, rent, and family composition.
- Tenant's right to use and occupy the premises.
- Housing authority's responsibility to maintain the premises and all building systems in decent, safe, and sanitary condition in accordance with all building codes, housing codes, and HUD regulations, including lead-based paint safety standards.
- Housing authority's responsibility to provide notice to tenant of grounds for any adverse action as well as tenant's right to grieve such actions.
- Tenant's obligations not to assign lease or house boarders, to abide by housing authority rules and regulations, to use the premises as a residence, to maintain the unit in clean and safe condition, to pay reasonable repair charges, to maintain peaceful enjoyment, to ensure the household and guests do not engage in criminal activity or alcohol abuse on the premises that threatens the health and safety of other tenants, and to ensure household and guests do not engage in drug-related criminal activity on or off the premises.
- Housing authority's duty to timely remedy conditions hazardous to the lives, health, or safety of tenants.
- Move-in and move-out requirements.
- Standards for housing authority access to tenant units.
- Notice and tenant housing authority communication requirements.

---

205. PUBLIC HOUSING OCCUPANCY GUIDEBOOK § 14.4 (2003).
206. See 24 C.F.R. §§ 966.4(l)–(2).
207. PUBLIC HOUSING OCCUPANCY GUIDEBOOK § 17 (2003).
208. 24 C.F.R. § 966.4 (2010).
209. 24 C.F.R. § 966.4a-2ii (2010). Community service and self-sufficiency requirements are discussed later in this chapter.

- Grounds for termination of tenancy.
- Eviction requirements and processes.
- Requirements for lease modification.
- Requirement of reasonable accommodation.

The following types of provisions may not be included in any lease between a housing authority and a tenant:[210]

- Tenant's agreement to automatic confession of wrongdoing.
- Tenant's agreement to have property held as pledge or security.
- Landlord hold-harmless language.
- Tenant's waiver of notice of legal action, right to jury trial, or right to appeal.
- Automatic charges to tenant for legal proceedings.

2. Tenant's Right to Grieve Housing Authority Actions

Pursuant to public housing regulations, tenants have a right to dispute or grieve any action or failure to act by the housing authority with respect to the lease or tenancy and that adversely affects the tenant's rights or duties.[211] Housing authorities have a right to exclude from the grievance process any termination of tenancy because of criminal activity threatening the health and safety of the tenant or other residents, any violent or drug-related activity, or a felony conviction.[212] Grievance procedures shall be included in tenant leases and the housing authority's admissions and continued occupancy policies.[213] Grievance procedures should provide for informal settlement processes and for formal grievance processes.[214] Formal grievance hearings must be conducted by an impartial person not involved in the dispute whose hearing findings must be rendered in writing within a reasonable time of the hearing.[215]

3. Community-Service and Economic Self-Sufficiency Requirements

Annually, each non-exempt[216] family member in a public housing household must do one of the following: complete eight hours of community service, spend eight hours participating in an economic self-sufficiency program, or spend eight hours completing a combination thereof.[217] Housing authorities must develop policies for administering community service and economic self-sufficiency requirements and can either self-administer the programs or make such activities available to tenants through third-party providers and social-service organiza-

---

210. 24 C.F.R. § 966.6 (2010).
211. 24 C.F.R. § 966.50 (2010).
212. 24 C.F.R. § 966.51a-2 (2010).
213. 24 C.F.R. § 966.52 (2010).
214. 24 C.F.R. § 966.56 (2010).
215. 24 C.F.R. § 966.55b (2010) & 24 C.F.R. § 966.57a (2010).
216. Exempt family members include the elderly, disabled, individuals who care for the disabled, and those who work. 24 C.F.R. § 960.601b (2000).
217. 24 C.F.R. § 960.603a (2000).

tions.[218] Some types of community-service activities that satisfy the community-service requirement include:[219]

- Volunteering with a nonprofit children's or seniors' organization.
- Volunteering as a member of the housing authority's resident advisory organization.
- Volunteering with the housing authority.
- Caring for another tenant's children so that tenant may work.

Eligible economic self-sufficiency programs include:[220]

- Job-training programs.
- Higher education.
- Apprenticeships.
- Credit counseling.

Non-exempt members of the tenant household must provide a certification documenting completion of the applicable requirements.[221] Should a housing authority determine that a non-exempt individual failed to complete the community service and economic self-sufficiency requirements, the housing authority must notify the tenant household of the noncompliance and advise the respective tenant that the lease will not be renewed unless the tenant enters into a written agreement outlining the measures tenant will take to remedy the noncompliance.[222]

4. *Pet Ownership in Public Housing*

Subject to compliance with reasonable requirements imposed by the housing authority, tenants are permitted to have pets in public housing.[223] Note that the standards discussed herein apply to pets but not to assistance or service animals that are required as a reasonable accommodation for persons with disabilities. Such service animals must be accommodated in accordance with Section 504 of the Rehabilitation Act of 1973 and the Fair Housing Act.[224] See Chapter 14, "Civil Rights Programs Administered and Enforced by HUD," for a discussion of the fair-housing requirements related to assistive animals. HUD has established separate standards for pets in elderly, disabled, mixed-population developments and those in family developments, but for the most part, the standards and requirements are quite similar.[225] In general, when establishing pet policies, a housing authority may do the following:[226]

---

218. 24 C.F.R. § 960.605b (2000).
219. PUBLIC HOUSING OCCUPANCY GUIDEBOOK § 15.2 (2003).
220. *Id.* § 15.3(2003).
221. 24 C.F.R. § 960.607a (2000).
222. 24 C.F.R. § 960.607b-c (2000).
223. 42 U.S.C. § 1437z-3(1998), 12 U.S.C. § 1701r-1 (1983), 24 C.F.R. pt. 5 & 24 C.F.R. § 960 subpt. G (2000).
224. 29 U.S.C.793 § (1992) & 42 U.S.C. §§ 3601–3619 (1988).
225. PUBLIC HOUSING OCCUPANCY GUIDEBOOK § 16.2 (2003).
226. *Id.*

- May establish a reasonable definition of what constitutes a household pet and which pets may reside in public housing.
- May establish reasonable limitations on the number of pets in a unit.
- May require tenants to pay a pet deposit to cover the reasonable costs of maintaining the common areas and repairing the unit as a result of damage caused by the pet.
- May require the pet to be registered or licensed.
- May prescribe standards of pet care.
- May bar pets from specified areas of the project so long as pet owners have adequate ingress in and egress from the building when accompanied by pets.

Two more applicable requirements for pet policies are as follows: a housing authority's pet policies may not require removal of a pet's vocal chords, and housing authorities must solicit and incorporate tenant input on the pet policies and rules.[227]

VII. DEMOLITION, DISPOSITION, AND CONVERSION OF PUBLIC HOUSING

Before a housing authority may demolish[228] structures or dispose of[229] land subject to an ACC with HUD, the housing authority must seek approval from the Special Applications Center (SAC), a division of HUD's Office of Public Housing Investments. The SAC application must include a number of certifications, resolutions, and documents that evidence the requisite consultation, processes, and approvals for the intended action.[230] An environmental review must be completed before disposition or demolition can be approved,[231] and HUD limits the use of proceeds received from disposition of public housing property.[232] HUD recently published a notice that provides guidance on additional requirements and limitations for conveyance of public housing property.[233]

In the late 1990s, HUD began requiring housing authorities to analyze their aging and distressed public housing stock to determine whether it would be more costly to revitalize the developments, or portions thereof, than to provide the tenants with tenant-based assistance under Section 8 of the U.S. Housing Act.[234] Housing authorities that determine it would be most cost-effective to provide replacement vouchers to current residents of the distressed developments than to redevelop the distressed development must prepare a conversion plan that outlines the processes and requirements for removing the distressed public housing units

---

227. *Id.*
228. HUD refers to "demolition" as the removal, by razing or other means, in whole or in part, of one or more permanent buildings of a public housing development. 24 C.F.R. § 970.5 (2006).
229. HUD defines "disposition" as the conveyance or other transfer by the housing authority, by sale or other transaction, of any interest in the real estate of a public housing development, subject to exceptions listed in 24 C.F.R. §§ 970.3, 5 (2006).
230. 24 C.F.R. §§ 970.7, 9, 11, 15, 17 (2006).
231. 24 C.F.R. § 970.13 (2006).
232. 24 C.F.R. § 970.19 (2006).
233. HUD Notice PIH 2012-7 (HA), Feb. 2, 2012.
234. 24 C.F.R. § 971 (1997).

from the housing authority's inventory and providing tenants with replacement housing choice vouchers instead.[235]

For fiscal year 2012, Congress authorized a program called the Rental Assistance Demonstration, which, when implemented, will result in the conversion of a potentially significant number of public housing units.[236] The Rental Assistance Demonstration provides funding to convert up to 60,000 public housing and other HUD-assisted units to Section 8–assisted units that can be used to finance debt and that could be used to fund capital improvements.[237] Although this program is in its early stages of development, it could result in a major overhaul and conversion of public housing stock.

VIII. MONITORING AND OVERSIGHT OF PUBLIC HOUSING

A. Enforcement through the Annual Contributions Contract and Grant Agreements

HUD's main enforcement mechanism against housing authorities that fail to comply with various public housing requirements is through the Annual Contributions Contract (ACC) HUD enters into with each respective housing authority, as described earlier in this chapter. Most public housing grants and funds that a housing authority receives are provided via amendments to the ACC and therefore incorporate the requirements of the ACC into the requirements for use of the funds. Should HUD determine that a housing authority has materially violated the terms of the ACC or its grant agreements,[238] HUD must follow the remedies provided for in the ACC, which requires that HUD provide notice to the housing authority of the substantial default and, in most cases, an opportunity for cure.[239] If the housing authority fails to cure the violations, HUD may require that the housing authority property be conveyed to HUD or that HUD take control of the projects through a receivership or other means.[240]

B. Monitoring through Public Housing Agency Plans

HUD requires housing authorities[241] to complete an annual plan every year and a five-year

---

235. 24 C.F.R. § 972 (2001).
236. Consolidated Appropriations Act of 2012, Pub. L. 112-074 (Dec. 23, 2011).
237. Id.
238. HUD considers a material violation the following: failure to maintain decent, safe, and sanitary housing; disposition of public housing units without HUD approval; violation of civil rights requirements; abandonment of a project; failure to complete modernization or development in a timely fashion; termination of PILOT. See Terms and Conditions Constituting Part A of a Consolidated Annual Contributions Contract Between Housing Authority and the United States of American, Form 53012A, § 17 (1995).
239. Terms and Conditions Constituting Part A of a Consolidated Annual Contributions Contract Between Housing Authority and the United States of American, Form 53012A, § 17 (1995).
240. Id.
241. Note that HUD also requires any local, regional, or state agency that receives funds to operate public housing or Section 8 programs to complete PHA Plans. PUBLIC HOUSING OCCUPANCY GUIDEBOOK 1 (2001).

plan every five years (each a PHA Plan).[242] The purpose of the PHA Plan is to summarize the housing authority's programs, policies, funding, and plans for meeting various federal requirements and local needs in connection with the housing functions administered by the housing authority.[243] All housing authorities must submit annual PHA Plans, except those considered "qualified" pursuant to the Housing and Economic Recovery Act of 2008,[244] which exempted housing authorities meeting all the following requirements from submitting annual plans:[245]

- Have 550 or fewer public housing units and Section 8 units, combined.
- Are not designated as "troubled" under HUD's Public Housing Assessment System.
- If applicable, have not received a failing score on the Section 8 management Assessment System for the past 12 months.

Housing authorities submit PHA Plans in a format and on templates established by HUD.[246] In addition to providing a good overview and snapshot of housing authority activities and operations, the PHA Plan serves as the housing authority's annual application for grants to support improvements to public housing buildings, i.e., Capital Funds and various grant funds.[247] Housing authorities that are required to submit annual plans and fail to do so will not receive Capital Funds or other applicable funds until the PHA Plan is submitted.[248] In developing the PHA Plan, housing authorities are required to engage residents through a housing authority-wide resident council or, if none exists, then through a resident advisory board to elicit feedback and input on the PHA Plan.[249] Once the draft PHA Plan is complete, the housing authority must, following a 45-day public notice and review period, hold a public hearing on the proposed PHA Plan[250] and then submit the PHA Plan to the housing authority's board of commissioners for approval. The PHA Plan is due to HUD 75 days before the beginning of the housing authority's fiscal year[251] and deemed approved 75 days after submission unless HUD provides specific written notice to the housing authority of its disapproval.[252]

---

242. 24 C.F.R. § 903.4a (2001).
243. 24 C.F.R. § 903.3 (2001).
244. Sections 2701 and 2702 of the Housing and Economic Recovery Act of 2008, Pub. L. 110-289, July 30, 2008
245. *Id.*
246. *See* HUD Form 50075, PHA Annual Plan and 5 Year Plan Templates; HUD Forms 50075.1, Annual Statement/ Performance and Evaluation Report, and 50075.2, Capital Fund Five Year Action Plan.
247. OFFICE OF PUBLIC AND INDIAN HOUSING, OFFICE OF POLICY, PROGRAM AND LEGISLATIVE INITIATIVES, U.S. DEP'T OF HOUSING AND URBAN DEVELOPMENT, PUBLIC HOUSING AGENCY PLAN DESK GUIDE 1 (2001) (hereinafter PUBLIC HOUSING AGENCY PLAN DESK GUIDE).
248. PUBLIC HOUSING AGENCY PLAN DESK GUIDE 1 (2001), p.14.
249. 24 C.F.R. § 903.13 (2001).
250. 24 C.F.R. § 903.17 (2001).
251. PUBLIC HOUSING AGENCY PLAN DESK GUIDE 1 (2001), p.15.
252. 24 C.F.R. § 903.23(c)(2) and (3).

C. Monitoring through the Public Housing Assessment System

HUD established the Public Housing Assessment System (PHAS) following passage of QHWRA to more effectively measure the performance of housing authorities. Following implementation of HUD's project-based asset-management reforms in 2008, the PHAS measurement system was revised to better align PHAS with the principals of asset management. HUD published the interim rule in February 2011.[253] The interim rule aims to simplify reporting as well as establish project-based versus authority-wide measurements. PHAS assesses the physical condition, financial condition, and management operations at each project, as well as the housing authorities' effectiveness in managing their Capital Fund programs.[254] PHAS scoring is based on a 100-point total score, dividied between the four indicators or components as follows:[255]

- Physical Condition: 40 points
- Financial Condition: 25 points
- Management Operations: 25 points
- Capital Fund: 10 points

Housing authorities undergoing a PHAS assessment will receive a performance designation based on the PHAS score.[256] Housing authorities will receive incentives or sanctions depending on their PHAS scores. Those receiving a combined score of 90 or better are designated as high performers.[257] High performers are eligible for less monitoring, public recognition, and bonus points in various funding competitions.[258] Housing authorities that score between 60 and 89 points will be designated as standard performers.[259] Those that score between 60 and 89 but that fail to score at least 60 percent on the physical condition, financial condition, and management operations indicators will be designated as a substandard performer.[260] Housing authorities that score less than 60 overall or that score less than five on the Capital Fund indicator will be designated as troubled performers.[261] Standard, substandard, and troubled housing authorities will be required to correct the deficiencies identified by the assessment.[262] Those who fail to correct the deficiencies in a timely fashion may be required to enter into a Corrective Action Plan that specifically outlines the actions to be taken and time frames for correcting the deficiencies.[263] Often, troubled housing authorities are subject to higher scrutiny on PHAS and other compliance and monitoring and are ineligible to apply for some HUD grants.

---

253. FR-5094-I-02.
254. 24 C.F.R. § 902.1c (2011).
255. 24 C.F.R. § 902.9b (2011).
256. 24 C.F.R. § 902.11 (2011).
257. 24 C.F.R. § 902.11a (2011).
258. 24 C.F.R. § 902.71a (2011).
259. 24 C.F.R. § 902.11b (2011).
260. 24 C.F.R. § 902.11c (2011).
261. 24 C.F.R. § 902.11d (2011).
262. 24 C.F.R. § 902.73a (2011).
263. 24 C.F.R. §§ 902.3, 73a (2011).

D. Physical Condition Assessment

The objective of this indicator is to determine whether the housing authority's housing stock is decent, safe, sanitary, and in good repair, as well as to identify any accessibility issues that may indicate noncompliance with the Fair Housing Act and/or Section 504 of the Rehabilitation Act of 1973.[264] HUD makes this assessment by having an independent inspector conduct inspections of the building's exterior, building systems, dwelling units, and common areas.[265] Once an initial assessment is conducted, the frequency of future physical condition assessments will be based on the score the authority receives on the physical condition assessment. Housing authorities[266] receiving a physical condition score of 90 or above will be assessed every three years.[267] Those receiving a physical condition score between 80 and 89 will be assessed every two years.[268] Housing authorities receiving a physical condition score of less than 80 or who are designated as troubled will receive an annual physical condition inspection.[269]

Under the physical condition indicator, a score will be calculated for both the housing authority's entire portfolio and per project, referred to as an asset management project (AMP).[270] Should the inspection yield serious health and safety concerns, the inspector will immediately notify the housing authority of such deficiencies, which will have 24 hours to correct the delinquency.[271] Housing authorities may have the sites reinspected following correction of the serious health and safety concerns to adjust the score.[272] To receive a passing score on the physical condition indicator, a housing authority must achieve a score of at least 24 out of 40 points or 60 percent of the total available physical condition points.[273] Housing authorities are encouraged to complete a housing authority-wide Uniform Physical Conditions Standards (UPCS) inspection prior to the pro forma PHAS inspection to identify and correct health, safety, and other structure-related issues prior to the PHAS inspection.

E. Financial Condition Assessment

The objective of the financial condition indicator is to determine the fiscal health of each project. This indicator evaluates whether the project's available financial resources are adequate

---

264. *See* 24 C.F.R. § 902.20a (2011) *and see* 24 C.F.R. § 5.703 for the definition of decent, safe, sanitary housing in good repair. *See also* Fair Housing Act, 42 U.S.C. §§ 3601–3619 and Section 504 of the Rehabilitation Act of 1973, 29 U.S.C. § 794 (2002). Note that should an inspector identify potential accessibility issues, it will refer the issue to HUD's Office of Fair Housing and Equal Opportunity for further investigation. *See* 24 C.F.R. § 902.22g (2011).
265. 24 C.F.R. § 902.21b (2011).
266. Title II of Division K, Consolidated Appropriations Act, 2008, Pub. L. 110-161, § 225 (Dec. 26, 2007).
267. 24 C.F.R. § 902.13b-2 (2011).
268. *Id.*
269. 24 C.F.R. § 902.13b-2 (2011) & 24 C.F.R. § 902.13b-3 (2011).
270. 24 C.F.R. § 902.25(a).
271. 24 C.F.R. § 902.22(f).
272. 24 C.F.R. § 902.26(a)(1).
273. 24 C.F.R. § 902.25(c)(2).

to maintain the project at suitable standards.[274] Note that mixed-finance projects are exempt from the financial indicator measurement.[275] As part of this indicator, HUD reviews a housing authority's unaudited and audited financial statements prepared in accordance with generally accepted accounting principles (GAAP)[276] to determine, by project, the following:[277]

- Quick ratio or current assets (cash or other assets, investments, and receivables easily convertible to cash)[278] measured against current liabilities (amounts due within the next 12 months).[279]
- Size and adequacy of reserves, referred to as months expendable net asset ratio.[280]
- Debt service coverage ratio or the net operating income available to make debt payments.[281]

Financial condition scores are issued both on individual projects and on the overall housing authority portfolio.[282] A housing authority must receive a score of at least 15 out of 25, or 60 percent of the available points, to pass the financial condition indicator.[283]

F. Management Operations Assessment

The PHAS management operations indicator measures the manner in which the housing authority operates each project.[284] Mixed-finance projects are excluded from the management operations indicator.[285] HUD analyzes the following three factors as part of this assessment:[286]

- Occupancy averaged across the fiscal year.[287]
- Accounts payable at the end of the fiscal year.
- Tenant accounts receivable.

HUD will adjust a housing authority's management operations score if factors such as age of the project[288] and high poverty rates in the area[289] exist. This indicator yields a total of 25 points.[290] Housing authorities must score at least 15 points to pass this indicator.[291]

---

274. 24 C.F.R. § 902.902.30(a).
275. 24 C.F.R. § 902.30(c).
276. 24 C.F.R. § 902.33(a).
277. 24 C.F.R. § 902.35(b).
278. Docket No. FR-5094-I-02.
279. Id.
280. Id.
281. Id.
282. 24 C.F.R. § 902.35(c).
283. 24 C.F.R. § 902.35(d)(2).
284. 24 C.F.R. § 902.43(a).
285. 24 C.F.R. § 902.40(b).
286. 24 C.F.R. § 902.43(a).
287. Occupancy is weighted most heavily in the management operations indicator, as it yields a potential of 16 of the total 25 points.
288. The units are over 28 years old. 24 C.F.R. § 902.44.
289. The project is in a Census tract in which over 40% of the families have incomes below the poverty rate. 24 C.F.R. § 902.44.
290. 24 C.F.R. § 902.45(c)(2).
291. Id.

G. Capital Fund Program Assessment

This indicator measures, on a housing authority-wide basis, versus by project, the timeliness of the housing authority's obligation of Capital Funds to make capital improvements as well as the housing authority's occupancy rate at the end of its fiscal year.[292] HUD determines a housing authority's obligation of Capital Funds by reviewing the electronic Line of Credit Control System (eLOCCS)[293] for each housing authority Capital Fund grant and assesses whether those funds are being expended in a timely manner.[294] This indicator carries a total of 10 points and housing authorities must receive at least five points to pass.[295] HUD allocates five points to timeliness of obligation and five points for occupancy rate.[296] If the housing authority obligates at least 90 percent of its Capital Fund grants by the obligation deadline, HUD will award five points.[297] No points are awarded to housing authorities that obligate less than 90 percent by the obligation end date.[298] With respect to occupancy, HUD will award the following for the respective occupancy rates: five points if a housing authority exceeds 96 percent occupancy; two points for 93 percent to 95.9 percent occupancy; and no points for less than 92 percent occupancy.[299]

H. HUD Office of Inspector General Audits

Housing authorities, as is the case for other recipients of HUD funding, are often subject to Office of Inspector General (OIG) audits. HUD audits of housing authorities often center on their procurement processes and their use of HUD funds. See Chapter 15, titled "Compliance and Enforcement" for a more detailed discussion of HUD OIG audits.

I. Voluntary Compliance Agreements

HUD's Office of Fair Housing and Equal Opportunity enforces fair-housing, accessibility, and civil rights requirements. Should HUD find that housing authorities are in violation of such requirements in administering or operating its public housing units, HUD often will require housing authorities to enter into a Voluntary Compliance Agreement that requires certain corrective actions and remedial measures to be taken to rectify the infractions within certain time frames. For a more detailed discussion of remedies to enforce fair-housing compliance, see Chapter 14, "Civil Rights Programs Administered and Enforced by HUD."

---

292. 24 C.F.R. § 902.50.
293. LOCCS is HUD's primary grant disbursement system. eLOCCS is an Internet-based version of LOCCS that currently is limited to housing authorities. *eLOCCS Getting Started Guide*, January 2003.
294. See 24 C.F.R. § 902.50(d).
295. 24 C.F.R. § 902.53.
296. Fed. Reg. 5094-I-02, Vol. 76, No. 36, p.10,138, Feb. 23, 2011.
297. *Id.*
298. *Id.*
299. *Id.*

IX. CONCLUSION

Although this chapter may be one of the longer ones in this book, it has only scratched the surface of many of the rules, requirements, and challenges that confront public housing today. While public housing continues to serve an important and necessary function in this country, the continued federal budget cuts and regulation make it a challenge for housing authorities to operate effectively. A few glimmers of hope have appeared on the horizon; should they come to fruition, they will likely change the face of much of public housing in the future.

The Section 8 Housing Assistance Program

10

Michael H. Reardon and Tatiana Gutierrez Abendschein

The Section 8 housing assistance program, administered by the U.S. Department of Housing and Urban Development (HUD), originated out of the Housing and Community Development Act of 1974,[1] a far-reaching piece of housing legislation that rewrote the United States Housing Act of 1937 (the Act).[2] Section 8 of the revised Act[3] created a program to subsidize private rental housing, with HUD paying the difference between a contract rent not exceeding fair market rent[4] and a specified percentage of a tenant's gross or adjusted income, which is generally the highest of the following amounts: (i) 30 percent of the family's monthly adjusted income, (ii) 10 percent of the family's monthly income, or (iii) a welfare payment that is specifically designated by a public agency to meet the family's housing costs.[5] The Section 8 program comprises two major components: (1) Section 8 project-based assistance programs,[6] and (2) Section 8 tenant-based assistance programs.[7] The project-based assistance programs are administered by the Assistant Secretary for Housing—FHA Com-

---

1. Pub. L. 93-383; 88 Stat. 633 (1974)
2. 42 U.S.C. § 1437a *et seq.*
3. 42 U.S.C. § 1437f *et seq.*
4. 42 U.S.C. § 1437f (c)(1).
5. 42 U.S.C. § 1437a (a)(1).
6. 42 U.S.C. § 1437f(b)(2). The authority for HUD to provide Section 8 project-based rental assistance to newly developed projects was repealed by Congress in section 202 of the Housing and Urban-Rural Recovery Act of 1983, Pub. L. 98-181 (1983).
7. 42 U.S.C. § 1437f (e)(1).

missioner in HUD's Office of Housing (Housing). The tenant-based programs are administered by the Assistant Secretary for Public and Indian Housing in HUD's Office of Public and Indian Housing (PIH).[8]

I. PROJECT-BASED ASSISTANCE PROGRAMS

The defining feature of the project-based assistance programs is that the Section 8 assistance is provided to housing projects and not to individual households. HUD or Public Housing Agency (PHA) contract administrators (through Annual Contributions contracts between HUD and the PHA) entered into long-term Section 8 Housing Assistance Payment (HAP) contracts with project owners.[9] As long as an eligible household resides in a Section 8 unit in the project, the owner will receive Section 8 assistance for that unit.[10] When the household moves from the unit, the household no longer receives the Section 8 assistance. If the owner rents the unit to a new eligible household, then the owner will continue to receive Section 8 assistance for the unit.[11]

Over the years, there have been five Section 8 project-based assistance programs administered by Housing. Starting in 1976, HUD provided Section 8 project-based assistance to new construction and substantial rehabilitation projects, including projects financed by state housing finance agencies.[12] These contracts generally had terms and appropriated budget authority for 20 years. State Agency contracts ran for 30 to 40 years.[13] Although, HUD and Section 8 contract administrators continue to administer these three Section 8 project-based programs for existing projects, the statutory authority for HUD to fund Section 8 New Construction/Substantial Rehabilitation and State Agency projects was repealed in October of 1983.[14] The Section 8 Loan Management Set Aside (LMSA) program was implemented by

---

8. As discussed in detail below, the basic legal requirements for the project-based programs and the tenant-based programs are quite similar, although there are some legal differences between the two programs and differences in administrative procedures as a result of the administration of the programs by two different HUD Offices. *See generally* HUD HANDBOOK 4350.3, Occupancy Requirements of Subsidized Multifamily Housing Programs for the section 8 project-based program, and HUD GUIDEBOOK 7420.10, Housing Choice Voucher Guidebook for the section 8 tenant-based program.

9. 42 U.S.C. § 1437f(b)(2) prior to repeal in 1983. *See* 24 C.F.R. § 880.311; 24 C.F.R. § 881.311 and 24 C.F.R. § 883.407 as set forth in Title 24 of C.F.R. pts. 800 to 1699 (revised as of April 1, 1981).

10. *See* 24 C.F.R. § 880.101(b), 24 C.F.R. § 881.101(b), and 24 C.F.R. § 883.602(c) as set forth in Title 24 of C.F.R. pts. 800 to 1699 (revised as of April 1, 1981).

11. *Id.*

12. *See generally* 24 C.F.R. pt. 880, Section 8 Housing Assistance Payments Program for New Construction; 24 C.F.R. pt. 881, Section 8 Housing Assistance Payments Program for Substantial Rehabilitation; and 24 C.F.R. pt. 883, Section 8 Housing Assistance Payments Program–State Agencies, all as set forth in Title 24 of C.F.R. pts. 800 to 1699 (revised as of April 1, 1981). The Section 8 New Construction, Substantial Rehabilitation programs were initially implemented by HUD through regulations issued at 41 Fed. Reg. 17,488, April 12, 1976.

13. *Id.*

14. Section 202 of the Housing and Urban-Rural Recovery Act of 1983, Pub. L. 98-181 (1983).

HUD in 1976 and continued to receive separate funding from Congress until 1997.[15] Section 8 LMSA contracts were provided to projects with FHA-insured or HUD-held mortgages that were in financial difficulty. The initial contract term for most LMSA projects was for five years with two five-year renewal terms.[16] The Section 8 Property Disposition (PD) program was implemented by HUD in 1976 and its contracts were provided to projects when HUD was selling formerly FHA-insured multifamily properties that HUD acquired through foreclosure.[17] The contract term for most PD projects was 15 years.[18] The Section 8 PD program was implemented by HUD regulation in 1979. The regulations for the LMSA and PD programs are still contained in HUD regulations.[19]

Under the original Section 8 project-based assistance program, Congress appropriated and HUD contracted with the owner for the full amount of the funds needed for the entire contract term in the first year of the contract. Since all of the funds were under contract, there was essentially no possibility that political or budget pressures could eliminate funding at any point during the original term of the Section 8 contract. In the mid-1990's, the early Section 8 project-based contracts began expiring. In response, Congress enacted the Multifamily Assisted Housing Reform and Affordability Act of 1997 (MAHRA),[20] which was amended significantly in the FY 2000 HUD Appropriations Act.[21] MAHRA provides the statutory basis for the renewal of Section 8 project-based assistance contracts upon expiration or termination of the contract.[22] As discussed in more detail below, MAHRA established rules governing contract terms,[23] rent levels,[24] and rent adjustments[25] for Section 8 renewal contracts. Technical changes in federal appropriation and budget rules since 1990 generally now disallow

---

15. The LMSA program was originally implemented by HUD by an interim regulation at 41 Fed. Reg. 12,170 (March 23, 1976), which was followed by a final regulation implemented at 42 Fed. Reg. 5603 (Jan. 28, 1977).

16. 24 C.F.R. § 886.111, as set forth in Title 24 of C.F.R. pts. 800 to 1699 (revised as of April 1, 1981).

17. The PD program was originally implemented by HUD for immediate effect at 41 Fed. Reg. 13,603 (March 31, 1976) and by final rule implemented by HUD at 41 Fed. Reg. 32,687 (Aug. 4, 1976). 24 C.F.R. pt. 886, subpt. B. A second PD program was implemented by HUD at 44 Fed. Reg. 70,365, Dec. 6, 1979). 24 C.F.R. pt. 886, subpt. C, which was intended "to use section 8 housing assistance in connection with the sale of HUD-owner housing in order to increase and maintain the amount of decent, safe and sanitary housing affordable to low-income families, to minimize displacement of tenants, to preserve and revitalize residential neighborhoods, and to dispose of projects in a manner consistent with HUD's disposition objectives." 24 C.F.R. § 886.301 as set forth in Title 24 of C.F.R. pts. 800 to 1699 (revised as of April 1, 1981).

18. 24 C.F.R. § 886.213 and 24 C.F.R. § 886.311, as set forth in Title 24 of C.F.R. pts. 800 to 1699 (revised as of April 1, 1981). Although there has been no repeal or rescission of HUD's legal authority to provide Section 8 PD assistance, HUD has in recent years not sold HUD-owner properties with Section 8 PD assistance.

19. 24 C.F.R. pt. 883, subpt. C, Section 8 Housing Assistance Program for Disposition of HUD-Owned Projects. *See* Title 24 of C.F.R. pts. 700 to 1699 (revised as of April 1, 2011).

20. Pub. L. 104-204; 110 Stat. 2874 (1977); codified as amended at 42 U.S.C. § 1437f note.

21. Pub. L. 106-74; 110 Stat. 1047 (1999); codified as amended at 42 U.S.C. § 1437f note.

22. MAHRA § 524(a)(1) (2011).

23. *Id.*

24. MAHRA § 524(a)(4) (2011).

25. MAHRA § 524(c) (2011).

forward funding of any type of multi-year federal contract, including Section 8 contracts. All Section 8 contracts now are funded at a maximum term of one year subject to annual appropriations.[26] While this change in policy introduces "annual appropriations risk," Congress has never failed to provide continued funding for all families being assisted with Section 8 project-based assistance.[27] Project-based voucher contracts also subject the assisted properties to the National Environmental Policy Act and to the Davis-Bacon Act.[28]

II. TENANT-BASED ASSISTANCE PROGRAMS

The Section 8 tenant-based assistance program is administered by PHAs under Section 8 Annual Contributions Contracts (ACCs) with HUD.[29] Utilizing funding from the ACC, the PHA enters into Section 8 HAP contracts with owners of existing housing on behalf of eligible households.[30] As long as an eligible household resides in the project, the owner receives Section 8 payments from the PHA on behalf of the eligible household.[31] When the household moves from the project, the Section 8 assistance to the owner is terminated.[32] As long as the household remains eligible, the household may use the Section 8 assistance for any other unit approved by the PHA.[33]

The original tenant-based program was called the Section 8 Certificate Program.[34] Eligible households received a certificate from the PHA that allowed them to rent an apartment that met HUD's Housing Quality Standards and which had rent no higher than the Fair Market Rent (FMR).[35] HUD annually publishes FMR's for all housing markets in the country.[36] The FMR is intended to represent the amount needed to pay the rent for privately owned, decent, safe, and sanitary non-luxury rental housing.[37] FMR's for a given market area are based on local user rent surveys conducted by HUD and PHAs.[38] Under current rules, FMRs are generally set at the 40th percentile of all market rents surveyed.[39] HUD may set rents at the 50th percentile[40] for areas that meet certain criteria, such as the FMR area that has at least 100 census tracts, the gross rents of two-bedroom units in the census tracts, and the concentration of assisted housing in certain census tracts.

---

26. *See* Housing Programs Project Based Rental Assistance Account, FY 2012 HUD Appropriations Act.
27. *Id.*
28. 24 C.F.R. § 983.4 imposes Davis-Bacon and NEPA cross reference. 24 C.F.R. § 983.58 imposes NEP directly. NEPA is codified at 42 U.S.C. 4321–4370d (2012). Davis-Bacon Act is codified at 40 U.S.C. 3141–3148 (2012).
29. 42 U.S.C. § 1437f (b)(1).
30. *Id.*
31. 24 C.F.R. § 982.309; 24 C.F.R. § 982.451.
32. 24 C.F.R. § 982.309.
33. 24 C.F.R. § 982.355.
34. *See* 24 C.F.R. § 982.501.
35. *See* 24 C.F.R. § 882.106, as set forth in Title 24 of C.F.R. pts. 800 to 1699 (revised as of April 1, 1981).
36. 42 U.S.C. 1437f (c)(1); 24 C.F.R. § 888; *see* 76 Fed. Reg. 60,698 (Sept. 30, 2011).
37. *Id.*
38. *See* 76 Fed. Reg. 60,698 (Sept. 30, 2011).
39. 24 C.F.R. § 888.113(b).
40. 24 C.F.R. § 888.113(c).

The Section 8 Voucher Program (Voucher Program) was a variation on the Section 8 Certificate Program.[41] The defining feature of the Voucher Program is that a household can rent a unit with a rent greater than the FMR or the "payment standard" adopted by the PHA for its Voucher Program.[42] The PHA administering the Section 8 Voucher Program establishes a payment standard for each unit size within its jurisdiction, between 90 percent and 110 percent of the FMR.[43] If an assisted household chooses a unit with a PHA-approved rent greater than the payment standard, the household must pay the difference between the payment standard and the rent for the unit even if the tenant payment exceeds the standard 30 percent of adjusted income, subject to a requirement that the initial rent for the unit may not exceed 40 percent of the family's adjusted income.[44]

In 1998, Congress merged the Certificate and Voucher programs into a single program, the Housing Choice Voucher (HCV) Program, which generally followed the rules of the Voucher Program rather than the Certificate Program.[45] The HCV regulations are at 24 C.F.R. Part 982.

In 1978, Congress added a Section 8 Moderate Rehabilitation (Mod Rehab) Program to the Section 8 statute.[46] Although the Mod Rehab Program was essentially project-based assistance, it was enacted within the tenant-based provisions of the Section 8 statute, and funds for the program were provided under the Section 8 tenant-based assistance appropriation.[47] The purpose of the Mod Rehab program was to provide Section 8 assistance to owners of existing projects that needed rehabilitation of at least originally $1,000 per unit.[48] Although the authority for the Mod Rehab program was repealed in 1990,[49] owners may renew Section 8 Mod Rehab contracts under MAHRA.[50]

Section 8 Project-Based Vouchers (PBVs) are a subcomponent of the Section 8 tenant-based assistance program.[51] Under the PBV program, PHAs are allowed to use up to 20 percent of their Section 8 tenant-based ACC budget authority to enter into project-based contracts with property owners.[52] The Section 8 PBV program is the only component of Section 8 currently available (at the discretion of the administering PHA) to fund new Section 8 project-based contracts.[53] Congress authorized the PBV program under Section 8(o)(13) of the Act, as significantly amended by the FY 2001 HUD Appropriations Act.[54] The 2001

---

41. *See generally* 68 Fed. Reg. 23,836 *et seq.* (April 30, 1998).
42. *Id.*
43. 24 C.F.R. § 983.503(b).
44. 24 C.F.R. § 983.508.
45. *See generally* 68 Fed. Reg. 23,836 *et seq.* (April 30, 1998).
46. Pub. L. 95-557; 92 Stat. 2080 (Oct. 31, 1978); s*ee* 44 Fed. Reg. 26,660 (May 4, 1979); 24 C.F.R. § pt, 882.
47. *Id.*
48. *See* 44 Fed. Reg. § 26,670 (May 4, 1979).
49. § 289(a) of Pub. L. 101-265 (Nov. 28, 1990).
50. MAHRA § 524(b)(3).
51. 42 U.S.C. § 1437f (o)(13); *see generally* 24 C.F.R. § pt. 983.
52. 42 U.S.C. § 1437f (o)(13)(B).
53. 24 C.F.R. § 983.5.
54. Cranston-Gonzalez National Affordable Housing Act, Pub. L. 106-377—Appendix A; 114 Stat. 1411A-3.

changes by Congress were intended to facilitate PHAs' ability to use PBVs in conjunction with other affordable and preservation activities being undertaken in a PHA's jurisdiction. The PBV program allows the PHA to use amounts already provided under its Annual Contributions Contract (ACC) with HUD for the HCV program to enter into project-based HAP contracts with owners of units in existing, newly constructed, or rehabilitated housing.[55] A PHA has discretion whether or not to operate a PBV Program.[56] With the exception of a Subsidy Layering Review performed by HUD[57] to assure that the assistance being provided to an individual project is not excessive, HUD approval is not required for the PHA to operate a PBV Program or to fund a particular project. A PHA must determine the amount of budget authority available for the PBV Program and ensure that the amount of assistance is within the amounts available under the ACC.[58] The PHA may use up to 20 percent of its HCV inventory for the PBV program,[59] and it must limit the number of PBVs in a project to no more than 25 percent of the units in the project,[60] with exceptions for units for elderly or disabled families or families receiving supportive services.[61]

A PHA must select PBV proposals by one of two methods.[62] One method allows the PHA to request that PBV proposals be submitted in accordance with competitive selection criteria established by the PHA, which criteria may not limit proposals to a single site and without practically precluding owner submission of proposals for PBV housing on different sites.[63] The other method allows the PHA to select specific properties that have been assisted under a federal, state, or local government housing assistance; community development; or supportive services program that requires competitive selection of proposals within three years of the PBV selection as long as the earlier competitive selection proposal did not involve any consideration that the project would subsequently receive PBV assistance.[64] One competitive program that has been specifically recognized by HUD as meeting the PBV selection criteria is the selection of a project to receive an allocation of 9 percent low-income housing tax credits (LIHTC) by the state LIHTC allocating agency.[65]

In addition, the PHA must comply with the PBV site selection standards in the regulations,[66] which can generally be summarized as follows: (1) the site supports the PHA goal of de-concentrating poverty and expanding housing and economic opportunities; (2) the site is

---

55. *See generally* 24 C.F.R. § 983.
56. 24 C.F.R. § 983.5(c).
57. *Id.*; 24 C.F.R. § 983.55.
58. 24 C.F.R. § 983.5(b).
59. 42 U.S.C. § 1437f (o)(13)(B); 24 C.F.R. § 983.6.
60. 42 U.S.C. § 1437f (o)(13)(D); 24 C.F.R. § 983.56. It should be noted that Congress amended the provision limiting the percentage of PBVs so that the percentage limitation is now based on the project and not on a building. § 2835(a)(1) of Pub. L. 110-289 (July 30, 2008). However, there has not yet been an amendment to the regulation. HUD implemented the change through publication in the *Federal Register.* 73 Fed. Reg. 71,037 (Nov. 24, 2008).
61. 24 C.F.R. § 983.6.
62. 24 C.F.R. § 983.51.
63. 24 C.F.R. § 983.51(b)(1).
64. 24 C.F.R. § 983.51(b)(2).
65. *Id.*
66. 24 C.F.R. § 983.57.

suitable to facilitating further compliance with Title VI and the implementing HUD regulations; and (3) the site meets or upon completion of improvements will meet HUD's Housing Quality Standards (HQS).[67] The plan must establish a policy for selection of sites in accordance with these requirements, and the PHA must select proposals in accordance with the plan.[68] For existing and rehabilitated properties, additional site selection standards include: (1) adequacy of size, exposure, and contour of the buildings and adequate utilities and streets; (2) promotion of greater housing choice opportunities and poverty de-concentration; (3) accessibility to social, recreational, education, commercial, health, and municipal facilities and services; and (4) accessibility to cost-effective transportation to jobs targeted to the relevant population. In addition to these site selection standards, new construction also requires no minority concentration (with exceptions).[69]

In addition to the standards noted above, for a new construction project the site must meet the following standards: (1) the site must not be located in an area of minority concentration, except as allowed under the regulation, or be in a racially mixed area, if the project will cause a significant increase in the proportion of minority to non-minority residents in the area; (2) a project may be located in an area of minority concentration only if: (i) there are sufficient comparable opportunities for minority families to live outside of areas of minority concentration, or (ii) the project is necessary to meet overriding housing needs that cannot be met in that market area as evidenced by or in accordance with criteria established in the regulations.[70]

Once the PHA selects a proposal, it must give prompt notice to the owner and the public.[71] After the PHA conducts the pre-HAP contract inspection for an existing property, the PHA and the owner enter into a HAP contract for the property.[72] In the case of newly constructed or rehabilitated housing, the project will be developed under an Agreement to Enter into Housing Assistance Payments Contract (AHAP) and become part of a HAP contract upon completion of construction or rehabilitation.[73]

Rents for PBV units cannot exceed 110 percent of FMRs,[74] except: (i) if HUD has approved an exception payment standard;[75] or (ii) if the property is a LIHTC property not located in a qualified census tract, rents are only subject to comparable non-Section 8 LIHTC units in the same property.[76] If the LIHTC unit rents are less, the PHA has the discretion to approve the higher Section 8 rents. Absent LIHTCs or an exception payment standard, rent to the owner must not exceed the lowest of 110 percent of the applicable fair market rent, the rent of a comparable unassisted unit (reasonable rent),[77] or the rent requested by the owner.[78]

---

67. 24 C.F.R. § 982.401(l).
68. 24 C.F.R. § 983.51(a).
69. 24 C.F.R. § 983.57(d).
70. 24 C.F.R. § 983.57(e).
71. 24 C.F.R. § 983.51(d).
72. 24 C.F.R. § 983.204(b).
73. 24 C.F.R. § 983.204(c).
74. 24 C.F.R. § 983.301(b)(1).
75. *Id.*
76. 24 C.F.R. § 983.301(c).
77. 24 C.F.R. § 983.303.
78. *See generally* 24 C.F.R. § 983.301.

III. COMMON FEATURES OF ALL SECTION 8 PROGRAMS

Generally, in order to be eligible for Section 8 assistance, households must earn 80 percent or less of Area Median Income (AMI).[79] However, income-targeting requirements limit most participants to households that are "very low-income"[80] (at or less than 50 percent of AMI).[81] Specifically, in the Section 8 Project-Based Program, projects first made available prior to October 1, 1981, are required to rent at least 75 percent of units to very low-income families,[82] and units in projects first made available after October 1, 1981, are required to rent at least 85 percent of units to very low- income families.[83] Exceptions are possible if the owner demonstrates a need for a broad range of incomes, insufficient very low income families, state requirements, or that an exception is necessary to prevent displacement.[84] Additional income targeting provisions require that 40 percent of Section 8-assisted units that are made available for occupancy in any year must be rented to extremely low-income families,[85] i.e., families with incomes at or less than 30 percent of AMI.[86] A comparable requirement is also present in the tenant-based program.[87]

Households participating in the Section 8 project-based assistance programs pay 30 percent of adjusted income as the tenant payment, and the Section 8 program pays the difference between the tenant payment and the rent.[88] In the HCV Program, a household may pay more than 30 percent of adjusted income if it chooses an apartment with rent above the PHA's payment standard.[89] However, in the HCV program, the tenant payment initially may not exceed 40 percent of the household's adjusted income.[90] PHAs and owners may collect minimum rent payments from tenants.[91] In the tenant-based programs, PHAs may allow owners to charge a minimum rent up to $50 per month.[92] In project-based programs, owners may charge a minimum rent up to $25 per month.[93]

---

79. *See, e.g.*, 24 C.F.R. § 5.653(b)(2) (2011) (provides income limitations for the Section 8 project-based assistance programs excluding the project-based voucher program, with "low income" being defined at 24 C.F.R. § 5.603 (2011)), 24 C.F.R. § 982.201(b)(ii)–(vi) (2011) (provides income limitations for the Housing Choice Voucher tenant-based program, with "low income" being defined, per 24 C.F.R. § 982.4(a)(3), in 24 C.F.R. pt. 5, subpt. F, *i.e.*, 24 C.F.R. § 5.603 (2011)).

80. *See, e.g.*, 24 C.F.R. § 5.653(c)–(d)(2011)(for the Section 8 project-based assistance programs, excluding the project-based voucher program), 24 C.F.R. § 982.201(b)(i) (2011) (for the Housing Choice Voucher program).

81. 24 C.F.R. § 5.603 (2011).
82. 24 C.F.R. § 5.653(d)(1) (2011).
83. *See* 24 C.F.R. § 5.653(d)(2) (2011).
84. 24 C.F.R. § 5.653(d)(3) (2011).
85. 24 C.F.R. § 5.653(c)(2011).
86. 24 C.F.R. § 5.603 (2011).
87. *See* 24 C.F.R. § 982.201(b)(2)(2011).
88. *See* 24 C.F.R. § 5.628(a) (2011) (for the Section 8 project-based assistance programs), 24 C.F.R. § 982.1(a)(4)(ii) (2011) (for the Housing Choice Voucher program).
89. 24 C.F.R. § 982.1(a)(4)(ii) (2011).
90. 24 C.F.R. § 982.508 (2011).
91. *See generally* 24 C.F.R. § 5.630 (2011).
92. 24 C.F.R. § 5.630(a)(2) (2011).
93. 24 C.F.R. § 5.630(a)(3) (2011).

IV. SECTION 8 PROJECT-BASED CONTRACT RENEWALS

In 1997, the first Section 8 New Construction and Substantial Rehabilitation contracts were reaching the end of their original 20-year terms. At that time, HUD's Office of General Counsel determined that there was no extant statutory authority for HUD to renew Section 8 project-based assistance contracts that were reaching the end of their initial term. There was also a serious concern at HUD and in Congress that rents in some Section 8 projects greatly exceeded rents at comparable unassisted properties in the market area. Contract rents in the New Construction and Substantial Rehabilitation programs were adjusted annually by applying an automatic annual adjustment factor (AAF) to the rent.[94] The AAF was not tied to actual operating costs and resulted in the potential for rents in excess of the market.[95] In other projects, particularly LMSA properties, rents had the potential to be significantly below market because rent adjustments were provided under a "budget-based" approach.[96]

Congress enacted MAHRA to both provide HUD with the authority to renew Section 8 project-based contracts upon expiration and to require that renewal rents generally be set at levels comparable to unassisted market rents.[97] FHA-insured projects with Section 8 rents above market are subject to the mortgage restructuring provisions of MAHRA,[98] which authorize HUD to reduce the outstanding FHA mortgage balance on a project to an amount that can be supported by rents that are reduced to comparable market levels.[99] Section 8 project-based HAP contracts that are not FHA-insured or do not have rents above comparable market rents are not subject to mortgage restructuring.[100] They are renewed under Section 524 of MAHRA, which states:

> . . . upon termination or expiration of a contract for project-based assistance under Section 8 for a multifamily housing project . . . the Secretary shall, at the request of the owner of the project and to the extent that sufficient amounts are made available in appropriation Acts, use amounts available for the renewal of assistance under Section 8 of the Act to provide such assistance for the project.[101]

Provided that funds are appropriated by Congress, existing law is not changed, the project is not subject to mortgage restructuring, and the project and the owner are not in violation of

---

94. 24 C.F.R. § 880.609(a) (2011) (for the New Construction program), 24 C.F.R. § 881.601 (2011) (for the Sub Rehab program, which makes applicable § 880.609(a) to the Sub Rehab program). *See generally* 24 C.F.R. §§ 888.201–888.204 on Automatic Annual Adjustment Factors generally.

95. *See generally* 24 C.F.R. § 888.203 (2011).

96. *See generally* 24 C.F.R. § 886.112(b) (for general rules on LMSA program rent increase provisions). *See also* 24 C.F.R. § 236.730 (as properties insured and/or assisted under Section 236 of the National Housing Act, as amended, were recipients of LMSA contracts, this is the reference to the Section 236 program rules regarding rental assistance annual increases).

97. *See generally* MAHRA § 511 (2011).

98. *See generally* MAHRA §§ 512(2) and 514(g) (2011).

99. *See generally* MAHRA § 517(a) (2011).

100. *See* MAHRA § 512(2) (2011).

101. MAHRA § 524(a)(1) (2011).

the Section 8 program requirements, HUD is obligated to renew Section 8 project-based HAP contracts at their expiration upon the request of the owner.[102] Separately, HUD also is obligated to renew Section 8 renewal contracts on projects that have had mortgages restructured under MAHRA.[103]

There is no detailed legal or regulatory guidance explaining the terms of a renewal contract. In practice, renewal contract terms have ranged from one to 20 years. Except for an Option 1 renewal (defined below), in which the contract renewal term must be at least five years,[104] the owner may request a contract term between one and 20 years, subject to the approval of HUD.[105] HUD has typically approved the contract terms requested by owners, with some exceptions for contracts in the middle of Option 3 and Option 5 renewals.[106]

HUD issued the *Section 8 Renewal Policy Guide* (*Renewal Guide*) in 2000 to implement the MAHRA provisions on contract renewals. In 2010, HUD published on its website a proposed revision to the *Renewal Guide*.[107] However, HUD has not finalized the revised *Renewal Guide,* but has updated guidance through amendments to the *Renewal Guide* and through issuance of memoranda providing additional guidance, which is usually published on the HUD website.[108]

V. MAHRA RENEWAL OPTIONS

The *Renewal Guide* sets forth six renewal options.[109] Market rents under most of the renewal options discussed below are generally determined based on a rent comparability study (RCS) commissioned by the owner.[110] The purpose of the RCS is to establish a comparison between the current Section 8 rents and unassisted market rents in the project area.[111] Chapter 9 of the *Renewal Guide* establishes procedures for the preparation of the RCS. The owner must commission an appraiser to complete an RCS in accordance with HUD's requirements.[112]

If an owner requests a mark-up-to-market renewal, HUD will contract with a third party appraiser to undertake a second RCS in addition to the owner's RCS.[113] When HUD's RCS comparable gross rent potential is higher than the owner's, the final comparable market rents will be the rents from the owner's RCS.[114] When HUD's RCS rents are lower than the owner's, then: (i) if the owner's rents are less than 105 percent of HUD's rents, the owner's rents will

---

102. *See* MAHRA § 524(a)(1) (2011) ("... the Secretary shall, at the request of the owner of the project and to the extent sufficient amounts are made available in appropriation Acts, use amounts available for the renewal of assistance under section 8 of such Act to provide such assistance for the project.").
103. *See id.*
104. Renewal Guide § 3-7.D. (January 2012).
105. *See generally* Renewal Guide § 2-3.A.
106. *See, i.e.,* Renewal Guide § 7-3.B.
107. The link to the proposed Section 8 Renewal Guide is no longer active on the HUD website.
108. http://portal.hud.gov/hudportal/HUD?src=/program_offices/housing/mfh/mfhsec8.
109. Renewal Guide § 2-2.A.
110. *See generally* MAHRA § 511; Renewal Guide § 1-1; Renewal Guide Ch. 2 introduction.
111. *See generally* Renewal Guide Ch. 2 introduction; Renewal Guide Ch. 9.
112. *See generally* Renewal Guide Ch. 9.
113. Renewal Guide § 3-7.F.1.d.
114. Renewal Guide § 3-7.F.2.a.

be used; (ii) if the owner's RCS rents are greater than 105 percent of HUD's RCS rents, then the owner's rents will be 105 percent of the rents from HUD's RCS.[115] An owner has no right to appeal HUD's RCS findings,[116] although an owner may bring to HUD's attention errors that may be contained in the HUD RCS, such as mathematical errors, incorrect utility information, and other factual inconsistencies.

A. Option 1: Mark-Up-to-Market

A project whose current Section 8 rents are below comparable market rents is potentially eligible to renew under the Option 1 mark-up-to-market example in the *Renewal Guide*.[117] Generally, these properties could be renewed at the lesser of comparable market rents (as determined by the HUD process) and 150 percent of FMRs,[118] although renewals at rents above 150 percent of FMRs are also possible with HUD approval.[119] A project can mark-up-to-market at any time once it has renewed initially under MAHRA,[120] including in the middle of a contract term, although HUD's current practice is not to allow a project to mark-up-to-market in the middle of an Option 1 renewal term. The owner must enter into a Section 8 renewal contract with a term of at least five years,[121] although the owner may request a longer term contract up to HUD's current policy maximum limit of 20 years.[122]

In order to renew under Option 1, the project must also be in good physical condition, owned by a profit-motivated or limited distribution entity, not be subject to a low or moderate income use restriction that cannot be unilaterally terminated by the owner, and have comparable market rents between 100 percent and 150 percent of FMRs.[123] If the project meets these requirements, it is eligible to renew as an "entitlement" mark-up-to-market project.[124] If the project does not meet all four "entitlement" conditions, HUD has discretionary authority to provide mark-up-to-market renewal rents.[125] HUD may approve a discretionary mark-up-to-market rent increase if the project meets at least one of the following three characteristics: (i) serves vulnerable populations, e.g., elderly, disabled, or large households, (ii) is located in a low-vacancy or rural area, or (iii) has evidence of community support as demonstrated by state or local funding.[126] Projects subject to low or moderate income use restrictions that cannot be unilaterally terminated by the owner are eligible for "discretionary" mark-up-to-market.[127] Generally, nonprofit owners are not eligible to mark-up-to-market under Option 1,[128] but do have comparable options under Chapter 15 of the Renewal

---

115. RENEWAL GUIDE § 3-7.F.2.b.
116. *See* RENEWAL GUIDE § 3-7.F.2.
117. *See generally* RENEWAL GUIDE § 3-1.
118. *See* RENEWAL GUIDE § 3-1.C; RENEWAL GUIDE § 3-2.C.
119. *See* RENEWAL GUIDE § 3-3.B.
120. RENEWAL GUIDE § 3-2.E.
121. RENEWAL GUIDE § 3-7.D.
122. *See, e.g.,* Willie Spearmon 2010 Memo.
123. *See generally* RENEWAL GUIDE § 3-2.
124. *See id.*
125. *See* RENEWAL GUIDE § 3-3.A.
126. *See* RENEWAL GUIDE § 3-3.B.
127. *See id.* § 3-2.D. note.
128. *See id.* § 3-2.F.

Guide which provides for a mark-up-to-budget process for eligible nonprofit owners that are refinancing and rehabilitating projects.[129] HUD has recently issued guidance that allows for-profit owners to obtain a mark-up-to-budget renewal in accordance with Chapter 15 and Option 2, discussed below.[130]

B. Option 2: OCAF or Budget-Based

If an expiring contract has rents at or below market comparables, the owner can elect to renew under Option 2 of the *Renewal Guide*.[131] Under this option, an owner can get a renewal contract at the current contract rents adjusted by the current-year operating cost adjustment factor (OCAF) or at budget-based rents, provided that the renewal rents do not exceed comparable market rents.[132] HUD annually issues OCAFs for each state that are used to annually adjust Section 8 project-based rents.[133] The budget-based rent method is described in Chapter 7 of *HUD Handbook 4350.1*.[134] This Chapter 7 budget-based method does not allow the use of "new" debt service,[135] which significantly affects its usefulness in preservation transactions.

C. Option 3: Referral to OAHP

Projects with FHA-insured mortgages and rents that are above comparable market rents are referred to HUD's Office of Affordable Housing Preservation (OAHP).[136] Depending on the circumstances, OAHP may determine that the project is eligible for a Section 8 renewal contract at the lower comparable market rents and thus does not need mortgage restructuring.[137] In other instances, OAHP may determine that the project is eligible for a mortgage restructuring, but the restructuring does not occur, either because the owner disagrees with the determination, refuses to change his/her election, refuses to execute a full restructuring commitment, or refuses to close on a full restructuring. These properties are issued "watch list" Section 8 contract renewals.[138] HUD believes these properties should be watched more carefully because the rents have been reduced but the mortgage debt has not been restructured, and therefore the mortage has a higher risk of default and imposing a burden on the FHA insurance fund.[139] If the risk to the FHA insurance fund is eliminated through a refinancing of the FHA-insured mortgage loan, the owner can request that the watch list contract

---

129. *See generally* RENEWAL GUIDE Ch. 15.
130. Memorandum dated February 22, 2010, from Carol J. Galante, Deputy Assistant Secretary for Multifamily Housing Program at the U.S. Dep't of Housing and Urban Development to Multifamily HUB and Program Center Directors and Contract Administrators regarding Waivers to the Section 8 Regulations and the Section 8 Renewal Guide (the Carol Galante 2010 Memo).
131. *See* RENEWAL GUIDE § 4-1.1.
132. *See id.* § 4-3.H.1.
133. 24 C.F.R. § 888.202 (2011).
134. RENEWAL GUIDE § 4-2.D.
135. *Id.* § 4-2.D. note.
136. *Id.* § 5-1.A.
137. *See* RENEWAL GUIDE § 5-1.F.
138. *See generally id.* § 5-6.A.
139. *See id.* § 5-6.C.

be transferred to a basic renewal contract, since HUD no longer has an interest in protecting its insurance fund.[140] Provisions particular to watch list contracts include: (1) a reduction of rents to market; (2) limitation to only a one-year term; and (3) a requirement that the owner submit monthly accounting reports to Housing.[141] Watch list properties are not classified as troubled or potentially troubled, but HUD requires senior project managers to prepare quarterly status reports, monitoring the physical condition, property management and financial performance, on all watch list properties for the term of the watch list contract and any subsequent renewals.[142]

If OAHP determines the project is eligible for mortgage restructuring and the owner agrees and closes on a full mortgage restructuring, the FHA-insured first mortgage is reduced to an amount that can be supported by the lower market rents.[143] The balance of the insured mortgage amount is structured as typically bifurcated subordinate financing held by HUD.[144] These properties are required to enter into a long-term use agreement and a 20-year HAP contract.[145]

D. Option 4: Exception Projects

Certain projects are not eligible for mark-to-market even though the Section 8 rents may exceed comparable market rents.[146] The rents on these projects can be renewed at above comparable market rents.[147] These "exception" projects include:

- Section 202 elderly housing;
- Section 515 rural housing;
- Projects financed by state and local governments that are not FHA-insured; and
- Projects financed by state or local governments with FHA insurance, which cannot be prepaid due to state or local law.[148]

The renewal contract rents for exception projects are the lesser of the existing rents plus an operating cost adjustment factor, or a budget-based rent, even if the resulting rent exceeds

---

140. *Id.* § 5-6.B.4, § 5-6.F.
141. *See* form of Watch List Renewal Contract, *available at* http://portal.hud.gov/hudportal/HUD?src=/program_offices/housing/mfh/exp/guide/s8guideatt.
142. RENEWAL GUIDE § 5-6.C; Memorandum from Frederick Tombar III, Acting Deputy Assistant Secretary for Multifamily Housing, dated Sept. 27, 2001, to all Multifamily HUB Directors, Program Center Directors, Performance-Based Contract Administrators, Property Disposition Centers, OMHAR Regional Offices, and OMHAR Participation Administrative Entities, regarding Revised Guidance on Monitoring OMHAR Watch List Properties.
143. *See generally* RENEWAL GUIDE § 5-4.
144. *See generally* M2M OPERATING PROCEDURES GUIDE, dated Sept. 30, 2004, *available at* http://portal.hud.gov/hudportal/documents/huddoc?id=DOC_19447.pdf.
145. *See generally id.*
146. MAHRA § 524(a)(2) (2011); RENEWAL GUIDE § 6-1.
147. *See* MAHRA § 524(a)(2) (2001); RENEWAL GUIDE § 6-2.B.
148. *See* RENEWAL GUIDE § 6-1.

comparable unassisted market rents.[149] At each subsequent renewal under Option 4, the project will be subject to this "lesser of" test.[150]

E. Option 5: Preservation and Demonstration Projects

The fifth renewal option in the *Renewal Guide* applies to projects that had FHA-insured mortgages under the Section 236 and Section 221(d)(3) below-market interest rate FHA mortgage insurance programs, whose owners entered into long-term use agreements with HUD under either the Emergency Low Income Housing Preservation Act (ELIHPA) or the Low Income Housing Preservation and Resident Homeownership Act (LIHPRHA).[151] The LIHPRHA program was the successor to ELIHPA and enacted in 1990 to preserve affordable housing projects whose owners had the right to prepay their FHA-insured mortgages without HUD approval.[152] The LIHPRHA program provided owners with incentives such as equity take-out loans and increased Section 8 rents in return for long-term affordability restrictions.[153] Although the LIHPRHA program still exists in law, changes to the program in the FY 1996 and FY 1997 HUD Appropriations Acts have resulted in its disuse.[154] MAHRA provides that upon expiration of Section 8 contracts on LIHPRHA projects, renewal rents will be set to provide owners with the same incentives and benefits provided for under the initial LIHPRHA agreements known as Plans of Action.[155] Option 5 also applies to certain projects that were restructured under Section 8 restructuring "Demonstration" programs in the FY 1996 and 1997 HUD Appropriations Acts that preceded MAHRA.[156] Generally, ELIHPA and LIHPRHA properties will not be able to opt out of their Section 8 HAP contract.[157]

F. Option 6: Opt Out

Although HUD is generally required to offer a contract renewal upon expiration of any project-based Section 8 contract, the owner is not necessarily required to accept the renewal contract.[158] An owner may choose to opt out of the Section 8 program as long as the owner has provided a one-year notice to HUD and the tenants.[159] Short-term renewals are generally offered by HUD in order to facilitate meeting the one-year notice requirement.[160]

---

149. *Id.* § 6-2.B.
150. *Id.* § 6-4.A.
151. *See id.* § 7-1.
152. 42 U.S.C. § 4101(a) (2011).
153. *See generally* 42 U.S.C. § 4109 (2011).
154. *See* 104 Pub. L. 134, Title II, codified at 42 U.S.C. § 4101 note (limiting plans of action to nonprofits, resident associations, and other priority purchasers, and allowing the secretary to impose a moratorium on applications). *See* 104 Pub. L. 204, Title II, Preserving Existing Housing Investment ("That with the exception of projects described in clauses (1), (2), or (3) of the preceding proviso, the Secretary shall, notwithstanding any other provision of law, suspend further processing of preservation applications which have not heretofore received approval of a plan of action.").
155. MAHRA § 524(e)(1); *see* RENEWAL GUIDE § 7-5.
156. *See* MAHRA § 524(e)(2); RENEWAL GUIDE § 7-2.
157. *See, e.g.,* RENEWAL GUIDE § 7-5.C.
158. *See* RENEWAL GUIDE Ch. 8 introduction.
159. *See* RENEWAL GUIDE § 8-1.A.
160. *Id.* § 8-1.B.

It should be noted that a number of states have imposed additional notice requirements for owners that intend to opt out of their Section 8 HAP contracts.[161] When an owner chooses not to renew a Section 8 project-based contract, then the eligible tenants in the project will receive Section 8 Housing Choice Vouchers.[162] Tenants may elect to remain in the project with their vouchers.[163] If the unassisted market rents for the project are higher than the local PHA's payment standard, the tenant may remain in the unit and the PHA must use the higher market rent as its payment standard for as long as the tenant remains in the unit.[164] In such circumstances, the vouchers are referred to as "enhanced vouchers."[165] In the event that HUD terminated a Section 8 contract, which could occur in response to serious and repeated violations by the owner of the HAP contract obligations, tenants would receive vouchers, though not enhanced vouchers,[166] and in practice these typically could not be used in the abated property on a permanent basis.

VI. CHAPTER 15

Under the Renewal Guide, nonprofit owners are eligible to renew Section 8 project-based contracts under any of the six renewal options, except for Option 1.[167] Chapter 15 carves out two additional types of rent increases originally available only to nonprofit owners: (1) Mark-Up-to-Market for Nonprofit Transfers (the Transfer Program), and (2) the Budget-Based Rent Increase for Capital Repairs by Nonprofit Owners (the Cap Needs Program),[168] which has now been extended to for-profit owners as well.[169] Under the Transfer Program HUD can use its discretionary authority to mark rents up to market to facilitate a change in ownership from a for-profit or limited dividend owner to a nonprofit owner or from one nonprofit owner to another nonprofit owner.[170] Under the Cap Needs Program, an owner can request a budget-based rent increase with a budget reflecting capital needs, new debt financing, recapitalization of the replacement reserve escrow,[171] and/or provision of at least a 6 percent return on initial equity.[172] There is a 10 percent cap on rent increases for non-Section 8 units in both programs.[173] The eligible costs for the Cap Needs Program are: (1) capital repairs and rehabilitation including the recapitalization of the replacement reserve escrow, *or* (2) substantial rehabilitation, including the new financing needed to cover the cost of repairs and rehabilitation.[174] The Transfer Program requires that the applicant address the cost of recapitalizing the replacement reserve account if the original HAP contract was old regulation or LMSA, or

---

161. *E.g.*, California, District of Columbia.
162. Section 8(t), codified at 42 U.S.C. § 1437f(t); *see generally* PIH Notice 01-41.
163. *See generally* PIH Notice 01-41 § 2.
164. *See* PIH Notice 01-41 § 2.
165. *Id.*
166. PIH Notice 01-41 Part I.A. regarding "Enforcement Actions."
167. *See generally* RENEWAL GUIDE.
168. *Id.* § 15-1.
169. *See* Carol Galante 2010 Memo, *supra* note 129.
170. RENEWAL GUIDE § 15-14.
171. *Id.* § 15-11.
172. *See* Carol Galante 2010 Memo, *supra* note 129.
173. RENEWAL GUIDE § 15-7.A.
174. *Id.* § 15-11.

establish the adequacy of the replacement reserve account if the original HAP contract is new regulation.[175] Chapter 15 does not currently treat nonprofit distributions. However, HUD's current policy is that while HUD changes to the Section 8 regulations and the *Renewal Guide,* all Multifamily Hub and Program Centers are allowed to recommend waivers of certain portions of the regulations and the Guide to Headquarters, including nonprofit owners with "new regulation" new construction or substantial rehabilitation Section 8 HAP contracts may request a regulatory waiver to receive a distribution of 6 percent on initial equity investment for projects for elderly families, a 10 percent distribution for projects for non-elderly families, or unlimited distributions for Chapter 15 preservation renewals.[176] Also, for-profit owners that wish to comply with Chapter 15's requirements for budget-based increases for capital improvements may request a waiver of the provision limiting Chapter 15 rent increases to nonprofits.[177] Such a waiver also would inform the owner and its debt and equity providers in advance of the approved post-rehab rents.[178] Owners may request a waiver of the requirement that a project have a REAC score greater than 30.[179]

VII. ANNUAL INCREASES

Section 524(c) of MAHRA provides that after the initial renewal of a Section 8 contract, the Secretary shall annually adjust rents by an Operating Cost Adjustment Factor (OCAF) or on a budget basis upon the request of the owner and approval by HUD. OCAFs are published annually by HUD for all states. OCAFs are based on aggregate statewide data for inflation in the major operating cost categories such as utilities, labor and insurance.[180] Rents may not be reduced by HUD, even if OCAFs indicate deflation in operating expenses.[181] For projects that were renewed under Options 1 and 2, at the expiration of each five-year period, the rents are subject to another rent comparability analysis and the rents may be adjusted up or down to keep them in line with the comparable market rents.[182]

VIII. OTHER HUD RENTAL ASSISTANCE PROGRAMS

A number of other HUD programs involve Section 8 assistance or similar rental assistance. These programs are much smaller than the Section 8 programs discussed above.

The Section 8 Moderate Rehabilitation Single Room Occupancy (SRO) Program[183] helps very low-income, single, or homeless persons obtain housing in projects rehabilitated for this purpose. The SRO Program has been funded since 1990 and is still funded today. The regulations for the Section 8 SRO program are at 24 C.F.R. § part 882, subpart H. The SRO

---

175. *Id.* § 15-18.
176. *See* Carol Galante 2010 Memo, *supra* note 129.
177. *See id.*
178. *See id.*
17. *See id.*
180. *See, e.g.,* Fed. Reg. 66,319–20 published on Oct. 26, 2011.
181. MAHRA § 524(c)(1) (2011).
182. *Id.*
183. 42 U.S.C. § 1437f(e)(2) and Title IV of the McKinney-Vento Homeless Assistance Act, Pub. L. 100-77; 101 Stat. 482 (July 22, 1987); 24 C.F.R. pt. 882, subpt. H.

Section 8 rental assistance contract is provided to the owner for a period of 10 years[184] and must provide the PHA administrator the option to renew the contract for an additional 10 years.[185] During the term of the Section 8 SRO contract, rents are adjusted by the application of the HUD-published Annual Adjustment Factor (AAF)[186] and the projects are also eligible for special adjustments in accordance with 24 C.F.R. § 882.410.[187] Section 8 SRO projects generally do not qualify for FHA mortgage insurance.[188] They are eligible for renewal under Option 4 of MAHRA as exception projects.[189]

The Shelter Plus Care (S+C) Program links rental assistance with supportive services for homeless persons with disabilities, primarily those with serious mental illness, chronic problems with alcohol and/or drugs, and AIDS.[190] The S+C Program has been funded since 1990 and is still funded today.[191] The program provides grants for rental assistance for permanent housing for homeless persons with disabilities. While the grants for the rental assistance are not technically Section 8, the S+C regulations at 24 C.F.R. part 582 impose a number of Section 8 requirements on the rental assistance under the program, including income requirements, tenant payments, rent reasonableness, and Housing Quality Standards.[192] The initial contract term may be for five years or 10 years, depending on rehabilitation level.[193] Recipients of S+C grants frequently contract with PHAs to administer the rental assistance, and the PHAs generally follow the Section 8 requirements.[194] The S+C Program is a grant program to participating city and state governments, which in turn make grants to housing providers.[195] Funds for the full initial contract term are made available at the commencement of the contract.[196] Following the initial term of the S+C Contract, Congress has been appropriating one-year renewal funds.[197] The S+C Program is one of several programs designed to reduce homelessness under the McKinney-Vento Homeless Assistance Act (42 U.S.C. § 11403).[198]

In 1990, Congress changed the Section 202 elderly housing program from a loan program to a capital grant program.[199] In the same legislation, Congress provided for rental assistance to new Section 202 projects to be made under a Project Rental Assistance Contract (PRAC) rather than a Section 8 HAP contract.[200] Also in 1990, Congress established the

---

184. 24 C.F.R. § 882.807.
185. Id.
186. 24 C.F.R. § 882.807(e) and 24 C.F.R. § 882.410.
187. Id.
188. See generally 24 C.F.R. pt. 200, subpt. S.
189. MAHRA § 524(b) (2011).
190. Title IV, Subtitle F, of the Stewart B. McKinney Homeless Assistance Act (42 U.S.C. § 11403–07(b); 24 C.F.R. pt. 582.
191. FY 2012 HUD Appropriations Act, Homeless Assistance Grants Heading. H.R. 2112.
192. 24 C.F.R. pt. 582, subpt. D.
193. 24 C.F.R. § 582.100(b).
194. See generally HUD Homeless Resource Exchange, www.hudhre.info/index.cfm.
195. See 24 C.F.R. pt. 582, subpt. C.
196. See generally HUD Homeless Resource Exchange, www.hudhre.info/index.cfm.
197. FY 2012 HUD Appropriations Act, Homeless Assistance Grants Heading. H.R. 2112.
198. See generally HUD Homeless Resource Exchange, www.hudhre.info/index.cfm.
199. Title VIII of the Cranston-Gonzalez Affordable Housing Act, Pub. L. 101-625, 104 Stat. 4297 (Nov. 28, 1990).
200. Id.

companion Section 811 program for persons with disabilities including PRAC rental assistance.[201] Although the statutes provide that the PRACs shall be for 20-year terms, since the late 1990s, Congress has authorized HUD to limit the initial PRAC term, which under current policy is for three years.[202] Consequently, Section 202 and Section 811 projects funded until approximately 1996, received PRACs that had appropriations for the initial 20-year term of the PRAC. Thereafter, Section 202 and Section 811 projects received PRACs with initial funding for five-year or, more recently, three-year terms.[203] The PRAC is administered by HUD under essentially the same rules as Section 8 project-based assistance.[204] Rents in PRAC contracts are adjusted through a budget-based rent increase request.[205] Since the funding for PRAC is not appropriated under Section 8, the Section 8 renewal requirements do not apply to Section 202 and Section 811 PRAC projects.[206] Each year the HUD Appropriations Act provides funding for new capital grants for Section 202 and Section 811 projects.[207] Congress also provides annual funding for the renewal of expiring PRAC contracts for additional one-year periods.[208]

The requirements addressed in this memorandum are based on HUD statutory and regulatory provisions and reference certain HUD administrative guidance and policy positions, which are subject to occasional changes. This chapter is not a substitute for review of actual project documents and applicable regulations with regard to specific projects or circumstances.

---

201. Form HUD 90173-A-CA (12/2005); Form HUD 90173-B-CA (12/2005).
202. FY 2012 HUD Appropriations Act, Housing for the Elderly Heading. H.R. 2112.
203. *Id.*
204. Form HUD 90173-A-CA (12/2005); Form HUD 90173-B-CA (12/2005).
205. *Id.*
206. MAHRA § 524(a).
207. For the first time since the inception of the capital advance fund programs for the elderly and persons with disabilities, Congress did not fund appropriations for new capital advances for the development of housing for the elderly and persons with disabilities. FY 2012 HUD Appropriations Act, Housing for the Elderly Heading. H.R. 2112.
208. *Id.*

11
Looking to the Future—
The Heat Is On: Trimming HUD's Energy Bill for Public and Privately Owned Assisted Housing

N. Linda Goldstein*

As this book goes to print, the annual energy bill for housing programs administered by the U.S. Department of Housing and Urban Development (HUD) is an estimated $6 billion.[1] This sum includes energy costs incurred by public housing agencies and privately owned HUD-assisted multifamily properties. As we look to the future, we can expect that efforts to control these costs will directly impact both our clients and their tenants.

Beyond HUD, the federal government as a whole is the single largest consumer of energy in the nation.[2] Soon after entering office, President Obama signed an Executive Order establishing sustainability goals for federal agencies under the Administration's Greening of Government program.[3] Federal officials were directed to *lead by example*. To reemphasize his earlier message, on December 2, 2011, President Obama signed a Presidential Memorandum direct-

---

* Ms. Goldstein wishes to thank the following individuals for their participation in the review of this chapter: Stuart Davis, Fannie Mae; Charlie Harak, National Consumer Law Center; Denise Muha, National Leased Housing Association; and Theodore K. Toon, U.S. Department of Housing and Urban Development.

1. *Livable Communities, Transit Oriented Development, and Incorporating Green Building Practices into Federal Housing and Transportation Policy U.S. Department of Housing and Urban Development: Hearing before the H. Subcomm. on Trans., HUD and Related Agencies, Comm. on Appr.*, 111 Cong. (2009) (statement of Shaun Donovan, HUD Sec.)

2. White House, Office of the Press Secretary, President Obama Signs an Executive Order Focused on Federal Leadership in Environmental Energy, and Economic Performance (Oct. 5, 2009). *See also* Letter from U.S. Senator Ben Cardin to the Joint Select Committee on Deficit Reduction (Oct. 21, 2011).

3. Exec. Order No. 13,514, 3 C.F.R. (2009).

ing all federal agencies to "maximize existing authorities" to use performance-based contracting for undertaking energy retrofits on federal buildings.[4] This means that administrative officials at HUD's offices in Washington, and elsewhere, have been engaged in rehabilitating HUD offices to make them more energy efficient. As HUD shrinks its own energy bill, we can expect program officials will grow increasingly more mindful concerning the cost of energy for programs they administer. Our clients, whether owners of HUD-assisted housing or public housing, will undoubtedly feel the pressure to bring down energy bills. The impact of this shift will likely take effect in numerous ways. In part, the requirement to reduce energy-related expenditures results from requirements of law.

The Energy Policy Act of 2005 requires HUD to "develop and implement an integrated strategy to reduce utility expenses through cost-effective energy conservation and efficiency measures and energy efficient design and construction of public and assisted housing."[5] The HUD Secretary is required to report to Congress every two years concerning the action taken by the Department in implementing the strategy.[6] The first report was filed in 2005, when then HUD Secretary Alphonso Jackson reported that the Department's energy bill had swelled to more than 10 percent of the entire HUD budget.[7] HUD's most recent report was filed in December 2008, at which time HUD advised that its energy bill had jumped to $5 billion, "representing a 13.5 percent increase since the Department's initial report."[8] As this book goes to print, HUD's next report to Congress is in the final stages of review within the Department. As we await this report, it's likely that the cost of energy has continued to rise.

The challenge for HUD will be accomplishing the mission with limited funding for implementation of energy-efficient improvements. Some public-interest groups have criticized HUD for failing to aggressively pursue opportunities to reduce its energy bills. In one noteworthy report, the National Consumer Law Center (NCLC) identified numerous ways HUD can dramatically reduce its energy costs.[9] The author presents actions HUD can take toward more efficient use of energy—without cost to the government or new legislation. These recommendations include "tapping into the $4.5 billion spent annually by utility companies on energy efficiency so that low-income multifamily housing gets its fair share of that funding," "providing assistance to smaller housing authorities so they can utilize 'energy performance contracts' that are now almost exclusively used by large, well-staffed housing authorities to improve their energy efficiency," and "facilitating greater use of energy efficient 'utility allowances,' thereby providing better incentives for housing authorities and

---

4. The White House, Office of the Press Secretary, Memorandum For the Heads of Executive Departments and Agencies, Implementation of Energy Savings Projects and Performance-Based Contracting for Energy Savings (2011).

5. Energy Strategy for HUD, Pub. L. No. 109-158, 42 U.S.C.A. 15842 (2005).

6. Id.

7. HUD Office of PD&R, Promoting Energy Efficiency at HUD in a Time of Change 2 (2006). Submitted pursuant to Section 154, Energy Policy Act of 2005, Energy Policy Act of 2005, Pub. L. 109-58, 119 Stat. 594 (2008).

8. HUD, Implementing HUD's Energy Strategy, 1–74, (2004). Submitted Pursuant to Section 154, Energy Policy Act of 2005, Pub. L. 109-58, 119 Stat. 594 (2008).

9. CHARLIE HARAK, NATIONAL CONSUMER LAW CENTER, UP THE CHIMNEY: HOW HUD'S INACTION COSTS TAXPAYERS MILLIONS AND DRIVES UP UTILITY BILLS FOR LOW-INCOME FAMILIES 5 (2010).

private, subsidized owners to invest in energy efficiency."[10] The author complains that "HUD's failure thus far to significantly reduce its energy bill represents a costly failure for taxpayers, for those living in assisted housing, and for our much needed efforts to reduce greenhouse gas emissions" and notes that the bulk of HUD's energy savings have come from energy performance contracts entered into by some of the larger public housing authorities.[11] The author opines that HUD has barely scratched the surface of what can be accomplished: "Given the age and nature of most of HUD's assisted housing stock, HUD should be aiming for hundreds of millions of dollars in energy savings."[12] He concludes that the Department's failure to develop energy usage reduction goals—despite a clear congressional mandate to do so—reflects "an alarming lack of urgency."[13]

As the Department's annual fuel bill continues to rise, pressure from internal government financial watchdogs and outside housing and consumer groups will undoubtedly intensify. For instance, beyond NCLC, the pressure mounts for HUD to unleash utility resources to assist in retrofitting affordable housing. As noted above, at issue are the utility energy-efficiency programs available in most states and funded through charges included in customer utility rates. The National Housing Trust, a housing nonprofit, has joined NCLC in educating the housing industry about this potential source of funding. NHT advises that these programs are a significant and growing resource for residential energy retrofits—and remain largely untapped by the multifamily sector.[14]

While the Secretary of HUD has yet to actively advocate that utility resources be directed to multifamily housing, there are several state-level initiatives directing these funds toward multifamily energy efficiency.[15]

HUD appears to be more receptive concerning other recommendations from NCLC. For instance, HUD is directing attention to the needs of small housing authorities. Specifically, it is reported that the Department is working on regulatory changes that will help small housing authorities access savings through energy performance contracts.[16] Also, there are hints that the utility allowance is under review. A recent HUD memorandum advises that "energy efficiency goals will be addressed in the future and may result in regulatory clarification and or change."[17]

There is other change on the horizon. Recently, the Obama Administration convened an interagency working group for the purpose of identifying ways to better align federal policies related to rental properties. This included a review of energy-efficiency requirements.[18]

---

10. *Id.*
11. Energy Strategy for HUD, Pub. L. No. 109-158, 42 U.S.C.A. 15842 (2005).
12. *Id.*
13. *Id.*
14. National Housing Trust, *Utility-Funded Energy Efficiency Programs: An Untapped Resource for Affordable Housing,* Sept. 2011, http://www.nhtinc.org/green_affordable_housing_preservation.php.
15. *Id.* The website of the National Housing Trust references programs in Iowa, New Jersey, Massachusetts, and Oregon.
16. *See* "Donovan Opposes House Bill's Cut in Section 8 Administrative Fees," *in Housing and Development Reporter*, CURRENT DEVELOPMENTS, Sept. 26, 2011, Vol. 39, No. CD-19, at p. 581.
17. Carol J. Galante, Deputy Assistant Secretary for Multifamily Housing Programs, Utility Allowance Regulations (June 20, 2011), http://www.oregon.gov/OHCS/APMD/HCA/docs/2011/2011-08-22_01_HUD_Clarification_of_UA_Regs.pdf?ga=t.
18. Federal Rental Alignment, Administrative Proposals, Dec. 31, 2011.

While programmatic consistency will be a welcome improvement, as legal advisors we need to be alert to coming change and ensure that any new requirements advance through proper administrative procedure. While we all have an interest in bringing down the government's energy bill, it is important to ensure that the burdens and responsibilities are assigned consistent with contractual agreements and related obligations.

During the coming years we should expect new opportunities for financing energy efficient improvements. HUD, owners (public and private) and housing attorneys need to be ready to embrace this change. For instance, recently Connecticut became the first state in the nation to create a green bank. The bank will allocate $48 million in initial capital for low interest loans for clean energy projects and energy efficiency projects. Other states are considering formation of similar institutions. As a community, we need to be prepared to deploy these resources.

In this chapter, we provide affordable housing attorneys with an overview of HUD's efforts to control energy costs with respect to both assisted housing and public housing. To assist in providing this overview, I called on some of my colleagues from the National Leased Housing Association (NLHA) Green/Energy Committee.

Inez Tremain considers the early Mark-to-Market "Green Initiative" and the Green Retrofit Program of the American Recovery and Reinvestment Act (ARRA), two greening programs for assisted housing. *Michael Johnson* provides an overview of Fannie Mae's new Green Refinance Plus Program, a mortgage with more flexible loan underwriting that can generate additional proceeds for energy-conservation improvements. *Kevin McMahan* and *Robert Hazelton* provide important background concerning the green assessment and briefings on the utility allowance and federal weatherization program. Finally, *George Weidenfeller* and *Mattye Goulsby Jones* offer an overview of HUD requirements related to energy-savings projects at public housing authorities.

I. THE MARK-TO-MARKET'S GREEN INITIATIVE AND THE GREEN RETROFIT PROGRAM—EARLY EFFORTS TO MAKE HUD-ASSISTED HOUSING ENERGY EFFICIENT

Inez Tremain

HUD has administered two green programs for its assisted housing stock. Specifically, the multifamily projects addressed in this subsection are privately owned, HUD-subsidized (through Section 8), multifamily properties.

In 2007, HUD expanded its preservation initiative—Mark-to-Market (M2M)—to include the "Green Initiative."[19] This was followed by the HUD Green Retrofit Program as part of the

---

19. Multifamily Assistance & Housing Reform and Affordability Act of 1997 § 42, U.S.C. § 1437f. Regulations are at 24 C.F.R. pt. 401 and 402. *See also* HUD, Office of Affordable Housing Preservation, *M2M Green Initiative, The Greening of the M2M Portfolio* (July 2007):

> The M2M program has resulted in restructuring of more than 1600 properties. Through this program has HUD resized and restructured the property debt to account for changed market rent levels, to pay for rehabilitation costs and 20 years of estimated repairs and replacements. The objective is to establish a financially viable project for the longer term.

government-wide stimulus program under the American Recovery and Reinvestment Act of 2009 (ARRA).[20] Undoubtedly, the lessons learned from these programs will affect decision making as HUD advances its efficiency initiatives. For instance, these programs serve as the backdrop for the emerging Energy Innovation Fund addressed below.

The M2M program offered a unique platform for establishing an energy-efficiency initiative. HUD was able to implement this new effort under existing statutory and regulatory authority. The Department's concept was straightforward: to implement green building principles in connection with certain M2M restructurings. Because these projects were undergoing renovation, this offered an obvious platform for change. The Green Initiative provides incentives to owners to rehabilitate projects in an energy-efficient manner. For instance, HUD offers a reduced owner financial contribution, incentive fees to support an owner's ongoing maintenance of the property utilizing green efficiencies, and general flexibility to include green elements in the restructuring (such as utilizing above-market rents).

Under ARRA's Green Retrofit Program, owners received loans and grants for energy/green-related retrofits. Recipients of these funds committed to long-term management plans and extension of affordability requirements for 15 years. In return, some were given the opportunity to pursue innovative plans for energy efficiency—for instance, retrofits including wind, solar, and geothermal power. Of course, many owners used their funding for more conventional green retrofit, such as improved insulation and installation of new windows.

Based on early reviews, HUD reports the energy savings from the Green Retrofit Program are in the range of 27.5 percent.[21] The lessons learned for this program, and the Green Initiative, will inform future efforts to make HUD's housing stock more energy efficient. For instance, as earlier noted, the Department brings lessons learned from these programs to its administration of the emerging Energy Innovation Fund. The Consolidated Appropriations Act of 2010 authorized $25 million to be used for this energy pilot program.[22] As this book goes to print, HUD is reviewing responses to its Notice of Funding Availability for this program. The purpose of the Energy Innovation Fund is to catalyze innovations in the multifamily energy-efficiency sector that have promise of replicability and can help standardize the retrofit market. It is significant that both assisted housing owners and public housing authorities have competed for this funding—perhaps marking the beginnings of a more integrated approach to identifying solutions for more energy-efficient affordable housing. Many hope that participants in this new program will identify new sources of funding for energy efficiency, including use of utility funds.

One of the more significant lessons learned by the Department in administering the Green Initiative and Green Retrofit Program related to the assessment made in preparation for renovation work. The Department determined that the conventional physical condition assessment (PCA) was not satisfactory. For greening initiatives, the physical assessment of the property

---

20. American Recovery and Reinvestment Act of 2009, Pub L. No. 111-5, 123 Stat. 115 (2009). *See* section titled Assisted Housing Stability and Energy and Green Retrofit Investments, under Housing Programs. Presentation by Theodore Toon, HUD's Office of Affordable Housing Preservation, at Meeting of Council for Affordable and Rural Housing (Jan. 24, 2011).
21. *Id.*
22. Consolidated Appropriations Act of 2010, Pub L. No. 111-117, 123 Stat. 3034 (2009).

is central to defining the scope of work. Accordingly, the Department determined that there was need for an enhanced PCA. Thus emerged the Green Physical Condition Assessment (GPCA). This assessment tool produces a list of green improvements that the property budget can support—and generates green measures for future investment that are tailored for the property. Later in the chapter, Kevin McMahan and Robert Hazelton explain the central importance of the GPCA for energy-efficiency improvements.

Faced with the reality that near-term budgetary constraints make unlikely the possibility of additional new greening programs for HUD-assisted properties, the Department has cooperated with Fannie Mae to launch a new mortgage program for older properties. Michael Johnson describes this program.

II. FANNIE MAE'S GREEN REFINANCE PLUS MORTGAGE PROGRAM

Michael Johnson

In a speech before the 2010 GreenBuild International Conference, HUD Secretary Shaun Donovan introduced a new Fannie Mae program for refinancing certain older multifamily properties and making energy-related improvements.[23] This new program is known as the Fannie Mae Green Refinance Plus Mortgage Program. However, the reader should be forewarned: Fannie Mae officials advise that the program may be renamed soon, to assist with marketing initiatives. More significant, and intriguing, officials at Fannie Mae and HUD are already considering changes to the program to encourage greater participation.

This Fannie Mae program is an enhancement to the standard FHA Risk-Sharing Program.[24] This program is structured to encourage owners to incorporate energy-efficiency and water-efficiency measures when renovating their affordable housing properties. This is accomplished by permitting 4 percent to 5 percent of additional loan proceeds for such improvements for eligible properties.

---

23. Shaun Donovan, HUD Secretary, Prepared Remarks at the Greenbuild International Conference and Expo Closing Plenary (Nov. 19, 2010), http://portal.hud.gov/hudportal/HUD?src=/press/speeches_remarks_statements/2010/Speech_11192010.

24. The HUD Risk-Sharing program is authorized by the Housing and Community Development Act of 1992, Section 542(b), Pub. L. 102-550, 106 Stat. 3672, 12 U.S.C. § 1707. Sec. 235 of HUD's FY 2001 Appropriations Act, Pub. L. 106-377, 114 Stat. 1441 (2000), amended Section 542, making the program permanent. To determine eligible properties for the risk-share program, *see* authority at 12 U.S.C. § 1707. There are no HUD program regulations for the Green Refinance Mortgage. The requirements for the program are set forth in risk-sharing agreements with qualified participating entities, such as Fannie Mae. The Secretary of HUD may establish and enforce standards for eligibility. (Within HUD, the risk-sharing program is administered by the HUD Office of Multifamily Housing.) Agreements under this authority may provide for mortgage insurance through the FHA of loans for affordable multifamily housing originated by or through, or purchased by, qualified participating entities, and reinsurance, including reinsurance of pools of loans, on affordable multifamily housing. In entering into risk-sharing agreements, the Secretary may give preference to mortgages that are not already in the portfolios of qualified participating entities. Multifamily housing securing loans insured under this subsection shall qualify as affordable only if the housing is occupied by families and bears rents not greater than the gross rent for rent-restricted residential units as determined under section 42(g) of the Internal Revenue Code of 1986 [26 U.S.C. 42(g)].

HUD and Fannie Mae will share the risk on these loans. To encourage participation, the loan pricing is set to be highly competitive, with rates below the normal Fannie Mae DUS[25] pricing. Lenders use the standard DUS forms. This is a "one-stop" program handled entirely by the DUS lender who will structure, underwrite, and service the mortgage loan.

The basic requirements for this Fannie Mae program are as follows:

a. Properties must be at least 10 years old.
b. Income restrictions will run at least through the term of the mortgage loan.
c. The four percent to five percent of additional loan proceeds are to be used for energy-efficiency and water-efficiency retrofits or other renovations recommended in the Physical Needs Assessments.

Under this loan program, renewable energy sources can be financed. For example, solar panels can be financed. Also of note, the loan parameters for this program exceed those normally available through the Fannie Mae DUS program. Those parameters are:

Loan-to-Value (LTV): The maximum loan-to-value for this program is 85 percent. (Normal DUS ceilings are 80 percent.) As noted above, the program provides 4 percent to 5 percent of additional loan proceeds for energy retrofit and targeted improvements.

Debt-Service Coverage: The minimum debt-service coverage is 1.15 percent. This is 5 percent lower than standard multifamily affordable DUS financing.

Loan Term and Interest: The loan term is a minimum 10 years with amortization based on a 30-year fixed rate. Variable-rate and interest-only loans are not available in this program.

Nonrecourse: Loans under this program are nonrecourse.

Subsidy Layering: Subsidy layering reviews are required and performed on all properties using "new" low-income housing tax credits, soft debt from a state or local government (i.e., HOME funds), IRP, or project-based Section 8.

To obtain a loan under the program, borrowers must procure a "green physical needs assessment" (GPNA).[26] (The GPCA, required by HUD for its energy-related assisted-housing programs, was described above by Inez Tremain. Below, Kevin McMahan and Robert Hazelton further explain the green assessment. Additionally, George Weidenfeller and Mattye Goulsby Jones describe energy-related changes expected with respect to assessments of certain housing authority projects.)

Fannie Mae has specific requirements for the GPNA prepared in connection with its Green Refinance Plus program. Moreover, they have direction concerning contractor qualifications. Lenders are required to follow set procedures in reviewing the GPNA.

The renovation and/or physical improvements that the borrower elects to make, based on the GPNA, must be made within 12 months of the loan disbursement. Moreover, the borrower must track energy and water usage using the Energy Star Portfolio Manager.

---

25. DUS stands for Delegated Underwriting and Servicing. Approved lenders are preapproved to underwrite, close, and service loans on behalf of Fannie Mae.

26. Bob Simpson, Vice President, Multifamily Mortgage Business Affordable Housing, *Green Refinance Plus Physical Needs Assessment Requirements* (July 8, 2011), https://www.efanniemae.com/mf/guidesforms/lendermemos.jsp.

It is clear that the physical assessment plays a key role with each of the greening programs described so far (the HUD and Fannie Mae programs). For more on this topic, we turn to Kevin McMahan and Robert Hazelton—consultants to HUD who have been actively engaged with the development of the Department's standards for green assessment. Additionally, these authors provide a briefing concerning the utility allowance and describe recent federal efforts to make the weatherization program more useful for the multifamily sector.

III. PRACTICAL GUIDANCE FOR COUNSEL—MORE ON GREEN ASSESSMENTS; UNDERSTANDING UTILITY ALLOWANCES; IMPLEMENTATION OF THE HUD/DOE MEMORANDUM OF UNDERSTANDING RELATED TO WEATHERIZATION

Kevin McMahan and Robert Hazelton

A. Understand the Green Assessment

In July of 2007, HUD became a pioneer in the multifamily building assessment by introducing its Green Initiative—an initiative to encourage owners of affordable, multifamily properties to rehabilitate and operate their properties using sustainable green building principles. Inez Tremain described this program above and briefly touched on the importance of the physical property assessment, including HUD's requirement for the GPCA. Additionally, Michael Johnson noted that the new Fannie Mae loan program requires a GPNA.

In structuring the Green Initiative, HUD better came to grips with the impact of operating a green property. What emerged was the concept of "healthy housing"—an integrated approach to green building principles—taking into consideration energy efficiency and water efficiency, recycling, indoor air quality, and related concerns. Indeed, there have been some notable examples of buildings owners taking a holistic approach that combines energy efficiency upgrades and other building improvements that lead to significantly improved health outcomes for low-income tenants. In some cases, the post-renovation health gains have been dramatic. For example, in the case of one renovation, prior to the improvements 10% of adult residents reported having chronic bronchitis. Post-renovation, none of the adults reported having bronchitis.[28]

More than 85 percent of our multifamily housing stock was constructed prior to 1990 at a time prior to adoption of statewide energy building codes.[28] For this reason, evaluation of conservation measures is an essential component of any physical and financial assessment of such older properties. As noted earlier in the chapter, HUD is projecting an average 27 percent utility savings for properties benefiting from the Green Retrofit Program. The HUD-required GPCA allows the department to systematically plan for such savings. Moreover, this tool can provide invaluable information for lenders engaged in underwriting loans.

In the simplest of terms, the GPCA has three parts:

---

27. Case Study: Crating Green and Healthy Affordable Homes for Families at Viking Terrace, Worthington, Minn., Enterprise Community Partners, National Center for Healthy Housing, page 16.

28. U.S. Census, *American Housing Survey for the United States (2009)*, http://www.census.gov/housing/ahs/.

1. *A physical condition assessment that analyzes traditional and green requirements.*
   The GPCA evaluates all components of the building and property, comparing more conventional efforts to rehabilitate properties with viable green alternatives.
2. *An energy audit (EA).*
   The EA documents prudent energy-related improvements and considers the cost of the improvements (applying a financial payback analysis).
3. *Integrated pest management (IPM) inspection.*
   The IPM inspection identifies current pest infestation, inspects the property for improvements needed to reduce entry points and to make the property less attractive to harboring pests, documents existing pest-control practices, and recommends actions to adopt an IPM plan for the property.[29]

The reports generated in preparation of the GPCA provide concrete guidance for the owner, thus permitting a move to improved energy efficiency and water efficiency and a healthier project. Additionally, as noted, the GPCA provides information on the costs and benefits of green retrofits. This is an important tool for lenders in underwriting loans, as the energy-conservation and water-conservation measures resulting from the GPCA can be viewed as a form of risk reduction.

The scope of work for a conventional PCA is derived from the ASTM E-2018-08 Standard Guide for Property Condition Assessments.[30] However, the GPCA reaches beyond the conventional PCA and requires a contractor with special qualifications.[31]

To some extent, various industry standards and initiatives may influence the scope of the HUD GPCA or Fannie Mae GPNA. For instance, in the fall of 2010, Enterprise Green Communities released their audit protocol intended to help standardize green audits.[32] Also, Qualified Allocation Plans (QAP) issued by the state finance housing agencies that allocate low-

---

29. More specifically, HUD-required GPCA includes:
- A standard PCA that exceeds ASTM 2018 standards and includes a 20-year capital needs replacement reserve analysis.
- A green PCA recommendation by an accredited industry professional that includes a 20-year green capital needs replacement reserve estimate.
- A comparison of conventional and green capital needs.
- An energy analysis, including utility bill review, systems analysis, and property benchmarking.
- Energy modeling (e.g., ASHRAE Manual J, TREAT, E-Quip, etc.).
- Retrofit recommendations with recognized financial metrics, including net present value (NPV), internal rate of return (IRR), and savings to investment ratio (SIR).
- A Simple Payback and Life Cycle Cost Analysis for each retrofit.
- Diagnostic testing as necessary (e.g., Integrated Pest Management (IPM) inspection, indoor air quality analysis, thermography/infrared photos, etc.).

30. ASTM International is a membership organization that provides a forum for development of voluntary standards for materials, products, systems, and services.

31. Mark-to-Market Program, *Draft Green Guide*, Ver. 9 (Sept. 2008), http://www.hud.gov/offices/hsg/omhar/paes/green/owner/giguidv9.pdf.

32. Enterprise Green Communities, *Enterprise Retrofit Audit Protocol to Standardize Green Audits* (Feb. 4, 2010).

income-housing tax credit (LIHTC) funds contain either green point scoring or have green threshold criteria. Indeed, some states have their own green scopes of work and energy-audit requirements. Yet, despite a common commitment to energy conservation, the industry remains fractured with respect to property assessment standards.[33] There is no single, dominant accrediting organization (no single assessment). Indeed, there is no common agreement concerning the acronym for such assessment (e.g., GPCA, GPNA, GCNA). Accordingly, at present, there is no commonly agreed-on standard for affordable multifamily housing retrofits. That said, it is reasonable to predict that soon all needs assessments will include reviews of energy and water consumption.

B. Understanding Utility Allowances

The utility allowance is intended to cover a reasonable consumption of utilities "by an energy-conservative household of modest circumstances consistent with the requirements of a safe, sanitary, and healthful living environment."[34] In most cases, the resident's share of rent and utilities in federally assisted housing and public housing is pegged to 30 percent of the household's adjusted monthly income.[35] The utility allowance is the amount necessary to cover a resident's reasonable utility costs.[36]

The utilities for which allowances may be provided include electricity, natural gas, propane, fuel oil, wood or coal, and water and sewage service, as well as garbage collection. The functions, or end uses, covered by an allowance may include space heating, water heating, cooling, refrigeration, lighting, or appliances.

When evaluating a utility allowance, understanding the type of subsidy is imperative, including the following guidance:

---

33. LISC GREEN DEVELOPMENT CENTER, PRIMER: GREEN PHYSICAL NEEDS ASSESSMENT (PNA) and GREEN CAPITAL NEEDS (June 16, 2010).

34. 24 C.F.R. § 965.505 (a); 24 C.F.R. § 5.603 (b) (Westlaw 2011).

35. 24 C.F.R. § 965.505 (a); 24 C.F.R. § 5.603 (b); 24 C.F.R. § 982.517; 26 C.F.R. § 1.42-10 (Westlaw 2011).

36. For greater information, see U.S. DEP'T OF HOUSING AND URBAN DEVELOPMENT, UTILITY ALLOWANCE GUIDEBOOK (Sept. 1998).

Property/Unit Type	Utility Allowance Guidance
U.S. Department of Agriculture/Rural Development (USDA RD) units	Use USDA RD utility allowance schedule
HUD Section 8, project-based units	Use HUD utility allowance schedule
HUD Section 8, housing choice voucher units	Use HUD Public Housing Authority utility allowance schedule
Low-Income Housing Tax Credit (LIHTC) Section 42 rent-restricted units	Use one of three acceptable methods (see below)

State Finance Housing Agencies have varying utility allowance guidance for low-income housing tax credit rent-restricted units that are not subsidized by HUD or USDA RD. However, the three generally recognized methods for completing a utility analysis include the following:

- Compiling utility samples from residents and submitting them with an owner certification form. Utility allowances are calculated using estimates obtained from the local utility providers.
- Completion of the HUD utility model. Owners calculate utility estimates using the HUD Utility Schedule Model accessed at http://www.huduser.org/portal/resources/utilmodel.html. Also, the IRS uses this model to determine utilities for its LIHTC program.
- Contracting with an experienced consultant who prepares an analysis, as applicable, pursuant to:
  - The Low-Rent Public Housing Program[37] and
  - The HUD Section 8 Housing Choice Voucher Program.[38]

Please keep in mind the following when considering utility allowances:

1. Unit gross rents include the applicable utility allowance.
2. Cable television, telephone, and Internet costs are excluded from utility allowance calculations.
3. Only utility costs paid directly by the resident(s) and not by or through the owner are included in the utility allowance calculation.
4. The per-unit cost for master-metered utilities must be part of the tenant's rent and cannot exceed the maximum gross rent for that unit. The tenant's pro rata share of the master-metered utility cost will be determined based on the PHA estimate. The owner will need to indicate on all leases that the master-metered utility is included in the rent.
5. Utility allowances are applied individually to each building in the development. Therefore, depending on the development, an owner or manager could have buildings in the same development using different utility allowances.

---

37. 24 C.F.R. § 965 subpt. E (Westlaw 2011).
38. 24 C.F.R. § 982.517 (Westlaw 2011).

6. Rents may need to be adjusted twice in a year because the release of median income figures and utility estimates may occur at different times.

The level of utility allowances, and the methods by which they are adopted or revised, can provide either incentives or disincentives for owners of affordable housing to implement energy efficiency measures. They can also lead to support or opposition from tenants for installing energy improvements. Since tenants pay an actual rent that is calculated as the nominal (gross) rent minus any utility allowances, owners will want to make sure that the utility allowances are revised downward if significant energy efficiency measures are installed in buildings where tenants (not owners) pay the energy bills—assuming, of course, that the pre-improvement level of those allowances was in fact fair and adequate. Downward adjustments in utility allowances result in higher net rents paid to owners, without increases in total costs to tenants (again assuming allowances are fair and reasonable). Owners have little financial incentive to invest in energy efficiency if they see no counterbalancing gain.

On the other hand, owners should be sensitive to the fact that existing utility allowances may be inadequate, that is, lower than the actual, reasonable costs incurred by tenants who pay their own energy bills. This can result from the owner (or housing authority) using a utility allowance calculation method that does not produce reasonable results, or using inaccurate tenant consumption or utility cost data, or simply the result of the owner (or PHA) not increasing the energy prices. To the extent utility allowances are inadequate (or widely perceived as inadequate), it may be hard to work cooperatively with tenants in terms of installing energy efficiency upgrades or ensuring that tenant behavior supports reductions in non-essential energy use.

There have been some limited examples of models under which energy savings resulting from efficiency upgrades are split between the owners and tenants, to ensure that all parties work together and see the advantages of energy efficiency. These models are worthy of consideration.[39]

C. Implementation of the HUD/DOE Memorandum of Understanding Related to Weatherization

The U.S. Department of Energy (DOE) administers the low-income Weatherization Assistance Program (WAP). This program, first authorized in 1976, has as its purpose the reduction of energy costs for low-income households by increasing the energy efficiency of their homes.[40] Historically, the program targeted low-income single-family households and the

---

39. *See* CHARLIE HARAK, NATIONAL CONSUMER LAW CENTER, UP THE CHIMNEY: HOW HUD'S INACTION COSTS TAXPAYERS MILLIONS AND DRIVES UP UTILITY BILLS FOR LOW-INCOME FAMILIES (2010), pages 10-11 and 27. The authors thank Mr. Harak for his guidance and insights in preparing this subchapter.

40. Title IV, Energy Conservation and Production Act, as amended, authorized the Department of Energy to administer the Low-Income Weatherization Assistance Program. Grant awards made under this program must comply with applicable law, including regulations contained in 10 C.F.R. pt. 440 (issued Feb. 1, 2002), the Energy Policy Act of 2005, Pub. L. No. 109-58, 119 Stat. 594 (2005), the Energy Independence and Security Act of 2007, Pub. L. No. 110-140, 121 Stat. 1492 (2007), and the American Recovery and Reinvestment Act of 2009, Pub L. No. 111-5, 123 Stat. 115 (2009).

funding for the program was not significant. The program grabbed headlines when some $5 billion was provided under ARRA.[41] With this funding the federal government took a new look at how best to include multifamily properties.

HUD and DOE published a Memorandum of Understanding aimed at reducing impediments regarding the use of weatherization funds in public and assisted multifamily housing.[42] This effect was intended to streamline the weatherization eligibility process for residents in approximately 1.1 million public housing units, another 1.2 million privately owned federally assisted units, and some 950,000 units financed with the LIHTC.[43] DOE published a final rule in 2010 that provided needed clarification related to administration of this program.[44] Prior to this new rule, verification that a multifamily property was eligible for weatherization assistance presented a burdensome task. The new rule posted a list of properties determined to meet certain eligibility criteria under WAP. Of course, the new rule did not result in automatic eligibility for the identified buildings, nor did it establish a priority for the weatherization of the identified buildings. Indeed, states were not required to establish a particular prioritization with regard to weatherization of multifamily buildings. Since the release of the MOU and the new rule, a number of states have set aside funds to target multifamily housing.[45]

It is important to note for those who might seek to use DOE's WAP to help pay for energy efficiency upgrades in subsidized housing that the ARRA funds for WAP originally had an expenditure deadline of March 2012. While many states have received extensions of 3 to 6 months, as of this writing it would be close to impossible for an assisted, multifamily property to access the ARRA funding for WAP. Moreover, the federal government has sharply curtailed regular (annual appropriations) funding for WAP in FY 2012. Owners may be better off seeking assistance from their local utility company, in states that have utility funding for energy efficiency improvements.

Notwithstanding the progress described here and in the prior sections by Inez Tremain and Michael Johnson, the department has a long way to go in making its assisted-housing stock more energy-efficient. As noted by N. Linda Goldstein in her introduction, it is the efforts by larger public housing authorities that have contributed significantly to reducing HUD's housing bill. In the final section, George Weidenfeller and Mattye Goulsby Jones explore the Department's requirements related to energy-savings projects at housing authorities.

---

41. American Recovery and Reinvestment Act of 2009, Pub L. No. 111-5, 123 Stat. 115 (2009). 42 U.S.C. § 6861 *et seq.*

42. Memorandum of Understanding between DOE and HUD, An Opportunity for Agencies to Collaborate and Help Working Families Weatherize Their Homes in Multi-Unit Buildings (May 6, 2009). *See also* Memorandum of Understanding between DOE and HUD, Building Energy Programs and Energy-Efficient Mortgages (Jan. 13, 2010).

43. HUD-DOE, Weatherization Partnership Fact Sheet: Streamlining Weatherization Assistance in Affordable Housing (Mar. 05, 2010), http://portal.hud.gov/hudportal/documents/huddoc?id=factsheet_doe_weatherize_3.pdf.

44. 10 C.F.R. § 440.22 (Westlaw 2011).

45. National Housing Trust, *Multifamily Weatherization State Best Practices* (Mar. 2010), http://www.nhtinc.org/green_affordable_housing_preservation.php.

IV. HUD REQUIREMENTS FOR IMPLEMENTING ENERGY-SAVINGS PROJECTS AT HOUSING AUTHORITIES

George Weidenfeller and Mattye Goulsby Jones

Public housing consists of approximately 1.2 million units in 13,000 properties, managed by some 3,100 local public housing authorities.[46]

Utility expenditures are tracked and reported in the HUD Financial Assessment Subsystem for Public Housing.[47] The overall cost of PHA-paid utilities in public housing (including water and sewer) for 2006 totaled $1.4 billion, and this represented approximately 23 percent of total operating expenses.[48] Without a doubt, these costs are significantly higher as this book goes to print—and we await HUD's next report to Congress.

To address statutory requirements and concern about rising costs, HUD's Energy Action Plan[49] for Public Housing includes the following:

1. **Energy Star**

    Appliance/product purchases in public housing must be based on Energy Star standards, unless the purchases are not cost-effective. HUD field offices are required to conduct Energy Star "events" annually directed toward public housing authorities (PHAs) and residents.[50]

2. **HOPE VI—Choice Neighborhood Initiatives**

    HUD has required development of HOPE VI and now Choice Neighborhood Initiative (CNI) developments to achieve a high level of energy efficiency.[51] HUD promotes energy efficiency through HOPE VI grant incentives and requires a survey of

---

46. U.S. Dep't of Housing and Urban Dev., Implementing HUD's Energy Strategy, H.R. Doc. No. 110 at 1–74 (2008).

47. *Id.* at 9. *See* references to this data, last reported.

48. *Id.* at 9. When combined with the then most recent available estimate of tenant-paid utilities, total estimated energy-related utility expenditures in public housing were $1.85 billion. For PHA fiscal years ending between June 30, 2007, and March 31, 2008, PHA-paid utilities had risen to $1.5 billion annually or 24 percent of the cost to operate public housing. For PHA fiscal years ending between June 30, 2008, and March 31, 2009, PHA-paid utilities had risen to $1.6 billion.

49. Office of Policy Development and Research et al., HUD's Energy Action Plan Implementation Plan, H.R. Doc. No. 110 at 1–13 (2007).

50. On October 12, 2010, HUD issued HUD Notice PIH-2010-41, which updated previous HUD guidance encouraging Energy Star as the standard for PHAs. On March 5, 2009, HUD issued Notice PIH 2009-9, which was a reissuance of HUD Notice PIH 2007-30 on "Using Energy Star to Promote Energy Efficiency in Public Housing" and HUD Notice PIH 2005-25. The most recent notice states that when purchasing original or replacement (as needed) equipment, in accordance with 24 C.F.R. § 965.306, PHAs shall acquire only equipment that meets or exceeds the minimum efficiency requirements set by the Department of Energy, provided they are within the cost requirements of 24 C.F.R. § 941, the procurement requirements of 24 C.F.R. § 85.36, and HUD *Procurement Handbook* 7460.8 Rev. 2. *See also* Audit Report, July 21, 2010, *The Hartford Housing Authority's Plan to Replace Boilers Did Not Meet Recovery Act and Federal Efficiency Requirements.*

51. *See* Annual Notifications of Funding Availability.

HOPE VI projects to ensure that energy-efficient standards are being used. The Energy Independence and Security Act of 2007 required that HUD raise the standard for new construction of public housing to the 2006 International Energy Conservation Code (IECC). Field offices are required to monitor 10 percent of the HOPE VI inventory of construction projects to ensure implementation of energy-conservation measures.[52]

3. Monitoring for Energy Efficiency

Rather than management at the agency level, HUD has transitioned to asset management of public housing projects.[53] In part, this was done to better measure utility consumption and costs. Additionally, HUD has implemented utility benchmarking. The HUD Office of Public and Indian Housing website provides links to the benchmarking tools.

As part of their on-site review each year, the HUD field office is required to determine that the PHA has an energy audit on file.[54] Also, at the time of review, the HUD field offices will consider the utility allowances provided by the authority.[55]

4. Energy Performance Contracting

HUD has issued guidance to streamline energy performance contracting (EPC) by public housing authorities (and ease oversight by the HUD field office).[56] The EPC is a financing technique that uses cost savings from reduced energy consumption to repay the cost of installing equipment for energy conservation. The EPC usually is made available by an Energy Service Company (ESCO). Generally, the cost of installation is covered by the ESCO and subsequently paid back over time through energy savings.

Additionally, HUD will permit Power Purchase Agreements (PPAs) to be arranged in conjunction with EPCs. Under a PPA, the supplier of a renewable-energy system pays most or all of the cost of system installation and maintenance, and the housing authority (as the owner of the property on which the energy-generating equipment is located) pays reduced electric rates. According to HUD Notice PIH 2009-43, PPAs can be negotiated to include lease/purchase agreements that permit a

---

52. The Energy Independence and Security Act of 2007, 42 U.S.C. 42 § 17001 (2007).
53. 24 C.F.R. § 990 (Westlaw 2011).
54. 24 C.F.R. § 965.302 (Westlaw 2011).
55. 24 C.F.R. § 965.505 (Westlaw 2011).
56. U.S. Dep't of Housing and Urban Dev. Field Office Review Procedure, Energy Performance Contracting (2005); HUD Notice PIH 2006-06, HUD Notice PIH 2008-22, and HUD Notice 2009-16. *See also* 24 C.F.R. § 965.308, which addresses energy performance contracts. Consistent with HUD financial regulation, 24 C.F.R. § 990.185; utility regulation, 24 C.F.R. § 965; and HUD procurement regulations, 24 C.F.R. § 85.36, HUD Field offices are expected, through streamlined procedures, to review EPCs within 45 days, consistent with a standardized review protocol. The following charts reflect the streamlined process for development of an Energy Performance Contract, development of an ESCO, and the HUD Field office approval process:
http://portal.hud.gov/hudportal/documents/huddoc?id=developement-epc-pha-man.pdf
http://portal.hud.gov/hudportal/documents/huddoc?id=developement-epc-esco.pdf
http://portal.hud.gov/hudportal/documents/huddoc?id=epc-approvalprocess.pdf

housing authority to assume ownership of the renewable-energy system—and receive related benefits and maintenance responsibilities.[57]

5. **Energy Conservation and Green Construction Practices**

    HUD encourages the use of renewable-energy and green-construction practices in public housing.[58] Housing authorities are encouraged to use solar, wind, geothermal/ground-coupled heat pumps, and other renewable energy sources, and employ "green" construction and rehabilitation techniques whenever they procure for construction or modernization. For HUD, green building includes low-impact development, as well as improvements for indoor air quality and water conservation or modernization.[59]

6. **Green Assessments and Energy Audits**

    Increasingly, HUD is taking a more proactive role and actively encouraging energy efficiency by public housing authorities. A recently published proposed rule would require public housing authorities to project the current modernization and life-cycle replacement repair needs of its projects over a 20-year period rather than a five-year period.[60] Moreover, the rule proposes to integrate the performance of the property needs assessment with the performance of any energy audit. Another proposed rule revises HUD's energy-audit requirements, for public housing authorities, by identifying certain energy-efficient measures that need to be addressed in an audit.[61] This rule also would improve coordination with the physical needs assessment process. These proposed rules are intended to integrate so that eventually there is a coordinated approach to physical needs assessments and energy audits.

****

---

57. For information concerning the Boston Housing Authority's $63 million ESCO transaction *see* CHARLIE HARAK, NATIONAL CONSUMER LAW CENTER, UP THE CHIMNEY: HOW HUD'S INACTION COSTS TAXPAYERS MILLIONS AND DRIVES UP UTILITY BILLS FOR LOW-INCOME FAMILIES (2010), pp. 10-11.

58. HUD Notice 2009-43, a reissuance of HUD PIH Notice 2008-25.

59. 24 C.F.R. § 85.36 (Westlaw 2011), 24 C.F.R. § 941 (Westlaw 2011), 24 C.F.R. § 965.302 (Westlaw 2011), 24 C.F.R. § 965.305 (Westlaw 2011), 24 C.F.R. § 965.306 (Westlaw 2011), 24 C.F.R. § 965.308 (Westlaw 2011), 24 C.F.R. § 990.170 (Westlaw 2011), 24 C.F.R. § 990.180 (Westlaw 2011), 24 C.F.R. § 990.185 (Westlaw 2011), 24 C.F.R. § 990.225 (Westlaw 2011), HUD PIH Notice 2005-25, Using Energy Star to Promote Energy Efficiency in Public Housing (2008); HUD PIH Notice 2007-30, Using Energy Star to Promote Energy Efficiency in Public Housing; HUD PIH Notice 2009-09, Using Energy Star to Promote Energy Efficiency in Public Housing; HUD PIH Notice 2010-41, Using Energy Star to Promote Energy Efficiency in Public Housing; HUD PIH Notice 2006-06, Guidance on Energy Performance Contracts with terms up to 20 Years; HUD PIH Notice 2008-22, Guidance on Energy Performance Contracts with terms up to 20 Years; HUD PIH Notice 2009-16, Guidance on Energy Performance Contracts with terms up to 20 Years; HUD PIH Notice 2008-25, Guidance on Energy Performance Contracts with terms up to 20 Years; HUD PIH Notice 2009-43, Renewable energy and green construction practices in Public Housing; HUD, PROCUREMENT HANDBOOK 7460.8 Rev.2. Also, the HUD ENERGY DESK BOOK and the HUD Office of Public and Indian Housing website offer very useful information on the latest changes and updates to HUD public housing energy innovation, including the Public Housing Environmental and Conservation Clearinghouse.

60. Fed. Reg., Vol. 76, No. 139 (July 20, 2011).

61. Fed. Reg., Vol. 76, No. 222 (Nov. 17, 2011).

V. IN SUMMARY

It is likely that few disagree that HUD should reduce its energy bill. As we look to the future, the challenge is how best to accomplish this goal in a way that is cost-efficient and fair to all. As attorneys, we are uniquely positioned to identify those administrative requirements that discourage energy efficiency, and it is incumbent on each of us to identify creative ways to encourage energy efficiency.

Resolution of Troubled or Defaulted HUD-Insured Multifamily and Health-Care Loans

12

La Fonte Nesbitt and Stephen D. Niles

I. INTRODUCTION

Pursuant to various sections of the National Housing Act of 1934, as amended,[1] the Department of Housing and Urban Development (HUD), acting through the Federal Housing Administration (FHA),[2] insures mortgage loans made to finance construction, rehabilitation, acquisition, and refinancing of multifamily rental[3] and certain types of residential health-care facilities.[4] Overall, HUD has an enviable track record of having only a small percentage of its insured loans that are troubled or in default as compared to other sources of multifamily or health-care financing, but in recent years, defaults have been increasing.[5]

---

1. National Housing Act, Pub. L. No. 73-479, 48 Stat. 1246. Section 203(b), 12 U.S.C.A § 1709; Section 213, 12 U.S.C.A. § 1715 e.
2. FHA became part of HUD in 1965. For simplicity, throughout this chapter, references to HUD will include FHA.
3. Multifamily rental generally means projects containing five or more rental units. Multifamily rental does not include loans made on for-sale projects such as condominiums.
4. In this chapter, health-care loans refer to loans made to finance board and care, assisted-living facilities, nursing homes, and other residential facilities under Section 232. Health-care loans do not include hospitals and other treatment facilities financed under Section 242.
5. According to *Recommendations Regarding HUD's Proposed Changes [to] FHA Multifamily Mortgage Insurance Programs Underwriting Requirements March 2010,* published by the National Multi-housing Council, HUD reports that mortgage insurance claim rates have increased from 0.6% in FY 2007 to 1.2% in FY 2009, and

This chapter discusses various ways in which a HUD-insured multifamily or health-care loan or mortgage[6] that is troubled (i.e., the project is struggling to fund its operating costs and pay the full amounts due under the loan) or in default might be resolved to either put the project back on solid operating footing or cure the default.

II. OVERVIEW OF HUD MULTIFAMILY AND HEALTH-CARE LOAN PROGRAMS

A complete description of HUD's various multifamily rental and residential health-care loan programs is beyond the scope of this chapter, but before beginning a discussion of possible ways in which defaulted or troubled multifamily or health-care loans insured by HUD might be resolved, it is useful to review the basic details of HUD's most widely used multifamily and health-care loan programs.

- **Section 207/223(f)** insures mortgage loans to facilitate the purchase or refinancing of existing multifamily rental housing. These projects may have been financed originally with conventional or FHA insured mortgages. The property must been completed or substantially rehabilitated for at least three years prior to the date of the application for mortgage insurance.[7] The program allows for non-critical repairs that generally must be completed within 12 months of loan closing, but projects requiring substantial rehabilitation are not acceptable under this section, and loans may not involve the replacement of more than one major system. The mortgage term cannot exceed the lesser of 35 years or 75 percent of the remaining economic life of the physical improvements. The maximum mortgage amount for a purchase transaction is the lesser of: (i) 85 percent of HUD appraised value; (ii) 85 percent of the acquisition cost; (iii) Section 207 statutory per-unit limits, adjusted by the local Field Office high cost percentage for the locality; or (iv) a mortgage amount supported by 85 percent of net income. The maximum mortgage amount for a refinance transaction is the lesser of: (i) 85 percent of HUD appraised value; (ii) Section 207 statutory per unit limits, adjusted by the local Field Office high cost percentage for the locality; (iii) the mortgage amount supported by 85 percent of net income; or (iv) the greater of the cost to refinance or 80 percent of HUD appraised value.[8]

---

further reports that HUD Hub directors, in reviewing their portfolios, project claim/partial payment of claim rates of 2.4% in FY 2010. *See* http://www.nmhc.org/Content/ServeFile.cfm?FileID=8042.

6. We will use HUD mortgage and HUD loan interchangeably to refer to a loan insured by HUD.

7. HUD has briefly instituted a policy that permits waiver of the so-called three-year rule due to dislocations in the multifamily finance markets. But that policy was set to expire in February 2012. *See* Mortgagee Letter 2011-13.

8. Adapted from description of Section 207/223(f) loan programs at http://portal.hud.gov/hudportal/HUD?src=/program_offices/housing/mfh/progdesc/purchrefi223f. Section 223(f) of the National Housing Act was added by Section 311(a) of the Housing and Community Development Act of 1974. Regulations are found at 24 C.F.R. pt. 200. For processing and underwriting instructions, refer to *HUD Handbook 4565.1- Mortgage Insurance for the Purchase of Existing Multifamily Housing Projects*, available on HUDclips.

- **Section 220** insures mortgage loans on new or rehabilitated multifamily housing located in designated urban renewal areas, in areas with concentrated programs of code enforcement, and in other areas where local governments have undertaken designated revitalization activities. Section 220 has statutory mortgage limits that may vary according to the size of the unit, the type of structure, and the location of the project. For new construction projects, the maximum mortgage loan may not exceed 90 percent of the estimated replacement cost. For substantial rehabilitation projects, the maximum mortgage amount is 90 percent of the estimated cost of repair and rehabilitation and the estimated value of the property before the repair and rehabilitation project. The maximum mortgage term is the lesser of 40 years or 75 percent of the remaining economic life of the project.[9]
- **Sections 221(d)(3) and 221(d)(4)** insure mortgage loans to facilitate the new construction or substantial rehabilitation of multifamily rental or cooperative housing. Single Room Occupancy (SRO) projects may also be insured under this section. Section 221(d)(3) is used by nonprofit borrowers and Section 221(d)(4) is used by profit-motivated borrowers. The program has statutory mortgage limits that vary according to the size of the unit, the type of structure, and the location of the project. The principal difference between the (d)(3) and (d)(4) programs is the amount of the insured mortgage available to nonprofit and profit-motivated borrowers. Under Section 221(d)(3), nonprofit borrowers or cooperatives may receive an insured mortgage up to 100 percent of HUD/FHA estimated replacement cost of the project. All types of borrowers under Section 221(d)(4) can receive a maximum mortgage of 90 percent of the HUD/FHA replacement cost estimate.[10]
- **Section 231** insures mortgage loans to facilitate the construction and substantial rehabilitation of multifamily rental housing for elderly persons (62 or older) or persons with disabilities. Few projects have been insured under Section 231 in recent years; nonprofits have opted to use Section 221(d)(3), while profit-motivated developers have used Section 221(d)(4). Projects under Section 231 must consist of eight or more dwelling units. For nonprofit borrowers, the maximum loan amount is 100 percent of the estimated replacement cost of the building (or 100 percent of project value for rehabilitation projects). For all other borrowers,

---

9. Adapted from description of Section 220 loan program at http://www.hud.gov/offices/hsg/mfh/progdesc/renturbanhsg220.cfm. This program is authorized by Section 220(a) and (h), National Housing Act (12 U.S.C. 1715k). Regulations are in 24 C.F.R. pt. 200 *et seq.*, 24 C.F.R. pt. 220.1 *et seq.* The basic program instructions are in *HUD Handbook 4555.1.—Rental Housing in Urban Renewal Areas for Project*, available on HUDclips.

10. Adapted from description of Section 221(d)(3) and 223(d)(4) loan program at http://portal.hud.gov/hudportal/HUD?src=/program_offices/housing/mfh/progdesc/rentcoophsg221d3n4. The 221(d)(3) and 221(d)(4) programs are authorized by the National Housing Act (12 U.S.C. § 17151(d)(3) and (d)(4). Program regulations are found at 24 C.F.R. § 221, subpts. C and D. Basic TAP program instructions are in HUD HANDBOOK 4560.01—MORTGAGE INSURANCE FOR MULTIFAMILY MODERATE INCOME HOUSING PROJECTS, available on HUDclips.

the maximum loan is 90 percent of the replacement cost (or 90 percent of project value for rehabilitation projects).[11]
- **Section 232** provides mortgage insurance for construction or rehabilitation and purchase or refinancing of multifamily residential care facilities, such as assisted-living facilities, nursing homes, intermediate care facilities, and board and care homes. Section 232 loans for construction or rehabilitation generally follow the loan limits applicable to Section 221(d)(4), and Section 232 loans for acquisition or refinancing generally follow the loan limits applicable to Section 223(f).

All of these loan programs share the following basic features:

1. The lender (typically called the "mortgagee" by HUD in various regulations, statutes, handbooks, and other HUD issuances) must be approved by HUD to make and service the loans.
2. The loan must be originated and serviced in accordance with the applicable regulations and other guidance issued by HUD. The majority of multifamily loans must be originated, and serviced in part, in accordance with HUD's *Multifamily Accelerated Processing (MAP) Guide, Handbook* 4430.G[12] Until HUD issues its *Section 232 Handbook*, which is expected to be issued at some point during calendar year 2012, health-care loans must be originated and serviced in accordance with the 2002 version of the *MAP Guide,* the instructions on HUD's Section 232 webpage, and so-called "LEAN Email Blasts."[13]
3. The lender prepares a loan application and various underwriting materials and information that are submitted (a) to the HUD Field Office or Multifamily Hub with jurisdiction over the property location for multifamily loans and (b) to the location designated by Office of Healthcare Programs in the case of Section 232 health-care loans. Once HUD approves a loan, HUD issues a loan commitment to the lender and borrower that details the loan amount and other conditions under which HUD agrees to insure the loan. The time between loan application and loan closing varies, among other things, based on the type of loan (e.g., construction or substantial rehabilitation loans take longer than acquisition or refinancing loans), the quality of the borrower and other loan participants, HUD's workload, and other factors. As of the date of this chapter, in our experience, from loan application to closing often takes three to six months for Section 223(f) loans, six to nine months for Section 232 acquisition or

---

11. Adapted from description of Section 231 loan program at http://www.hud.gov/offices/hsg/mfh/progdesc/renthsgeld231.cfm. Section 231 is authorized by the National Housing Act, as amended, Pub. L. 86-372 (73 U.S.C. § 654 and 12 U.S.C. § 1715 (V)). Program regulations are found in 24 C.F.R. § 231. The basic program instructions are in HUD HANDBOOK 4570.1—HOUSING FOR THE ELDERLY FOR PROJECT MORTGAGE, available on HUDclips.

12. *See* http://portal.hud.gov/hudportal/HUD?src=/program_offices/administration/hudclips/guidebooks/hsg-GB4430. HUD's revised *MAP Guide* became effective on Nov. 1, 2011.

13. *See* http://portal.hud.gov/hudportal/HUD?src=/federal_housing_administration/healthcare_facilities/section_232/lean_processing_page/underwriting_guidance_home_page. Until such time that OHP's *Section 232 Handbook* is published, and for guidance not contained in our Email Blasts, please visit the *Original MAP Guide.*

refinancing loans, and 12 months or more for construction or substantial rehabilitation loans under any of various applicable loan programs.

4. Subject to certain restrictions and compliance with applicable requirements by the lender, HUD's mortgage insurance covers 99 percent of the outstanding principal amount of the loan, plus accrued and unpaid interest, which is paid to the lender as a mortgage insurance claim following a default by the borrower under the loan and the assignment of the defaulted loan by the lender to HUD.[14]

5. HUD loans are non-recourse, except for certain limited exceptions to non-recourse, as provided in the loan documents, primarily in the Regulatory Agreement that is executed by the borrower and HUD.[15]

6. HUD-insured loans are considered to be in default if a payment required to be made under the loan is not paid in full within 30 days of date it was due.[16] However, the borrower has the right to reinstate the mortgage, and it shall not be considered to be in default if reinstatement occurs,[17] and the lender and borrower, with HUD's consent, may extend the time to cure a default or modify the mortgage or the payment terms of the mortgage.[18]

7. The lender must notify HUD of a default within 30 days of its occurrence[19] and must notify HUD within 45 day after the date of default (or, in other words, 75 days after the payment was due in full) whether the lender wants to assign the loan to HUD in exchange for the payment of a mortgage insurance claim or foreclose on the mortgage, acquire title to the property, and then convey title to the property to HUD.[20]

III. OVERVIEW OF GOVERNMENT NATIONAL MORTGAGE ASSOCIATION'S ROLE IN HUD'S MULTIFAMILY AND HEALTH-CARE LOAN PROGRAMS

The overwhelming majority of HUD lenders are mortgage companies that borrow money from warehouse banks to initially fund HUD loans and then sell the economic interests in the loan to obtain funds to repay their warehouse bank. While not all HUD-approved lenders are approved as issuers of mortgage-backed securities (MBS) guaranteed by the Government National Mortgage Association (Ginnie Mae),[21] almost all HUD loans are funded through the

---

14. *See* 24 C.F.R. § 207.259.
15. NOTE: With the introduction of its revised multifamily loan documents effective Sept. 1, 2011, for multifamily loans, one or more persons or entities identified in the HUD loan commitment will be required to expressly acknowledge potential personal liability for certain specified actions under both the HUD Regulatory Agreement and the Note. *See* Multifamily Note (HUD-94001M - Rev. 04/11) and Regulatory Agreement (HUD-92466M - Rev. 04/11), posted at http://portal.hud.gov/hudportal/HUD?src=/program_offices/administration/hudclips/forms/.
16. *See* 24 C.F.R. § 207.255.
17. *See* 24 C.F.R. § 207.256a.
18. *See* 24 C.F.R. § 207.256b.
19. *See* 24 C.F.R. § 207.256.
20. *See* 24 C.F.R. § 207.258
21. Ginnie Mae was created in 1968 as a wholly-owned government corporation within the U.S. Department of Housing and Urban Development (HUD). Ginnie Mae guarantees the principal

issuance of Ginnie Mae MBS. Ginnie Mae claims to securitize more than 97 percent of HUD multifamily mortgages.[22]

Ginnie Mae guarantees the timely payment of principal and interest on the security to the holder of a Ginnie Mae MBS backed by a HUD loan, regardless of whether the borrower on the underlying loan has made the payments required under its note or whether the lender, as issuer of the MBS, has fulfilled its obligation under Ginnie Mae requirements to advance the principal and interest—again, regardless of whether the borrower has made its underlying payment. The Ginnie Mae guaranty essentially "wraps" the HUD mortgage insurance to create the soundest and most creditworthy mortgage investment available.[23]

The lender remains the record owner of the HUD mortgage and the mortgagee and servicer from HUD's perspective. However, the holder of the Ginnie Mae MBS owns the economic interest in the loan, and the loan must be serviced in accordance with the *Ginnie Mae Mortgage-Backed Securities Guide* (Ginnie Mae Guide)[24] in addition to following HUD's other servicing requirements. In exchange for its guarantee, Ginnie Mae receives a guaranty fee that is currently 13 basis points, and Ginnie Mae requires the lender to receive a servicing fee of at least 12 basis points. Both the servicing fee and guaranty fee are included within the interest rate on the HUD loan, meaning that the interest rate on the HUD loan is 25 basis points higher than the rate on the Ginnie Mae MBS.[25]

This means that in the case of virtually all HUD loans, in addition to gaining approval from HUD and the lender, in order to resolve a troubled or defaulted FHA-insured loan, the borrower often also needs to obtain approval from the Ginnie Mae MBS investor who actually owns the economic interest in the loan. This also means that the resolution of the loan must comply with the requirements of *The Ginnie Mae Guide*.

IV. OPTIONS

So let us now consider possible alternatives for the borrower whose loan is troubled or has gone into default. Those options are: (i) refinancing using HUD's Section 223(a)(7) loan

---

and interest payments on mortgage-backed securities (MBS) issued by program participants. The securities are collateralized by the cash flows from loans insured or guaranteed by the Federal Housing Administration (FHA), Department of Veterans Affairs Home Loan Program for Veterans (VA), Office of Public and Indian Housing (PIH), and the U.S. Department of Agriculture Rural Development (RD). The Ginnie Mae guaranty assures investors that they will receive their monthly principal and interest payments on outstanding securities in a timely manner. The Ginnie Mae MBS guaranty is the only MBS guaranty explicitly backed by the full faith and credit of the U.S. government.

22. *See* http://www.ginniemae.gov/issuers/programs.asp?subTitle=Issuers. In FY 2008, Ginnie Mae securitized more than 97% of eligible FHA multifamily mortgages.

23. *See* http://www.ginniemae.gov/about/about.asp?Section=About. Ginnie Mae securities are the only MBS to carry the full faith and credit guaranty of the U.S. government, which means that even in difficult times an investment in Ginnie Mae MBS is one of the safest an investor can make. In addition, Ginnie Mae MBS are fully modified pass-through securities guaranteed by the full faith and credit of the U.S. government. Regardless of whether the mortgage payment is made, investors in Ginnie Mae MBS will receive full and timely payment of principal as well as interest.

24. Ginnie Mae 5500.3, Rev. 1. *See* http://www.ginniemae.gov/guide.

25. Ginnie Mae 5500.3, Rev. 1, chs. 31–33.

program; (ii) mortgage modification; (iii) Partial Payment of Claim (PPC); and (iv) purchasing the defaulted loan under HUD's Note Sale program.

V. REFINANCING UNDER § 223(A)(7)

It may seem counterintuitive, but given some of the requirements that HUD currently imposes on mortgage modifications, as discussed below in Section VI, refinancing a troubled or defaulted loan with a HUD Section 223(a)(7) loan carrying a sufficiently lower interest rate may be the most attractive option if a project can be carried long enough to get through the refinancing process.

Although a troubled or defaulted HUD loan could be refinanced with a non-HUD loan, HUD's Section 223(a)(7) loan program is in many respects a natural vehicle for this purpose. Section 223(a)(7) is limited to refinancing loans that are already insured by HUD under many of its various loan programs. As stated in HUD Mortgagee Letter 06-03, "the objective of Section 223(a)(7) is to stabilize the FHA insured portfolio through refinancing of existing debt and completion of necessary repairs, which result in lower debt service and improved mortgage security." Underwriting and closing a loan under Section 223(a)(7) is done on an expedited basis and can sometimes be accomplished in as few as three to four months. Especially with interest rates at or near historic lows over the last several years, a number of borrowers have taken advantage of Section 223(a)(7) to provide just such lower debt service and improved project cash flow.

Under Section 223(a)(7):

- The maximum loan amount may not exceed the lowest of (i) the original principal amount of the existing insured mortgage that is being refinanced, (ii) the unpaid principal amount of the existing insured mortgage that is being refinanced plus certain HUD-approved items (e.g., repairs, cost of refinance) or (iii) the amount that can be amortized by 90 percent of net operating income.
- The term of the new Section 223(a)(7) mortgage may not exceed the remaining term of the existing mortgage except when HUD determines an extension is needed for project feasibility, not to exceed 12 years beyond the remaining term of the existing mortgage being refinanced.[26]

Several obstacles do present themselves, however, in refinancing troubled or defaulted loans under Section 223(a)(7). The HUD loan being refinanced cannot be in default, meaning that any past-due payments must be brought current at or before closing on the Section 223(a)(7) loan. In addition, depending upon when in the term of the existing loan a refinancing plan is being contemplated, there may be a prepayment lock-out or prepayment premium that must be addressed.

HUD permits, but does not impose, prepayment restrictions on insured loans, and prepayment restrictions cannot require that HUD consent to prepayment of the loan by the borrower.[27] But based on the demands of loan investors, the vast majority of HUD loans (and

---

26. *See* HUD Mortgage Letter 06-03 and HUD HANDBOOK 4567.1, chs. 2-2 and 2-4.
27. *See, e.g.*, Chapter 3.4E of the MAP GUIDE.

virtually all loans funded with Ginnie Mae MBS) have some combination of a period during which voluntary prepayment is prohibited—the so-called "lock-out period"—and also require the payment of a "prepayment premium" for some period of time after the lock-out period has expired. Compared to the complicated defeasance provisions or yield maintenance provisions of other types of financing, the prepayment provisions of a typical HUD loan are refreshingly straightforward, however.

For loans funded with Ginnie Mae MBS, the typical prepayment provision covers a period of not more than 10 years following the commencement of amortization (or the construction period stated in the HUD-approved construction contract) and provides for a prepayment premium equal to a percentage of the principal being prepaid based on scale that begins at not more than 10 percent in the first year and declines by 1 percent per year until the loan is prepayable without any prepayment at the end of the tenth year.[28] For example, a fairly widespread prepayment provision in use at the preparation of this chapter prohibits voluntary prepayment for a period of two years, followed by a prepayment premium of 8 percent, which declines 1 percent per year until the prepayment premium is zero in year 10.

If a loan becomes troubled or defaults *after* the end of its prepayment period, the prepayment issues are moot. But if a loan becomes troubled or defaults *during* the prepayment period, the parties need to address the prepayment lock-out and premium provisions of the loan by, for example, negotiating a discounted prepayment premium with the investor or paying the prepayment premium in full. Thankfully, HUD has recognized the issues created generally by prepayment premiums on refinancing and, with disclosure, under Section 223(a)(7) HUD allows any "trade premium" received from the loan investor generated by having an interest rate on the Section 223(a)(7) that is above the current market (but still low enough to make the loan sound from an underwriting perspective) to be shared by the lender with the borrower to offset, in whole or part, a prepayment premium that is due on the loan that is being paid off.

If the proposed refinancing transaction does not produce sufficient funds, even with a trade premium, in theory there is another possibility for addressing the prepayment lock-out or premium issues—HUD's invocation of its so-called "prepayment override." As a condition to permitting the typical prepayment provision, HUD requires the inclusion of the following "override" provision in the note allowing HUD to override the prepayment lock-out and/or prepayment premium provisions in the event of a default during the period where a prepayment premium is greater than 1 percent.[29]

> Notwithstanding any prepayment prohibition imposed and/or penalty required by this Note with respect to prepayments made prior to _____, 20__, [enter first date on which prepayments may be made with a penalty of one percent or less] the indebtedness may be prepaid in part or in full on the last or first day of any calendar month without the consent of the mortgagee and without prepayment pen-

---

28. In fact, HUD prohibits prepayment periods of longer than 10 years following the date of the first payment of principal (i.e., commencement of amortization) or the construction period stated in the construction contract and under which the prepayment premium is more than 1 percent at the end of the tenth year following the construction period stated in the construction contract or commencement of amortization. *See* Chapter 11.7.B.4. of the MAP GUIDE.

29. *See, e.g.,* Chapter 11.7.C.1 of the MAP GUIDE.

alty if HUD determines that prepayment will avoid a mortgage insurance claim and is, therefore, in the best interest of the Federal Government.

Unfortunately, although we are not aware of any regulatory or statutory prohibitions that prevent its use in these circumstances, we are also not aware of any instance in which HUD has exercised its override to facilitate a Section 223(a)(7) refinancing.[30] Moreover, given the conditions imposed by HUD as a condition to exercise of its prepayment prohibition override, as discussed in Section VII below, it may rarely be a good choice for a borrower, even if HUD were so inclined.

VI. MORTGAGE MODIFICATION

As indicated above, a lender and borrower are permitted to modify a HUD mortgage with HUD's approval. This presents a possible method to address a defaulted or troubled project by modifying the interest rate on a mortgage to lower the interest rate and resultant debt service where the original interest rate is higher than current rates and the loan can be fully serviced using current interest rate.

In prior years, HUD seemingly made mortgage modifications to address troubled projects or cure defaults easier to obtain. See, for example, the following language from HUD Mortgagee Letter 93-39 concerning proactive use by HUD of Section 223(a)(7) loans to reduce HUD's risk on insured loans: "NOTE: Reduction in interest rate alone, agreed upon between the mortgagor and mortgagee, may be handled by a modification of the mortgage documents rather than using 223(a)(7)." More recently, however, HUD has greatly increased the requirements for a mortgage modification.

HUD requirements for approving a mortgage modification of a HUD multifamily loan[31] are currently set forth in (i) Chapter 14 (Partial Payment of Claims Loan Modifications) of *HUD's Asset Management Handbook* 4350.1 Rev. 2, November 2010 (*Revised PPC and Modification Handbook*) and (ii) HUD Mortgagee Letter 2010-32 (Revision to Policy for Partial Payment of Claims and Mortgage Modifications) (Mortgagee Letter 2010-32). As stated in the *Revised PPC and Modification Handbook*:

> A loan modification may be appropriate when an adjustment in the current mortgage terms, such as a reduction in the interest rate, may cure or prevent a default absent owner contribution. If the mortgage is under a lock-out and/or a penalty provision, the requirements of Mortgagee Letter 87-9 are met by following the requirements of this Chapter. The process for requesting, reviewing and approving a mortgage modification (or refinancing per Mortgagee Letter 87-9) will be the same as a PPC, except for the closing process.

Given the language above about "preventing" a default, a mortgage modification could possibly be approved by HUD prior to the loan actually going into default as a way of

---

30. *See, e.g.*, the following language from HUD Mortgagee Letter 93-39: "NOTE: Mortgagors may not violate prepayment restrictions and lock-out provisions in the existing mortgage documents to refinance under 223(a)(7)."

31. Section 232 health-care loans are not eligible for a mortgage modification under Chapter 14. *See* Chapter 14.23 of HANDBOOK 4350.1 Rev. 2, Nov. 2010.

preventing the payment of a mortgage insurance claim. However, the conditions prescribed in the *Revised PPC and Modification Handbook* anticipate that the loan is already in default.

HUD's threshold requirements for approving a mortgage modification (which are very similar to the threshold requirements for approving a Partial Payment of Claim as discussed in Section VII below) are as follows:

- The owner (and its affiliates) must not have any other loans in any of HUD's multi-family housing programs that are in default (unless the owner demonstrates that the default was caused by circumstances beyond the owner's control).
- The owner must not be in violation of any HUD regulatory or business agreements, including any Housing Assistance Payments (HAP) contracts or HUD Use Agreements.
- The owner must provide a statement by a certified public accountant or independent public accountant indicating that, during the period after final endorsement, a net capital contribution of 5 percent or more of the project's loan's original mortgage amount was made to the project. (Note: If sufficient capital contributions were not previously made, they may be made at the time of the mortgage modification closing). As a general matter, accrued but unpaid payments to parties having an identity-of-interest with the owner (e.g., management fees paid to an affiliated management agent) will not be considered. However, for a nonprofit owner, in-kind services may be considered towards the capital contribution requirement.
- The owner's cash flow projections must reflect the project's cash flow can support 100 percent of the modified mortgage at a current market interest rate. In order to allow borrowers to confirm whether they satisfy the financial requirements, HUD has made a PPC Analysis Model available on the Internet.[32]
- The mortgagee must submit a letter to HUD agreeing to accept a mortgage modification consistent with HUD's requirements.
- The owner must have submitted and continue to submit all net cash monthly to the mortgagee from and after the loan default.[33]

The process for the borrower and lender submitting a modification proposal to HUD and HUD's approval of a mortgage modification proposal are the same as for a PPC, as discussed below in Section VII.

In one truly curious development, especially given that one of the purposes of the mortgage modification is to reduce risks to the mortgage insurance fund, as a condition to a mortgage modification, HUD is requiring the owner to execute a 20-year Use Agreement that imposes affordability requirements on the project. That appears to be true even for "market rate" projects (i.e., projects whose rents are not regulated by HUD), which represent the majority of projects financed by HUD-insured loans, and even though the original HUD financing did not require any affordability restrictions. The Use Agreement will have a term of 20 years following the date of the mortgage modification closing, and it requires the owner

---

32. *See* http://hudatwork.hud.gov/po/h/hm/fog/misc.cfm.
33. *See* Revised PPC HANDBOOK, Section 14-4.

to (i) reserve at least 30 percent of the project's units for residents with incomes at or below 80 percent of the Adjusted Median Income (AMI), and (ii) charge such residents rents not to exceed 30 percent of 80 percent of AMI.[34]

As indicated above, in addition to gaining approval from HUD and the lender, the borrower often also needs to obtain approval from the Ginnie Mae MBS investor who actually owns the economic interest in the loan. For a HUD loan that is not in default but merely troubled, approval of the Ginnie Mae investor is required in order for the loan to be modified. Thus, there is often negotiation among the lender,[35] the Ginnie Mae investor, and the borrower concerning any potential mortgage modification.

For example, assume a troubled HUD loan has an interest rate of 6.5 percent and current market rates are 5 percent for that type of loan. Further assume that modifying the interest rate to 5 percent would enable the project to comfortably service the modified HUD loan. Clearly, the borrower is interested in modifying the interest rate. So too is the lender, in order to both keep the servicing fee it earns on the HUD loan and avoid having a default on a HUD loan it services (and, perhaps, also underwrote and originated). HUD is also likely to support the modification so it can avoid a possible mortgage insurance claim. However, in this example, the Ginnie Mae investor may not be very interested in losing a yield of 6.25 percent on its Ginnie Mae MBS in order to reinvest its funds in a market where the current yield on a similar Ginnie Mae MBS is only 4.75 percent.[36] As a result, it would not be atypical as a condition to its approval of the mortgage modification for the Ginnie Mae investor to want: (i) a cash payment or the contribution of additional equity from the borrower or (ii) an interest rate on the loan that is less than 6.5 percent but more than 5 percent in order to keep a somewhat above market yield on its investment. Conversely, the borrower will argue that without a mortgage modification to current market rates, the loan will eventually go into default and be assigned to HUD for the payment of a mortgage insurance claim, in which case the Ginnie Mae investor would lose its entire yield in any event. And there you have the parameters for the negotiation.

For loans that are actually in default, the road to a mortgage modification from the Ginnie Mae perspective is perhaps somewhat easier. Chapter 18 of the Ginnie Mae Guide governs the servicing of defaulted HUD loans that are funded with Ginnie Mae MBS. Under Chapter 18, loans in default may, under certain circumstances, be repurchased from their Ginnie Mae pool if they remain in default and then be "repooled" for the sale of a Ginnie Mae MBS backed by the new or modified loan to a new investor.[37]

There are somewhat different thresholds for repurchase and repooling, depending on when the loan was closed and the related Ginnie Mae MBS was issued. If those conditions are met, the loan may be repurchased without approval from Ginnie Mae or the Ginnie Mae MBS investor. As you will see from the excerpt of Chapter 18 of the *Ginnie Mae Guide* below, the standards have tightened slightly for loans with securities issued on or after January 1, 2003.

---

34. *Id.* at Section 14-7.H and HUD Mortgagee Letter 2010-32, Para. C.
35. Under the Ginnie Mae Guide, lenders are called "Issuers."
36. There is a minimum 25-basis-point servicing fee on loans funded by Ginnie Mae MBS; hence the 25-basis difference in the rate on the HUD loan and the Ginnie Mae MBS.
37. Ginnie Mae 5500.3, Rev. 1, ch. 18. *See* http://www.ginniemae.gov/guide/pdf/chap18.pdf.

A. Requirements for Repurchase

1. ***Loans Backing Securities Issued before January 1, 2003***
   For loans backing a Ginnie Mae security with an issue date before January 1, 2003, Issuers may repurchase any pooled loan without written permission from Ginnie Mae if (1) the borrower fails to make any payment for three consecutive months or (2) for four consecutive months one missed payment remains uncured.

2. ***Special Repooling Restrictions on Loans Backing Securities Issued between August 1 and December 1, 2002***
   Special repooling restrictions are imposed on loans repurchased under paragraph 18-3 (B)(1)(a)(2) above [i.e., loans where for four consecutive months one missed payment remains uncured] and that back securities issued between August 1 and December 1, 2002: (1) These loans may only be repooled once, even if the loan is sold to a new Issuer; and (2) these loans may only be repooled if (i) the loan becomes current and remains current for six months, or (ii) if the loan undergoes formal loss mitigation and is otherwise eligible to be placed in a Ginnie Mae pool.

3. ***Loans Backing Securities Issued on or after January 1, 2003***
   For loans backing a Ginnie Mae security with an issue date on or after January 1, 2003, Issuers may repurchase any pooled loan without written permission from Ginnie Mae if the borrower fails to make any payment for three consecutive months. For example, no payments are made for the months of March, April, and May. The Issuer may purchase the loan out of the pool on or after June 1.

4. ***Loans Subject to a Trial Modification Period***
   In connection with each agency's own program requirements, an Issuer shall also be permitted to repurchase a loan from a pool if the borrower is approved for a trial modification and the loan is in a continuous period of default for 90 days or more. Until the loan is repurchased from the pool, however, the Issuer remains obligated to make full payments of principal and interest to investors, as required by the security.

B. Procedures for Repurchase

The Issuer shall repurchase any pooled loan for an amount equal to 100 percent of the loan RPB, less the principal payments advanced by the Issuer on the loan. The repurchased loan's principal amount must be included in the payment made to security holders following the reporting month in which the loan was removed. The removed loan must not be included in the RPB reported in the month in which the proceeds of the repurchase are paid to security holders.

C. Permissible Loan Modifications

While Issuers are prohibited from modifying the terms of loans held in Ginnie Mae pools that affect the amount or duration of loan payments, certain loss mitigation strategies, such as Special Forbearance and Partial Claim options described in FHA loss mitigation guidance do not alter the terms of the loan. These loss mitigation strategies may be accomplished without repurchasing the delinquent loan from the pool.

As described above, the lender (Issuer) needs to find a source of money to purchase the defaulted loan "at par" (i.e., 100 percent of the loan's outstanding principal balance). While it is not required, typically the lender will want to issue a new Ginnie Mae MBS backed by the modified loan. Following approval of the mortgage modification by HUD, the loan investor and Ginnie Mae, if required, the lender arranges to sell a Ginnie Mae MBS backed by the modified HUD loan to an investor and effectively uses the money from the sale of that new Ginnie Mae MBS to repurchase the original Ginnie Mae MBS.

VII. PARTIAL PAYMENTS OF CLAIM (PPC)

HUD's Partial Payment of Claim (PPC) procedures represent a valuable tool to remedy financially troubled multifamily projects and Section 232 health-care facilities with HUD-insured loans that are in default. The PPC approach is typically used where a project's financial difficulties cannot be effectively addressed by a mortgage modification or a refinancing. Among other things, the PPC process often allows project owners to cure existing loan defaults, stabilize project operations for the long term, ameliorate future 2530 clearance problems, and avoid potential foreclosure (and bankruptcy). From HUD's perspective, the PPC process also permits HUD to reduce its losses on defaulted HUD-insured loans assigned to HUD and preserve affordable housing.

The typical PPC transaction involves restructuring an existing HUD-insured loan (the Original Loan) that is in default into two loans: (i) a modified first lien HUD-insured loan that can be supported by the project's existing operations (the Modified First Loan), and (ii) a new HUD-held "cash-flow" loan in an amount that equals the difference between the Original Loan and the Modified First Loan (plus accrued interest) and which is payable out of a portion of the project's available surplus cash (the PPC Loan). For example, a project with an Original Loan having an outstanding principal balance of $10 million might be divided into a $6 million Modified First Loan and a $4 million PPC Loan (and the accrued but unpaid interest amount would then be added to the PPC Loan).

To apply for a PPC transaction, the project owner must submit a PPC proposal to the HUD Field Office with jurisdiction over the project, and a copy of the proposal to the related HUB Office. HUD's guidance indicates that the proposal must be submitted to HUD within 60 days of the loan default.[38] However, in the past, HUD has generally been willing to consider PPC proposals that are submitted to HUD after (and sometimes, well after) such 60-day period. A further discussion of HUD's requirements for the PPC proposal is included in Section 3 below.

Applicable HUD regulations indicate that HUD may ask a mortgagee to participate in a PPC transaction whenever HUD receives notice from the mortgagee of the mortgagee's intention to file an insurance claim on a defaulted loan.[39] Before HUD will authorize a PPC transaction, HUD must determine that the PPC "would be less costly to the Federal Government than other reasonable alternatives for maintaining the low- and moderate-income character of the project." To make this determination, HUD will consider, among other things, whether (i) the default was caused by circumstances beyond the mortgagor's control; (ii) the

---

38. *See* Revised PPC HANDBOOK, Section 14-7.
39. *See* 24 C.F.R. § 207.258b(b).

relief resulting from the PPC, when considered with other available resources, would be sufficient to restore the financial viability of the project; (iii) the management of the project is satisfactory to HUD; and (iv) the mortgagee is entitled, under HUD regulations, to assign the mortgage to HUD in exchange for a claim payment.[40]

1. The Recent Reemergence of HUD's PPC Approach

While HUD has long had authority to implement PPCs, HUD largely terminated the use of PPCs when it began selling defaulted loans through its loan auction program. Under the auction program, HUD holds public auctions two or more times each year to dispose of the defaulted insured loans (including loans on some partially subsidized projects) previously assigned to HUD. The auctions have been effective for purposes of removing defaulted loans from HUD's portfolio of HUD-held loans. However, in recent years, HUD has incurred substantial losses at the auctions where loans are often sold at 35 percent to 50 percent, if not less, of their unpaid loan balances. Also, because the winning bidders often pursue or threaten to pursue foreclosure against the borrowers, the end result can mean substantial disruption—and potential displacement—for low- and moderate-income tenants (and the loss of much-needed affordable housing).

In the past few years, in response to the substantial losses incurred by the federal government through the HUD auction program, HUD has reinstituted—and refined—its PPC procedures. The revised procedures are set forth in the following HUD issuances: (i) a modified Chapter 14 (Partial Payment of Claims Loan Modifications) of *HUD's Asset Management Handbook* 4350.1 Rev. 2, November 2010 (*Revised PPC Handbook* or *Handbook*), (ii) HUD Mortgagee Letter 2010-32 (Revision to Policy for Partial Payment of Claims and Mortgage Modifications) (Mortgagee Letter 2010-32), and (iii) HUD Mortgagee Letter 2011-15 (Revision to Policy for Partial Payment of Claims of Section 232 Mortgages) (Mortgagee Letter 2011-15). For purposes of this chapter, the focus will largely be on the revised PPC requirements impacting multifamily projects as set forth in the *Revised PPC Handbook*.

2. Qualifying for a PPC

Eligible Mortgages: PPCs may be used to remedy loan defaults on loans originated under most of HUD's most active multifamily loan programs, as well as the Section 232 health-care facility loan program. The multifamily programs eligible for PPCs include Section 207 projects (Multifamily Housing), Section 213 projects (Cooperative Housing), Section 220 projects (Urban Renewal), certain Section 221(d) projects (Low-Cost and Moderate Income Housing), certain Section 223(f) and 223(a)(7) projects (Refinanced Housing), and Section 542(c) projects (HFA Risk Share).[41]

Regulatory Requirements: *The Revised PPC Handbook* indicates that owners of projects with eligible mortgages must satisfy several "threshold requirements" in order to qualify for a PPC. They include the following:

---

40. *Id.*
41. *See* Revised PPC HANDBOOK, Section 14-2.

A. The owner must not have any other loans in any of HUD's multifamily housing programs that are in default (unless the owner demonstrates that the default was caused by circumstances beyond the owner's control).
B. The owner must not be in violation of any HUD regulatory or business agreements, including any Housing Assistance Payments (HAP) contracts or HUD Use Agreements.
C. The owner must provide a statement by a certified public accountant or independent public accountant indicating that, during the period after final endorsement, a net capital contribution of 5 percent or more of the project's loan's original mortgage amount was made to the project (Note: if such contribution were not previously made, they may be made at the time of the PPC closing).[42] As a general matter, accrued but unpaid payments to parties having an identity-of-interest with the owner (e.g., management fees paid to an affiliated management agent) will not be considered. However, for a nonprofit owner, in-kind services may be considered.
D. The owner's cash flow projections must reflect the project's ability to support a recast new insured mortgage of at least 50 percent of the current outstanding mortgage with a debt service coverage ratio of 1.2.[43] In order to allow borrowers to confirm whether they satisfy the financial requirements, HUD has made a PPC Analysis Model available on the Internet at http://hudatwork.hud.gov/po/h/hm/fog/misc.cfm.
E. The mortgagee must submit a letter to HUD agreeing to accept a PPC consistent with HUD's requirements.
F. The owner must have submitted and continue to submit all net cash monthly to the mortgagee from and after the loan default.
G. The owner must agree to repay HUD an amount equal to the partial payment, with the obligation secured by a second mortgage prescribed by HUD.[44]

3. PPC Proposal

The *Revised PPC Handbook* provides a relatively detailed description of the various items that the project owner must include in its PPC proposal submission to the applicable HUD Field Office (and with a copy to the HUB). The *Handbook* indicates that the submission should include: (a) a cover letter describing the terms and conditions of the owner's request (e.g., a discussion of the problems leading to the default and a description of how the existing debt would be restructured in accordance with HUD's PPC requirements); (b) a statement identifying the net owner contributions made to the project; (c) copies of various financial information relating to the project's past financial performance and 10-year projections reflecting the terms of the proposed PPC; (d) a discussion of the property's condi-

---

42. Prior to issuance of the *Revised PPC Handbook*, HUD limited the size of the PPC claim payment to three times the amount of the owner's contribution. This limitation was eliminated, however, under the *Revised PPC Handbook*.
43. Although the limitation is subject to waiver, HUD generally requires the original principal amount of the Modified First Loan to be at least 50% of the existing balance of the Original Loan immediately prior to the PPC closing.
44. *See* REVISED PPC HANDBOOK, Section 14-4.

tion, the adequacy of replacement reserves and, in certain instances, a Project Comprehensive Needs Assessment (PCNA); (e) information relating to recent management reviews and physical inspection reports relating to the project; (f) information demonstrating that the project is providing or will provide needed affordable housing; and (g) a statement that the owner and all lienholders will accept the HUD-prescribed Use Agreement applicable to PPC transactions.[45]

Because the submission of an incomplete PPC proposal can greatly delay the HUD processing, owners are strongly encouraged to use the PPC checklist included as Appendix A to the *Handbook*—and to follow the various directions included in Sections 14-5 through 14-8 of the *Handbook*. It is also important for owners to remain in regular contact with the HUD officials responsible for processing the PPC proposal to ensure that any questions raised by HUD are promptly addressed. Because some HUD Field Offices are less familiar with PPCs than others, a project owner pursuing a PPC should also try to determine, at an early point in the process, whether the PPC will be processed primarily by the HUD Field Office or by the HUB. If the HUB will be responsible for the processing, the owner should also try to establish regular contact with the HUB officials.

4. Loan Restructuring Issues

As indicated above, if a project owner is eligible for a PPC, and HUD, the owner, and the lender can agree on the terms of the restructuring, the transaction will typically result in a Modified First Loan and a cash-flow PPC Loan. In addition, HUD will typically require the owner to execute a 20-year HUD Use Agreement that imposes affordability requirements on the project. Some of the primary elements of the Modified First Loan and the PPC Loan, as well as the HUD-required Use Agreement, are described below.

Modified First Loan: The *Revised PPC Handbook* indicates the Modified First Loan will be underwritten based upon an interest rate that is 125 basis points over the 10-year Treasury Rate at the time of the HUD approval. If the loan is ultimately closed at a lower rate, HUD will not re-underwrite the Modified First Loan. However, if the loan is closed at a higher rate, the original principal amount of the Modified First Loan will be reduced to maintain the minimum required debt service coverage ratio (including mortgage insurance premium) of 1.20.[46]

The Modified First Loan will have the same maturity date as the Original Loan, and the monthly payments will be re-amortized over the remaining term based upon the original principal balance of the Modified First Loan and the new interest rate.[47]

As a general matter, accrued late fees and closing costs cannot be included in the transaction or paid by the project. However, funds held by the mortgagee can be used at closing to pay certain closing attorney fees, title and recording fees, escrow shortages, bond or GNMA fees, and interest for the remainder of the closing month.[48]

---

45. *See id.*, Section 14-7.
46. *See* Revised PPC HANDBOOK, Section 14-4.
47. *Id.* at Section 14-10.
48. *Id.* at Section 14-6.

Per the *Revised PPC Handbook*, the mortgagee must agree that any prepayment lock-out and/or penalty provisions are overridden by the PPC or approved mortgage modification.[49] The Guidance also indicates that the mortgagee is prohibited from charging the project a fee for processing a PPC or mortgage modification.[50]

PPC Mortgage Loan: The PPC Loan amount is typically equal to (i) the difference between the outstanding principal balance of the Original Loan and the original principal balance of the Modified First Loan, plus (ii) the amount of interest accruing on the Original Loan from the "paid through date" through the PPC closing deadline date established by HUD (or the actual closing date, if earlier).[51]

The *Revised PPC Handbook* indicates that the PPC Mortgage Loan shall provide for:

- an interest rate equal to the Applicable Federal Rate (AFR) for the month of the PPC closing;
- a maturity date co-terminus with the Modified First Loan;
- a minimum annual payment of 75 percent of annual surplus cash, as computed in accordance with the HUD Regulatory Agreement (the 25 percent remainder belongs to the owner);
- a due-on-sale provision in the event of sale, refinancing, or termination;
- a service charge (so long as the PPC Loan is held by HUD) calculated at an annual rate of 0.5 percent of the unpaid principal balance; and
- a call provision that permits the holder of the PPC Loan, at the loan's 20-year anniversary, to require full payment of amounts then owing on the loan.[52]

Use Agreement: The *Revised PPC Handbook* adds a new wrinkle to PPC transactions involving multifamily projects. According to the *Revised PPC Handbook,* in order to obtain a PPC, the owner must agree to the terms of a HUD-mandated Use Agreement that is superior to all liens on the project, including the Modified First Loan. The Use Agreement has a term of 20 years following the date of the PPC closing and requires the owner to: (i) reserve at least 30 percent of the projects units for residents with incomes at or below 80 percent of the Adjusted Median Income (AMI), and (ii) charge such residents rents not to exceed 30 percent of 80 percent of AMI.[53]

Prior to issuance of the *Revised PPC Handbook,* most market-rate projects that underwent a PPC never had to satisfy any HUD-imposed affordability requirements as a condition of the PPC. Moreover, such market-rate projects typically had no reason to collect the information required to ensure compliance with such affordability requirements. This may explain, at least in part, why the Use Agreement provides for a limited grace period for the project owner to come into compliance with the Use Agreement's requirements.

---

49. As discussed above, the party agreeing that any prepayment provisions have been overridden is not really the mortgagee, but the loan investor.
50. *Id.* at Section 14-6.
51. *Id.*
52. *Id.* at Section 14-10.B.
53. *Id.* at Section 14-7.H.

It is also important to note that Mortgagee Letter 2011-15, which applies to PPCs on Section 232 health-care projects, does not impose a Use Agreement requirement.

Additional Terms and Conditions of PPC Transaction: The *Revised PPC Handbook* imposes a number of additional terms and conditions on PPC transactions that are worth noting, including the following:

- The Sources and Uses of Funds Statement for the transaction may not show disbursement of funds to the owners. Furthermore, no funds may be paid to identity-of-interest persons.
- The monthly deposit to the Reserve for Replacement Account will resume with the first payment of the Modified First Loan. However, previous deposits will not have to be made up, unless the RFR balance has been found by HUD to be inadequate.
- All escrows, such as tax, hazard insurance, and MIP, must be fully funded at closing.
- All payables older than 30 days must be paid by the owner prior to closing or converted to notes payable that can be repaid only from the owner's share of surplus cash.
- If HUD determines that there has been an uncorrected material violation of the project's Regulatory Agreement, HAP Contract, Use Agreement, or any other regulatory requirement, the interest rate on the PPC Loan will revert to the rate on the Original Loan, retroactive to the date of the PPC closing.
- Project operating income may not be used to pay financing fees, attorney fees, consultant fees, other professional fees, or any costs of the restructuring transaction.[54]

While the *Revised PPC Handbook* does not expressly indicate that these terms and conditions are negotiable, HUD has shown some limited flexibility on a case-by-case basis.

5. Tax Considerations

As may be expected, HUD does not take any position on the tax implications of restructuring HUD-insured debt as contemplated by the PPC process. Some owners and their tax counsel have expressed concern that, among other things, the IRS might characterize the transaction as a "tax avoidance" scheme and assess income taxes on the indebtedness transferred to the PPC Loan. HUD officials have on occasion referred owners inquiring about the tax aspects of PPCs to IRS Revenue Ruling 98-34—a ruling that pertains to the restructuring of HUD-insured debt in the context of mark-to-market transactions under the Multifamily Assisted Housing Reform and Affordability Act of 1997, as amended (MAHRAA). Revenue Ruling 98-34 addresses the situation in which an existing HUD-insured loan is bifurcated under MAHRAA, and the interest rate charged on the resulting soft-second loan is reduced below the Applicable Federal Rate (AFR). In the Revenue Ruling, the IRS indicated that even though the proposed restructuring under MAHRAA converted part of an existing HUD-insured, market-rate loan into a cash-flow second loan with an interest rate below the AFR, the transaction was not structured with a principal purpose of avoiding federal tax—and it did not create "cancellation of indebtedness income" for the participating owner.

---

54. *Id.* at Section 14-10.C.

While Revenue Ruling 98-34 is closely tied to specific aspects of MAHRAA, the Ruling potentially provides some helpful insights for owners considering PPCs. At the same time, owners must consult with their counsel to address whether, among other things, the specific facts and circumstances of the relevant PPC Loan meets all of the qualifications for valid indebtedness under applicable law. For example, for the PPC Loan to be deemed "real debt," there must be a reasonable likelihood of repayment. Because the PPC Loan provides for no scheduled repayment of principal or interest, and it is payable only from excess cash flow from the project, the "real debt" analysis can be problematic. Again, owners are advised to consult on these issues with their tax counsel before undertaking a PPC transaction.

6. PPC Processing and Closing Process

The PPC processing and closing process moves "relatively" quickly, at least as compared with other refinancing/restructuring transactions involving HUD. The HUD Field Office (or HUB) generally notifies a project owner applying for PPC within 30 to 45 days whether the applicant's proposal meets HUD requirements. If the PPC transaction is approved by HUD, a PPC approval letter is often issued by HUD within 30 to 75 days after the request for such approval was first made. The approval letter may be issued by the HUD Field Office or by the related HUB Office.

HUD's guidance indicates that HUD will, within five business days of the owner's acceptance of the PPC approval, coordinate with HUD Office of General Counsel and HUD's Multifamily Claims Branch to provide the owner with a projected closing date. HUD indicates that the closing must occur within 60 days from the date of notification of PPC approval.[55] Timing the closing is critical because HUD takes the position that, once the amount of the PPC Loan is determined, "any increase in the funds required to close (i.e., interest) must be funded by the owner at closing."[56] Therefore, if the closing delay is beyond 60 days, the borrower will likely have to pay the added interest expense (and any other expenses) from such delay.

HUD requires the PPC closing documents to be submitted to HUD for review at least 10 days prior to the scheduled closing date.[57] HUD has issued form documents for, among other things, the Modified First Loan, the PPC Loan, and the Use Agreement. As might be expected, HUD permits relatively few modifications to the form documents, except to the extent required to satisfy applicable State law requirements.

One critical aspect of closing a PPC transaction is ensuring that HUD's Office of Asset Management, HUD's Multifamily Claims branch, the lender, and the borrower agree on the outstanding loan balance, the escrow/reserve balances, and the proposed loan amounts for the Modified First Loan and the PPC Loan. Borrowers and lenders are encouraged to make sure that everyone is in agreement on the projected numbers as soon as practicable—and to resolve any discrepancies promptly.

Of course, the HUD Field Office may also reject an owner's request for a PPC. According to the *Revised PPC Handbook*, if HUD rejects the PPC request, the owner has 15 calendar days from receipt of a rejection letter to provide additional information to the HUD Field

---

55. *Id.* at Section 14-13.
56. *Id.*
57. *Id.* at Section 14-11.

Office Director and request reconsideration of the request. If the request is again rejected, the owner has five business days to submit an appeal to HUD Headquarters. HUD indicates that after any appeals have expired, the lender will be instructed by HUD to process a full claim if the mortgage is not reinstated.[58]

7. PPC Conclusion

HUD's PPC process is now playing an important role in addressing the needs of financially troubled multifamily projects with HUD-insured loans. As discussed above, the procedures have enabled many owners to retain their properties, stabilize project operations, and avoid potentially significant adverse tax consequences. PPCs have also permitted HUD to reduce insurance losses and preserve much-needed affordable housing. While the PPC process may not be the best solution to address a project in financial distress, it certainly warrants serious consideration by owners and HUD as they both look to make the best out of a bad situation.

VIII. HUD NOTE SALES

What if all else fails and none of the options suggested above are successful, and the defaulted HUD loan is assigned by the lender to HUD?

As mentioned above, despite what might be regarded as less than stellar prices in recent auctions,[59] HUD continues to have a regular practice of selling multifamily and health-care loans that have been assigned to it, as conducted by the FHA Office of Asset Sales.[60] HUD engages a contractor such as a real estate advisory firm, investment bank, or other company experienced in the sale of loans to work with the FHA Office of Asset Sales in conducting a competitive auction of its so-called "HUD-held loans."

So if a borrower's loan is put into one of these so-called "note sales," the borrower might want to consider bidding on its loan against other participants in the loan auction. (Of course, the borrower (or its principals or affiliates) could lose their loan to another bidder who is willing to pay more for their loan, or, depending on the way in HUD has structured the particular loan sale in question, the borrower could lose to a bidder who is not willing to pay more for its loan, but whose aggregate bid for a portfolio of loans, including the borrower's loan, provides the best overall value to HUD.)

As part of its bid, the borrower (or parties owning interests in the borrower or otherwise affiliated with the borrower) will be required to execute one or more documents disclosing its relationship to the loan, will be limited to bidding on just its loan, and will have to make a number of other certifications and be subject to additional conditions and qualifications that are not imposed on other bidders. See, for example, the provisions below from the Bidder's Qualification Statement used in connection with HUD's Multifamily and Healthcare Loan Sale 2012-1:[61]

---

58. *Id.* at Section 14-9.
59. HUD reported that the average bid for its MHLS 2012-1 note sale conducted in December 2011 was 48.75%. See http://portal.hud.gov/hudportal/documents/huddoc?id=mhls2012-1rr.pdf.
60. *See* http://portal.hud.gov/hudportal/HUD?src=/program_offices/housing/comp/asset/gen/sofc.
61. *See* http://www.debtx.com/doc/MHLS percent202012-1.pdf.

II. Purchaser Qualification.

The undersigned understands that if it is determined to be a "qualified bidder" for the Loan Sale, its status as such does not necessarily mean that it will be a "qualified bidder" for any other loans or assets offered in any other HUD sale. The undersigned also understands that its status as a "qualified bidder" for any other HUD sale does not necessarily mean that it will be a "qualified bidder" for the Loan Sale. Purchaser hereby certifies, represents and warrants to HUD that it is a "qualified bidder" based upon Purchaser's satisfaction of one or more of the following qualifying statements 1 through 8. Purchaser must check one or more of the following qualifying statements 1 through 8 to qualify as a "qualified bidder" for the Mortgage Loans being sold in the Loan Sale. (**Check all that are appropriate**):

(___) 7. Purchaser is a mortgagor or operator with respect to one or more of the Mortgage Loans being offered in the Loan Sale and as such has the requisite knowledge and experience with respect to those Mortgage Loans and the properties securing those Mortgage Loans to enable it to evaluate the merits and risks of a purchase of and to make an informed decision with respect to those Mortgage Loans. The projects securing the Mortgage Loans with respect to which Purchaser is the mortgagor or the operator are listed below. (**Checking only this box and meeting the requirements in Paragraphs B–K inclusive, below, will enable Purchaser to be qualified to bid only on Purchaser's Mortgage Loans as identified below.**) If Purchaser checked Number 7, please indicate the appropriate Mortgage Loans below:

FHA Project No.   Project Name
_____   _____
_____   _____

(___) 8. Purchaser is a limited partner or non-managing member (including tax credit investors) with respect to one or more of the Mortgage Loans being offered in the Loan Sale. Purchaser certifies that Purchaser has the requisite knowledge and experience with respect to such Mortgage Loans and the properties securing those Mortgage Loans to enable Purchaser to evaluate the merits and risks of a purchase of and to make an informed decision with respect to those Mortgage Loans. The projects securing the Mortgage Loans with respect to which Purchaser is a limited partner or non-managing member (including tax credit investors) are listed below. (**Checking only this box and meeting the requirements in Paragraphs B–H inclusive, L, and M below will enable Purchaser to be qualified to bid only on the Mortgage Loans identified below.**) If Purchaser checked Number 8, please indicate the appropriate Mortgage Loans below:

FHA Project No.   Project Name
_____   _____
_____   _____

Unless otherwise stated herein, by executing this Qualification Statement, Purchaser certifies, represents and warrants to HUD that EACH of the following statements (A through and including M) is true and correct as to such Purchaser:

I. If Purchaser is a mortgagor or operator with respect to any of the Mortgage Loans being offered in the Loan Sale, Purchaser has identified such Mortgage Loans under Number 7 above. If Purchaser has only checked Number 7 under Part II above, Purchaser acknowledges and agrees that Purchaser will only be permitted to review information concerning the Mortgage Loans identified under Number 7 above and to bid on the Mortgage Loans identified under Number 7 above.

J. If Purchaser is a mortgagor or operator with respect to any of the Mortgage Loans being offered in the Loan Sale, before executing this Qualification Statement, Purchaser has submitted to HUD, in accordance with HUD's regulations and the regulatory agreements relating to the projects securing such Mortgage Loans, the required annual financial statements for each such project for fiscal years 2007–2010 (or for such time as the Project has been in operation or the Purchaser has served as operator, if less than three (3) years). If any of the required annual financial statements for a project securing a Mortgage Loan have not already been submitted to HUD, Purchaser must meet the requirement for electronic submission of the annual financial statements. **If HUD does not receive the required annual financial statements by November 30, 2011, Purchaser will be ineligible to bid in the Loan Sale.** Purchaser agrees to provide any additional information relating to such a Mortgage Loan or project as HUD may reasonably request in connection with the Loan Sale.

K. If Purchaser or any Related Party, as defined below, is a mortgagor in any of HUD's multifamily housing programs or health-care programs (regardless of whether such mortgage loan is included in the Loan Sale), Purchaser represents and warrants that: (i) neither Purchaser nor any of its Related Parties is in default (whether monetary or nonmonetary) under any HUD loan, and neither Purchaser nor any of its Related Parties has been notified by HUD that it is in violation of, or not in compliance with, any regulatory or business agreements with HUD; or (ii) if such a default or violation exists, Purchaser shall cure such default or violation on or before November 30, 2011. **If Purchaser does not cure such default or violation on or before November 30, 2011, Purchaser will be ineligible to bid in the Loan Sale.**

If Purchaser or any Related Party, as defined below, is an operator in any of HUD's health-care programs (regardless of whether such mortgage loan is included in the Loan Sale), Purchaser represents and warrants that: (i) neither Purchaser nor any of its Related Parties has been notified by HUD that it is in violation of, or not in compliance with, any regulatory or business agreements with HUD; or (ii) if such a violation exists, Purchaser shall cure such violation on or before November 30, 2011. **If Purchaser does not cure such violation on or before November 30, 2011, Purchaser will be ineligible to bid in the Loan Sale.**

If Purchaser or any Related Party is in default under any HUD loan or in violation of any HUD regulatory or business agreement, please check the following line _____ and on an attachment submitted with this Qualification Statement either (A) indicate the FHA loan number, the name of the project, the name of the mortgagor, and the nature of the default or violation; or (B) provide a complete listing or organizational chart of known Related Parties or affiliates which HUD will review, pursuant to its 2530 Previous Participation process, to determine whether Purchaser or any Related Party is in default under or has violated any HUD loan, regulatory agreement or business agreement.

For purposes of this Qualification Statement, Related Parties shall include any principal of Purchaser, any affiliate of Purchaser, and any principal of any affiliate of Purchaser. An affiliate is any party that controls, is controlled by, or is under common control with Purchaser. A principal in a partnership is any general partner, or a limited partner with a 25 percent or greater equity or ownership interest. A principal in a corporation is any officer or director, and any stockholder with a 10 percent or greater equity or ownership interest. A principal in a limited liability company is any manager, officer or director, and any owner with a 10 percent or greater equity interest. Purchaser represents and warrants that each of its Related Parties that is a mortgagor in a HUD multifamily housing program or a mortgagor and/or operator in a HUD health-care program is identified on an attachment submitted with this Qualification Statement.

L. If Purchaser is a limited partner or non-managing member (including tax credit investors) with respect to any of the Mortgage Loans being offered in the Loan Sale, Purchaser has identified such Mortgage Loans under Number 8 above. If Purchaser has only checked Number 8 under Part II above, Purchaser acknowledges and agrees that Purchaser will only be permitted to review information concerning, and bid on, the Mortgage Loans identified under Number 8 above.

M. Notwithstanding the definition of Related Party above, if Purchaser checked Number 8 under Part II above, with respect to those Mortgage Loan(s), Purchaser represents and warrants that: (i) prior to the loan becoming a HUD-held asset, Purchaser's involvement in the property securing the Mortgage Loan was solely financial, and (ii) Purchaser did not participate directly or indirectly in the ongoing management of the property securing the Mortgage Loan.

So while HUD's note sale program presents "one last chance" for a borrower with a defaulted loan, given the conditions detailed above, participation in the loan sales may not be a particularly viable alternative for a borrower seeking resolution of its defaulted mortgage. If a borrower is unsuccessful in its bid, or chooses not to bid, the borrower will be left to negotiate with the investor who acquired the defaulted loan at a discount, often with the intent of foreclosure.

IX. CONCLUSION

While the choices are limited, and some of the policy decisions made by HUD in implementing the possible methods of resolutions are open to question, the hopeful news is that after years of virtually not entertaining any requests to resolve troubled or defaulted loans and choosing to rely almost solely on note sales, the owner of a project subject to a troubled or defaulted HUD loan has at least a few possible solutions to put its HUD project back on a sound financial footing or to cure a default.

Cross-Cutting Requirements: Federal Requirements Impacting HUD Programs

13

Mary Grace Folwell, Amy M. Glassman, Amy M. McClain, Joy C. O'Brien, Nydia M. Pouves, Margaret H. Tucker, and Sharon Wilson Géno

I. INTRODUCTION

Many federal requirements that originate outside of HUD apply to the implementation of HUD-funded projects. These requirements include government-wide rules promulgated by various federal agencies intended to unify and standardize the expenditure of federal dollars. Most often, these requirements are intended to protect the public interest and include topics such as procurement, protection of the environment, energy efficiency, and rights of tenants and owners displaced by a federally funded project. When implementing these rules, practitioners can often refer to HUD regulations at Title 24 of the Code of Federal Regulations and related guidance, but often there is a wider body of law available interpreting the implementation of these rules. This chapter contains sections covering: 1. Procurement, 2. Labor provisions, 3. Environmental requirements, 4. Relocation requirements, 5. Subsidy layering, 6. Funding and grant issues, 7. Regulatory waivers, 8. Energy Star/energy-efficiency programs, and 9. Section 3. Because of space limitations, please note that the following is provided as a basic overview, and readers are advised to undertake additional review and research as individual situations dictate.

II. PROCUREMENT BY HUD GRANTEES AND SUBGRANTEES

With limited exceptions, a HUD grantee and, at times, a subgrantee must use a competitive process and follow other federal requirements when purchasing goods or services.[1] Different procurement requirements apply depending on whether the HUD grantee is a public or private entity. The uniform administrative rules for federal grants and cooperative agreements and subawards to public grantees such as state, local, and Indian tribal governments can be found in the federal regulations at 24 C.F.R. Part 85. The uniform administrative rules for federal grants and agreements awarded to private grantees such as institutions of higher education, hospitals, and other nonprofit organizations can be found in the federal regulations at 24 C.F.R. Part 84. This section focuses on common rules that apply to both public and private HUD grantees in establishing procedures for the procurement of supplies, equipment, real property, and services with federal funds.[2] These requirements apply to grantees, the governmental entity that receives funds from HUD, and subgrantees, government, or other entities that receive funds from a grantee.

A. Procurement Standards and General Requirements

HUD grantees and subgrantees must comply with and navigate multiple layers of procurement requirements, including federal regulations and guidance, state and local procurement laws, and requirements imposed by contractual agreements between HUD and grantees or between grantees and subgrantees. If state or local requirements conflict with or are different than HUD requirements, HUD grantees are generally expected to follow the more stringent requirement. Contracts cannot abrogate applicable federal, state, or local laws but may impose additional procurement-related obligations on recipients of HUD funds.[3] Examples of common contractual terms that augment federal, state, and local regulations are those involving resolution of disputes, claims, protests of award, and termination for convenience or cause.[4]

All HUD grantees must have a procurement policy. When procuring goods or services under a grant, a state may use the same policies and procedures it uses for procurements from its non-federal funds. The state must ensure that every purchase order or contract includes the HUD-required clauses further described in Section 1(f) below.[5] Other HUD grantees and subgrantees must ensure that their procurement policies and procedures reflect all applicable

---

1. Procurement requirements apply to solicitation of all goods and services by a HUD grantee, including financial *services*. Procurement requirements, however, do not apply to financial *transactions*, such as the process to qualify a grantee as a borrower, although other requirements, including a determination that fees are reasonable pursuant to 2 C.F.R. § 225, apply. For further explanation, *see, e.g.*, HUD guidance at http://portal.hud.gov/hudportal/HUD?src=/program_offices/public_indian_housing/programs/ ph/capfund/fintrns.

2. Where parallel citations do not appear for both public and private grantees, the HUD requirement applies to the particular grantee as cited. Please additionally review the federal regulations and other HUD guidance for a complete set of the HUD requirements for public and private grantees.

3. 24 C.F.R. § 84.41 (2010); 24 C.F.R. § 85.36(b)(11) (2010).
4. 24 C.F.R. § 84.41 (2010); 24 C.F.R. § 84.36(b)(11) (2010).
5. 24 C.F.R. § 85.36(a) (2010); 24 C.F.R. § 84.5 (2010).

federal, state, and local laws and regulations.[6] The procurement standards described in this section are generally applicable to both public and private HUD grantees.

Features of a grantee's or subgrantee's procurement policy and procedures should include the following:

- A contract administration system intended to ensure that contractors perform in accordance with the terms, conditions, and specifications of their contracts or purchase orders.[7]
- A written ethics code that includes standards of conduct for the performance of their employees engaged in the award and administration of contracts.[8] Included in the policy should be a prohibition on the participation in the selection, award, or administration of contracts by employees, officers, or agents who have a conflict of interest, real or apparent.[9] Conflict of interests arise when the employee, officer, or agent; any member of his or her immediate family; his or her partner; or an organization that employs, or is about to employ, any of the above, has a financial or other interest in the firm selected for award.[10] Additionally, a grantee or subgrantee may not solicit or accept gratuities, favors, or anything of monetary value from persons seeking or awarded contracts with the grantee/subgrantee.[11] However, grantees and subgrantees may set minimum rules where the financial interest is not substantial or the gift is an unsolicited item of nominal intrinsic value.[12] The standards of conduct must provide for disciplinary actions to be applied for violations of such standards by officers, employees, or agents of the recipient.[13]
- Protest procedures to handle and resolve disputes relating to procurements, with information regarding a protest always disclosed to HUD.[14]
- A requirement to take all necessary, affirmative steps to assure that minority firms, women's business enterprises, and small businesses are used when possible.[15]
- Maintenance of procurement records that include, but are not necessarily limited to, the rationale for the method of procurement, selection of contract type, contractor selection or rejection, and the basis for the contract price.[16]
- A limitation on making awards only to responsible contractors possessing the ability to perform successfully under the terms and conditions of the proposed procurement. Consideration should be given to factors such as contractor integrity, compliance with public policy, record of past performance, and financial and technical resources.[17]

---

6. 24 C.F.R. § 85.36(b)(1) (2010); 24 C.F.R. § 84.48 (2010).
7. 24 C.F.R. § 85.36(b)(2) (2010); 24 C.F.R. § 84.47 (2010).
8. 24 C.F.R. § 85.36(b)(3) (2010); 24 C.F.R. § 84.42 (2010).
9. 24 C.F.R. § 85.36(b)(3) (2010); 24 C.F.R. § 84.42 (2010).
10. 24 C.F.R. § 85.36(b)(3) (2010); 24 C.F.R. § 84.42 (2010).
11. 24 C.F.R. § 85.36(b)(3) (2010); 24 C.F.R. § 84.42 (2010).
12. 24 C.F.R. § 85.36(b)(3) (2010); 24 C.F.R. § 84.42 (2010).
13. 24 C.F.R. § 85.36(b)(3) (2010); 24 C.F.R. § 84.42 (2010).
14. 24 C.F.R. § 85.36(b)(12) (2010); 24 C.F.R. § 84.41 (2010).
15. 24 C.F.R. § 84.44(b) (2010); 24 C.F.R. § 85.36(e) (2010).
16. 24 C.F.R. § 85.36(b)(9) (2010); 24 C.F.R. § 84.46 (2010).
17. 24 C.F.R. § 85.36(b)(8) (2010); 24 C.F.R. § 84.44(d) (2010).

- Awards and subcontracts cannot be made to contractors that are debarred or suspended by the federal government. The Excluded Parties List System (EPLS), operated by the General Services Administration and available online,[18] lists all parties debarred, suspended, or otherwise excluded from participation in HUD-funded and other federally funded activities. Grantees and subgrantees are responsible for checking EPLS prior to executing agreements with a contractor.

B. Competition

All procurement transactions should be conducted in a manner that provides, to the maximum extent practical, open and free competition.[19] This section provides some general principles with which HUD grantees must comply to ensure open and free competition in procuring contracts.

In the federal regulations, HUD sets forth situations considered to be restrictive of competition. They include, but are not limited to, the following: (1) placing unreasonable requirements on firms in order for them to qualify to do business, (2) requiring unnecessary experience and excessive bonding, (3) noncompetitive pricing practices between firms or between affiliated companies, (4) noncompetitive awards to consultants that are on retainer contracts, (5) organizational conflicts of interest, (6) specifying only a brand-name product instead of allowing an equal product to be offered, or (7) any arbitrary action in the procurement process.[20]

With limited exceptions, HUD grantees and subgrantees cannot use geographical preferences in the evaluation of bids or proposals. To the extent federal statutes expressly mandate or encourage geographic preference, then such preferences may be used.[21] This requirement also does not preempt state licensing laws, and geographic preferences *may* be used in certain circumstances for procurement of architectural or engineering firms.[22]

Solicitations must incorporate a clear and accurate description of the technical requirements for the material, product, or service to be procured and must identify all requirements that offerors must fulfill and all factors to be used in evaluating bids or proposals.[23] HUD grantees have the discretion to reject bids when it is in their best interest to do so.[24]

To ensure objective contractor performance and eliminate unfair competitive advantage, contractors that develop or draft specifications, requirements, statements of work, invitations for bids, and/or requests for proposals cannot compete for such procurements.[25] HUD grantees and subgrantees must ensure that all prequalified lists of persons, firms, or products that

---

18. *See* www.epls.gov (last visited Oct. 13, 2011).
19. 24 C.F.R. § 84.43 (2010); 24 C.F.R. § 85.36(c)(1) (2010).
20. 24 C.F.R. § 85.36(c)(1) (2010); 24 C.F.R. § 84.44(a)(3)(i) (2010).
21. 24 C.F.R. § 85.36(c)(2) (2010).
22. 24 C.F.R. § 85.36(c)(2) (2010). When HUD grantees contract for architectural and engineering services, geographic location may be a selection criterion as long as an appropriate number of qualified firms, given the nature and size of the project, compete for the contract.
23. 24 C.F.R. § 85.36(c)(3) (2010); 24 C.F.R. § 84.43 (2010).
24. 24 C.F.R. § 84.43 (2010).
25. *Id.*

are used in acquiring goods and services are current and include a sufficient number of qualified sources to maximize open and free competition.[26]

C. Methods of Procurement

There are several procurement methods that public HUD grantees may employ in purchasing goods and services. Below is a brief description of those methods and their applicability.

- *Procurement by small purchase procedures.* Small purchase procedures are relatively simple and informal procurement methods for securing services or supplies valued at no more than $100,000 under federal law.[27] If this method is used, price or rate quotations must be obtained from an adequate number of qualified sources.
- *Procurement by sealed bids.* Bids are publicly solicited and a firm-fixed-price contract, in the form of a lump sum or unit price, is awarded to the responsible bidder whose bid, conforming with all the material terms and conditions of the invitation for bids, is the lowest in price.[28] The sealed-bid method is the preferred method for procuring construction, where certain conditions apply.[29]

  Where sealed bids are used, the invitation for bids must be publicly advertised and bids must be solicited from an adequate number of known suppliers.[30] The invitation for bids also must include any specifications and pertinent attachments and define the items or services such that the bidder may properly respond.[31]
- *Procurement by competitive proposals.* The competitive proposal method is generally used when conditions are not appropriate for the use of sealed bids and, in particular, when price may not be the primary determining factor for the contract award.[32] Requests for proposals must be publicly advertised and the solicitations must identify all evaluation factors as well as their relative importance.[33] Proposals must be solicited from an adequate number of qualified sources.[34] HUD grantees also must have a process for conducting technical evaluations of the proposals received and for selecting awardees.[35] This is usually achieved through appointment of an evaluation committee or similar reviewing body. Awards are made to the responsible firm whose proposal is most advantageous to the program, with price and other factors considered.[36]

---

26. 24 C.F.R. § 85.36(c)(3) (2010).
27. 41 U.S.C. § 403(11) (2010); 24 C.F.R. § 84.48 (a)–(b) (2010).
28. 24 C.F.R. § 85.36(d)(2) (2010).
29. 24 C.F.R. § 85.36(d)(2)(i) (2010). In order for sealed bidding to be feasible, the following conditions should be present: (1) a complete, adequate, and realistic specification or purchase description is available; (2) two or more responsible bidders are willing and able to compete effectively and for the business; and (3) the procurement lends itself to a firm-fixed-price contract and the selection of the successful bidder can be made principally on the basis of price.
30. 24 C.F.R. § 85.36(d)(2) (2010).
31. *Id.*
32. 24 C.F.R. § 85.36(d)(3) (2010).
33. *Id.*
34. *Id.*
35. *Id.*
36. *Id.*

- When procuring architectural/engineering (A/E) professional services, HUD grantees and subgrantees may use a competitive, qualifications-based procurement process.[37] With this method, only qualifications are considered; price is not used as a selection factor.[38] The most common use of requests for quotations (RFQs) is for A/E contracts, although RFQs can also be used to select development partners for mixed-finance public housing projects or when specifically authorized by HUD.[39]
- *Procurement by noncompetitive proposals.* The method of noncompetitive procurement involves the solicitation of a proposal from only one source.[40] This method may also be employed after the solicitation of a number of sources results in inadequate competition.[41] Procurement by noncompetitive proposals may be used only when the award of a contract is infeasible under the other procurement methods and one of the following circumstances applies: (1) the item is available only from a single source, (2) the public exigency or emergency for the requirement will not permit a delay resulting from competitive solicitation, (3) HUD authorizes noncompetitive proposals, or (4) solicitation of a number of sources results in inadequate competition.[42]
- *Interagency or Intergovernmental Agreements.* To foster greater economy and efficiency, HUD encourages grantees and subgrantees to enter into state and local intergovernmental purchasing agreements without competitive procurement.[43] These agreements are generally entered into by and between a HUD grantee or subgrantee that is a governmental entity and another governmental entity such as a state or local government office. Certain restrictions apply to these agreements. For example, HUD's *Procurement Handbook for Public Housing Authorities*, Chapter 14, outlines the prerequisites, process, and documentation required for such agreements.[44]

D. Bonding Requirements

The federal regulations provide minimum bonding requirements for contracts for construction or facility improvements. Unless otherwise approved by HUD,[45] contracts or subcontracts exceeding the simplified acquisition threshold (currently set at $100,000) are subject to the following bonding requirements:

- A bid guarantee equivalent to five percent of the bid price;[46]
- A performance bond for 100 percent of the contract price;[47]

---

37. *Id.*
38. *Id.*
39. HUD Procurement Handbook for Public and Indian Housing Authorities, HUD HB 7460.8, Rev-2 (Mar. 2, 2007) § 7.3(a), (c).
40. 24 C.F.R. § 85.36(d)(4) (2010).
41. *Id.*
42. *Id.*
43. 24 C.F.R. § 85.36(b)(5) (2010).
44. Procurement Handbook for Public and Indian Housing Authorities, HUD Handbook 7460.8, Rev-2 (Mar. 2, 2007).
45. 24 C.F.R. § 85.36(h) (2010); 24 C.F.R. § 84.48(c) (2010).
46. 24 C.F.R. § 85.36(h)(1) (2010); 24 C.F.R. § 84.48(c)(1) (2010).
47. 24 C.F.R. § 85.36(h)(2) (2010); 24 C.F.R. § 84.48(c)(2) (2010).

- A payment bond on the part of the contractor for 100 percent of the contract price;[48]
- Separate payment and performance bonds each for 50 percent or more of the contract price;[49]
- A 20 percent cash escrow; or[50]
- A 25 percent irrevocable letter of credit.[51]

E. Cost and Price Analysis

As part of the procurement process, HUD grantees and subgrantees must engage in some form of cost or price analysis for every procurement action.[52] The method and degree of analysis depends on the particular procurement situation.[53] Price analysis may be accomplished in different ways, such as the comparison of price quotations submitted by offerors, the comparison of market prices, and the comparison of other similar factors.[54] Independent estimates must be completed before receiving bids or proposals.[55] A cost analysis must be performed when the offeror is required to submit the elements of his or her estimated cost, for instance, with professional, consulting, and architectural engineering services contracts.[56] A cost analysis is also required where there is inadequate price competition and for sole-source procurements, unless price reasonableness can be established based on the methods described above or based on prices set by law or regulation.[57] All cost analysis should be documented in the procurement files for every procurement action.[58]

F. Required Contract Provisions

HUD grantees and subgrantees must include certain provisions in all contracts. While most of the provisions below are applicable to both public and private HUD grantees, certain provisions are only required for certain types of grantees. The required provisions relate to remedies for contract breaches and termination; compliance with various federal laws, such as those pertaining to payment of prevailing wage rates and environmental protection; access to books and other documentation by the grantee, HUD, the Comptroller General of the United States, and their authorized representatives; and records retention. The specific provisions can be found at 24 C.F.R. § 84.84(i) and App. (for private grantees) and 24 C.F.R. § 85.36(i) (for governmental entity grantees).

---

48. 24 C.F.R. § 85.36(h)(3) (2010); 24 C.F.R. § 84.48(c)(3) (2010).
49. *See* HUD PROCUREMENT HANDBOOK, *supra* note [43], Section 6-11(D)(1).
50. *Id.*
51. *Id.*
52. 24 C.F.R. § 85.36(f) (2010); 24 C.F.R. § 84.45 (2010).
53. 24 C.F.R. § 85.36(f)(1) (2010); 24 C.F.R. § 84.45 (2010).
54. 24 C.F.R. § 84.45 (2010).
55. 24 C.F.R. § 85.36(f)(1) (2010).
56. 24 C.F.R. § 85.36(f)(1) (2010).
57. 24 C.F.R. § 85.36(f)(1) (2010); 24 C.F.R. § 84.46 (2010).
58. 24 C.F.R. § 85.36(f) (2010); 24 C.F.R. § 84.46 (2010).

III. LABOR PROVISIONS

Several federal statutes apply to wages paid to workers employed under contracts supported with HUD funds. This section summarizes the applicability of Davis-Bacon and HUD-determined prevailing wage requirements, the Contract Work Hours and Safety Standards Act (CWHSSA), the Copeland Act, and the Fair Labor Standards Act to HUD-funded programs.

A. Davis-Bacon Statute

Davis-Bacon prevailing wage requirements apply to federal contracts and subcontracts in excess of $2,000 for the construction, alteration, or repair of public buildings or public works.[59] Contractors subject to Davis-Bacon wage requirements must pay their laborers and mechanics no less than the locally prevailing wages and fringe benefits for corresponding work on similar projects in the area as determined by the Department of Labor (DOL).

The Davis-Bacon Act does not apply directly to HUD-funded housing programs. However, Davis-Bacon Related Acts (DBRA) in various federal housing statutes apply Davis-Bacon wage requirements to the use of federal funds authorized by these statutes. DBRA can be found in the Housing and Community Development Act of 1974 (HCDA),[60] the National Affordable Housing Act of 1990 (NAHA),[61] the U.S. Housing Act of 1937 (USHA),[62] and the Native American Housing Assistance and Self-Determination Act of 1996 (NAHASDA).[63] The language of the DBRA is slightly different in each statute, resulting in different applications of the rule for each funding source. For a project receiving funding from multiple sources that apply Davis-Bacon wage rates, the strictest guidelines must be followed.

B. APPLICATION OF DAVIS-BACON RELATED ACTS

The applicability of a DBRA depends on the language of the statute, implementing regulations, and HUD and DOL guidance. As discussed in this section, the differences in statutory language result in different rules of application.

C. Community Development Block Grant Program

The DBRA for the Community Development Block Grant (CDBG) and related programs is at Section 110 of the HCDA, as amended.[64] The HCDA authorizes the CDBG program, Section 108 loan guaranty, and Economic Development Initiative funds, among other programs.

The CDBG DBRA states that Davis-Bacon wages are required for "construction work financed . . ." by CDBG funds. Thus, any CDBG funds used to finance construction will

---

59. *See* 40 U.S.C. § 3142(a) and 29 C.F.R. pts. 1, 3, 5, 6, and 7.
60. 42 U.S.C. § 5301 *et seq.*
61. 42 U.S.C. § 12701 *et seq.*
62. 42 U.S.C. § 1437 *et seq.*
63. 25 U.S.C. § 4101 *et seq.*
64. "All laborers and mechanics employed by contractors or subcontractors in the performance of construction work financed in whole or in part with assistance received under this chapter shall be paid wages at rates not less than those prevailing on similar construction in the locality as determined by the Secretary of Labor in accordance with [the Davis-Bacon Act, as amended]: Provided, That this section shall apply to the rehabilitation of residential property only if such property contains not less than 8 units . . . ." 42 U.S.C. § 5310(a).

trigger Davis-Bacon. In addition to construction advances of CDBG funds, any CDBG funds used to pay the interest rate or points charged on a construction loan or to provide permanent financing used to take out construction financing will be construed to be financing of construction work, triggering Davis-Bacon wage requirements. Conversely, CDBG funds used to finance non-construction activities or items such as real property acquisition, purchase of equipment, or accounting or architectural fees do not trigger Davis-Bacon wage requirements.[65]

Given the phrase in the CDBG DBRA "in whole or in part," Davis-Bacon standards are applicable to the entire project even if CDBG finances only a small part of a project. CDBG DBRA does not apply to employees of the grantee but to "all laborers and mechanics employed by contractors or subcontractors." Finally, Davis-Bacon will apply only to property that includes eight or more units. These eight units must be included within a "property" typically understood to be "one or more buildings on an undivided lot or on contiguous lots or parcels which are commonly-owned and operated as one rental, cooperative or condominium project."[66]

D. HOME

The DBRA in the NAHA, as amended, appears at Section 286.[67] NAHA authorizes the HOME Investment Partnership Program. The HOME DBRA is triggered by "units assisted" by HUD funds applying Davis-Bacon wage requirements whether HOME funds that support the units are used for construction or non-construction uses.[68] Once 12 or more units are assisted with HOME funds, Davis- Bacon applies to the entire project.[69]

A HOME project cannot be divided into multiple different construction contracts solely to avoid the application of Davis-Bacon wage requirements.[70] Likewise, a construction contract with 12 or more HOME units will require Davis-Bacon wages, even if the construction contract involves more than one separately funded HOME project.[71]

HOME provides for a sweat equity program, in which such sweat-equity participants may contribute labor in exchange for acquisition or property for home ownership or to reduce rental payments. Sweat-equity participants are exempt from Davis-Bacon.[72]

---

65. *See* U.S. DEPT OF HOUS. & URBAN DEV., MAKING DAVIS-BACON WORK—A PRACTICAL GUIDE FOR STATES, INDIAN TRIBES, AND LOCAL AGENCIES 17 (June 2006).
66. *Id.*, Exhibit 2, p. 17.
67. Any contract for the construction of affordable housing with 12 or more units assisted with funds made available under this part shall contain a provision requiring that not less than the wages prevailing in the locality, as predetermined by the Secretary of Labor pursuant to [the Davis-Bacon Act], shall be paid to all laborers and mechanics employed in the development of affordable housing involved, and participating jurisdictions shall require certification as to compliance with the provisions of this section prior to making any payment under such contract. 42 U.S.C. § 12836(a).
68. *See* U.S. Dep't of Hous. & Urban Dev., *supra* note 65 at 18, 24 C.F.R. 92.354(a)(2).
69. *See id.*
70. *See id.*
71. *See* HUD LR-96-02 (Aug. 21, 1996).
72. *See* U.S. Dep't of Hous. & Urban Dev., *supra* note 65 at 18.

E. Public Housing and Section 8/Housing Choice Voucher Programs

The DBRA for public housing and the Section 8/housing choice voucher programs is incorporated at Section 12 of the USHA, as amended.[73] The USHA authorizes public housing capital funds, replacement housing factor funds, public housing operating funds, HOPE VI funds, voucher funds used for "project-basing," and Section 8 project-based rental assistance contracts attached to multifamily housing.

The USHA DBRA applies prevailing wage rates through provisions required in "any contract for loans, contributions, sale, or lease pursuant to this Act. . . ." The "contract" referred to in the USHA most often is the Annual Contributions Contract between HUD and a public housing agency. It can also refer to an Agreement to Enter into a Housing Assistance Payments Contract for a housing project that will receive Section 8 rental assistance. HUD Guidance notes that the application of prevailing wages to a project under Section 12 is "not tied to a funding source nor to specific use of any funds."[74] Therefore, the federal funds themselves are not a prerequisite to the application of prevailing wages to a project.

USHA DBRA can be distinguished from DBRA for HOME and CDBG in two significant aspects. First, Section 12 of the USHA applies prevailing wages to "all laborers and mechanics," not just those employed by contractors and subcontractors. Thus, force account laborers (workers employed directly by the agency) are subject to prevailing wages. HUD guidance states that the prevailing wage provisions apply to force account labor whether on a full-time, part-time, permanent, or temporary basis.[75] Second, Section 12 applies *HUD-determined prevailing wages* to "maintenance laborers and mechanics employed in the operation" of a low-income housing project extending wage requirements beyond construction. HUD-determined prevailing wages are similar to the DOL-determined wage rates, but they must be issued by HUD in accordance with HUD requirements. HUD has provided some guidance on compliance with its prevailing wage requirements, which are similar to DBRA compliance requirements.[76]

Determining when a project is development or maintenance can be challenging. Various HUD statutes, regulations, and guidance provide some clarification on how HUD defines "development," "operation," "maintenance," and "non-routine maintenance." HUD statute

---

73. "Any contract for loans, contributions, sale, or lease pursuant to this [Act] shall contain a provision requiring that not less than the wages prevailing in the locality, as determined or adopted (subsequent to a determination under applicable State or local law) by the Secretary, shall be paid to all architects, technical engineers, draftsmen, and technicians employed in the development, and all maintenance laborers and mechanics employed in the operation, of the low-income housing project involved; and shall also contain a provision that not less than the wages prevailing in the locality, as predetermined by the Secretary of Labor pursuant to [the Davis-Bacon Act], shall be paid to all laborers and mechanics employed in the development of the project involved (including a project with nine or more units assisted under Section 8 of this Act, where the public housing agency or the Secretary and the builder or sponsor enter into an agreement for such use before construction or rehabilitation is commenced), and the Secretary shall require certification as to compliance with the provision of this section prior to making any payment under such contract." 42 U.S.C. § 1437j(a).
74. U.S. Dep't of Hous. & Urban Dev., *supra* note 65 at 19.
75. *See* HUD LR-04-01 (Rev. 1) (Oct. 26, 2006).
76. *See* HUD LR-04-01; HUD LR-04-02 (Sept. 8, 2004).

defines "development" as "any or all undertaking necessary for planning, land acquisition, demolition, construction, or equipment in connection with a low-income housing project . . . [c]onstruction activity in connection with a low-income housing project may be confined to the reconstruction, remodeling, or repair of existing buildings."[77] In contrast, "operation" means "any or all undertakings appropriate for management, operation, services, maintenance, security (including the cost of security personnel), or financing in connection with a low-income housing project."[78] "Maintenance" is not defined in HUD statute or regulations; however, HUD guidance defines maintenance as:

> [W]ork that involves the regular upkeep and preservation of buildings, grounds, and facilities. Maintenance may include but is not limited to groundskeeping, janitorial work, patching, and/or finishing of interior and exterior walls and other surfaces, and the preservation, inspection, and general upkeep of electrical, plumbing, and heating and air-conditioning systems. Maintenance work is subject to HUD-determined prevailing *maintenance* wage rages.[79]

Maintenance includes both "routine maintenance" and "non-routine maintenance"[80] and HUD issues separate wage decisions for each.[81] "Routine maintenance" is not defined in HUD statute, regulations, or guidance, but its definition can be derived from HUD regulations that define "nonroutine maintenance" as:

> [w]ork items that ordinarily would be performed on a regular basis in the course of upkeep of a property but have become substantial in scope because they have been put off, and that involve expenditures that would otherwise materially distort the level trend of maintenance expenses. Nonroutine replacement of equipment and materials rendered unsatisfactory because of normal wear and tear by items of substantially the same kind does qualify, but reconstruction, substantial improvement in the quality or kind of original equipment and materials, or remodeling that alters the nature or type of housing units does not qualify.[82]

Additional guidance is available through a HUD guide that lists approximately 75 examples of work items classified as either maintenance or development.[83]

Section 8 voucher funds and Section 8 project-based rental assistance trigger Davis-Bacon for a development project if nine or more units are subsidized with Section 8 funds, and where a Section 8 contract is entered into before the commencement of construction. If the allocation of Section 8 funds is approved by the funding agency before the commencement of construction, the Davis-Bacon wage requirement applies even if an Agreement to

---

77. 42 U.S.C. § 1437a(c)(1).
78. 42 U.S.C. § 1437a(c)(2).
79. HUD Labor Relations Letter, 1993-01 at p. 3 (Jan. 11, 1993). (Emphasis included in the original.)
80. *See* HUD Labor Relations Letter, 2004-01 at pp. 1–2.
81. *See* HUD LR 93-01 at p. 3.
82. 24 C.F.R. § 968.105.
83. *See* HUD Public and Indian Housing Comprehensive Improvement Assistance Program, HUD HANDBOOK 7485.1, Appx. 14.

Enter into a Housing Assistance Payments Contract is not executed. Similar rules apply to public housing operating funds. If, at the outset of the construction, the housing authority and developer, if applicable, have acknowledged that the project to be developed will be subsidized with public housing operating funds, then Davis-Bacon wages will apply to the entire development process.[84]

F. Indian Housing Block Grants/NAHASDA

The DBRA applicable to Indian Housing Block Grants is at Section 104(b) of NAHASDA, as amended.[85] Assistance for Native Hawaiian Housing Block Grants Housing is included in Section 805(b) of NAHASDA, as amended.[86]

The language of the DBRA for both Indian Housing Block Grants (IHBG) and Native Hawaiian Housing Block Grants (NHHBG) is exactly the same as the USHA, so the application to force account workers and maintenance workers will be the same as described in the analysis of the U.S. Housing Act in this section of this chapter. However, there is an exception at Section 104(b)(3) of NAHASDA, allowing any applicable regulations adopted by an Indian tribe to prevail over the IHBG DBRA. This exception does not exist for NHHBG.

G. Demolition

Davis-Bacon wage rates may not always apply to demolition work funded with HUD funds. Demolition is not considered "construction," and, therefore, Davis-Bacon wage rates are not

---

84. *See* HUD PIH Notice for Mixed-Finance Development of Operating Subsidy-Only Projects, Notice PIH 2004-05 (Apr. 9, 2004).

85. "(1) In general. Any contract or agreement for assistance, sale, or lease pursuant to this chapter shall contain a provision requiring that not less than the wages prevailing in the locality, as determined or adopted (subsequent to a determination under applicable State, tribal, or local law) by the Secretary, shall be paid to all architects, technical engineers, draftsmen, and technicians employed in the development, and all maintenance laborers and mechanics employed in the operation, of the affordable housing project involved; and shall also contain a provision that not less than the wages prevailing in the locality, as predetermined by the Secretary of Labor pursuant to [the Davis-Bacon Act, as amended], shall be paid to all laborers and mechanics employed in the development of the affordable housing involved, and the Secretary shall require certification as to compliance with the provisions of this paragraph before making any payment under such contract or agreement. . . . (3) Application of tribal laws. Paragraph (1) shall not apply to any contract or agreement for assistance, sale, or lease pursuant to this chapter, if such contract or agreement is otherwise covered by one or more laws or regulations adopted by an Indian tribe that requires the payment of not less than prevailing wages, as determined by the Indian tribe."

86. "(b)(1) In general. Any contract or agreement for assistance, sale, or lease pursuant to this subchapter shall contain— (A) a provision requiring that an amount not less than the wages prevailing in the locality, as determined or adopted (subsequent to a determination under applicable State or local law) by the Secretary, shall be paid to all architects, technical engineers, draftsmen, technicians employed in the development and all maintenance, and laborers and mechanics employed in the operation, of the affordable housing project involved; and (B) a provision that an amount not less than the wages prevailing in the locality, as predetermined by the Secretary of Labor pursuant to [the Davis-Bacon Act, as amended] shall be paid to all laborers and mechanics employed in the development of the affordable housing involved." 25 U.S.C. § 4225(b).

triggered by demolition, as long as that demolition occurs as a stand-alone project. If subsequent construction is planned as part of the same contract or if subsequent construction is planned for the site of the demolished properties, then the demolition is considered to be a part of the overall "construction" or "development" of the project, and Davis-Bacon wages required by the source of federal funds will apply to the entire development project.[87]

Thus, Davis-Bacon coverage of demolition requires knowledge that there will be subsequent construction *and* that the subsequent construction work will be covered by Davis-Bacon. This implies that there is "documented evidence" of the expected subsequent construction, which may include contract specifications, disposition plans, budgets, funding applications, requests for proposals, and/or information in an agency or municipal planning document.[88]

H. Character of the Work

Davis-Bacon wage determinations generally are issued for four different categories of work: residential, building, highway, or heavy.[89] Each of these wage decisions has a different set of wage rates that apply to all the work performed under the contract. A "residential" wage decision applies to single-family homes or apartments four stories or less in height.[90] A "building" decision applies to an apartment building greater than four stories, an office building, parking garage, or community center.[91] A "highway" wage decision would apply to parking lots, streets, or sidewalks.[92] A "heavy" wage decision would apply to an outdoor swimming pool.[93]

Often a project will include work that could be classified under more than one category—residential, building, highway, or heavy. However, there is a strong bias by HUD and DOL to classify a project as belonging in only one of the four categories.[94] HUD and DOL only issue separate wage decisions if the work of a different character is substantial, and the different elements are not incidental to one another. Incidental work would not "alter the overall character of the project" and is functionally related to the purpose of the total project.[95] For example, items incidental to residential construction include site work, parking areas, utilities, streets, and sidewalks.[96] A mixed-use project is most likely to justify multiple wage schedules, as such projects often include "elements of different construction characters [that] . . . are *not incidental* to each other."[97] For example, a mixed-use project that included both

---

87. *See* HUD Labor Relations Letter 2009-01 (Aug. 12, 2009).
88. *See id.*
89. *See* HUD Labor Relations Letter 1996-03 (Dec. 2, 1996) (Rev. 1).
90. *See* HUD Labor Relations Letter 1996-03 (Dec. 2, 1996) (Rev. 1); Dep't of Labor All Agency Memorandum #130 (Mar. 17, 1978).
91. *See* U.S. Dep't of Labor All Agency Memoranda #130 (Mar. 17, 1978) and #131 (July 14, 1978); HUD Labor Relations Letter 1996-03 (Rev. 1) (Dec. 2, 1996); Labor Relations Letter 2009-01 (Aug. 12, 2009).
92. *See id.*
93. *See id.*
94. *See id.*
95. HUD-LR-96-03.
96. *See* AAM #130 and HUD LR-96-03.
97. *Id.*

low-rise housing and a high-rise elderly building could be issued separate wage decisions. Likewise, a four-story apartment building with commercial use on the first floor would justify separate wage decisions. In these two examples, the different elements each "have their own purpose—they are not merely supportive of another element's function."[98]

A project starting with demolition introduces unique considerations for determining the character of the work. The nature of the development project will determine the wage decision applicable to the demolition.[99] For example, the demolition of two-story townhouses that results in the construction of an eight-story apartment building would be subject to a building wage decision, while the demolition of an office building that is followed by the construction of a parking lot would be subject to a highway wage decision.[100] HUD guidance advises that if the nature of the final development project is not known at the time of the demolition, but it is known that Davis-Bacon will apply, a heavy wage decision is applicable.[101] For example, even if the unknown character of the final project is whether an apartment building will be four stories (residential wage decision applicable) or five stories (building wage decision applicable), a heavy wage decision still will apply.[102]

I. Contract Work Hours and Safety Standards Act

The Contract Work Hours and Safety Standards Act (CWHSSA) requires time and one-half pay for any hours worked over 40 in any workweek.[103] The CWHSSA applies to direct federal contracts and to indirect federally assisted contracts except where the assistance is solely in the nature of a loan guarantee or insurance. In addition, certain safety standards apply to projects.[104] CWHSSA does not apply to prime contracts of $100,000 or less or to projects that are subject to federal prevailing wage rates. However, even though CWHSSA overtime pay is not required for certain categories of contracts, Fair Labor Standards Act overtime requirements are likely still applicable.[105]

J. Copeland Act

The Copeland "Anti-Kickback" Act requires the submission of weekly certified payroll reports for projects paying Davis-Bacon wages and regulates permissible payroll deductions.[106] Under the Copeland Act, it is a federal crime for anyone to induce, by any means, any laborer or mechanic to give up or pay back (i.e., "kick back") any part of his or her wages.[107]

---

98. *Id.*
99. *See* HUD LR-09-01.
100. For additional examples, *see* HUD LR-09-01.
101. *See* HUD LR-09-01.
102. *See id.*
103. *See* U.S. Dept. of Hous. & Urban Dev., *supra* note 65 at 1-1.
104. *See* 40 U.S.C. § 3701 et seq. and 29 C.F.R. Parts 4, 5, 6, and 8 and 70 to 120.
105. *See* U.S. Dept. of Hous. & Urban Dev., *supra* note 65 at 1-1.
106. *See* 40 U.S.C. § 3145.
107. *See* 18 U.S.C. § 874 and 29 C.F.R. pt. 3.

K. Fair Labor Standards Act

The Fair Labor Standards Act (FLSA) generally applies to any labor performed, and it sets standards for minimum wage, overtime, recordkeeping, and youth employment.[108]

IV. ENVIRONMENTAL REQUIREMENTS

A. Overview

The National Environmental Policy Act (NEPA) requires federal agencies to incorporate environmental considerations in planning and decision making and to prepare detailed assessments of the environmental impact of and alternatives to major federal actions significantly affecting the environment.[109] Such "federal actions" include activities and projects supported with HUD funds. Part 58 of Title 24 of the federal regulations (Part 58) implements NEPA requirements for most HUD-funded projects and also includes requirements to confirm compliance of HUD-funded projects with a number of other environmental laws and authorities.

There are three levels of analysis under NEPA for HUD-funded programs. First, a project is evaluated to determine whether it is exempt or categorically excluded from an NEPA analysis.[110] Second, if the project is not exempt or categorically excluded, it is analyzed through a written environmental assessment (EA) to determine whether the project will have a significant impact on the environment.[111] If an EA determines that a project will have a significant impact on the environment, then an environmental impact statement (EIS) is prepared for the project, which is a more detailed analysis of the impact of the project and the alternatives to the project.[112] HUD-funded projects rarely require an EIS.[113]

For each HUD funding source, Part 58 describes what entity is responsible for conducting an environmental review, referred to as the "responsible entity" (RE). The responsible entity is usually the recipient of the funds, or it may be the state, the unit of general local government, an Indian tribe, or an Alaskan native village. Part 58 provides guidance regarding what entity is the RE for various HUD funding sources. Each responsible entity should designate a certifying officer and an environmental officer. The certifying officer is the chief elected official, executive officer, or other official designated by formal resolution of the governing body of the responsible entity.[114] The environmental officer is the person responsible for coordinating the environmental review process and ensuring documentation of the process is saved in the environmental review record.[115]

---

108. *See* 29 U.S.C. § 201 et seq.
109. The National Environmental Policy Act (42 U.S.C. § 4321 *et seq.*) is implemented by Exec. Order 11,514 of March 5, 1970 (3 C.F.R., 1966-1970, Comp., p. 902), as amended by Exec. Order 11,991 of May 24, 1977 (3 C.F.R., 1977, Comp., p. 123) and by the Council on Environmental Quality Regulations, 40 C.F.R. pts. 1500–1508.
110. 24 C.F.R. pt. 58, subpt. D.
111. 24 C.F.R. § 58.36.
112. *See* 24 C.F.R. § 58.40(g)(2).
113. *See* 24 C.F.R. § 58.22.
114. *See* Basically CDBG, section 15-2, HUD, Office of Block Grant Assistance (Nov. 2007).
115. *Id.*

The environmental review process must be complete before HUD funds are committed to the project or any choice limiting actions are taken.[116]

B. Environmental Review Process

The responsible entity must maintain a written record of the environmental review for each project, called an "environmental review record."[117] Before HUD funds can be committed to a project, HUD or the state, as applicable, must approve the recipient's Request for Release of Funds (RROF). If a project is exempt or categorically excluded, then no RROF is necessary. The responsible entity must assemble and review all materials required for an environmental assessment and must confirm that the project is in compliance with other environmental laws and authorities. If the responsible entity determines that the project will not result in a significant impact on the quality of the human environment, then the responsible entity may make a "finding of no significant impact" (FONSI). On finding no significant impact, the responsible entity must publish a FONSI notice, providing opportunity to the public for comment.[118] On review and response to comments, the responsible entity must publish a Notice of Intent to Request a Release of Funds (NOI/RROF).[119] After applicable requisite comment periods have tolled for both notices and the responsible entity has reviewed and responded to any comments, the certifying officer of the responsible entity may sign the RROF and include a certification that the responsible entity has complied with all applicable environment requirements of Part 58.[120]

C. Exempt Activities

Certain activities are so unlikely to have any impact on the environment that these activities are exempt from the requirements of an environmental review and an RROF. Such activities include environmental studies, information services, financial services, administrative and management activities, public services that will not have a physical impact or result in any physical changes, inspections and testing of properties for hazards or defects, purchase of insurance, purchase of tools, engineering or design costs, technical assistance and training, payment of principal and interest on loans made or guaranteed by HUD, and improvements intended to address effects from disasters or imminent threats to public safety. In addition, any of the categorically excluded activities are exempt from environmental review and an RROF provided that there are no circumstances that require compliance with other federal laws and authorities cited in 58.5.[121]

---

116. *Id.* at 15.1.9.
117. *See* 24 C.F.R. § 58.38.
118. *See* 24 C.F.R. §§ 58.43–58.47. The length of the comment period is 15 days when published or, if no publication, 18 days when mailing and posting.
119. *See* 24 C.F.R. § 58.43–58.47. The length of the comment period is 7 days when published or, if no publication, 10 days when mailing and posting.
120. *See* 24 C.F.R. §§ 58.2(a)(2), 58.5, and 58.71.
121. *See* 24 C.F.R. § 58.34(a) and the discussion, below, on "categorical exclusion" for more detail on exempt activities.

D. Categorical Exclusion

Some activities are categorically excluded under NEPA but may still require review under other environmental laws and authorities.

- Acquisition, repair, improvement, reconstruction, or rehabilitation of public facilities and improvements (other than buildings) when the facilities and improvements are in place and will be retained in the same use without change in size or capacity of more than 20 percent (e.g., replacement water or sewer lines, construction of curbs and sidewalks, repaving of streets).[122]
- Special projects directed to the removal of architectural barriers that restrict the mobility of and accessibility to elderly and handicapped persons.[123]
- Rehabilitation of residential buildings with one to four units, as long as the density is not increased beyond four units, the land use is not changed, and the footprint of the building is not increased in a floodplain or in a wetland.[124]
- Rehabilitation of residential buildings with five or more units as long as unit density is not changed more than 20 percent, there is no change in land use to non-residential, and the estimated cost of rehabilitation is less than 75 percent of the total estimated cost of replacement after rehabilitation.[125]
- Rehabilitation of non-residential structures as long as size or capacity will not change more than 20 percent and the activity does not involve a change in land use, such as from non-residential to residential, commercial to industrial, or from one industrial use to another.[126]
- New construction, development, demolition, acquisition, disposition, or refinancing on up to four units of residential housing.[127]
- New construction, development, demolition, acquisition, disposition, or refinancing on five or more housing units developed on scattered sites when the sites are more than 2,000 feet apart and there are no more than four housing units on any one site.[128]
- Acquisition, leasing, disposition, or providing loans on an existing structure or acquisition or leasing of vacant land, as long as the same use applies after the HUD-supported action.[129]

E. Other Environmental Laws and Authorities

Unless a project is exempt from environmental review, the responsible entity should confirm whether any additional review is required under other environmental laws and authorities. Other environmental laws and authorities that may apply to HUD-funded projects are de-

---

122. 24 C.F.R. § 58.35(a)(1).
123. 24 C.F.R. § 58.35(a)(2).
124. 24 C.F.R. § 58.35(a)(3)(i).
125. 24 C.F.R. § 58.35(a)(3)(ii).
126. 24 C.F.R. § 58.35(a)(3)(iii).
127. 24 C.F.R. § 58.35(a)(4).
128. *Id.*
129. 24 C.F.R. § 58.35(a)(5).

scribed at 24 C.F.R. § 58.5 and § 58.6, which address the following areas of environmental compliance:

- Historic properties,[130]
- Floodplain management and wetland protection,[131]
- Coastal zone management,[132]
- Sole-source aquifers,[133]
- Endangered species,[134]
- Wild and scenic rivers,[135]
- Air quality,[136]
- Farmland protection,[137]
- HUD environmental standards,[138]

---

130. *See* 24 C.F.R. § 58.5(a), *citing* The National Historic Preservation Act of 1966 (16 U.S.C. § 470 *et seq.*), particularly §§ 106 and 110 (16 U.S.C. § 470 and 470h-2); Exec. Order 11,593, Protection and Enhancement of the Cultural Environment, May 13, 1971 (36 Fed. Reg. 8921), 3 C.F.R., 1971–1975 Comp., p. 559, particularly § 2(c); 36 C.F.R. pt. 800 with respect to HUD programs and 36 C.F.R. pt. 801 with respect to Urban Development Action Grants; The Reservoir Salvage Act of 1960 as amended by the Archeological and Historic Preservation Act of 1974 (16 U.S.C. § 469 *et seq.*), particularly § 3 (16 U.S.C. § 469a-1).

131. *See* 24 C.F.R. § 58.5(b), *citing* Exec. Order 11,988, Floodplain Management, May 24, 1977 (42 Fed. Reg. 26,951), 3 C.F.R., 1977 Comp., p. 117, as interpreted in HUD regs. at 24 C.F.R. pt. 55, particularly § 2(a) of the order; Exec. Order 11,990, Protection of Wetlands, May 24, 1977 (42 Fed. Reg. 26,961), 3 C.F.R., 1977 Comp., p. 121, particularly §§ 2 and 5.

132. *See* 24 C.F.R. § 58.5(c), *citing* The Coastal Zone Management Act of 1972 (16 U.S.C. § 1451 *et seq.*) as amended, particularly § 307(c) and (d) (16 U.S.C. § 1456(c) and (d)).

133. *See* 24 C.F.R. § 58.5(d), *citing* The Safe Drinking Water Act of 1974 (42 U.S.C. § 201, 300(f) *et seq.*, and 21 U.S.C. § 349) as amended, particularly § 1424(e) (42 U.S.C. § 300h-3(e)); Sole- Source Aquifers (40 C.F.R. pt. 149).

134. *See* 24 C.F.R. § 58.5(e), *citing* The Endangered Species Act of 1973 (16 U.S.C. § 1531 *et seq.*) as amended, particularly § 7 (16 U.S.C. § 1536).

135. *See* 24 C.F.R. § 58.5(f), *citing* The Wild and Scenic Rivers Act of 1968 (16 U.S.C. § 1271 *et seq.*) as amended, particularly § 7(b) and (c) (16 U.S.C. § 1278(b) and (c)).

136. *See* 24 C.F.R. § 58.5(g), *citing* The Clean Air Act (42 U.S.C. § 7401 *et seq.*) as amended, particularly § 176(c) and (d) (42 U.S.C. § 7506(c) and (d)); Determining Conformity of Federal Actions to State or Federal Implementation Plans (40 C.F.R. pts. 6, 51, and 93).

137. *See* 24 C.F.R. § 58.5(h), *citing* Farmland Protection Policy Act of 1981 (7 U.S.C. § 4201 *et seq.*), particularly §§ 1540(b) and 1541 (7 U.S.C. §§ 4201(b) and 4202); Farmland Protection Policy (7 C.F.R. pt. 658).

138. *See* 24 C.F.R. § 58.5(i). HUD environmental standards include those criteria and standards specified in 24 C.F.R. pt. 51. It is HUD policy that all properties that are proposed for use in HUD programs be free of hazardous materials, contamination, toxic chemicals and gases, and radioactive substances, where a hazard could affect the health and safety of occupants or conflict with the intended utilization of the property. Evaluation of previous uses of the site is mandatory for multifamily dwellings (five or more units) and non-residential properties. Particular attention should be given to any proposed site on or in the general proximity of such areas as landfills, industrial sites, or other locations that contain or may have contained hazardous wastes.

- Environmental justice considerations,[139]
- Special flood hazards,[140] and
- Property in a runway clear zone.[141]

When the certifying officer of the responsible entity provides a certification of compliance, the officer is complying with NEPA and with these environmental laws and authorities.[142] Documentation of the RE's review of compliance should be included in the environmental review record for that project.[143] The HUD website, under the Office of Community Planning and Development, Environmental Review, has suggested forms and checklists and additional guidance on compliance with each of the above-referenced additional environmental laws and authorities.[144]

F. Environmental Assessment

If a project is not exempt or categorically excluded, and as long as the scope of the project does not require an EIS (as described in more detail below), then the responsible entity must prepare an EA. The environmental assessment must address the following:

- Determine existing conditions and describe the character, features, and resources of the project area and its surroundings; identify the trends that are likely to continue in the absence of the project.[145]
- Identify all potential environmental impacts, whether beneficial or adverse, and the conditions that would change as a result of the project. Identify, analyze, and evaluate all impacts to determine the significance of their effects on the human environment.[146]
- Examine and recommend feasible ways in which the project or external factors could be modified to eliminate or diminish adverse environmental impacts.[147]
- Examine alternatives to the project itself, if appropriate, including the alternative of no action.[148]
- Complete the environmental review necessary for the project's compliance with other environmental laws and authorities, as applicable cited in 24 C.F.R. § 58.5 and § 58.6, as described in more detail above.[149]

---

139. *See* 24 C.F.R. § 58.5(j), *citing* Exec. Order 12898—Federal Actions to Address Environmental Justice in Minority Populations and Low-Income Populations, Feb. 11, 1994 (59 Fed. Reg. 7629), 3 C.F.R., 1994 Comp., p. 859.
140. *See* 24 C.F.R. § 58.6.
141. *See* 24 C.F.R. § 58.6.9(d).
142. *See* 24 C.F.R. 58.13, basically CDBG, § 15.1.2, U.S. Dept. & Hous. Dev. (Nov. 2007).
143. 24 C.F.R. § 58.38.
144. *See* www.hud.gov/offices/environment/review (last visited Oct. 13, 2011).
145. 24 C.F.R. § 58.40(a).
146. 24 C.F.R. § 58.40(b), (c).
147. 24 C.F.R. § 58.40(d).
148. 24 C.F.R. § 58.40(e).
149. 24 C.F.R. § 58.40(f).

The HUD website, under the Office of Community Planning and Development, Environmental Review, has a suggested format for completion of an environmental assessment.

G. Environmental Impact Statement

An EIS is required when a project is determined to have a potentially significant impact on the environment.[150] An EIS would be rare for most HUD-funded projects. An EIS is required for the following:

- Any project that would provide a site or sites or result in the construction of a hospital or nursing home containing 2,500 or more beds.[151]
- Any project that would remove, demolish, convert, or substantially rehabilitate 2,500 or more existing housing units.[152]
- Any project that would result in the construction or installation of 2,500 or more housing units or provide sites for 2,500 or more housing units.[153]
- Any project that would provide additional water and sewer capacity to support 2,500 or more housing units.[154]
- A finding of significant impact is found as a result of the environmental assessment.[155]

The HUD website, under the Office of Community Planning and Development, Environmental Review, has a suggested format for completion of an environmental impact statement.

H. HUD as Responsible Entity

Part 50 of Title 24 of the federal regulations describes HUD's responsibility for environmental review under NEPA and other applicable environmental laws and authorities. This law applies to HUD's direct expenditure of its own funds and includes HUD's review of its policy actions. Occasionally, HUD may serve as the responsible entity when the recipient that is regulated under Part 58 claims the lack of legal capacity to assume environmental review responsibilities and the claim is approved by HUD. HUD may determine that it should conduct the environmental review in the place of a non-recipient responsible entity.[156]

---

150. 24 C.F.R. § 58.37(a).
151. 24 C.F.R. § 58.37(b)(1).
152. 24 C.F.R. § 58.37(b)(2).
153. 24 C.F.R. § 58.37(b)(2).
154. 24 C.F.R. § 58.37(b)(3).
155. 24 C.F.R. § 58.37(a).
156. *See* 24 C.F.R. §§ 50.1 and 58.11.

V. RELOCATION REQUIREMENTS

A. Federal Relocation Law

1. Overview

A number of different laws protect the interests of tenants and property owners when federal funds are used to acquire property or displace residents. The Uniform Relocation Assistance and Property Acquisition Policies Act of 1970 (the Uniform Relocation Act, or URA) applies to all acquisitions of real property or the displacement of persons because of federally assisted projects.[157] The URA applies to the actions of 18 federal agencies, including HUD.[158] The Uniform Relocation Act applies to most HUD acquisitions. Section 104(d) of the Housing and Community Development Act of 1974 (Section 104(d)) includes additional requirements above and beyond the URA for projects assisted with CDBG, HOME, and other HUD programs.[159] The URA does not apply to residents of public housing displaced as the result of an approved application for demolition or disposition under Section 18 of the USHA.[160] Additionally, the Protecting Tenants at Foreclosure Act, discussed in Chapter 7, provides protections for occupants in rental properties that are subject to foreclosure action, who may be displaced.

Either the local agency funding the project or the developer of the project will coordinate relocation. URA expenses are an eligible use of most federal funds for a project. Although either a public agency or a developer may conduct the relocation activities, this chapter will use the term "agency."

The U.S. Department of Transportation promulgated the uniform rule implementing the URA at 49 C.F.R. Part 24, which was last revised at this writing in 2005.[161] HUD has published a very helpful handbook on interpreting the application of the URA to HUD programs that also includes numerous forms and links to laws, guidance, and other forms at www.hud.gov/relocation.[162] Individual HUD programs may have specific requirements in addition to the URA.[163] States and localities may also have laws that apply to displaced tenants or owners.

2. Relocation Plans and Surveys

The URA requires that agencies plan for relocation, although often a formal plan is not required as long as the planning efforts address the needs of the occupants.[164] Relocation

---

157. *See* 42 U.S.C. § 4601 *et seq.*
158. *See* 70 Fed. Reg. 590 *et seq.* (Jan. 4, 2005).
159. 42 U.S.C. § 5304(d); *see also* 24 C.F.R. § 42 (2010) and HUD HANDBOOK 1378, ch. 7.
160. *See* 42 U.S.C. § 1437p; 24 U.S.C. pt. 970; HUD HANDBOOK 1378, Appx. 33, describing the relocation requirements applicable to the demolition and/or disposition of public housing land.
161. *See* 70 Fed. Reg. 590 *et seq.* (Jan. 4, 2005). The publication of the final rule includes useful guidance in interpreting the rule at Appx. A, included in the *Federal Register* notice.
162. *See Tenant Assistance, Relocation, and Real Property Acquisition*, HUD HANDBOOK 1378.0, Change 11 (Sept. 1, 2011).
163. Agencies should review program regulations. HUD HANDBOOK 1378 includes chapters summarizing unique requirements of specific HUD funding programs.
164. 49 C.F.R. § 24.205(a) (2010).

planning may include surveys of the occupants' needs and research regarding available services to meet those needs. Individual HUD programs or specific Notices of Funding Availability may specify required planning activities, budgets, and/or plan documentation.

3. Notice Requirements

Agencies must comply with certain notice requirements, which are among the services and benefits provided to displaced occupants under the Uniform Relocation Act. Notices required by the regulations vary depending on the eligibility of the occupant. An agency may send out a Notice of Intent to Acquire, a General Information Notice, a Notice of Eligibility, a Notice of Non-displacement, a 90-Day Notice, and a Move-In Notice.[165]

a. General Information Notice

The General Information Notice informs the tenant or owner about the expected acquisition of the property and relocation of the occupants. Although the contents of the notice vary depending on whether the relocation is expected for a particular occupant, all occupants should receive the notice.[166] The general notice should be distributed "as soon as feasible" in accordance with federal law.[167] For tenants not lawfully present in the United States, the General Information Notice must indicate that such persons are ineligible for relocation benefits unless their ineligibility would result in extreme hardship to a spouse, parent, or child who is eligible for relocation benefits.[168] In addition to the required notices, HUD also has a number of information brochures available on its website.[169]

b. Notice of Eligibility or Notice of Non-displacement

Following the General Information Notice, the agency must deliver either a Notice of Eligibility or a Notice of Non-displacement promptly after the date the occupants or owners are eligible for relocation benefits.[170] The Notice of Eligibility provides details regarding the relocation benefits and services that will be made available to occupants.[171] For HUD-funded programs, the date an occupant becomes eligible for relocation benefits is set by statute or regulation. The Notice of Eligibility for relocation is triggered by the "initiation of negotiations."[172] Most often, the "initiation of negotiations" is the date the agency signs the agreement for federal funding for the project.

---

165. 49 C.F.R. § 24.203 (2010).
166. 49 C.F.R. § 24.203(a) (2010).
167. *Id.*
168. 49 C.F.R. § 24.203(a)(4) (2010).
169. *See* www.hud.gov/relocation. These notices are also available as appendices to HUD HANDBOOK 1378.
170. 49 C.F.R. § 24.203(b) (2010).
171. 49 C.F.R. § 24.2(a)(15)(ii) (2010); 49 C.F.R. § 24.203(b) (2010); HUD HANDBOOK at Section 2-3(C).
172. The *HUD Handbook* has compiled this information for most HUD programs. *See* HUD HANDBOOK 1378, Ch. 1, Exhibit A.

The agency must deliver a Notice of Non-displacement promptly after the initiation of negotiations.[173] A Notice of Non-displacement would most often be provided to tenants who will not displaced or who will only be displaced temporarily.[174]

c. 90-Day Notice

Agencies must provide a 90-day notice that includes specific information regarding the relocation, including the earliest date by which the occupant will be required to move, not less than 90 days from the date of the notice. [175] There are certain instances where a 90-day notice is not required. For a HUD-funded program, the most likely reason that a 90-day notice would not be required include when an occupant vacates the property prior to receipt of a 90-day notice or an occupant is not considered a "displaced person," as discussed in more detail in Section 4(b) below.[176]

d. Other Notices

If new occupants move into a property within 90 days prior to the initiation of negotiations, the agency must provide new occupants a notice of non-eligibility for relocation benefits before the occupant moves into the property. This notice, called a "Move-In Notice," informs the occupants that they are ineligible for relocation benefits and that they will not be considered a "displaced person" for the purpose of determining the applicability of any relocation benefits.[177]

It is also important for developers to keep in mind that occupants retain their rights under local landlord-tenant law and their leases during the relocation process. As such, developers must make sure all relocation efforts comply with local laws and lease requirements.

B. Displaced Persons

When a person moves from a project covered by the URA, he or she may be considered displaced or non-displaced, depending on the facts and circumstances of the move. A displaced person is eligible for relocation benefits under the URA, while a non-displaced person is not eligible. Under federal law, a displaced person is one who moves because of the acquisition, rehabilitation, or demolition of a property by an agency or after receipt of a notice of

---

173. HUD HANDBOOK at Section 2-3(D).
174. Temporary displacement is defined as displacement for less than one year. A tenant who is displaced for more than one year is eligible for full relocation benefits. *See* HUD HANDBOOK Sections 1-4 (II), 2-3(D); 49 C.F.R. Appx. A, discussion under 24.2(a)(9)(ii)(D).
175. 49 C.F.R. § 24.203(c) (2010). The 90-day period may be shortened where it is impracticable to give 90 days; however, this will occur only as a result of unusual circumstances—for instance, where continued occupancy would threaten the health or safety of occupants.
176. HUD HANDBOOK at Section 2.3(E).
177. 49 C.F.R. § 24.2(a)(9)(ii)(B) (2010). *See* also HUD HANDBOOK at Section 1-4(J)(2) and 1-4(Y). Note, however, that such occupants remain entitled to receive comparable replacement housing within their financial means. *See* 49 C.F.R. § 24.2(a)(b)(viii)(C). As such, these occupants may be eligible to receive payments for replacement housing of last resort. *See* Section 4(d)(iii) *infra*.

intention to acquire by a public agency.[178] An agency's refusal to renew a lease to avoid paying relocation benefits does not negate that person's status as a displaced person eligible for relocation benefits.

An occupant may be considered a displaced person if he or she moves out before the agency takes title to the property but after negotiations begin for the acquisition of a property.[179] In this instance, the occupant may be able to establish that relocation was the result of the impending acquisition of the property.[180] Upon the agency's decision not to acquire the property, occupants should be notified that the acquisition will not occur and they will not be displaced. Any occupants who move on such notice will not be considered displaced for the purposes of receiving relocation benefits.[181]

C. Exclusions from Displaced Persons Definition

Under federal law, there are certain occupants who are excluded from the definition of "displaced persons." Persons who are not "displaced" are not eligible for URA benefits. These occupants include the following: unlawful occupants, post-acquisition tenants, persons not required to move, owner-occupants who voluntarily sell, persons who move as a result of code enforcement, persons who are temporarily displaced, and unqualified aliens.

An unlawful occupant is one who occupies the property without right, title, or payment of rent.[182] Unlawful occupants also include persons legally evicted from the unit without any rights under state law to occupy the unit.[183]

Post-acquisition tenants include persons who first occupy the property after its acquisition by a public agency or private party receiving funds from a public agency or after the owner enters into a contract for federal funds.[184] To ensure that post-acquisition tenants are not considered displaced and eligible for relocation benefits, they must be notified of the impending displacement.[185]

An occupant who is not required to move as a result of an acquisition and who was provided notice of such but moves nevertheless does not qualify as a displaced person. A person who is not required to move, however, may qualify as a displaced person if the project results in a significant change in the use or character of the property.[186]

An owner-occupant who moves after a voluntary sale to a developer does not qualify as a displaced person if the owner-occupant receives written notice that the developer will not acquire the property if a negotiated agreement cannot be reached.[187] The developer must

---

178. 42 U.S.C. § 4601(6)(A)(i)(I) (2010); 49 C.F.R. § 24.2(a)(9) (2005); HUD HANDBOOK at Section 1-4(I).
179. HUD HANDBOOK at Section 1-4(I).
180. *Id.*
181. HUD HANDBOOK at Section 1-4(I).
182. 49 C.F.R. § 24.2(a)(9)(ii)(K) (2010).
183. 49 C.F.R. § 24.2(a)(29) (2010).
184. 49 C.F.R. § 24.2(a)(9)(ii)(B) (2010).
185. 49 C.F.R. § 24.2(a)(9)(ii)(B) (2010); HUD HANDBOOK at Section 1-4(J)(2).
186. 49 C.F.R. § 24.2(a)(9)(ii)(D) (2010); HUD HANDBOOK at Section 1-4(I)(7).
187. 49 C.F.R. § 24.2(a)(9)(ii) (2010).

inform the seller of the market value of the property and that the property will not be acquired if an agreement cannot be reached for the transaction to qualify as a voluntary sale.[188]

Occupants who move because of routine health or housing code enforcement activities of a public agency do not qualify as displaced persons. However, if the public agency commences such activities to displace occupants for an impending project, occupants may be considered displaced.[189]

An occupant who is temporarily displaced qualifies for temporary benefits but is not considered a displaced person under federal law.[190] Under federal law, temporary relocation may not extend beyond 12 months.[191] If temporary relocation extends beyond 12 months, the displacing agency must offer the occupant permanent relocation assistance, in addition to any temporary relocation assistance already received.[192] The URA regulations require that occupants being temporarily displaced receive certain benefits. Occupants must be relocated to decent, safe, and sanitary housing and must be reimbursed for all out-of-pocket moving and increased housing costs.[193] Under reasonable terms and conditions, occupants also have the right to move back into a unit in the same building or complex. Before moving out, occupants also must receive a "Notice of Nondisplacement" that indicates the ability to move back into the same building or complex.[194] Lastly, occupants must receive reasonable notice, usually 30 days, of the relocation.[195] A displacing agency's failure to comply with the aforementioned requirements will result in the occupant being considered a displaced person eligible for full relocation benefits.[196] When an occupant may not be able to return to the same building or complex on account of a reduced number of units, for instance, permanent relocation benefits should be given to the occupant.[197]

Certain federal housing programs impose additional requirements for occupants who are temporarily displaced. For instance, the CDBG program and HOME program require that, on an occupant's return to the property, rent cannot exceed the greater of the monthly rent plus utility allowance before displacement or 30 percent of the household income, for a period of at least 12 months.[198]

Aliens not lawfully present in the United States are not considered displaced persons and therefore are ineligible for relocation benefits, except where the denial of relocation benefits would impose undue hardship on the alien and the alien is the parent, spouse, or child of a displaced person who is a citizen or lawful resident.[199]

---

188. 49 C.F.R. § 24.101 (b)(1)-(2) (2010).
189. HUD HANDBOOK at Section 1-4(J)(3).
190. 49 C.F.R. § 24.2(a)(9)(ii)(D) (2010).
191. 49 C.F.R. § 24 App. A (2010).
192. Id.
193. Id.
194. HUD HANDBOOK at Section 2-4.
195. HUD HANDBOOK at Section 2-3(E)(3).
196. 49 C.F.R. § App. A (2010); HUD HANDBOOK at Section at Section 1-4(II).
197. HUD HANDBOOK at Section 2-7.
198. 49 C.F.R. § 570.606(2)(D)(1) (2010); 24 C.F.R. § 92.353(b) (2010).
199. 42 U.S.C. § 4605 (2010); 49 C.F.R. § 24.2(a)(9)(ii)(L) (2010).

D. Relocation Benefits

Generally, there are three types of relocation benefits available once it is determined that an occupant is a displaced person in accordance with federal law: (1) advisory assistance, (2) moving assistance, and (3) housing or reestablishment assistance.

Advisory assistance includes the delivery of the various notices described above and may include counseling and similar services to assist occupants in securing new housing.[200] Moving assistance includes payment of all relocations expenses.[201] Housing assistance for residential occupants includes providing for replacement housing. Business occupants are eligible for reestablishment assistance that is intended to provide sufficient payment to reestablish the business elsewhere.[202] Below is a more detailed description of the relocation benefits available to commercial and residential occupants.

1. Business Occupants

Businesses that are displaced because of activities that are federally funded are eligible for advisory and moving assistance.[203] Businesses are also eligible for reestablishment assistance if they qualify as a small business under federal law.[204]

Moving expenses include, but are not limited to, transporting and storing items; disconnecting, removing, or reinstalling machinery; searching for a new location; relettering signs; and replacing stationery.[205] Businesses have the option of moving themselves, in which case they receive reimbursement based on the lowest bid received for the cost of the move.[206]

A small business, defined as a business with no more than 500 employees, receives reestablishment expenses in an amount not to exceed $10,000.[207] Reestablishment expenses include the costs for repairs or improvements to the replacement property, signage, advertisements, professional services for the purchase or lease of the replacement property, and the estimated increase in operating costs at the replacement site for first two years.[208] Reestablishment expenses do not include purchase of capital assets, manufacturing materials used in the normal course of business, and aesthetic improvements to the replacement property.[209]

Instead of receiving moving and reestablishment assistance, a displaced business may opt to receive a fixed payment in the amount of the average annual net earnings of the business.[210]

---

200. 49 C.F.R. § 24.203 (2010); 49 C.F.R. § 24.205 (2010); HUD Handbook at Section at Section 2-4.
201. 49 C.F.R. § 24.301–.305 (2010); HUD Handbook at Section 3-2, 4-2.
202. 49 C.F.R. § 24.304 (2010); 49 C.F.R. § 24.401–.403 (2010).
203. 49 C.F.R. § 24.301 (2010); 49 C.F.R. § 24.303–.305 (2010); HUD Handbook at Section 4-1 through 4-7.
204. 49 C.F.R. § 24.301 (2010); 49 C.F.R. § 24.303–.305 (2010); HUD Handbook at Section 4-1 through 4-7.
205. 49 C.F.R. § 24.301(d) and (g) (2010); 49 C.F.R. § 24.303–.305 (2010); HUD Handbook at Section 4-3.
206. 49 C.F.R. § 24.301(d)(2) (2010).
207. 49 C.F.R. § 24.304 (2010); 49 C.F.R. § 24.2(a)(24) (2010); HUD Handbook at Section 4-6.
208. 49 C.F.R. § 24.304 (2010); HUD Handbook at Section 4-6.
209. 49 C.F.R. § 24.304 (2010).
210. 49 C.F.R. § 24.305 (2010); HUD Handbook at Section 4-7.

Businesses that choose this option must substantiate their requests with the applicable tax returns, certified financial statements, or other similar documentation.[211] Nonprofit organizations, however, are presumed to meet the requirements for the fixed payment and therefore do not have to substantiate their requests unless the public agency determines otherwise.[212] In requesting the fixed fee, certain limitations apply. The fixed payment may not be less than $1,000 or exceed $20,000.[213] The fixed payment is allowed only where the business cannot be relocated without losing substantial business and if such business is not a part of a chain.[214] In addition, the fixed payment is allowed only if the business owns or rents personal property that must be moved as part of the relocation and the business would otherwise be eligible for moving assistance.[215] Nonprofit organizations may receive the fixed payment where the business cannot be relocated without losing substantial business and if such business does not have more than three other locations.[216]

2. Residential Occupants

a. Tenants

Displaced residential occupants are eligible for moving and housing assistance, as well as the advisory assistance discussed above.

A displaced occupant chooses between two types of moving assistance: (1) payment of the person's actual and reasonable moving and moving-related expenses or (2) a fixed moving expense allowance.[217] For displaced occupants who choose actual and reasonable moving-related expenses, the federal regulations provide which expenses are reimbursable and which are not.[218] A displacing agency has discretion to reimburse expenses that are not specifically included in the regulations but are reasonable.[219]

To comply with housing assistance requirements, a displacing agency must provide displaced occupants with at least one comparable dwelling unit.[220] When it is possible, the displacing agency must provide three or more comparable replacement dwellings.[221] A replacement dwelling is comparable if the displaced person: (1) is informed of its location; (2) has sufficient time to negotiate and enter into a purchase agreement or lease for the property; and (3) is assured of receiving the relocation assistance and acquisition payment in sufficient time to complete the purchase or lease of the property.[222] A comparable dwelling unit also must be

---

211. 49 C.F.R. § 24.305(e) (2010).
212. 49 C.F.R. § 24.305(d) (2010).
213. 49 C.F.R. § 24.305(a) (2010).
214. *Id.*
215. 49 C.F.R. § 24.305(a)(1) (2010).
216. 49 C.F.R. § 24.305(d) (2010).
217. 49 C.F.R. § 24.301 (2010); HUD HANDBOOK at Section 3-2.
218. 49 C.F.R. § 24.301 (2010); HUD HANDBOOK at Section 3-2.
219. 49 C.F.R. § 24.301 (2010); HUD HANDBOOK at Section 3-2.
220. 49 C.F.R. § 24.204 (2010).
221. *Id.*
222. 49 C.F.R. § 24.204(a) (2010).

safe, decent, and sanitary, and comparable in size.[223] The federal agency funding the project may waive the comparable housing requirement in the event of a major disaster, a presidentially declared national emergency, or another emergency when continued occupancy of the displacement dwelling would pose a substantial danger to the health or safety of the occupants or the public.[224]

For persons receiving public assistance that makes the unit affordable, specific rules apply to what is considered a comparable replacement dwelling. A public housing unit may be considered a comparable replacement dwelling for a person being displaced from a public housing unit.[225] A privately owned unit with a program subsidy tied to the unit may be considered a replacement dwelling for a person being displaced from a similar unit or from a public housing unit.[226] A housing choice voucher may be included in an offer for a replacement dwelling unit for a person occupying a public housing unit, a privately owned unit with a program subsidy tied to the unit, or a similar type of tenant-based subsidy.[227] For occupants of housing that is not subsidized, a "comparable replacement dwelling" does not include a unit subsidized by a government housing program.[228] However, an agency may offer, and an occupant may accept, assistance under a government housing program.[229]

Displaced occupants who have occupied the displacement property for 90 days before the initiation of negotiations are eligible for a long-term replacement housing payment.[230] The payment is calculated so that the replacement housing will be affordable for a period of 42 months.[231] For displaced occupants who are considered low-income in accordance with federal Section 8 regulations, affordability requires that they pay no more than 30 percent of their income towards rent. For displaced occupants who are not low income, affordability requires that the occupant pay no more rent at the replacement dwelling than at the displacement dwelling.[232] The regulations impose a $5,250 limit on replacement housing payments.[233] In lieu of receiving the replacement housing payment, a displaced occupant may receive a payment to assist in the purchase of a replacement dwelling.[234]

Under Section 104(d) of the Housing and Community Development Act, when a developer uses CDBG or HOME program funds to demolish a unit occupied by low-income persons at a rent below Section 8 fair market rent, the affordability period for the replacement housing payment is 60 months rather than 42 months.[235] However, the displaced occupant may choose to receive the replacement housing payment under Section 104(d) or under the URA regulations.[236]

---

223. 49 C.F.R. § 24.2 (2010); HUD Handbook at Section 1-4(F).
224. 49 C.F.R. § 24.204 (2010).
225. 49 C.F.R. pt. 24, Appx. A, discussion of Section 24(a)(6)(ix).
226. Id.
227. Id.
228. 49 C.F.R. pt. 24, Appx. A, discussion of Section 24(a)(6)(vii).
229. 49. C.F.R. pt. 24, Appx. A, discussion of Section 24(a)(6)(ix).
230. 49 C.F.R. § 24.402 (2010).
231. 49 C.F.R. § 24.402(b) (2010).
232. Id.
233. 49 C.F.R. § 24.402(a) (2010); HUD Handbook at Section 3-4.
234. 49 C.F.R. § 24.402(c) (2010); HUD Handbook at Section 3-5 and 3-6.
235. 42 U.S.C. § 5304(d) (2010).
236. Id.

b. Homeowners

Similar to tenants, displaced occupants who are homeowners are eligible for the reimbursement of actual and reasonable moving costs and comparable replacement housing that meets the criteria mentioned above.

In addition, homeowners also may receive a replacement housing payment not to exceed $22,500.[237] The amount of the payment is limited to the amount necessary to relocate to a comparable replacement dwelling within one year from the date the displaced homeowner is paid for the displacement dwelling or the date a comparable replacement dwelling is made available to such person, whichever is later.[238] The payment is the sum of (1) the amount by which the cost of a replacement dwelling exceeds the acquisition cost of the displacement dwelling, (2) the increased interest costs and other debt service costs that are incurred in connection with the mortgage(s) on the replacement dwelling, and (3) the reasonable expenses incidental to the purchase of the replacement dwelling.[239]

To receive the one-time replacement housing payment, homeowners must have owned and occupied the home for at least 180 days before the initiation of negotiations.[240] A homeowner who has owned and occupied the home for at least 90 days before the initiation of negotiation receives the same relocation benefits as a displaced tenant, as described above.[241]

3. Last-Resort Housing

In the event that the displacing agency cannot provide comparable housing for displaced tenants and homeowners without exceeding the maximum replacement housing payments described above, the displacing agency may provide last-resort housing assistance.[242]

Before providing such assistance, the displacing agency must determine that the project cannot be completed without last-resort housing and that the housing can be provided in a cost-effective manner.[243] The regulations specify various ways for providing last-resort housing, including, but not limited to: (1) replacement housing payments that exceed the regulatory limits, (2) rehabilitation or construction of replacement dwellings, (3) direct loans to displaced occupants, (4) purchase of land and/or replacement dwellings, and (5) change displaced occupants status from tenant to homeowner.[244]

Displaced occupants who do not qualify for the standard replacement housing payment because they did not live in the displacement dwelling for the requisite number of days are eligible to receive last-resort housing payments.[245]

---

237. 49 C.F.R. § 24.401 (2010); HUD Handbook at Section 3-9.
238. 49 C.F.R. § 24.401(a) (2010).
239. Id.
240. Id.
241. 49 C.F.R. § 24.401–.505 (2010); HUD Handbook at Section 3-8.
242. 49 C.F.R. § 24.404(a) (2010).
243. 49 C.F.R. § 24.404(a) (2010).
244. 49 C.F.R. § 24.404(c) (2010);
245. 49 C.F.R. § 24.404(c)(3) (2010);

E. Grievances and Waivers of Benefits

The federal regulations provide a process for displaced occupants to appeal their relocation determinations and benefits.[246] The displacing agency's executive director reviews the determination of relocation benefits and issues a decision.[247] Displaced occupants also have the option of pursuing judicial review if the decision of the executive director does not resolve their concerns.[248]

A displacing agency cannot request that a displaced occupant waive relocation benefits.[249] However, a displaced occupant may provide a written waiver on being informed of all relocation benefits.[250]

F. Section 104(d)

As mentioned above, Section 104(d) of the Housing and Community Development Act of 1974 includes additional requirements above and beyond the URA for projects assisted with CDBG, HOME, and other HUD programs.[251] Persons eligible for relocation assistance under Section 104(d) are also eligible for relocation assistance under the URA and may choose to receive either type of assistance. The differences between the URA and 104(d) are summarized by the *HUD Relocation Handbook*.[252] Only low-income tenants are eligible for relocation assistance under 104(d). A significant difference between the URA and 104(d) is the obligation to replace demolished or converted units affordable to low-income tenants under the CDBG, HOME, and other programs covered by Section 104(d) on a one-for-one basis.[253] Not only must the replacement units account for every demolished or converted unit, they must remain affordable for a minimum of 10 years.[254] To facilitate the one-for-one requirement, units constructed one year before or three years following the demolition or conversion will count as replacement units.[255] HUD field offices have the discretion to determine that the one-for-one replacement requirement is inapplicable where there is a sufficient number of vacant low-income housing in the surrounding area.[256]

VI. SUBSIDY LAYERING

For all housing projects that receive assistance or subsidy from HUD that is combined with any "other government assistance,"[257] a subsidy-layering review (SLR) must be performed,

---

246. 49 C.F.R. § 24.10 (2010).
247. *Id.*
248. 49 C.F.R. § 24.10 (2010); HUD Handbook at Section 1-10.
249. 49 C.F.R. § 24.207(f) (2010).
250. 49 C.F.R. § Appx. A (2010).
251. *See* 24 C.F.R. pt. 42; HUD Handbook 1378, Ch. 7.
252. *See* HUD Handbook 1378, Ch. 7.
253. 24 C.F.R. § 42.375 (2010).
254. 24 C.F.R. § 42.375(b) (2010).
255. *Id.*
256. *Id.*
257. "Other government assistance" includes any form of direct or indirect assistance from any federal, state, or local government, or any agency or instrumentality thereof, including a loan, grant, guaranty, insurance, payment, rebate, subsidy, credit, or tax benefit.

and HUD is responsible for certifying that the project is not using any more assistance than necessary to provide affordable housing.[258] The SLR must determine that the project is financially feasible, based on a consideration of the total of HUD and other government assistance. The factors to be evaluated to determine the project's feasibility include the rate of return to owners of and investors in the project; the project's long-term needs; the usual and customary fees for a similar project; and the resident population of the assisted project.

For certain HUD programs or where certain forms of other government assistance are involved, another government entity may perform the subsidy-layering review and provide the required certification instead of HUD:

- **Low-Income Housing Tax Credits.** If low-income-housing tax credits (LIHTCs) awarded under Section 42 of the Internal Revenue Code are a source of assistance in the project, a state housing credit agency (HCA) is permitted to perform the review.[259] HUD issued instructions in 1995 that provide guidance to HUD Field Offices for delegating authority to an HCA to perform an SLR and for conducting an SLR in the event HUD does the analysis itself.[260] The HUD guidance requires a determination by the HCA that the amount of investor equity generated by the sale of the LIHTCs is not less than the amount that would be expected to be generated in the current market conditions and that the project costs are within a reasonable range.[261]
- **HOME Funds.** If an applicant applies to a participating jurisdiction (PJ) for HOME funds that will be combined with other government assistance, including Community Development Block Grant (CDBG) funds, the PJ must perform an SLR and certify that "the combination of federal assistance provided to any housing project shall not be any more than is necessary to provide affordable housing."[262] Under the HOME program, there are four components to the SLR evaluation: (1) the sources and uses of the project, including documented verification of the sources and uses; (2) certification of federal assistance from the applicant for HOME funds; (3) the project's development budget, to ensure the reasonableness of the costs; and (4) the operating pro forma to evaluate the rate of return on the equity investment.[263]
- **Section 8/Project-Based Vouchers.** Prior to the passage of the Housing and Economic Recovery Act of 2008 (HERA), HUD was required to conduct a SLR prior to approving Section 8 project-based voucher (PBV) assistance and certify that the PBV assistance was not excessive, after considering other types of governmental assistance in the project.[264] HERA eliminated the requirement that HUD perform an SLR for existing housing projects financed under the Section 8 program.[265]

---

258. Section 102(d), Dep't of Housing and Urban Development Reform Act of 1989 (HUD Reform Act); 24 C.F.R. § 4.13(d) (2010).
259. Section 911(a), Housing Community Development Act of 1992.
260. HUD Notice H 95-4 (issued Jan. 20, 1995).
261. Section 911(b), Housing Community Development Act of 1992. The project costs to be considered include developer fees, and the HCA must take into account certain factors, including the project's location, risk factors, and size.
262. Section 212(f), Cranston-Gonzales National Affordable Housing Act.
263. HUD Notice CPD 98-01 (issued Jan. 22, 1998).
264. 24 C.F.R. § 983.55 (2010).
265. Section 2835(a)(1)(F), Housing Economic Recovery Act of 2008.

HERA also eliminated the requirement for HUD to perform an SLR for newly constructed and substantially rehabilitated buildings if the applicable state or local agency had performed an SLR for the project.[266] In 2010, HUD released administrative guidelines implementing this provision, stating that the SLR requirement for newly constructed and substantially rehabilitated buildings with PBV housing assistance payment contracts is satisfied if an HCA has performed an SLR with respect to the LIHTCs, HOME funds, or other government assistance in the project and the HCA considered the Section 8 PBVs in its SLR evaluation.[267] To perform the SLR, the HCA must notify HUD of its intent to do so and certify to HUD that it will perform the SLR in accordance with the HUD guidelines, which provide specific standards that the project must meet.

- **Federal Housing Administration (FHA) Mortgage Insurance**. HERA amended the SLR requirement and specifically excludes FHA mortgage insurance issued pursuant to Section II of the National Housing Act[268] from the list of programs under HUD jurisdiction for which an SLR must be performed.[269]

VII. FUNDING AND GRANT ISSUES

The HUD Reform Act of 1989, P.L. 101-235,[270] included a set of reforms intended to ensure greater accountability and integrity in the Department's administration of federal funds. Reforms included specific requirements for awards of HUD competitive grants and sanctions for HUD employees that fail to comply. Two additional statutes significantly restrict HUD's ability to fund programs and expend grant funds: the Anti-deficiency Act and the Cash Management Improvement Act. This section discusses the intersection of HUD funding processes with these three important statutes.

A. Grant Application Requirements

When HUD plans to make federal assistance available through a competition, HUD must publish in the *Federal Register:* (1) a notice of availability of assistance;[271] (2) a description of the form and procedures by which applicants can apply for assistance and the deadlines associated with the award;[272] and (3) no less than 30 days before any submission deadlines, the criteria for selection.[273] The foregoing requirements may be waived only if the Secretary of HUD determines that a waiver is required to respond to an emergency.[274] HUD may award or allocate assistance only in response to written applications, except where other procedures are specified in the statute.[275] For example, formula funding to public housing authorities pursu-

---

266. *Id.*
267. Fed. Reg. Notice, Docket No. FR–5417–N–01, issued July 9, 2010.
268. 12 U.S.C. § 1707 *et seq.*
269. Section 2834(a), Housing Economic Recovery Act of 2008.
270. The regulations implementing the HUD Reform Act are at 24 C.F.R. pt. 4.
271. 42 U.S.C. § 3545(a)(1); 24 C.F.R. § 4.5(a).
272. 42 U.S.C. § 3545(a)(2); 24 C.F.R. § 4.5(a).
273. 42 U.S.C. § 3545(a)(3); 24 C.F.R. § 4.5(a).
274. 42 U.S.C. § 3454(a)(5).
275. 42 U.S.C. § 3545(a)(4).

ant to the Capital Fund or Operating Fund is not subject to the process described in this paragraph, because distribution of those funds is made by regulatory formula, not competition. HUD must publish at least quarterly its decisions related to competitive or discretionary (non-formula, non-demand) funding.[276]

All applicants for HUD assistance—regardless of whether the assistance is allocated competitively or by other means—must disclose the following information via Form HUD 2880 if an aggregate amount of assistance for the project/activity in excess of $200,000 is anticipated during the federal fiscal year during which the application was submitted: (1) other governmental assistance that is expected to be made available with respect to the project or activities that are the subject of the application for HUD funds; (2) the name and pecuniary interest of any interested party; and (3) expected sources and uses of funds for the project/activity, including both governmental and non-governmental funds.[277] Completion of the Form HUD 2880 is typically required with all competitive funding applications, Moving to Work annual plan submissions, and other funding requests. Although the form must be completed, disclosures described in (1), (2), and (3) in this paragraph are not required with respect to requests for formula funding requests (e.g., Capital Funds, Operating Funds, CDBG, etc.). HUD will indicate in its application instructions or regulations whether submission of the form is required. In the event of a substantial change in the information provided in Form HUD 2880 during the application process or the period in which assistance is provided, applicants must update the form within 30 days of the change.[278] The type of change triggering an updated disclosure may vary based on the specific housing program.[279]

If a violation of the disclosure rules occurs, HUD may halt pending selection processes or void selection decisions that have been made.[280] Sanctions and funding recapture may be pursued.[281] HUD also may seek civil money penalties of up to $16,000 per violation against persons or entities that knowingly and materially violate the disclosure requirements.[282]

B. Funding Decisions

During the selection process for assistance, HUD employees and consultants representing HUD in the process are prohibited from disclosing certain information to unauthorized persons within or outside of the Department.[283] This prohibition is intended to avoid situations in which one applicant gains an unfair advantage over others through obtaining information that is otherwise unavailable to applicants or the public.[284] The prohibition begins at the point that a HUD official awarding the assistance, or his or her designee, "makes a written request (which includes the selection criteria to be used in providing the assistance) to the [HUD] Office of General Counsel (OGC) to prepare the [Notice of Funding Availability], solicita-

---

276. 42 U.S.C. § 3545(a)(4)(C)(ii); 24 C.F.R. § 4.7.
277. 42 U.S.C. § 3545(b); 24 C.F.R. § 4.9.
278. 42 U.S.C. § 3545(c); 24 C.F.R. § 4.11.
279. See 24 C.F.R. § 4.11(b).
280. 42 U.S.C. § 3545(e.
281. 42 U.S.C. § 3545(e.
282. 42 U.S.C. § 3545(f); 24 C.F.R. § 30.25.
283. 42 U.S.C. § 3537a(a); 24 C.F.R. § 4.20-4.22.
284. 24 C.F.R. § 4.20.

tion, or request for application for assistance" and the prohibition ends once the selection of recipients is announced.[285]

The following types of selection-related disclosures are *not* prohibited during a selection process:

- Information and technical assistance related to requirements of a HUD program, including unpublished policy statements, provided that the disclosure is made to any applicant or potential applicant who requests it;[286]
- The date by which a decision in the selection process will be made;[287]
- Any information published in the *Federal Register* or which has otherwise been made public;[288]
- Information requested by an auditor or investigator authorized by the HUD Inspector General that is necessary to the audit or investigation;[289] or
- Legal, including litigation-related, disclosures to counsel to HUD or that is otherwise responsible to HUD.[290]

The following types of selection-related disclosures *are* prohibited during a selection process:

- Advance disclosure of funding decisions;[291]
- Information on an applicant's relative standing;[292]
- The amount of assistance requested by an applicant;[293]
- Any information contained in an application;[294] and
- Prior to submission of applications, the disclosure of an applicant's identity or the number of applicants.[295]

A HUD employee who improperly discloses selection information may be subject to civil money penalties of up to $16,000 per violation.[296] The recipient of the unauthorized disclosure may also be sanctioned.[297] HUD regulations specify a procedure by which violations of the disclosure rules may be disclosed to HUD, investigated, and remedied.[298]

---

285. 24 C.F.R. § 4.22
286. 24 C.F.R. § 4.26(a)(1).
287. 24 C.F.R. § 4.26(a)(2).
288. 24 C.F.R. § 4.26(a)(3)–(4).
289. 24 C.F.R. § 4.26(a)(5).
290. 24 C.F.R. § 4.26(a)(6).
291. 24 C.F.R. § 4.26(c)(1).
292. *Id.*
293. *Id.*
294. *Id.*
295. 24 C.F.R. § 4.26(c)(2).
296. 42 U.S.C. § 3537a(c); 24 C.F.R. §§ 4.20, 4.28, 30.20. For more information on civil money penalties, including the process by which they may be assessed or challenged, *see* 24 C.F.R. pt. 30.
297. 24 C.F.R. § 4.20.
298. *See* 24 C.F.R. §§ 4.30–4.38.

C. The Anti-Deficiency Act

The Anti-Deficiency Act of 1906 (ADA) prohibits the federal government from obligating or expending federal funds before an appropriations measure has been enacted.[299] By law, Congress sets a federal agency's budget authority, and the agency is then required to limit its obligations and expenditures within that authority. The Office of Management and Budget (OMB) issues circulars, which set forth instructions and policies for executive branch agencies to follow in properly controlling their budget authority. For example, OMB Circular A-11, "Preparation, Submission, and Execution of the Budget," provides instructions and guidance for budget formulation;[300] OMB Circular A-123, "Management Accountability and Control," requires agencies to take proactive measures to develop and implement appropriate, cost-effective management controls for results-oriented management;[301] and OMB Circular A-127, "Financial Management Systems," requires agencies to issue and maintain agencywide financial management system directives to reflect the policies defined therein.[302]

HUD incorporates the standards prescribed in the OMB Circulars and sets forth its own policies and procedures for compliance with the ADA in the *HUD Budget and Accounting Handbook* (the Handbook). The Handbook provides that "all obligations shall be for the purpose authorized by law, within amounts authorized, executed before the end of the period of availability of the appropriation, and supported by documentary evidence that is in writing and approved by a duly authorized official."[303] Furthermore, "an obligation may not be authorized before enactment of the applicable appropriation, unless otherwise provided by law" and "a prevalidation of the availability of funds should be performed before an obligation is incurred."[304]

The ADA imposes certain reporting requirements on HUD for ADA violations. Agencies who violate the ADA "shall report immediately to the President and Congress all relevant facts and a statement of actions taken."[305] Moreover, an officer or employee who violates the ADA can face stiff administrative and/or criminal penalties, including suspension from duty without pay or removal from office, and, in some cases, a fine of not more than $5,000, imprisonment of not more than two years, or both.[306]

D. The Cash Management Improvement Act

The Cash Management Improvement Act of 1990, 31 U.S.C. 6501 (Pub. L. 101-453) (CMIA), as amended, sets forth the general guidelines for the transfer of financial assistance from the federal government to the states, territories, and the District of Columbia (collectively, the States). The purpose of the CMIA is "to ensure greater efficiency, effectiveness, and equity in the exchange of funds between the federal government and the States."[307] The intent of the

---

299. 31 U.S.C. §§ 1341, 1517(a) (2010).
300. OMB Circular No. A-11 (2011).
301. OMB Circular No. A-123 (2006).
302. OMB Circular No. A-127 (2009).
303. HUD BUDGET AND ACCOUNTING HANDBOOK, POLICIES AND PROCEDURES § 2.2(B).
304. *Id.*
305. 31 U.S.C. §§ 1351, 1517(b) (2010).
306. 31 U.S.C. §§ 1349–1350, 1518–1519 (2010).
307. H.R. 4279, 101st Cong. (1990).

CMIA is for federal assistance programs to be interest-neutral, resulting in no interest gained or lost by either federal or state governments. Prior to the enactment of the CMIA, States were drawing federal funds in advance of a need, resulting in the federal government losing interest revenue.[308] In addition, the federal government was providing late grant awards to States, causing States to advance their own funds for federal purposes and to lose interest revenue.[309]

The CMIA and its implementing regulation, 31 C.F.R. part 205.12, require the timely transfer of federal funds from the government to the States and the payment of interest to the States in the event that such transfers are delayed.[310] In addition, the federal government is entitled to interest from the States for the period that federal funds are in State accounts, pending payment. Pursuant to the "Three-Day Rule," States receiving federal funds are required to spend such funds within three days of receipt.[311]

The CMIA applies to all programs and functions where the state pays out federal funds for program purposes where such funds are transferred from the federal government. The interest payment provisions, however, apply only to "major" federal assistance programs.[312] States establish a Treasury-State Agreement (TSA) with the U.S. Department of the Treasury to detail their implementation of the CMIA. Each State's TSA identifies the major federal assistance programs covered by the CMIA and documents the accepted funding techniques and methods for calculating interest agreed on by both parties.[313]

E. Grant Disbursements

The Line of Credit Control System, the Integrated Disbursement and Information System, and the Grants Management Process System are HUD's primary grant disbursement systems. The purpose of these systems is to allow grantees to draw down approved funds and for HUD to monitor grantee obligation and expenditure progress against funds disbursed by HUD.[314] These systems permit HUD to make automatic payments on specific dates, ensuring that loan or bond repayments are made accurately, on time, and without costly errors. When advances are made by electronic transfer of funds methods, grantees are required to "make drawdowns as close as possible to the time of making disbursements."

---

308. *See* Financial Management Service, *Cash Management Improvement Act (CMIA): Common Questions*, http://www.fms.treas.gov/cmia/questions.html (last visited Oct. 31, 2011).

309. *See* Financial Management Service, *Cash Management Improvement Act (CMIA): Common Questions*, http://www.fms.treas.gov/cmia/questions.html (last visited Oct. 31, 2011).

310. 31 U.S.C. § 6503(a)(1), (2) (2010).

311. 31 C.F.R. § 205.12(b)(4).

312. *See HUD Policy to comply with the Cash Management Improvement Act*, available at http://www.hud.gov/offices/cfo/policies/cfopol1.cfm (last visited Oct. 31, 2011).

313. *See id.*

314. *See Line of Credit Control System (LOCCS) for HUD staff*, *available at* http://www.docstop.com/docs/7480963/Line-of-Credit-Control-System-(LOCCS)–For HUD-Staff (last visited Oct. 31, 2011); *see also Integrated Disbursement and Information System (IDIS) OnLine Quick Tips User Guide*, *available at* http://www.hud.gov/offices/cpd/systems/idis/IDIS_Online_Quick_Tips_User_Guide_v3.pdf (last visited Feb. 27, 2012).

The regulations at 24 C.F.R. part 84 and 24 C.F.R. part 85 (collectively, Parts 84 and 85) govern the implementation of federal grants and agreements with various types of institutions, organizations, and governments. These regulations set forth uniform requirements for financial management systems, reports, and records, and grant closeouts for recipients of federal grant funding. Subjects covered in Parts 84 and 85 include financial management standards, budget controls, accounting controls, cash management, and procurement and contracting.

VIII. REGULATORY WAIVERS

The Secretary of HUD, or his or her designee, has authority to waive any HUD regulations at Title 24 of the *Code of Federal Regulations* pursuant to the HUD Reform Act of 1989 on determination of good cause and subject to statutory limitations.[315] Unless specified in the statute, the Secretary is not authorized to waive statutory provisions.

Any waiver of HUD regulations must be in writing and specify the grounds for approving the waiver.[316] The Secretary may, and generally does, delegate the waiver authority to an individual of Assistant Secretary or equivalent rank.[317] The Secretary also must notify the public of all waivers of regulations approved by HUD through publication in the *Federal Register* at least quarterly.[318]

HUD Field Office program directors also have the authority to waive provisions of HUD Handbooks without the Secretary's approval. Any waiver of a provision of a HUD Handbook must be in writing and must specify the grounds for approving the waiver.[319] All waivers must be maintained in indexed form and made available for public inspection for at least three years beginning on the date of the waiver.[320] HUD Guidebooks need not be waived, as they are considered suggested policies, and adherence to them is not mandatory.

Notice PIH-2009-41, for example, sets forth the current processing procedure for public housing–related waiver requests.[321] The waiver request and good-cause justification must be presented to the HUD Field Office, which then completes a checklist and makes a recommendation.[322] HUD Headquarters then prepares a final determination, which is reviewed by the HUD OGC and then submitted for execution by the Assistant Secretary for Public and Indian Housing.[323] A more streamlined procedure is used for mixed-finance waivers that are processed by the Office of Public Housing Investments.[324]

IX. ENERGY STAR/ENERGY-EFFICIENCY PROGRAMS

The Energy Star program, also discussed in Chapter 15, was started in 1992 by the U.S. Environmental Protection Agency (EPA) and currently operates as a joint program with the

---

315. 42 U.S.C. § 3535(q) (2010); 24 C.F.R. § 5.110 (2010).
316. *Id.*
317. *Id.*
318. *Id.*
319. *Id.*
320. *Id.*
321. Notice PIH-2009-41.
322. *Id.*
323. *Id.*
324. *Id.*

U.S. Department of Energy (DOE).[325] The goal of the Energy Star program is the reduction of greenhouse gas emissions by providing information about the energy efficiency of consumer goods through the implementation of a labeling program.[326] The Energy Star program originally labeled computers and computer monitors to identify energy-efficient models and it has been expanded to include the labeling of office equipment, residential heating and cooling equipment, major appliances, lighting, and home electronics.[327] The Energy Star label also can be earned by new homes[328] and commercial buildings.[329]

In 2005, HUD partnered with the EPA and the DOE to form the Partnerships for Home Energy Efficiency (PHEE), a program aimed to reduce home energy costs by 10 percent over 10 years.[330] A key component of PHEE is the promotion of energy efficiency in affordable housing.[331] HUD promotes the Energy Star program and energy efficiency in several of its affordable housing grant programs, as well as in the Public and Indian Housing program, by encouraging the use of Energy Star–qualified products and practices when HUD grantees or Public Housing Authorities or Indian Housing Authorities (PHA/IHAs) rehabilitate existing housing or construct new homes.[332] HUD provides several tools for grantees and PHA/IHAs to utilize when developing rehabilitated or newly constructed affordable housing.

A. Public and Indian Housing

HUD offers incentives to PHA/IHAs to develop energy-efficient housing by permitting authorities to use funds to pay for other capital expenses that would otherwise be used to pay for energy costs. There are several methods for PHA/IHAs to take advantage of HUD's cost-saving programs:

- Under the Three-Year Rolling Base incentive, PHA/IHAs can phase out utility cost savings from energy conservation over a four-year period, resulting in the PHA/IHA retaining 150 percent of the value of the first year's cost savings.[333]
- PHA/IHAs can enter into an Energy Performance Contract (EPC), under which a PHA/IHA installs energy-conservation measures (ECMs) to improve energy efficiency. HUD will freeze the three-year rolling base utility consumption at the level of the PHA/IHA prior to installation of the ECMs, and the PHA/IHA uses the cost savings to

---

325. *See* Energy Policy and Conservation Act § 324a, 42 U.S.C. § 6294a (2010).
326. *Id.*
327. *See* History: ENERGY STAR, http://www.energystar.gov/index.cfm?c=about.ab_history (last visited Sept. 12, 2011).
328. *See* Qualified New Homes, http://www.energystar.gov/index.cfm?c=new_homes.hm_index (last visited Oct. 31, 2011).
329. *See* The ENERGY STAR for Buildings & Manufacturing Plants, http://www.energystar.gov/index.cfm?c=business.bus_bldgs (last visited Oct. 31, 2011).
330. *See* Energy Policy Act of 2005 § 154, 42 U.S.C. § 15842 (2010); *see also* U.S. Dep't of Housing and Urban Development Notice PIH 2005-25 (PHA) (issued July 13, 2005).
331. *See Partnerships for Home Energy Efficiency: An Overview*, http://www.energystar.gov/ia/home_improvement/PHEE_Overview_final.pdf (last visited Oct. 31, 2011).
332. *See* Energy Policy Act of 2005 § 152, 42 U.S.C. § 15842 (2010).
333. *See* 24 C.F.R. § 990.180(c) (2011).

pay off the cost of the installation of the ECMs. PHA/IHAs who enter into an EPC can also request additional subsidy from HUD, which would be applied to amortizing payments under the EPC, so long as the cost savings from the ECMs exceeds the amount of the "add-on" subsidy. The term of the EPC must not exceed 20 years.[334]

- If a PHA/IHA realizes cost savings from actions it has taken that result in lower payments for utilities, the PHA/IHA may retain half of the first year's cost savings with HUD approval.[335]

B. Affordable Housing Grant Programs

HUD encourages grantees of several of its affordable housing grant programs, including the CDBG program, HOPE VI, and the HOME program, to include energy-efficiency measures in their affordable housing efforts. Affordable housing built with CDBG, HOPE VI, or HOME funds can incorporate Energy Star into the new construction or substantial rehabilitation of affordable housing by specifying Energy Star–qualified products. To assist in this effort, HUD provides information to grantees about how to find rebates in their local areas for Energy Star–qualified projects.[336] Grantees also are encouraged to develop residential buildings that meet the Energy Star building standards.[337] For a residential building to meet Energy Star building standards, it must be verified to be at least 30 percent more energy-efficient than homes built to the 1993 national Model Energy Code, or at least 15 percent more energy-efficient than the state energy code, whichever is more rigorous.[338]

X. SECTION 3

Section 3 of the Housing and Urban Development Act of 1968 (Section 3) and its implementing regulations[339] help foster local economic development, neighborhood economic improvement, and individual self-sufficiency.[340] Section 3 requires that recipients of certain HUD

---

334. *See* U.S. HUD Notice PIH-2011-36 (HA) (issued July 8, 2011); *see also* 24 C.F.R. § 990.185 (2011).
335. *See* 24 C.F.R. § 990.185(b) (2011).
336. *See* How to Promote ENERGY STAR Through CDBG, http://hud.gov/energystar/cdbg.cfm (last visited Aug. 29, 2011); How to Promote ENERGY STAR Through HOME Investment Partnership Program, http://hud.gov/energystar/home.cfm (last visited Aug. 29, 2011); How to Promote ENERGY STAR Through HOPE VI, http://hud.gov/energystar/hope.cfm (last visited Aug. 29, 2011); How to Promote ENERGY STAR Through HOME Investment Partnership Program, http://hud.gov/energystar/home.cfm (last visited Aug. 29, 2011); How to Promote ENERGY STAR Through Public and Indian Housing, http://hud.gov/energystar/pih.cfm (last visited Aug. 29, 2011).
337. *Id. [au: to which?]*
338. *See* How to Promote ENERGY STAR Through CDBG, http://hud.gov/energystar/cdbg.cfm (last visited Aug. 29, 2011); How to Promote ENERGY STAR Through HOME Investment Partnership Program, http://hud.gov/energystar/home.cfm (last visited Aug. 29, 2011); How to Promote ENERGY STAR Through HOPE VI, http://hud.gov/energystar/hope.cfm (last visited Aug. 29, 2011); How to Promote ENERGY STAR Through HOME Investment Partnership Program, http://hud.gov/energystar/home.cfm (last visited Aug. 29, 2011).
339. *See* 24 C.F.R. § 135.
340. 12 U.S.C. § 1701u (2010).

financial assistance and their contractors, to the greatest extent feasible, provide job training, employment, and contracting opportunities to low-income and very low-income residents and businesses that substantially employ these persons in connection with projects and activities in their neighborhoods.[341] Recipients of HUD funds are expected to make every effort to comply with the regulatory requirements of Section 3 by implementing effective notification procedures for employment and contracting opportunities that specifically target Section 3 residents and businesses.

A. Applicability

Before complying with Section 3 requirements, recipients of HUD funds must verify the applicability and scope of such requirements. Section 3 requirements apply to a broad range of HUD recipients and activities.

Section 3 is applicable to all direct and indirect recipients of HUD funds, including, but not limited to, public housing authorities, private agencies and institutions, units of state or local government, property owners, developers, public or private nonprofit organizations, and resident councils.[342] Recipients also include any successors, assignees, or transferees of any entity mentioned above, but do not include any ultimate beneficiaries under the HUD program to which Section 3 applies or contractors.[343]

Section 3 covered assistance includes Public and Indian Housing development, operating, and modernization assistance and certain housing and community development assistance.[344] Section 3 projects and activities involve the construction or rehabilitation of housing or other public construction, including buildings or improvements assisted with housing or community development assistance.[345]

Section 3 is triggered when the completion of construction and rehabilitation projects, as described above, creates the need for new employment, contracting, or training opportunities.[346] However, recipients of HUD funds are not required to hire Section 3 residents or award contracts to Section 3 businesses, other than what is needed to complete construction and rehabilitation projects and activities.[347] Therefore, if the expenditure of Section 3 covered assistance does not result in new employment, contracting, or training opportunities, the requirements of Section 3 have not been triggered. In addition, Section 3 requirements apply to the entire project or activity that is funded with Section 3 assistance, regardless of whether the activity is fully or partially funded with Section 3 covered assistance.[348]

---

341. 24 C.F.R. § 135.1(a) (2010). Low- and very low-income household limits are determined annually by HUD. These limits are typically established at 80% and 50%, respectively, of the median income for each locality by household size.
342. 24 C.F.R. § 135.5 (2010).
343. *Id.*
344. 24 C.F.R. § 135.3(a)(1), (2) (2010).
345. 24 C.F.R. § 135.5 (2010).
346. Annual Section 3 Summary Reporting Requirements for Recipients of HUD Community Planning and Development Funding, Technical Assistance on Form HUD-60002.
347. *Id.*
348. 24 C.F.R. § 135.3(b) (2010).

B. Thresholds

For certain types of HUD assistance, threshold expenditure amounts trigger the applicability of Section 3. In other cases, there is no expenditure threshold.

There is no threshold amount for the applicability of Section 3 covered public housing assistance.[349] As such, Section 3 requirements apply whenever a HUD recipient or its contractor generates new employment, training, or contracting opportunities for construction or rehabilitation projects.

Threshold amounts do apply, however, for HUD-funded housing and community development assistance. Section 3 requirements apply to recipients of housing and community development funds exceeding $200,000 combined from all sources in any one year.[350] Any recipient that receives community development funds exceeding $200,000 must comply with Section 3 requirements regardless of the actual dollar amount of covered assistance that is invested in the individualized project or activity. All contracts or subcontractors that receive covered contracts in excess of $100,000 for Section 3 covered projects and activities, as described in Section 9(a) above, also must comply with Section 3 requirements.[351]

C. Compliance Requirements

To meet Section 3 requirements, HUD recipients and their contractors must hire a certain percentage of Section 3 residents and contract with a certain percentage of Section 3 businesses.

Section 3 residents include public housing residents or low-income or very low-income persons residing in the metropolitan area or non-metropolitan county where the Section 3 covered assistance is expended.[352] Section 3 businesses include businesses that (1) are 51 percent or more owned by Section 3 residents, (2) employ Section 3 residents for at least 30 percent of their full-time permanent staff, or (3) provide evidence of a commitment to subcontract 25 percent or more of the dollar amount of the awarded contracts to Section 3 business concerns.[353]

HUD considers recipients and contractors in compliance with Section 3 if they meet the minimum numerical goals set forth in the regulations: (1) 30 percent of the aggregate number of new hires must be Section 3 residents; (2) 10 percent of the total dollar amount of all covered construction contracts must be subcontracted to Section 3 business concerns; and (3) three percent of the total dollar amount of all covered nonconstruction contracts must be awarded to Section 3 business concerns.[354]

---

349. 24 C.F.R. § 135.3(a)(3) (2010).
350. *Id.* Housing and community-development programs include the following: CDBG; Home Investment Partnership Assistance, Housing Opportunities for Persons with Aids (HOPWA); Economic Development Initiative (EDI); Brownfield Economic Development Initiative (BEDI); Emergency Shelter Grants; Homeless Assistance; University Partnership Grants; Neighborhood Stimulus Program (NSP); Certain Grants Awarded under HUD Notices of Funding Availability (NOFAs).
351. 24 C.F.R. § 135.3(a)(3) (2010).
352. 24 C.F.R. § 135.5 (2010).
353. *Id.*
354. 24 C.F.R. § 135.30(b)–(c) (2010).

HUD recipients must ensure their own compliance and the compliance of their contractors and subcontractors with Section 3 requirements. This responsibility includes, but is not limited to, the following: (1) designing and implementing procedures to ensure that all parties, including residents, businesses, contractors, and subcontractors, comply with Section 3; (2) facilitating the training and employment of Section 3 residents; (3) facilitating the award of contracts to Section 3 businesses; (4) ensuring contractor and subcontractor awareness of Section 3 requirements; (5) ensuring compliance with numerical goals by assessing the hiring and subcontracting needs of contractors, regularly monitoring contractor compliance, assisting and actively cooperating with the Secretary of HUD in obtaining the compliance of contractors, penalizing noncompliance, providing incentives for good performance, and refraining from entering into contracts with any contractor that previously failed to comply with the requirements of Section 3; and (6) documenting all actions taken to comply with Section 3 requirements.[355]

HUD recipients and contractors who meet the numerical goals above are considered to have complied with Section 3 requirements.[356] HUD recipients or contractors who fail to meet the numerical goals have the burden of demonstrating why compliance was not feasible.[357]

The types of opportunities available under Section 3 include job training, employment, and contracts. These opportunities encompass a broad range from architecture to information technology to marketing. Section 3 does not apply to contracts for the purchase of supplies and materials, unless the contract also provides for the installation of the materials.[358] HUD recipients and their contractors are encouraged to provide all types of employment opportunities, including permanent and long-term jobs.

For training and employment opportunities, the following Section 3 residents receive priority: (1) persons in public and assisted housing, (2) persons in the areas where the HUD funds are expended, (3) participants in HUD YouthBuild programs, and (4) homeless persons.[359] For contracting opportunities, businesses that meet the definition of "Section 3 business," as described above, receive priority.[360]

Businesses may recruit Section 3 residents in public housing developments and in neighborhoods where HUD assistance is being spent. Effective ways to do so include: contacting resident organizations and local community development employment agencies, distributing flyers, posting signs, and placing ads in local newspapers. The regulations provide an extensive list of examples of efforts to offer training and employment opportunities to Section 3 residents, examples of efforts to award contracts to Section 3 businesses, and examples of procurement procedures that provide for preference for Section 3 business concerns.[361]

---

355. 24 C.F.R. § 135.32 (2010).
356. 24 C.F.R. § 135.30(d)(1) (2010).
357. 24 C.F.R. § 135.30(d)(2) (2010).
358. 24 C.F.R. § 135.5 (2010).
359. 24 C.F.R. § 135.34(a) (2010).
360. 24 C.F.R. § 135.36(a)(1)(i) (2010).
361. 24 C.F.R. § 135 Appx. (2010).

D. Reporting and Monitoring

To ensure compliance with Section 3 requirements, HUD receives annual reports from recipients and monitors the performance of contractors. HUD examines employment and contract records for evidence of actions taken to train and employ Section 3 residents and to award contracts to Section 3 businesses.[362]

E. Complaints

Section 3 residents, businesses, or their representatives may file written complaints with their local HUD Field Offices or the Assistant Secretary for Fair Housing and Equal Opportunity for alleged violations of Section 3 requirements. A written complaint should contain (1) the name and address of the person filing the complaint, (2) the name and address of the HUD recipient, contractor, or subcontractor that is the subject of the complaint, (3) a description of acts or omissions in alleged violation of Section 3, and (4) a statement of the corrective action sought. A complaint that cannot be resolved voluntarily may result in an administrative hearing.

XI. CONCLUSION

A wide range of affordable housing and community development funding opportunities are available through HUD. With each of these opportunities comes a variety of regulatory requirements to layer on the project. Diligence in analyzing applicable requirements and confirming compliance helps ensure a successful project. To that end, our hope is that the foregoing may provide a helpful foundation.

---

362. 24 C.F.R. § 135.90 (2010).

Civil Rights Programs Administered and Enforced by HUD

14

Harry Carey

This chapter examines the civil rights programs administered and enforced by the Department of Housing and Urban Development (HUD or Department). The chapter describes the historical context of civil rights in the area of housing; discusses the non-discrimination requirements in current civil rights laws; summarizes the enforcement of civil rights under the Federal Fair Housing Act and other civil rights authorities; and outlines other civil rights requirements applicable in HUD programs and activities.

I. HISTORY OF CIVIL RIGHTS IN HOUSING

The right of persons to be free from discrimination in real estate transactions and contracts begins with post–Civil War legislation known as the Civil Rights Act of 1866.[1] These protections against racial discrimination are based on the constitutional protections in the Thirteenth and Fourteenth Amendments.

In 1896, in the case of *Plessy v. Ferguson*,[2] the United States Supreme Court established the doctrine of "separate but equal." In its decision, the Court held that a State of Louisiana statute requiring railroad companies to provide separate (but equal) accommodations for white and colored passengers was not in conflict with the Thirteenth and Fourteenth Amendments.

The doctrine of "separate but equal" remained until the 1954 decision in *Brown v. Board of Education*.[3] However, during the almost 60 years where

---

1. *See* 42 U.S.C. §§ 1981 and 1982.
2. Plessy v. Ferguson, 163 U.S. 537 (1896).
3. Brown v. Bd. of Educ., 347 U.S. 483 (1954).

separate but equal was the rule, three noteworthy Supreme Court decisions were issued pertaining to the area of protections from discrimination in housing.

In *Buchanan v. Warley*,[4] the Supreme Court struck down a criminal ordinance in Louisville, Kentucky, prohibiting blacks and whites from occupying houses on blocks in which their race did not predominate. The Court held that "the Fourteenth Amendment and these Statutes (42 U.S.C. sections 1981 and 1982) enacted in furtherance of its purpose operate to qualify and entitle a colored man to acquire property without state legislation discriminating against him solely because of color." However, the Court also distinguished between its decision and the "separate but equal" doctrine in *Plessy* providing for separation where equal privileges are provided. Thus, this decision only made a partial inroad into the *Plessy* doctrine.

In *Shelley v. Kraemer*,[5] the Supreme Court examined state judicial enforcement of restrictive covenants on privately owned property that limited the use or occupancy of the property to white persons. The Court found that, as long as the restrictions are effectuated by voluntary adherence to their terms, there would not be state action involving a violation of the Fourteenth Amendment. However, the Court did hold that judicial enforcement of restrictive covenants did involve State action and that such enforcement activity would violate the constitutional protections provided under the Fourteenth Amendment. In a companion case, *Hurd v. Hodge*,[6] involving the judicial enforcement of restrictive covenants in federal court in the District of Columbia, the Court also found that federal judicial enforcement of racially restrictive covenants in federal courts violated the Civil Rights Act of 1866.

The decade of the 1960s saw advances to civil rights in a number of areas.

In the area of housing, these actions began with Executive Order 11,063.[7] In this Executive Order, President Kennedy prohibited discrimination in certain housing provided through or owned by the federal government. During this decade, Congress also enacted the Civil Rights Act of 1964[8] and the Civil Rights Act of 1968.[9]

The 1964 Civil Rights Act prohibited discrimination in places of public accommodation; required desegregation in public facilities; provided for equal employment opportunities; and prohibited discrimination based on race, color, and national origin in federally assisted programs.[10]

The 1968 Civil Rights Act prohibited interfering with persons engaged in federally protected activities. Title VIII[11] and Title IX[12] of the Civil Rights Act of 1968 provided civil and criminal protections for discrimination against individuals relating to housing based on race,

---

4. Buchanan v. Warley, 245 U.S. 60 (1917).
5. Shelley v. Kraemer, 334 U.S. 1 (1948).
6. Hurd v. Hodge, 334 U.S. 24 (1948).
7. Exec. Order 11,063, Equal Opportunity in Housing, 27 Fed. Reg. 11,527, Nov. 20, 1962, as amended by Exec. Order 12,259, Leadership and Coordination of Fair Housing in Federal Programs, 46 Fed. Reg. 1253, Jan. 6, 1980.
8. Civil Rights Act of 1964. Pub. L. 88-352, 78 Stat. 241, 42 U.S.C. § 2000a.
9. 42 U.S.C. § 3601 *et seq.*
10. 42 U.S.C. § 2000a.
11. 42 U.S.C. § 3601 *et seq.*
12. 42 U.S.C. § 3631.

color, religion, or national origin in most public and private transactions relating to housing.[13] In the fair housing provisions of the Civil Rights Act of 1968, Congress also recognized the critical role that state and local agencies can assume when they administer laws that the Secretary of HUD determines provide rights and remedies substantially equivalent to those in the federal law.[14]

The expansion of civil rights protections from discrimination also continued in the early 1970s.

In 1973, Congress extended the protections from discrimination in federal financial assistance programs to persons with disabilities. Specifically, in Section 504 of the Rehabilitation Act of 1973, Congress made it unlawful to discriminate against otherwise qualified persons over their access to or participation in programs of federal financial assistance solely because of disability.[15]

Also, in consolidating many of the Department of Housing Urban Development categorical grant programs into a Community Development Block Grant (CDBG) program in the Housing and Community Development Act of 1974,[16] Congress included protections from discrimination for participants and beneficiaries of funding in Section 109 of Act.[17]

In the Age Discrimination Act of 1975, Congress added protections to persons who are subject to limitations and discrimination based on age.[18]

Finally, Congress enacted the Fair Housing Amendments Act of 1988.[19] The Fair Housing Amendments Act of 1988 created a new administrative enforcement mechanism, added two new protected classes of persons, and strengthened the penalties that can be assessed where violations are found. The measure also adopted a common term for Title VIII of the Civil Rights Act of 1968 and the Fair Housing Amendments Act (the Fair Housing Act[20]).

The passage of the Fair Housing Amendments Act of 1988 was the most important development in housing discrimination law in 20 years.

The Fair Housing Amendments Act of 1988 created a new enforcement mechanism for handling administrative complaints under the Fair Housing Act.[21] The Act added families with children and people with disabilities to the groups protected by the law,[22] created "housing for older persons," and exempted such housing from the familial status provisions of the Act.[23]

---

13. In 1974, the classes of groups protected under Title VIII of the Civil Rights Act of 1968 expanded to include protections from discrimination based on sex. Pub. L. 93-383.
14. 42 U.S.C. § 3610(f).
15. § 504 of the Rehabilitation Act of 1973 (29 U.S.C. § 794).
16. Pub. L.93-383; 88 Stat. 633; 42 U.S.C. § 530 *et seq.*
17. Section 109 of the Act (42 U.S.C. § 5309) now prohibits discrimination based on race, color, national origin, religion, or sex in any activities funded in whole or in part with CDBG funds. This section also mandates that recipients of CDBG funds also comply with the Age Discrimination Act of 1975 and Section 504 of the Rehabilitation Act of 1973.
18. 42 U.S.C. § 6101.
19. Fair Housing Act Amendments, Pub. L.100-430, 102 Stat. 1619 (1988).
20. *See* 42 U.S.C. § 3601 note.
21. 42 U.S.C. § 3610.
22. 42 U.S.C. §§ 3604, 3605, 3606, and 3618.
23. 42 U.S.C. § 807(b)(2).

The Fair Housing Amendments Act of 1988 also clarified the ban on discrimination in residential financing on a wide range of "real-estate related transactions,"[24] and it expanded the definition of "discriminatory housing practice" to include interference and intimidation claims under Section 818.[25]

The Act created a new administrative enforcement process, extended the statute of limitations in private lawsuits from 180 days to two years, eliminated the $1,000 cap on punitive damages in private lawsuits, liberalized the attorney's fees provision in private lawsuits, and strengthened the damages that can be awarded in both administrative and federal lawsuits brought by the Secretary of HUD and the Department of Justice.[26]

The Act also authorized the Secretary of HUD to seek prompt judicial action and provided for civil penalties and damage awards to persons aggrieved in administrative proceedings brought by the government.[27]

Further, the Act required HUD to submit annual reports to Congress about the nature and extent of housing discrimination in the United States and about the demographic makeup of people residing in federally assisted housing.[28] HUD was then directed to promptly issue regulations to implement and interpret the Fair Housing Act, as amended.[29]

The Secretary of Housing and Urban Development published implementing regulations that took effect on the day that the Fair Housing Amendments Act of 1988 became effective. The HUD substantive regulations are codified in 24 C.F.R. Part 100.[30]

One final legislative change to the Fair Housing Act occurred in 1996, when Congress amended the Act and the Equal Credit Opportunity Act to permit lenders to conduct self-testing of their practices.

II. CURRENT CIVIL RIGHTS REQUIREMENTS IN HOUSING AND COMMUNITY DEVELOPMENT PROGRAMS AND ACTIVITIES

A. Title VI of the Civil Rights Act of 1964

The Civil Rights Act of 1964[31] prohibits discrimination in a broad range of activities, including the denial of federal assistance in programs and activities receiving funds based on race, color, or national origin.[32] Title VI makes it unlawful to exclude persons from, deny the benefits of, or discriminate in any manner in federally assisted programs and activities on the basis of race, color, or national origin.

Title VI, generally, is enforced by the federal agency dispensing the federal funding. An individual lawsuit may be brought under Title VI, which requires every federal department

---

24. 42 U.S.C. § 3605.
25. 42 U.S.C. § 3602.
26. 42 U.S.C. § 3613(c).
27. 42 U.S.C. § 3610(e).
28. 42 U.S.C. § 3608 (e)(6).
29. 42 U.S.C. § 3601 note.
30. The Supreme Court has held that these regulations are substantive and are to be accorded *Chevron* deference. Meyer v. Holley, 537 U.S. 280 (2003).
31. 42 U.S.C. § 2000 *et seq.*
32. 42 U.S.C. § 2000(a).

and agency to promulgate rules and orders of general applicability consistent with their programs of assistance.[33] To provide a basic framework for describing the general responsibilities and enforcement procedures for all federal agencies, the President directed all federal agencies to adopt uniform regulations of a lead agency.

The regulations HUD issued implement the general provisions of Title VI,[34] describe the nondiscrimination requirements of Title VI of the Civil Rights Act of 1964, and contain specific examples of the conduct that would constitute a violation of Title VI in HUD programs and activities.[35]

When uniform regulations were published, they included provisions relating to the need for corrective actions to both ameliorate present issues and remedy past conduct. The regulations contained corrective action to address past discrimination through affirmative action. They also included a requirement that recipients of agency assistance in programs that had previously discriminated against persons on the ground of race, color, or national origin, take affirmative action to overcome the effects of prior discrimination. The uniform regulations also stated that even in the absence of such prior discrimination, a recipient in administering a program should take affirmative action to overcome the effects of conditions that resulted in limiting participation by persons of a particular race, color, or national origin.[36]

The issuance of Executive Order 11063, the passage of the Civil Rights Act of 1964, and the publication of a common rule for federal agencies resulted in efforts to make significant changes in the Federal Public Housing Program. These efforts were designed to address discrimination in all federal programs.

B. Section 504 of the Rehabilitation Act of 1973

In the Rehabilitation Act of 1973, Congress extended protections in federal programs and activities to persons with disabilities. Specifically, Section 504 of the Rehabilitation Act prohibited discrimination in programs and activities receiving federal financial assistance. As with the implementation of Title VI of the Civil Rights Act of 1964, agencies were charged with publishing uniform rules tailored to agency programs and activities, designed not only to prohibit discriminatory denials of benefits but also to ensure that programs and activities were accessible to, and usable by, persons with disabilities.

The Department of Housing and Urban Development published its final rules implementing Section 504 in June of 1988.[37] Like the HUD regulations under Title VI of the Civil Rights Act of 1964, the HUD Section 504 regulation[38] covers both the discriminatory conduct that is prohibited[39] and specific requirements for program accessibility.[40]

The program accessibility requirements in the regulation describe a recipient's obligation to make housing accessible with regard to new construction,[41] alterations of existing hous-

---

33. 42 U.S.C. § 2000(d)(1).
34. See 24 C.F.R. pt. 1.
35. 24 C.F.R. § 1.4.
36. 24 C.F.R. § 1.4(b)(6).
37. 53 Fed. Reg. 20,214, June 2, 1988. These regulations are codified in 24 C.F.R. pt. 8.
38. 24 C.F.R. pt. 8.
39. 24 C.F.R. § 8.4.
40. 24 C.F.R. subpt. C.
41. 24 C.F.R. § 8.22.

ing,[42] and operation of existing housing programs.[43] The regulation indicates that the accessibility standards for compliance with regard to design, construction, or alteration of buildings will be the Uniform Federal Accessibility Standards (UFAS).[44]

In addition, the regulation contains requirements for making reasonable accommodations to policies and alterations to facilities to assure equal use and enjoyment of the facility and the individual dwelling units. With regard to alterations, the definition of accessibility provides:

> When a unit in an existing facility is being made accessible as a result of alterations intended for use by a specific qualified individual with handicaps (e.g., a current occupant of such unit or another unit under the control of the same recipient, or an applicant on a waiting list), the unit will be deemed accessible if it meets the requirements of applicable standards that address the particular disability or impairment of such person.[45]

HUD and the Department of Justice have taken the position that the responsibility for the cost of alterations to an existing facility receiving federal financial assistance must be borne by the recipient of the assistance (the housing or service provider). With regard to structural changes to a unit or common area in housing that receives federal financial assistance the agencies have concluded that the responsibility for making the alterations rests with the housing provider.[46]

C. Section 109 of the Housing and Community Development Act of 1974[47]

Prior to 1974, the Department of Housing and Urban Development provided grants and loans for a wide range of community development activities, including major programs such as the Model Cities Program and the Urban Renewal Program, and others such as Community Planning Development Grants and Water and Sewer Grants. Many of the community development programs had selection procedures for making awards that included civil rights consid-

---

42. 24 C.F.R. § 8.23.
43. 24 C.F.R. § 8.24.
44. 41 C.F.R. subpt. 101-19.6 Appx. A.
45. 24 C.F.R. § 8.3. *See* definition of "accessible."
46. http://www.justice.gov/crt/about/hce/documents/reasonable_modifications_mar08.pdf. Question and answer 31 in part states:

> Housing that receives federal financial assistance is covered by both the Fair Housing Act and section 504 of the Rehabilitation Act of 1973. Under regulations implementing section 504, structural changes needed by an applicant or resident with a disability in housing receiving federal financial assistance are considered reasonable accommodations. They must be paid for by the housing provider unless providing them would be an undue financial and administrative burden or a fundamental alteration of the program or unless the housing provider can accommodate the individual's needs through other means.

47. 42 U.S.C. § 5309.

erations. These programs, like the public housing program and the subsidized housing programs, were determined to constitute federal financial assistance and were thus subject to Title VI of the Civil Rights Act of 1964 and Section 504 of the Rehabilitation Act of 1973,[48] and, to the extent that they involved housing, they were also subject to Title VIII of the Civil Rights Act 1968.

In 1974, Congress enacted the Housing and Community Development Act of 1974 (HCDA), which rescinded several of the categorical grant programs and consolidated many others into a single grant in the Community Development Block Grant Program. In addition to the CDBG Program, the statute created the Home Investment Partnership, the Emergency Shelter Grant Program, and Housing Opportunities for Persons with AIDS.

All the programs and activities in the HCDA are considered to involve federal financial assistance and, thus, Title VI of the Civil Rights Act of 1964 applied. Further, Section 109 of the HCDA contained a nondiscrimination provision that was almost identical to the one in Title VI, except that Section 109 covers sex, age, and disability discrimination and provides for protections against discrimination in employment.

The CDBG Program not only states that activities must be conducted in accordance Title VI and Title VIII, but since 1983 also requires grantees to certify that they will affirmatively further fair housing in programs and activities funded. The HOME Program regulations also states that the statutory requirement from the Community Housing Affordability Strategy that funded HOME jurisdictions must affirmatively further fair housing.

D. The Fair Housing Act

1. Prohibited Conduct under the Fair Housing Act

The Fair Housing Act[49] prohibits unlawful discrimination in the sale, rental, advertising, financing, and brokering[50] of dwellings[51] based on race, color, religion, sex, national origin, familial status,[52] or handicap (although the Act refers to handicap, the term "disability" is

---

48. 42 U.S.C. § 2000(d) and 29 U.S.C. § 794.
49. 42 U.S.C. §§ 3601–3600, The Fair Housing Act or "The Act."
50. *See* §§ 804, 805, and 806. 42 U.S.C. §§ 3604–3606.
51. The Act defines a dwelling as "any building, structure, or portion thereof which is occupied as, or designed or intended for occupancy as, a residence by one or more families, and any vacant land which is offered for sale or lease for the construction or location thereon of any such building, structure, or portion thereof." 42 U.S.C. § 3602(b).
52. "'Familial status' means one or more individuals (who have not attained the age of 18 years) being domiciled with—
    (1) a parent or another person having legal custody of such individual or individuals, or
    (2) the designee of such parent or other person having such custody, with the written permission of such parent or other person.
    The protections afforded against discrimination on the basis of familial status shall apply to any person who is pregnant or is in the process of securing legal custody of any individual who has not attained the age of 18 years."
42 U.S.C. § 3602(k)

used to describe the protected class and individuals therein).[53] The Act also makes it unlawful to interfere, coerce, or intimidate persons engaged or assisting others to engage in activities protected under the Act.[54]

With regard to disability, the Act makes it unlawful to fail to make reasonable accommodations or to fail to permit reasonable modifications that permit disabled persons the opportunity to have full use and enjoyment of a dwelling; the Act also makes it unlawful to fail to design and construct certain new multifamily housing with several features of adaptive design.[55] The following discussion reviews the nondiscrimination provisions, the accommodation and modification provisions, the design and construction requirements, and the five exemptions to the coverage of the Act.

a. Sale, Rental, and Advertising Practices

The six provisions applying to sale, rental, and advertising practices are:

1. *Discrimination in the sale or rental of housing and other prohibited practices.*[56]
   The sale or rental protections deal with refusals to sell or rent, after the making of a bona fide offer, or to otherwise make unavailable or deny housing based on a person's membership in a protected class. The subsection is not limited to outright refusals, but extends to sales and rental techniques that make housing unavailable, including a failure to communicate an offer effectively, or denial of a bona fide offer upon learning of a person's protected status.

2. *Discrimination in the terms, conditions, or privileges of sale or rental of a dwelling.*[57]
   This subsection prohibits discrimination in the provision of services to tenants and purchasers after a sale or rental has occurred; and it prohibits a seller, landlord, or rental or sales agent from imposing—prior to or after the sale or rental—discriminatory privileges, terms, or conditions on prospective purchasers or renters who are members of a protected class, or associated with members of a protected class.

3. *Discrimination in advertisements, notices, and statements with respect to the sale or rental of a dwelling.*[58]
   This subsection makes it unlawful to "make, print, or publish, or cause to be made, printed, or published any notice, statement, or advertisement, with respect to the sale or rental of a dwelling that indicates any preference, limitation, or discrimination based on [membership in a protected class], or an intention to make any such prefer-

---

53. "'Handicap' means, with respect to a person—
    (1) a physical or mental impairment which substantially limits one or more of such person's major life activities,
    (2) a record of having such an impairment,
    (3) being regarded as having such an impairment. . . ."
42 U.S.C. § 3602(h)
54. 42 U.S.C. § 3617.
55. 42 U.S.C. § 3604(f)(3).
56. 42 U.S.C. § 3604.
57. 42 U.S.C. § 3604(b).
58. 42 U.S.C. § 3604(c).

ence, limitation, or discrimination." This prohibition applies both to verbal statements and to written statements, and it applies to the person or entity that makes the statement and to the entity that publishes it. It applies to advertisements and statements made in all types of media, including newspapers, magazines, television, radio, and the Internet.

4. *Misrepresentation that a dwelling is not available for inspection, sale, or rental, when such dwelling is in fact so available.*[59]

    This provision makes it unlawful to "represent to any person, because of [their protected status] that any dwelling is not available for inspection, sale, or rental when such dwelling is in fact so available." This rather simply worded provision has been recognized as providing a basis for testers to file complaint and civil actions.

5. *Engaging in panic peddling or blockbusting.*[60]

    This subsection prohibits, for profit, attempting to induce a person to sell or rent any dwelling by representations regarding the entry or prospective entry into a particular neighborhood. This subsection makes it unlawful "for profit, to induce or attempt to induce any person to sell or rent any dwelling by representations regarding the entry or prospective entry into the neighborhood of a person or persons [who is (are) a member (s) of a protected class]." The purpose of this section is "to prevent persons from preying on the fears of property owners and inducing panic selling resulting in monetary loss to the sellers and instability in the neighborhoods involved."

6. *Discrimination in the sale or rental of housing to any person based on disability.*[61]

    Section 804(f) of the Fair Housing Act contains additional prohibited conduct against persons because of disability related to the sale or rental of housing. Sections 804(f)(1) and (2) make it unlawful to discriminate because of a person's disability in the sale or rental of housing, or in the provision of services or facilities. The intent of these provisions is to provide persons with disabilities all of the same protections that are recognized for members of the traditional protected classes. In this respect, it should be noted that persons with disabilities are included in the protections regarding advertising, false information about availability, and blockbusting in Sections 804(c), (d), and (e).

b. Reasonable Accommodations and Reasonable Modifications[62]

The reasonable accommodations and reasonable modifications requirements augment the nondiscrimination protections for persons with disabilities in the sale or rental of housing by further defining actions and conduct that will be unlawful when taken on the basis of disability. These provisions reflect the concept that mere nondiscrimination may not provide a person with disabilities the same use and enjoyment of housing.

First, a landlord or housing provider must permit a disabled tenant or owner to make, at his expense, reasonable modifications or changes to the premises that are necessary to afford

---

59. 42 U.S.C. § 3604(d).
60. 42 U.S.C. § 3604(e).
61. 42 U.S.C. § 804(f)(1) & (2).
62. 42 U.S.C. § 804(f)(3)(A) & (B).

the handicapped persons full enjoyment of the premises. Such modifications might include installment of grab bars in the bathroom, lowering kitchen cabinets, widening a doorway to the tenant's laundry room, and installing a visual doorbell. However, these modications can also include changes to any of the facilities and services provided at the housing.

With regard to structural changes, Congress made it unlawful for a housing provider to refuse to permit reasonable modifications to premises, at the expense of a person requesting the modification, where the structural changes may be necessary to afford a person full enjoyment of the premises. A landlord may, where it is reasonable, require a tenant to restore the interior of the unit to its original condition, reasonable wear and tear excepted.[63]

On March 5, 2008, the Department of Housing and Urban Development and the Department of Justice issued a joint statement on the reasonable modifications provision in the Act. The joint statement is written in Question and Answer format and can be obtained on the Department of Justice, Civil Rights Division Website.[64]

Second, a landlord or housing provider cannot refuse to make reasonable changes in rules, policies services, or practices, when these accommodations are necessary to allow a person with a disability an equal opportunity to use and enjoy the housing.

With regard to policies, Congress made it unlawful for a housing provider to fail to make reasonable accommodations in rules, policies, practices, or services that may be necessary to afford a disabled person an equal opportunity to use and enjoy a dwelling.[65]

The Department of Housing and Urban Development and the Department of Justice have also issued a joint statement explaining their interpretation of the operation of the reasonable accommodations provision of the Act. This May 17, 2004, joint statement can be found on the Department of Housing and Urban Development, Office of Fair Housing and Equal Opportunity Website.[66] Under this guidance, a reasonable accommodations request must be granted unless there is an undue financial and administrative burden or there would be a fundamental alteration of the housing provider's program.

c. Failure to Design and Construct Certain New Multifamily Housing to Be Accessible to and Usable by Persons with Disabilities

The Act also contains a requirement for accessibility in the construction of new multifamily dwelling units.[67] Specifically, the Act makes unlawful the design and construction of certain multifamily dwellings[68] for first occupancy after March 13, 1991, that do not include enumerated adaptive features for disabled persons. The design and construction requirements include accessible and usable public and common use portions of the premises, doors that permit passage by persons in a wheelchair, an accessible route into and through dwellings,

---

63. 42 U.S.C. § 3604(f)(3)(A).
64 http://www.justice.gov/crt/about/hce/documents/reasonable_modifications_mar08.pdf.
65. 42 U.S.C. § 3604(f)(3)(B).
66. http://www.hud.gov/offices/fheo/library/huddojstatement.pdf.
67. 42 U.S.C. § 3604 (f)(3)(C).
68. 42 U.S.C. § 3604(f)(7) defines the multifamily dwellings covered as being all units in a building consisting of 4 or more units with one or more elevators or ground-floor units in other building consisting of four or more units.

accessible controls, reinforcements in bathroom walls for later installation of grab bars and usable kitchens and bathrooms.[69]

d. Discrimination in Residential Real Estate–Related Transactions

The provisions of the Fair Housing Act relating to discriminatory real estate related transactions in the Fair Housing Amendments Act were designed to clarify the provisions of the Civil Rights Act of 1968. The Act now more clearly describes the nature and scope of the discriminatory practices prohibited under the Act with regard to all aspects involved in the financing of housing and its rehabilitation.[70]

The provision describes residential real estate–related transactions as the "marking or purchasing of loans or providing other financial assistance (a) for purchasing, constructing, improving, repairing, or maintaining a dwelling; or (b) [that are] secured by residential real estate." Residential real estate transactions are also defined to include "the selling, brokering or appraising of residential real property." The activities covered also extend to activities in the secondary mortgage market as well as those in the primary mortgage market.

e. Discrimination in the Provision of Brokerage Services

The Act prohibits discrimination in provision of brokerage services with respect to membership or participation in multiple listing or other brokerage services, organizations or facilities, or the terms or conditions of participating in such activities.

f. Unlawful Interference, Coercion, and Intimidation[71]

This provision makes it unlawful to coerce, intimidate, threaten, or interfere with any person's exercise of his or her rights that are protected under sections 803, 804, 805, and 806 of the Act or to engage in such conduct with another person or organization that is assisting a person exercising fair housing rights.

2. Exemptions to the provisions of the Fair Housing Act

The Act contains five limited exemption to certain types of conduct made unlawful.

The first two exemptions relate to the coverage of sale or rental activities made unlawful under the Act. The exemptions, under Section 803(b) of the Act,[72] apply to the sale or rental of certain single-family dwellings by an owner[73] and to dwellings containing living quarters for no more than four families in which the owner occupies one of the units.[74] However, this exemption does not protect exempt owners from liability for making or publishing discrimi-

---

69. 42 U.S.C. § 3604(f)(3)(C)(i)–(iii). A detailed description of the requirements for the design and construction of newly constructed multifamily dwellings under the Act can be found at www.fairhousingfirst.org.
70. 42 U.S.C. § 3605.
71. 42 U.S.C. § 3617.
72. 42 U.S.C. § 3603(b).
73. 42 U.S.C. § 3603(b)(1).
74. 42 U.S.C. § 3603(b)(2).

natory notices advertisements or statements in connection with sales or rentals.[75] In addition, owners or renters who qualify for the single-family exemption can be liable to individual civil actions brought under the Civil Rights Act of 1866.[76]

Section 807 of the Act contains the remaining three exemptions. The first two limited exemptions relate to how certain housing religious organizations and private clubs operate.[77] The final exemption provides that the familial status protections[78] of the Act do not apply to housing for older persons.[79]

III. THE HUD PROCESS OF ENFORCEMENT IN CIVIL RIGHTS CASES

A. Programs of Federal Financial Assistance

The process for enforcement of Civil Rights requirements in programs receiving federal financial assistance is generally uniform for Title VI of the Civil Rights Act of 1964 (race,

---

75. *See* introductory language in 42 U.S.C. § 3603(b) (42 U.S.C. § 3603(b) and § 3604(c) of the Act.
76. *See* Jones v. Mayer, 392 U.S. 409 (1968).
77. 42 U.S.C. § 3607(a) provides:

> Nothing in this subchapter shall prohibit a religious organization association, or society or any nonprofit institution or organization operated, supervised or controlled by or in conjunction with a religious organization, association, or society from limiting the sale, rental or occupancy of dwellings which it owns or operates for other than a commercial purpose to persons of the same religion, or from giving preference to such persons, unless membership in such religion is restricted on account of race, color, or national origin.

With regard to private clubs, the section goes on to provide:

> Nor shall anything in this subchapter prohibit a private club, not in fact open to the public, which as an incident to its primary purpose or purposes provides lodgings which it owns or operates for other than a commercial purpose, from limiting the rental or occupancy of such lodgings to its member or from giving preference to its members.

78. 42 U.S.C. § 3607(b)(1) provides that nothing in the Act limits the applicability of any reasonable local, state, or federal restrictions regarding the number of occupants permitted to occupy a dwelling. Although not an exemption, this provision caused confusion because there are few occupancy codes beyond those restricting the maximum number of persons (e.g., unrelated adults or fire safety limits). In 1991, then HUD General Counsel Frank Keating issued a memorandum describing the manner in which the Office of General Counsel would evaluate occupancy restriction for dwellings. The Keating Memo indicates that a policy of two persons per bedroom is presumed reasonable subject to a number of considerations, such as the unit type and size. The Occupancy Guidance Keating memo can found on the FHEO website at www.hud.gov/fheo/library under Policy and Guidance or at 63 Fed. Reg. 70,983, Dec. 22, 1998.
79. 42 U.S.C. § 3607(b)(2) defines three classes of housing for older persons. The first is provided under a state or federal program the Secretary of HUD determines is specifically designed and operated to assist elderly persons. The second is housing intended for, and solely occupied by, persons over the age of 62. The third is housing for occupancy by at least one person 55 or older. The housing must be occupied by at least 80% of 55 and older persons, be marketed as housing to serve age-qualified persons, and must use age-verification procedures for admission and occupancy.

color, and national origin), Section 504 of the Rehabilitation Act of 1973 (disability) and Section 109 of the Housing and Community Development Act of 1974 (race, color, sex, and national origin).[80] In November of 2004, HUD published a list of programs and activities involving federal financial assistance.[81]

The regulations for each civil rights authority applicable to federal assistance indicate that the responsible Department official[82] can accept and investigate complaints of discrimination and, subject either to a complaint or on his or her own initiative, conduct a compliance review of recipients of operation of one or more funding programs or activities to determine whether they are in compliance with the nondiscrimination and other regulatory provisions in the law and regulations.[83]

If the responsible Department official finds that there may be a failure or threatened failure to comply with the civil rights requirements, the regulation requires notification of the recipient of apparent findings of noncompliance and the provision of an offer to respond to the apparent finding and to resolve the issues through informal efforts to achieve voluntary compliance through the execution and implementation of a Voluntary Compliance Agreement (VCA).[84]

If efforts to resolve the apparent findings cannot be resolved informally, the responsible Department official can make a formal finding of noncompliance and initiate formal enforcement action. The formal enforcement process includes initiation of either a formal administrative enforcement proceeding before an administrative tribunal seeking to terminate, limit, or reduce payments to the recipient, or a referral to the Department of Justice for the initiation of appropriate sanctions to terminate assistance or achieve compliance.[85]

B. The Fair Housing Act

The Fair Housing Act places the responsibility for administering and enforcing the Act on the Secretary of HUD.[86] The administrative enforcement process is for the receipt of complaints,

---

80. Section 109 also contains provisions making Age Discrimination Act and § 504 parts of the conduct prohibited in programs and activities funded in whole or in part with assistance.

81. 69 Fed. Reg. 6899, Nov. 24, 2004. The notice contains a listing of 60 active HUD programs and 14 inactive programs. The inactive programs are listed because the nondiscrimination requirements apply for as long as the housing or facility is operated for the purpose for which funding was provided to the recipient.

82. The Assistant Secretary for Fair Housing and Equal Opportunity is designated as the responsible Department official for Title VI, § 504, the Age Discrimination Act and § 109 of the Housing and Community Development Act of 1974.

83. See 24 C.F.R. § 1.7 (race, color, and national origin), 24 C.F.R. § 8.56 (disability), 24 C.F.R. § 146.35 and 36 (age), and 24 C.F.R. § 6.11 (nondiscrimination in programs and activities in programs and activities funded under Title I of the Housing and Community Development Act of 1974).

84. See 24 C.F.R. § 1.8, 24 C.F.R. § 8.57, 24 C.F.R. § 8.57.

85. See 24 C.F.R. pts. 1, 6, 8, and 146.

86. 42 U.S.C. § 3608(a). The Secretary, with the exception of final decision making and limited assignment of authority to the General Counsel, has delegated full authority with regard to the administration and enforcement of the Fair Housing Act to the Assistant Secretary for Fair Housing and Equal Opportunity.

as investigations and informal efforts to conciliate complaints are statutorily mandated.[87] The receipt and investigation of complaints is described in section 810.

Section 810 of the Fair Housing Act contains the requirement for the Secretary to engage in informal efforts to resolve complaints throughout the investigation process and directs that conciliation agreements between the parties be approved by the Secretary.[88] The statute also requires notification to respondents within 10 days of the filing of complaints[89] and completion of investigations within 100 days of receipt of the complaint as far as practicable.[90]

The Fair Housing Act[91] continues to provide for the referral of complainants to State and local agencies administering laws that, the Assistant Secretary for Fair Housing and Equal Opportunity determines, provide substantially equivalent rights and remedies to those provided in the revised Fair Housing Act. Where a state or local law is determined to have substantially equivalent rights and remedies, the Assistant Secretary is required to refer complaints under the Fair Housing Act to that agency for processing.

The Fair Housing Act provides that HUD take no action with respect to referred complaints unless:

- a certified agency failed to commence proceedings within 30 days of referral,
- having commenced proceedings, the agency failed to carry them forward with reasonable promptness, or
- HUD determines that the certified agency is no longer qualified for certification.

Under the statute and HUD regulations,[92] the determination of the Secretary to certify an agency is based on affirmative determinations in a two-part analysis. First, the Assistant Secretary must determine that the substantive rights, procedures, and remedies provided in the law or ordinance and their availability are substantially equivalent to those in the Fair Housing Act. Second, the Secretary must determine that the current practices and past performance of the agency demonstrate that, in operation, the law, in fact, provides rights and remedies that are substantially equivalent to those in the Fair Housing Act.

The Act requires that, at the close of an investigation, and if conciliation is not successful, the Secretary must issue a determination based solely on the facts as to whether there is "reasonable cause" to believe that a discriminatory housing practice has occurred.[93] The Secretary is also required, in the event of a determination that discrimination has occurred, to issue a Charge of Discrimination.[94]

---

87. 42 U.S.C. §§ 3610 and 3611.
88. HUD regulations (24 C.F.R. pt. 103, subpt. E) indicate that an approvable conciliation agreement should resolve all issues in the complaint; provide appropriate relief, such as out-of-pocket expenses, lost housing opportunities, and emotional damages; and contain relief in the public interest.
89. 42 U.S.C. § 3610(a)(1)(B).
90. 42 U.S.C. § 3610(a)(1)(C).
91. 42 U.S.C. § 3610(f).
92. 24 C.F.R. pt. 115.
93. 42 U.S.C. § 3610(f)(1).
94. 42 U.S.C. § 3610(f)(2).

After issuance, all parties to a complaint have the option of electing to have the case tried in federal court rather than before a HUD administrative law judge (ALJ). If a case proceeds before a HUD ALJ, the General Counsel of HUD brings the case on behalf of the complaint. If any party elects to go to federal court rather than to an ALJ, the Attorney General files the case in federal district court.

The Act authorizes the Secretary and the Department of Justice to seek extraordinary relief through prompt judicial action and the issuance of Temporary Restraining Orders in appropriate cases.[95]

The Act provides authority for the Secretary to issue subpoenas and order discovery in aid of investigations, and provides criminal penalties against persons who fail or neglect to cooperate or comply with the Secretary's investigation.

The Fair Housing Act provides a broad range of options where reasonable cause findings have been made. The Act describes the enforcement options available.[96] These options are designed to enhance the ability of complainants to seek enforcement in a case where they believe discrimination has occurred. Generally, the Fair Housing Act provides options for persons to seek relief administratively[97] and/or judicially[98] and to initiate their own civil actions,[99] and provides a federal opportunity to initiate or support enforcement of the Act.[100]

The Fair Housing Act established a new administrative enforcement mechanism for the trial of allegations of discrimination under the Act.[101]

---

95. 42 U.S.C. § 3610(e).
96. See 42 U.S.C. §§ 3612, 3613, and 3614.
97. After the issuance of a Finding of Reasonable Cause and a charge of discrimination, all parties (including each complainant and each respondent) have a 20-day opportunity to elect to have the case tried in federal court. If no election is filed, the case is tried before a HUD-designated ALJ. In the case of an election, HUD will refer the case to the Department of Justice to bring the civil action in federal district court on behalf of the complainant. (42 U.S.C. § 812).
98. Under the Fair Housing Act, a complainant or any person may commence a civil action in federal district court alleging a violation of the Act. A private civil action can be brought or maintained under the Act even if a finding of reasonable cause or an administrative proceeding has been commenced, as long as the administrative proceeding has not come to a hearing. (42 U.S.C. § 3613).
99. Section 813 provides for private enforcement in federal courts for persons aggrieved. Private individuals can bring civil actions with or without filing a complaint with HUD. In these cases the complainant can seek actual and punitive damages. The court may also appoint an attorney to represent the complainant. However, the court may award attorney's fees to a prevailing party in these proceedings. The statute of limitations for these cases is two years from the date of the last act of discrimination, except for the period of a pending administrative complaint tolls the limitation period. As discussed above, section 812 provides for elections for judicial enforcement where there is a determination of reasonable cause. However, this section also provides an opportunity for private individuals to file federal actions on their own under section 813.
100. Section 814 authorizes the Attorney General of the United States to file suit where one or more of the parties to a reasonable cause determination elects to seek federal district court action. This section also provides authority for the Attorney General to file cases where he has reasonable cause to believe that there is a "pattern or practice" of discrimination, where violations raise issues of "general public importance," or where civil actions are necessary to enforce HUD investigatory activity.
101. 42 U.S.C. § 3612.

Where no party to a charge of discrimination makes an election to have the case heard in federal district court, the fair housing case will be tried in an administrative proceeding before an administrative law judge.[102] In such a proceeding, the Act requires that the Federal Rules of Evidence will apply,[103] and the Department of Housing and Urban Development will prosecute the case on behalf of the aggrieved person(s).[104]

The Act requires the ALJ to commence a hearing within 120 days following the issuance of a charge unless it is impracticable to do so,[105] and to issue findings of fact and conclusions of law within 60 days of a hearing.[106]

When the ALJ finds that a respondent has engaged in a discriminatory housing practice, the Act provides for the issuance of an order for such relief as may be appropriate, including actual damages[107] and injunctive or other equitable relief, and may, to vindicate the public interest, assess a civil penalty against the respondent.[108]

The Secretary of Housing and Urban Development can review the decision of an ALJ, but unless the decision is revised within 30 days of issuance, the ALJ's decision becomes the final agency decision.[109]

Judicial review of the final decision of the Secretary of Housing and Urban Development is in the United States Court of Appeals where the discriminatory act occurred, and petitions for review must be filed within 30 days after the final order.[110]

In 1996, the Department adopted the administrative enforcement process for the Fair Housing Act to apply for complaints and compliance actions under Title VI of the Civil Right Act of 1964, Section 109 of the Housing and Community Development Act of 1974, the Age Discrimination Act of 1975, and Section 504 of the Rehabilitation Act of 1973.[111]

---

102. 42 U.S.C. § 3612(b).
103. 42 U.S.C. § 3612(c).
104. 42 U.S.C. § 3610(g)(2)(A).
105. 42 U.S.C. § 3610(g)(1).
106. 42 U.S.C. § 3610(g)(2).
107. Actual damages have generally been categorized in three distinct areas: out-of-pocket expenses, those quantifiable expenses associated with the discriminatory act; lost housing opportunities, those non-quantifiable damages associated with the specific dwelling, such as its location or amenities; and finally, emotional distress, such as humiliation and pain or suffering.
108. 42 U.S.C. § 3612(g)(3). The civil penalties permitted under the Act increase based on whether there have been additional violations within specified time periods.
109. This unique review procedure was intended to ensure that the administrative process speed would be an incentive to the federal court enforcement.
110. This procedure emphasizes the need for aggrieved persons and complainants to become parties to preserve their right to appeal, since the Secretary is not an appropriate party to appeal his or her own final decision in the administrative proceeding.
111. 24 C.F.R. pt. 180. While the Fair Housing Act process applies to federally assisted programs and activities, the consolidated hearing regulation recognizes that the sanctions and remedies available for federal assistance programs may be different from those available under the Fair Housing Act. 24 C.F.R. § 180.670.

IV. ADMINISTRATION OF HUD PROGRAMS AND ACTIVITIES

A. Executive Order 11,063

Executive Order 11,063 requires agencies, insofar as their programs relate to the provision of housing, to take all action necessary and appropriate to prevent discrimination because of race, color, religion, sex, or national origin. The Executive Order covers the sale, rental, leasing, or other disposition of residential property and related facilities owned and operated by the government, provided with loans or grants from the government, or provided with loans insured, guaranteed, or secured by the credit of the government.[112] The Executive Order also covers lending practices of institutions relating to loans insured or guaranteed by the government.[113]

Under the HUD regulations implementing the Executive Order,[114] the principal responsibility for implementing and enforcing the Executive Order is vested in the Assistant Secretary for Fair Housing and Equal Opportunity through complaint investigations and compliance reviews.[115]

Where the Assistant Secretary finds apparent noncompliance and cannot resolve the findings through voluntary efforts,[116] the violation can be sanctioned through the contract for the benefits provided or through the program sanctions contained in the statute or regulations under which the benefits are provided.[117]

In addition, the regulation provides for the initiation and conduct of an investigation or compliance review where the subject of the alleged Executive Order violations would also constitute a violation of Title VI of either the Civil Rights Act of 1964 or the Fair Housing Act.[118]

B. Affirmatively Furthering Fair Housing

The discussion of current fair housing laws and their enforcement highlighted the scope of Department of Housing and Urban Development's responsibility under civil rights laws and Executive Orders as extending beyond enforcement of nondiscrimination requirements and covering efforts to promote equal opportunity for the classes of persons protected under the statutes.

The Civil Rights Act of 1964[119] prohibited discrimination in a broad range of activities, including the denial of federal assistance in programs and activities receiving federal funds to persons based on race, color, or national origin.[120] Title VI makes it unlawful to exclude persons from, deny the benefits of, or discriminate in any manner in federally assisted programs and activities on the basis of race, color, or national origin.

---

112. *See* § 101 (a) of Exec. Order 11,063.
113. *See* § 101 (b) of Exec. Order 11,063.
114. 24 C.F.R. pt. 107.
115. 24 C.F.R. § 107.35.
116. 24 C.F.R. § 107.55.
117. 24 C.F.R. § 107.60.
118. 24 C.F.R. § 107.11.
119. 42 U.S.C. § 2000 *et seq.*
120. 42 U.S.C. § 2000(a).

Title VI required every federal department and agency to promulgate rules and orders of general applicability consistent with their programs of assistance. In order to provide a basic framework for describing the general responsibilities and enforcement procedures, the President directed all federal agencies to adopt uniform regulations of a lead agency.

When uniform regulations were published, they contained not only corrective action to address discrimination, but also included a requirement that recipients of agency assistance, in programs where a recipient has previously discriminated against persons on the ground of race, color, or national origin must take affirmative action to overcome the effects of prior discrimination. The uniform regulation also stated that even in the absence of such prior discrimination, a recipient in administering a program should take affirmative action to overcome the effects of conditions that resulted in limiting participation by persons of a particular race, color, or national origin.

As a result of the enactment of Title VIII of the Civil Rights Act of 1968, discrimination was prohibited both in federally assisted housing and in most private housing. However, not only discriminatory actions were included in the law. Under Title VIII, the Secretary of Housing and Urban Development also is charged with the responsibility to "administer the programs and activities relating to housing and urban development in a manner affirmatively to further the policies of this [Act]."[121]

Thus, the administration of the Civil Rights Acts of 1964 and 1968,extends beyond merely prohibiting discrimination. They both pointed to efforts to provide opportunities and prevent further discrimination and segregation.

The Third Circuit Court of Appeals in 1970, in *Shannon v. HUD,* 436 F. 2d 809 (3d Cir. 1970), clearly indicated the impact of the Fair Housing Act and Title VI of the Civil Rights Act of 1964 on federal programs beyond the principle of nondiscrimination. In that case, a group of residents in a Philadelphia neighborhood challenged the location of a HUD-subsidized project in its neighborhood, claiming that the project would result in a dramatic shift in the racial and economic character of their community.

At the time of the lawsuit, the HUD Title VI regulation provided only for consideration of the provision of nondiscriminatory housing for tenants. Specifically, the regulation required that project sites or locations should not be selected with the purpose or effect of excluding persons or denying them the benefits of federal assistance (24 C.F.R. § 1.4(b)(3)), Further, the policy of HUD then regarding siting of projects was that there should be a balanced distribution of projects within a locality in order to provide opportunities for persons outside as well as inside areas of racial concentration.[122]

---

121. 42 U.S.C. § 3608(e)(5).
122. The court of appeals recognized that subsidized housing in the City of Philadelphia was evenly and well dispersed. However, the court found this was not the test for siting subsidized housing projects. The court noted that:

> [A]t least under the 1968 Civil Rights Act and probably under the 1964 Civil Rights Act more is required of HUD than the determination that some rent supplement housing is located outside ghetto areas. . . . Possibly before 1964 the administrators of the federal housing programs could, by concentrating on land use controls, building code

The court did recognize that, in limited situations, the need for rehabilitation or additional housing could clearly outweigh the disadvantages of increasing or perpetuating racial concentrations. However, the court, in reading Title VI of the Civil Rights Act of 1964 and the Fair Housing Act as a combined entity, directed that HUD:

> [m]ust use some institutionalized method whereby, it has before it the relevant racial and socio-economic information necessary for compliance with its duties under the 1964 and 1968 Civil Rights Acts.

1. HUD Project Site-Selection Criteria

On January 7, 1972, the Department of Housing and Urban Development published Project Selection Criteria for its subsidized housing projects. The regulations, published as 24 C.F.R. § 200.700, advised that HUD would rate and rank projects for funding using eight criteria. Six of the eight related to program operations, such as the need for low- and moderate-income housing, the ability of the applicant to perform efficiently, and the provision of sound housing management. However, the two remaining criteria related to civil rights.

Projects would receive a rating of Superior, Adequate, or Poor on each factor. A project receiving a Poor rating on any factor would result in disapproval, and the priority groups were established based on the number of adequate ratings. (A project with all Superior ratings would be in the first priority for funding. A project with one Adequate rating would be in the second priority.)

The first civil rights criterion related to the impact of the project on minority housing opportunities, and the second related to the creation of employment and business opportunities.

With respect to housing opportunities, the criteria objective was to provide minority families with opportunities for housing in a wide range of locations and to open up nonsegregated housing opportunities that would help decrease the effects of past housing discrimination.

2. Affirmative Fair Housing Marketing

In addition to the Project Site Selection Regulation, in January 1972, HUD promulgated Affirmative Fair Housing Marketing (AFHM) Regulations (24 C.F.R. § 200.600), which were drawn up to ensure that individuals eligible for housing have a like range of housing choices available to them throughout their housing market area regardless of their race, color, religion, or national origin. The objective of the regulations was based on the description of equal housing opportunities in the President's 1971 statement, and the authority for the regulations resided in the Secretary of HUD to affirmatively advance fair housing in programs and activities relating to housing and urban development under Section 808(e)(5).

The AFHM regulation applied to all HUD-assisted and all FHA-insured projects of more than five units. The requirements applied to initial marketing and throughout the term of the project participation in the HUD program.

---

enforcement, and physical conditions of buildings, remain blind to the very real effect that racial concentration has had in the development of urban blight. Today, such color blindness is impermissible. Increase or maintenance of racial concentration is prima facie likely to lead to urban blight and is thus prima facie at variance with national housing policy.

Pursuant to the AFHM regulation, applicants and participants in covered programs were required to develop and implement a HUD-approved Affirmative Fair Housing Marketing Plan. These plans must be designed to attract buyers and renters of all majority and minority groups to assisted or insured dwellings that were being marketed.

There were two essential elements required in formulating an acceptable plan.

The first element involved identifying segments of the population eligible for the housing who are least likely to be aware of or to apply for the housing without special outreach because neighborhood customs, price, institutionalized discrimination in the housing market, and other factors have had the effect of denying or limiting housing choice.

The second element involved the development of an outreach program that included special measures designed to attract those groups identified as least likely to apply and other efforts designed to attract persons from the total eligible population.

Affirmative Fair Housing Marketing Plans and their implementation and revisions are subject to HUD review through the Office of Fair Housing and Equal Opportunity. Complaints can be accepted and compliance can be conducted. A failure to comply with affirmative marketing requirements subjects program participants to the imposition of sanctions within the program under which the housing application was made.[123]

In adopting tenant selection and assignment practices applicable to HUD-funded public housing programs in 1973, the Department adopted a rule requiring assignment of units based on a community-wide waiting list on a first-come, first-served basis.

3. *Affirmatively Furthering and Public Housing Tenant Selection*

The enactment of the Fair Housing Act in 1968 also had a clear impact on HUD programs. An example of that impact can be seen in the Public Housing Program tenant selection and assignment policy developed under Title VI of the Civil Rights Act of 1964, published in 1967.

In 1970, HUD considered revising the public housing tenant selection and assignment procedures to permit housing authorities to offer an applicant all available units and allow the applicant to choose from the available units. As recounted in General Counsel Knapp's testimony, the Assistant Secretary for Equal Opportunity did not agree to this proposal. In addition, a letter from the Assistant Attorney General for Civil Rights strongly objected to the inclusion of applicant project choice in assignment. The February 6, 1970 letter from the Assistant Attorney General to the Under Secretary of HUD questioning the proposed change stated:

> In general, prior to 1967, your Department approved unrestricted freedom of choice, as an appropriate method of tenant assignment, irrespective of racial patterns in the community or of the existence or nonexistence of pressures or other choice influencing factors which tend in some areas to perpetuate segregation. In 1967, your tenant assignment regulations were changed to eliminate unrestricted freedom of choice and to require, in general that tenants be assigned on a first come first served basis.

---

123. The procedures governing affirmative marketing compliance can be found at 24 C.F.R. pt. 108

The revised regulations allowed authorities, however, to adopt plans under which tenants had the right to a limited number of locations without loss of priority. In practice, this refusal system, which was adopted by most Authorities at least in the South, allowed a certain degree of freedom of choice, and, as applied, it permitted a substantial number of projects to remain completely segregated.... Consequently, it is apparent under the current regulations, which were designed to be nonracial, the elements of flexibility have been applied by many housing authorities in such a way as to maintain prior racial patterns.

Since the 1967 changes, the passage of the 1968 Fair Housing Act has expressed a national commitment to desegregated housing. The development of the law in other areas of civil rights enforcement has simultaneously tended to invalidate desegregation procedures based on freedom of choice, where, because of choice influencing factors, such measures have not resulted in significant desegregation. The courts have also held that proof of past discrimination creates a duty to take affirmative action to correct the continuing effects of past discrimination. Under these circumstances we believe that those authorities, north and south, which assigned tenants or selected locations racially in the past, to the extent that wholly or largely racially segregated projects persist, are required to do more to desegregate public housing than to offer applicants freedom of choice. Just as the above principles of law apply to private citizens, so to they should apply to governmental bodies. It is my view that in order for the government to be consistent and even-handed in the enforcement of Title VIII of the 1968 Act, it cannot be more lenient with public housing authorities which have discriminated in the past than with private landlords who have done so.[124]

4. Community Development Programs

Prior to 1974, the Department of Housing and Urban Development provided grants and loans for a wide range of community development activities, including major programs such as the Model Cities Program, Urban Renewal Program, and others such as Community Planning Grants and Water and Sewer Grants. Many of the community development programs had selection procedures for making awards that included civil rights considerations.

As indicated above, these programs, like the public housing program and the subsidized housing programs, were determined to constitute federal financial assistance and were thus subject to Title VI of the Civil Rights Act of 1964, and, to the extent that they involved housing, were also subject to Title VI of the Civil Rights Act 1968. In 1974, Congress enacted the Housing and Community Development Act of 1974, which rescinded several of the categorical grant programs and consolidated many others into a single grant in the Community Development Block Grant Program. In addition to the CDBG Program, the statute created the Home Investment Partnership, the Emergency Shelter Grant Program, and Housing Opportunities for Persons with AIDS.

---

124. Letter from Jerris Leonard, Assistant Attorney General, Civil Rights Division, to Richard C. Van Dusen, Under Secretary, Feb. 6, 1970. Quoted in written testimony of John J. Knapp, General Counsel before the Subcommittee on Housing and Community Development of the Committee on Banking, Finance and Urban Affairs, House of Representatives, Nov. 21, 1985. [Serial No. 99-83] Part 1, pp. 200–04.

The CDBG Program not only states that activities must be conducted in accordance Title VI and Title VIII, but since 1983 also requires grantees to certify that they will affirmatively further fair housing in programs and activities funded.[125] The HOME Program regulations also states that the statutory requirement from the Community Housing Affordability Strategy (CHAS) that funded HOME jurisdictions must affirmatively further fair housing.

5. Fair Housing Poster

In the implementation of the Fair Housing Act the Assistant Secretary for Fair Housing and Equal Opportunity has developed a fair housing poster for use in connection with the sale, rental of housing, and other activities covered under the Fair Housing Act.

The Assistant Secretary provides the poster to persons involved in housing transactions for their use in expressing their commitment to promote equal housing opportunity and to comply with the provisions of the Fair Housing Act.[126]

The regulation indicates that in an investigation under the Act, the Office of Fair Housing and Equal Opportunity will deem the failure to display the poster appropriately as prima facie evidence of a discriminatory housing practice.[127]

6. Economic Opportunities for Low- and Very Low-Income Persons

In the Housing and Urban Development Act of 1968 Congress established a policy to promote training, employment, and business opportunity for low- and very low-income persons in the areas of HUD-financed and -assisted housing.[128] Currently, the emphasis on Section 3 under the statute is directed toward ensuring that, to the greatest extent feasible, employment and other economic opportunities generated by federal financial assistance be directed toward low- and very-low income persons, particularly those who are recipients of government assistance for housing.[129]

HUD regulations implementing Section 3 provide for the investigation of complaints, determinations of violations, and informal and formal methods for achieving compliance in programs and activities, particularly public and Indian programs, but also in other HUD assistance programs.[130] Additional information on Section 3 can be obtained through HUD publications.[131]

---

125. 42 U.S.C. § 5304.
126. 24 C.F.R. pt. 110.
127. 24 C.F.R. § 110.30.
128. Section 3 of the Housing and Urban Development Act of 1968. 12 U.S.C. § 1701u.
129. 12 U.S.C. § 1701u (b).
130. 24 C.F.R. pt. 135.
131. *See* http://www.hud.gov/offices/fheo/section3/section3.cfm.

Compliance and Enforcement 15

Margarita Maisonet

> There is, however, a limit at which forbearance ceases to be a virtue.
> Sir Edmund Burke
> *Observations on a Late Publication on the*
> *Present State of the Nation* (1769)

I. INTRODUCTION

At the U.S. Department of Housing and Urban Development (HUD), program violations are almost always addressed through compliance efforts rather than through enforcement actions. With an overall budget that has not significantly increased in the past 30 years, HUD has increased its compliance and enforcement efforts over the years by implementing technological changes that allow for greater consistency in data collection, analysis, and monitoring. HUD has also increased reliance on industry partners (such as fair-housing partners, state agencies, and Section 8 contract administrators) or third-party resources (such as fee-based inspectors) to help ensure program compliance. Finally, HUD continues to set forth new regulations and directives that require program participants such as lending institutions, state and local governments, and grantees to self-monitor and improve the oversight of projects and more closely monitor subrecipients.

Given that most enforcement actions at HUD are discretionary rather than statutorily mandated, the level and type of enforcement actions have varied over the years. While compliance is always the first goal, there are times when enforcement becomes necessary. External influences are common reasons why the focus and level of enforcement vary. In November 2011, the Department announced proposed new regulatory requirements under its Home Investment Partnerships Program (HOME) designed to strengthen the program's performance and accountability. Earlier in 2011, the *Washington Post* published a series of articles that detailed alleged patterns in stalled or delayed projects (sometimes spanning years) funded by the HOME program after a yearlong investigation.[1] The newspaper cited lack of HUD oversight as one of the reasons why projects were not completed as required. While HUD's press release stated that efforts were made to rewrite some of HOME's compliance rules in 2009, which was before the *Washington Post* began its investigation, the press release was issued two days after a second congressional hearing was held in response to the newspaper articles.

Market conditions also drive changes in compliance and enforcement activities. In the past 25 years, HUD's Federal Housing Administration (FHA) single-family market share of newly originated mortgages has increased from approximately 3 percent to 35 percent.[2] While FHA institutionalized its monitoring and quality assurance activities years ago, the significant increase in market share predicated in great part by the collapse of the housing market (and the increased use of FHA financing rather than the use of subprime lenders) also caused the FHA to strengthen its lender indemnification process and increase monitoring of lender performance.[3] Similarly, record increases in multifamily loan volume during fiscal year 2011[4] coincided with increased lender monitoring and changes to lender approval requirements as well as changes to underwriting standards.

Finally, administrative priorities greatly influence the scope and depth of enforcement and compliance activities undertaken by any government agency. This was especially true when then Secretary Andrew Cuomo announced the HUD 2020 Management Reform Plan in response to congressional calls for action after the Government Accountability Office (then the Government Accounting Office) listed HUD as the first and only agency in its entirety named to its "High Risk" list—a dubious honor typically reserved only for specific government programs. Appearing at a Senate hearing on May 7, 1998, Cuomo said:

> Recognizing HUD's failures, both internal and external, Congress, in 1996, gave HUD an ultimatum: Reinvent or die! Based on promises of reinvention, reorganization, and streamlining—a HUD transformation—elimination was avoided—but it was a harbinger of things to come. HUD had been given a reprieve by the Congress, but the clock was still ticking.

In addition to streamlining HUD's operations into two basic job categories (Community Builders and Public Trust Officers) and consolidating numerous functions into fewer offices,

---

1. *See* note 161 in the "Community Development" chapter. Additional related articles were published by the *Washington Post* on November 6, 17, and 29, 2011, and on December 11 and 16, 2011.
2. David Hintz, *An Encyclopedia of FHA Enforcement*, MORTGAGE BANKING, March 2011.
3. On October 8, 2010, HUD published a proposed rule in the *Federal Register* with the most significant change affecting increased guidance on mortgagee indemnification to HUD of insurance claims in the instances of fraud, misrepresentation, or noncompliance with HUD's requirements. *See* http://gpo.gov.
4. http://portal.hud.gov/hudportal/HUD?src=/press/press_releases_media_advisories/2011/HUDNo.11-172.

Secretary Cuomo created the Departmental Enforcement Center (DEC), which began operations in 1998.

This chapter discusses compliance and enforcement activities for HUD's program offices followed by a section on the Departmental Enforcement Center, its role in the Office of General Counsel, and how it works with HUD's program offices. The chapter concludes with an overview of the Office of Hearings and Appeals and the Office of the Inspector General.

II. OFFICE OF COMMUNITY PLANNING AND DEVELOPMENT

The Office of Community Planning and Development (CPD) administers myriad programs in the form of grants (entitlement as well as non-entitlement) and loan guarantee programs designed to assist urban communities, rural communities, Native American tribes, homeless populations, and special-needs populations, such as persons with AIDS. This section of the chapter focuses on the compliance and enforcement activities of CPD's two largest programs, the Community Development and Block Grant program (CDBG) and the Home Investment Partnerships Program (HOME), because together they account for more than 73 percent of CPD's budget in fiscal year 2010. A comprehensive list of program and technical area sanction references for each of CPD's programs can be found in *HUD Handbook 6509.2 Rev-6, CPD Monitoring*.[5]

A. Community Development Block Grant (CDBG)

In conducting performance reviews,[6] HUD primarily relies on information obtained from the recipient's performance report, records maintained, findings from monitoring, grantee and sub-recipient audits, audits and surveys conducted by the HUD Inspector General, and financial data regarding the amount of funds remaining in the line of credit plus program income. HUD also may consider relevant information pertaining to a recipient's performance gained from other sources. A recipient's failure to maintain records in the prescribed manner may also result in a finding that the recipient has failed to meet the applicable requirement to which the record pertains. Monitoring activities for CDBG are primarily centered on the following areas:

- Compliance with the primary and national objectives;
- Determination if CDBG-funded activities are being carried out in a timely manner (and assessment of continuing capacity to carry out these responsibilities in a timely manner);
- Compliance with consolidated plan responsibilities;
- Compliance with equal opportunity and fair housing requirements; and
- Cooperation between urban counties and local participating governments funded by the county.

---

5. *See* http://www.hud.gov/adm/hudclips/handbooks/cpdh/.
6. *See* 24 C.F.R. pt. 570, subpt. O.

Corrective and remedial actions HUD may take include:

- Issuing a letter of warning advising that additional action may be taken if the deficiency is not corrected;
- Recommending or requiring the recipient to submit a corrective action plan;
- Requiring recipients to submit evidence beyond a certification that the matter has been resolved;
- Requiring the recipient to suspend disbursements;
- Advising the recipient to reimburse the program account or letter of credit and reprogram the funds accordingly;
- Changing the method of payment to the recipient from a letter of credit to a reimbursement basis;
- Instituting collection procedures in the case of claims payable;[7] or
- Conditioning the use of funds from a succeeding fiscal year's allocation on the required appropriate action for entitlement and insular recipients.

Grant funds may also be reduced, withdrawn, or adjusted; grantees are provided an opportunity for an informal consultation with HUD before these actions are taken. In the case of nondiscrimination violations, HUD will notify the governor of the state and the head of the local government and ask them to secure compliance. Referrals are made to the Attorney General for any matters not resolved in a reasonable amount of time. Other enforcement actions that can be taken include termination, reduction, or suspension of payments; recipients are allowed to request a hearing before an administrative law judge before these actions are instituted.[8]

B. Home Investment Partnerships Program (HOME)

As with CDBG, HUD completes performance reviews for the HOME program.[9] Corrective and remedial actions are substantially similar to those cited above; participating jurisdictions may also be withdrawn from participation in allocations or reallocations of funding contained in 24 C.F.R. Part 92, Subparts B and J. In the event HUD proposes to take actions pursuant to the regulations, the respondent will be the participating jurisdiction or, at HUD's option, the state recipient.[10]

III. OFFICE OF FAIR HOUSING AND EQUAL OPPORTUNITY

The Fair Housing Act covers most housing.[11] In some circumstances, the Act exempts owner-occupied buildings with no more than four units, single-family housing sold or rented without the use of a broker, and housing operated by organizations and private clubs that limit occupancy to members.

---

7. *See* 24 C.F.R. § 570.910.
8. *See* 24 C.F.R. § 570.913.
9. *See* 24 C.F.R. § 92.551.
10. Proceedings are conducted in accordance with 24 C.F.R. pt. 26, subpt. B.
11. Summaries of the Fair Housing Laws and related Executive Orders can be found on HUD's website at http://portal.hud.gov/hudportal/HUD?src=/program_offices/fair_housing_equal_opp/FHLaws.

FHEO Charges from 2007 to 2011	
Year	No. of Charges
2007	17
2008	40
2009	27
2010	30
2011	46
2012	6

Source: http://portal.hud.gov/hudportal/HUD?src=/program_offices/fair_housing_equal_opp/enforcement

HUD investigates complaints of housing discrimination based on race, color, religion, national origin, sex, disability, or familial status. Complainants have one year after the alleged violation to file a complaint. HUD also may refer complaints to state or local agencies if it determines that the agency has substantially equivalent fair-housing powers as HUD and notify the complainant of the referral. The state or local agency must begin work on the complaint within 30 days or HUD may take it back.

In investigating fair-housing complaints, HUD first tries to conciliate the matter with both parties. If conciliation fails, HUD will determine whether "reasonable cause" exists to believe that a discriminatory housing practice has taken place. If HUD has a finding of "no reasonable cause," the complaint is dismissed. If HUD finds reasonable cause, HUD will issue a charge of discrimination and schedule a hearing before a HUD administrative law judge (ALJ). The case will be heard in an administrative hearing within 120 days, unless the complainant or respondent wants the case heard in federal district court. In either situation, the hearing/case is held at no cost to the complainant.

For administrative hearings, HUD attorneys litigate on behalf of the complainant unless the complainant chooses to have his or her own attorney. If heard in federal district court, the Department of Justice pursues the case on behalf of the complainant. The decisions of the ALJ are subject to Secretarial Review; the decisions of the federal district court are subject to review by the U.S. Court of Appeals. Successful complainants can be awarded for actual damages including pain and suffering, injunctive or other equitable relief (such as making the housing available), and reasonable attorney's fees and costs. Civil penalties payable to the federal government also may be assessed. The maximum penalties are $16,000 for a first violation and $65,000 for a third violation within seven years. If the case is heard in federal district court, the court can also award punitive damages.

Complainants can also file suit, at their expense, in federal district court or state court within two years of an alleged violation. The court may appoint an attorney if the complainant cannot afford one. A suit may be filed even after filing a complaint as long as the complainant has not signed a conciliation agreement and an ALJ has not started a hearing.

IV. OFFICE OF HEALTHY HOMES AND LEAD HAZARD CONTROL

HUD's Office of Healthy Homes and Lead Hazard Control (OHHLHC) was established to eliminate lead-based paint hazards in America's privately owned and low-income housing and to address other housing-related health hazards that threaten vulnerable residents. The OHHLHC is charged with enforcing HUD's lead-based paint regulations.[12] OHHLHC's enforcement activities center primarily around two rules, the Lead Disclosure Rule and the Lead Safe Housing Rule. The Lead Disclosure Rule is found at 24 C.F.R. Part 35, Subpart A: Disclosure of Known Lead-Based Paint and/or Lead-Based Paint Hazards upon Sale or Lease of Residential Property. The Lead Safe Housing Rule is contained in 24 C.F.R. Part 35, Subparts B through R: Lead-Based Paint Poisoning Prevention in Certain Residential Structures.

A. Lead Safe Housing Rule

Sections 1012 and 1013 of this rule apply to all target housing that is federally owned and target housing that receives federal assistance. Depending on the nature of the work and the dollar amount of federal investment in the property, certain requirements must be complied with in handling lead-based paint.[13] Requirements that may be enforced include:

- Provision of a pamphlet,
- Lead-based paint inspection,
- Risk assessment,
- Notice to occupants of results or clearance,
- Response to elevated blood levels in a child,
- Paint stabilization,
- Ongoing lead-based paint maintenance,
- Interim controls, and
- Safe work practices during rehabilitation.

Remedies for failure to comply include civil money penalties as well as program-specific remedies based on the type of assistance the housing receives. For example, violations under this rule at FHA-insured multifamily properties could result in the imposition of civil money penalties, declaration of a violation under a Regulatory Agreement or Housing Assistance Payment Contract, and/or administrative sanctions.

B. Lead Disclosure Rule

The Residential Lead-Based Paint Hazard Reduction Act of 1992, also known as Title X, was passed to protect families from exposure to lead from paint, dust, and soil. Section 1018 of this law directed HUD and the Environmental Protection Agency (EPA) to require the disclosure of known information on lead-based paint and lead-based paint hazards before the sale or lease of most housing built before 1978. Before ratification of a contract for housing sale or lease, sellers and landlords must:

- Give an EPA-approved information pamphlet on identifying and controlling lead-based paint hazards.

---

12. Links to lead regulations and statutes can be found at http://portal.hud.gov/hudportal/HUD?src=/program_offices/healthy_homes/enforcement/regulations.

13. Information on requirements by subpart of the rule can be found at http://portal.hud.gov/hudportal/HUD?src=/program_offices/healthy_homes/enforcement/lshr_summary.

- Disclose any known information concerning lead-based paint or lead-based paint hazards. The seller or landlord must also disclose such information as the location of the lead-based paint and/or lead-based paint hazards and the condition of the painted surfaces.
- Provide any records and reports on lead-based paint and/or lead-based paint hazards that are available to the seller or landlord (for multi-unit buildings, this requirement includes records and reports concerning common areas and other units, when such information was obtained as a result of a building-wide evaluation).
- Include an attachment to the contract or lease (or language inserted in the lease itself) that includes a Lead Warning Statement and confirms that the seller or landlord has complied with all notification requirements. This attachment must be provided in the same language used in the rest of the contract. Sellers or landlords, and agents, as well as homebuyers or tenants, must sign and date the attachment.
- Sellers must provide homebuyers a 10-day period to conduct a paint inspection or risk assessment for lead-based paint or lead-based paint hazards. Parties may mutually agree, in writing, to lengthen or shorten the time period for inspection. Homebuyers may waive this inspection opportunity.

Failure to comply with the rule can result in the following remedies:

- Civil money penalties,
- Adjunctive relief,
- Triple damages for knowing violations, or
- Court costs, reasonable attorney fees, and expert witness fees.

V. OFFICE OF HOUSING

A. SINGLE-FAMILY HOUSING

Primary responsibility for ensuring compliance with HUD's Federal Housing Administration (FHA) requirements resides in the Quality Assurance Division (QAD). QAD develops and implements the compliance programs for loan origination, servicing, and loss mitigation. QAD staff performs on-site and off-site reviews of lenders. Compliance reviews combine the review of actual origination and servicing files, as well as the review of operational processes and the lender's quality assurance program.[14] Written responses to QAD's reviews are required and lenders may be required to submit revised quality control plans or even provide HUD with indemnification against actual or potential claims. Based on the nature of the findings, the reviews may be closed out by the local office or matters may be referred to the Mortgagee Review Board or the Office of the Inspector General or, for administrative sanctions, to the Departmental Enforcement Center (DEC).

---

14. David Hintz, *An Encyclopedia of FHA Enforcement*, MORTGAGE BANKING, March 2011.

B. Multifamily Housing

A significant percentage of compliance-related and enforcement-related actions undertaken by the Office of Multifamily Housing is coordinated with the DEC and/or the Office of General Counsel. Additional information on DEC actions is described later in this chapter. Non-DEC compliance and enforcement actions include:

- Issuance of Notice of Violations under Regulatory Agreements and/or Housing Assistance Payment contracts for matters not referred to the DEC;
- Referrals to the Mortgagee Review Board for failure by Multifamily FHA lenders to perform physical inspections when required; and
- Follow-up to monitoring visits performed by Section 8 contract administrators or HUD staff under the Management and Occupancy Review procedures.

A unique tool that the Office of Multifamily Housing has is the Active Partners Performance System (APPS).[15] The APPS process requires submission of certain participant data for individuals and companies wishing to participate in *multifamily* FHA, direct loan, grant and project-based Section 8 programs. Participants can receive a "flag" in the system for certain instances of noncompliance or for substandard performance. For example, property owners may be flagged in the system when they score below 60 points on an inspection conducted by the Real Estate Assessment Center. Flags are also placed when a property receives a less than satisfactory score on a Management and Occupancy Review or whenever there is a default under the Mortgage or Regulatory Agreement. Flags can be appealed either at the local field office or, when participation has been denied, at HUD Headquarters.[16]

C. Mortgagee Review Board[17]

The Mortgagee Review Board (MRB) is authorized to take administrative action against FHA-approved lenders that are not in compliance with FHA lending requirements. The board reviews cases that are referred. Referrals may come from the Office of Housing's divisions and offices, such as Single Family Homeownership Centers, Lender Approval Division, Quality Assurance Division, and the Office of Multifamily Housing. The Office of Fair Housing and Equal Opportunity and HUD's Inspector General also can make referrals. The cases before the board typically involve lenders who knowingly and materially violate HUD/FHA program statutes, regulations, and handbook requirements now collectively known as "program obligations." For serious violations, the board can withdraw a lender's FHA approval so the lender cannot participate in FHA programs. In less egregious cases, the board enters into settlement agreements with lenders to bring them into compliance. The board can also impose

---

15. APPS is still often referred to as 2530 because that was the form number participants were required to submit prior to July 1, 2006, when APPS was fully implemented. Note that while APPS is now operational, it is not mandatory. Participants still have the option to submit the paper 2530 in accordance with the Preservation Approval Process Improvement Act of 2007.

16. *See* http://www.hud.gov/offices/adm/hudclips/handbooks/hsgh/4065.1/40651c4HSGH.pdf.

17. *See* MRB website, http://portal.hud.gov/hudportal/HUD?src=/program_offices/housing/sfh/mrb.

civil money penalties, probation, and suspension and issue letters of reprimand. Board actions are published in the *Federal Register*.[18]

D. Limited Denials of Participation (LDPs)[19]

This is an action taken by a HUD Field Office or the Deputy Assistant Secretary for Single Family or Multifamily Housing that excludes a party from further participation in a HUD program area. The scope of the LDP is limited to the geographic area of the office that sent the notice to the party. An LDP generally expires in one year. In most cases, the causes of an LDP action could be remedied by the party. LDP actions include provisions for an appeal process with a speedy conference at the HUD office that issued the LDP as the first step. LDPs are tracked by the Departmental Enforcement Center's Compliance Division.

E. Other Tools

An approved lender's origination authority may be revoked by HUD under Credit Watch. Termination is based in geographic areas where a lender has a high rate of early defaults and claims. HUD can also revoke a lender's Direct Endorsement authority because of early default and high claims rates. Terminations for both types of authority are published regularly in the *Federal Register*.[20]

VI. OFFICE OF PUBLIC AND INDIAN HOUSING

On February 23, 2011, HUD published a final rule in the *Federal Register* promulgating the criteria and determination for substantial default by a public housing authority (PHA).[21] While other statutory and regulatory authorities exist that allow HUD to take action against a PHA that is in substantial default, this new rule was developed to establish that there are additional violations besides troubled performance or violation of HUD's Public Housing Assessment System (PHAS) regulations that could lead to a declaration of substantial default.

HUD's Real Estate Assessment Center (REAC) develops a composite score on each PHA's performance based on four components: physical, financial, management, and resident satisfaction. Based on this composite score, HUD determines whether a PHA is a higher performer, standard performer, or troubled performer. Troubled performers are required to enter into a memorandum of agreement (MOA) with HUD designed to help the PHA substantially improve performance.

A. PHAS Designations[22]

A PHA will receive a status designation corresponding to its final PHAS score as follows:

---

18. MRB decisions can also be found at http://portal.hud.gov/hudportal/HUD?src=/program_offices/housing/sfh/mrb/mrbhome.
19. See http://portal.hud.gov/hudportal/HUD?src=/program_offices/enforcement/theecmemo2.
20. *See* Mortgage Letter 10-03 at http://portal.hud.gov/hudportal/HUD?556=/program_offices/administration/hudclips/letter/mortgagee.
21. *See* 24 C.F.R. pt. 907.
22. Source: http://portal.hud.gov/hudportal/documents/huddoc?id=DOC_26295.pdf.

- **High Performer:** A PHA that achieves a score of at least 60 percent of the points available under each of the four PHAS Indicators described in the final rule and achieves an overall PHAS score of 90 percent or greater of the total available points under PHAS shall be designated a High Performer. A PHA shall not be designated a High Performer if it scores below the threshold established for any indicator.
- **Standard Performer:** A PHA that is not a High Performer shall be designated a Standard Performer if (1) the PHA achieves a total PHAS score of not less than 60 percent of the total available points under PHAS and (2) the PHA does not achieve less than 60 percent of the total points available under PHAS Indicators #1, #2, or #3. Standard Performers must correct reported deficiencies. A PHA that achieves a total PHAS score of less that 70 percent but not less than 60 percent is required by the Hub/Program Center to submit an Improvement Plan to correct identified deficiencies. A PHA that achieves a total PHAS score of less than 70 percent but not less than 60 percent is at risk of being designated Troubled.
- **Overall Troubled:** A PHA that achieves an overall PHAS score of less than 60 percent or achieves less than 60 percent of the total points available under more than one of PHAS Indicators #1, #2, or #3 shall be designated Troubled and referred to the Hub/Program Center.
- **Troubled in One Area:** A PHA that achieves less than 60 percent of the total points available under only one of PHAS Indicators #1, #2, or #3 shall be considered a Substandard Financial, Substandard Management, or Substandard Physical Performer and referred to the Hub/Program Center.

The regulations contain several bases for substantial default, including violations of laws and agreements or failure to act. Violations of laws and agreements include federal statute, federal regulation, or one or more terms of an Annual Contributions Contract, or other covenants to which the PHA is subject. "Failure to act" provisions include failing to execute an MOA, failing to comply with the terms of the MOA, or failing to show substantial improvement.

B. Declarations of Substantial Default

If a PHA is found in substantial default, HUD provides a written determination that:

- Identifies the specific statute, regulation, covenant, condition, or agreement violated;
- Identifies the specific events, occurrences, or conditions that constitute the violation;
- Specifies the time period (at least 10 days but no more than 30 days) during which the PHA has an opportunity to demonstrate that the determination or finding is not substantively accurate, if required;
- Provides (if HUD determines it to be appropriate) an opportunity to cure with a specific cure period; and
- Notifies the PHA that if the PHA fails to provide a satisfactory response, HUD will take appropriate actions.

HUD Receiverships as of April 2011

Administrative	
PHA Name	Start Date
East St. Louis HA	March 1985
Wellston HA	July 1996
HA of New Orleans	February 2002
Virgin Islands HA	August 2003
Detroit HC	July 2005
Philadelphia HA	March 2011
HA City of Lafayette	March 2011
Judicial	
HA of Kansas City	July 1993
Chester HA	August 1994

Source: http://www.hud.gov/offices/pih/oro/rec.cfm

PHAs may respond in writing as to why they believe the default determination is in error or why the violation does not constitute noncompliance with the cited provisions, or that the violations have been cured or will be cured in the time period allotted. An important exception to the right of a PHA to respond to a written determination is if HUD determines that conditions exist that post an imminent threat to the life, health, or safety of public housing residents or residents of the neighborhood or if the events or conditions precipitating the default are determined to be the result of criminal or fraudulent activity. PHAs also may waive their right to respond, and HUD will proceed with the remedies described below.

C. Remedies for Substantial Default

On determination that events have occurred or conditions exist that constitute a substantial default, HUD may take any of these actions sequentially or simultaneously in any combination:

- Take any action provided for in Section 6(j)(3) of the Act;[23]
- Provide technical assistance for existing PHA management staff; or
- Provide assistance deemed necessary, in HUD's discretion, to remedy emergency conditions.

In the case of a substantial default where intervention is deemed necessary,[24] HUD may petition for the appointment of a receiver. For a PHA with 1,250 or more units or for PHAs

---

23. *See* 42 U.S.C. § 1437d, 42 U.S.C. 353d.
24. *See* 24 C.F.R. 902.83.

with fewer than 1,250 units, HUD will either petition for the appointment of a receiver or take possession of the PHA (including all or part of any project or program of the PHA), and appoint, on a competitive or noncompetitive basis, an individual or entity as an administrative receiver to assume the responsibilities of HUD for the administration of all or part of the PHA (including all or part of any project or program of the PHA).[25] HUD (or its agent) may serve as the Executive Director/Administrator, the Commissioners, or both.

To the extent feasible, while a PHA is operating under any of the actions that may have been taken by HUD, all services to residents will continue uninterrupted. HUD also may limit remedies to one or more of a PHA's specific operational areas (such as maintenance, capital improvement, occupancy, or financial management), to a single program or group of programs, or to a single project or a group of projects.

Finally, it should be noted that HUD may also seek administrative sanctions, such as suspension or debarment or, in the case of a PHA with Section 8 units, the imposition of civil money penalties.

VII. DEPARTMENTAL ENFORCEMENT CENTER

The Departmental Enforcement Center (DEC) was created in 1998 to consolidate most of HUD's compliance and enforcement activities into one office, thus allowing program offices to focus on other functions, such as technical assistance, customer service, and program administration. In 2003, the DEC was merged into the Office of General Counsel in part to help streamline the Department's various offices (the Real Estate Assessment Center merged into the Office of Public Housing at this time as well) and also to further strengthen the existing relationship between DEC and HUD attorneys. Staff in DEC Headquarters is supported by OGC's Office of Program Enforcement, and staff in the five satellite offices is supported by Regional Counsel attorneys.

DEC Headquarters includes the Office of the Director and two divisions, Compliance and Operations. The DEC Director also serves as HUD's Debarring Official. Besides overseeing the two Headquarters divisions, the DEC Director also oversees five satellite offices. The five offices, located in Atlanta, Chicago, Fort Worth, Los Angeles, and New York, are led by a Satellite Office Director.

A. Compliance Division

The DEC's Compliance Division processes suspensions and debarments against HUD's program participants who do not comply with departmental requirements and can even process sanctions against HUD employees. Sanctions result in their exclusion from further participation in HUD and, generally, all other federal executive branch non-procurement programs; in limited cases, sanctions may be limited to HUD programs only.[26]

The Compliance Division receives referrals from HUD offices, including:

- Office of the Inspector General,
- Office of Multifamily Housing,

---

25. *See* note 9.
26. *See* 2 C.F.R. pts. 180 and 2424 for information on suspensions and debarments.

- Office of Single Family Housing,
- Office of Public and Indian Housing, and
- Office of Community Planning and Development.

Suspensions are imposed for a temporary period pending the completion of an investigation or legal proceedings, such as an indictment. Suspensions also may be imposed based on adequate evidence to support claims of serious program violations. Suspensions result in immediate exclusion from participation in further government transactions. Suspensions usually lead to debarment.

Debarments are serious actions imposed by HUD. The general duration of a debarment is three years, but it could be longer, even for an indefinite period of time, depending on the seriousness of the violation. Respondents seeking a hearing after receiving a notice of suspension or debarment may request a hearing held by the debarring official's Hearing Officer. Respondents may be represented by counsel or they may appear pro se. Attorneys from HUD's Office of Program Enforcement represent the Department. Hearings may be held in person and often are held over the phone. After the hearing, the Hearing Officer makes a recommendation to the debarring official. Appeals are heard by HUD's Office of Hearings and Appeals.

The federal government maintains information on sanctioned individuals and companies on the Excluded Parties List System (EPLS).[27] Many federal programs require a review in EPLS before program participants can be deemed eligible to participate.

B. Operations Division

The Operations Division is responsible for policy development of existing enforcement responsibilities and policy development for new initiatives. The Operations Division also helps manage the day-to-day recovery and enforcement strategies along with the Satellite Offices. The Operations Division assists with the development of reporting tools and administrative functions and also processes its own enforcement cases.

C. Satellite Offices

The DEC's Satellite Offices primarily focus on properties with physical and financial deficiencies that are referred from HUD's Real Estate Assessment Center (REAC), the Office of Multifamily Housing, and, for health-care properties, the Office of Healthcare Programs. For physical referrals, REAC assesses the physical condition of HUD's Multifamily Housing inventory. Properties with a REAC inspection score of 30 points or less are automatically referred to the DEC. Multifamily Housing may choose to electively refer properties scoring between 31 and 59 points.

The DEC also handles financial referrals when the annual financial statements (AFS) reflect compliance discrepancies. AFS statements are submitted electronically to REAC through the Financial Assessment Subsystem. Once the statements are received, they go through various system checks and review by REAC analysts. If certain conditions are noted either by the system or the REAC analyst, a referral is made to the Office of Multifamily Housing, the Office of Healthcare Programs, or the DEC.

---

27. *See* https://www.epls.gov/.

D. Office of Program Enforcement[28]

The Office of the Associate General Counsel for Program Enforcement provides legal assistance to the DEC and to other HUD offices. Attorneys initiate and litigate administrative and civil actions and sanctions against individuals referred to the DEC. The Office also provides affirmative counsel, guidance, and support to HUD program offices and is composed of two divisions: Administrative Proceedings and Program Enforcement.

The Administrative Proceedings Division handles affirmative administrative litigation for the Department. (OGC's Office of Ligation, under the direction of the Associate General Counsel for Litigation, handles defensive litigation.) Attorneys handle MRB sanctions, suspensions and debarments, CMP actions, Program Fraud Civil Remedies Act (PFCRA) actions, and federal litigation with the Department of Justice that results from any of these actions.

In MRB and CMP actions, attorneys evaluate potential cases for legal sufficiency and litigate cases on behalf of the government. In suspension and debarment actions, attorneys evaluate proposed sanctions recommended by the DEC's Compliance Division and represent the government in cases. In PFCRA actions, attorneys evaluate potential cases, consult with the Department of Justice, and litigate cases on behalf of the government. When matters handled by the Administrative Proceedings Division reach federal court, the attorneys assist the Department of Justice.

The Program Enforcement Division provides a significant amount of assistance to the DEC Satellite Offices and the OGC Regional Counsel Offices that support the DEC. Program Enforcement attorneys handle enforcement actions to enforce business agreements, including Regulatory Agreements and Housing Assistance Payment contracts, and assist on CMP matters. The division also handles certain enforcement actions for the Office of Public and Indian Housing (i.e., on receivership issues) and the Office of Community Planning and Development (i.e., grant reductions or terminations). Attorneys also assist the Department of Justice in bringing False Claims actions and the Office of Multifamily Housing's Multifamily Participation Review Committee when APPS/2530 decisions are appealed.

E. Civil Money Penalties[29]

Owners who do not file timely annual financial statements with REAC are referred to the DEC. The DEC's primary goal has been to obtain owner compliance in filing the required statements. However, the DEC has authority to impose civil money penalties (CMPs) against owners with HUD-imposed CMPs for other violations. HUD may seek a CMP against numerous multifamily housing participants, such as mortgagors, general partners of mortgagors, officers or directors of corporate mortgagors, identity-of-interest management agents, and certain members of limited liability corporations. CMP rules also cover Section 8 owners, general partners, and identity-of-interest management agents.

The current maximum penalty that may be imposed on an FHA mortgagor of a multifamily property (or on any person in a relationship with the mortgagor as described in the regulations) is $37,500 per violation. If the property has only a Housing Assistance Payment

---

28. *See* http://www.hud.gov/offices/enforce/office_cc1.cfm?&lang=en.
29. *See* 24 C.F.R. pt. 30.45.

(HAP) contract, the maximum penalty is $25,000 per violation. In no case can project funds be used to pay the penalty. As previously noted, the Mortgage Review Board also can impose CMPs against program participants who violate HUD's requirements.[30]

VIII. OFFICE OF HEARINGS AND APPEALS

The Office of Hearings and Appeals (OHA) is an independent adjudicatory office within the Office of the Secretary whose administrative judges and administrative law judges conduct hearings and make determinations for HUD in accordance with existing statutes and departmental policies, regulations, and procedures. The Secretary may also delegate any matter in controversy to the OHA requiring findings of fact and conclusions of law, and such other quasi-judicial matters that the Secretary deems appropriate consistent with existing regulations. The OHA is headed by a Director, appointed by the Secretary, who supervises the administrative judges of the Office of Appeals, the administrative law judges of the Office of Administrative Law Judges, and OHA support staff.

Both the Office of Appeals and the Office of Administrative Law Judges encourages the use of alternative dispute resolution (ADR) procedures. Both offices work to provide the most suitable location for a hearing to accommodate small businesses and pro se litigants, while also providing the most convenient and economical forum for witnesses.

A. Office of Appeals

The Office of Appeals conducts independent and impartial hearings and reviews of the record on behalf of the Department consistent with authorizing statutes and departmental regulations. The administrative judges of this Office are Departmental Hearing Officers in the Office of Hearings and Appeals who conduct hearings, make determinations, and issue impartial decisions, the majority of which are final agency decisions.

The administrative judges of the HUD Office of Appeals conduct mandated reviews of administrative wage garnishments[31] and cases involving administrative offset of various federal payments due to indebted public and private parties.[32] Decisions of the administrative judges in these cases are final agency decisions. In addition, the administrative judges hear cases relating to limited denial of participation, debarment, and suspension cases.[33] (Additional information on suspension and debarments can be found in this chapter in the section on the Departmental Enforcement Center.)

B. Office of Administrative Law Judges

The Office of Administrative Law Judges conducts independent and impartial hearings on behalf of this agency consistent with authorizing statutes and departmental regulations. The judges are appointed pursuant to the Administrative Procedure Act[34] and are independent of agency influence in their proceedings and decisions.

---

30. *See* 12 U.S.C. § 1734f-14.
31. *See* 24 C.F.R. § 17.170 and 31 C.F.R. § 285.11(f).
32. *See* 24 C.F.R. § 17.150–.161.
33. *See* 2 C.F.R. pt. 180 and 24 C.F.R. pt. 26, subpt. A.
34. *See* 5 U.S.C. § 551.

The administrative law judges hear and decide cases under certain sections of the Code of Federal Regulations (CFR).[35] The administrative law judges also have jurisdiction to hear and decide certain cases involving fair housing, interstate land sales, departmental sanctions, and community block grants.

IX. OFFICE OF THE INSPECTOR GENERAL (OIG)

The HUD Inspector General is one of the original 12 Inspectors General authorized under the Inspector General Act of 1978, as amended.[36] While OIG is located within HUD, it operates as a separate organization with its own budgetary authority and even its own strategic plan. This independence was designed to facilitate clear and objective reporting of agency deficiencies to the Secretary and the Congress.[37] It is not HUD's enforcement arm; rather, its primary role is to conduct internal and external audits and perform investigations. In doing so, it works closely with the Office of General Counsel, the Departmental Enforcement Center, and program offices to achieve its mission. OIG senior staff is routinely called on to testify before congressional oversight committees.

The mission statement of the OIG is as follows:

- Promotes the integrity, efficiency, and effectiveness of HUD programs and operations to assist the Department in meeting its mission.
- Detects and prevents waste, fraud, and abuse.
- Seeks administrative sanctions, civil recoveries, and/or criminal prosecution of those responsible for waste, fraud, and abuse in HUD programs and operations.

OIG's primary activities are to:

- Promote efficiency and effectiveness in programs and operations;
- Detect and deter fraud and abuse;
- Investigate allegations of misconduct by HUD employees; and
- Review and make recommendations regarding existing and proposed legislation and regulations affecting HUD.

In addition to an Executive Office, OIG consists of the Offices of Audit, Investigation, and Management and Planning, with staff located in Headquarters, eight regions, and numerous field offices. OIG also has its own Counsel, and the Inspector General serves as an advisor to the FHA's Mortgagee Review Board as a non-voting member.

---

35. *See* http://portal.hud.gov/hudportal/HUD?src=/program_offices/hearings_appeals.
36. *See* 5 U.S.C. Appx. 3.
37. OIG's Semiannual Reports to Congress are *available at* http://www.hudoig.gov/reports/sars.php. The reports include highlights for the reporting period on significant audits, investigations, and other matters, as well as the status of audits and whether or not recommendations have been resolved.

A. Office of Audit[38]

Led by an Assistant Inspector General for Audit, the Office of Audit plans and conducts reviews of HUD activities and operations that include:

- HUD program and operations offices in Headquarters and the field,
- Hundreds of HUD programs and initiatives, and
- Thousands of program participants and contractors doing business with HUD.

OIG routinely publishes Audit Plans[39] that outline the areas OIG intends to audit based on several factors, including its strategic plan goals and HUD management challenges that OIG previously identified and reported to Congress. Additional audits are often performed in response to requests received from Congress and HUD. Audit reports are almost always made publicly available unless there are specific security or confidentiality concerns. Reports are grouped by internal and external audits performed and are available online. Finally, the Office of Audit also publishes audit guides for use by program participants and HUD staff.[40]

The audit process begins with an entrance interview with the auditee. An audit schedule and an audit scope are provided. OIG auditors may spend days, weeks, or months working on-site and/or off-site on a single audit. The Office of Audit has subpoena authority to obtain documents but not witness subpoena authority. Audits are performed in accordance with professional industry and government accounting standards. A draft audit report is provided to the auditee once the audit work has been completed. Auditees are provided an opportunity to comment on the draft audit before it is finalized.

If the audit report includes recommendations from OIG, one or more HUD offices is assigned responsibility for developing an audit resolution action plan regardless of whether the audit was an internal audit (HUD program or office) or external audit (non-HUD program participant). For example, if a public housing authority is the auditee and OIG has recommendations in its report, the local HUD public housing field office could be assigned responsibility for working with the housing authority to clear any programmatic audit findings. Additionally, if OIG recommends sanctions in the audit report, the Departmental Enforcement Center could be assigned responsibility for closing those recommendations. A significant percentage of audit reports have recommendations, but it is not unusual for there to be no recommendations made by OIG.

B. Office of Investigation[41]

The Office of Investigation initiates investigations about possible violations of laws or regulations in the administration of HUD programs and activities, or misconduct on the part of HUD employees and/or the recipients of HUD funds. OIG has sole jurisdiction over criminal

---

38. Office of Audit's website, http://www.hudoig.gov/reports/audit.php.
39. Office of Audit's website at http://www.hudoig.gov/reports/auditplan.php.
40. Audit reports and audit guides are *available at* http://www.hudoig.gov/reports/auditreports.php.
41. Office of Investigation's website: http://www.hudoig.gov/fraud/investigation.php.

and fraud cases. The Office of Investigation works closely with the Department of Justice, HUD's Office of General Counsel, and the Departmental Enforcement Center when possible criminal violations occur and civil and/or administrative actions are contemplated. The Office of Investigations has subpoena authority for documents and witnesses.

Special agents in the Office of Investigation are authorized to:[42]

- Carry a firearm while engaged in official duties as authorized under the Inspector General Act or other statute, or expressly authorized by the Attorney General;
- Make an arrest without a warrant while engaged in official duties as authorized under this Act or other statute, or as expressly authorized by the Attorney General, for any offense against the United States committed in the presence of such Inspector General, Assistant Inspector General, or agent, or for any felony cognizable under the laws of the United States if such Inspector General, Assistant Inspector General, or agent has reasonable grounds to believe that the person to be arrested has committed or is committing such felony; and
- Seek and execute warrants for arrest, search of a premises, or seizure of evidence issued under the authority of the United States on probable cause to believe that a violation has been committed.

OIG usually receives reports of fraud, waste, or abuse by written correspondence, calls to the OIG Hotline, referrals from HUD offices or law enforcement agencies, congressional requests, and as a result of independent audits. OIG evaluates each allegation based on its connection to HUD and if it involves criminal or civil fraud. Once a preliminary review of an allegation is completed, the complaint is either converted to an investigation, referred to the appropriate program office, or closed.

OIG does not provide status reports on investigations in progress to Department managers or interested parties unless or until it is completely necessary. It is also OIG policy not to release the details of an ongoing investigation. It is not unusual for HUD program offices to be notified that a complaint is being evaluated or even that an investigation has been started and HUD program staff not notified of pending actions until an investigation is closed or a legal action such as an indictment, information, or arrest is imminent.

The Office of Investigation includes the Inspections and Evaluations Division, which conducts activities[43] that are designed to promote economy, efficiency, and effectiveness in the administration of HUD programs; detect and deter fraud and abuse in HUD programs and operations; and ensure compliance with applicable laws and regulations. This office uses various study methods and evaluative techniques and provides information to improve policies, programs, and procedures. The division publishes annual plans available online that outline the planned work activities for the year.[44]

---

42. From the Office of Investigation's Frequently Asked Questions website, http://www.hudoig.gov/fraud/oifaqs.php.
43. OIG website. http://www.hudoig.gov/reports/IandE.php.
44. Office of Investigation website, http://www.hudoig.gov/reports/IEannual.php.

Epilogue—Looking to the Future 16

HUD is poised for change—if not tomorrow, then in the not-too-distant future. Whether change results from pressure on the HUD budget, advances in technology, or modification to law and regulation, practitioners' ability to provide legal services related to affordable housing and community and economic development requires agility, flexibility, attention to detail, and a focus on the ever-shifting regulatory environment.

Going forward, HUD must demonstrate its commitment to serve as a meaningful participant in the public discussion regarding the appropriate role of the federal government in housing triggered by the 2008 federal takeover of the two government-sponsored entities (GSEs), Fannie Mae and Freddie Mac.[1] This discussion occurs in the face of both expected budget cuts and increased need. For example, the 2013 HUD budget *request* totals approximately $44 billion, down $11.9 billion (or almost 20 percent) from the enacted 2012 budget.[2] Meanwhile, housing affordability for lower-income households has decreased over

---

1. For a detailed discussion of the this issue, *see* Douglas J. Elliott, *The Federal Role in Housing Finance: Principal Issues and Policy Proposals* (Brookings Institute) (undated), at http://www.brookings.edu/~/media/Files/Press/Books/2011/thefutureofhousingfinance/thefutureofhousingfinance_chapter.pdf. This article indicates a consensus that the GSEs should shift the affordable housing portion of their mandates to FHA. *Id.* at p.2.

2. HUD, 2013 HUD Budget, Budget Authority by Program: Comparative Summary Fiscal Years 2011–2013, at B-5.

the last decade. For example, the Joint Center for Housing Studies of Harvard University calculates that as of 2009, the "share of 'severely burdened' owners climbed from 9.3 percent to 12.4 percent over the past decade, while the share of 'severely burdened' renters increased from 20.7 percent to 26.1 percent."[3] We will see this balance between mission and cost play out in the upcoming years, along with an almost inevitable side effect of regulatory and programmatic change.

Some changes can already be seen on the horizon. As FHA addresses increasing demand for its products, it has attempted to adjust its approach with respect to development, preservation, and asset management. The stress on FHA's resources is likely to increase until the housing market stabilizes, and those pressures will be impacted by action within HUD, the U.S. Department of Treasury, the Federal Housing Finance Agency, the GSEs, the White House, and the U.S. Congress. FHA is expected to further streamline its processing techniques as part of FHA's transition to a more user-friendly entity, with initiatives such as increased coordination with the low-income housing tax credit program. The contributions of practitioners working with these programs will be invaluable in assisting FHA in developing and implementing these changes.

CPD, PIH, and FHEO are expected to be active as well. CPD has proposed significant revisions to its HOME regulations,[4] in part to incorporate policy determinations reached through administration of the NSP programs. PIH is grappling with a declining but still large inventory of aging and underfunded public housing projects and has begun experimenting with the idea of converting public housing to Section 8 assistance through the Rental Assistance Demonstration program (RAD).[5] Regardless of whether RAD is implemented nationally beyond the initial demonstration program, HUD can be expected to continue seeking new vehicles to fund and transform public housing. Similarly, FHEO is expected to publish a proposed rule updating the obligation regarding practices to affirmatively further fair housing.

As shown by making sustainability one of HUD's six policy priorities in recent years, HUD has also indicated its interest in continuing to develop energy initiatives to reduce the utility costs of subsidized housing, partnering with other governmental agencies through the Office on Sustainable Development, and otherwise moving full force to address 21st-century issues.[6] Sustainability, energy, and place-based development have become increasingly central to allocation of funds in HUD's discretionary programs, as may be seen, for example, in the Choice Neighborhoods Program to revitalize public and assisted housing, which states as

---

3. JOINT CENTER FOR HOUSING STUDIES OF HARVARD UNIVERSITY, THE STATE OF THE NATION'S HOUSING (2011) at 27.

4. Docket No. FR-5563-P-01, Proposed Rule: HOME Investment Partnerships Program: Improving Performance and Accountability; and Updating Property Standards.

5. See HUD, PIH Notice 2012-18, Rental Assistance Demonstration—Partial Assistance and Request for Comments (March 8, 2012).

6. Of note, HUD has, for the second year in a row, included Sustainability as one of the key policy priorities that are used in rating and ranking all applications for discretionary funding. See HUD, Docket No. 5600-N-01, Notice of HUD's FY 2012 NOFA Policy Requirements and General Section to HUD's FY 2012 NOFAs for Discretionary Programs, at http://portal.hud.gov/hudportal/documents/huddoc?id=2012gensecNOFA.pdf.

one of its four objectives housing that is "energy efficient, sustainable, accessible, connected and free from discrimination."[7]

As HUD comes under greater pressure to reduce its budget, a thorough understanding of both new and old programs may become essential to developers, governmental entities, lenders, investors, and others using or competing for these resources. Our hope is that this book provides a framework for this understanding and a platform for meaningful participation in shaping future HUD programs, policies, and practices.

---

7. *See* HUD, HUD's Fiscal Year 2012 NOFA for the Choice Neighborhoods Initiative—Planning Grants, at 3, http://portal.hud.gov/hudportal/HUD?src=/program_offices/public_indian_housing/programs/ph/cn/fy12funding.

Index

A

Abandoned properties in neighborhood stabilization programs, 209–10, 214–15
Accounts receivable financing, 112–13
Acquisition or refinancing loans
  under Section 223(a)(7), 45
  under Section 223(f), 40–44, 58–60
Active Partners Performance System (APPS), 156, 166, 171–72, 452
Activity delivery costs, 204–05
Additional Deposit Amount, 43, 44
Additional Units projects in Section 202 Mixed-Finance transaction, 135
Administrative law judge (ALJ), 437, 438, 449, 459–60
Admissions policies for public housing, 303–05
Advisory assistance in relocation, 404
Affiliate relationships for Section 242 loans, 126
Affiliates as mixed-finance owners, 269–70
Affirmative Fair Housing Marketing (AFHM) regulations, 441–42
Affordable Housing and Self-Sufficiency Improvement Act of 2012, 302
Affordable Housing Program (AHP), 136–37, 146–54
Affording housing grant programs and energy efficiency programs, 417
Age Discrimination Act of 1975, 425
Agreement and Certification (HUD-93305M), 16, 71
Agreement to Enter into Housing Assistance Payments Contract (AHAP), 325
Allocation housing plan, 305
ALTA/ASCM Land Title Surveys, 62
American Dream Downpayment Initiative (ADDI), 187

American Homeownership and Economic Opportunity Act of 2000 (AHEO), 131, 138–40
American Reinvestment and Recovery Act of 2009 (ARRA), 196, 249, 268, 340, 341, 349
Annual Adjustment Factor (AAF), 327, 335
Annual Contributions Contract (ACC), 263, 285, 288–89, 312, 324, 388
Anti-Deficiency Act of 1906 (ADA), 413
Anti-Kickback Act, 392
Appeal process in 2530 Previous Participation Certification and Approval Process, 175
Application fee, FHA, 19–20
Approval process for new construction/substantial rehabilitation
  acquisition or refinancing under Section 223(f), 58–60
  Firm Commitment, 54–58
  letter of invitation, 53–54
  pre-application, 49–53
Approval process to participate in HUD's programs, 155–76
Architecture/engineering exhibits (A/E Exhibits), 49–50, 54–55, 58–59, 384
Area benefit activities, 181
Asset management, 299
  issues with Section 232 loans, 114–16
Asset Management Handbook, 363
Asset management project (AMP), 315
Asset-repositioning fees, 301
Assistant Secretary for Fair Housing and Equal Opportunity, 439
Assisted-living facilities (ALF)
  decreasing energy costs, 337–53
  eligibility for Section 232 loan, 103
Assumable FHA-insured mortgages, 21–23
Assurance of completion, 33
ASTM E-2018-08, 345

Audited financial statements, 60, 66–67
Auditing process, 461
Audits by Office of Inspector General (OIG), 317

B

Backlog need in public housing funding, 294
Base Rent, 114
Basic Rent, 86
Bauer, Catherine, 232
Below-market interest rate, 83
Block grant program, characteristics, 178–83
Block grants, 193
    for homeless programs, 188
Blockbusting, 431
Board-and-Care Facility
    eligibility for Section 232 loan, 102–03
    financing, 100
Bond financing in mixed-financed projects, 277
Bond obligations, 14
Bonding requirements in procurement requirements, 384–85
Borrower equity in insurance of advances, 30–33
Borrowers for mortgage insurance, 6–7
Borrower's organizational documents, 61
Brokerage services and discrimination, 433
Brooke, Edward, 38, 239
Brooke Amendment, 239
Brown v. Board of Education, 423
Buchanan v. Warley, 424
Budget Authority, 85–86
Budget-Based Rent Increase for Capital Repairs by Nonprofit Owners, 333
Budget line items (BLIs), 296–97
Builder's and sponsor's profit and risk allowance (BSPRA), 28–29
Building Loan Agreement (HUD-92441M), 34, 68–69
    for insurance of completion, 40
Building wage decision, 391
Business occupants and relocation benefits, 404–05
Business Partners Registration System, 172
Buy American requirements, 215, 267–68
Byrd Amendment certification, 105

C

Cap Needs Program, 333
Capital Fund Financing (CFF) Program, 250, 294–95, 298
    for mixed-financed projects, 277–80
Capital Fund Formula (CFF), 248–49
Capital fund program assessment for public housing, 317
Capital funds, 313, 314, 317
    leveraging, 298
    for public housing, 248–50, 293–97
    use of, 298
Cash Management Improvement Act of 1990 (CMIA), 413–14
Cash out refinance, 42–43
Ceiling rents, 307
Certificate of Actual Cost, 16
Certificate of Need (CON)
    for Section 232 loans, 111–12
    for Section 242 loans, 123–25
Certificates of actual cost, 16–17
Change orders, 34–35
Chief Principal, 161–62, 163, 167
Choice Neighborhood initiatives, 248, 285
    and energy efficiency initiatives, 350–51
Civil money penalties, 458–59
Civil Rights Act of 1866, 423
Civil Rights Act of 1964, 182, 424, 426–27, 439–40
Civil Rights Act of 1968, 182, 197, 227, 424–25
Civil rights in housing, 426–34
    and community development programs, 443–44
    enforcement, 434–38
    history of, 423–26
    and project site-selection criteria, 441
    and public housing tenant selection, 442–43
Civil rights programs administered by HUD, 423–44
Closing documents, 62–71
    building loan agreement, 68–69
    construction contract, 69–70
    lender's certificate/request for endorsement, 68
    Note, 64–65
    Opinion of Borrower's Counsel, 70

Regulatory Agreement, 65–68
security instrument, 62–64
Closing Guide, 4–5
Closing process, 60–71
Co-operation agreement for rental developments, 264
Commercial space, loans for, 26–27
Community Based Development Organizations (CBDOs), 180, 202
Community Development Block Grant (CDBG) program, 198, 386–87, 425, 429, 443–44
 characteristics of, 179
 compliance and enforcement activities, 447–48
 eligible activities, 179–80
 program administration, 182
 program requirements, 182–83
 programmatic eligibility, 180–81
 sources of guidance for, 191
Community development programs, 177–93
 and civil rights in housing, 443–44
Community Housing Affordability Strategy (CHAS), 444
Community Housing Development Organizations (CHDOs), 184–85
Community Planning Development Grants, 428
Community Planning Grants, 443
Community-service requirements for public housing, 309–10
Comparable replacement dwelling, 405–06
Competition in procurement transactions, 382–83
Competitive, qualifications-based procurement process, 384
Competitive proposals as a procurement method, 38
Completion Assurance Agreement (HUD-92450M), 33, 71
Compliance and enforcement of HUD programs, 445–65
Compliance division of Departmental Enforcement Center, 456–57
Comprehensive Grant Program, 250, 294
Comprehensive Improvement Assistance Program, 250, 294
Concept meeting for approval of new construction/substantial rehabilitation projects, 49

Conditioned contracts in neighborhood stabilization programs, 224
Condominium projects eligibility for mortgage, 7–8
Conflict of interest, 289
ConPlan, 182, 184, 185
Consolidated Appropriations Act of 2010, 247–48, 341
Consolidated Plan (ConPlan), 182, 184, 185
Consortium members in neighborhood stabilization programs, 203–04
Construction commencement for Section 242 loans, 123
Construction Contingency Amount, 31–32, 34, 40
Construction Contract, 33, 69–70
Construction Contract-Cost Plus (HUD-92442M), 29
Construction initiation for Section 242 loans, 126
Construction loan securities, 94
Construction period, 71
Contingency reserve in substantial rehabilitation projects, 29
Contract administration system, 381
Contract Authority, 85–86
Contract provisions for procurement by HUD grantees, 385
Contract types for public housing programs, 290–93
Contract Work Hours and Safety Standards Act (CWHSSA), 392
Contractors in neighborhood stabilization programs, 206
Contractor's Requisition for Project Mortgages (HUD-92448), 34, 36, 69
Conversion of public housing, 311–12
Cooperation Agreement, 288–89
Copeland Act, 392
Corporate Buyout in 2530 Previous Participation Certification and Approval Process, 160
Cost and price analysis in procurement process, 385
Cost-based loan programs, 9
Cost Breakdown (HUD-2328), 55, 69
Cost certification
 by contractors, 16–17
 for mortgage insurance, 15–16

Cost plus percentage of construction cost contracts, 292–93
Cost plus percentage of cost contracts, 292
Cost-reimbursement contracts, 291
Cost review
  during approval process, 59
  for new construction/substantial rehabilitation, 55
Court Order/Inheritance in 2530 Previous Participation Certification and Approval Process, 161
Covenant events of default, 21
Covenants for Section 242 loans, 125
Covered Project, 167, 172
CPD Monitoring Handbook, 209
Cranston-Gonzalez National Affordable Housing Act of 1990, 130, 138, 157, 183, 271
Critical Findings Memorandum, 156
Cuomo, Andrew, 446, 447
Cure period for defaults, 21

D

Date of Full Availability (DOFA), 276
Davis-Bacon Act, 182, 267, 386
Davis Bacon prevailing wage requirements, 23–24, 40, 386
Davis-Bacon Related Acts (DBRA), 386–92
Debt restructuring plans, 92–93
Debt service coverage, 343
Debt service coverage ratio (DSCR), 10–11
Debt service savings, 138–39
Declaration of Restrictive Covenants, 263
Declaration of Trust, 263, 279, 289
Declarations of substantial default, 454–55
Defaulted loans, 20–21
  resolving, 360–78
Definite quantity contracts, 291–92
Demolition
  and Davis-Bacon wage rates, 390–91
  as eligible use for neighborhood stabilization programs, 215–17
  of public housing, 311–12
Demolition escrow, 33
Department of Energy, 348–49
Department of Housing and Development. *See* HUD
Department of Housing and Urban Development Appropriations Act (2012), 81
Department of Housing and Urban Development Reform Act of 1989, 188
Department of Veterans Affairs and Housing and Urban Development, and Independent Agencies Appropriations Act (1997), 80
Departmental Enforcement Center (DEC), 169, 456–59
Deposit Account Control Agreement (DACA), 110–11
Design-build facilities eligibility for Section 242 loans, 119
Designated housing for elderly or disabled, 305
Developers in neighborhood stabilization programs, 205–06
Diaz, Nelson, 245
Diaz Opinion, 245
Direct Endorsement authority, 453
Disabled designated housing, 305
Disabled persons and housing discrimination, 425, 427–28, 431–33
Discriminatory housing practice, 423–26
  in provision of brokerage services, 433
  in residential real estate-related transactions, 433
  in sales, rental and advertising practices, 430–31
  and unlawful interference, coercion, and intimidation, 433
Displaced persons
  exclusions from definition of, 402–03
  and relocation benefits, 401–02
Disposition/demolition in mixed-finance projects, 257–58
Distressed assets in Section 232 loans, 115–16
Distributions from project income, 66
Dodd-Frank Act, 196, 217
Donovan, Shaun, 342
Due diligence in 2530 Previous Participation Certification and Approval Process, 169–71

E

Early start procedures in insurance of advances, 29–30
Economic self-sufficiency requirements for public housing, 310
Economic stimulus of U.S. Housing Act of 1937, 233–34, 284

Elderly housing, 84, 305
　insuring, 38–39
　low-income, 129–54
Elderly housing loan programs, 335, 357–58
Eligible projects for acquisition or refinancing loans, 41
Elimination of slums and blight prong, 181
Emergency Low Income Housing Preservation Act of 1987 (ELIHPA), 90, 332
Emergency Shelter Grant Program (ESG), 188, 429, 443
End of Initial Operating Period (EIOP), 276
Energy Action Plan for Public Housing, 350
Energy audits, 345, 351, 352
Energy conservation measures (ECMs), 416–17
Energy efficiency
　improvements for assisted housing, 337–53
　monitoring for, 351
Energy efficiency programs, 415–17
　for affordable housing grant programs, 417
　for public and Indian housing, 416–17
Energy Independence and Security Act of 2007, 351
Energy Innovation Fund, 341
Energy Performance Contract (EPC), 339, 351, 416
Energy Policy Act of 2005, 338
Energy retrofits, 339
Energy savings projects for public housing, 350–52
Energy Service Company (ESCO), 351
Energy Star program, 215, 350, 415–16
Enhanced vouchers, 333
Enterprise Communities, 190
Enterprise Green Communities, 345
Entity Flag Report, 171
Environmental assessment (EA), 393, 397–98
Environmental Assessment and Compliance Findings for the Related Laws (HUD-4128), 52
Environmental impact statement (EIS), 393, 398
Environmental Policy Act of 1969, 223
Environmental requirements for HUD grantees and subgrantees, 393–98
Environmental review, 267, 311, 394
　for neighborhood stabilization programs, 223–24

Equal Credit Opportunity Act, 426
Equity funding, 94–97
　for Section 242 loans, 122
Escrow, 19
　for latent defects, 40
Escrow Agreement for Incomplete Construction, 70
Escrow Agreement for Non-Critical, Deferred Repairs (HUD-92476.1M), 42
Escrow Agreement for Noncritical Repairs, 71
Escrow Agreement for Offsites or Demolition, 70
Escrow Agreement for Operating Deficit, 70
Escrow Agreement for Working Capital, 34, 70
Escrow requirements in insurance of advances, 30–33
　demolition escrow, 33
　front-money escrow, 30–31
　off-site escrow, 32
　operating deficit escrow, 32
　working capital escrow, 31–32
Ethics code, 381
Events of defaults, 20–21
Evidentiary Materials, 260–61, 265–67
Evidentiary review in mixed finance projects, 260–61, 265–67
Exception rents, 92
Excess amenities in elderly housing, 136–37
Excess Rents, 89
Excluded Parties List System (EPLS), 382
Executive Order 11,063, 424, 427, 439
Existing loan refinancing for Section 242 loans, 122
Existing modernization needs in public housing funding, 294

F

Fair Deal, 285
Fair housing
　affirmatively furthering, 439–44
　complaints, 448–49
　provisions in Civil Rights Act of 1968, 425
Fair Housing Act of 1968, 310, 429–34, 442–43
　and enforcing civil rights requirements, 435–38
　exemptions to, 433–34
　reasonable accommodations and modifications, 431–32

Fair Housing Amendments Act of 1988, 425–26
Fair Housing and Equal Opportunity (FHEO), 464
Fair Labor Standards Act (FLSA), 393
Fair Market Rent (FMR), 218–19, 322–23
  in HOME housing program, 186
Faircloth Limit, 249
Fairness opinion requirement, 279
Fannie Mae Green Refinance Plus Mortgage Program, 342–44
Federal admissions preferences in public housing, 240–41, 246
Federal Emergency Administration of Public Works, 232, 284
Federal financial assistance programs, 434–35
Federal financing of U.S. Housing Act of 1937, 234
Federal Home Loan Bank (FHLB), 136–37
Federal Housing Act of 1949, 285
Federal Housing Administration. *See* FHA
Federal Housing Finance Agency (FHFA), 197
Federal real property to assist homeless, 188
Federal Register, 410, 415
Federal relocation law, 399
Federal requirements impacting HUD programs, 379–421
  energy efficiency programs, 415–17
  funding and grant issues, 410–15
  labor provisions, 386–93
  procurement by HUD grantees and subgrantees, 380–85
  regulatory waivers, 415
  relocation requirements, 399–08
Federal Rules of Evidence, 438
FHA, 197, 285, 446
  application fee, 19–20
  inspection fee, 20
  multifamily programs, 1–5
FHA mortgage insurance, 1–5, 73
  backed by full faith and credit of the United States, 75
  contesting, 74
  funding for claims, 75–76
  funding source transfers, 81–82
  loan funding sources, 94
  NHA Section 207, 78–80
  NHA Section 220, 82–83
  NHA Section 221, 83–84
  NHA Section 223, 76–78
  NHA Section 231, 84
  NHA Section 236, 84–85
  NHA Section 241, 87
  NHA Section 250, 87–88
  preservation of rental assistance payments, 81
  and subsidy layering review, 410
  transfer of physical assets, 21–23
FHA Office of Asset Sales, 374
FHA Risk-Sharing Program, 342
50-75 percent Rule, 29
Final closing, 71
  for Section 202 Supportive Housing for the Elderly, 133
Final endorsement, 35–36
  for Section 242 loans, 126
Financial condition assessment for public housing, 315–16
Financial feasibility study for Section 242 loans, 124–25
Financial reporting
  requirements, 66
  for Section 242 loans, 126
Financing mechanisms as eligible use for neighborhood stabilization program, 213–14
Finding of no significant impact (FONSI), 394
Firm Commitment, 3, 4, 48–49, 73, 125
  application fee, 19–20
  for insurance of completion, 39–40
  issuance of, 60
  for new construction/substantial rehabilitation, 54–58
  and reserve for replacements, 17
  for Section 202 Supportive Housing for the Elderly, 133
  for Section 242 loans, 126
  and transfer of physical assets (TPA), 23
First-lien interest for Section 242 loans, 122–23
First-lien requirement, 7
Fixed moving allowance, 405
Fixed-price contracts, 291
Flags in 2530 Previous Participation Certification and Approval Process, 169–71
Flat, market-based rent, 307
Flexible Subsidy program, 88–90

Foreclosed properties in neighborhood stabilization programs, 207–09, 214–15
Foreign nationals participating in 2530 Previous Participation Certification and Approval Process, 168–69
Form 2530, 156, 171–72
Form 52722, 300
Form 52723, 300
Form HUD 2880, 411
Formula income for determining operating subsidy, 301
Fourteenth Amendment, 423, 424
Front-money escrow, 30–31
Fund allocation for HOME housing program, 183–84
Fund Reservation for Section 202 Supportive Housing for the Elderly, 133
Funding and grant issues, 410–15
Funding decisions, 411–12
Funding source transfers, 81–82

G

General Conditions for Construction Contracts, 293
General Conditions for Non-Construction Contracts, 293
General information notice for relocation, 400
Ginnie Mae mortgage-backed securities, 4, 14, 75
  repurchase of, 363–67
Ginnie Mae Mortgage-Backed Securities Guide, 359–60
Ginnie Mae Tandem Program, 84
Government Health-Care Receivables Deposit Account Agreement (DAISA), 110–11
Government National Mortgage Association (Ginnie Mae), 4, 94, 359–60
Grant application requirements, 410–11
Grant disbursements, 414–15
Grant Manager, 259–60
Grantees in neighborhood stabilization programs, 202–03
Grants Management Process System, 414
Green assessments, 344–46, 352
Green bank, 340
Green construction practices, 352
Green Initiative, 344
Green Physical Condition Assessment (GPCA), 342, 344–46

Green Physical Needs Assessment (GPNA), 343
Green Refinance Plus Mortgage Program, 342–44
Green Retrofit Program, 340–41
Greening of Government program, 337
Grievance procedures for tenants, 309
  for mixed-finance projects, 266

H

Handbook 4571.2, 131
Handbook 4571.4, 132
Harvard cost study, 286, 299
Health-care facility financing, 99–16, 157–58
Health care loans, 358
  resolving troubled or defaulted, 360–78
Healthy housing, 344
Heavy wage decision, 391
High-rise developments, 244
Highway wage decision, 391
HOME housing program, 183–87, 387, 429, 443, 444, 446
  and Community Housing Development Organizations (CHDOs), 184–85
  compliance and enforcement activities, 448
  eligible activities, 184
  fund allocation for, 183–84
  home ownership, 186–87
  program administration, 185–86
  sources of guidance for, 191
  and subsidy layering review, 409
Home Investment Partnerships Program. *See* HOME housing program
Home ownership in HOME housing program, 186–87
Home ownership mixed finance development, 271–73
  Mixed-Finance Addendum to Grant Agreement, 264
Homeownership units restrictions in neighborhood stabilization programs, 219–22
Homebuyer counseling, 222
Homeless programs, 187–90
  legal and policy issues, 189–90
Homeowners, displaced
  and relocation benefits, 407
Homeownership and Opportunity for People Everywhere (HOPE) program, 244–45

HOPE VI program, 256, 285
　and "Choice Neighborhoods" initiative, 247–48
　deconcentration of poverty, 252
　and energy efficiency initiatives, 350–51
　mixed finance approach to, 245–47
　origins of, 244–45
Hopkins, Harry, 233
Hospitals
　eligibility under Section 242 loans, 118–20
　financing, 116–28, 157–58
　refinancing of, 120
Housing Act of 1949, 178, 237–38
Housing Act of 1954, 238
Housing Act of 1959, 100
Housing and civil rights requirements, 423–44
Housing and Community Development Act of 1974, 179, 319, 386, 399, 425, 428–29, 443
Housing and Community Development Act of 1979, 240–41
Housing and Community Development Act of 1987, 100, 120, 271
Housing and Community Development Amendments of 1978, 80, 88
Housing and Development Act of 1968, 268
Housing and Economic Recovery Act of 2008 (HERA), 131, 195, 409–10
Housing and Home Finance Agency, 178
Housing and Urban Development Act of 1965, 82, 89
Housing and Urban Development Act of 1968, 241, 417, 444
Housing and Urban Development Act of 1969, 239
Housing and Urban-Rural Recovery Act of 1983, 241
Housing Assistance Payment (HAP) contracts, 192, 320
Housing authorities, 287–88
　procurement requirements for, 290
Housing authority contracts, 290–93
Housing Choice Voucher (HCV) program, 323, 326
Housing for working poor, 235–37
Housing Notice, 4–5, 90
Housing Notice 95-18, 137
Housing Notice 96-102, 132
Housing Notice 99-7, 137

Housing Notice 2002-16, 138, 139
Housing Notice 2011-18, 132
Housing Opportunities for Persons with AIDS (HOPWA), 190, 429, 443
Housing Quality Standards, 115
HUD
　civil rights programs, 423–44
　energy efficiency initiatives, 337–53
　and fair housing, 439–40
　as responsible entity for environmental review, 398
HUD 2020 Management Reform Plan, 446
HUD Addendum to Operating Lease, 108
HUD Asset Management Handbook, 368
HUD Budget and Accounting Handbook, 413
HUD-determined prevailing wages, 388
HUD grantees and subgrantees
　energy efficiency programs, 415–17
　and environmental requirements, 393–98
　　environmental assessment, 397–98
　　environmental impact statement, 398
　　environmental review process, 394
　　exclusions, 395
　funding and grant issues, 410–15
　and procurement requirements, 380–85
　　bonding requirements, 384–85
　　competition, 382–83
　　cost and price analysis, 385
　　methods of procurement, 383–84
　　procurement requirements, 380–82
　　required contract provisions, 385
　and relocation requirements, 399–08
　　notice requirements, 400–01
　　relocation plans, 399–400
　subsidy layering, 408–10
HUD-held loans, sale of, 374–78
HUD Mortgagee Letter 2010-32, 363, 368
HUD Mortgagee Letter 2011-15, 368
HUD note sales, 374–78
HUD programs. *See also* Specific programs
　compliance and enforcement, 445–65
　federal requirements impacting, 379–421
HUD Reform Act of 1989, 410
HUD Relocation Handbook, 408
HUD reviewing 2530 applications, 173–75
HUD Utility Schedule Model, 347
HUD's Survey Instructions (HUD-92457A-M), 62
Hurd v. Hodge, 424

I

Imposition Deposits, 63–64
Income-based rent, 274, 306–07
Income limits for eligibility in neighborhood stabilization programs, 217–18
Income targeting, 185
　provisions, 326
Indefinite delivery contracts, 291–92
Indefinite quantity contracts, 291–92
Independent Agencies Appropriations Act of 1996, 302
Indian Housing Block Grants (IHBG), 390
Individual Taxpayer Identification Number (ITIN), 168
Initial Closing for Section 202 Supportive Housing for the Elderly, 133
Inspection fee, FHA, 20
Instrumentalities as mixed-finance owners, 269–70
Insurance claims, funding for, 75–76
Insurance of advances, 27–39
　assurance of completion, 33
　borrower equity and escrow requirements, 30–33
　change orders, 34–35
　early start procedures, 29–30
　final endorsement, 35–36
　Minimum Property Standards, 33
　mortgage increases, 35
　procedures for advances, 34
　program variations, 36–39
Insurance programs
　insurance of advances, 27–39
　new construction, 27–29
　substantial rehabilitation, 27–29
Insurance requirements for Section 242 loans, 125
Insurance upon completion (IUC), 39–40
Integrated Disclosure and Information System, 414
Integrated pest management inspection, 345
Interagency agreement as a procurement method, 384
Interest, mortgageable, 7–9
Interest rate, 64
Interest Reduction Payment (IRP), 82, 85, 87, 158
Intergovernmental agreement as a procurement method, 384

Intermediate-Care/Board-and-Care facilities (IC Facilities)
　eligibility for Section 232 loan, 102
Intermediate-care facility financing, 100
International Energy Conservation Code (IECC), 351

J

Jackson, Alphonso, 338
Joint-venture parties involvement with Section 202 Supportive Housing for the Elderly, 132

L

Labor-hour contracts, 292
Labor provisions impacting HUD programs, 386–93
Land banking as eligible use for neighborhood stabilization programs, 215–16
Land survey, 62
Large loan limits, 12–13
Last-resort housing, 407
Latent defects escrow, 40
Lead-based paint hazards, 449–51
Lead Disclosure Rule, 450–51
Lead Safe Housing Rule, 450
LEAN 232 program, 100–01
LEAN processing for Section 232 loans, 105
Lease Addendum (HUD-92070M), 8–9
Leased hospitals eligibility for Section 242 loans, 119–20
Leasehold mortgages, 8–9
Lender selection for Section 242 loans, 123
Lender's Certificate (HUD-92434M), 62, 68
Lender's origination authority, 453
Letter contracts, 292
Letter of invitation for new construction/substantial rehabilitation, 53–54
Licenses for health-care facilities requirement for Section 232 loans, 111–12
Liens, 61
Limited clientele activities, 181
Limited Denials of Participation (LDPs), 453
Limited-liability corporate investors participating in 2530 Previous Participation Certification and Approval Process, 166–67

Line of Credit Control System, 414
LLCI Memorandum, 157, 167
Loan auction program, 368
Loan funding sources, 94
Loan guarantee program, 180
Loan ratio (LR), 9
Loan restructuring issues, 370–72
Loan structure in Section 202 Mixed-Finance transaction, 134, 143–45
Loan-to-cost limitations for construction loans, 28–29
Loan-to-value (LTV), 343
Loan transactions, 2
Loans
   backing securities, 366
   for commercial space, 26–27
Low-income elderly housing, 129–54
Low Income Housing Preservation and Resident Homeownership Act of 1990 (LIHPRHA), 90–91, 332
Low-Income Housing Tax Credits (LIHTCs), 51, 54–55, 83, 94–97, 214, 277
   combined with Section 202 program, 130–34
   and energy efficiency initiatives, 345–46
   and subsidy layering review, 409
Low income persons, training of, 444
Low/moderate income benefit test, 181

M

M2M. *See* Mark-to-Market Program
Maintenance wage rates, 389
Major Organization Change in 2530 Previous Participation Certification and Approval Process, 159–60
Management agent requirements in Section 232 loans, 109–10
Management agreement, 67
   for mixed-finance projects, 265–66
Management improvement operating plan (MIOP), 89
Management operations assessment for public housing, 316
Management review
   for acquisition or refinancing, 60
   for new construction/substantial rehabilitation, 57–58
Management Review Score (MOR), 164
MAP Guide, 5

Mark-to-Market Program, 92, 158
Mark-to-Market's Green Initiative, 340–41
Mark-Up-to-Market for Nonprofit Transfers, 333
Mark-Up-to-Market renewal of rents, 328–30
Market rents, 86, 328–33
Market study, 59
Maximum insurable loan amounts, 9–11
Maximum insurable mortgage
   under Section 223(d), 46–47
   under Section 241, 47–48
Maximum Insurable Mortgage (HUD-92580), 71
Maximum insurable mortgage for acquisition or refinancing, 41–42
Maximum per-unit subsidy in HOME housing program, 186
McKinney-Vento Homeless Assistance Act, 335
Minimum Property Standards, 33
Minor Organization Change in 2530 Previous Participation Certification and Approval Process, 160–61
Mixed-Finance ACC amendment, 263–64
Mixed-Finance Addendum to Grant Agreement for home ownership, 264
Mixed finance approach to public housing, 245–47, 250–53
   educating funders, 280–81
   evidentiary review and funding, 260–61, 265–67
   financial impact of program limitations, 273–77
   guidance to, 254–57
   key documentation, 262–64
   other legal requirements, 267–69
   PHAs as principals, 269–70
   processing projects, 257–61
   project proposal, 258–60
   use of project-based vouchers, 280, 323–25
Mixed Finance Guidebook (HUD), 255
Mixed-finance home ownership development, 271–73
Mixed Finance Owner, 134
Mixed-Finance Ownership Term Sheet, 258–59
Mixed-Finance Protocol, 258–60
Mixed-Finance Regulations, 253, 258
Mixed-Finance Rental Term Sheet, 258

Mixed-Finance Term Sheets, 259
Mixed-population housing projects, 305
Model Cities Program, 178, 428, 443
Modified First Loan, 367, 370–71
Modified transfer of physical assets (TPA), 23, 160
Monetary event of default, 20
Mortgage-based securities (MBS), 94, 359–60
   repurchase of, 363–67
Mortgage credit review, 52–53, 56–57
   for acquisition or refinancing, 60
Mortgage increases, 35
Mortgage insurance
   cost certification, 15–16
   eligible borrowers, 67
   eligible projects, 5
   first-lien requirement, 7
   large loan limits, 12–13
   maximum loan amounts, 9–11
   prepayment restrictions, 14–15
   term of mortgage, 13–14
Mortgage insurance premiums (MIP), 1–2
   escowing for, 19
   payments due dates and rates, 18
Mortgage insurance programs, 1–5
   See also Specific programs
Mortgage modification for troubled and defaulted loans, 363–67
Mortgage reduction, 17
Mortgage Reserve Fund, 124
Mortgage Reserve Trust Fund Agreement, 124
Mortgage Restructuring and Rental Assistance Sufficiency Plans, 92
Mortgage Review Board (MRB), 452
Mortgage term, 13–14
Mortgageable interest, 7–9
Move-In Notice for relocation, 401
Moving assistance, 404
Moving to Work (MTW) program, 302
MTW Act, 302
Multifamily Accelerated Processing (MAP) Guide, 3, 48, 358
Multifamily Assisted Housing Reform and Affordability Act of 1997 (MAHRA), 92–93, 139, 321–22, 372
   renewal contract options, 328–33
Multifamily assisting housing redevelopment, 248
Multifamily energy efficiency, 339, 341–44
Multifamily housing
   accessible to disabled, 432–33
   compliance and enforcement activities, 452
   preservation, 73–97
   weatherization of, 349
Multifamily loan programs
   approval process, 48–60
   closing process, 60–72
   Insurance of Advances, 27–38
   Insurance Upon Completion, 39–40
   overview, 356–57
   overview of, 6–27
   resolving troubled or defaulted, 360–78
   Section 223(a)(7), 45
   Section 223(d), 46–47
   Section 223(f), 40–44
   Section 241, 47–48
Multifamily mortgage loan programs, 1–5
Multifamily Participation Review Committee, 174
Multifamily projects eligible for 2530 Previous Participation Approval Process, 158

N

National Affordable Housing Act of 1990, 386
National Commission on Severely Distressed Public Housing, 251
National Consumer Law Center (NCLC), 338
National Environmental Policy Act (NEPA), 267, 393–97
National Housing Act of 1934, 73, 76, 99
National Housing Trust, 339
National Industrial Recovery Act of 1933, 231–32, 284
National Loan Committee, 39, 48
Native American Housing Assistance and Self-Determination Act of 1996, 190, 386, 390
Native Hawaiian Housing Block Grants (NHHBG), 390
Natural person borrowers, 7
Negative rent, 275
"Negro removal," 178
Nehemiah Housing Opportunity Grants Program (NHOP), 271
Neighborhood Stabilization Program 1 (NSP1), 195, 197–99
Neighborhood Stabilization Program 2 (NSP2), 196, 199–200

Neighborhood Stabilization Program 3 (NSP3), 196, 200–01
Neighborhood Stabilization Program Resource Exchange, 201
Neighborhood stabilization programs, 195–229
　abandoned properties, 209–10, 214–15
　affordability restrictions, 217–23
　combined with other funding sources, 222–23
　consortium members, 203–04
　contractors, 206
　developers, 205–06
　eligible partners for, 202–06
　eligible properties for, 206–11
　eligible uses of properties, 212–17
　federal requirements, 223–27
　overview, 197–202
　sources of guidance for, 201–02
　subrecipients, 203–04
　timing considerations, 211–12
　vacant properties, 210–11
New construction and substantial rehabilitation projects, 16–17
New construction insurance programs, 27–29, 83
　approval process, 48–58
　insurance of advances, 27–39
　insurance upon completion, 39–40
NHA Section 206A, 79
NHA Section 207, 78–80
NHA Section 220, 82–83
NHA Section 221, 83–84
NHA Section 221(d)(3)/(5), 89, 90
NHA Section 223, 76–78
NHA Section 231, 84
NHA Section 236, 84–85, 89, 90
NHA Section 241, 47–48, 87
NHA Section 241(f), 90–91
NHA Section 250, 87–88
90-day notice for relocation, 401
90 Percent LTV (Loan to Value), 122
Non-profit or limited dividend borrowers, 37
Noncompetitive proposals as a procurement method, 384
Nonrecourse provisions in regulatory agreement, 68
Note (HUD-94001M), 2–3
Note as closing document, 64–65
Note sales, 374–78
Notice of eligibility for relocation benefits, 400
Notice of Funding Availability (NOFA), 132, 141, 199
Notice of Intent to Request a Release of Funds (NOI/RROF), 394
Notice of non-displacement, 401
Notice PIH-2009-41, 415
November Miller Memorandum, 156, 162
NSP Policy Alerts, 201
NSP Toolkits, 201
NSP1, 195, 197–99
NSP2, 196, 199–200
NSP3, 196, 200–01
Nursing homes
　eligibility for Section 232 loan, 102
　financing, 100

O

Obama, Barack, 337, 338
Occupancy documents for mixed-finance projects, 266
Occupancy standards and requirements in public housing, 308–11
Off-site escrow, 32
Office of Administrative Law Judges, 459–60
Office of Affordable Housing Preservation (OAHP), 330
Office of Appeals, 459
Office of Audit, 461
Office of Community Planning and Development (CPD), 195, 196, 201–29, 447–48
　programs, 177–87
Office of Fair Housing and Equal Opportunity, 317, 448–49
Office of General Counsel, 123, 124, 261
Office of Healthcare Programs (OHP), 99, 105, 114–15
Office of Healthy Homes and Lead Hazard Control (OHHLHC), 449–51
Office of Hearings and Appeals (OHA), 459–60
Office of Hospital Facilities (OHF), 99, 116–17, 123–24
Office of Housing (HUD), 320
　compliance and enforcement activities, 452–53
Office of Inspector General (OIG) audits, 317

Office of Insured Healthcare Facilities (OIHCF), 99
Office of Investigation, 461–62
Office of Multifamily Housing, 453
Office of Program Enforcement, 458
Office of Public and Indian Housing (PIH), 320
  compliance and enforcement activities, 453–56
Office of Public Housing Investments, 246
Office of Residential Programs (ORP), 99
Office of the Inspector General (OIG), 460–62
OMB Circulars, 413
Operating Cost Adjustment Factor (OCAF), 93, 330, 334
Operating deficit escrow, 32
Operating deficit reserve requirements, 12–13
Operating Fund Formula, 300, 301
Operating Fund Rule, 276
Operating Funds for public housing, 293, 299
Operating lease requirements in Section 232 loans, 108–09, 113–14
Operating lessee requirements in Section 232 loans, 109
Operating Loss Loan, 46–47
Operating subsidy, 285, 299–302
  in mixed-finance projects, 275–77
Operating subsidy formula, 262
Operations division of Departmental Enforcement Center, 457
Operator security agreement, 109–10
Opinion of Borrower's Counsel, 70
Opinion of Counsel in mixed-finance projects, 265
Opportunity for cure, 312
Option contracts in neighborhood stabilization programs, 224
Organization Change Submissions, 159–60, 173–74
Organization structure changes and 2530 Previous Participation Certification and Approval Process, 159–61
Organizational and financing documents for mixed-finance projects, 266
Ownership structure
  for hospital financing, 121–22, 133–34, 142
  in Section 202 Mixed-Finance transaction, 133–34, 142

P

Panic peddling, 431
Parks, insuring construction of, 36
Part 85, 268, 270
Partial Payment of Claim (PPC), 115–16, 367–74
  loan restructuring issues, 370–72
  processing and closing process, 373–74
  proposal, 369–70
  qualifying for, 368–69
  tax considerations, 372–73
Participating Administrative Entities (PREs), 92
Participating jurisdictions, 183–85
Particularly urgent community development needs prong, 181
Partnerships for Home Energy Efficiency (PHEE), 416
Pass-through securities, 4
Passive Investor Memorandum, 156, 167–68
Passive investors participating in 2530 Previous Participation Certification and Approval Process, 167–68
Payment and Performance Bonds, 33, 70–71
Payment in lieu of taxes (PILOT), 288
Permission to Occupy (HUD-92485), 71
Pet ownership in public housing, 310–11
PHA Plan, 312–14, 416–17
Phase I Environmental Site Assessment (Phase I Report), 51–52
Physical condition assessment (PCA), 315, 341–42
Physical Inspection Report, 58, 59
Physician owned/investor owned hospitals eligibility for Section 242 loans, 119
Plans of Action, 90–91, 332
Plessy v. Ferguson, 423, 424
Policy Alert, 256
Portfolio Reengineering Programs (Pre), 91–92
Portfolio Restructuring Agreements (PRAs), 92
Portfolio transactions review for Section 232 loans, 106–07, 114
Power Purchase Agreements (PPAs), 351–52
PPC Mortgage Loan, 371
Pre-application for new construction/substantial rehabilitation, 49–53
Preleasing of commercial space, 27

Prepayment
    override, 362
    restrictions, 14–15, 89
    under Section 202 Direct Loans program, 138–40
Prepayment lock-out period, 362
Prepayment premium, 362
Preservation Approval Process Improvement Act of 2007, 166
Preservation of FHA subsidized projects, 87–88
Prevailing wage requirements, 23–24, 40
Previous Participation Certificate (PPC) disclosure, 169
Previous Participation Certification (HUD-2530), 52–53, 56, 156, 161
Principal, 172
    definition in 2530 Previous Participation Certification and Approval Process, 161–63
    disclosure of participation history, certification, and signature for 2530 Previous Participation Certification and Approval Process, 163–66
Priority watch list for Section 242 loans, 127
Private rental housing, 319
Procedures for advances, 34
Procurement Handbook for Public Housing Agencies (HUD), 290
Procurement methods, 383–84
Procurement requirements
    for housing authorities, 290
    for HUD grantees, 380–85
Programmatic eligibility of Community Development Block Grants (CDBG), 180–81
Project-Based Vouchers (PBVs), 323–25, 333
    for mixed-financed housing projects, 280
    and subsidy layering review, 409–10
Project Capital Needs Assessment (PCNA) Report, 43, 58
Project Expense Level (PEL), 275–76
Project Expense Level (PEL) Estimator, 259
Project Owner's/Management Agent's Certification (HUD-9839), 57, 110
Project Rental Assistance Contract (PRAC), 130, 135, 335–36
Project Review Panel Protocol, 258–60
Project site-selection criteria, 441

Projects, housing, 238–39, 246
Property insurance premiums, escowing for, 19
Property submissions for 2530 Previous Participation Certification and Approval Process, 158–59
Property tax exemption for rental developments, 264
Protecting Tenants at Foreclosure Act of 2009 (PTFA), 225, 399
Protest procedures, 381
Pruitt-Igoe development, 242
Public housing
    admissions and tenant selection policies, 303–05
    capital fund program assessment, 317
    community-service and economic self-sufficiency requirements, 309–10
    conversion of units to Section 8 funded units, 286
    deconcentration of poverty, 251–52
    demolition, disposition and conversion of, 311–12
    designated housing by elderly or disabled, 305
    determining tenant rent and income, 305–06
    energy-saving projects, 350–52
    financial condition assessment, 315–16
    green construction practices, 352
    income mixing of participants, 251–52
    increase in units, 285
    labor provisions, 388
    management operations assessment, 316
    mixed finance approach to, 245–47, 250–53, 255–57
    monitoring and oversight of, 312–17
    occupancy standards and requirements, 308–11
    operation of, 303–11
    pet ownership in, 310–11
    physical condition assessment, 315
    proportionality of public housing funding, 252–53
    reduced density of, 251–52
    severely distressed, 251–52
    tenant utility expenses, 307–08
    voluntary compliance agreements, 317
Public Housing Agencies (PHAs), 234–53
    declarations of substantial default, 454–55

participating in MTW, 302
as principals of mixed-finance owners, 269–70
processing mixed-finance projects, 257–81
remedies for substantial default declarations, 455–56
and Section 8 housing assistance program, 322–25
status designations of, 453–54
Public Housing Agencies (PHAs) Plan, 312–14
Public Housing Assessment System (PHAS), 278, 295, 314, 453
Public housing authorities, 287–89
Public Housing Capital Fund Program, 248
Public housing capital funds in mixed-finance projects, 277
Public housing demolition, 211, 215–16, 235, 237, 245, 301
Public housing development, 231–81
new models of, 243–53
Public Housing Development Program, 250, 294
Public housing funding
proportionality of, 252–53
Public housing programs, 231–53, 283–18
contracts and required provisions, 290–93
financial impact of program limitations, 273–77
funding of, 293–302
history of, 284–87
procurement requirements for housing authorities, 290
statutory and regulatory changes in, 237–43
structure of public housing authorities, 287–89
Public housing redevelopment
in 21st century, 253–73
capital funds, 248–50
regulatory and sub-regulatory guidance, 254–57
statutory regulations, 253–54
Public housing tenant leases, 308–09
Public housing tenant selection, 442–43
Public Works Administration (PWA), 232, 284
Purchase and rehabilitation of foreclosed and abandoned properties, 214–15

Q

Qualified Allocation Plans (QAP), 345–46
Qualified Certification for 2530 Previous Participation Certification and Approval Process, 165
Quality Assurance Division (QAD), 451
Quality Housing and Work Responsibility Act of 1998 (QHWRA), 243, 246–47, 286

R

Rate lock agreement, 3
Real Estate Assessment Center (REAC), 453
inspections, 115
physical inspection scores, 164
Real estate-related transactions and discrimination, 433
Reasonable accommodations and modifications in Fair Housing Act, 431–32
Recapture provisions in neighborhood stabilization programs, 221–22
Redevelopment of demolished or vacant property as eligible use for neighborhood stabilization programs, 216–17
Reestablishment assistance, 404–05
Refinancing, 17, 40–44
in Section 202 Mixed-Finance transaction, 138–40
under Section 223(a)(7), 45, 361–63
under Section 223(f), 58–60
Regulatory Agreement, 2, 65–68, 109
and transfer of physical assets, 21–23
Regulatory and Operating Agreement for rental developments, 262
Regulatory waivers, 415
Rehabilitation Act of 1973, 227, 310, 425, 427–28
Relocation benefits
for business occupants, 404–05
grievances and waivers of benefits, 408
last-resort housing, 407
for residential occupants, 405–07
under Section 104(d), 408
Relocation requirements for HUD grantees and subgrantees, 399–408
displaced persons, 401–03
last-resort housing, 407
notice requirements, 400–01

relocation benefits, 404–07
relocation plans, 399–400
Renewal grants in homeless programs, 188
Rent comparability study (RCS), 328
Rent increases for Section 8 housing assistance program, 333–34
Rent limitations in HOME housing program, 186
Rent requirement in mixed-finance projects, 273–75
Rent Supplement Payments, 82, 158
Rent types in public housing, 305–07
Rental Assistance Demonstration, 286, 287, 312, 464
Rental Assistance Payments, 86, 158
   preservation of, 81
Rental assistance programs, 253, 334–36
Rental developments
   co-operation agreement, 264
   Mixed-Finance ACC amendment, 263–64
   regulatory and operating agreement for, 262
Rental housing, 5, 44
   loan program, 356
   restrictions in neighborhood stabilization programs, 218–19
   subsidize private, 319
Rents
   annual increases, 334
   increase of, 327
   renewal of, 328–33
Repair Estimate Amount, 43, 44
Repairs Escrow, 42–44
Replacement Housing Factor (RHF) Funds, 249–50, 285, 297–98
Replacement housing payment, 406, 407
Repurchase requirements for loans, 366–67
Request for Construction Changes (HUD-92437), 34
Request for Endorsement of Credit Instrument (HUD-92455M), 62, 68
Request for Final Endorsement of Credit Instrument (HUD-92023M), 35
Request for Release of Funds (RROF), 224, 394
Requirements contracts, 291–92
Resale requirements in neighborhood stabilization programs, 220
Reserve
   for repairs, 43–44
   for replacements, 17–18, 42–44, 66

Residential Lead-Based Paint Hazard Reduction Act of 1992, 450
Residential occupants and relocation benefits, 405–07
Residential wage decision, 391
Residual receipts, 24, 66
Residual Receipts Note, 26
Responsible entity (RE), 393, 398
Restrictive covenant, 424
Retsinas, Nicholas, 245
Revised PPC and Modification Handbook, 363–64
Revised PPC Handbook, 368–70
Riders for Affordable Housing Program (AHP) and Section 202 Funds, 146–54
Riis, Jacob, 232
Rural Hospitals, critical-access Hospitals (CAHs) eligibility for Section 242 loans, 119
Rural Housing Service (RHS), 163, 165

S

Sales, rental and advertising practices and fair housing, 430–31
Sales price restrictions in neighborhood stabilization programs, 219–22
Sealed bids as a procurement method, 383
Secondary financing, 24–26
   for Section 202 Mixed-Finance transaction, 136–38
Secondary Financing Rider, 25–26
Secretary of State, 61
Section 3 of Housing and Urban Development Act of 1968, 417–21
   applicability, 418
   complaints, 421
   compliance requirements, 419–20
   reporting and monitoring, 421
   threshold expenditure amounts, 419
Section 8, 389–90
Section 8 Annual Contributions Contracts (ACCs), 322
Section 8 Certificate Program, 322
Section 8 funded housing units, 280, 286–87
Section 8 housing assistance program, 319–36
   Chapter 15, 333–34
   common features of, 326
   contract renewals, 327–33
   opting out of, 332–33

Index

project-based assistance programs, 320–22, 327–28
Section 8 Loan Management Set Aside (LMSA) program, 320–21
Section 8 Moderate Rehabilitation (Mod Rehab) Program, 323
Section 8 Moderate Rehabilitation Single Room Occupancy (SRO) Program, 334–35
Section 8 New Construction/Substantial Rehabilitation program, 320, 327
Section 8 of U.S. Housing Act of 1937, 91–93, 253
Section 8 project-based assistance programs, 319–22, 389–90
Section 8/Project-Based Vouchers (PBVs), 323–25, 333, 389–90
 and subsidy layering review, 409–10
Section 8 Property Disposition (PD) program, 321
Section 8 Renewal Policy Guide (HUD), 328
Section 8 rental subsidy program, 232
Section 8 tenant-based assistance programs, 319, 322–25
Section 8 Voucher Reform Act (SEVRA), 302
Section 9 funds in mixed-financed housing projects, 280
Section 32 homeownership development, 273
Section 42 of Internal Revenue Code of 1986, 94
Section 104(d), 408
Section 108 loan guarantee program, 180
Section 109 of the Housing and Community Development Act of 1974, 428–29
Section 202 Direct Loan program, 138–40
Section 202 housing assistance program, 335
Section 202 Mixed-Finance transaction, 131–38
 additional unit projects, 135
 addressing structural issues, 136
 ownership structure, 133–34, 142
 refinancing and preservation of projects, 138–40
 secondary financing, 136–38
 structure of loan to partnership, 134
Section 202 of Housing Act of 1959, 157
Section 202 Supportive Housing and Elderly Act of 2010 (2010 Act), 131

Section 202 Supportive Housing for the Elderly, 129–54
 application and closing process, 132–33
 mixed financing of, 133–38
 programmatic guidance and authorities, 132
 regulatory authority, 131–32
 statutory authority of, 130–31
Section 207/223(f) loan program, 356
Section 207 loans, 36, 41
Section 220 loans, 36–37
Section 220 program, 357
Section 221(d)(3) program, 37, 357
Section 221(d)(4) program, 357
Section 223(a)(7), 45
 and refinancing loans, 361–63
Section 223(d)(Operating Loss Loan), 46–47
Section 223(f) (Acquisition or Refinancing), 40–44, 58–60
 cash out refinance, 42–43
 eligible projects, 41
 maximum insurable mortgage, 41–42
 other requirements and restrictions, 44
 reserve for replacements, 43–44
Section 231 program, 38–39, 357–58
Section 232/223(a)(7) loans, 104
Section 232/223(f) loans, 103–04
Section 232/241 loans, 104–05
Section 232 Handbook, 358
Section 232 loans, 100–16, 358
 accounts receivable financing, 112–13
 asset management issues, 114–16
 collateral, 111–12
 commitment and closing, 106
 eligible facilities for financing, 102–03
 general terms and requirements, 101–02
 LEAN processing for, 105–07
 master lease requirement for portfolio transactions, 113–14
 review for portfolio transactions, 106–07
 security for, 110–12
 types of, 103–05
 underwriting and closing issues, 108–14
Section 232 New Construction and Substantial Rehabilitation loans, 103
Section 232 of the National Housing Act of 1934, 99
Section 241 loans, 121
Section 242/223(a)(7) loans, 120–21
Section 242/223(f) loans, 120

Section 242 loans, 116–28
  application process, 123–26
  asset management issues, 126–27
  eligible facilities for financing, 118–20
  final endorsement, 126
  general terms and requirements, 118–21
  governance of, 116–18
  interim reporting and certifications, 127
  preliminary review of, 121–23
  priority watch list, 127
  problem solving, 127–28
  processing and underwriting issues, 121–26
  regulatory and operational requirements, 125–26
  risk mitigation, 127
  transfers of physical assets (TPA), 127
  types of, 120–21
  underwriting and financing issues, 124–25
Section 242 New Construction/Substantial Rehabilitation, 120
Section 242 of National Housing Act, 157
Section 242 of the National Housing Act of 1934, 99
Section 504 of the Rehabilitation Act of 1973, 427–28
Section 811 Capital Advance program, 138–40
Section 811 housing assistance program, 336
Section 811 of Cranston-Gonzalez National Affordable Housing Act, 157
Security for Section 232 loans, 110–12
Security instrument, 62–64
Security Instrument (HUD-94000M), 2
Selection-related disclosures, 412
Separate but equal doctrine, 423–24
Shannon v. HUD, 440
Shelley v. Kaemer, 424
Shelter Plus Care (S+C) Program, 188, 335
Short form cost certification, 17
Single-family housing
  compliance and enforcement activities, 451
Single Room Occupancy (SRO) Program, 334–35, 357
Site control documentation for mixed-finance projects, 266–67
Skilled-Nursing Facilities (SNF)
  eligibility for Section 232 loan, 102
Slum clearance, 232–34, 284
  in the 1940s and 1950s, 237–38

Small purchase procedures as a procurement method, 383
Special Application Center (SAC), 257, 311
Sponsor-based housing, 302
Sponsor's profit and risk allowance (SPRA), 28–29
Stable occupancy, 44
Start-Up Hospitals eligibility for Section 242 loans, 119
Subordinate, Non-Disturbance, and Attornment Agreement (SNDA), 108–09, 114
Subordinate financing, 24–26
Subordination Agreement, 25
Subrecipients in neighborhood stabilization programs, 204–05
Subsidy Contract, 158
Subsidy layering, 343, 408–10
  analysis, 268–69
  review, 324, 408–09
Substantial default of PHA
  declarations of, 454–55
  remedies for, 455–56
Substantial rehabilitation insurance programs, 27–29, 83
  approval process, 48–58
  insurance of advances, 27–39
  insurance upon completion, 39–40
Supplemental Loan, 47–48
Supportive Housing for the Elderly Act of 2010 (SHEA), 139–40
Supportive Housing program, 188–89
Surplus cash, 24, 66
Surplus Cash Note, 26
Survey, land, 62
Sweat equity program, 387

T

Tax credit equity, 31
  in Section 202 Mixed-Finance transaction, 136
Taxes, escowing for, 19
Temporary relocation for displaced persons, 403
Tenant-based assistance program, 319, 322–25
Tenant-based rental assistance (TBA), 184
Tenant-in-common borrowers, 7
Tenant lease documents for mixed-finance projects, 266

Tenant leases for public housing, 308–09
Tenant protection requirements in neighborhood stabilization programs, 225–26
Tenant rent, 273–75, 305–06
Tenant rent payments, 86
Tenant selection policies for public housing, 303–05
Tenant utility expenses, 307–08
Tenants, displaced
 and relocation benefits, 405–06
Tenant's right to grieve housing authority actions, 309
Three-Day Rule, 414
Three-pronged test, 181
Three-Tier Rule, 162
Three Year Rule, 78
Threshold expenditure amounts for Section 3, 419
Time and material contracts, 292
Title 42 of U.S. Code, 232
Title I of Housing Act of 1949, 178
Title II of Cranston-Gonzalez National Affordable Housing Act, 183
Title II of National Housing Act, 157
Title policy, 61–62
Title VI of the Civil Rights Act of 1964, 426–27, 434–35, 440, 442
Title VIII of the Civil Rights Act of 1964, 424, 429
Title VIII of the Civil Rights Act of 1968, 440
Title X, 450
24/9 mixed-finance home ownership program, 271
24 C.F.R. part 901, 254
25 percent set-aside requirement, 226
2530 Handbook, 156
2530 Previous Participation Certification and Approval Process, 155–76
 appeal process, 175
 covered projects, 157–58
 definition of principal, 161–63
 disclosure of principal participation history, certification, and signature, 163–66
 due diligence in, 169–71
 issues with, 175–76
 legal authority of, 156–57
 and limited-liability corporate investors, 166–67
 participation by foreign naturals, 168–69
 participation by passive investors, 167–68
 property submissions for, 158–59
 review by HUD, 173–75
 submission form, 171–73
2530 Regulations, 156
202 Capital Advance, 130–31
 timing of, 134–35
202 Capital Advance Upon Completion (CAUC), 135
Traditional Application Processing (TAP), 3
Transfer of physical assets (TPA)
 for FHA-insured mortgages, 21–23
 for Section 232 loans, 115
 for Section 242 loans, 127
Transfer Program, 333
Treasury-State Agreement (TSA), 414
Trip Report (HUD-95379), 71
Troubled loans, resolving, 360–78
Turbov, Mindy, 245–46

U

Underwriting issues for Section 242 loans, 124–25
Uniform Federal Accessibility Standards (UFAS), 428
Uniform Physical Conditions Standards (UPCS), 315
Uniform Relocation Act (URA), 399, 408
Uniform Relocation Assistance and Real Property Acquisition Policies Act of 1970, 180, 182–83, 225, 268, 399
United States Housing Authority (USHA), 234
Unsecured promissory notes, 26
Urban Empowerment Zones, 190
Urban hospitals eligibility for Section 242 loans, 118–19
Urban redevelopment in the 1940s and 1950s, 237–38
Urban renewal, 178
Urban Renewal Program, 428, 443
U.S. Department of Housing & Urban Development. *See* HUD
U.S. Housing Act of 1937, 89, 180, 232–37, 253, 284, 319
 federal financing of, 234
 Section 8, 91–93
U.S. Housing Act of 1974, 386
U.S. Housing Authority (USHA), 284

Use Agreement, 364–65
  for partial payment of claims, 371–72
User Guide (2530 Process), 157
Utility allowances, 307–08, 345–48, 351
  in mixed-finance projects, 274–75
Utility Expense Level (UEL), 275–76, 300

V

Vacant properties
  as eligible use for neighborhood stabilization programs, 216–17
  in neighborhood stabilization programs, 210–11, 214–15
Valuation review, 50–52, 55–56
  for acquisition or refinancing, 59–60
Value-based loan programs, 9
Value limitation of mortgage insurance, 79
Very low income persons, training of, 444
Voluntary compliance agreements for public housing, 317

W

Wage rate requirements, 386–93
Wagner-Steagall Act, 232
Waiting list for admissions to public housing, 304–05
Waiver of commercial income limits, 26
Waiver of commercial space limits, 26
Wall Street Reform and Consumer Protection Act of 2010, 196
Warranted price of land, 55
Watch list contracts, 330–31
Weatherization, 348–49
Weatherization Assistance Program (WAP), 348–49
Web Access Secure System (WASS), 172
Williams Memorandum, 156
Working Capital Amount, 31–32
Working capital escrow, 31–32
Working poor, housing for, 235–37

Z

Zoning compliance for mixed-finance projects, 266–67